Israel's God and Rebecca's Children

Israel's God and Rebecca's Children

Christology and Community
in Early Judaism and Christianity

Essays in Honor of Larry W. Hurtado
and Alan F. Segal

edited by

David B. Capes
April D. DeConick
Helen K. Bond
Troy A. Miller

BAYLOR UNIVERSITY PRESS

Cover Design: Pamela Poll

Images of coins in Foster's article are used by permission of the Classical Numismatic Group, Inc.

    Figure 18.1 is found at
        http://members.verizon.net/vze3xycv/Jerusalem/confFirstRevolt.htm
    Figure 18.2 is found at
        http://homepages.luc.edu/~advande1/jerusalem/views/titusArch.htm
    Figure 18.3 is found at
        http://www.jewishencyclopedia.com/view.jsp?artid=183&letter=F

Library of Congress Cataloging-in-Publication Data

Israel's God and Rebecca's children : christology and community in early Judaism and Christianity : essays in honor of Larry W. Hurtado and Alan F. Segal / edited by David B. Capes [... et al.].
    p. cm.
  ISBN-13: 978-1-60258-026-8 (cover : alk. paper)
  1. Church history--Primitive and early church, ca. 30-600. 2. Christianity--Origin. 3. Jesus Christ--Person and offices. 4. Community--Religious aspects. 5. Judaism--History--Post-exilic period, 586 B.C.-210 A.D. I. Capes, David B.
  BR165.I87 2007
  270.1--dc22
                        2007034698

In memory of Donald H. Juel (1942–2003)
an absent but never forgotten founding member of EHCC

Contents

Introduction

This volume of essays celebrates the friendship and scholarship of two unique people, Larry W. Hurtado and Alan F. Segal. As we all have experienced at one time or another, academic life can be a solitary existence. Whether it is conducting research, grading, or negotiating the troubled, political waters inside a university, seminary, or divinity school, the reality for many inside academia is isolation. It is a rare and beautiful thing indeed to find a community of friends and scholars, diverse yet like-minded, who contribute to both the professional guilds and our own personal lives. All who have contributed essays in this tribute to Alan and Larry have benefited in many, positive ways by our associations with them.

The decision to produce a single volume dedicated to both Larry and Alan reflects our desire to honor them and to underscore the valuable friendship they share with each other and with us. This friendship was birthed in scholarly interaction and continues to grow in that same environment; yet their mutual admiration extends well beyond those bounds. The Early High Christology Club, an informal group of scholars with similar research interests, was cofounded by Alan and Larry. This club reflects and embodies a unique cocktail of scholarship, friendship, and fellowship (as well as spirits!). Many of the contributors to this volume have enjoyed the friendly association in annual gatherings during the American Academy of Religion (AAR) and Society of Biblical Literature (SBL) national conventions. All this made the current tribute not only possible but also appropriate and fitting. Finally, we as the editors, in a mischievous moment, thought it would be fun, not to say challenging, to have Larry write an essay for Alan and Alan write for Larry,

only for them to discover at the release—a true apocalyptic moment—
that they were being honored in the same book.

When several of us began to conspire about this project, we concluded that 2007 would be an appropriate time to release of this essay
collection for several reasons. First, as we pondered the inevitable separation of the AAR and the SBL in 2007, we wondered where the children
of the divorce would spend Thanksgiving (so to speak). For many the
annual pilgrimage to the AAR and SBL in November has been a high
point of the year, connecting us not only with the latest and greatest in
scholarship but also with friends whom we seldom, if ever, see outside of
professional meetings. Because of stronger ties some have with one
organization over the other, it appeared likely that the divorce would
result in the loss of full participation in both meetings. Therefore, it
seemed that the final joint meeting of SBL and AAR (San Diego 2007)
would provide the appropriate occasion to express our admiration for
Larry and Alan together.

Second, although when this book is released, neither of our honorees
will have reached the golden age of retirement; the fact is that day is
looming on the horizon. Still they will reach the age of 65 at separate
times, on separate continents, and in some ways separated from many
friends who would wish to celebrate that milestone with them. This
book anticipates and shares in that celebration.

Third, while a birthday or retirement is an important milestone, the
publication of a significant book serves as an equal, if not greater,
moment in the career of a scholar. In the case of our honorees, the recent
publications of Larry's *Lord Jesus Christ* and Alan's *Life After Death* are
monumental achievements that have situated them among scholars of
first rank in religious studies.

Finally, on a somber note, the untimely death of our colleague and
friend Donald Juel has caused us to reflect on our own mortality and to
wonder with the prophets and sages of old about the impermanence of
life. "All flesh is like grass, and all of its loveliness is like the flower of the
field" says the prophet (Isa 40:6-8). With these essays we wish to celebrate life, health and friendship while those gifts are still at hand.

The volume contains three distinct sections. The first part is composed
of a collection of essays that reconceptualize Christology and community
in early Judaism and Christianity. In the first essay **April D. DeConick**
(chapter 1) argues that the categories traditionally employed to discuss

christological developments from the New Testament era to Chalcedon (e.g., "incarnational," "adoptionistic," "subordinationist") distort our understanding of this period because they derive historically from the Nicene and post-Nicene christological debates. She offers an alternative model that takes seriously how geographically distinct communities in Jerusalem, Antioch, and Alexandria developed "peculiar christological descriptors that were attended by equally peculiar soteriologies." In another programmatic essay **Paula Fredriksen** (chapter 2) advocates that scholars retire four over-used terms: conversion, nationalism, religio licita, and monotheism. Although these terms provide easy handles for discussion, she argues that they lead to inexact generalizations and misleading anachronisms that are the inevitable result of reading ancient texts with modern sensibilities. **Richard Bauckham** (chapter 3) analyzes the frequency and significance of the title "the Most High" in Jewish literature dating from 250 B.C.E. to 150 C.E. Bauckham is convinced that progress in understanding the nature of Jewish monotheism can proceed most effectively by tracking the ways early Jewish writers speak about God. More studies of the literary and epigraphic evidence of divine titles and names found in early Jewish literature are needed. **Adela Yarbro Collins** (chapter 4) responds to one of Larry's recent books, *How on Earth Did Jesus Become a God?* She offers a new approach to this question and the development of devotion to Christ that recognizes the cultural and religious diversity that characterized the Mediterranean world. The starting point for faith in and devotion to Jesus, she thinks, begins with the confession "Jesus is the Messiah." **Pheme Perkins** (chapter 5) brings the works of Alan and Larry into conversation. She investigates the way in which resurrection and Christology are configured in Paul. Resurrection, she argues, "appears to be a factor in, but not the catalyst for" Paul's basic christological insights relating to the saving death of God's Messiah. It is "part of a linguistic complex that understands God, humanity's plight, the destiny of God's people and salvation through faith in Christ in an apocalyptic perspective." In his essay **Eldon Epp** (chapter 6) reconsiders the value of the abundance of manuscripts for NT textual criticism. The predominance of the essay is dedicated to a meticulous "visual accounting" of the manuscript data by period. In the end, Epp reasserts the significance of the early and more extensive manuscripts for text criticism.

Part two of this volume focuses the conversation on particular questions related to Christology. **Maurice Casey** (chapter 7) argues that the conflicts which characterized Jesus' ministry can be understood best by recognizing his prophetic identity. As a prophet, he attacked the central features of Jewish observance, which pit him against more "orthodox" forms of Jewish identity—Pharisees, Herodians, and scribes—and the nation's priestly leaders. In particular, Jesus' enacted prophecy against the Temple endangered his life, an eventuality Jesus likely expected. **David B. Capes** (chapter 8) focuses on Rom 9:30–10:13, a passage not typically considered as evidence for the divine preexistence and incarnation of Jesus. His exegesis shows that the proper interpretation of this passage actually assumes and reflects upon incarnational convictions. **Carey Newman** (chapter 9) tackles Paul's "Christophany" from the perspective of literary theories developed by Jacques Lacan, Peter Brooks and Marianna Torgovnick, as a "pure signifier." He offers a semiotic reading of the Christophany that reveals the significance of the powerful sign within Paul's narrative worlds. It wields power for him, Newman argues, because it is "the end." **James D. G. Dunn** (chapter 10) asks "When Did the Understanding of Jesus' Death as an Atoning Sacrifice First Emerge?" After considering the pre-Pauline formula preserved in 1 Corinthians 15:3b, Jesus' self-understanding and the early Christians' continuing participation in the temple, Dunn speculates that the view of Jesus' death as "for our sins" may well have emerged amongst Hellenist believers who were driven from Jerusalem and instructed Paul in the faith in Damascus. **Helen K. Bond** (chapter 11) reviews several attempts to explain Jesus' robe in John 19:23-24 and concludes that the likeliest explanation is that John wants his readers to make a connection between Jesus and the Jewish high priest. Contrary to general opinion, she argues, high priestly Christology is not alien to the Fourth Gospel. **Larry W. Hurtado** (chapter 12) underscores a feature present in the intra-canonical Gospels, i.e., all identify the risen, glorified Jesus with the historic figure, Jesus of Nazareth. In this essay he turns his attention to the Gospel of John (GJohn) and draws three conclusions: (a) compared with the Synoptics, the GJohn distinguishes more sharply between Jesus' pre- and post-Easter significance; (b) the GJohn emphasizes the agency of the Holy Spirit/Paraclete in guiding Christ believers into the fuller truth about Jesus; and (c) the GJohn employs distinctive language of "remembering" to describe the Paraclete's role in further, post-resurrection revelations of the earthly Jesus' transcendent significance. **Marianne Meye Thompson** (chapter 13) highlights yet another aspect of John's "high" Christology in Jesus' role as the sole "eyewitness" of God. In privileging "seeing" over "hearing," John's Jesus has not merely seen God's glory, but in being preexistent with God, has seen the Father directly thus uniquely authenticating his testimony. **Charles Gieschen** (chapter 14) examines the characterization of Jesus as the "lamb" on the throne instead of the "man" (Rev 5:5-14). According to Gieschen, by placing the "slaughtered-yet-standing" lamb on the throne, the writer includes the crucified Jesus in the worship of the one God, a strategy that both follows and expands earlier traditions on the worship of the enthroned YHWH.

Part three of this volume investigates issues regarding community and identity in early Judaism and Christianity. With his essay **John (Jack) Levison** (chapter 15) aims to recapture the textures of Ezekiel's vision of a "new creation." He contends that spiritual renewal in Ezekiel is a protracted process that cannot be isolated to the visions in chapters 36–37. Ezekiel appears to have adapted his view of renewal by the spirit as the circumstances of Israel deteriorated in the sixth century BCE. This more nuanced and comprehensive representation of "new creation" is one that demands closer attention in works on Ezekiel and Pauline pneumatology. **Jonathan Klawans** (chapter 16) highlights how little we know about the Sadducees and Zadokites and challenges both the common link between them and whether Zadokite descent was as important to ancient Jews as scholars have often imagined. He explores the connections between Sadducees and the wisdom literature and finds "precise analogues" in the Wisdom of Ben Sira to much of what we know from Josephus of Jesus' aristocratic contemporaries. **Rachel Elior** (chapter 17) focuses on the question of community in terms of sacred space (in Jerusalem and in heaven) and the communal meanings surrounding it. Her main interest is to describe how "alternative" understandings of sacred space emerge through the years within different communal settings. **Paul Foster** (chapter 18) investigates Vespasian's introduction of the *fiscus Judaicus* and its influence on Jewish and Christian identity. The pericope regarding the temple tax (Matt 17:24-27), he proposes, was preserved by the Matthean community because the strategy it suggests was useful in regard to the fiscus Judaicus. Written in the time of Domitian, the advice to comply with authorities was both subversive and politically astute in that it gave the Matthean community a certain degree of freedom in their religious practices. In his essay **Alan F. Segal** (chapter 19) acknowledges Larry Hurtado's contributions to the study of the role of religious experience in the ancient world. Generally, Segal notes, modern Jewish scholarship on Paul over the last century has given only scant attention to the nature and dynamic of religious experience as a factor in understanding the former Pharisee's faith. Most Jewish scholars have been more interested in the politics of Paul's identity than in his spiritual experience. **Troy Miller** (chapter 20) examines the Hellenistic Synagogal

Prayer 5 to assess its contribution to our understanding of the character as evidence of the nature of early Syrian Christianity. The distinctive Jewish tone of the prayer (1) controverts the claim that Gnosticism was the primary shaping force for early Christianity in Syria and (2) reveals a community that has not "parted ways" but intentionally maintains its identity within Judaism. Fittingly, we end our tribute to Larry and Alan with an essay by **John T. Fitzgerald** (chapter 21) on friendship and reconciliation. Fitzgerald considers Matthew's redaction of the sayings material in Matthew 5:21-26 in light of Hellenistic and Jewish moralists. In the ancient world—and in our own—anger and angry words pose a grave danger to the bonds of friendship that can and must be remedied by seeking reconciliation with others and with God.

———

We wish to thank Carey Newman and his staff at Baylor University Press (BUP) for publishing these essays as a tribute to Alan and Larry. Carey's initiative and experience has helped this volume take on the shape needed to appropriately represent and express our gratitude, honor, and respect for these two scholars and friends. BUP has become one of the premiere university publishing houses in the United States, much to the tireless efforts and talents of Carey, and we are glad to have partnered with them in this. We also wish to thank Mr. Ryan Wiley, whose computer expertise and willingness to serve helped us work out many of the technical problems we faced in receiving essays from all over the world.

David B. Capes
April D. DeConick
Helen K. Bond
Troy Miller

Larry W. Hurtado

Larry W. Hurtado was born December 29, 1943, in Kansas City, Missouri. He earned a B.A. in Biblical Studies (with highest honors) in 1965 from Central Bible College in Springfield, Missouri. From there he enrolled in Trinity Evangelical Divinity School (Deerfield, Illinois) and earned a M.A. in New Testament (*cum laude*) in 1967. He continued his studies at Case Western Reserve University (Cleveland, Ohio) and wrote his dissertation under the supervision of Eldon J. Epp. The title was: "Codex Washingtonianus in the Gospel of Mark: Its Textual Relationships and Scribal Characteristics." He received the Ph.D. in Religion with an emphasis in New Testament and Christian Origins in 1973.

From 1975 to 1978 Larry served as Assistant Professor of New Testament at Regent College, Vancouver, British Columbia. In 1978 he moved to Winnipeg, Manitoba, and took a post in the Department of Religion at the University of Manitoba. Ten years later (1988) he was promoted to full professor. He served there with distinction until August 1996 when he moved to Edinburgh, Scotland, and became Professor of New Testament Language, Literature and Theology at the School of Divinity (New College), University of Edinburgh. In 1997 Larry founded, and today serves as, Director of the Centre for the Study of Christian Origins. In January 2006 he became Director of Postgraduate Studies in Divinity. Larry maintains active memberships in Studiorum Novi Testamenti Societas, The Society of Biblical Literature and the British New Testament Conference.

Larry's publication record is impressive. As even a casual survey of his full curriculum vitae will show, he has a broad range of academic interests. Among his best known publications are the following: *Text-Critical Methodology and the Pre-Caesarean Text: Codex W in the Gospel of*

Mark. "Studies and Documents," (vol. 43; Grand Rapids: Eerdmans, 1981); *Mark: A Good News Commentary* (New York/San Francisco: Harper & Row, 1983); revised and published as *Mark: New International Biblical Commentary* (Peabody, Mass.: Hendrickson Publishers, 1989); *One God, One Lord: Early Christian Devotion and Ancient Jewish Monotheism* (Philadelphia: Fortress Press, 1988; British edition by SCM Press; Second edition, Edinburgh: T&T Clark, 1998; reprint edition, London: T&T Clark [Continuum], 2003); *At the Origins of Christian Worship: The Context and Character of Earliest Christian Devotion* (The 1999 Didsbury Lectures; Carlisle: Paternoster Press, 1999; US edition, Grand Rapids: Eerdmans, 2000); and *Lord Jesus Christ: Devotion to Jesus in Earliest Christianity* (Grand Rapids: Eerdmans, 2003). This last title was listed number two in the Academy of Parish Clergy Top Ten Books of 2004 and among the "Books every preacher should read in 2004" in *Preaching*. Indeed, some have described *Lord Jesus Christ* as a true magnum opus, a distillation of decades of research and discussion with friends and critics of an early, high Christology. A more popular and condensed version of this book is available in *How on Earth Did Jesus Become a God?* (Grand Rapids: Eerdmans, 2005).

Larry investigates the material evidence of early Christian culture in numerous scholarly articles. Many of his insights are available in *The Earliest Christian Artifacts: Manuscripts and Christian Origins* (Grand Rapids: Eerdmans, 2006). In 2006 he was invited by the Smithsonian to assist in coordinating an effort to commemorate the 100th anniversary of the Freer collection, biblical manuscripts of the NT and LXX dating from the third to fifth centuries CE. Larry edited the volume of published essays: *The Freer Biblical Manuscripts: Fresh Studies of an American Treasure Trove* (Decatur, Ga.: Society of Biblical Literature, 2006).

Larry has lectured all over the world. He has given invited presentations and/or lectures at the universities of Cambridge, Oxford, Durham, London, Edinburgh, Aberdeen, St. Andrews, Glasgow, Manchester, and Exeter in Britain, Ben Gurion University (Israel), Zurich (Switzerland), Otago (Dunedin, New Zealand), National University of Singapore, and at the universities of Leipzig, Halle and Gottingen in Germany. He is an internationally recognized expert in the fields of New Testament and Christian origins, the religious environment of early Christianity, the Jewish religion during the second temple period, New Testament textual criticism and early Christian manuscripts. He even dabbles in modern theology and is a regular participant in Jewish-Christian dialogue.

Alan F. Segal

Alan F. Segal is professor of Religion and Ingeborg Rennert Professor of Jewish Studies at Barnard College, Columbia University in Manhattan. When appointed he was the youngest full professor in the humanities in the university. He chaired the Department of Religion from 1981 to 1984.

Alan was born in Worcester, Massachusetts, educated at Worcester Academy, Amherst College (B.A. 1967), Brandeis University (M.A. 1969), Hebrew Union College–Jewish Institute of Religion (B.H.L. 1971) and Yale University (M.A. 1971, M.Phil. 1973, Ph.D. 1975). His studies included English Literature, Psychology, Anthropology, Comparative Religion, Judaica, Christian Origins, and Rabbinics.

Before moving to Columbia University, Alan was appointed to Princeton University for two three-year terms and to the University of Toronto with tenure. He received tenure at the University of Toronto in 1977, three years after beginning his teaching career.

Alan was also invited to the Aspen Institute for Humanistic Studies in Aspen, Colorado, and to leadership training at Aspen's Wye Plantation in Maryland. While living in Israel in 1977–1978 on a Guggenheim Fellowship, he lectured at the Hebrew University of Jerusalem, Tel Aviv University, and Bar Ilan University. He has served as guide on trips to Egypt, Turkey, and Israel and traveled extensively in Europe. He has held fellowships from the Woodrow Wilson Foundation, the American Council of Learned Societies, the National Endowment for the Humanities, The Annenberg Institute, and the J. S. Guggenheim Foundation.

In the summer of 1988 at the Jubilee celebration in Cambridge England, Alan became the first Jewish member of the *Studiorum Novi*

Testamenti Societas to address the society. He was elected into member-
ship of the American Society for the Study of Religion and the American
Theological Association. He was also the first American to be elected
president of the Canadian Society for Biblical Studies while living
abroad. He has also written many scholarly articles for journals in the
United States, Canada, and Europe.

Alan's publications include *Jews and Arabs: A Teaching Guide*
(UAHC Press); *Two Powers in Heaven: Early Rabbinic Reports about
Christianity and Gnosticism* (Studies in Judaism in Late Antiquity, vol.
25; Leiden: Brill, 1977; reprint, 2002); *Rebecca's Children: Judaism and
Christianity in the Roman World* (Cambridge, Mass: Harvard University
Press, 1986); *The Other Judaisms of Late Antiquity* (Brown Judaic
Studies, No. 127; Scholars Press, 1987). *Paul the Convert: The Apostasy
and Apostolate of Saul of Tarsus* was published by Yale University Press in
Spring 1990 and was the Editor's Choice, the main selection of the
History Book Club's summer list. It is also a selection of The Book of
the Month Club.

His latest book is *Life After Death: A History of the Afterlife in Western
Religion* (New York: Doubleday, 2004). It was a selection of the History
Book Club, the Book of the Month Club, and the Behavioral Science
Book Club. It has been featured on the Leonard Lopate Show, Talk of
the Nation, "A Show of Faith" (Houston) and was the cover article of the
Globe and Mail Book Review Supplement of Toronto.

Alan has given presentations and lectures internationally. He has
spoken at the universitites of Brandeis, Brown, Calgary, Claremont,
Chicago, Columbia, Emory, Fordham, Houston Baptist, Illinois
Wesleyan, John Hopkins, Miami, McGill, Michigan, Northwestern,
Ohio State, Pennsylvania, Princeton, Purdue, Quebec, Stanford, St.
Andrews, St. Olaf, St. Thomas, Toronto, Tulane, Washington and Lee,
Wright State, and Yale. He has traveled widely, participating in confer-
ences and congresses across the globe. He has a reputation of excellence
in scholarship. His expertise covers a wide range of fields including
Second Temple Judaism, the New Testament, Pauline Studies, Early
Christianity, Jewish-Christian relations in antiquity, Rabbinism, Early
Jewish Mysticism, and comparative relations in antiquity. He is a found-
ing member of the Society of Biblical Literature section on Early Jewish
and Christian Mysticism, a group in which he regularly contributes. He
also was a founding member and frequent contributor of the Divine
Mediators in Antiquity Group.

PART I

RECONCEPTUALIZING CHRISTOLOGY AND COMMUNITY

Chapter 1

How We Talk about Christology Matters

April D. DeConick

A miscellany of categories and descriptors has come to dominate our discussions of Christology over the years, labels and definitions we have inherited from our predecessors: "adoptionist," "high" versus "low," "subordinationist," "incarnational," and so forth.[1] While there is nothing inherently wrong with such theologically sympathetic labels, I fear that they have done more to hamper our understandings of early Christology and its development from the New Testament to Chalcedon than they have aided us. They represent post-Nicene mentalities and, in essence, have boxed us into artificial Catholic and Protestant corners.

If a Christology has been described as "adoptionist," it also has been understood to be "low" because, by the definition of "adoptionist," Jesus is not God, but is a man adopted by God at his baptism. Because it is found in our earliest gospel, Mark, we tend to see this Christology as early and connect it with "low" christological titles such as "prophet" and "Messiah." If we talk about "incarnational" Christology, we frame it as "high" because, by the definition of "incarnational," God becomes the human Jesus. Because it is discovered in our latest New Testament gospel, John, we tend to view it as a "later" development and associate it with titles like "Logos" and "Sophia."

As for the material that does not fit neatly into either of these categories—Paul's testimonies, the virgin birth stories, and angelic associations—we just do not seem to know what to do with it. So we attempt to carve out some kind of in between language to include it—"preincarnational," "on the verge of divinity," "angelomorphic," "theomorphic," "functional," "ontic," and so on. Then we have that really thorny evidence that has been nearly impossible to manage in this model— early

1

references suggesting devotion to Jesus and early passages attributing the divine Name to Jesus. This evidence has sparked heated debates about whether such a thing as "early high Christology" could have existed, a discussion entirely dependent on the works of Alan Segal and Larry Hurtado to whom this volume and this essay are dedicated.[2] This discussion has stressed the old model to the point of fracture. Furthermore, the model completely fails us in our discussions of second, third, and fourth centuries Christology. If the Ebionites, for instance, are adoptionist, then what do we do with the fact that they believed without reservation that Jesus was God? Or Arius? He is explicit in his letters that even though the Son will always be a Son subordinate to the Father and a creature like the angels, he is still God.

The construction of an alternative model is needed, I believe, to move us beyond the fractures and corners that have trapped us. Rather than making the starting point of this new model (as it was with the old) definitions sympathetic to post-Nicene theology, I think the new model must be built coherently and consistently out of the textual evidence gleaned from New Testament period literature. At the same time, it must make sense out of the later christological debates that led to Chalcedon, debates largely trying to explain the biblical evidence in terms beyond the biblical. When this is done, it is evident that certain geographical centers developed peculiar christological descriptors that were attended by equally peculiar soteriologies, so that it becomes possible to reconstruct three metaparadigms that dominated the Christian landscape for centuries (and frankly still do).

The Impulse toward Christology

What exactly happened between the years immediately following Jesus' death and the composition of John's gospel is anything but certain. What is most certain, however, is that Christianity either was initially very diverse or became so very quickly. I tend to favor the latter because the literary evidence supports the fact that most, if not all, of the varieties of early Christianity formed post-Jerusalem, including the *Gospel of Thomas* and Quelle.[3] The only references I know that might marshal some evidence for pre-Jerusalem forms of Christianity are found in Mark 9:38–41 and Acts 18:24–19:7. The first is a reference to a nondisciple casting out demons in Jesus' name and presumes an apocalyptic worldview. In Acts, we are told about Apollos, a native Jew from Alexandria, who brought a version of Christianity to Ephesus that taught a baptism for cleansing of sins, not for the reception of the Holy Spirit in the name of Jesus. This form of Christianity also seems to be known and criticized by the author of the Gospel of John. This is very interesting and may be evidence for an early variety of pre-Jerusalem Christianity. Or it may represent a very early moment in the mission of the Jerusalem Church before baptism with the Holy Spirit had developed in their praxis. The latter appears to me to be the better solution, especially given John's familiarity with it and indirect references to it in Mark 1:8, Matthew 3:11, and Luke 3:16.

So although it is certainly possible that early pre-Jerusalem forms of Christianity took root, if they did, they did not leave a big enough imprint in our texts to recover their footsteps with any certainty. It looks like the formation of Christianity in Jerusalem took place very early. Since mission work appears to have been a large part of its agenda, the Christian message and praxis were dispersed geographically and were translated under a number of other influences into the varieties we find in our literature. Paul's personal correspondences indicate that for decades following Jesus' death the church in Jerusalem was powerful enough and respected enough to be considered the authority in all matters Christian. Jerusalem controlled much of the discourse, something which Paul confronted when he broke away from Antioch and began preaching his own agenda.

When did Christianity begin? Certainly no singular point of origin or one event mobilized all others into some linear or romantic progression, as Luke would lead us to believe in Acts. A complex of impulses worked together to bring about the formation of Christianity. The christological impulse to give meaning to the troubling death of Jesus appears to me to have been one of these foundational impulses, given the allusions and interpretations of his death across the early literature. Jesus' death was very troubling for his first followers caught unawares by his crucifixion. Why had their prophetic leader been killed as a criminal? Why did God allow this to happen? What did it mean that Jesus was appearing to his closest followers even after his death? Where was Jesus now? What would happen next?

These and other similar questions captured their attention for quite some time, as we can infer from their writings. And being first-century Jews living in Palestine under the harsh imperial rule of Roman colonizers, their responses were not only shaped by their religious, cultural, social, and political expectations, but earlier expectations were remolded and older traditions given meanings in such a way that *only* made sense within their present crisis. Their communal memory had been severely threatened. The connection between their past and their present had ruptured. This situation is one that sociologists and anthropologists have shown forces communities to transform their social memory—their beliefs, expectations, and hopes—in such a way that their present crisis is explained or averted, and the crisis is avoided in the future.[4]

One of the main ways that communities succeed in this remodeling, is hermeneutically, healing the fissure seamlessly by shifting or developing explanatory schema and practices which change the original cognitive holdings of the group. But that is not all. Both baseline traditions *and* their understanding of contemporary events are reinterpreted so that the offending cognitions are dampened, expunged, or forgotten. The contemporary event becomes the foil through which the past is remembered and retold. The new hermeneutic controlled by the contemporary event becomes the lens through which traditional texts, rituals, and beliefs are now filtered and understood.

An equally significant impulse toward the creation of Christology appears to have been religious experience, a point that, thankfully, Larry Hurtado has discussed at some length in terms of social scientific studies.[5] This religious experience is evidenced in our literature by reports drifting from the first followers that they were having visions of Jesus after his death. This impulse toward reflectivity was a retrospective and hermeneutical process that resulted in christological developments almost immediately in the tradition.

The Jerusalem Paradigm

Although we may not be able to recover the very first attempts at making christological sense of Jesus, we can construct from the literature three general paradigms that resulted from this process, the earliest model having its roots in the Jerusalem church under the leadership of Jesus' brother James. This paradigm spread quickly north and east into Antioch and eastern Syria. It formed the foundation for continued speculation and the later development of the two other paradigms, as we will see later.

Resurrected from the Dead

The early Christian literature showcases this reflective and hermeneutical process well, and, in the case of explaining Jesus' postmortem appearances, reports two responses, the one typical and the other not so typical. The typical response is recorded in Luke: Jesus' followers thought they had seen his ghost (Luke 24:37). But as conventional as this explanation is, it is not the one that they embraced. Instead, they interpreted the appearances as religious experiences bolstering their Jewish beliefs and eschatological expectations—that the end of the world was at hand, just as they remembered Jesus had taught them (Mark 9:1; *Gos. Thom.* 111.1). Jesus had been resurrected from the dead as the first of the righteous heroes released from their graves (1 Cor 15:20; Matt 27:52-53).[6]

So his appearances were explained in terms of the glorified eschatological body to be raised out of the grave at the end of time. It was an angelic body, a heavenly body, a glorified, imperishable form whose flesh and blood had been transfigured into a nature and a body that was immortal. It could be described in terms of a body of gigantic portions (*Gos. Pet.* 10:39-40), unrecognizable at first (Luke 24:13-31; John 20:14), able to walk through doors (John 20:19) but still be touched (Luke 24:39; John 20:27), eat fish (Luke 24:42-43), break bread (Luke 24:30), vanish into thin air (Luke 24:31), and float up into the sky (Acts 1:9). The conventional explanation—it was his ghost—was dismissed in favor of an explanation that worked to align the community's memory of Jesus' teaching about the Eschaton's imminence and its memory of the Jewish eschatological dream with the challenge that present circumstances dictated. The proclamation that Jesus was "raised from the dead" must have entered the liturgy very early indeed (e.g., Acts 2:24; 2:32; 3:15; 4:2; 4:10; 4:33; etc.). This old Jerusalem teaching emerges in a liturgical passage in Romans 1:3-4, when Paul reminds his audience that he preaches "the gospel concerning the son, who was descended from David according to the flesh, and designated Son of God in power according to the Holy Spirit by his resurrection from the dead, Jesus Christ our Lord. . . ."

Righteous One

At the same time that this interpretation of the postmortem appearances was becoming the accepted communal hermeneutic, the standard, other questions about Jesus were being discussed among the first Christians in Jerusalem. Why had Jesus died the way he had? If Jesus had been resurrected from the dead, what did this mean about his identity while alive? It would not have taken more than seconds for these Jews to attach this event to the traditions of the righteous men of Israel, particularly the

Maccabean martyrs who died horrific deaths while maintaining their innocence and faithfulness to God and his laws. Alan Segal discusses this christological identification at length in his already classic work on resurrection.[7] These martyrs were the faithful, the holy ones, who would be rewarded by God in the last days for their righteousness by being bodily resurrected and returned to Paradise (2 Macc 7:9; 7:23; Wis. Sol. 3:1-9; 4:20–5:6; 5:15-16). As long as a righteous man lived, God had promised that he would not destroy the world, a covenant shaped by their memory of the Noah story.

It appears that one of the first Christian titles attached to Jesus was "Holy and Righteous One" (Acts 3:14; 7:52), a title which also is given to his brother James ("the Just"), the person who emerges as the leader of the Jerusalem Christians following Jesus' death. These early Christians concluded that, just as the deaths of the Maccabean martyrs had atoned for the sins of Israel (2 Macc 6:12-16; 7:38; 4 Macc 6:27-29; 17:20-22), so too the martyrdom of the Righteous One, Jesus, provided repentance to Israel and the forgiveness of its sins (Acts 5:31). The primacy of this title is certain, I think, given the fact that it is one that later Christians (like the author of Acts) no longer applied to Jesus. So the association of Jesus' death with Jewish martyrdom patterns probably was not late or original to the author of the Gospel of Mark as has been suggested.[8] It was, in fact, an association made quite early in the tradition by the followers of Jesus in Jerusalem and reused by Mark in his gospel story.

This association brought with it a complex of other traditions that Jesus' followers also used to explain the difficult fact that Jesus had suffered and died unexpectedly as a criminal condemned by Rome. Associated with these Maccabean stories were the Psalms of Lament (e.g., Pss 22, 35, 69) and the Songs of the Suffering Servant (Isa 52:13–53:12), songs about the suffering of righteous Jews at the hands of foreign oppressors or from illnesses. So they understood Jesus sufferings to have been foreshadowed in the Laments as part of God's plan. Interpretation of the Laments in this way influenced early on how the story of Jesus' passion was remembered and retold, as is frequently attested in the Synoptics, John and the *Gospel of Peter*. The Songs of the Suffering Servant appear to have been an early "proof text" used by missionaries as they tried to convert people to the faith (Acts 8:32-33; cp. Matt 8:17, 26:19; Mark 15:28; Luke 22:37; John 12:38; Rom 10:16; 1 Pet 2:22-24).

The creation of this new hermeneutic allowed the first followers of Jesus to conclude that God had meant for Jesus to suffer and die, that they had simply failed to recognize until now that this had been foretold in the scripture. Jesus was God's Righteous Holy One who had carried out God's plan to redeem Israel through his death. Because of his faithfulness, Jesus had been resurrected and exalted to God's right hand in heaven, something which also had been forecast in the Psalms (Acts 2:23-36; cf. Ps 16:8-11; 110:1; 132:11). His resurrection set into motion the events of the Eschaton. Judgment was sure to be swift.

Prophet-Like-Moses

While this new hermeneutic was developing, the first followers of Jesus were also trying to make sense of Jesus' life and teachings. There is no doubt that the early followers of Jesus understood him in prophetic terms, as a prophet in a long line of Jewish prophets who had been rejected (Acts 2:23; 3:17-18; 7:51-53; Mark 6:4-5; Matt 13:57-58; Luke 4:23-24; John 4:44). I imagine that this reflected Jesus' own self-understanding since it is multiply attested in all layers of the tradition (i.e., Matt 13:57; Mark 6:4; Luke 4:23-24; John 4:44; *Gos. Thom.* 31; cp. Acts 7:52). By applying Psalm 118:22, the "rejected stone which has become the head of the corner," they provided further scriptural proof for their burgeoning speculations (Acts 4:11; Mark 12:10-11; Matt 21:42; Luke 20:17; 1 Pet 2:4-8; *Gos. Thom.* 66).

Whether or not Jesus understood this role in terms of a prophetic Messiah or whether its identification was only made by the first Christians themselves is difficult to know. Clearly, very early in the tradition, he was identified with a particular prophet, the Messianic Prophet-Like-Moses predicted in Deuteronomy 18:15-16 (Acts 3:19-26; 7:51-53), an identification which undergirds independently the Synoptic tradition (Mark 6:4; 6:15; 8:28; Luke 4:24; 7:16; 9:8; 13:33; 24:19), the Gospel of John (1:19-27; 4:19; 4:25; 6:14), and Hebrews (3:5). The identification of Jesus with this figure gave him messianic credentials as the prophet who would come in the last day to restore God's Law to its original intent, preparing the faithful for the final Judgment.[9]

The stories of the descent of the Holy Spirit at Jesus' baptism worked to explain his "anointing" as God's prophet, a concept also supported by their investigation of scripture (cf. *Wis. Sol.* 7:27). So Mark's gospel again preserves this old tradition that Jesus was installed into his prophetic office at his baptism, possessed by God's Spirit as were all the prophets before him. This means that the oldest tradition portrays him as fully human, but his soul augmented with God's Spirit. This characterization of Jesus is sympathetic with the earliest understanding of his birth.

Matthew and Luke preserve genealogies that trace Jesus' lineage through his father Joseph, genealogies that Matthew and Luke conveniently rewrote later in light of the myths of the virgin birth (Matt 1:16; Luke 3:23). Jesus' biological connection to Joseph is an early concept retained by the Ebionites, eastern Jewish Christians who carried on in the second century many of the main aspects of the earlier Jerusalem tradition.

The identification of Jesus with the prophet-like-Moses provided another paradigm to talk about his exaltation since Jewish tradition contained a significant amount of speculation that Moses had been given an exalted position in heaven, even seated on God's throne as his viceroy and mediator (cf. *Sir* 45:1-5; *Test. Mos.* 1:15; *Ezek. Trag.* 68–69; Philo, *Vit. Mos.* 1.155-59; *Sac.* 9; *Post.* 27–31; *Gig.* 49). In the Samaritan tradition, there is an enormous amount of evidence that Moses is so exalted and glorified that he was vested with God's Name.[10] This type of Jewish speculation about the exaltation of patriarchs and their investiture with the Tetragrammaton was not uncommon. We see it also with Enoch (*1 En.* 37–71; *2 En.* 22.5-10; 24:1-3; *3 En.* 10–12) and Jacob (*Prayer of Joseph* quoted by Origen, *Comm. Joh.* 2.31).[11] It is very important to the development of Christology because, I believe, it is how Jesus' exaltation, very early in the tradition, was linked with his investiture of the Divine Name, "Jesus is Lord (=Yahweh)" (Κύριος Ἰησοῦς: i.e., 1 Cor 12:3; Phil 2:9-11; Rev 17:14; 19:16; cf. Acts 2:38).[12]

Angel of the Lord

Once the link had been forged between Jesus' exaltation and the investiture of the Divine Name, there was no turning back. His resurrected angelic body could be none other than that of the Angel of the Lord, God's principal angel and bearer of his Name and Image, and connected to his *kavod* or Glory (i.e., Matt 18:15; 18:20; 28:19; John 1:12; 2:23; 3:18; 5:43-44; 10:25; 14:10-11, 12-13; 12:28; 15:21; 17:6, 11, 26; 20:31; Acts 2:21; 2:38; 5:41; 9:16; 15:26; 21:13; Phil 2:9; James 2:7; Heb 1:4, 13:15; cf. Acts 2:17-21, 38; 9:14; 22:16; Rom 10:9–13; 1 Cor 1:2; 2 Tim 2:22).[13] With this identification, his exaltation and enthronement as God was complete since, in Jewish tradition, this particular angel is God's visible manifestation and, as such, he is either indistinguishable from God or operating with God's power and authority.[14] It was this early identification that was invoked at the initiatory rite, baptism (Acts 2:38), and healings (Acts 3:6, 16; 4:30; cf. 16:18; 19:13, 17) because it was this Name that had power.

This association also brought with it the attribution of the title "Judge," created through a pesher of images from scriptural passages. An interpretation of Zechariah 3:1-7, Isaiah 66:15-16, and Malachi 3:1-5 fostered the opinion that at the Eschaton a great angel of Yahweh would judge the world with fire. Such images related to Jesus are found embedded in several early Christian texts (Luke 12:49; *Gos. Thom.* 10; Matt 10:34; Luke 12:51; *Gos. Thom.* 16:1-3; Rev 8:5; 19:11-16; 2 Pet 3:7-14). Our earliest liturgies contained references to Jesus as the "Judge of the living and the dead" (Acts 10:40, 42). Paul knows this tradition well, referencing to Jesus as the eschatological Judge (whom he does not know as the "Son of Man") in his letters (Rom 2:16; 14:10; 1 Cor 4:5; 11:32). This line of thinking is born out in the *Pseudo-Clementine* literature associated with the Ebionites. Jesus is appointed by God as the greatest of the archangels, the "god of princes, who is Judge of all" (*Ps.-Clem. Rec.* 2.42).

Possession Christology

Looked at collectively, this evidence means that the first followers of Jesus developed within the first decade of Christianity what can be called "Possession Christology," the schema that understands Jesus to have been born a complete human being to human parents. Mary and Joseph are his biological parents—just as Matthew's and Luke's genealogies relate—and is preserved by a branch of the Ebionites in the second century (Eus., *Eccl. Hist.* 3.27; 6.17; Hipp., *Ref.* 7.22; Epiph., *Pan.* 30.2.2; 34.6). At his baptism, the Holy Spirit descends, taking up residence in him (εἰς: Mark 1:10), possessing him.

Jesus is a full human being, body and soul, possessed by the Holy Spirit, sometimes God's Wisdom. This anthropology is quite natural in the ancient world where human beings were constantly bombarded with spirits, mostly demonic, attempting to possess their souls and corrupt their bodies. Guardian or holy spirits were a blessing, since they aided people from otherwise succumbing to demonic invasion.

As God's Prophet, Jesus called the people to repentance, taught people how to interpret correctly and follow the Laws so that they could live righteously (as he did) and be prepared to stand before God at the Judgment. Ultimately, he was rejected and suffered a horrific death as foretold in the scripture, a death that atoned for the past sins of Israel. Immediately before his death, the Holy Spirit left him. But because of his righteousness and faithfulness, God resurrected him from the dead, transforming his physical body into an angelic body and exalting him to

God's right hand as the principal angel of Yahweh, vested with the powerful Name and enthroned as God. In this capacity, he will return to Judge the living and the dead. As a result the doctrine of the Second Coming was born, as well as the divinization of Jesus. Jesus was not divine during his lifetime, but a human being possessed by the Holy Spirit, exalted to divinity after his death.

A Behaviorial Soteriology

This christological pattern was developed by the Jerusalem Christians within ten years after Jesus' death, and it had ramifications for ritual performance and soteriological beliefs. Baptism, the initiatory ritual, was performed by invoking the Name, cleansing the initiate from past sins so that the soul could receive the Holy Spirit (Acts 2:38-42). There is evidence that the anointing ceremony was a later addition to the original baptism ceremony, creating a ceremony apart from baptism for the reception of the Holy Spirit (Acts 8:14-17). The later Ebionites preserve this understanding of baptism and so develop daily baths as a means to cleanse themselves from postbaptismal sin. The cleanliness of the soul was of utmost importance because a purified soul was a prerequisite for the indwelling of the Holy Spirit. The Spirit aided the person—just as it did Jesus—to live righteously in imitation of Jesus and his teachings, so that, after death, the person would be resurrected as a glorious immortal being, like Jesus. The human being attains immortality by imitating a divine being, conforming his or her soul (with the help of the Spirit's indwelling) to the sacred template.

This emphasis on perfecting oneself through righteous living is the undercurrent sustaining soteriological claims in the Gospel of Matthew (cf. 5:48), as well as the thesis of the epistle of James (1:4) and the older sources retained by the authors of the *Didache* (1–6) and the *Epistle of Barnabas* (18–21). Although it is conventional to date James to the beginning of the second century—because it is not mentioned by our earliest church fathers—this is unreasonable given the letters' content, which promotes the old Jerusalem soteriological pattern of righteous life. The epistle's content fits into the religious landscape of the early Jerusalem church, concerned about Paul's rebellious agenda which promoted that "faith," rather than one's responsible and moral actions, leads to "righteousness" and justification (Jas 2:14-26). In my view, a date no later than 60 C.E. is justifiable for the composition of James's epistle.

As for other ritual activities, apparently the first performances of the Lord's Supper—the thanksgiving meal or Eucharist—were joyous occasions, celebrating the imminent return of Jesus and anticipating the heavenly Messianic banquet. This performance of the meal is preserved in Mark 14:25 and Matthew 26:29 ("Truly, I tell you, I will never again drink of the fruit of the vine until the day when I drink it new in the Kingdom of God"), as well as the old formulae in *Didache* 9 ("Maranatha"; cf. 1 Cor 16:22; Rev 22:20). The meal may also have had a covenantal aspect, affirming the Christians as the New Israel through the death of the Righteous One, Jesus (Luke 22:14-18). Paul, too, is aware of this performance-type since he tells us that every time the eucharist is celebrated, Christians proclaim the death of the Lord "until he comes" and presents the "cup" as the "new covenant" (1 Cor 11:25–26). He is uncomfortable, in fact, with the festive party nature of the eucharist meal as the Corinthians were celebrating it, and works to turn its performance into more of a wake, during which Jesus is mourned, than a banquet anticipating his return (1 Cor 11:17-22).

The Antiochean Paradigm

If Jesus had been exalted to the right hand of God as the principal Angel of Yahweh, what did this suggest about the appearances of this angel in scriptural stories that took place prior to Jesus' birth? This logical question must have crossed the minds of the early Christians who were familiar with the Jerusalem Paradigm. To judge exactly when the first Christians raised this perplexing question is difficult, but certainly the answer was discussed in literature associated with Antioch. The answer was known also by Paul, who was at one time a primary leader and missionary for the Antiochean Church. So I think it safe to say that this paradigm was developed and promulgated by Antiochean Christians in western Syria and eventually taken up by Paul and the communities in Asia Minor and Greece before becoming the dominant meta-paradigm in Rome and the West.

Born of Woman (or Virgin)

If the first Christians believed that Jesus had been elevated to the status of God's Namesake Angel, then passages about this Angel in the Jewish scripture (cf. Gen 16:7; 22:15; Exod 3:2-14; 23:20-21) must have been intriguing, indeed! The Antiochean Christians must have reasoned, if

Jesus had been exalted at his death, becoming the Angel of Yahweh, who was the Angel of Yahweh before Jesus was born? The only logical solution would have been "Jesus." Since the scriptures clearly related that the Angel existed before Jesus' earthly advent, the Antiochean Christians concluded that this Angel must have descended from heaven and somehow embodied Jesus at Jesus' conception or birth.

We find in Paul's letters the old Antiochean hymnal fragments relating that Jesus had been "in the form of God" and "did not count equality with God a thing to be grasped," a likely reference to an angel, probably the Angel of the Name. This divine being "empties" himself and is "born in the likeness of men" (Phil 2:5-7). Jesus is the "image of the invisible God, the first-born of creation" (Col 1:15). In Jesus, "the fullness of God was pleased to dwell" (Col 1:19). The references to "form" and "image" and "first-born of creation" all carry angelomorphic connotations.[15] Paul himself relates that "God sent forth his son" and he was "born of woman" (Gal 4:4), a concept mentioned elsewhere in his letters as well (Rom 8:3). Paul's use of the word "son" in this regard probably reflects the association between angels and sonship in Judaism.[16] Although this incremental shift occurred in Antiochean Christianity prior to Paul, it appears to have had an enormous impact on early Christian traditions after Paul and developed in fascinating directions.

In this regard, we might recall the fragment from the *Gospel of the Hebrews*. It relates that the Father summoned the angel Michael and gave to him the Power called Christ. Michael descended into the world and was "called Mary." So Christ was in her womb "seven months" (Cyril of Jerusalem, *Discourse on Mary Theotokos* 12a). The tradition as it stands appears to be bowdlerized, altered in its transmission so that it has become nonsensical. But what might it have been? A teaching that the angel Christ descended into Mary's womb at the time of quickening with the assistance of Michael? It is noteworthy that the ancients believed that angels helped deliver the child's soul into the womb at the time of quickening or before (cf. Clem. Alex., *Ecl.* 50.1–3; Maim., *Guide* II 6, Munk 2, 17ab; Hildegard of Bingen, *Scivias* illuminations). So there appears to be an allusion to this belief in the Hebrew fragments. This teaching, in fact, aligns with what we know of some Ebionites who taught that Christ "was not begotten of God the Father, but created as one of the archangels" and that "he rules over the angels and all the creatures of the Almighty" (Epiph., *Pan.* 30.16.4–5). This branch of the Ebionites thought that Jesus was "born of a virgin and the Holy Spirit" (but denied his preexistence as "Logos" or "Sophia"; see Eus., *Eccl. Hist.* 3.27). This type of teaching appears to have been possible because "spirits" and "angels" functioned sometimes as equivalents in Jewish and Christian thought, as well as an Angel as the Spirit.[17] The same appears to be the case for the word Power (*Dynamis*).[18] This ability to understand "spirit" as "angel," who like a demon can possess a human being, is likely the result of a synthesis between Jewish angelology and ancient beliefs about spirit or demon possession. The angel, since it could be described as a spirit, took on activities, such as possession, of spirits.

The Ebionites further developed this idea by teaching that this angel's advent as Jesus was not unique, but one in a long line of prophets beginning with Adam.[19] The Ebionites taught, according to Epiphanius, that the son acquired a Power from God at the time he "put on Adam," as well as the subsequent bodies of the patriarchs (Epiph., *Pan.* 34.6). This teaching appears to be known in Syria since the language of cyclic embodiment is also found in the Syriac *Acts of Thomas*. The Christians argue here that Christ, the Great Power, put on the first man (cf. Symmachians in Marius Victorinus, *ep. ad Gal.* 1.15; *Ps.-Clem. Rec.* 1.28.4).

It appears to me that this christological shift in Christian Judaism to possession in the womb was forced by hermeneutics. If the Angel of Yahweh existed before Jesus' advent, then this Angel who was God's "equal" in terms of bearing his Name and functioning as his manifestation on earth, must have descended and been embodied in the human Jesus. The human Jesus, a complete man with body and soul, was possessed by this Angel at the moment of his conception or quickening.

The virgin birth stories, in fact, appear to be similar (but not identical) adaptations of this story, that a divine being possesed a fetus in the womb. The story of womb-possession is very prominent in Luke's gospel, which parallels John the Baptist's conception to Jesus'. Of the former's conception, Luke relates "he will be filled with the Holy Spirit, even from his mother's womb" (Luke 1:15; πνεύματος ἁγίου πλη‑σθήσεται ἔτι ἐκ κοιλίας μητρὸς αὐτοῦ). When the process of Jesus' conception is explained by the angel Gabriel, it is in these words: "The Holy Spirit will come upon you, and the power of the Most High will overshadow you; therefore the child to be born will be called holy, the Son of God" (Luke 1:35; πνεῦμα ἅγιον ἐπελεύσεται ἐπὶ σὲ καὶ δύναμις ὑψίστου ἐπισκιάσει σοι· διὸ καὶ τὸ γεννώμενον ἅγιον κληθήσεται υἱὸς θεοῦ). If we reread Jeremiah 1:5—"Before I formed you in the womb, I knew you, and before you were born I consecrated you; I appointed you a prophet to the nations"—and Isaiah 49:1—"The Lord called me from the womb, from the body of my mother he named my name"—and even Galatians 1:15—"when he who had set me apart before I was born"—we see in the Lukan virgin birth narrative an attempt to understand Jesus' birth in light of his prophetic career, that in him the Spirit was indwelling even in the womb, that the descent of the divine angel or spirit occurred long before his baptism, even as early as his conception because he was God's Prophet chosen before his birth.

In the Gospel of Matthew the relationship of Jesus to the Holy Spirit is framed in terms of agency with the prominence of the preposition ἐκ. Mary is found "having [a fetus] in her womb *from* the Holy Spirit" (Matt 1:18; ἐν γαστρὶ ἔχουσα ἐκ πνεύματος ἁγίου). This appears to me to be yet another incremental shift in this christological pattern, moving the theology from spirit possession at conception to divine parentage, a shift that may have made more sense to Hellenistic audiences familiar with stories of gods siring heroes. Since the embodiment of the Spirit has occurred at conception, it is significant that both Matthew and Luke independently shift the Markan baptism account of possession of the Spirit "in" Jesus (εἰς: Mark 1:10), to "upon" (ἐπ': Matt 3:16; Luke 3:22).

The person who has preserved the paradigm shift in its entirety, incorporating both the Angel of Yahweh traditions and the virgin birth stories, is the early second century Roman teacher, Justin Martyr. In his writings, we find the survival of the teaching that the manifestations of the Angel of Yahweh according to the scriptures were essentially manifestations of Jesus before his birth.[20] The son is the Angel of Yahweh who speaks from the burning bush, visits with Abraham, wrestles with Jacob (Justin Martyr, *Dial. Trypho* 59.1; 56.1-23; 58.4-13). He appears to Joshua as a warrior angel (62.5). Justin says with conviction, "Therefore, neither Abraham, nor Isaac, nor Jacob, nor any man saw the Father . . . but only him who, according to his [God's] will, is both God, his son, and angel, from the fact that he ministers to his purpose. Whom he also has willed to be born through the virgin, and who once became fire for that conversation with Moses in the bush" (Justin Martyr, *Dial. Trypho* 127.4). The great Angel of Yahweh embodied the man Jesus, born from a virgin womb.

Embodiment Christology

Hermeneutics appears to have forced a shift in the Jerusalem paradigm, particularly in terms of Jesus' origin as a divine being. If he were Yahweh's angel upon exaltation at his resurrection, then he must have preexisted as this angel whose activities are recounted in the scripture. Already at his conception or quickening, he embodied the angel or spirit. So he was a complete human being with his own body and soul that functioned as a container or vessel for the resident angel or spirit.

The rest of the Jerusalem paradigm remains intact, however. At Jesus' death, he returns to heaven and is (re)installed. His exaltation at his resurrection to the Name above all names continues to reverberate in this literature (Rom 1:3-4; Phil 2:10-11; cf. 1 Cor 15:20-22; Phil 3:20-21). As this great angel, he will be revealed in the heavens, descending with "a cry of command, with the archangel's call, and with the sound of the trumpet of God" (1 Thess 4:16). He will come "with his mighty angels in flaming fire, inflicting vengeance upon those who do not know God and upon those who do not obey the gospel of our Lord Jesus" (2 Thess 1:7-8). He will usher in God's Kingdom after he destroys his enemies (1 Cor 15:24-28). He will sit in the Judgment seat and mete out rewards and punishments (1 Cor 8:6). This tradition is carried on in Ebionism. According to Epiphanius, the Ebionites taught that Christ was "created like one of the archangels" and was appointed by God to rule over the future age (Epiph., *Pan.* 30.16.2-4).

A Sacrificial Soteriology

The Jerusalem paradigm taught that Jesus' transformation into a glorified, divine being happened as the result of his righteous actions and piety, which brought about the indwelling of the Holy Spirit and his gradual perfecting. Thus at death, God raised him and exalted him, giving him a transformed body and angelic role. True, this idea was Jewish apocalypticism gone wild, but it made perfect sense given the environs and conditions. It also meant that anyone who imitated Jesus, particularly in terms of righteousness and piety, could expect a similar gradual transformation and eventual resurrection.

This soteriology worked until Jesus was considered to be born already special, already embodying an angel or spirit, a condition the rest of humanity could not imitate. Jesus did not work for his divinity, but had it from the womb of Mary. This meant that the road to salvation had to shift as well. It had to engage the power of the divine Jesus rather than that of the human, promising redemption because of a divine action rather than a human one. This shift occurred on several levels, but the most prominent was the full engagement with martyrological interpretations of Jesus' death in terms of atonement, particularly as Mark relates it in his gospel. The Christians developed the Jerusalem Christology in this regard, which as we saw earlier, explained Jesus' death in terms of patterns of the Jewish martyrs, patterns which included beliefs about the efficacy of their deaths for sin atonement, especially for Israel's disobedience and sins against the Torah.

This shift, however, does not mean that the behavioral soteriology from the Jerusalem paradigm vanished or was replaced by the divine redemptive action. What happened was a fusion of the two soteriologies so that the sacrificial emerged dominant while the behavioral receded to the background. In many ways, this shift disabled the behavioral—if a divine action redeemed the human being, then what was the benefit of good behavior? Paul faces and tries to explain this very problem in Romans 12–13, where good behavior is the *outcome* of a person's redemption and transformation, rather than the *cause*.

The earliest development of this shift can be traced in Paul's letters, particularly in Romans (e.g.., 3:23-24; 4:24-25; 6:23) where he assumes that God operates as a great judge and lawmaker. The penalty for breaking God's laws is death. Since all humans, Jews and Gentiles alike, have broken his laws, everyone is guilty in God's courtroom. Everyone receives the death penalty. The solution Paul teaches is the heavenly righteous man Jesus, who did not sin and did not deserve the death penalty. But he dies anyway. His undeserved death provides vicarious payment for everyone else's death sentence. This efficacious atonement is not something earned by deeds or piety, but rather a benevolent act accomplished by Jesus. I might mention that this act was understood in cosmic terms, as part of God's plan at the end of time to defeat Satan and his army of angels that have been battling against the archangels since the beginning of time. The defeat of these powers began when they crucified Jesus (1 Cor 2:6-7; Col 2:15; cf. 1 Cor 15:23-28).

The believer reaped the benefits of Jesus' death through participation in ritual activities. According to Paul, the initiate actually was baptized into Jesus' death (Rom 6:1-11; cf. Col 2:12-15). This shift in the meaning of baptism developed the older form of baptism as it had been earlier performed by those Christian Jews from the Jerusalem Church by insisting that one was united with Christ, that the spirit one received was not any holy spirit, but Jesus' own spirit (Gal 2:20; 4:19; 1 Cor 1:12-13; 2 Cor 4:11; Phil 2:5; Rom 8:29). Because the person possesses Jesus' spirit, the person has become Jesus, even now participating in his death and atonement (Phil 3:1-21; Rom 8:15-21). Instead of the convert paying the death penalty for his own sins, he shares Jesus' death. So through Jesus' death, the penalty for the convert's sins was paid (2 Cor 5:16-21; 1 Cor 6:20; 15:2). The person has been resurrected provisionally by partaking in Jesus' resurrection, although the full glory of the resurrected body could only be wholly achieved at the eschaton (2 Cor 3:18; Phil 3:12, 20-21). In this way, the believer was experiencing a bodily transformation as the old mortal body of sin was being replaced (Rom 12:1-2).

Given this interpretative trajectory, the meaning of the Eucharist also had to shift. The Jerusalem model understood it to be a meal that they were sharing with the exalted Jesus who was called to "come" (e.g, 1 Cor 16:22, *maranatha*) and sit at their table to sup with them. The joyous meal was anticipatory of the great Messianic banquet, which they believed would be hosted by Jesus at the Eschaton. For Paul, whose writings reveal another interpretation, the Eucharist is about ingesting the sacrificed body of Jesus (1 Cor 10:1-5, 16-17) and a memorial service for his death (1 Cor 11:23-26). The meal became a reperformance of his death, a sacrificial meal to which all were invited. The believer, by ingesting his sacrificed body, repeatedly and regularly shares in that death and its atoning benefits. as Paul writes, "Consider the people of Israel. Are not those who eat the sacrifices partners in the altar?" (1 Cor 10:18).

The Alexandrian Paradigm

This paradigm is preserved by the author of the Gospel of John, and it becomes the dominant hermeneutic in Alexandria by the mid-second century. At about the same time, a version of this paradigm also emerges in east Syrian literature like the Gospel of Thomas. Consequently, it is not at all clear where it originated. Was it conceived in Syria and transported to Alexandria or vice versa? One of the difficulties I face in answering this question hinges on the fact that the geographical location of the Gospel of John has never been worked out to my satisfaction. Its traditional location as a gospel written in Ephesus appears to be based on very slim evidence interpreted from Acts 19:1-7, that the followers of John the Baptist were present in Ephesus and were converted to Christianity there. This is connected with the Johannine polemic against John the Baptist (John 1:6-8; 1:19–34; 3:22-36; 5:36) and the conversion of many of the Baptist's believers (10:40-42). Although this makes some sense, is it not equally likely (based on the same argument) that the Gospel of John could have been written in Alexandria? How did the Christian Baptists come to be in Ephesus? A Jew named Apollos, a native of Alexandria, had received instruction about Jesus based on scriptures, while knowing only the baptism of John. He moved to Ephesus (Acts 18:24) where he spoke openly (and with some success) in the synagogue before the arrival of Priscilla and Aquila (Acts 18:25-28). So the Christian Baptists in Ephesus may have originated out of Apollos's mission from Alexandria, which could place the authorship of John in Alexandria rather than Ephesus.

Pretemporal Jesus

Retrospective thinking about Jesus is at its height in this paradigm. Jesus is not a great Angel or a spirit who descends and embodies a human being in the womb. His preexistence is moved a step back, to a time *before* creation. He is God's Logos, his Reason. He is with God before the world is created (John 1:1-2) and is involved in creating the world before he *becomes flesh* (σὰρξ ἐγένετο) (John 1:3; 1:14). This language (ἐν σαρκί) is also present in the Gospel of Thomas (*Gos. Thom.* 28: P.Oxy. 1.13).

Since the work of J. Rendel Harris and Rudolph Bultmann, there has been much discussion about how this preexistent figure can have its roots in Sophianology.[21] Although there are many uncanny parallels between these traditions, it remains to explain the identification of the Logos with God who existed from the beginning.[22] As a result, Jarl Fossum has offered an alternative explanation, one that makes an enormous amount of sense given the development of the three paradigms I am suggesting. He shows us that the Johannine author could be relying on traditions about the Angel of Yahweh who is indistinguishable from the Tetragrammaton. The Name of God in Jewish traditions, Fossum demonstrates, was understood to be a hypostasis of God's eternal nature, and, thus, equivalent to him. It helped with creating the world and was present in the Angel of Yahweh.[23] If Fossum is correct (and I think he is), then what we are seeing in this paradigm is retrospective thinking about the embodiment model. Jesus' identification with the Angel of Yahweh is pushed back pretemporally, from preexistent to precosmogonic.

Another aspect of Jesus' pretemporality must be mentioned. The Logos' cohabitation with God means that he alone "saw" God (John 1:18; 6:46; cf. 5:37). This exclusive vision has made the Logos extraordinarily special. He not only is the only one who truly knows the Father because he is the only one who has seen the Father, but he also participates in and is God (John 1:1). Once the Logos has descended from heaven (John 3:13, 31-32; 7:29; 8:23; cf. 17:5) and "tabernacled" with us, he, as Jesus, can claim that "the Father and I are one" (John 10:30) and "believe me that I am in the Father and the Father in me" (John 14:11). Jesus has God's Name and, thus, is one with God (John 17:11).

This Christology appears to me to result from the fusion of traditional Jewish thinking about the Angel of Yahweh, the Name, and Hellenistic cosmogony, particularly the origin of the rational aspect of the human being. The synthesis of these traditions results in the Johannine portrayal of the pretemporal Jesus that embraces elements from the previously independent traditions: he is God's Reason and at the same time he is the Angel of Yahweh. The Logos and Angel traditions conflate in such a way that the Reason of God takes on the characteristics of the Angel of Yahweh.[24]

Ensoulment Christology

Is the descent of the Logos into the flesh not equivalent to the descent of the Angel or Spirit into the human Jesus as was the case in the embodiment paradigm? The short answer is, "No." His descent is not described in terms of a divine being assuming a full human being, a person with his own body and soul. His descent is described in very different terms, that is, as the descent of the Reason of God into human flesh, so that the Logos becomes a human being. This means that God's *psyche* descends into the flesh and functions as the soul of Jesus. The divine aspect is not an appendage to Jesus' soul; it is Jesus' soul! One of the reasons for the fusion of Logos language with Angel of Yahweh traditions must be due to the fact that the paradigm is using the christological platform that it has received from the embodiment model while embracing a different anthropological argument—that Jesus' soul was God's Logos. The word "Logos" was appropriate because it would have been understood by the Hellenistic populace to describe a substitute *psyche*. God's Reason is ensouled in Jesus.

What is the result of his descent? Literally, it means God is walking around on earth as a human being. It is fascinating to me how the Johannine author preserves a play on this tradition by presenting us with a Jesus whose body is the New Temple in which God's presence dwells.[25] He is the Glory (δόξα or כבוד)—God's manifestation, visible in his person (John 1:14), his signs and wonders (John 2:11; 11:40; 17:4) and his crucifixion (John 12:23, 28; 13:32; 17:1, 5). In 1:14, the claim is made, "We have seen his Glory, the Glory of the Only Begotten from the Father." The background of this vision may be found in Moses' vision of the Glory in Exodus 33:18–34:8.[26] But because this is an ensoulment paradigm, the *kavod* is made to assert characteristics of Reason, characteristics that would otherwise be foreign to its tradition, that is, it is made to function as Jesus' soul. It is personalized, so that a particular person becomes the earthly visible manifestation of the hidden God (John 1:18). Remarkably, this paradigm says that God has been manifested in history.

Transmutative Soteriology

Because the Christology is such that God and flesh meet, forming an extraordinary sacred human being, the goal of this paradigm is for all humans to experience the same transmutation, a perfecting that alters their humanity in the same way that it had altered Jesus'. This process is truly a process of personal transmutation and *theosis*; as many of the Eastern Church Fathers grasped, "God became man so that man can become God."

How did the devotee achieve this transmutation? Largely, it is accomplished through the sacraments, although the Gospel of Thomas also allows for contemplative activity that leads to transforming visionary experiences.[27] Initially, it begins through baptism when one is "reborn of water and spirit" (John 3:5). The baptism is a rebirth; the person's soul literally is born anew. Those who developed this interpretation of baptism must have operated within the thought-world of middle Platonism, seemingly arguing that their postbaptismal souls were no longer in the degraded state associated with their first birth (John 3:4). This appears to have been achieved by the purificative effects of the water ritual, as well as the infusion of the soul at the same time with a holy spirit (John 3:5-8). It is fascinating how the language of baptism in John is a language of birth, not of the flesh, but of the spirit (John 3:6). The water is "living water" that wells up to "eternal life" (John 4:7-15). The result is a new creation, a transmutation of person.

This transmutation is maintained through the devotee's participation in the Eucharist. In John 6, the Johannine author is not speaking about cannibalism, eating the flesh and drinking the blood of the historical Jesus. Rather the devotees consume a sacred or divinized body, the extraordinary body of God on earth. His body is "the bread of life," which has "come down from heaven" (John 6:35, 41, 51). This heavenly bread is his "flesh," and if the devotee consumes it, he or she will live forever (John 6:51). This is expanded to include Jesus' blood that must be drunk by the faithful in order to have life everlasting (John 6:53-55). The incorporation of the sacred body worked like divine medicine, immortalizing the person over time. The devotee literally has incorporated Jesus, and the result is his or her transmutation or immortalization (John 6:56).

This mystical understanding of the Eucharist can be characterized in the catchphrase "at-one-ment" in contrast with the sacrificial model of "atonement." The devotee incorporates the sacred elements to imitate the ensoulment of Jesus, since at the moment of consumption a unification between God and the human is experienced. When this happens regularly, a process of transmutation is undergone, and eventually *theosis* will be achieved.

Results

Paradigms are only successful if they have heuristic value. The value of the model I have set in place here is that it neither depends upon theologically sympathetic labels nor does it serve to justify or condemn them. The model recognizes the incremental development of traditions fostered by the communal memory of living religious groups whose experiences influence their preservation. At all times, the model operates within the parameters of Second Temple Judaism and requires no mutation of thought or practice—no unique moment—to explain *how* Christology quickly developed and how, almost immediately, Jesus became God.

This model helps expose the fact that the Christians within the first few years following Jesus' death had exalted him and identified him with Yahweh's Angel. Because he had Yahweh's Name and Power, this identification ultimately allowed for his worship. The relatively quick growth of three different christological Paradigms appears to result from the intersection of hermeneutics and experience, forcing Christians in various locales to update their collective memories, to make present sense of their receding past and burgeoning future.

Last, the model is very useful as a device to examine later christological developments and understand the conflicts involved. In the case of Arius, for instance, it shows us a man influenced by two of the paradigms—the old Jerusalem and the Alexandrian. Although he is an Egyptian priest in the Alexandrian diocese, Arius himself implies that Lucian of Antioch was his teacher as well as Eusebius of Nicomedia (*ep. ad. Euseb. Nicom.* 5; cf. Alexander, *ep. ad. Alex.* 35–36; Philostorgius, *hist. eccl.* 1), who, in turn, was a pupil of Paul of Samosata, a Dynamic Monarchianist familiar with the Jerusalem Paradigm. In fact, this old

Paradigm formed the basis of Paul of Samosata's Christology. Jesus was understood by him to be a human being (Eusebius, *hist. eccl.* 7.27.2). The divine element that came to dwell within the righteous man Jesus was the impersonal Logos, God's rational power (Epiphanius, *haer.* 65.1.5-8). This possession and eventual union of God's Logos with Jesus' soul came about because Jesus' human will desired it. The more obedient Jesus was to God's commandments, the more he conformed himself with God's Logos until he achieved complete union with it and attained full divine status. In this way, the morally perfected man was *homoousios* with the Father (Athanasius, *de. syn.* 45; Hilary, *de. syn.* 81; Basil, *ep.* 52.1). Jesus' perfecting provided the template for all believers to use. If they conformed their wills to God's, following Jesus' example, they would become divine themselves.

Now Arius's understanding of Christology is based on this teaching, but it has distinct differences due to the fact that Arius was familiar also with the Alexandrian Paradigm and its high regard for the pretemporal Son. About this Son, Arius taught that he was a "creature" (κτίσμα or ποίημα) whom God made from nothing (Arius, *ep. ad. Euseb. Nicom.* 4–5). He was an entity separate from God's Logos and Wisdom, and distinct from the Father's *hypostasis* (Arius, *ep. ad. Alex.* 4). This explanation is probably an allusion, couched in philosophical garb, to the old Jerusalem teaching that Jesus was the Angel of Yahweh. Given this, it should not surprise us that an Arian at a conference admitted that the Son might have fallen as the angel Satan did (Alexander, *ep. en cyc.* 10).

Arius's genius, in my mind, is that he welded Paul of Samosata's teaching about the moral development of Jesus into the Alexandrian Paradigm. Thus, it is the pretemporal Son who conforms his own will or Logos to that of the Father's, perfecting himself before time. This welding brought with it also the behavioral soteriology of the Jerusalem Paradigm. Believers, Arius thought, could conform to God's will, just as the Son had done, and progressively over their lifetimes become divine themselves.

As for the human Jesus, Arius preferred the Alexandrian Paradigm, insisting that the perfected spiritual Son who had conformed himself to the Logos, took the place of Jesus' soul. Because the Son as the Logos was a creature, he was susceptible to change. So Jesus could be ignorant at times, grow in wisdom, and need help with temptation.

History has unfairly remembered Arius as a heretic priest who thought Jesus was a demigod. As we have seen, this is a far cry from the truth. For Arius, Jesus was God, but became so through a complex process of conformation of his will, a conformation that we can imitate. As such, Arius's Christology and Soteriology are closer to earlier Christian expressions than those of his orthodox contemporaries like Alexander and Athanasius, who rely completely on the later Alexandrian Paradigm. My *doktorvater* once told me that if I wanted to learn about the earliest forms of Christianity, I should study the heretics, because many of their views represent early Jewish thinking that, within this developing Christian landscape, has grown out-dated or become a liability, views that many second century Christians were replacing with what they considered to be fresher perspectives from the Gentile population. With Arius, this appears to be the case. It may also be true for Nestorius who resurrected certain aspects of the old Jerusalem Paradigm himself. Perhaps really to understand the earliest forms of Christianity, it is necessary to step away momentarily from our orthodox post-Nicene heritage and grasp the forbidden fruit.

Chapter 2

Mandatory Retirement
Ideas in the Study of Christian Origins
Whose Time Has Come to Go

Paula Fredriksen

I would like to propose the speedy retirement of four much-used terms that routinely appear in scholarship on Christian origins.[1] These terms serve scholars of ancient Christianity both as a kind of academic short-hand and as interpretive concepts. Their use affects historical reconstruction in similar ways. They lead us down the path of anachronism and abstraction, ultimately obscuring the lives and concerns of the ancient people whom we seek to understand. In exploring how this is so, I will, of course, be offering my own descriptions of religious life in the ancient Mediterranean. I constructed these descriptions in the course of think-ing through what description itself is like once we try to avoid using these terms. This effort was inspired in part by my realization that con-tinuing to think in these terms was making it progressively harder to work with what primary evidence we have. In brief, I must confess openly what I have just implied: every error of judgment, every distortion of the historical environment, every inadvertent anachronism that I am about to sketch, I have gone into print with myself.

I begin by offering some ideas to hold in mind while I present my arguments. These are generalizations that I find helpful when thinking about and looking at the ancient Mediterranean and tracking the interre-lations of its two main populations, gods and humans. In antiquity:

- Gods run in the blood.
- Cult is an ethnic designation; ethnicity is a cultic designation.
- Cult makes gods happy.
- Unhappy gods make for unhappy humans.

With these ideas in mind, I come to my first term: "conversion." In the field of New Testament studies, the question whether this term can properly be applied to the apostle Paul has especially been debated. Earlier scholarship, which had seen the first generation of the Christian movement as a community already distinct (indeed, self-consciously distinct) from Judaism, had no problem with this term or with its application to Paul: after all, Paul had rejected Judaism in favor of Christianity, and he had condemned his former allegiance as servitude to the "works of the Law." This scholarly understanding both of Paul the convert and of the term "conversion" cohered easily with a classic definition, presented in A. D. Nock's great study, which held that conversion is "a deliberate turning . . . which implies that a great change is involved, that the old was wrong and the new is right."[2]

A generation later, Krister Stendahl, among others, urged that scholars adopt the term that Paul himself had used to describe his shift of allegiance toward the ἐκκλησία: not "conversion," but "call."[3] Seeing Paul's transformation as his call to be an apostle to the Gentiles, argued the advocates of this position, had a double benefit. It was both true to Paul and true to Paul's historical context. Besides the advantage of this term's being anchored in Paul's own text (Gal 1:15, θεός . . . καλέσας), "call" did not suggest, as "conversion" did, the idea of a rupture with Judaism. Rather, it places Paul and his idea of himself within a trajectory of Israel's continuing prophetic role vis-à-vis the nations. In other words, "call" had the virtue of implying or presupposing no sharp contrast between the native religion of Paul, of the first apostles, and of the makeup of the movement that they dedicated themselves to spreading in the Diaspora. "Conversion" too readily facilitated imagining the Jesus movement circa 34 as already something other than Judaism; "call" more readily allowed imagining the Jesus movement as a *type* of Judaism.

Against this view, indeed perhaps in response to it, other scholars more recently have brought arguments urging that "convert," after all, be kept. These scholars emphasize the benefits of using modern methodologies (whether derived from social science or psychology or cultural anthropology) when reconstructing ancient figures. Thus, though they do regard earliest Christianity as a species of late Second Temple Judaism, they emphasize the contrast—sociologically or psychologically or behaviorally—between Paul as a persecuting outsider and Paul as a committed, indeed, as a missionizing, insider. The virtue of the term "convert," these scholars claim, is not historical so much as *functional*: only "conversion" seems to express adequately the degree of difference between Paul's old life and his new one. The term's analytic utility, in this view, offsets any supposed problem with descriptive anachronism.

Besides (as these scholars rightly point out), historians routinely rely upon words developed well beyond the time frame of the phenomena that they analyze. If economic historians, for example, can speak without anguish of "inflation" in the third century, why should New Testament historians not speak without anguish of Paul's "conversion"?[4]

I have never been persuaded by these last arguments. This is, in part, because I routinely work on another ancient figure, Augustine, who really does conform much more readily to the definition of a "convert" than does Paul (whom Augustine recasts as his own theological model of a convert). "Conversion" necessarily implies something about the person's environment as much as about his mental state: a convert goes from A to B. In 386 C.E., for example, Augustine converted *from* something (Manichaean Christianity) *to* something else (that is, to Catholic Christianity). But if B cannot be said to exist yet in any way that would distinguish it from A, we have a problem. Thus, while Augustine does indeed convert to Catholicism, can we say similarly of Luther? Does he convert to Protestantism? And if not, then for that same reason, can we speak of Paul "the convert"?[5]

The problems with using the word "conversion" for this first generation of the Christian movement become even more confounding when it describes a seemingly much less controversial case: not that of Paul himself, but that of Paul's Gentiles. These folk are routinely identified as Paul's "converts." Here is a genuine and clear case of a move from A to B, namely from the worship of traditional or native gods with all their pomps and ways—that is, with all their cult and images—to the aniconic worship of the god of Israel, who in the Diaspora, in principle, received no offerings. What could possibly be the problem with using "convert" to describe these people?

The problem, once again, is the confusion that leads to anachronism. Both Paul (certainly) and his apostolic colleagues (probably; cf. Gal 2:7) imagined their universe as composed of two religious communities: Israel and everybody else, that is, "the nations" (Heb. *goyim*, Gk. *ta ethnê*; cf. Paul's division of humanity into τῆς περιτομῆς or τῆς ἀκροβυστίας in Gal 2:7). These apostles expected the return of Jesus and the establishment of God's kingdom within their own lifetimes: they were not establishing institutions for the *longue durée*. The convenient distinction between "pagan" and "Gentile" had not yet occurred to anyone. So firmly is Paul set within this dual-option universe that he is reduced, when scolding his Gentiles in Corinth, to telling them that they are acting worse than Gentiles (1 Cor 5:1).[6]

Recall now Paul's argument in his letter to the Galatians. In that letter, Paul rails against other Christian missionaries who attempt to persuade his Gentiles-in-Christ to receive circumcision. If the Galatian Gentiles do so, he warns, they will be responsible for the whole Law (Gal 5:3). Circumcision—and then keeping the Law—is thus tantamount to saying that these Gentiles would become Jews; that is, they would convert. (I will discuss conversion to Judaism in antiquity shortly.) But what distinguishes Paul's mission from that of these other apostles—quite precisely—is that he in principle *opposes* conversion. His Gentiles are to stay Gentiles. True, they must cease the worship of their own gods and instead worship only the god of Israel. But, insists Paul, they are not to convert, and, therefore, they must not consent to circumcision. In other words, the only potential Christian converts in the Diaspora scenario presupposed by the letter to the Galatians are those Gentiles who heed Paul's rivals. And in that case, they would be converts to *Judaism*, motivated to become such by their commitment to Christ.

The point about Paul's Gentiles—the ones of whom he still approves—is precisely that they are not converts. If we slip into calling them "converts" —as I, alas, have routinely done—then we confuse the very situation that we are trying to describe. The term "converts" entangles us in anachronism, letting in by the back door the idea that Christianity is somehow already a *tertium quid*, something that exists for these people to convert *to*.[7] But would the participants at this moment of the movement, whether they were Jews or Gentiles, think of Christianity as anything other than the true form of Judaism, or as the right way to read the Jewish scriptures, or as the latest and best revelation from Israel's god in keeping with his ancient promises to his people?[8] In short, if Paul insists that his Gentiles *not* convert to Judaism, then, circa 50 C.E., there is nothing else to which they can convert. Paul, in other words, was working with a different idea. So should we.

Using "convert" or "conversion" to describe either Paul or his Gentiles implicitly but necessarily posits that Christianity was already something other than Judaism. Thus, it pulls our analysis into a future that, whether circa 34 C.E. for Paul or circa 50 C.E. for his Gentiles, does not yet exist. Before continuing on this topic, however, it might be well to look at the way that other ancients spoke about "conversion to Judaism," that is, about Gentiles becoming ex-Gentiles by becoming Jews.

Conversion was not that coherent an idea. The disapproving descriptions that we find in Greek and Roman authors who refer to what we call "conversion to Judaism" attest first of all to a fundamental construction of the relation of ancient gods and their humans. For the majority culture, as for Jewish culture, gods and their humans formed kinship groups. Phrased somewhat differently, kinship groups in Mediterranean antiquity were organized around the worship of that family's god(s). We see this idea stated both early and late. Specifically, Herodotos, in *Hist.* 8.144.2, defines "Greekness" (τὸ Ἑλληνικόν) in terms of shared blood (ὅμαιμον), language (ὁμόγλωσσον), sanctuaries and cult (θεῶν ἱδρύματά τε κοινὰ καὶ θυσίαι), and customs (ἤθεά τε ὁμότροπα). Mid-first century, Paul in Romans 9:3-5 presents "Jewishness" similarly: his συγγενοὶ (a "blood" term) share sonship, sanctuary (δόξα, a reference both to the Jewish god and to his temple in Jerusalem), laws, and cult (λατρεία).[9]

In ancient Mediterranean culture, ethnicity and antiquity indexed proper religion, the correct attitude toward which—for the members of whatever group—was "piety." "Piety" meant observing acknowledged and inherited protocols of enacting respect, first of all for one's own tradition. Put slightly differently, what we think of as religion, ancient people, whether Jews or non-Jews, identified as "ancestral custom": *Mos maiorum, religiones patriis, ta nomima,* παράδοσις πατρικῶν (Gal 1:14). Please note: One did not "believe" or "believe in" these customs; one "respected" them, meaning that one kept them and (perhaps just as important) that one was seen to keep them. One might also, of course, show respect to the gods of others, too; and in many circumstances—situations calling for political politesse; military or diplomatic engagements; visions of or visitations from divinities other than one's own—such a show of respect was simply a matter of courtesy and common sense.[10] After all, any god is more powerful than any human.

Showing respect to the gods of others—a commonplace concern and a commonplace occurrence in a world so filled with gods—did not under normal circumstances require ceasing to show respect to one's own gods. We have evidence in antiquity of Jews "showing respect" to foreign gods, while identifying and being identified as Jews (more on this below). And we have complimentary evidence of Gentiles, whether as tourists to Jerusalem's famous temple or as interested outsiders in Diaspora synagogues, present in Jewish communities and showing respect to the Jews' god. In both cases, arrangements were voluntary and ad hoc. And particularly in the instance of those Gentiles who chose to participate in Jewish assemblies, such people were under no obligation to make a unique commitment to Israel's god. Indeed, we know from various donor inscriptions

that some of these interested Gentiles—often designated as "godfearers"—were also very active publicly in their own native cults: Julia Severa,
the Roman lady who built a προσευχή (place of prayer) in Acmonia, was
also a priestess of the imperial cult; the nine godfearers who sponsored the
Jews' fund-raiser in Aphrodisias, were also, as members of the town council, highly identified pagans. To whatever degree these people chose to
participate in synagogue functions, they participated as pagans.[11]

In the instance of conversion to Judaism, however, this situation
becomes more complicated because of the Jewish avoidance of foreign
cult. (I will speak more of this in a moment, when I ruminate on the difficulties with "monotheism" in this context.) The act of this extreme form
of affiliation, given the normal ethnicity of religious groups, was most
often and most easily expressed in terms of forging a political alliance:
Gentiles become members of the Jews' πολιτεία (e.g., Philo, *leg spec.*
4.34.178).[12] Hostile pagans complained that these people thereby dis-
owned their own families. Their abandonment of native obligations was
seen as disrespectful and disloyal. Spurning one's own laws for foreign
laws was akin to treason (thus Juvenal, *Sat.* 14; Tacitus, *Hist.* 5.1–2). Or
to atheism and treason (thus Domitian's response to members of the ruling class who assumed foreign customs, the ἔθη τῶν Ἰουδαίων, Dio
67.14.1-2).

Paul's Gentiles, and obviously other Gentiles in the first-century
Jesus movement such as those in Rome, fit neither category. They are
certainly not converts (at least, according to Paul, they better not be!).
But neither, surely, are they godfearers: if they were, Paul would not be
so insistent that they cease worshipping their native deities. (Again, synagogues made no such demand of interested Gentiles. Probably, though,
this first wave of Gentiles joining the ἐκκλησία had been godfearers
before contact with Paul or other apostles, otherwise they would not
have understood the biblical building-blocks of the εὐαγγέλιον. This
prior and less demanding degree of affiliation might also have contributed to their confusions when, after Pauline baptism, some resumed
worship of their own gods, 1 Cor 5:11.) When Paul describes what
Gentiles-in-Christ are doing, he uses two other images: that of turning,
and that of being adopted.

"Turning" is a good biblical and postbiblical prophetic locution.
According to an articulate stream of apocalyptic tradition, turning is
what the Gentiles will do once God's kingdom comes. "Turn
(ἐπιστράφατε) to me!" (Isa 45:22 LXX, addressed to the nations). "All
the nations will turn (ἐπιστρέψουσιν) in fear to the Lord God . . . and

will bury their idols," (Tobit 14:6; frequently elsewhere). Eschatological Gentiles (not quotidian Gentiles) will turn from the images of their own gods and turn to Israel's god.[13] However, in part because of the accidents of translation (Greek into Latin into English), this idea becomes garbled. The notes at the bottom of the RSV for Tobit, at 14:6, for example, comment that, in this passage, postexilic Jews expressed the belief that at the end of days Gentiles will "turn" (a στρέφω word) to "Judaism." Not quite. "Turning to" the god of the universe is not the same thing as "turning to" the παράδοσις πατρικῶν of Israel; worshipping Israel's god is not the same thing as becoming a Jew. So also Paul says in 1 Thessalonians 1:9 : "You turned (ἐπεστρέψατε) to God from idols, to worship the true and living God."

Alas, all these στρέφω-words come into Latin as *converso*-words (thus, 1 Thess 1:9 is *conversi estis*); and *converso*-words come into English as "convert" and "conversion." But again, these Gentiles do not convert. They do not turn to Judaism. They turn to Israel's god. They do not assume responsibility for ancestral Jewish customs. Israel is not their family, and they are not so obligated.[14]

According to Paul, however, the Holy Spirit does effect a fictive family connection for these people. Here Paul uses a very Roman idea: adoption. Roman adoption was both a legal and a religious act. Since entering a new family entailed taking on obligations to new gods and new ancestors (much as conversion to Judaism did), the protocols effecting adoption were superintended by a *pontifex*.[15] Paul's pneumatic adoptees, however, are less encumbered than Roman ones. They are *not* responsible for patriarchal paradosis. Nonetheless, they count as sons: they can inherit, and they can cry, "Abba: Father" (Rom 8:15; cf. Gal 4:6, where the spirit of Jesus effects the adoption). The father whom they invoke, however, is neither Abraham (the primal patriarch of Israel) nor Moses (through whom God gave Israel the Law). Abba in early Christian proclamation, whether for Jesus or for his adopted Gentiles siblings, is the god of Israel, thus the god of the universe.

This is the context within which we should try to understand Paul's statements on Jewish observance, especially circumcision. And this brings me, briefly, to another word and concept that I would like to retire: "nationalism" (and its derivative, derogatory adjectival form, "nationalistic"). I shall leave to one side for now the ways that "nationalism" cannot help but conjure Bismarck, nation-states, and other political formations to which the modern period has been heir. Those connotations glimmer in some New Testament scholars' discussions of

Jesus and the Temple.[16] Scholars who look at Paul sometimes explain his aversion to Gentile circumcision as his renouncing of "ethnic boundary markers." This explanation seems to me simply to put a social-anthropological spin on the same idea of Jewish ancestral custom as "too Jewish."[17] But Paul thinks that being Jewish is terrific (Rom 3:1–2), and he also thinks that he is a terrific Jew (Phil 3:4–6).

To say that Paul rejects Jewish practices for his Gentiles because he is opposed to Jewish nationalism or to ethnic superiority or to ethnic distinctions of any sort (often by appeal to Gal 3:28) begins again to blur our picture. Cult in his period *is* an ethnic designation. Ancient gods run in the blood. A γένος or *natio* is precisely a birth connection. (Paul's συγγενοί in Romans become *cognati* in Latin.) To claim that Paul condemns his Jewish ancestral practices as too "national" or as "nationalistic" can only mean, in his historical context, that he condemns them as "too Jewish." But in a world where cult, tradition and deities are ethnic, this is nonsense. And Israel's god is no exception to this rule. He may be the master of the whole universe, but he is not a generic divinity such as, for instance, the high god of middle and late Platonism. He is the lord of Jewish history and the god of the fathers, Abraham, Isaac, and Jacob (Rom 15:8).

To sum up, Paul insists that his Gentiles-in-Christ should act as if they were eschatological Gentiles (which, given his convictions, they are). They should eschew the worship of their native deities and the practice of their own ancestral traditions. They should turn away from their own gods and turn to Israel's god. This is because, through the Spirit, they live in a prolepticly eschatological state, in the brief wrinkle in time between the Resurrection and the Parousia. They have been swept up, through Christ, into Israel's redemptive history. They are included in that redemption, but they are not thereby turned into Jews: they are saved as Gentiles. Both this Gentile redemption and the redemption of Israel, however, are known (and correctly understood by Paul, as Paul says) according to God's promises to Jewish patriarchs and to Jewish prophets as preserved in Jewish books (Rom 15:4-9). Is this "nationalism" or "anti-nationalism"? How can this concept possibly help us here?

These thoughts lead me to a third term that I would like to see retired: *religio licita*, "legal religion." This phrase usually appears in scholarly discussions of pagan anti-Christian persecutions, where it supposedly describes a statutory distinction between Christianity and Judaism. Rome (so goes the argument) legally recognized Judaism; it did not so recognize Christianity.

There are several problems with the term *religio licita*. The first, and perhaps the least significant, is the false impression it gives (because it is rendered in Latin) of actually being a term of Roman law. Its origins, rather, go back no further than to the late second/early third century C.E., and not to Roman law, but to that great ecclesiastical sound-bite meister, Tertullian. In his *Apology*, Tertullian complains that pagans say of Christians, *"Non licet esse vos!"* "You're not legit!" (4.4). By contrast, the Jewish religion is *"certe licita"* (21.1). From these slight beginnings, *religio licita* has grown into a mighty academic idée fixe, invoked to explain why the Empire went after the Church, or why it did not go after the synagogue.[18] From there, historians chase after the wild goose of trying to figure out why Christianity was *not* a legal religion, when we have no record of any laws that render it specifically illegal—nor any record of any laws, of course, that identify any religion as specifically legal.

Apart from (and only implicitly in) Tertullian, *religio licita* is nowhere attested in any ancient source. But its usefulness as a term of historical analysis is compromised not because of this slight attestation, but because of its utter wrong-headedness, its utter obscuring of the essential connection in antiquity between cult and ethnicity. Thus, to begin with the issue of pagan anti-Christian persecution, we note first that the main cause of such aggression was the anxiety felt by those of majority culture when the Tiber overflowed or the Nile did not (Tertullian again; *Ap.* 40.2). Offering to the gods was important for public security, for the maintenance of the *pax deorum*, the concordat between heaven and earth that guaranteed the well-being of city and empire.[19]

The problem, then, in the view of the major culture, was not that Gentile Christians were Christians. The problem was that, whatever religious practices these people chose to assume, they were still, nonetheless, Gentiles, that is, members of their native γένος or *natio*, with standing obligations to their own gods, who were the gods of the majority. From roughly the end of the first century until 250 C.E., these Gentile Christians could be the object of local resentments and anxieties precisely because they were not honoring the gods upon whom their city's prosperity depended. (Recall: cult makes gods happy. If deprived of cult, gods can grow resentful, then angry. Unhappy gods make for unhappy humans.) But *Jewish* Christians were not so persecuted, because as Jews their exemption from public cult was ancient, traditional, and protected by long precedent. Ancestral obligation, not legal status, is what mattered.[20]

Popular fear of this strange new group fed also on rumor, which attributed terrible antisocial crimes to Christians—infanticide, cannibalism,
incestuous intercourse—all accusations that the different Christian sects
also made against each other, and that Graeco-Roman protoracist thought
routinely attributed to outsiders.[21] Such stories about Christians eventually
lost their force: courts discounted and disproved them (e.g., Pliny, *ep.* X).
Once a Christian stood before the governor, the matter turned upon showing respect both for imperial authority and for the *mos Romanorum*.
Would the accused defer to the governor's request? Would he honor the
emperor's image? Would she eat meat offered to the gods? Many Christians
complied; others refused. The stalwart might end their days in the arena,
robed as characters from classical mythology, sacrificed in spectacles recalling the stories of the same gods whom these Christians had refused more
conventionally to honor.[22]

This first phase of anti-Christian persecution was random, sporadic,
and local. The contributing role of social factors seems clear, though the
actual charges that brought Christians to trial remain foggy. Evidence of
significant freedom of movement—Christians visiting and supporting
those arrested in jail (such as we see in the case of Perpetua), or Christians
in custody visiting churches despite having been arrested (as we see in the
case of Ignatius of Antioch)—implies what the correspondence between
Pliny and Trajan clearly states: simply *being* a Christian did not suffice for
having action brought. The admiring many, who recorded and preserved
acts of the martyrs, surely outnumbered the heroic, and perhaps voluntary, few.[23]

With Decius, in the mid-third century, both the issues and the evidence are clearer. In response to the decades of turmoil that had gripped
the empire, Decius mandated that all citizens participate in public cult.
The protocols most especially emphasized blood sacrifices and honoring
the emperor.[24] The emperor did not forbid the practice of Christianity.
Rather, he ordered that Gentile Christians, whatever their peculiar practices, *also* observe those rites that ensured the gods' good will. His goal was
not universal religious uniformity, much less persecution of Christianity,
but the preservation of the commonwealth. Once again, Jews—and thus
Jewish Christians—were exempt.[25] Their exemption makes the point that
ethnic or ancestral obligation—not religious affiliation—was what mattered. If Christianity itself were *illicita*, Decius would not have given
Jewish Christians a pass.

The chief problem with the term *religio licita*, then, is not merely
that it misdescribes Judaism and, by extension, Christianity, and not

merely that it conjures chimerical explanations for pagan anti-Christian activity. The essential problem is that it beclouds our view of what we think of as religions, and how these were commonly constituted, in antiquity. *All subject peoples within both the Hellenistic empires and the later Roman Empire normally had the right to observe and to preserve their ancestral customs.*[26] Religions (various ancestral practices) simply existed because their subject peoples did. Ancient empire meant the greatest number of peoples, and thus the greatest number of gods, beneath the umbrella of imperial authority. Rome was not "tolerant"—another anachronistic term drawn from our own liberal political context. Religious pluralism was simply the native and normal condition of ancient society. As long as frontiers were quiet, internal peace maintained, and taxes and tribute collected, all was well as far as the imperial government was concerned. And as a final consideration—and a practical one in a culture where any god was presumed to be more powerful than any human—Rome had little reason to want to alienate the gods of its subjects.[27]

Let me restate this last point: In antiquity, all gods exist. And this observation brings me to the fourth and final term on my list of words that I wish would disappear: "monotheism." This word and this concept are enjoying something of a vogue in scholarship just now. Big books and long articles have appeared analyzing the sudden and early development of high christological claims by imputing an austere and exclusive monotheism to late Second Temple Judaism.[28] Jews are distinguished from pagan contemporaries on the basis of their cultic exclusivism, a consequence of this monotheism. The persecution of Gentile Christians, in turn, is explained as the result of their commitment, inherited from Judaism, to this sort of monotheism. Meanwhile, the higher the christological claims, the more ingenious the various and scholarly reassurances that these claims do not, in fact, compromise monotheism.

All this raises the question, What do we mean by "monotheism"? In the modern context of its origin, the word denotes belief in a single god who is the only god. When modern scholars transpose the term to antiquity, the definition remains constant. And that is a large part of the problem.

Ancient monotheism spoke to the imagined architecture of the cosmos, not to its absolute population. Ancient monotheism means "one god on top," with other gods ranged beneath, lower than, and in some sense subordinate to the high god. People of sufficient education who thought philosophically about relations between levels of divinity might see these lower gods as ontologically contingent on the high god; less philosophical monotheists were content simply to assert that their own god was the biggest, the most powerful, or the best god. The Bible itself—prime textual residence of the god of Israel—of course acknowledges frequently the existence of other gods, who are the deities of "the nations." "All the peoples walk, each in the name of its god," says the prophet Micah, "but we will walk in the name of the Lord *our* god forever and ever" (4:5; and frequently elsewhere, especially in Psalms). Exodus 22:28 (LXX) taught that Israel was not to revile τοὺς θεούς, "the gods."

That these other gods existed was a matter of experience, not a question of belief. Paul, for example—often identified as an exclusive monotheist—complains about lesser divinities who try to frustrate his mission (2 Cor 4:4, the θεὸς τοῦ αἰῶνος τούτου). The divinities formerly worshipped by his congregations in Galatia are not gods by nature, he tells them, but mere στοιχεῖα, cosmic light-weights unworthy of fear or of worship (Gal. 4:8-9. Note that Paul only demeans the cosmic status of these beings, but does not deny their existence.) "Indeed, there are many gods and many lords," he says to his Gentiles in Corinth; but they are to worship only the god of Israel through his son (1 Cor 8:5-6). These lower cosmic powers whom the nations worship through cultic acts performed before idols will themselves acknowledge the superior authority of the god of Israel once Christ returns to defeat them and to establish his father's kingdom (1 Cor 15:24-27). They, too, will bend their knees to Jesus (Phil. 2:10). Through Christ, in brief, Paul's Gentiles have been spared *two* sorts of divine wrath: that of their native deities, whose anger at now being neglected cannot harm the Gentile-in-Christ; and that of the god of Israel, whose wrath they have averted by turning from the images ("idols") of these lower divinities (1 Thess 1:9-10). Note that Paul certainly "believes in" these other gods, meaning that he knows that they exist and that they can have and have had real effects.[29] He just does not worship them. Neither, he insists, should his Gentiles.

Second-century Gentile intellectuals who joined the Christian movement—Valentinus, Marcion, Justin—twined together two originally separate strands of monotheism. From the pagan side, they brought the monotheist principles of *paideia*, influenced by Platonism.[30] From the Jewish side they took over biblical monotheism, whether through the LXX or through Paul's letters and the gospels or from both. This double heritage—and its shared commitment to the idea that the high god had revealed himself through Christ his son—nonetheless still left broad scope for disagreement.

All three theologians concurred that the busy god described as making the material world in Genesis *ipso facto* could not be the high god. According to their philosophical principles, the high god does not create: he is instead radically stable, perfect, and changeless. The work of organizing matter was relegated to a lower deity, the *kosmokrator* or *demiurge*. To anyone with a decent philosophical education, that was clearly the figure described in the opening chapters of the Septuagint. Valentinus and Marcion both held that this lower deity, the creator god, was the god of the Jews. He was also the opponent of Christ and of his father, the high god. Justin also held that the ἕτερος θεός of the Septuagint's theophanies was properly the god of the Jews (*Dial.* 56). But Justin identified this god not as Christ's opponent, but rather as Christ himself, the Logos or messenger (*angelos*) of the high god his father. (The role of the opponent passed to yet lower divine personalities, those fallen messengers who inspired pagan pantheons.)[31] All three theologians have one single high god, whom they see as uniquely revealed in Jesus. And all three envisage a cosmos thick with multitudes of other divine personalities, to whom they refer as θεοί, "gods." (Cf. Philo, another ancient, philosophically sophisticated biblical monotheist, who quite unselfconsciously designated the heavenly firmament as "the most holy dwelling-place of the manifest and visible gods," [θεῶν ἐμφανῶν τε καὶ αἰστήτων] *de opificio mundi* 7.27.) My point, quite simply, is that ancient monotheists were polytheists.

Some scholars rightly note that a) Jews were monotheists and b) some Christian Jews, such as Paul or the author of the Gospel of John, imputed divinity to Jesus. The correct inference from these observations is not, I think, the tortured Chalcedonianism *avant la lettre* that we now see assigned to first-century figures, who supposedly "identified" Christ with the Father in some unique, binitarian way. Multiple divine personalities are native to ancient monotheism. John could (and did) designate Christ as θεός and remain an ancient monotheist, because of the hierarchical arrangement of his heaven: λόγος is subordinate to ὁ θεός, just as "son" is to "father." As long as one god reigned supreme at the peak of the theo-ontological pyramid, the base could be as broad as needed. (The Christian Basilides conjectured 365 divine entities; other Christian thinkers made do with fewer.) And the theologians of the generation of Chalcedon (451 C.E.), who complicated Christian monotheism to the point of paradox with their creed, still thought easily in terms of multiple lesser gods. After all, in their period, the emperor, too, was divine.[32]

Our unthinking dependence on the word "monotheism" confuses not only our view of ancient Christians, but also our view of ancient Jews. Pagan complaints of Jews as "unsociable" (*akoinonetoi*) or "separate" (living an *amixia bios*) are interpreted as reinforcing anachronistic ideas of Jews as exclusive monotheists. Consequently, we have no place to put all our evidence for Jews who did show respect for foreign gods, whether in manumission inscriptions, or through funding or participating in dedicated games, or through building temples to emperors.[33] For that matter, the Jewish mastery of the Hellenistic curriculum measures precisely the penetration of Jews into the polytheistic universe of the gymnasium. Every time we find a Jewish ephebe, a Jewish town councilor, a Jewish soldier, a Jewish actor, or a Jewish athlete, we find a Jew identified as a Jew who also obviously spent part of his work day showing courtesy toward gods not his.[34]

Scholars of an earlier generation came up with the term "henotheism" in order to accommodate all this evidence of a comfortable polytheism that is found within ancient texts or populations habitually regarded as monotheist. But what henotheism describes is really just normal ancient monotheism. Modern monotheism—the belief that only one god exists—arose only with the disenchantment of the universe in the modern period. Modern science swept away a lot of cosmic clutter, reducing radically the number of divine personalities needed earlier to account for the way the world worked. As a result, the god of modern monotheist imagination is a lonely punctum in a relatively underpopulated metaphysical heaven. The ancient world, by contrast, was filled with gods, and the people who lived in it—even members of Jewish and of Christian communities—knew this to be the case. They encountered these lower gods and felt their effects fairly often. They developed techniques and ritual protocols to cope with this fact. We would cope with it better, too, if "monotheism" were retired as a term of art for thinking about ancient religion.

Conversion, nationalism, *religio licita*, monotheism. These terms, I think, are ripe for retirement. The problem with them, as I hope I have demonstrated, is that they obscure more than they clarify, usually by inviting us along the path of anachronism. They too easily permit or even encourage us to project our own thoughts and values onto ancient people. But the ancient dead are radically independent of us, and they lived in a world different from ours. We understand them better by respecting that difference.

Chapter 3

The "Most High" God
and the Nature of Early Jewish Monotheism

Richard Bauckham

Larry Hurtado and Alan Segal have both made important contributions to the discussion of the nature of Jewish monotheism in the early Jewish period.[1] That discussion continues.[2] It can now make significant progress mainly, in my view, through careful study of the ways Jewish writers of the period talk about God. There is a huge amount of evidence, but little study of it. For example, to have complete listings of the use of various divine names and titles in early Jewish literature would be extrememly useful, because only then can we observe which were popular, which were not, and in which types or categories of literature. Then we shall be able to write the kind of close studies of such terms in early Jewish literature that *Theological Dictionary of the Old Testament* provides for the Hebrew Bible. The present chapter is a step in that direction. Table 3.1 at the end of the chapter lists all the occurrences, as far as I have tracked them, of the title "the Most High" in early Jewish literature. The chapter attempts to account for this title's relatively high frequency, asks about its significance, and seeks, thereby, to shed some light on the nature of early Jewish monotheism.

In order to situate the discussion, some preliminary comments on the distinction between exclusive and inclusive monotheism will be helpful. The terms are used by William Horbury in a recent study of "Jewish and Christian Monotheism in the Herodian Age."[3] He states the argument of his paper thus:

> It is argued overall that the interpretation of Judaism as a rigorous monotheism, "exclusive" in the sense that the existence of other divine

beings is denied, does less than justice to the importance of mystical and messianic tendencies in the Herodian age—for these were often bound up with an "inclusive" monotheism, whereby the supreme deity was envisaged above but in association with other spirits and powers.[4]

The problem here is the meaning of "other divine beings," a term that Horbury apparently equates with "other spirits and powers." If such a meaning supposed that "rigorous" or "exclusive" monotheism must deny the existence of any supernatural or heavenly beings besides God, then clearly such monotheism never existed until the modern period. Traditional monotheism in the Jewish, Christian, and Islamic traditions has always accepted the existence of vast numbers of supernatural beings: angels who serve and worship God, demons who oppose God within an overall sovereignty of God above all. But such beings have been considered creatures, created by and subject to God, no more a qualification of monotheism than the existence of earthly creatures is. With this view of their nature, we can properly and, in my view, still usefully speak of "rigorous" or "exclusive" monotheism.

Misunderstanding of this point has recurrently muddied the waters of recent discussion of early Jewish monotheism.[5] The key question is how the uniqueness of the one God is understood. In inclusive monotheism, the one God is the highest member of a class of beings to which he[6] belongs. He is unique only in the sense of the superlative: he is the most powerful of the gods (and can, therefore, subject them to his will), he is the wisest, he resides highest in the cosmos, and so forth. He is unique in the sense of being supreme. Something like this view of God and the gods developed in antiquity out of an older polytheism in which the gods acted independently and competitively. It developed over much of the Near Eastern and, later, the Hellenistic and Roman worlds in antiquity.[7] This perspective takes a gradient view of reality that does not draw sharp ontological distinctions between the supreme God and other gods or between gods and humans.[8]

By contrast, exclusive monotheism understands the uniqueness of the one God in terms of an absolute difference in kind from all other reality. We could call it "transcendent uniqueness." It means that God belongs to no class of beings of which he can be the supreme instance. Instead, it takes a binary view of reality.[9] In my view, early Jewish literature (with few, if any, exceptions) is strongly committed to such a view in the way it constantly understands the uniqueness of the God of Israel as that of the one Creator of all things and the one sovereign Ruler of all things.[10] Because these definitions of God's uniqueness drive an absolute difference of kind between God and all things, they override any older gradient features of the Israelite-Jewish worldview (such as survive in some of the vocabulary used) and create an essentially binary view of reality. This does not and need not deny the existence of many heavenly beings but simply insists that they are created by God and subject to the sovereign will of God. In early Judaism, the binary distinction between God and all other reality was observed and inculcated—in daily religious observance—by monolatry. In a gradient world view (such as the pagan, inclusive monotheism of antiquity), many beings are accorded honor, each to a degree appropriate to its rank in the cosmic scale. Early Judaism turned monolatry (which had originally been a concomitant of henotheism) into a powerful symbol of exclusive monotheism. While appropriate honor might be accorded high-ranking creatures (but not in contexts where it might be mistaken for divine worship, and so usually not granted to angels or to rulers who claimed divinity), worship was different because it was acknowledgement of the transcendent uniqueness of the God of Israel. Study of Jewish God-talk in the Second Temple period must be alert to these distinctions if it is to achieve more than superficial understanding.

The investigation of the divine title or name "the Most High" should be important for the nature of early Jewish monotheism for several reasons. In the first place, it was remarkably common. In the Hebrew Bible, excluding Daniel,[11] it occurs thirty-one times.[12] According to my calculations, set out in the Table, there are no fewer than 284 occurrences in literature we can with certainty or reasonable probability date to the period from 250 B.C.E. to 150 C.E.[13] This figure is the more impressive when we notice that the voluminous works of Philo and Josephus— much the largest corpora of Jewish literature from this period—account for only fourteen of these 284 occurrences. Second, another comparison with the usage of the Hebrew Bible is illuminating. There, with the only partial exception of Genesis 14:18-22,[14] the title is found exclusively in poetic passages, mostly Psalms (which account for twenty-one of the thirty-four instances). In the literature of early Judaism, on the other hand, this title occurs across all the main genres of literature that were used. Clearly, the title came into much more general use in the later Second Temple period than had been the case previously. But, third, this conclusion appears correct only with regard to Palestinian Jewish literature. Of the 284 occurrences, 250 are in Palestinian Jewish literature,[15] only thirty-four in literature from the western Diaspora.[16] This difference demands some explanation.

In addition to the pattern of usage, there are also reasons why the use of this title in particular may throw light on the question of the nature of the Jewish monotheism of the period. In the first place, the Hebrew term עליון (sometimes אל עליון), meaning "the Most High," is usually thought to designate this god as the highest god, supreme over other gods.[17] This title is also commonly associated with the idea of a council of the gods at which Elyon presides. We might therefore expect it, in early Judaism, to be associated with an inclusive monotheism that envisages many divine beings among whom the one God is supreme. However we should then notice how easily this inclusive monotheistic sense could attach itself to the usual Greek translation of the term. In the Septuagint the divine title עליון is always translated as ὁ ὕψιστος (אל עליון as ὁ θεος ὁ ὕψιστος). This word was in widespread, non-Jewish use to designate the supreme God. For example, Celsus, the second-century pagan critic of Christianity, says that "it makes no difference whether we call Zeus the Most High (Ὕψιστον), or Zen, or Adonai, or Sabaoth, or Amoun like the Egyptians, or Papaeus like the Scythians" (*apud* Origen, *C. Cels.* 5.41).[18] Celsus accepted a supreme God, the Most High God, known by various names to various peoples, including the Jews, but thought the Jews quite mistaken in abandoning the worship of other gods (1.23).

Interpretation of Deuteronomy 32:8-9

An important biblical text about the Most High that has played a prominent part in discussion of Jewish monotheism is Deuteronomy 32:8-9. There are important differences between the Masoretic Hebrew, the Septuagint Greek, and Hebrew texts from Qumran (4QDeutj).[19] The Masoretic Text reads

> When the Most High (עליון) apportioned the nations,
> when he divided humankind (בני אדם),
> he fixed the boundaries of the peoples
> according to the number of the sons of Israel (בני ישראל);
> for YHWH's portion is his people,
> Jacob his allotted share.

In place of "the sons of Israel," the Qumran text reads "the sons of God" (בני אל[20]), and the Septuagint "the angels of God" (ἀγγέλων θεοῦ). "The angels of God" in the Greek is doubtless a translation of the Hebrew as attested by the Qumran manuscript. The Masoretic looks like a modification of the text motivated by concern for monotheism, but both forms of the text were evidently extant in the Second Temple period.

As far as the relationship of the two divine names (Most High, YHWH) goes, there are two possible ways of reading the text. On one reading, the Most High apportions the nations to his sons ("the sons of God" in 4QDeutj), of whom YHWH is one. According to the other reading, the Most High and YHWH are the same. In his exercise of universal sovereignty over the nations (as the Most High), he allocates them to the heavenly beings of his entourage ("the sons of God" in 4QDeut) but reserves Israel for his own direct rule (as YHWH the covenant God of Israel).

Some scholars have claimed the former reading as the original meaning of the text,[21] but it is hard to believe that in its present context in Deuteronomy 32 it could ever have been read in this way (cf. YHWH's words in 32:39, which hardly leave room for his subordination to another god).[22] Margaret Barker is obliged to admit: "[H]ow such a 'polytheistic' piece came to be included in Deuteronomy, with its emphasis on monotheism, is a question we cannot answer."[23] But this reading of the text is the foundation for her argument that in the preexilic Temple cult YHWH was worshipped as the son of the high God and that this belief survived to become the source of early Christology, in which Jesus was identified with YHWH and God his Father with the Most High. Deuteronomy 32:8-9 seems indispensable to this case, since scarcely any other text in the Hebrew Bible can be read as designating YHWH a son of God.[24]

Moreover, Barker's argument that this ditheistic reading of Deut 32:8-9 survived to become available to the first Christians in the Judaism they knew ignores the good evidence we have for the interpretation of this text in early Judaism:

> He appointed a ruler (ἡγούμενον) for every nation,
> But Israel is the Lord's own portion (Sir 17:17).[25]

> And he sanctified them [Israel] and gathered them from all the sons of man because (there are) many nations and many people, and they all belong to him, but over all of them he caused spirits to rule so that they might lead them astray from following him. But over Israel he did not cause any angel or spirit to rule because he alone is their ruler and he will protect them and he will seek for them at the hand of his angels and at the hand of his spirits and at the hand of all his authorities so that he might guard them and bless them and they might be his and he might be theirs henceforth and

forever (*Jub.* 15:31-32).[26]

But from the sons of Isaac one would become a holy seed and he would not be counted among the nations because he would become the portion of the Most High and all his seed would fall (by lot) to the Lord, a (special) possession from all, people, and so that he might become a kingdom of priests and a holy people (*Jub* 16:17-18).[27]

When God divided and partitioned off the nations of the soul, separating those of one common speech from those of another tongue, and causing them to dwell apart; when he dispersed and put away from himself the children of earth, then did he fix the boundaries of the offspring of virtue corresponding to the number of the angels. . . . But what are the portions of his angels, and what is the allotted share of the All-sovereign Ruler (τοῦ παντάρχου καὶ ἡγεμόνος)? The particular virtues belong to the servants, to the Ruler the chosen race of Israel (Philo, *Post.* 91–92).[28]

Marvel not at all, then, if the title of special portion of God the universal Ruler, to whom sovereignty over all pertains (τοῦ πανηγεμόνος θεοῦ τὸ ἐφ' ἅπασι κράτος), is bestowed upon the company of wise souls, whose vision is supremely keen. . . . Is not this the explanation of that utterance in the Greater Song [Deut 32:7-9]? (Philo, *Plant.* 58–59).[29]

It is clear that all these interpretations of Deueronomy 32:8-9, including Philo's allegorical interpretations (which presuppose a literal reading), take the Most High and YHWH in the text to be one and the same. They derive from three very different forms of early Judaism. The passages from Philo are of particular interest in revealing Philo's understanding of the title Most High. He took it to refer to God's sovereign rule over all things—one of the essential elements in the early Jewish understanding of God.

Early Jews and early Christians were, of course, capable of innovative exegesis. Given an appropriate theology, it was possible for any such exegete to adopt a ditheistic interpretation of this text, but we have no evidence that anyone did so before Eusebius of Caesarea in the early fourth century C.E.[30] This is not a text that features in the rabbinic discussion of the "two powers in heaven" heresy.[31]

William Horbury does not accept Barker's idea of a Jewish ditheism based on Deuteronomy 32:8-9, but he does call that biblical text, along with the interpretations of it in Sirach 17:17 and *Jubilees* 15:31, "clear expressions of an inclusive monotheism."[32] But this begs the question of the nature of those beings to whom the Most High allotted the Gentile nations. We should note that all these postbiblical texts, like the

Septuagint, avoid calling them "sons of God" (as in 4QDeutʲ). Philo, following the Septuagint, calls them "angels," while Ben Sira calls them "rulers," and Jubilees "his angels," "his spirits" and "his authorities." There is nothing to suggest their "divinity." In all cases, they are entirely subject to God, while in Jubilees, at least, they are unequivocally beings created by God (2:2). *Jubilees* and perhaps Sirach understand them to be beings worshipped as gods by the Gentile nations, but this acceptance that the gods of the nations exist does not entail that they exist *as* gods, as in any way comparable with YHWH the Most High God, who created and rules over them. Deuteronomy, in fact, calls the gods of the nations "nongods" (32:17: לא אלה, οὐ θεῷ; 32:21: לא אל, οὐ θεῷ): they exist, no doubt, but are not fit to be called "gods,"[33] any more than human rulers are. The mere existence of supernatural beings does not make inclusive monotheism.

"The Most High" in Early Jewish Literature

It is not possible to explain why specifically this divine title is used in every one of its occurrences. Sometimes, no doubt, it is used for the sake of variation, especially in poetic parallelism, and some writers use it more habitually than others. Nevertheless, a large percentage of the occurrences belong to three identifiable fields of associations.[34]

Temple, Cult, and Prayer

Often, the Most High is the God to whom one has access in the temple rituals. The repeated use of this title in Ben Sira's description of Temple worship (Sir 50:1-21: significantly seven times) corresponds to usage in many other texts. The Temple itself can be called the house or temple of the Most High.[35] This title is commonly associated with sacrifice,[36] with worship, praise and thanksgiving,[37] and with blessing (i.e., pronouncing God's blessing on people).[38] Prayer, whether or not offered in the Temple, is often to the Most High and it is the Most High who answers prayer.[39] A select few (Melchizedek, Levi, and the Hasmoneans) are called "priests of the Most High (God)."[40]

God's Sovereign Rule over All Things

The holy of holies in the Temple on earth corresponds to the throne-room of God in the heights of heaven. This is why, the God who is accessible to his people in the Temple is called "the Most High." Praise and prayer are addressed to him as the one who is supreme over all things. In many cases, the use of the title "Most High" is accompanied by other indications that this God is the universal ruler.[41] Closely related is the use of this title in connexion with God's judgment.[42]

Use by or to Gentiles

Evidently, this title, "Most High," was thought appropriate for Gentiles to use when referring to the God of Israel as the supreme God (thirty-two occurrences)[43] or for Jews (and heavenly beings) to use when addressing Gentiles (nineteen occurrences).[44] Some of the uses by Gentiles are undoubtedly authentic (notably those by the emperor Augustus in Josephus, *Ant.* 16:163; Philo, *Leg. Gai.* 157, 317),[45] but probably the usage also became a Jewish literary convention. Some of these instances overlap with others: for example, Philo addressing Gentiles calls the Jerusalem Temple "the temple of the Most High God" (Philo, *Flacc.* 46; *Leg. Gai.* 278), while Pseudo-Solomon tells Gentile kings: "[Y]our dominion was given you from the Lord, and your sovereignty from the Most High" (Wis 6:3). Indeed, it was this connotation of universal sovereignty that made this title for the Jewish God appropriate for Gentiles. Over the course of the Second Temple period it took the place of the title "God of heaven" that played this role in early postexilic Jewish literature.[46]

One feature of the evidence that these fields of association do not entirely explain is the very frequent use of the title "Most High" in the two Apocalypses, *2 Baruch* and *4 Ezra*, both from the end of the Second Temple period and closely related to each other. In *4 Ezra*, this title is overwhelmingly dominant (sixty-eight occurrences), except in the seer's direct address to God, where he uses "Lord" (*domine*: eleven occurrences)[47] or "Sovereign Lord" (*dominator domine*: nine occurrences).[48] God is never called "the Lord" in third-person usage. The term "the Mighty One" (*fortis*) occurs five times, four of these in parallelism with "the Most High" (6:32; 10:24; 11:43; 12:47) where another divine title was needed for literary reasons.[49] God is called "God" only four times (7:19, 21, 79; 9:45), two of these in parallel with "the Most High" (7:19, 79). This overwhelming dominance of the title "the Most High" in 4 Ezra has been mentioned but apparently never discussed.[50] In *2 Baruch* the pattern is different in that this writer uses "the Mighty One" much more often than "the Most High" (forty-three occurrences of "the

Mighty One";[51] four of "the Mighty God";[52] twenty-four of "the Most High"). But here also "Lord" occurs only in the seer's direct address to God (twenty-two times, sometimes "my Lord," sometimes "Lord, my Lord"), while the word "God" is hardly used at all (10:1; 54:12).

In general, it could be said that the titles "the Most High" and "the Mighty One" are both appropriate in these works where God is presented overwhelmingly as the one who is sovereign over history and the nations. But it may also be that these titles fill the gap left in Jewish God-talk by, on the one hand, the avoidance of the Tetragrammaton, as normally in this period (and with it avoidance of divine titles including YHWH, such as YHWH Sabaoth), and, on the other hand, a tendency to avoid also the word אלוהים, because of its ambiguity as a term referring very generally to all the gods of all the nations. The major writings of the Qumran sect also avoid using אלוהים of God, while using אל.[53] This avoidance of the ordinary word for "god" is very significant for our understanding of early Jewish monotheism. It indicates a recognition of the transcendent uniqueness of the one God who cannot belong with others to a class of gods. "The Most High," on the other hand, is appropriate to the uniqueness of the God of Israel as the one who alone is sovereign over all things.

"The Most High" and the Gods

For scholars of the Hebrew Bible, the divine title "the Most High" (עליון) suggests the divine council in which Elyon presides over other gods, variously called "gods," "sons of God/gods," and "holy ones." Nonetheless, it is important to note that few biblical texts explicitly bring the title "the Most High" into connection with lesser gods, however described. This is really only the case in Deuteronomy 32:8-9 (discussed above); Psalm 97:9 ("For you, YHWH, are the Most High over all the earth; you are exalted far above all gods"); and Psalm 82:6 ("You are gods, sons of the Most High")[54] where the context is explicitly the divine council.[55] For an early Jewish reader of scripture, these would be unusual cases that would not necessarily influence his or her own understanding or use of the title "the Most High." He or she would be much more likely to be influenced by many passages in which the title is associated with YHWH's transcendent supremacy over all other reality, and especially over the nations. Moreover, we should note that the word עליון itself by no means necessarily conveys the meaning "highest of the gods." As Randall Garr puts it, "[T]he superlative degree of the epithet

עליון is not morphologically marked but semantically inferred."[56] It merely situates God "on high." Finally, we should note that even in Psalm 82:8, the most polytheistic of passages in the Hebrew Bible, the idea of a real kinship of nature between "the Most High" and his "sons," the gods, is already contradicted by the former's judgment that the latter "will die like humans" (Ps 82:7). The strong impulse to draw an absolute distinction of kind between YHWH and all other reality, characteristic of Second Temple Judaism, is here already at work, despite the use of the very old terminology that was not designed to express this idea.

It is important to avoid reading forward from the way passages in the Hebrew Bible are understood by modern scholars in search of their original meaning to assumptions about the way such passages would have been read by Jews in the late Second Temple period or the way they would have used the terminology of such passages. This mistake is commonly made in arguments that early Judaism—or parts of it—was not monotheistic or did not espouse exclusive monotheism. Early Jewish readers of scripture read it in the context of a monotheizing dynamic that was already at work in the formation of the Hebrew canon.[57] They were not in search of diversity but of uniformity and consistency. They read the nonmonotheistic or less monotheistic passages in the light of the strongly monotheistic ones. Language that may originally have had polytheistic significance was refunctioned in early Jewish use in the service of monotheism. The divine title "the Most High" is a significant case in point.

If there are few passages in the Hebrew Bible that bring this title into relationship with explicit reference to lesser gods, it is even harder to find such passages in the postbiblical literature of early Judaism. One might, for example, cite the *Genesis Apocryphon* (1QapGen 2:4-5) where Lamech, suspecting his son Noah may be a child of the Watchers, adjures his wife "by the Most High, by the Great Lord, by the King of all ages" to tell him the truth, and refers to the Watchers as "the sons of heaven." But this periphrasis is surely meant to avoid the term "sons of God," used in Genesis 6:2, 4, and, thus, to dissociate them from kinship with "the Most High." This title, in the literature of early Judaism, does not function to evoke YHWH's presidency of a council of other gods.

Imagery of height is pervasive in early Jewish picturing of God.[58] It pictures God's transcendent supremacy over all things, in heaven or on earth. The very lofty throne of God[59] is situated in the highest of the heavens,[60] or even "above the heavens,"[61] far above all the many ranks of angels that worship and serve him. It represents the absolute sovereignty of God over the whole cosmos. It is compatible with one of the essential aspects of the uniqueness of the one God that is repeated everywhere in early Jewish literature:[62] that God is the only sovereign ruler over all things, while all other beings are his creatures, subject to his will.[63] Sometimes this idea of God's unlimited sovereignty is explicitly expressed in the context of use of the title "the Most High" (e.g., Dan 4:34-35; 1QapGen 20:12–13; *Jub.* 22:27; 3 Macc 6:2; *Ps-Aeschylus*). But, in the context of Second Temple Judaism, the title itself must have evoked this pervasive idea of God. This is surely what explains its widespread popularity.

However, we must notice again that this popularity, as far as the extant literature goes, is largely confined to the writings of Palestinian Judaism. We can now further specify the evidence that almost all the uses in literature from the western Diaspora fall within the third of the three fields of association we identified above: Use by or to Gentiles. The only exceptions[64] are 1 Esdr 9:46 ("Ezra blessed the Lord God Most High, the God of hosts, the Almighty"), 3 Macc 6:2 (Eleazar the priest prays: "King of great power, Almighty God Most High, governing all creation with mercy"), Philo the Epic Poet fragment ("the Most High, great Lord of all"), and the few occasions on which Philo quotes and discusses those texts in the Greek Pentateuch that use the title.[65] It may not be accidental that in the three exceptions other than Philo and in several of the exceptions in the works of Philo (*Post.* 91–92; *Plant.* 58–60; *Leg. All.* 3:82), "the Most High" is accompanied by other divine titles or descriptions that reinforce the significance of the title "the Most High" as indicating the uniquely divine sovereignty over all things. Perhaps, in the Diaspora context, this unpacking of the title was necessary, as it does not seem to have been in Palestine.

The difference of use between Palestinian and Diaspora Jewish literature must be related to the fact that the title "the Most High" (ὕψιστος with or without θεός) was in widespread use by non-Jews.[66] Consequently, it became a term for the God of Israel that Gentiles would readily understand and a term that could, for apologetic purposes, connect with Gentile usage. This likelihood accounts for its regular use by or for Gentiles in Diaspora Jewish literature. As Dodd comments,

> [T]he tendency to exalt and worship a supreme God above all other gods is one of the ways in which Greek religious thought approached monotheism. In the Hellenistic world it met Jewish monotheism half-way. The Jews were conscious of this.[67]

But the same currency of the term in Gentile use also made for serious ambiguity. Unlike עֶלְיוֹן, ὕψιστος is morphologically a superlative, which might be used in an elative sense ("very high"), but can also be taken as a true superlative, meaning "the highest" in a series.[68] The latter was its meaning in ordinary Hellenistic religious usage. The god so called was the highest of the gods. This must be why Diaspora Jewish literature, for the most part, avoided it as a properly Jewish usage.

Its absence from the voluminous works of Philo and Josephus is especially striking. Josephus uses it only once when he is quoting the emperor Augustus (*Ant.* 16.163). His reluctance to use it is conspicuous, for example, when he retells the story of Abraham's meeting with Melchizedek (*Ant.* 1.180; cf. *War* 6.438). In Genesis 14 the title "the Most High God" is very prominent, and it is only to be expected that Palestinian Jewish retellings of the story retain it (*Jub* 13:29; *Pseudo-Eupolemus fragm.* 1:5.) Josephus, however, does not.

Philo, as we have noted, uses the title only when addressing Gentiles or when he quotes and discusses biblical texts that use it. But one of these latter instances is very illuminating. With reference to the phrase "priest of the Most High God," used of Melchizedek in Genesis 14:18, Philo explains:

> not that there is any other [god] not Most High—for God being One "is in heaven above and on earth beneath, and there is none besides him" [Deut 4:39]—but to conceive of God not in low earthbound ways but in lofty terms, such as transcend all other greatness and all else that is free from matter, calls up in us a picture of the Most High (*Leg. all.* 3.82).

Philo here deploys a classic Jewish monotheistic formula,[69] both in his own formulation ("not that there is any other") and in a peculiarly appropriate biblical version (Deut 4:39 LXX: "the Lord your God, he is God in heaven above and in the earth beneath, and there is none besides him"), as well as an echo the *Shema'* ("for God being One"). The Most High is not the highest of a pantheon of gods active throughout the heavens and the earth; he is the utterly unique One, the only one in heaven or on earth. The misunderstanding of θεὸς ὕψιστος as the highest but not the only true God—a misunderstanding easily encountered in a Hellenistic religious context—is what Philo is careful to avert. The rarity of the term in his writings and in those of most other Jewish writers in the Mediterranean Diaspora must be for this reason. As in many other instances, we find Second Temple Jewish writers deliberately dissociating their monotheism from the common pagan pattern of belief in the divine monarchy of a high God who rules as chief of the many gods.

We have confined this discussion to literature. The epigraphic evidence requires separate discussion, since there is so much uncertainty and disagreement about the extent to which Jewish usage is reflected in the inscriptions, and whether there was something like a "cult of Theos Hypsistos" that spanned the distinctions among Jews, pagans, and Christians.[70] At this point, we can only leave open the possibility that in some popular Jewish usage in the Greek-speaking Diaspora, the title was rather more freely used than it is in the extant literature.

TABLE 3.1
God "Most High" in Early Jewish Literature (250 B.C.E.–150 C.E.)

Note: Works which can with reasonable confidence be identified as (non-Christian) Jewish works and dated before 150 C.E. are included in the main lists below, and divided into works written in Palestine (or, in a few cases, perhaps the Mesopotamian Diaspora) and those written in the western Diaspora. Supplementary lists contain works that many scholars cite as evidence of early Judaism, but about which there are serious doubts as to their early date and/or their non-Christian Jewish provenance.[71]

Palestine (and eastern Diaspora)	*Number of Occurrences*
4 Ezra[72]	68
Sirach[73]	47
2 Baruch[74]	24
Jubilees[75]	23
1 Enoch[76]	17
Daniel[77]	14
Genesis Apocryphon (1QapGen)[78]	10
Prayer of Nabonidus (4Q242)[79]	4
Psalm 154 (3, 9, 10, 14; = 11Q5 18:1, 6, 7, 14)	4
Qumran War Rule[80]	4
Tobit[81]	3
Qumran Community Rule (1QS 4:22; 10:12; 11:15)	3
4QApocryphon of Joshuaᵃ (4Q378 26:1, 3, 4)[82]	3
Pseudo-Philo, *Biblical Antiquities* (33:14; 53:2)	2
Testament of Moses (6:1; 10:7)[83]	2
Qumran Thanksgiving Hymns (1QH 12:31; 14:33)[84]	2
Cairo Geniza Testament of Levi (Bodleian b 5-6; d 16)	2

TABLE 3.1
(continued)

Ladder of Jacob (5:12; 6:8)[85]	2
4QEschatological Hymn (4Q457b 2 3 5, 6)	2
1QBook of Noah (1Q19 2 2)	1
Judith (13:18)	1
Apostrophe to Zion (11Q5 22:15)	1
Compositions of David (11Q5 27:11)[86]	1
Damascus Rule (CD 20:8)	1
4QWork Containing Prayers A (4Q291 1 3)	1
4QAramaic Apocalypse (4Q246 2 1)[87]	1
4QBeatitudes (4Q525 2 24)	1
4QParaphrase of Genesis and Exodus (4Q422 2–6 2: 9)	1
4QProto-Esther[d] (4Q550c 3 1)[88]	1
4QKingdoms[a] ar (4Q552 4 2)[89]	1
4QNarrative Work and Prayer (4Q460 5 1:3)	1
4QAramaic C (4Q536 1 8)[90]	1
Pseudo-Eupolemus (fragm 1:5)[91]	1

Palestine (early date and non-Christian Jewish provenance uncertain)

Lives of the Prophets (4:3)	1

Western Diaspora

Philo[92]	13
1 Esdras (2:2[3]; 6:31; 8:19, 21; 9:46)[93]	5
Sibylline Oracles book 3 (519, 574, 580, 719)[94]	4
Sibylline Oracles book 1 (179, 200)[95]	2
3 Maccabees (6:2; 7:9)[96]	2
Wisdom of Solomon (5:15; 6:3)	2
Sibylline Oracles fragment 1 (4)	1
2 Maccabees (3:31)[97]	1
Philo the Epic Poet (frag. 3)[98]	1
Ezekiel the Tragedian (239)	1
Josephus (*Ant.* 16.163)[99]	1
Pseudo-Aeschylus[100]	1

Western Diaspora (early date and/or non-Christian Jewish provenance uncertain)

Joseph and Aseneth[101]	35
Testament of Abraham[102]	10
Greek Apocalypse of Zephaniah[103]	1

Works of doubtful provenance (geographical provenance uncertain, early date and/or non-Christian Jewish provenance uncertain)

Testaments of XII Patriarchs[104]	17
Latin Life of Adam and Eve (15:3; 28:1)[105]	2
Prayer of Manasseh (7)	1

Chapter 4

"'How on Earth Did Jesus Become a God?'
A Reply"

Adela Yarbro Collins

Wilhelm Bousset argued in 1913 that it was only when the gospel was accepted among Greek-speaking Gentiles in a Hellenistic cultural context that Christ began to be worshiped as Kyrios (Lord), that is, as a divine being.[1] Hurtado agrees with Bousset that Paul's letters provide the earliest evidence for devotion to Christ, but argues that this devotion began in the earliest Jewish Christian communities.[2] Hurtado rightly characterizes the approach of Bousset and his followers as "evolutionary or incremental."[3] In my view such an approach is not wrong, but it is too simple. Regardless of when one dates the first attribution of divinity to Jesus and the earliest cultic or liturgical devotion to him, a more adequate theoretical model is necessary. A better approach is one that recognizes cultural and religious diversity in most ancient contexts, especially urban locations, including Jerusalem.[4] Such an approach would also recognize that the mix of cultures differed from city to city and that the dominance of particular cultures also varied from place to place. This model accepts the post-Bousset view that no simple evolution from Jewish to Hellenistic culture took place.[5] At the same time, it recognizes that the proclamation of the gospel was probably formulated differently in contexts in which ethnic Jews dominated and in those dominated by ethnic Gentiles. When Gentiles dominated, Gentile ideas and practices were likely to play a greater role.[6] Another feature of a more adequate model is that full recognition of cultural diversity and pluralism entails the assumption of regular contact and mutual influence. At the same time, however, language of syncretism is to be rejected, at least when it presupposes that each culture is pure and homogenous and that the influence of other cultures can be avoided.[7]

An example of such cultural interaction and influence is, as William Horbury has shown, the impact of ruler-cult on Jewish messianism.[8] Biblical scholars today are more familiar with opposition on the part of Jews to ruler-cult than with its influence on them: "Yet opposition was not the only Jewish attitude. Ruler-cult inevitably attracted attention and imitation because it symbolized the focus of power."[9]

Horbury has made a good case for the view that "messianism, as a counterpart to contemporary ruler-cult and the ideas surrounding it" shaped the messianic hope of Second Temple Jews as much as "its roots in biblical tradition."[10] He also argued persuasively that:

> As the focus of governmental power [ruler-cult] attracted attention and imitation; among Jews, such imitation influenced the praise of their rulers and depictions of their messianic king. Ruler-cult was therefore an important factor in the continuing vigor and centrality of monarchy and monarchic ideas in the messianism of the Greek and Roman periods.[11]

What Is "Devotion"?

Hurtado also agrees with Bousset to a significant extent about what constitutes devotion to Jesus. They agree that "calling upon the name of the Lord (Jesus)" had cultic significance.[12] In his commentary on 1 Corinthians 1:2, Conzelmann argues that "calling upon the name of the Lord" is an expression taken from the Greek Old Testament. Christians apply it to Jesus instead of to Yahweh, and it even becomes a technical term for "Christians."[13] Conzelmann interprets the activity reflected in this phrase as "acclamation" and not as "prayer."[14] Like him, even Bousset concluded that, although the name of the Lord (Jesus) was invoked in worship, prayer was still addressed to God in Gentile Christian communities and "the boundary between God and Christ was observed."[15]

Even if the invocation of the exalted Christ presupposed his divinity in a functional or (limited) ontological sense,[16] the evidence suggests that such ideas did not compromise ancient views of monotheism. As Horbury puts it:

> Apotheosis raised the monarch into the company of spirits and divinities themselves subordinate to transcendent divine majesty; Jews and Christians, whatever their attitude to the honor, could readily share the view of the cosmos within which it was envisaged.[17]

Bousset and Hurtado also agree that the celebration of the Lord's Supper and baptizing and exorcising in the name of Jesus had cultic or devotional significance. For Bousset these activities point to the Christian cult and the spiritual gifts derived from it.[18] For Hurtado, such activities, including healing and prophesying in the name of Jesus, express the intention of executing divine power.[19]

One of Hurtado's key criteria for his thesis that the earliest Jewish Christians were already thinking and worshipping in binitarian terms and that they were involved in a mutation of Second Temple Jewish monotheism is that these early followers of Jesus worshipped him or expressed devotion to him in public, corporate, cultic, or liturgical contexts. This activity contrasted with the alleged refusal of devout Second Temple Jews to worship any being, including exalted patriarchs and principal angels, other than the God of Israel. Now the Lord's Supper seems to qualify as a corporate and cultic or liturgical event, if not a public one. Whether the rest of these activities qualified, in the time of Paul and earlier, as "public, corporate and cultic or liturgical" is debatable.[20] The more important question, however, is whether they necessarily implied the divinity of Jesus, and if so, what kind of divinity was intended.

What Is Meant by "Divinity"?

Second Temple Jewish and early Christian texts speak of or imply two different kinds of divinity. One is functional. The "one like a son of man" in Daniel 7:13-14, "that Son of Man" in the Similitudes of Enoch, and Jesus in some Synoptic passages are divine in this sense when they exercise (or are anticipated as exercising) divine activities like ruling over a universal kingdom, sitting on a heavenly throne, judging human beings in the end-time or traveling on the clouds, a typically divine mode of transport. The other sense is ontological (but not in a later creedal sense).[21] The hymn in Philippians 2 expresses this sense in describing the preexistent Christ as "in the form of God." I take this to mean that he was god-like in appearance or nature, that is, a heavenly being as opposed to a human being.[22]

Baptizing, healing, exorcising, and prophesying in the name of Jesus may imply that Jesus "has transcendent authority."[23] But that authority may be understood primarily as functional. In other words, Jesus is invoked because he is God's chosen agent. God chooses to endow the Spirit and to grant the power to heal, exorcise, and prophesy through the mediation of Jesus.

What Kind of Mediator Did the Earliest Christians Believe Jesus to Be?

What kind of agent or mediator did the earliest Jewish Christians believe Jesus to be? In his discussion of the ode in Philippians 2:6-11, Hurtado notes that the verb "highly exalt" (ὑψόω) is used both in Philippians 2:9 and Psalm 96:9. He points out that Psalm 96 (LXX; 97 in Hebrew and English) praises "God's supremacy 'far above all gods.'" Analogously, God "gave to Jesus 'the name above every name'." This means that God vindicated Jesus and exalted him "to a unique status."[24]

Hurtado does not mention that Psalm 96 is what form-critics used to call an "enthronement Psalm," that is, one that celebrates God as king.[25] The opening line of the Greek version is "The Lord is king, let the earth rejoice!" (Ὁ κύριος ἐβασίλευσεν, ἀγαλλιάσθω ἡ γῆ). If, as Hurtado rightly observes, this psalm transfers the state of being highly exalted (v. 9) from God to Jesus, then it would seem that kingship and the term "Lord" (v. 1) are also applied to Jesus. This intertextual relationship suggests that Paul and his audience agree that Jesus is exalted as the Messiah.[26]

Interestingly, in summarizing his earlier work, *One God, One Lord,* Hurtado uses the category "principal agent."[27] Yet neither in *One God, One Lord* nor in *How on Earth Did Jesus Become a God?* does he pay much attention to the Messiah as God's principal agent.[28] He argues that it was primarily "Jesus' uniquely exalted status" that evoked the persecution by Paul and the opposition of other devout Jews to the followers of Jesus. It would be more convincing for the early period, at least, to argue that it was the proclamation of Jesus' messiahship that was the major contention.

As Hurtado points out, what transformed Paul from a persecutor to a proclaimer of the faith was the event in which, as Paul wrote to the Galatians, God revealed "his son to me."[29] Hurtado infers that this event convinced Paul that Jesus had "a uniquely exalted status."[30] He also infers that the fact that Paul "ceased acting against Jewish Christians precisely as a result of a revelation of Jesus' exalted status" suggests "that exalted christological claims and associated religious practices were the major objectionable features of the Christian movement that drew Paul's ire prior to conversion."[31] But this may be an overinterpretation. The major issue may have been whether Jesus was the Messiah or rather a false prophet.[32] That Acts depicts Paul as proclaiming the Way that he once persecuted is noteworthy: his proclamation is that Jesus is the Messiah (Acts 9:22).

Hurtado also points out that the pre-Christian Paul of Acts directed "his efforts 'against the name of Jesus of Nazareth,' which included attempts to force Jewish Christians to 'blaspheme,' which probably means demanding [that they] curse Jesus (Acts 26:9, 11)."[33] The term βλασφημεῖν in v. 11 should perhaps be translated "revile" or "insult," rather than "blaspheme,"[34] but the argument that cursing Jesus was involved is plausible in light of 1 Corinthians 12:3 and Galatians 3:10-14.[35] The point may have been, however, from the perspective of non-Christian Jews including the persecuting Paul, that Jesus cannot be the Messiah because he was crucified and, therefore, under a (divine) curse. As Hurtado points out, this curse "represents divine judgment against the false teacher in the spirit of Deuteronomy 13:1-5; 18:20."[36] Thus, Paul's original view may have been that Jesus was a false prophet, and he may have persecuted the followers of Jesus because they proclaimed this accursed person as the Messiah.

With regard to the conflicts between Christian Jews and other Jews, Hurtado concludes that they were due to the latter's concern "with the uniqueness of God."[37] In his view, "in the eyes of at least some devout Jews," the main problem was adding "open cultic devotion" to the acceptably honorific rhetoric. "In these cases, charges of 'blasphemy' connoted an accusation of infringement on the uniqueness of God, the most important teaching of the Torah among devout Jews of the Roman period."[38]

Another way of approaching the matter is to infer that non-Christian Jews feared that the proclamation of Jesus as the Messiah would put all Jews in danger from the Roman authorities.[39] The messiahship of Jesus implied that, from a Roman point of view, an unauthorized king of the Jews was competing with Caesar and his appointees. Even if the Messiah was safely in heaven, excitement about his kingship could lead to revolt. The proclamation of Jesus as the Messiah was both religious and political, in our terms. Jews who did not accept Jesus as the Messiah, both in Palestine and in the diaspora, may well have believed that the spread of his message would destabilize the power-relations that characterized Jewish life under the sway of Roman imperial power, including the civil rights of the various Jewish communities.[40]

Was the Messiah Believed to Be Divine?

Did the proclamation of the risen Jesus as Messiah imply or entail his divinity? The key here seems to be the ambiguity of the phrase "son of God," which in the Jewish scriptures is a royal title or epithet.[41] It is likely that the king of Israel was believed to be divine during the period of the monarchy.[42] Second Temple Jews may have recognized the vestiges of that idea in the scriptures, both in the Hebrew and in the Greek version.[43]

The Messiah is apparently portrayed as the son of God in two passages from the Dead Sea Scrolls. One is "the son of God text" or 4QAramaic Apocalypse.[44] The other, the Rule of the Congregation or the Messianic Rule, includes a description of how the Community should assemble for the common meal "when God begets the messiah."[45] The reading is uncertain, but if the text does read יוליד, it probably alludes to Psalm 2:7, in which God says to the king, "You are my son; today I have begotten you." The primary significance of the Qumran text is that God will choose or raise up the Messiah of Israel in the last days. The passage, however, is open to a reading according to which the Messiah is divine, in at least a limited ontological sense, as the offspring of God.[46]

Another important text for this topic is the Jewish apocalypse known as *2 Esdras* 3–14 or *4 Ezra*. In its original form, this work probably portrayed God as referring to the Messiah as "my son" in 7:28-29; 13:32, 37, 52; 14:9. Although the expression "my servant" is attested in some versions, the allusion to Psalm 2 in 13:8-9 makes it likely that the reading "my son" is original.[47]

In a Greek or Roman (Gentile) context, the epithet or title "son of God" had clearly divine connotations. Thus Celsus, according to Origen, criticized the use of it for Jesus:

> If you should tell them that Jesus is not the Son of God, but that God is the Father of all, and that He alone ought to be truly worshipped, they would not consent to discontinue their worship of him who is their leader in sedition. And they call him Son of God, not out of any extreme reverence for God, but from an extreme desire to extol Jesus Christ.[48]

Similarly, Plutarch considered the epithet "son of God" (παῖς θεοῦ) to be false and vain praise:

> For to him who declines the greater honors envy is not displeased to grant the more moderate, and does not cheat of true praise those who reject what is false and vain. Hence those kings who were unwilling to be proclaimed a god or son of a god, but rather Philadelphus or Philometor or Euergetes or Theophiles, were ungrudgingly honored by those who gave them these noble yet human titles.[49]

For Paul, those who are "in Christ" are "sons [and daughters] of God."[50] Being sons (and daughters) of God means sharing in the glory of Christ:

For those who are led by the spirit of God, these are sons of God. For you did not receive a spirit of slavery again so that you should fear, but you have received a spirit of sonship in which we cry, "Abba, Father." The same spirit testifies with our spirits that we are children of God. If then children, also heirs. And as heirs of God, [we are] also fellow heirs with Christ, provided that we suffer with him in order that we may be glorified with him.[51]

Being glorified with Christ means "sonship, the redemption of our bodies,"[52] which ultimately means resurrection to or transformation into a heavenly body and eternal life, events described by Paul in 1 Thessalonians and 1 Corinthians.[53]

Paul's view of an ethical and bodily process of transformation is summed up as follows:

For those whom he knew beforehand, he also predetermined to be conformed to the appearance[54] of his son, in order that he might be the firstborn among many brothers.[55]

The goal in the plan of God is that human beings become like the resurrected and glorified Christ, that is, that they attain a heavenly, eternal existence. This conferral of "sonship" or "adoption" (υἱοθεσία) upon all those who are "in Christ" fits with the idea, expressed in Romans 1:4, that Jesus "was appointed son of God in power in accordance with a spirit of holiness by[56] his resurrection from the dead, Jesus Christ our Lord." This interpretation is supported by Acts 13:32-33. In this passage, a line from Psalm 2:7, "today I have begotten you," is interpreted with reference to Jesus' being raised from the dead.

The Preexistence of the Messiah

The divine sonship of Christ Jesus, however, is distinct from that of his followers in that Paul attributes preexistence to him alone. The idea of the preexistence of the Messiah was already current in Second Temple Jewish texts. Psalm 109:3c Septuagint (Psalm 110 in Hebrew and English) reads:

before the Morning-star I begot you
(πρό ἑωσφόρου ἐξεγέννησά σε).[57]

This psalm originally concerned the king, but was interpreted messianically by followers of Jesus. It is plausible that it was understood messianically by at least some Jews of the Second Temple period.

The Similitudes of Enoch clearly attribute preexistence to the figure called "the Son of Man," who is elsewhere called "the Messiah":

> For from the beginning the Son of Man was hidden,
> and the Most High preserved him in the presence of his might,
> and he revealed him to the chosen.[58]

4 Ezra also portrays the Messiah as preexistent. In the last days, the Messiah is to be "revealed" (7:28). The Most High "has been keeping him for many ages" (13:26).

In two passages, Paul seems to identify Christ with preexistent, personified Wisdom.[59] The only passage that explicitly attributes preexistence to Christ in the undisputed letters of Paul is the prose hymn in Philippians 2:6-11. There, in v. 6 as noted above, the preexistent Christ is described as being "in the form of God" (ἐν μορφῇ θεοῦ). Hurtado rightly rejects James Dunn's view that this phrase is an allusion to the creation of Adam "in the image of God" (κατ᾽ εἰκόνα θεοῦ) and that there is no implication of Christ's preexistence.[60] Others have argued that the figure "in the form of God" is an angel or is angel-like.[61]

As proposed above, the allusion to Psalm 96 in the account of the exaltation of Christ in Philippians 2:9 suggests that Christ is exalted as the Messiah. This reading is supported by the book of Acts which associates the exaltation of Jesus with his proclamation as Messiah.[62] It is also supported by the fact that the name "Lord" (κύριος) is bestowed upon the exalted Jesus Christ in v. 11. Hurtado has pointed out that at least for some of those familiar with the Septuagint, the name "Lord" would evoke the divine name, the Tetragrammaton.[63] As Bousset showed, however, the epithet or title "Lord" was also used in the ancient ruler-cults.[64] It is even used in Acts 25:26 for Nero.[65]

Paul's presentation of the Messiah as "Wisdom" in 1 and 2 Corinthians and as a preexistent heavenly being in Philippians is analogous to the depiction of the heavenly Messiah in the Similitudes of Enoch:

> And in that hour that Son of Man was named in the presence of the Lord of Spirits, and his name, before the Head of Days. Even before the sun and the constellations were created, before the stars of heaven were made, his name was named before the Lord of Spirits. . . . And for this [reason] he was chosen and hidden in his presence before the world was created and forever.[66]

In both cases, the Messiah is portrayed as divine, both functionally and, to some degree, ontologically. But in neither case is the preexistent figure equal to God. Thus, we do not yet seem to have an expression of binitarianism in Paul's letters.

Equality with God

Hurtado also points out that Philippians 2:10 is an adaptation of Isaiah 45:23.[67] He infers from this allusion that:

> The monotheistic thrust of Jewish tradition that is stridently expressed in Isaiah 45:23 is adapted to express in equally strong terms a new and remarkable "binitarian" form of monotheism, with two closely linked but distinguishable figures: God and Jesus.[68]

But this inference seems to be an overinterpretation. The worship of the God of Israel alone can, in the Second Temple period, be combined with obeisance to God's primary agent, the Messiah.[69]

Hurtado's overinterpretation is based on his translation of οὐχ ἁρπαγμὸν ἡγήσατο τὸ εἶναι ἴσα θεῷ in Philippians 2:6 as "did not consider equality with God something to be exploited." Thus, in his view, Christ was already equal to God before "taking the form of a slave" (v. 7). In my view, as stated above, the Greek clause should be translated "did not consider equality with God something to be seized."[70]

Even if, for the sake of argument, one accepts Hurtado's translation, the ancient notion of being "equal to the gods" should not be taken in a binitarian sense. When Roman senators voted that Octavian "should be inscribed, on a par with the gods, in the hymns" (εἰς τοὺς ὕμνους αὐτὸν ἐξ ἴσου τοῖς θεοῖς ἐσγράφεσθαι),[71] presumably they did not think that the living Octavian was equal, for example, to Zeus in any strong sense. Their intention apparently was that he should be honored in the same way as the gods are honored because of his beneficial accomplishments. Furthermore, according to E. Badian, ancient people distinguished between *isotheoi timai* and deification.[72]

Jesus as Son of God in the Gospel according to John

As Hurtado has pointed out, Maurice Casey has argued that the full divinization of Jesus is first evident in the Gospel of John.[73] Analogously, James Dunn has argued that the Gospel of John provides the first clear evidence of the worship of Jesus.[74] As noted above, Paul affirmed only that the preexistent Jesus Christ was "in the form of God" (Phil 2:6). The prologue of John goes further in identifying Jesus with the incarnate

Word (ὁ λόγος) in verse 14 and in declaring that the Logos is "a god" or "God" (θεός) in v. 1. The statement in verse 2 that the Logos was in the presence of God "in the beginning" (ἐν ἀρχῇ) clearly implies preexistence. It is not clear, however, whether it implies that the Logos is eternal. If the Logos is taken as an aspect of God, it would seem to be eternal. Verse 3, however, states that "all things came into being through it (or him), and apart from it (or him), not a single thing came into being." This depiction of the Logos as the means or instrument of God's creation of all things implies an identification of the Logos with preexistent, personified Wisdom.[75] If Wisdom is taken as an aspect of God, then it (or she) is eternal. But the Greek version of Proverbs 8:22 clearly states that God created Wisdom (κύριος ἔκτισέν με). This recognition of ambiguity in the prologue of John is supported by the christological controversies of the fourth century. If the texts of the New Testament had been unambiguous, there would have been fewer disagreements about what the texts meant.

Clearly, the Gospel of John puts more emphasis on the divinity of Jesus than the Synoptics, especially Mark.[76] At first glance, the narrator's comment in 5:18 seems to imply that Jesus is equal to God in a stronger sense than that discussed above:[77]

> For this reason, therefore, the Jews (or Judeans) were seeking all the more to kill him, not only because he broke the Sabbath, but also said that God was his own father, making himself equal to God.

But such a conclusion might be too hasty. For one thing, talk about Jesus "breaking the Sabbath" is clearly spoken from the point of view of the opponents of Jesus, not necessarily from the vantage point of Jesus as a character in the narrative or of the audience of the gospel. Second, some Jews, Greeks, and Romans opposed the ruler-cults and the imperial cults for making human beings equal to God or a god in a less than binitarian sense.[78]

The climax of the dialogue in 8:31-59 between Jesus and "the Jews (or Judeans) who had believed in him" (so v. 31) makes an important, though ambiguous, statement about Jesus and his relation to God:

> Then the Jews (or Judeans) said to him, "[Y]ou are not yet fifty years old and you have seen Abraham?" He said to them, "Truly, truly I say to you, before Abraham came into being, I am." They then picked up stones in order that they might cast them at him. But Jesus was hidden (from them) and went out of the temple-precinct.[79]

Even a minimalist reading of this passage seems to confirm that Jesus (as the Logos, in light of the prologue) is not only preexistent, but eternal.[80] Now this usage of the phrase "I am" (ἐγώ εἰμί) is absolute, that is, there is no predicate stated or implied.[81] It is difficult to find non-Christian, non-Jewish examples of this absolute usage.[82] Its source seems to be the use of the formula "I am Yahweh and there is no other" in certain prophetic passages of the Hebrew Bible.[83] An equivalent phrase is "I am He," and this phrase is always translated absolutely in the Septuagint (ἐγώ εἰμί). There is some evidence that this phrase came to be understood as a divine name.[84]

Readings that see the phrase "I am" (ἐγώ εἰμί) as an allusion to the relevant passages of the Septuagint and as signifying the divine name conclude that it is the clearest implication of divinity in the gospel tradition[85] or "that Jesus is in some direct way *associated with God*."[86] Hurtado comes to the latter conclusion and elaborates it later in the following terms:

> To speak of Jesus as invested with the divine name, as coming with and in the name of God, as given the name, and as manifesting God's name in his own words and actions, was to portray Jesus as bearing and exhibiting God in the most direct way possible in the conceptual categories available in the biblical tradition, and within the limits of the monotheistic commitment of that tradition.[87]

This statement implies that the author of John (and perhaps his predecessors) was straining to express "in the conceptual categories available in the biblical tradition" something that was only adequately expressed later on in the creeds, that is, in doctrinal, Trinitarian terms. Such an implication is in tension with Hurtado's claim to be approaching the question of Christology historically.[88]

Another, perhaps more accurately historical, way of reading this evidence in John is to conclude that the association of the divine name with Jesus is symbolic and rhetorical language that expresses the claim and the conviction that Jesus is the most authoritative agent of God, who reveals most fully God's nature and will for humanity. Such language is surely related to the conviction that Jesus is the Messiah.[89]

As indicated above, for Paul all those "in Christ" are sons (and daughters) of God. Yet Christ is distinctive in being preexistent. In John, Jesus (as the Logos) is the unique Son of God.[90] Therefore, in John, the royal and messianic epithet "son of God" has been interpreted in an even more distinctive way than it is in Paul's undisputed letters. The expression has strong connotations of divinity in John, yet the subordination of the Son to the Father is clear.[91]

Concluding Remarks

Larry Hurtado has contributed significantly to New Testament scholarship in his reconstruction and appreciation of various types of divine figures in Jewish texts of the Second Temple period: divine attributes and powers, such as Wisdom or the Logos; exalted patriarchs, such as Moses and Enoch; and principal angels, such as Michael and Yahoel.[92]

In my view, however, the starting point for both beliefs about Jesus and devotion to Jesus was the conviction that he was the Messiah. The Hebrew Bible and the Septuagint contained affirmations about the current or ideal king that implied his divinity. In Second Temple Jewish texts, including the Dead Sea Scrolls, the ideal king or Messiah was spoken of in ways that suggested at least functional divinity, if not ontological divinity. The Similitudes of Enoch and *4 Ezra* portray the Messiah as a preexistent being. Paul, and perhaps some of his predecessors, portrayed Jesus Christ as the preexistent Messiah and, like the Similitudes of Enoch, associated him with preexistent, personified Wisdom.[93]

Paul sometimes implies that Jesus became the son of God by his being raised from the dead. At other times, he implies that Jesus, as Wisdom, was preexistent. The gospel according to John more consistently and clearly attributes pre-existence to Jesus and perhaps even an eternal character. But it was only in the later christological controversies that "binitarianism"[94] and eventually "Trinitarianism" emerged in the teaching of Christian leaders.[95]

The idea of the divinity of Christ, in a limited sense, did emerge early and did have important precedents in biblical and Jewish traditions. But the successive reformulations and elaborations of this idea, and probably the earliest expressions of it as well, surely owed a great deal to interaction with and the influence of non-Jewish Greek and Roman ideas and practices, not least among them ruler-cults and imperial cults.

Chapter 5

Resurrection and Christology
Are They Related?

Pheme Perkins

Our two esteemed colleagues have published major volumes staking out new positions on views of the afterlife in Professor Segal's case[1] and Christology in Professor Hurtado's.[2] In an essay honoring both achievements, it seems appropriate to bring them into conversation in the arena where their interests overlap, namely the link between resurrection and Christology. Does an "early high Christology" such as that defended by Professor Hurtado shift the significance of beliefs about Jesus' resurrection away from the causal center that they occupy in other reconstructions of the origins of Christology? Even apart from hypotheses about when beliefs that treated Jesus as equivalent to God can be ascribed to Christians, can resurrection as it is understood by Jews of the first century C.E. bear the weight of generating christological claims for Jesus of Nazareth without some antecedent beliefs about his unusual or unique relationship with God?[3]

There is serious disagreement over the significance that the resurrection of Jesus is to be accorded in the origins of Christology. For some scholars, especially those who think that any form of preexistence or distinctive relationship to God comes late, it is the foundation stone for the whole edifice. J. D. G. Dunn writes in his discussion of Romans 1:3-4:

> [T]he resurrection of Jesus was regarded as of central significance in determining his divine sonship, either as his installation to a status and prerogatives not enjoyed before, or as a major enhancement of a sonship already enjoyed. What is also clear is that there is no thought of a pre-existent sonship here . . . . [T]he divine sonship of which the original formula speaks is a sonship which begins from the resurrection; something of tremendous significance for Jesus (the subject of the divine decree or appointment),

something of eschatological import (the beginning of the resurrection of the dead), took place in the resurrection of Jesus and it is characterized in terms of Jesus' divine sonship.[4] (italics Dunn's)

Contrast Joseph A. Fitzmyer on the same passage in Romans: "For Paul the resurrection made a difference in that process, but it did not make Christ the Son of God."[5] Fitzmyer insists that while resurrection is a key event in God's saving actions toward humanity, which culminate in Christ, it cannot generate such christological categories as "Messiah" or "Son of God." With his usual concern for precision, Fitzmyer also objects to the tendency to consider all christological titles messianic. He points out that there is no clear evidence that first century C.E. Jews would have understood "son of God" in that sense.[6] The unique relationship between Jesus and God suggested by the "Son of God" designation is to be correlated with Jesus' role in the economy of salvation. This role did not end with the Son's self-offering on the cross. As of the resurrection, he is the source of life for those who turn to him (1 Cor 6:14; Phil 3:10).[7]

Friedrich Schliermacher posed an even stronger challenge to the coupling of resurrection and Christology at the beginning of the nineteenth century. His dogma assumes that Jesus' own consciousness of God provides the basis for any truth associated with designations such as "Son of Man" and "Son of God."[8] Though few twenty-first-century exegetes or theologians would accept Schliermacher's formulation of Christology in terms of the God-consciousness of Christ, whether Christology can be grounded from the resurrection forward or must refer to claims made by Jesus himself is a fair question to ask. Schliermacher argues that there is no inherent connection between early Christian creedal statements about Jesus' resurrection, ascension, and coming in judgment and "the being of God in Him," which is the basis for redemption. He is an astute enough reader to recognize the ambiguity in the Pauline texts:

> It is true, on the one hand, Paul seems to attribute to the resurrection, just as much as to the death a share of its own in redemption; yet on the other, the way in which he brings it forward as a guarantee of our own resurrection shows that he in no sense thinks of it as having an exclusive connexion with the peculiar being of God in Christ. Also, it is never adduced as an evidence of the divine indwelling in Christ; for it is everywhere ascribed, not to Himself but to God. No more does John adduce the visible ascension as a proof of the higher dignity of Christ. Hence we may safely credit everyone who is familiar with dogmatic statements with a recognition of the fact that the right impression of Christ can be, and has been, present in its fulness without a knowledge of these facts.[9]

Schliermacher has put his finger on a key issue that is independent of his own solution to the problem: the logical and rhetorical use of resurrection claims. If they were as central to belief in Jesus as Messiah and Son of God as many recent exegetes have suggested, then they should have a more explicit role in establishing such claims. If resurrection is a contributing factor but not the catalyst, as Fitzmyer suggests, or nearly irrelevant to the issue of the presence of God in Christ, as in Scliermacher's view, then some other hypothesis for the origins of Christology must be advanced. In any case, resurrection cannot be presumed to explain the origins of Christology without explanation.

As a contribution to this problematic, we propose to investigate how resurrection and Christology are configured in Paul with reference to the work of Professors Segal and Hurtado. Does their work support the position that resurrection is of central significance to the belief that Jesus is Son of God? This position dominated Christology in the mid-twentieth century, though it has been criticized more recently. Liberation theologians seek a Christology grounded in the liberating praxis of Jesus of Nazareth, for example.[10] Thus a low Christology can be formulated which grounds its claims in Jesus' own project and understanding of God. Or does it suggest that one should view resurrection as an element in the story of salvation, but not the reason for referring to or worshiping—as in Hurtado's argument for early high Christology—Jesus as Son of God? Or is it marginal to the christological task as Schliermacher has concluded?

The question of religious experience(s) underlying early Christian confessional formulae and praxis that was essential for Schliermacher has reemerged in the work of both Segal and Hurtado.[11] The lynchpin in Hurtado's case for early high Christology is worship, not doctrine. Neither the belief that Jesus was Messiah nor adherence to halakah taught by Jesus can explain the involvement of Jewish leaders in Jesus' death or Paul's own vigorous persecution of the nascent Christian communities.[12] Resurrection of itself cannot explain Paul's change in allegiance. Hurtado (and Segal) credits the apostle with a dramatic, visionary experience. This Christophany (cf. 2 Cor 3:12–4:6) convinced him that Jesus is exalted with God and as such an appropriate object of worship.[13] Hurtado's critics find this category of "Christ devotion" too loosely defined.[14] Does devotion mean communal activities and rituals in which the Lord is felt to be present to the worshiper, comparable to some forms of Sufi song and/or dance today? Does it mean that prayers are addressed to Jesus as one able to orchestrate God's power on behalf of the faithful? Does it mean that early Christians organized themselves as a cult association?[15]

Hurtado begins with the postulate that any account of the origins of Christology will be multifaceted. What he considers to be odd and, hence, most in need of explanation is the binitarian pattern: ascription of divine attributes to Jesus without breaking loose from Jewish belief in the one God.[16] In his review, William Horbury points out that Hurtado is reshaping the landscape. In beginning with the question of monotheism, Hurtado has shifted the grounding of Christology away from Jewish messianism.[17] Weakening the ties between early Christology and prior convictions about the Messiah[18] places considerable weight on visions of the risen Lord. Horbury is skeptical of that piece of the structure. Rather than marking a genuinely new religious experience, such affirmations and even accounts might represent a group's existing loyalties to Jesus as God's agent.[19] That objection is hardly fatal to the argument, since later use of the topos must be distinguished from the role ascribed to visions of the risen Lord in generating christological claims about Jesus.

Segal correlates belief in bodily resurrection with the apocalyptic matrix out of which early Christianity emerged. He underlines the importance of religiously altered consciousness for the development of Christology. Paul stands within a Jewish mystical tradition that he has modified as a consequence of his Spirit-inspired visions:

> The specific nature of Paul's personal vision of Christ changed the quality of that apocalyptic prophecy in a characteristically christological way. It is not so much that Paul affected Christian apocalypticism as he exemplified Jewish apocalypticism with a single and important change—Jesus had ascended to be the Messiah and heavenly Redeemer, a part of God. This would be characteristic of Christian preaching ever afterward.[20]

This account places Segal squarely in the camp of scholars like Dunn, who insist that Christology originates with the resurrection understood to be Jesus' enthronement at God's right hand.[21] It also presumes that "Messiah" and "heavenly Redeemer" (or "Lord"?) are equivalent. This position cannot be sustained as Fitzmyer's analysis of the titles that Paul employs in Romans demonstrates.[22] The distinction is most evident precisely when Paul turns to the question of Israel's place in the story of salvation that is unfolding between Christ and the eschaton in Romans 9–11. As Messiah, Jesus belongs to the story of God's covenant with Israel (Rom 9:5). God raised him from the dead, not simply to confirm that designation. As risen, Jesus is Lord for the salvation of all humanity

(Rom 10:9b).[23] N.T. Wright's major study of the resurrection also cautions against a facile conclusion that "resurrection" entails installation as Messiah simply because the Jesus whom Christians see as exalted is expected to return in judgment. He points out that resurrection properly referred to a general resurrection of the dead. In admonishing the Corinthians that Christ's resurrection anticipates that of the faithful, Paul invokes that axiom. The resurrected dead are not, thereby, designated "Messiah" or "Lord." Therefore, Christians must have had other reasons for their claims about Jesus. Resurrection then appears in support of such convictions.[24]

Hurtado assumes that the revelation connected with visions of the risen and exalted Christ had a complex cognitive content. Christians generally assumed that some persons had ascended to see the exalted Christ (2 Cor 12:1-4; Acts 7:54–56; Rev 5:1-14).[25] He isolates four central motifs derived from these experiences:[26]

1. God has released Jesus from death.[27] Therefore, it is inappropriate to reduce resurrection to claims about the memory of Jesus or a vague influence of Jesus who lives.
2. Jesus is not similar to human figures like the emperor for whom *apotheosis* was asserted or such Jewish figures as Elijah, Enoch, or Moses or an angel. He has a unique, glorious existence.
3. Jesus is now immortal with a life enjoyed in bodily form.
4. Encounters with the risen Jesus are not solely about his existence. They involve a command to preach about this exalted figure to others.

On those occasions when Paul employs "Christ" in a titular rather than a nominal sense, he refers to Jesus' death and resurrection.[28] Most of the formulaic phrases concerning death and resurrection in Paul are weighted on the side of the saving significance of Jesus' death on the cross rather than on that of the resurrection. The death of Jesus requires resurrection to support the claim that it makes sinners righteous; it is God's response to the universality of sin.[29]

Despite the elaborate connections between resurrection and other elements of Pauline theology suggested by Hurtado's observations, the affirmation that Christ has been raised seems to have little traction with his non-Jewish audience. Though resurrection serves as a subordinate motif in the larger apocalyptic vision of how God's justice will be established at the judgment, its corporate connotations appear lost on that audience. The Thessalonians were troubled about the fate of the Christian dead (1 Thess 4:13-18), even though they had been taught to anticipate Jesus' return as judge (1 Thess 1:9-10). Paul mounts an elaborate defense of resurrection in 1 Corinthians 15 as a response to an indeterminate "some" who deny its possibility.[30] Both communities certainly engaged in what Hurtado refers to as devotion to Jesus. Both are also familiar with formulae in which Christians acknowledge that God raised Jesus from death. Paul opens his argument in 1 Corinthians 15:3b-5 by appealing to such a formula as inherited tradition, which he transmitted to the community. Since a general resurrection at the end-time is the primary meaning of the expression, how can believers confess the resurrection of Jesus while remaining clueless about the participation of the faithful deceased in resurrection (1 Thess 4:14-15)? One solution holds that this confusion points to a difference between transmitted formulae and actual instruction.

Not all religious activity—particularly as it involves devotion, cultic participation, and a specific pattern of life—demands the kind of belief system that scholars tease out of the texts as Pauline theology. In the case of Mithras devotees, a cult which communicated its vision of reality almost entirely in symbol and formulae, Roger Beck has mounted a persuasive case that scholars have been led astray by attempts to reconstruct a theological system.[31] Instead of doctrines, Beck proposes that one think of a collection of religious axioms known to members. Such axioms are not necessarily a bounded set. They are usually simple statements that can be invoked to sanctify or sanction an activity. They are not subject to verification or argument. They may appear attached to a variety of motifs. Beck compares the Mithras examples to early Christian views about covenantal nomism and Jesus as redeemer encapsulated in the phrase "Jesus is Lord."[32]

If Paul referred to Jesus' resurrection in expressions that functioned as religious axioms, he may never have provided any sort of elaboration. Though it is obvious that Paul comprehends resurrection within a more comprehensive, apocalyptic scenario as Segal argues,[33] there is no reason to infer that he instructed his non-Jewish converts in apocalyptic speculation.[34] The apocalyptic scenario which Paul employs to resolve the anxieties expressed by the Thessalonians weaves together additional elements of inherited apocalyptic symbolism without explanation. Paul presumes that the dead "sleep" prior to their resurrection on that last day (e.g., see Dan 12:2; 2 Macc 12:44-45; *1 Enoch* 92:3; *4 Ezra* 7:32).[35] Although Paul retains an apocalyptic scenario in 1 Corinthians 15, the argument is complicated with peculiar terminology used to distinguish the physical, mortal body from the spirit-determined body received at the resurrection.

Most scholars agree that some of the more intellectual Corinthians have introduced the anthropology of a religious Platonism into the discussion.[36] It had been employed to reinterpret the story of human origins in Genesis 1–2 as is evident in Philo of Alexandria.

Paul addresses those issues by introducing a new element of christological speculation: Christ as the final, "spiritual" Adam (15:21-22, 45-49). A Platonizing exegesis such as one finds in Philo would have given the priority to a first Adam, the spiritual image of God that belongs to the eternal world of ideas (Gen 1:27). That Adam serves as the model in the mind of God for creation of the mortal human Adam (Gen 2:7). The wise achieve immortality by assimilation to the spiritual image of God and dissociation from the material body.[37] Unlike his opponents, Paul's anchor in the biblical story is the apocalyptic defeat of death already exhibited in Christ's resurrection. As de Boer points out, the fact that death as the universal enemy has yet to be eradicated from the cosmos does not mean that Paul considers the victory of the exalted Lord to be incomplete or deferred.[38]

Though Paul's Christology remains firmly anchored in apocalyptic categories, the alternative suggested by his opposition will take on new life in the mythological recasting of Genesis by Gnostic Christians. The heavenly redeemer or archetype Adamas appears to the creator of the material world and his demons as a light image in the heavens above them or in the waters of the lower world. Adam's psychic nature, the basis for perception and emotion in the material world, is created first. Then Adam is secretly endowed with the Spirit from the divine "light world." When the powers perceive that he has become superior to them, they respond by encasing Adam in a material body and dividing the androgynous Adam/Eve from his feminine helper. Humanity remained deep in slavery to the creator god, ignorance, and darkness until the Savior descended to awaken the spiritual seed.[39] One need not determine the extent to which Paul's opponents in 1 Corinthians 15 had a Christology that divorced the true Christ as image of God from material embodiment. This type of speculation provides an example of the consequences of dissociating Christology from the resurrection.[40] Salvation moves to the mythic plane. The particularity of Jesus of Nazareth as a first-century Jew has been entirely erased in this primordial drama.

Not surprisingly, Gnostic mythographers have no place for the other side of the standard Pauline formula: death on the cross "for our transgressions" (Rom 4:25). Not only is the primordial redeemer entirely removed from implication in sin and death, even the true, inner humanity that

Gnostic initiation alleges to awaken, strengthen, and return to its divine source has no connection with its psychological, somatic, and material prison.[41] Karen King highlights the social and political implications of self-identification as the Other:

> The true self is represented as a kind of foreigner whose origin, essence and identity belongs to an other–place. This strategic identity works to decenter contemporary political claims by relocating the central locus of power form the mundane world and its gods to the transcendent Divine Realm. The world and all that belongs to it thereby becomes marginal to authentic reality; it is described as a false imitation of true Reality.[42]

It is unlikely that Paul's Corinthian audience was familiar with the full blown Adam myths that are stock-in-trade for Gnostics in the second century. However, some scholars detect a reading of Genesis that calls for recovering the primordial Adam within as the meaning of Jesus' kingdom preaching in the *Gospel of Thomas*.[43] If the core of this material goes back to first-century traditions as these scholars suggest, then the Adam speculation of 1 Corinthians 15 implied a full-fledged alternative soteriology with devotion to the divine Christ, the heavenly Adam at its core.

Although Paul may have adapted the speculative terminology of *psychikos* and *pneumatikos*, of "first" and "second" from his opponents, he makes no connection between Christ and myths about the primal human being.[44] As the reappearance of the Adam–Christ motif in Romans 5:12-21 demonstrates, Paul understands the connection in terms of a salvation history that perceives the actual, human death and resurrection of the Messiah as God's response to the deformation of creation by sin and death, which began with the first human being—not in the flaws of a female Wisdom figure in the hypercosmic divine world. Thiselton observes that Paul's formulaic reference to his view in 1 Corinthians 15:22 is not death over against (eternal) life, but the more explicitly apocalyptic, death over against resurrection. The expression "all are made alive" presumes that return from an intermediate stage of being dead is characteristic of resurrection. Humans do not possess some inner core of immortality that only needs activation. Instead, salvation exhibits an eschatological discontinuity, a new creation.[45] Because resurrection is embedded in the apocalyptic hope for a new creation, it could not be incorporated into a myth of return to the origins. Consequently, Thiselton concludes that Paul would be opposed in principle to any Christology based on speculation about an archetypal humanity.[46]

What does this example show about the relationship between resurrection and Christology? Resurrection as the promotion of a Jewish
healer, teacher, and prophet, Jesus of Nazareth to a new, unanticipated
status may be congenial to modern sensibilities, but it faces serious difficulties as a description of early Christology. Schliermacher's intuitions
that an adequate account must involve something unique about Jesus'
self and about Christian experience(s) of God have been sustained.
Consequently, the incorporation of religious consciousness in the work
of both Segal and Hurtado remains critical. However, the categories of
"religiously altered" and "religiously interpreted" consciousness used by
Segal or "Christ devotion" used by Hurtado remain problematic.
Religious axioms may be anchored in or directed toward such experiences, but theological reflection is not. Paul never argues from or
describes the content of his visions of the risen Lord. To that extent, resurrection appears to be a factor in but not the catalyst for his fundamental christological insights associated with the saving death of God's
Messiah.[47]

The Corinthian misunderstanding and the subsequent elaboration
of Adam Christologies in Gnostic speculation reverse direction. No one
denies the divine origins of the redeemer or the general axiom that salvation implies conformity to the divine image. The problem is whether
the concrete realities of a human life, a Jewish Messiah figure, Jesus of
Nazareth, have any significance. In denying that such "facts" as resurrection and ascension have any bearing on Christology, Schliermacher
comes closer to the Corinthian opponents and their Gnostic successors
than to Paul. For Paul resurrection is not an isolated axiom but part of a
linguistic complex that understands God, humanity's plight, the destiny
of God's people, and salvation through faith in Christ in an apocalyptic
perspective. Believers are not aliens in a hostile world, but persons in
whom the transforming power of the Spirit unleashed by the Messiah's
death and resurrection is already at work.

Chapter 6

Are Early New Testament Manuscripts Truly Abundant?

Eldon Jay Epp

Introduction

It has been said often, not only by others but by this writer as well,[1] that the manuscript witnesses to our New Testament writings are both more abundant and closer to the times of writing than are those of other ancient Greek literature. Nevertheless, many early manuscripts are highly fragmentary, and the extent of this phenomenon may not be fully appreciated. The purpose of this essay is to provide a visual accounting of the manuscript data period-by-period as a means of clarifying the age and extent of the textual variants available to New Testament textual criticism today.

Greek manuscripts that preserve the relatively few and often brief New Testament books now number nearly 5,500, plus an estimated 10,000 versional manuscripts. One Greek manuscript (P52 of the Gospel of John) has been dated as early as a quarter century after that gospel's likely composition; ten others are dated within about a century and a half after their contents are thought to have been penned. Yet eight of these eleven survive in a single small fragment or on a single leaf and another (P64+67) is extant in five fragments on three leaves, though the two other papyri, fortunately, are more substantial: P46 with eighty-six leaves and P66 with portions of seventy-five. This proportion of several highly fragmentary documents to a few more extensive ones may be thought typical of the earliest period, but does it persist later? That is a matter to be monitored, yet these and other early manuscripts (or fragments thereof) are great treasures because virtually all textual critics since the middle of the nineteenth century have valued the earlier manuscripts more highly than the later ones (with the exception of later manuscripts that preserve an earlier text). Altogether 71 percent of the Greek New Testament manuscripts date after the eleventh century, 84 percent after the tenth century, 90 percent after the ninth, and 94 percent after the eighth century.

The significance of this situation has been described in two contrasting ways. On the one hand, the large quantity of witnesses, it is claimed, assures success in the text-critical task, for the "original,"[2] or earliest attainable text of these writings, is to be found somewhere among the estimated third of a million variants in these thousands of manuscripts. All we have to do is find them! On the other hand, some have suggested that the huge cache of manuscripts does not assist the text-critical task nearly as much as is assumed, for the vast majority of manuscripts are late and the vast majority even of the earlier ones are fragmentary.

No matter how the situation is addressed, manuscripts of the New Testament writings have survived, in comparison with other ancient literature, in very significant numbers, including more early specimens than might have been expected. Yet, the precise nature of this abundance calls for assessment.

The Numerical Quantity of Greek New Testament Manuscripts

Counting New Testament Manuscripts

The first step in our exploration is to count the manuscripts themselves. The official list is maintained by the Institut für neutestamentliche Textforschung in Münster, currently headed by Holger Strutwolf (following the death of Kurt Aland in 1994 and the retirement of Barbara Aland in 2002). This basic list of manuscripts appeared in a revised edition in 1994, supplemented by published reports in 1998 and 2003 and on the Internet.[3] Together these manuscripts constitute the primary source for many of the analyses to follow. Counts of manuscripts, however, cannot simply be looked up, because duplications and items misplaced in the lists must be eliminated.[4] After such adjustments, the following quantities result (provided in the customary classifications):

Table 6.1
Quantity of Greek New Testament Manuscripts (data as of 2006)[5]

Type of Manuscript	Quantity in Official List	Adjustment for Duplication, etc.	Quantity of Different Manuscripts	Percent of all Manuscripts
Papyri	118	-3[6]	115[8]	2.1%
Majuscules	318	-40[7]	278	5.1%
Minuscules	2880	-117	2763	50.3%
Lectionaries	2436	-98	2338	42.5%
Totals	5752	-258	5494	100%

The next useful step is to sort the Greek New Testament manuscripts by century so as to obtain some sense of their distribution both by type and over time. We use the dating segments commonly employed in paleographical reporting, namely second century, second/third century, third century, and so forth, recognizing, of course, that certainty in dating, particularly of literary texts, has its numerous attendant difficulties. Table 6.2 carries the count into the eleventh century, thereby including all the papyri and majuscules known to date, as well as all minuscules and lectionaries in these periods. To extend the chart to include all extant New Testament manuscripts is unfeasible here, for the latest minuscule is doubtless 1775, a paper manuscript containing Revelation, with a date of 1847, and the latest lectionary is probably *l* 992, also a paper manuscript, with the date of 1762.[9] Since the earlier periods are the most significant for our purposes, this limitation of data is justified.

These data, of course, include only the manuscripts (or their remnants) that have survived, and they remind us that we know precious little about the actual quantity that might have been in use in the churches and schools in the respective timeframes. More significantly, these figures indicate that relatively few manuscripts are extant from the all-important first few centuries, when churches were formulating and solidifying worship practices, ethical standards, congregational polity, and doctrine. A further information barrier is the lack of knowledge about the provenance of manuscripts. For instance, those extant from the first three-and-a-half centuries of Christianity all come from Egypt,[10] which leaves us much in the dark about manuscripts from all the other vibrant areas of Christianity in that crucial period.

Table 6.2
Greek New Testament Manuscripts Sorted by Date through the Eleventh Century

Century	Papyri	Majus-cules	Minus-cules	Lection-aries	Totals	Cumulative Totals
1st	0	0	0	0	0	0
2nd	4	0	0	0	4	4
2nd/3rd	6	1	0	0	7	11
3rd	36	1	0	0	37	48
3rd/4th	12	3	0	0	15	63
4th	14	15	0	1	30	93
4th/5th	9	9	0	0	18	111
5th	2	39	0	2	43	154
5th/6th	5	10	0	0	15	169
6th	8	55	0	2	65	234
6th/7th	7	6	0	1	14	248
7th	9	30	0	1	40	288
7th/8th	1	5	0	0	6	294
8th	1	24	0	16	41	335
8th/9th	0	3	0	3	6	341
9th	0	55	19	111	185	526
9th/10th	0	2	34	8	44	570
10th	0	16	131	153	300	870
10th/11th	0	2	15	7	24	894
11th	0	1	403	273	677	1571
11th/12th	0	0	41	291	332	1903
Not dated[11]	1	1	0	0	2	1905
Totals	115	278	643	869	1905	

In actuality, then, the random nature of the survival of manuscripts, especially the early ones, casts a cloud of uncertainty over virtually all of our discussion, for we cannot know whether what has survived is an adequate basis for the information we seek or the conclusions we contemplate. There is, however, the clear witness of Origen in the early and mid-third century that there were "few," "other," "many," "most," or "almost all" manuscripts with various textual readings that he confronted as he wrote his commentaries and other treatises. For example, in some two dozen treatments of variants in the gospels and epistles, Origen (using the terms above) refers to the quantity of manuscripts supporting each variant in two-thirds of the cases. The other third involve exegetical or other content-related discussions.[12] Yet, there is no definitive way of knowing just what Origen meant by the relative terms "few" and "many" in terms of actual quantities of accessible manuscripts. Regardless of whether those numbers were limited or extensive, Origen is already two centuries removed from the beginning of Christianity, with greater obscurity characterizing the preceding period.

In this survey of the manuscript situation, the papyri dominate through the third and early fourth centuries, then all through the fourth and into the fifth century there is a fair balance between papyri and majuscules, with the latter rapidly overwhelming the papyri beginning with the fifth century. This eclipse of the papyri is complete by the ninth century due, of course, to the replacement of papyrus by parchment or vellum. When minuscule manuscripts appear in the ninth century they, in turn, soon supplant the uncial hand of the majuscules, replacing it with the more efficient (but, for us, more difficult to read!) cursive writing.

This gradual, smooth blending of the papyri and majuscules highlights an anomaly long recognized, namely, the separate classification employed for the papyri. After all, the papyri do not differ from the majuscules in their handwriting—both use uncial or upper case letters—but differ only in the material upon which they are written. The differentiation has historical reasons, mainly the discovery of New Testament papyri only after text-critical editions and handbooks of the New Testament had been established in the mid-nineteenth century without use—and, to a large extent, without knowledge—of the papyri. In addition, the first few papyri that came to light were dated later than the fourth-century majuscules upon which the critical editions of the day were based.[13] Hence, in lists of textual witnesses, the papyri at first were placed after all the other manuscripts. However, when early papyri began to appear—especially with the discovery of the Oxyrhynchus manuscripts and their publication beginning in 1898—the papyri as a group were moved to first place in the lists of manuscripts, a practice begun in 1923[14] and continuing today. Whether the anomaly should be remedied is an open question since the papyri as a group are distinctly earlier than the majuscules as a group, giving the papyri a deserved position of predominance.

Greek New Testament Papyri and Majuscules

Due to the separate category that the papyri have been given in official lists of New Testament manuscripts, and particularly first positions in such lists, it is commonly perceived that the papyri are, in their entirety, very ancient. To be sure, our oldest surviving New Testament manuscripts are written on papyrus, and a vast number of them—nearly sixty—do predate the grand parchment codices that appear in the fourth century. Yet, not only are many of the papyri of late date, but early majuscule manuscripts on parchment also exist, resulting in a considerable overlap in the two groups (compare tables 6.3 and 6.4).

Only five majuscules of the New Testament are extant from the period prior to Sinaiticus (ℵ) and Vaticanus (B), which were produced in the mid-fourth century. Thirteen or more fragmentary majuscules, however, appear in that same century, each containing no more than two dozen verses.

Despite our exclusion of minuscules and lectionaries from table 6.4, it should be noted that in the first seven centuries (see table 6.2), there also are seven extant lectionaries (portions of scripture for liturgical use): *l* 1604 (4th), *l* 1043 and *l* 1601 (5th), *l* 1347 and *l* 1354 (6th), *l* 2210 (6th/7th), and *l* 1348 (7th), with sixteen more dating into the eighth century. After that point, the numbers increase more rapidly. Still, through the eleventh century, lectionaries total only 869 or 31 percent of all known lectionaries. As for minuscule manuscripts, only from the ninth century and beyond are any extant, but through the eleventh century, they total 643 or 23 percent of all known minuscules.

All New Testament Manuscripts in Perspective, Century by Century to around 1100

A discussion of the quantity of New Testament manuscripts would not be complete without displaying the number of all extant manuscripts period-by-period in early Christianity. Ideally, of course, it would be most helpful to know how many manuscripts of each section of the New Testament were known in each generation and in each locality where churches existed. However, we are light-years away from such detailed knowledge. Indeed, it may forever be out of reach for obvious reasons, among them the current lack of adequate precision in dating the manu-

Table 6.3

All Greek New Testament Papyri, Century by Century

Century	Papyri	Total	Cumulative Total
1st	(none)	0	0
2nd	P52 P90 P98 (?) P104	4	4
2nd/3rd	P32 (ca. 200) P46 (ca. 200) P64+67 (ca. 200) P66 (ca. 200) P77 P103	6	10
3rd	P1 P4 P5 P9 P12 P15 P20 P22 P23 P27 P28 P29 P30 P39 P40 P45 P47 P48 P49 P53 P65 P69 P70 P75 P80 P87 P91 P95 P101 P106 P107 P108 P109 P111 P113 P114	36	46
3rd/4th	P7 P13 P16 P18 P37 P38 P72 P78 P92 P100 P102 P115	12	58
4th	P6 P8 P10 P17 P24 P25 P35 P62 P71 P81 P86 P88 P89 P110	14	72
4th/5th	P19 P21 P50 P51 (ca. 400) P57 P82 P85 P99 (ca. 400) P117	9	81
5th	P93 P112	2	83
5th/6th	P54 P56 P63 (ca. 500) P94 P105	5	88
6th	P2 P11+14 P33+58 P36 P76 P83 P84 P96	8	96
6th/7th	P3 P26 (ca. 600) P43 P44 P55 P97 P116	7	103
7th	P31 P34 P59 P60 P61 (ca. 700) P68 P73 P74 P79	9	112
7th/8th	P42	1	113
8th	P41	1	114
Not dated	P118	1	115
Total	(This includes all the different papyri known to date.)	115	

scripts and especially the uncertainty about the provenance of a great many. For example, there appears to be only one dated manuscript among the papyri and the majuscules: 028, dated 949 C.E.[15] The provenance of some seventy-two papyri is known or fairly certain. This large proportion (64 percent) is due primarily to the discovery of forty-seven papyri (plus twelve majuscules) at Oxyrhynchus and of thirteen others at

Table 6.4
All Greek New Testament Majuscules, Century by Century

Century	Majuscules	Total	Cumulative Total
1st/2nd	(none)	0	0
2nd/3rd	0189	1	1
3rd	0220	1	2
3rd/4th	0162 0171 (ca. 300) 0312	3	5
4th	ℵ B 058 0169 0185 0188 0206 0207 0221 0228 0230 0231 0242 0258 0308	15	20
4th/5th	W 057 059 0160 0181 0214 0219 0270 0315	9	29
5th	A C Dᵉᵃ I Q T 048 061 062 068 069 077 0163 0165 0166 0172 0173 0174 0175 0176 0182 0201 0216 0217 0218 0226 0227 0232 0236 0240 0244 0252 0254 0261 0264 0267 0274 0301 0313	39	68
5th/6th	071 072 076 088 0158 0170 0186 0213 0241 0247	10	78
6th	Dᵖ Eᵃ Hᵖ N O Pᵉ Z Ξ Σ φ 060 064 065 066 067 070 073 078 079 080 082 085 086 087 091 093 094 0143 0147 0159 0184 0187 0198 0208 0222 0223 0225 0237 0245 0246 0251 0253 0260 0263 0265 0266 0282 0285 0292 0293 0296 0302 0309 0310 (?) 0314	55	133
6th/7th	083 0164 0199 0294 0300 0318	6	139
7th	R 096 097 098 099 0102 0103 0104 0106 0107 0108 0109 0111 0144 0145 0167 0183 0200 0204 0209 0210 0239 0259 0262 0268 0275 0303(?) 0307 0316 0317	30	169
7th/8th	0157 0277 0281 0289 0291	5	174
8th	Eᵉ Lᵉ 047 054 095 0101 0116 0118 0126 0127 0134 0146 0148 0156 0161 0168 0229 0233 0234 0238 0250 0256 0280 0284	24	198
8th/9th	0279 0298 0311	3	201

9th	Fᵉ Fᵖ Gᵉ Gᵖ Hᵉ Hᵃ Kᵉ Kᵃᵖ Lᵃᵖ Mᵉ Pᵃᵖʳ U V Y Δ Θ Λ Π Ω 049 050 053 063 0120 0122 0128 0130 0131 0132 0133 0135 0136 0150 0151 0154 0155 0196 0197 0211 0248 0255 0257 0269 0271 0272 0273 0278 0283 0287 0288 0290 0295 0297 0304 0306	55	256
9th/10th	Ψ 0115	2	258
10th	S X Γ 046 051 052 056 075 0105 0121 0140 0141 0142 0177 0243 0249	16	274
10th/11th	0286 0299(?)	2	276
11th	055	1	277
Not dated	0305	1	278
Total	(This includes all the different majuscules known to date.)	278	

various specific sites, plus a dozen whose provenance was indicated by manuscript dealers or other sources.[16] Such information, however, is lacking for the remaining forty-one papyri and for the vast majority of the majuscules. Also, all except seven of the extant papyri[17] are from Egypt (though not all may have originated in Egypt), restricting our vision of the manuscript situation in virtually all other areas until the mid-fourth century, that is, until the advent of parchment. Our tabulation, therefore, cannot offer much information about actual manuscript use and distribution in churches and schools during the early years of Christianity. Nevertheless, tabulating the surviving manuscripts period-by-period is informative. A further limitation is the necessity of employing periods in our charts that extend, not to a couple of decades, but to a half-century or, in some displays, to a full century. A century, after all, includes more than three generations—more in antiquity when life expectancy was shorter. Yet, greater precision is precluded by the paucity of early, dated manuscripts and by the latitude that paleographical dating dictates.

The following table covers the first eleven centuries of Christianity (parallel to table 6.4, above). Note that manuscripts marked with double centuries (2nd/3rd, etc.) are treated with the preceding group, which is the reason for labeling each subsection as including the Greek New Testament manuscripts dating "up to and around" the year stated. (Undated manuscripts P118 and 0305 are not included.)

Table 6.5
Each Group of Surviving Greek NT Manuscripts as a Percentage of Those Extant in Each Century
(All numbers are cumulative from century to century)

Up to and around 200	*Up to and around 300*	*Up to and around 400*	*Up to and around 500*
10 Papyri = 91%	58 Papyri = 92%	81 Papyri = 73%	88 Papyri = 52%
1 Majuscule = 9%	5 Majuscules = 8%	29 Majuscules = 26%	78 Majuscules = 46%
0 Minuscules = 0%	0 Minuscules = 0%	0 Minuscules = 0%	0 Minuscules = 0%
0 Lectionaries = 0%	0 Lectionaries = 0%	1 Lectionary = 1%	3 Lectionaries = 2%
Total MSS for period: 11	**Total MSS for period: 63**	**Total MSS for period: 111**	**Total MSS for period: 169**
Up to and around 600	*Up to and around 700*	*Up to and around 800*	*Up to and around 900*
103 Papyri = 42%	113 Papyri = 38.5%	114 Papyri = 34%	114 Papyri = 20%
139 Majuscules = 56%	174 Majuscules = 59%	201 Majuscules = 59%	258 Majuscules = 45.3%
0 Minuscules = 0%	0 Minuscules = 0%	0 Minuscules = 0%	53 Minuscules = 9.3%
6 Lectionaries = 2%	7 Lectionaries = 2.5%	26 Lectionaries = 7%	145 Lectionaries = 25.4%
Total MSS for period: 248	**Total MSS for period: 294**	**Total MSS for period: 341**	**Total MSS for period: 570**

Up to and around 1000		*Up to and around 1100*	
114 Papyri = 13%		114 Papyri = 6%	
276 Majuscules = 31%		277 Majuscules = 14.6%	
162 Minuscules = 22%		643 Minuscules = 33.8%	
305 Lectionaries = 34%		869 Lectionaries = 45.6%	
Total MSS for period: 894		**Total MSS for period: 1,903**	

The data resulting from table 6.5 can now be summarized in table 6.6 (below), which highlights the percentage of all surviving Greek New Testament manuscripts (totaling 5,494 different manuscripts or their remnants) that were available for each of the periods covered in table 6.5. (Undated manuscripts P118 and 0305 are not included.)

Table 6.6
Total Extant Greek NT MSS up to around 1100 as a Percentage of All Greek NT MSS

Period Covered	Number of MSS (Cumulative)	Percent of All Extant MSS (5,494 different MSS)	Increase in Number of MSS over the Previous Period
MSS up to and around 200	11	.2%	11 (from inception)
MSS up to and around 300	63	1.2%	52
MSS up to and around 400	111	2.0%	48
MSS up to and around 500	169	3.1%	58
MSS up to and around 600	248	4.5%	79
MSS up to and around 700	294	5.4%	46
MSS up to and around 800	341	6.2%	47
MSS up to an around 900	570	10.4%	229
MSS up to and around 1,000	894	16.3%	324
MSS up to and around 1,100	1,903	34.7%	1,009
Totals	1,903	34.7% of 5,494 MSS	1,903

The most obvious finding from table 6.5 is that the early dominance of the papyri and majuscules slowly gives way to the lectionaries and minuscules until the all-important papyri and majuscule groups have shrunk to a much smaller percentage. If these charts were to follow through the nineteenth century—thereby including all extant manuscripts—the papyri and majuscules together would constitute a mere 7 percent of all extant New Testament manuscripts. This can be calculated from table 6.1: 393 papyri and majuscules divided by 5,494 extant manuscripts yields 7.2 percent. At the same time, of course, that brings the generally much later minuscules and lectionaries to a joint 93 percent majority. Obviously, however, these final statistics in no way diminish the number or nullify the antiquity of the papyri and majuscules—which both remain constant—in spite of being overwhelmed by the multitude of later manuscripts.

Also, table 6.6 clearly discloses the rate at which surviving manuscripts increased over time. From the century and a half after the earliest Christian writings appeared, eleven manuscripts are extant. Then, the quantity of extant manuscripts increases, century by century, at an average increment of fifty-five manuscripts per century through the eighth century. The increase during the ninth century is four times that rate; much larger still in the tenth; and in the eleventh century, eighteen times the earlier rate, accounting for 35 percent of all surviving Greek New Testament manuscripts as the twelfth century gets underway.

Naturally, the early periods are of greatest interest and importance in textual criticism, for manuscripts up to around 600 are primary in isolating the earliest attainable text, though a number of manuscripts to around 900 are also useful for this process, as are some minuscules that preserve earlier texts, such as 33 (ninth century), 1,739 (tenth century), and even 1,881 (fourteenth century).

If early manuscripts are most valuable, what value and how much abundance do we have in the mere eleven manuscripts that have survived from the period up to and around 200 C.E.? At that point, Christianity had been in existence for two hundred years! By the mid-third century, perhaps thirty or forty of our surviving manuscripts were in use in congregations. Then, in the mid-fourth century, the venerable majuscules, ℵ and B, appeared, and shortly thereafter Codex Washingtonianus (W). Of the surviving manuscripts, eighty-one papyri, twenty-nine majuscules, and one lectionary were in use by that time. From the period around 400, when the early churches had coped with extensive and sophisticated trinitarian and christological controversies with their alternating divisive and unifying influences, a total of 111 manuscripts survive.

The next century brought fifty-eight more, including the noteworthy codices Alexandrinus (A), Ephraemi Rescriptus (C), and Bezae (D^ea), for a total, around 500 C.E., of 169 survivors. While these numbers would appear to be substantial, nearly five centuries after the beginning of Christianity the manuscript survivors comprise only 3 percent of all extant New Testament manuscripts. Even a century later, around 600 C.E. the 248 surviving manuscripts constitute a mere 4.5 percent of all extant manuscripts, and when we reach the end of our survey, around 1100 C.E. and into the twelfth century—with the printing press only some two centuries in the future—still only 35 percent of our extant manuscripts had come into the picture. Of course, this is merely another way of emphasizing that the vast majority of all New Testament manuscripts are of a late date, but at the same time we learn, surprisingly perhaps, that the early manuscripts accessible to us are proportionately few in number.

A review of some obvious facts and factors reminds us, first, that it is impossible to know how many manuscripts of New Testament writings, in addition to those that have survived, were actually in existence in any given period. Second, though our statistics cover all areas of Christianity, there is no way to know, specifically or generally, the proportions in which manuscripts existed in various locations in these periods, except that common sense would dictate that the great Christian centers (for example, Antioch, Caesarea, Alexandria, Constantinople) would possess significant quantities. Third, our knowledge of the surviving manuscripts is skewed by the fact that all the earliest ones were found in Egypt or regions of similar climate, namely, dry areas where papyrus survives well unless subjected to repeated wetness and drying. The data, therefore, do not encourage generalizations about all—or any other—sections of earliest Christianity. Fourth, and finally, the quantity of early manuscripts, whether surviving or not, was affected by another factor. It is obvious that copies of Christian writings multiplied rapidly as scriptoria (professional copying centers) increased and as more and more congregations required more and more copies. The appearance of Christian scriptoria is debated; the Alands maintain that there were none before 200 C.E.,[18] though Harry Gamble, for example, argues in favor of earlier esstablishments.[19] In the earliest periods, however, manuscripts of Christian writings that were to become the New Testament likely would be copied by nonprofessional scribes, would circulate by informal means, and would total rather small numbers. So we might ask, if scriptoria were few and/or late and copying was largely by non-professional scribes, how many manuscripts would have been produced in the first two centuries of Christianity? Again, we cannot know, and we turn to perhaps the major issue regarding the quantity of surviving New Testament manuscripts.

The Extent of Text in Early Greek New Testament Manuscripts

Given the emphasis on abundance in this essay, we should remember that the term is relative and implicitly ask, "Compared to what?" The answer should involve simple numerical quantities, as in our preceding discussions. In the final analysis, however, the abundance of New Testament manuscripts involves not so much mere numbers of individual extant manuscripts, but primarily the quantity and quality of *text* in those manuscripts, and this clarification will reopen the issue in a new fashion. Once again, our emphasis will fall on the early manuscripts.

Circulation of Manuscripts in Standard Groups

A prior question, however, concerns what is designated by the term "manuscript" (or codex). The assumption by some may be that large portions of the New Testament are implied when a New Testament manuscript is mentioned or even that the entire collection of writings is thought to be present. As a matter of fact, only fifty-three out of the entire 5,494 manuscripts (see table 6.1), or 1 percent, are complete manuscripts in the sense of containing all twenty-seven books. There is no hint, either, that any surviving *papyrus* manuscript was a complete "New Testament," not least because the canon itself was not complete until more than half of the extant papyri had been produced, and later still in some areas of Christianity. Among the majuscules, only Codex Sinaiticus (ℵ, fourth century) and Codex Alexandrinus (A, fifth century) presently contain the complete New Testament in its final twenty-seven-book form (though ℵ also contains *Barnabas* and the *Shepherd of Hermas* and A lacks Matthew up to 25:7, portions of John and 2 Corinthians, but contains *1–2 Clement*).[20] Codex Ephraemi Rescriptus (C, fifth century) might well be included in this group, for undoubtedly it was complete, though over time it has lost about 65 percent of its New Testament leaves, yet has all books except 2 Thessalonians and 2 John. Technically, of course, it is not now complete. Among the minuscules, then, the remaining twenty-seven-book New Testaments occur, beginning with 1424 (ninth/tenth century), then 175 (tenth/eleventh), followed by others from the eleventh to the seventeenth centuries.

If "manuscript" only rarely designates a twenty-seven-book New Testament, what did manuscripts typically contain? It is clear, as time passed, that almost all manuscripts circulated in various groupings, usually described as nine or ten standardized combinations of New Testament writings (as listed in table 6.7), plus several other occasional units. At least that is the conventional assumption about how the Church's writings circulated—even in the early periods. Therefore, where a manuscript contains (or can be shown to have contained) all the writings of its particular unit or combination, it actually is a complete manuscript with respect to actual circulation practice. However, when a manuscript presently preserves only one or two books of the New Testament, the extent of its original contents is not always—indeed, not often—certain, especially in the case of the papyri and early majuscules.

Incidentally, adding the minuscules to table 6.7 would require sorting some 2,760 additional manuscripts into the standard units with no special contribution to the present essay except to show how the various circulating combinations solidified as the churches copied and recopied their sacred writings. The lectionaries are not included because they, of course, are not continuous-text manuscripts, but selections for liturgical use that have their own history of production and circulation.[21]

On the assumption that individual manuscripts commonly contained one of the listed combinations of writings, the extant papyri and majuscules have been assigned in table 6.7 to the varying categories that include their present contents. Following current custom, this has been done for all manuscripts, even those that consist of a mere fragment (a matter to be discussed presently). In addition to the ten groupings in table 6.7, a half dozen additional combinations exist, each found in fewer than a dozen manuscripts, all consisting of minuscules.[22]

When we look behind the data in table 6.7 to assess what actually survives that might be useful in establishing an early text of the New Testament, there are significant surprises. For example, the chart and its contents may be highly misleading, especially for the first several centuries, for they are open to two incorrect interpretations. First, they imply that the manuscripts in each category contain all the books in that category, and, second, they suggest—or at least do not discourage the notion—that the individual books themselves are complete in the manuscripts. In reality, of course, only a small percentage of the extant manuscripts contain portions of more than one New Testament writing, let alone all four gospels, or all Pauline letters, or Acts, plus all the Catholic Epistles, and so forth. Moreover, only a small fraction of manuscripts in the early centuries contains a large amount of text. The actual data will be instructive.

Table 6.7

All Extant Papyri and Majuscules Listed in the
Customary Circulating Combinations

Circulating Combination of Manuscripts	Papyri	Majuscules	Totals	Cumulative Totals
All twenty-seven books	0	3	3	3
All books except the gospels	0	1	1	4
All books except Revelation	0	2	2	6
Four gospels	55	169[23]	224	230
Acts, Catholic Epistles, and Pauline letters	0	9	9	239
The *Apostolos* = Acts and Catholic Epistles	20	30	50	289
Pauline letters only	31	55	86	375
Revelation of John alone	7	8	15	390
Gospels and Acts[24]	2	1	3	393
Totals	115	278	393	

Papyri and Majuscules Extant with More than One New Testament Book

Note that around 800 C.E. (when all the surviving papyri already have been written), extant New Testament manuscripts totaled 341: 114 papyri, 201 majuscules, and 26 lectionaries, and no minuscules (see tables 6.2 and 6.5). Since lectionaries are not relevant, the following analysis takes into account, first, only the 315 papyri and majuscules up to and around 800, and then the total 391 papyri and majuscules up to and around 1100 (when all the surviving majuscules had been written). The 643 minuscules known to have been produced between 900 and

1100 are omitted for space limitations and their lack of significance for our present purposes. Now observe table 6.8 on the next pages.

The subtotal reveals that during the first 800 years of Christianity only 58 manuscripts (out of the relevant 314[25] extant from that period), or about 18 percent, contain portions of more than a single book. In other words, the remaining 257 surviving manuscripts, or 82 percent, in this extensive period offer only one book. For the entire period to about 1100 C.E., 98 out of the relevant 391 manuscripts, or 25 percent, contain two or more books, the increase due obviously to the production of numerous, extensive codices as churches and scriptoria increased.

Yet, in the standard handbooks and manuscript lists used by all of us, the 293 extant papyri and majuscules carrying only a single book readily have been placed into the various circulating combinations, with the tacit assumption that most of them originally contained the writings appropriate to those several categories. In most cases, but especially in the early centuries, such an assumption is without firm evidence and—in spite of common practice—is generally unwarranted.

The Revelation of John appears to be an exception, for it often circulated alone, especially as time progressed. There are seven papyri and eight majuscules extant with only Revelation (partial or complete), but eighty-nine minuscules. The latter, however, are predominantly late: four are from the tenth century, with nineteen others through the thirteenth century, but then sixty-six stem from the fourteenth through the seventeenth centuries. No papyri and only four majuscules combine Revelation with other books, but 154 minuscules do so.

Natural groupings developed, of course, for the four gospels, the Pauline Letters, and the Catholic (or General) Epistles, and reasons are apparent for these and other combinations. For instance, the link of the Catholic Epistles to Acts can be rationalized because Acts purports to describe the activities of the apostles and the spread of the churches, and the General Epistles purport to be written by some major figures in that process and are addressed to the faithful more generally.

Nonetheless, placement of fragmentary manuscripts into the several groupings often has no basis except the combinations we know from later times. For example, papyri with one gospel or majuscules with one Pauline letter are placed, respectively, in the Four Gospels and in the Pauline Letters categories, and those containing only Acts or James or 1 John or Jude, join the *Apostolos* group. As can be calculated from table 6.8, among the 115 different papyri, 98 (or 87 percent) contain text from only one New Testament book; only 15 (or 13 percent) contain text from more

Table 6.8

Papyri and Majuscules Preserving Portions of Two or More NT Books, Listed Century by Century up to and around 1200

Date up to and around	Number of NT Books in Each Listed Manuscript									Total MSS in each century	Total copies of NT books preserved
	2	3	4	5	6	7	8	9	10–27		
200								P46		1	9
300	P30 P53 P92 0171 P75	P72		P45						7	18
400	P6 (1 Coptic)[26]		P99 W						ℵ (27) B (22)	5	59
500	Q T 088 0166 0247				D^ea				A (27) C (25) I (13) 048 (19)	10	100
600	P2 (1 Coptic) P44 P84 Σ Φ 064 067 070 083 093 0208 0251 0296	078 087	N P^e			0285		H^p	D^p (14)	20	70
700	P34 0104 0107 0209 0289	0209 0307				P61	P74			9	31

800	0234	0116	E^e L^e 047 0233 0250							7	25
Subtotals	[30]	[6]	[9]	[1]	[1]	[2]	[1]	[2]	[7]	[59]	[312]
900	0122 0130 0133 0196 0257	0135	F^e G^e H^e K^e M^e U V Y Δ Θ Π Ω 0211 0287						F^p (14) G^p (12) K^{ap} (21) L^{ap} (22) P^{apr} (23) ψ (25) 049 (22) 0150 (14) 0151 (14) 0278 (12)	30	248
1000	0121 0286	0243	S X Γ				0142		056 (22) 075 (13)	9	62
1200			055							1	4
Totals	37	8	27	1	1	2	2	2	19	99	626

than one book, and only six of the latter contain portions of more than two writings. This last group constitutes a mere 5 percent of all the papyri. Hence, if a papyrus fragment contains a few lines or even a few leaves of text from one gospel or one epistle, and even though we know (from writing on both sides of the leaf or leaves) that the fragments are from a codex, generally there is no certainty about what else may have been included in that codex. Often we have no way to assess its original size. The same situation applies to the fragmentary majuscules.

There is, to be sure, greater certainty about codices with multiple writings: P45 survived with portions of thirty leaves containing Matthew, Mark, Luke, John, and Acts; constructed of two-leaf quires, its original size is estimated as 220 leaves.[27] More certain is the size of P46, a single quire codex of 104 leaves, of which 86 survive; since most pages are numbered, the missing portion at the beginning can be calculated (seven leaves; therefore, seven missing also at the end) and the original size determined. The conclusion is clear enough: P46 was a codex of the Pauline letters, though no satisfactory solution has been reached as to what followed 1 Thessalonians 5:28.[28] P72 is an anomaly. Though it is treated as if it were a single codex containing 1–2 Peter and then Jude, the two were published as two separate Bodmer papyri (VIII and VII, respectively), for the manuscript in which they were found contained an odd collection of writings (including the *Apocalypse of James, 3 Corinthians*, Melito's *Homily on the Passover*, and others) and, both in the present codex and in an earlier one, 1–2 Peter were separated from Jude.[29] Incidentally, this lack of immediate connection with one another calls into question our treating P72 as a manuscript with three writings; in one sense, it is a single manuscript; in another it is not. Perhaps it should be treated as two manuscripts, one of which has two books, while the other has one. But we follow the conventional view on the matter, since in P72's history, 1–2 Peter as a unit and Jude have twice been parts of the same codex, albeit separated from one another in both.

The Amount of Text in Each New Testament Papyrus and Majuscule

The fragmentary nature of a large majority of the early New Testament manuscripts remains an unfortunate accident of history, and its exact proportions need to be assessed. Table 6.9 will facilitate that assessment, and, again, all the papyri and majuscules are included and listed by periods to provide perspective on the fragmentary or nonfragmentary nature of the manuscript materials. The term "fragmentary" is appropriate for describing a book surviving in ten or fewer leaves (a measure employed by the Alands[30]), and the term "highly fragmentary" might be used for manuscripts with one or two leaves. Counting leaves, however, still does not always clarify the actual amount of text in a manuscript, so on occasion a document might be described as consisting of five fragments on two leaves, and so forth. Table 6.9 reports the number of extant leaves (five or more) in parentheses following the manuscript designation.

This display covers the first millennium of Christianity and provides a dramatic demonstration of the fragmentary nature of a vast proportion of the manuscript evidence for the text of the New Testament. Visually, the multitudinous manuscripts surviving in only one or two leaves—often as a few tiny fragments—form a solid block in the left column, from the second to the ninth century, when finally a solid block of extensive manuscripts begins to form in the right columns.

An astounding 261 one-or-two-leaf manuscripts (that is, 66 percent of all papyri and majuscules) qualify as highly fragmentary, and they extend from the second into the eleventh century. They are joined by 43 more with three to ten leaves, for a total of 304 manuscripts (or 77 percent) in all the "fragmentary" categories. Of the remaining 89 papyri and majuscules, only 45 contain one hundred or more leaves, 12.5 percent of all manuscripts in these two most important groups.

Table 6.9 evinces a further observation: If it is surprising that highly fragmentary manuscripts are so numerous in the earliest three or four centuries of Christianity, it is doubtlessly more surprising that their presence continues, in equal and even larger numbers, in the fifth, sixth, seventh, and even in the eighth and ninth centuries. This wave of fragmentary materials is finally matched by more extensive manuscripts only in the ninth century.

To be exact, table 6.9 has not taken account of the minuscules, which appeared in the ninth century and by around 1100 C.E. had rapidly reached 643. In toto, of course, minuscules number 2,763 to date, and the statistics on fragmentary minuscules may be summarized, using the definition of "fragmentary" employed earlier, that is, a manuscript with ten or fewer leaves. The first such minuscules appear in the tenth century and the last in the eighteenth. During that period, 70 contain one or two leaves, 14 have three to four, and 42 consist of five to ten leaves, for a total of 126, with most coming from the twelfth century. The result is that fragmentary minuscules make up 4.5 percent of all minuscules with more than 95 percent,[31] therefore, in the nonfragmentary category. This compares with 77 percent fragmentary and only 23

Table 6.9
Amount of Textual Content in All Extant NT Papyri and Majuscules

Century	1–2 leaves	3–4 leaves	5–10 leaves	11–24 leaves	25–100 leaves	100+ leaves	Total MSS	Cumulative Total
2nd	P52 P90 P98 P104						4	4
2nd/3rd	P32 P77 P103 0189	P64+67			P46 (86) P66 (73)		7	11
3rd	P1 P9 P12 P15 P20 P22 P23 P27 P28 P29 P30 P39 P48 P49 P53 P65 P69 P80 P87 P91 P95 P101 P106 P107 P108 P109 P111 P113 P114 0220	P5 P40 P70	P4 (6) P47 (10)		P45 (30) P75 (50)		37	48
3rd / 4th	P7 P13 P16 P18 P37 P78 P92 P100 P102 0312	P38 0162 0171	P115 (9)		P72 (95)		15	63
Subtotals	**[48]**	**[7]**	**[3]**	**[0]**	**[5]**	**[0]**	**[63]**	**[63]**
4th	P8 P10 P17 P24 P25 P35 P71 P81 P86 P88 P89 P110 058 0169		P62 (6 frag.)	P6 (15)		ℵ (148) B (142)	29	92

	4th/5th	5th	5th/6th	6th
	110	151	166	229
	18	41	15	63
	W (187)	A (144) C (145) Dea (415)		Dp (533) Ea (227) N (231) Σ (188) Φ (190)
		T (32) I (84)		Hp (41) O (44) Pe (44) Z (32) Ξ (89) 070 (44)
		Q (13) 048 (21)		P11+14 (17 frag.) 064 (16) 086 (14) 0285 (22)
				P84 (9 frag.) 067 (6) 078 (6) 087 (8)
	P99	0274		P33+58 065 085 091 0225
	0185 0188 0206 0207 0221 0228 0230 0231 0242 0258 0308	P19 P21 P50 P51 P57 P82 P85 P117 057 059 0160 0181 0214 0219 0270 0315	P54 P56 P63 P94 P105 071 072 076 088 0158 0170 0186 0213 0241 0247	P2 P36 P76 P83 P96 060 066 073 079 080 082 093 094 0143 0147 0159 0184 0187 0198 0208 0222 0223 0237 0245 0246 0251 0253

Table 6.9
(continued)

Century	1–2 leaves	3–4 leaves	5–10 leaves	11–24 leaves	25–100 leaves	100+ leaves	Total MSS	Cumulative Total
	0260 0263 0265 0266 0282 0292 0293 0296 0302 0309 0310 0314							
6th/7th	P3 P26 P43 P55 P97 P116 0164 0199 0294 0300	P44	083 (10)	0318 (18)			13	242
7th	P31 P34 P68 P73 P79 096 097 098 099 0103 0108 0109 0111 0144 0145 0183 0200 0204 0210 0239 0259 0262 0268 0275 0303 0307 0316 0317	0104	P61 (7 0106 (10) 0107 (6) 0167 (6) 0209 (8)	P59 (14) P60 (20) 0102 (13)	R (48)	P74 (124)	39	281
7th/8th	P42 0157 0277 0291		0289 (8)		0281 (47)		6	287
8th	095 0101 0118 0126 0127 0134 0146 0148 0156 0161 0229 0234 0238 0256 0280 0284 (content unknown: 0168)		054(6)	P41 (11) 0116 (14)	0233 (93) 0250 (33)	E^e (318) L^e (257) 047 (152)	25	312

	[238]	[16]	[16]	[13]	[17]	[15]		
8th/9th	0279 0298 0311						3	315
Subtotals	[238]	[16]	[16]	[13]	[17]	[15]	[315]	[315]
9th	0122 0128 0132 0154 0155 0196 0197 0255 0269 0271 0288 0297 0304 0306	0131 0136 0272 0273 0295	0120 (6) 0130 (7) 0290 (8)	050 (20) 053 (14) 063 (22) 0135 (16) 0283 (15)	F^p (28) G^p (99) H^a (43) 0133 (36) 0248 (70) 0257 (47) 0287 (80)	F^e (204) G^e (252) H^e (194) K^e (267) K^{ap} (288) L^{ap} (189) M^e (257) P^{apr} (327) U (291) V (220) Y (309) Δ (198) Θ (249) Λ (157) Π (350) Ω (259) 049 (149) 0150 (150) 0151 (192) 0211 (258) 0278 (120)	55	370
9th/10th	0115					Ψ (261)	2	372

Table 6.9
(continued)

Century	1-2 leaves	3-4 leaves	5-10 leaves	11-24 leaves	25-100 leaves	100+ leaves	Total MSS	Cumulative Total
10th	0121 0140 0177 0249	052 0105	0243 (9)	046 (20)	051 (92)	S (235) X (160) Γ (257) 056 (381) 075 (333) 0141 (349) 0142 (381)	16	388
10th/11th	0286 0299						2	390
11th						055 (303)	1	391
No date	P118 (0305)				2	393		
Totals	*261*	*23*	*20*	*19*	*25*	*45*	*393*	

percent nonfragmentary among the papyri and majuscules. The vast improvement in preservation among the minuscules is obviously due to their generally much later dates and their better-surviving parchment or acid-free, cloth-content paper.[32]

As a matter of fact, however, the inclusion of the minuscules in our analysis effects no change in the actual numbers or percentages of fragmentary and nonfragmentary manuscripts up to and around 800. Of course, the 300 fragmentary papyri and majuscules begin to retreat into the background as the centuries pass. Yet, the periods from 900—and especially from 1100—forward are of little concern or value in seeking the earliest attainable text of the New Testament. This is not to rule out the minuscules entirely, for they are important in at least two ways: (a) Some minuscules carry texts much earlier than their times of copying, and (b) their textual variants, like all others, contribute meaningfully to our understanding of the churches, their real-life issues, their worship, and their thoughts and doctrines contemporary with the various manuscripts. Nonetheless, the statistics of fragmentary manuscripts in the early periods remain startling and significant.

Finally, table 6.10 in the appendix displays, century-by-century, the inclusion of various New Testament books in each papyrus and majuscule. Matching the data in table 6.9 (number of leaves or fragments) with table 6.10 (New Testament books represented in each manuscript) will indicate the general extent of material preserved in each manuscript. For example, in the second century, P52 and P90, each listed as surviving in one or two leaves, contain a portion of the Gospel of John. More precise data can be obtained from Kurt Aland's *Kurzgefasste Liste* and its supplements (see note 3) or from the Nestle-Aland *Novum Testamentum Graece*[27] (684–704). There we learn that each consists of one fragment and that the actual textual content of P52 is John 18:31-33 (*recto*) and 18:37-38 (*verso*); and of P90, John 18:36–19:1 (*recto*) and 19:2-7 (*verso*). Visually, table 6.10 is also a dramatic demonstration, century-by-century, of the density (or, more often, the lack thereof) of the preservation of the various New Testament writings in each period.

Conclusion

This extended quantitative and qualitative assessment of manuscripts available for constructing the earliest attainable text of the New Testament leaves a mixed picture of amplitude and fragmentation, especially in the first three centuries of Christianity. The amplitude improves markedly in the fourth century when two extensive majuscules appear. Further boosts come from several more major majuscules in the fifth century, and again from a few in the sixth. However, the high proportion of fragmentary documents persists, and only in the eighth century do the numbers of extensive manuscripts increase significantly (see tables 6.8 and 6.10).

Nonetheless, the raw quantity of early manuscripts is sizable—and abundant—in proportion to the relatively small collection of mostly brief New Testament writings from the latter half of the first century and the first quarter of the second. Up to and around 300 C.E., sixty-three manuscripts, as a group, contain all the New Testament books except 1–2 Timothy and 2–3 John. However, to a large extent—doubtlessly much greater than expected—we are dependent upon manuscripts with ten or fewer surviving leaves and upon documents containing only one or a few New Testament writings (tables 6.8, 6.9, 6.10). In fact, up to and around 300, forty-three out of the sixty-three manuscripts have only one to ten leaves (thirty-three of them with merely one or two leaves). In that same period, fifty-five out of sixty-three manuscripts contain only a single book (and usually a very small portion of it). Stating the matter more positively, prior to the influx of minuscule manuscripts in the ninth century and following, there are some 370 papyri and majuscules now extant with New Testament content, with 166, or 45 percent of them, available around 500 C.E., and the 63 mentioned earlier (that is, 17 percent) already in use around 300 C.E. All, of course, survive in varying degrees of completeness.

To describe this complex situation in terms of a metaphor, the textual transmission of the New Testament is a forest, thick with trees at the latter stages, but with trees thinning as we move backward toward the beginning of the process. In fact, only a few trees stand there, but the ground is randomly scattered with hundreds of leaves, and in many cases it is difficult to identify even the kinds of trees from which they have come.

What does this picture of our manuscripts mean for us? First, the very early and more extensive manuscripts (the "trees still standing": P46, P66, P45, P75, and P72) have an inherent significance, not only by virtue of their age and size—all with fifty to ninety-five leaves—but also for their importance in enlightening the text-critical process, each in a different fashion. Specifically, P75 (early third century), a text strikingly similar to that of Codex B (mid-fourth century), demonstrates dramatically the stability of one type of text through that century and a half, and beyond. P66 (ca. 200 C.E.) reveals early scribal activity with tendencies to abandon

Johannine style and to correct the exemplar's text toward (what is later called) the "Byzantine tradition." Hence, P66 reveals a scribe correcting difficulties and seeking the best sense without a rigid concern for preserving the exemplar.[33] P46 (ca. 200 C.E.) is an example of much less careful scribal attention, resulting in a text with numerous distinctive variations calling for explanation. P45, while showing extensive freedom in copying, presents a text midway between the P75 type of text (B-text) and the D-text, assisting scholars in the formulation of early text-types. Finally, P72, the earliest witness to the text of 1–2 Peter and Jude, because of the context in which it was found, raises intriguing questions about the intersection of the transmission process and issues of canon.

Second, the far more numerous fragmentary survivors are as valuable as they are frustrating. The papyri and majuscules that fit the stated definition of "fragmentary" are numerous (304), and that each fragment represents a full original manuscript that was in use somewhere by Christians in their worship and life is sometimes overlooked. And, indeed, we can recite a litany of insights gained from the fragmentary papyri. Some examples follow.

(a) *Perspective given by the earliest manuscripts:* P52 (a fragment of John 18, 3.5 by 2.25 inches, with fewer than sixty letters on each side) is undoubtedly our earliest New Testament papyrus, surviving from as early as twenty-five years after the time that the Gospel of John is thought to have been written. There are now two or three other second-century manuscripts: P90 (fragments of John 18–19); P104 (fragments of Matthew 21); and perhaps P98 (fragments of Revelation 1). Each survives on a portion of a single tattered leaf, and each provides an ancient connection between the earliest, most obscure phase and the later, more ample phases of the textual transmission of the eventual New Testament. This close continuity with the remote past is unusual in ancient text transmission.

(b) *Links with text-types:* Even small fragments can show connections with major representatives of the various text-types, often pushing back the functioning dates of those text-types. For instance, several one-to-four-leaf manuscripts such as P48, P38, P69, and 0171 (all third or third/fourth century) support a D-text akin to that in Codex Bezae (around 400 C.E.)—the leading representative of that text-type. Moreover, as many as twenty or more papyri (in addition to the extensive P75 and P66) can be linked to the later primary B-text representatives, B and ℵ, affirming a solid tradition from the earliest levels of transmission.[34] P115 (third/fourth century), extant in nine leaves, now is the earliest witness to the A/C type of text in the Revelation of John, and it will assist in more carefully reconstructing that text.[35]

(c) *Illuminating scribal behavior:* Scribal procedures can be observed in numerous fragmentary documents, though not as dramatically as in P45, P46, and P66 (the extensive documents described above).

(d) *Earlier support for known variants:* Fragmentary papyri are not conspicuous for furnishing a mass of new, meaningful variant readings. Rather, they frequently provide earlier attestation for variants well-established by later manuscripts. Some three dozen examples, taken only from the nine earliest fragmentary papyri and majuscules (see table 6.9), will make the point (see specifics in note[36]). The four fragments with multiple variant readings, P90, P32, P64+67, and 0189, show numerous textual connections with later manuscripts, but not simply by consistent agreement with one or more manuscripts (such as ℵ, B, or P66). Rather, the connections most often form a jumble of agreements and disagreements—a reading supported now by two or three manuscripts, then another supported by one or two versus a third, or by one versus one or two others, and so on. Significantly, the examples chosen—the earliest survivors—link most often with manuscripts that have been identified with one of the early text-types (notably, for P90 and P64+67, the B-text), yet numerous readings have divided support from the leading representatives of those text-types. The result is an array of connections with important later manuscripts, but not a simple, broad-scale continuity. Such a cross-mixture, as it might be described, is characteristic of the interrelationships among our early manuscripts, and it reveals the dynamic textual situation in early Christianity—the textual ferment in thought and practice in the churches. That is part of the excitement—and frustration—of working with these early manuscript remains.

(e) Detailing the history of the New Testament text: In these several ways, and by way of summary, both the more extensive and the fragmentary manuscripts of the New Testament assist scholars in writing the history of its textual transmission, due to both the content and greater age of these early documents. In such witnesses to the text, we glimpse also the dynamism of this living text—not always a rigid, mechanical, and perfunctory transfer of text from one copy to another, but a thoughtful, life-oriented, contextual interest in the material being transmitted.[37] Through the fragmented remains, we are carried, tantalizingly, to the very earliest reachable phases of our New Testament textual development. What these remnants lack in amplitude is made up by their provision of connection and continuity, and in that sense the New Testament manuscripts still may be understood as genuinely abundant.

Table 6.10
New Testament Books, Century by Century, in Papyri and Majuscules up to and around 800

Century	MSS	Mt	Mk	Lk	Jn	Act	Ro	1Co	2Co	Gal	Eph	Php	Col	1Th	2Th	Plm	1Ti	2Ti	Tit	Heb	Jas	1Pe	2Pe	1Jn	2Jn	3Jn	Jud	Rev
2nd	P52 P90				2																							
	P98																											1
	P104	1																										
2nd/3rd	P32																		1									
	P46						1	1	1	1	1	1	1	1						1								
	P64+67 P77 P103	3																										
	P66				1																							
	0189					1																						
3rd	P1 P70 P101	3																										
	P4 P69 P111			3																								
	P5 P28 P39 P80 P95 P106 P107 P108 P109				9																							
	P9																							1				
	P12 P114																			2								
	P15							1																				

Manuscript																			3rd/4th				
P20 P23									2														
P22	1																						
P27 P40 P48 P113 0220	5																						
P29 P91	2						1 1																
P30							1 1											1					
P45	1	1	1	1																			
P47			1																				
P49	1	1						1															
P53	1																						
P65		1	1																				
P75	1	1	1																				
P87							1																
P7 0312	2	2																					
P13													1										
P16						1																	
P18 P115																							
P37 P102	2																						
P38	1																						
P72					1 1													1					
P78					1 1															2			

Table 6.10
(continued)

Cent.	MSS	Mt	Mk	Lk	Jn	Act	Ro	1Co	2Co	Gal	Eph	Php	Col	1Th	2Th	Plm	1Ti	2Ti	Tit	Heb	Jas	1Pe	2Pe	1Jn	2Jn	3Jn	Jud	Rev
	P92										1					1												
	P100																				1							
	0162	1			1																							
	0171			1																								
MSS=63	**Subtotals**	12	1	8	16	6	6	2	1	1	3	2	1	3	2	1	0	0	1	4	3	1	1	1	0	0	2	4
4th	P6 0258				2																							
	P8					1																						
	P10 0221						2																					
	P17 P89 0228																											
	P24 0169 0207 0308																			3								4
	P25 P35 P62 P71 P86 058 0110 0231 0242	9																										
	P81 0206																					2						
	P88 0188		2																									
	)	1	1	1	1	1	1	1	1	1	1	1	1	1	1	1	1	1	1	1	1	1	1	1	1	1	1	1
	B	1	1	1	1	1	1	1	1	1	1	1	1	1	1					1	1	1	1	1	1	1	1	

0185																													1	
0230									1																					
4th/5th	P19 P21 0160	3	1																											
	P50 P57 057			3																									1
	P51					1																									
	P82 0181	2																													
	P85	1	1		1																										
	P99	1	1	1	1	1																									
	W	1	1	1	1	1	1	1	1	1	1	1	1	1	1	1	1	1	1	1	1	1	1	1	1	1	1	1	1	1
	059 0214 0315	3	3																												
	0219				1																										
	0270					1																									
5th	P93 068 0216 0217 0218 0264 0301			7																										
	P112 077 0165 0175 0236 0244		6																											
	A	1	1	1	1	1	1	1	1	1	1	1	1	1	1	1	1	1	1	1	1	1	1	1	1	1	1	1	1	1
	C	1	1	1	1	1	1	1	1	1	1	1	1	1	1	1	1	1	1	1	1	1	1	1	1	1	1	1		
	D^a	1	1	1		1	1	1	1	1	1	1	1	1	1										1					
	I	1	1																												
	Q	1	1																												

Table 6.10
(continued)

Cent.	MSS	Mt	Mk	Lk	Jn	Act	Ro	1Co	2Co	Gal	Eph	Php	Col	1Th	2Th	Plm	1Ti	2Ti	Tit	Heb	Jas	1Pe	2Pe	1Jn	2Jn	3Jn	Jud	Rev
5th	T			1	1																							
	048					1	1	1	1		1	1	1	1		1	1	1	1	1	1	1	1	1	1	1		
	061																1											
	062 0174 0176 0254 0261									5																		
	069 0274 0313		3																									
	0163																											1
	0166					1															1							
	0172						1																					
	0173 0227																				2							
	0182 0267			2																								
	0201							1																				
	0226													1														
	0232																								1			
	0240																		1									
	0252																			1								
5th/6th	P54																				1							

	C1	C2	C3	C4	C5	C6	C7	C8	C9	C10	C11	C12	C13	C14	C15	C16	C17	C18	C19	C20	C21	C22	C23	C24	C25	C26	C27
P56 076																							2				
P63																								1			
P94																						1				2	3
P105 071 0170																											
072 0213																							2				
088										1											1						
0158																			1								
0186																				1							
0241												1															
0247						1	1																				
Subtotals	13	6	6	5	6	7	9	12	14	8	5	7	6	6	10	7	8	11	14	9	12	17	25	34	20	17	33
P2 070																								2	2		
P11+14 0222																						2					
P33+58 E^a 066 086																							4				
P36 P76 060 065 091 0260 0302 0309 0314																								9			
P83 P96 O Z 073 085 094 0237 0293																										1	9
P84																								1			1

Left margin labels: MSS=165 (upper group through Subtotals); 6th (lower group).

Table 6.10
(continued)

Cent.	MSS	Mt	Mk	Lk	Jn	Act	Ro	1Co	2Co	Gal	Eph	Php	Col	1Th	2Th	Plm	1Ti	2Ti	Tit	Heb	Jas	1Pe	2Pe	1Jn	2Jn	3Jn	Jud	Rev
6th	D[p]	2					1	1	1	1	1	1	1	1	1	1	1	1	1	1								
	H[p]		2				1	1	1	1			1	1			1	1	1	1								
	N P[e] Ξ 079 0147 0253 0265 0266			2	2																							
	Σ Φ 064 067	4	4	6																								
	078	1		1	1																							
	080 0143 0184 0187 0263 0292		6																									
	082 0159				1						2																	
	087	1	1																			1						
	093					1																						
	0198												1															
	0208												1	1														
	0223 0225								2																			
	0245																							1				
	0246																				1							

		6th/7th						7th		
0251								1	1	
0282										
0285	1	1	1	1		1	1		1	
0296									1	
0310										
P3 P97	2									
P26						1				
P43	1									
P44	1									
P55	1									
P116		1	1						1	
083	2	1								
0164 0300					1					
0199			1							
0294		1								
P31				1	1					
P34			1	1						
P59 P60	2									
P61			1	1		1	1	1	1	1
P68		1								

Table 6.10
(continued)

Cent.	MSS	Mt	Mk	Lk	Jn	Act	Ro	1Co	2Co	Gal	Eph	Php	Col	1Th	2Th	Plm	1Ti	2Ti	Tit	Heb	Jas	1Pe	2Pe	1Jn	2Jn	3Jn	Jud	Rev
7th	P73 0102 0106 0200 0204 0275	6																										
	P74					1															1	1	1	1	1	1	1	
	P79																			1								
	R 0108 0239 0303			4																								
	096 097					2																						
	098								1																			
	099 0103 0144 0167		4																									
	0104 0107	2	2																									
	0109 0145 0210 0268				4																							
	0111															1													
	0183														1														
	0209						1		1										1										
	0259 0262																	2						1					
	0307	1	1	1																									
	0316																											1	

Date	MSS	1	2	3	4	5	6	7	8	9	10	11	12	13	14	15	16	17	18	19	20	21	22	23	24	25	26	27
7th/8th	P42 0291																									2		
	0157	1																										
8th	0277 0281																											2
	0289																			1		1						
	P41 095																							2				
	Eᵉ Lᵉ 047 0233 0250																								5	5	5	5
	054 0101 0127 0238 0256																								5			5
	0116																									1	1	1
	0118 0148 0161 0284																											4
	0126 0134 0146																										3	
	0156						1																					
	0229																								1			
	0234																								1			1
	0280																											
8th/9th	0279									1																1		1
	0298																											1
	0311																						1					
MSS=312	Totals	17	9	8	6	10	10	12	14	20	12	7	12	8	8	15	12	11	15	16	18	19	28	36	70	47	48	76

PART II

STUDIES IN CHRISTOLOGY

Chapter 7

Prophetic Identity and Conflict in the Historic Ministry of Jesus

Maurice Casey

At the time of Jesus, the prophetic form of Jewish identity was more than half a millennium old. Elijah, Isaiah, and other prophets prophesied in Israel long before the exile in Babylon: Jeremiah, Ezekiel, and Second Isaiah prophesied during the exilic period, and Haggai, Zechariah, and others did so later. Moreover, the works of these prophets occupied a large part of scripture. That the word of God himself came to these prophets was believed, and the words of the prophets were still relevant. Hence, Jesus preached on Isaiah 56 and Jeremiah 7 when he cleansed the temple.[1]

The most remarkable feature of prophetic Jewish identity is that it did not defend the outward features of normal Jewish identity. On the contrary, it was liable to attack central Jewish observances in the name of God. The two features most subjected to attack in the Bible were the state of Israel and the temple cultus. For example, Micaiah son of Imlah correctly prophesied the defeat of Israel, contrary to the lying spirit which informed Zedekiah and others (1 Kgs 22). Isaiah has God object to the people's sacrifices, tell them to stop trampling his courts, and reject their new moons, Sabbaths, and appointed festivals. Then he calls on them to cease to do evil, to do good, to seek justice (מִשְׁפָּט), and the like (Isa 1:11-17). Jeremiah predicted the destruction of the temple, if people did not repent (Jer 7). Hosea has God threaten the end of Israel's Sabbaths and major festivals (Hos 2:13). Jeremiah called upon people to circumcise themselves to the LORD (Jer 4:4) and declared that the house of Israel was uncircumcised in heart (Jer 9:26). It follows that the moral behavior of Jews was regarded as more important than physical circumcision. This was liable to cause great trouble for truthful prophets in Israel.

For example, Micaiah was imprisoned on reduced rations (1 Kgs 22:26-27). Uriah, son of Shemaiah, was put to death, which Jeremiah narrowly escaped, both for prophesying the conditional destruction of Jerusalem and the temple (Jer 26). By the time of Jesus, there were also stories of the deaths of other prophets. For example, the story was told of Isaiah being martyred by being sawn in half (*Mart. Isa.* 5). Jesus knew such traditions so well that he predicted his own death in a general statement that it would not do for a prophet to perish outside Jerusalem (Luke 13:33).[2]

In Israel, therefore, the prophetic form of identity was potentially damaging for many Jews, and lethal for prophets. In the Diaspora, it was potentially lethal for the Jewish community as a whole because of its central ability to attack Jewish observances in the name of God. In the Diaspora, Jewish observances protected Jewish identity. If a prophet had arisen in Alexandria and threatened, like Hosea, to end Israel's Sabbaths and major festivals, he would have reinforced existing threats from Gentiles and assimilating Jews to destroy the Jewish community. Moreover, there were no limitations to what a Diaspora prophet might have attacked, if he felt that observance of it was not centerd on God. Yet Diaspora observance was essential for the maintenance of Jewish identity. This reality is surely the reason why not a single prophet ever arose in the Diaspora. It was too dangerous a place for the prophetic spirit to attack aspects of normal Judaism.

The most recent prophet before Jesus was John the Baptist. The centre of John's prophetic ministry was baptism, which symbolised repentance. Mark's account briefly delineates a successful popular ministry (Mark 1:4-6). Mark also says that "everyone," that is, people in general as opposed to only the chief priests, scribes, and elders, believed that John was truly a prophet (Mark 11:32). Jesus believed that John fulfilled the prophecy that Elijah would come before the day of the Lord (Mal 3:23-24, see Mark 9:11-13; Matt 11:7-10//Luke 7:24–7).[3] Major points of John's ministry are confirmed by Josephus (*Ant.* 18.116–19), who effectively gives the popular success of John's prophetic ministry as the reason why Herod Antipas put him to death. This shows serious conflict between Jewish prophetic identity and the official Jewish leadership in Jerusalem followed by conflict with a Jewish tetrarch severe enough to lead to the prophet's death.

Jesus was the most important prophet of his time. Luke put into the mouth of Cleopas and another disciple the description of Jesus as ἀνὴρ προφήτης δυνατὸς ἐν ἔργῳ καὶ λόγῳ ἐναντίον τοῦ Θεοῦ καὶ παντὸς τοῦ λαοῦ (Luke 24:19). That is how Jesus was perceived. He preached powerfully throughout his ministry, he acted mightily in leading the Jesus movement and in his ministry of exorcism and healing, and in his final appearance in Jerusalem, he preached extensively and controlled, to a significant extent, the halakhah in parts of the temple. Consequently, he referred to himself as a prophet in two general statements. When he made a rather unsuccessful visit to his home town of Nazareth, he commented, "A prophet is not despised except in his home town and among his relatives and in his house" (Mark 6:4). The other statement followed from a report of a death threat from Herod Antipas. Jesus declared that he would keep his ministry going for the time being, concluding that "it would not be fitting for a prophet to perish outside Jerusalem" (Luke 13:33). Neither of these passages makes sense, unless Jesus believed that he really was a prophet. Other people also used the category of "prophet" to refer to him (Mark 6:14-16; 8:28). I turn next to the conflict which his prophetic ministry produced.

The first major dispute recorded by St. Mark concerns the observance of the Sabbath (Mark 2:23–3:6), a central facet of Judaism.[4] This dispute began when Jesus' disciples were walking on a path through the cornfields, plucking the ears of corn. Some Pharisees asked Jesus why they were doing what was not lawful *on the Sabbath*. The disciples, therefore, could not have been stealing other people's corn: they must have been taking *Peah*, the grain left at the edges of fields for poor people, which they could pluck by walking along the paths between the fields. Taking *Peah* on the Sabbath is not against the written law. Orthodox Jews had, however, been active in expanding the Sabbath halakhah to prohibit everything they felt should not be done. Some had already written down the following:

אל יאכל איש ביום השבת כי אם המוכן ומן האובד בשדה

A man shall eat on the Sabbath day only what has been prepared, and from what is decaying in the fields (CD X, 22–23).

This practice restricts people to prepared food and fruit which must have fallen off at least a day before, the opposite of what needs to be plucked. We should infer that the Pharisees took a similar view. This was a strict expansion of the Law from an orthodox perspective.[5] Hence, it was accepted neither by the ordinary Jews who were Jesus' disciples nor by Jesus himself.

Mark records two arguments used by Jesus in his disciples' defense. The first uses the example of David, who fed his men on the shewbread in the temple, because this was the only bread available (1 Sam 21:27). Jesus and the Pharisees alike would assume that the incident took place on the Sabbath because this is the day when the shewbread was changed and, hence, the day when it would be the only bread available. Jesus' second argument presupposed that God created the Sabbath for the benefit of people:

שבתא בדיל אנשא אתעבדת ולא אנשא בדיל שבתא: של יט נא הוא בר נש
אף בשבתא

The Sabbath was made for man, and not man for the Sabbath. [28]Surely, then, a/the (son of) man is master even of the Sabbath.

This passage uses a general statement containing the term (א)נש(א)בר rb, which refers especially to Jesus himself, a particularly idiomatic Aramaic idiom.[6] Both these arguments are based on scripture. They would have convinced Jesus' disciples, but not the Pharisees.

We are not told what the Pharisees said, but we are told what they did. In a synagogue meeting, they watched to see whether Jesus would perform a healing, so that they could accuse him (Mark 3:2). On what basis did the Pharisees consider that healing was a violation of the Sabbath? It was not against the written law. We have seen, however, that taking Peah was not against the written law either, and that these Pharisees belonged to the orthodox wing of Judaism. They were expanding the written law as they applied it to the whole of life. Just as they were shocked at the disciples plucking grain on the Sabbath, so they were shocked that Jesus should heal on the Sabbath. Later sources show concern that activities that are connected with healing should not be practiced on the Sabbath (*m. Sabb.* 14:30, with the major exception that saving life overrules the Sabbath. Jesus used this exception as the basis for his major argument in favor of healing on the Sabbath. He believed that in healing the man he was saving a person.

השל יט בשבתא למצבד מה טב או לאבאשה נפש לאחיה או למקטלה:

Is it permitted on the Sabbath to do what is good, or to do evil, to save life/a person or to kill him? (cf Mark 3:4).

The center of Jesus' argument is the expression "to save a life/ person." Whereas the Greek ψυχή is often translated "soul," the

Aramaic נֶפֶשׁ means both "person" and "life," and this range of meaning is essential to understanding Jesus' argument. Later rabbis wrote down the principle that saving life overrides the Sabbath (e.g. *m. Yoma* 8:6: ספק נפשות דוחה שבת). Jesus' argument makes sense only if we suppose that this principle was already accepted by the Pharisees. That the halakhic judgment was in this form is further shown by the sharp contrast with "to kill him": The penalty for Sabbath-breaking was officially death (Exod 31:14; 35:2). The combination of this fact with the normal ruling that saving life overrides the Sabbath explains this sharp contrast. We might suppose, and these Pharisees surely would have supposed, that Jesus was not saving the man's life, and that, therefore, his action was not covered by the halakhic agreement that saving life overrides the Sabbath. To understand Jesus' point of view, we need his argument in justification of another Sabbath healing, that of a sick woman who was also unable to make proper use of her limbs (Luke 13:10-17).

דא בת אברהם·דאסרה סטנא הא שנין עשרה ותמניה: לא יאי דאשתריתי
מן אסורא דנא ביומא דשבתא:

> This daughter of Abraham, whom Satan bound, look!, for eighteen years, (is/was) it not fitting that she should be released from this bond on the day of the Sabbath?[7]

Here we are in an area of overlap between demon possession and what we would regard as other forms of illness. Jesus took the view that this woman could not use her limbs properly because she had been bound by Satan. This view explains the strength of his commitment to healing on the Sabbath, his description of it as "to save life/a person," and the opposition between saving a life and "to kill him." He believed that he was saving people from the devil.

We can now return to the sharpness of "to kill him." We have seen that the official penalty for Sabbath-breaking was death. We shall shortly see the Pharisees taking counsel with the Herodians to bring about this penalty. Jesus is contrasting this action with his own action—he is saving a person, whereas they are bringing about death. Not only, therefore, is he innocent—they are guilty, and guilty of breaking the Law just when they think they are observing it. This wisdom explains the lead-in to this argument:

השליט בשבתא למצבד מה טב או לאבאשה ...

> Is it permitted on the Sabbath to do what is good, or to do evil. . . .

Jesus considered that he was doing good by saving the man from the bond of Satan. He did not regard this as work, in the sense of violating the commandment not to work on the Sabbath. We might have thought that doing evil was not in question, but it is more than a simple contrast with doing good. The Pharisees have every intention of doing evil on the Sabbath, and do so at the end of the passage when they take counsel with the Herodians to destroy Jesus.

The serious nature of this dispute is presented in the final verse, where the Pharisees went out with the Herodians and counseled how they might destroy him. The Herodians were supporters of Herod Antipas, who was in charge of Galilee at the time. He had recently had John the Baptist put to death (Mark 6:17-29; Josephus, *Ant.* 18.116–19).[8] This is the reason for Pharisees to contact the Herodians at that time, and to cooperate with them. We can see the aftermath of this event in Luke 13:31-33. Luke had an Aramaic source for this ancient tradition, with idiomatic and metaphorical uses of time intervals, and of "be perfected" as a metaphor for death.[9] This source may be translated as follows:

> [31] And in that hour Pharisees went and said to him, "Get out and go away from here, because Herod wants to kill you." [32]And he said to them, "Go tell that jackal, Look! I am casting out demons and performing healings today and tomorrow, and on the third day I am perfected. [33]But I am going to proceed today and day after day, for it would not be fitting for a prophet to perish outside Jerusalem."

Here we see the strains and stresses of the temporary alliance between Pharisees and Herodians. If Herod thought that John the Baptist was a threat to the Herodian state, he was likely to take the same view of Jesus. The alliance between Pharisees and Herodians, however, not only supplied Herod with a reason for killing Jesus, but also alienated some of the Pharisees. As such Pharisees were merely orthodox Jews. If some felt so strongly that taking *Peah* and healing on the Sabbath were, or should be, against the Law and that this infraction should be enforced with the death penalty, others are likely to have felt that their view of how the Law should be observed should not be imposed on everyone, especially not on a prophetic teacher who brought so many Jews back to basic observances. They are also likely to have been mindful of the sixth commandment. They, therefore, came and warned Jesus.

Jesus' response comes from the same context as the incident of Mark 3:1-6. He referred directly to his ministry of exorcism and healing and to his forthcoming death. The opposition to his ministry was so serious that he was already planning to die in Jerusalem. This underlines the seriousness of the conflict material in the gospels. In particular, the conflict between the orthodox and prophetic forms of Jewish identity was a matter of life and death. I have already noted the seriousness of the conflicts between prophetic and other forms of Jewish identity in previous centuries. I noted also that a major source of conflict was prophetic criticism of normal Jewish observances, Sabbath included. In Mark 2:23–3.6, we have a conflict that is at one level about a feature of normal Jewish observance, the Sabbath. But it is not normal Jewish observance of the Sabbath that is the subject of dispute at all. It is rather two orthodox expansions of the Sabbath halakhah that met serious opposition from the prophetic spirit. That this contention should lead to deadly struggle is in accordance with prophetic tradition.

I turn next to a major dispute over Jesus' ministry of exorcism.[10] This highly successful ministry ran into fierce opposition. Jesus was accused of casting out demons by the power of the devil himself. Our oldest source characterizes the opponents who made this accusation as "scribes who came down from Jerusalem" (Mark 3:22). These individuals must have been a group of powerful people. A group of scribes who took the trouble to come down from Jerusalem are likely to have included representatives of the chief priests, who were the central Jewish power group in Jerusalem. This gives us an important link to the final events of the ministry, when scribes and elders gathered together with the chief priests to plan Jesus' death.

Jesus responded vigorously with arguments that presuppose that the ministry of exorcism was part of a centrally important battle between the power of God and the power of Satan. One significant argument was a saying in which Jesus used the metaphor of the kingship of God to celebrate his triumph over the forces of evil:

וְהֵן בְּאֶצְבַּע אֱלָהָא אֲנָה מַפֵּק שִׁידַיָּא מְטָאת עֲלֵיכוֹן מַלְכוּתֵהּ דֵּאלָהָא:

But if I cast out demons by the finger of God, the kingship of God has come upon you (cf. Luke 11:20, with "finger" replaced by "spirit" at Matt 12:28).

Here both the "finger" and the "kingship" of God are images of God's powerful action. Jesus had no doubt that this power was moving through him.[11]

Jesus' appreciation of the seriousness of his opposition is especially clear in a Q saying which has not been properly understood because it does not make good sense in Greek, though it does in Aramaic.[12] Consequently, only a minority of early Greek manuscripts preserve the original Greek reading of με after σκορπίζει (Matt 12:30 א 1382* 33 Or et al., Luke 11:23 א*.[2] C² L Θ Ψ 33 579 et al.). The saying is a literal translation of an Aramaic saying of Jesus, which may reasonably be reconstructed as follows:

מן דלא עמי לקבלי הוא ומן דלא כנש עמי בדרני:

Whoever is not with me is against me, and whoever does not gather with me scatters me.

In Greek, as in English, one cannot scatter a person. In Aramaic, however, as in Hebrew, the same word (Aramaic בדר, Hebrew פרז) is used to express the separating of one creature from a group as is used for scattering a whole group—hence, the image of Israel as "a scattered sheep" (שה פרוזה, Jer 50:17). Jesus' whole ministry could reasonably be described as a gathering in of the lost sheep of the house of Israel (cf. Matt 10:6; 18:12-14//Luke 15:4-7). Scribes and Pharisees who were opposed to him were not merely refusing to gather with him. The accusation that he cast out demons by the power of the devil was so serious that it amounted to an attempt to isolate him from Israel altogether. This understanding is the very serious and precise sense of "he who does not gather with me scatters me."

The final argument transmitted from this dispute accused Jesus' opponents of an unforgivable sin. Its exact form is difficult to reconstruct because Jesus used an Aramaic idiom that has no literal Greek equivalent, and the content of the saying was not altogether congenial to some of the Christians who transmitted it. Bearing in mind that the Aramaic term (א)נש(א), literally "son of man," was used in general statements that referred particularly to the speaker, we may reconstruct an original saying like this:

וכל די ימלל מלה לבר אנשא ישתביק לה ומן דמלל מלה על רוחא קדישתא לא ישתביק לה לעלמין:

And everyone who speaks a word against a/the Son of Man, it will be forgiven him, and whoever speaks a word against the Holy Spirit, it will not be forgiven him for ever (cf. Mark 3:28-29, Matt 12:32, Luke 12:10).[13]

The first part of this saying is a general statement decreeing forgiveness to people who oppose or even slander other people. The use of the term "Son of Man," however, is the particular idiom whereby the statement refers particularly to Jesus himself. The saying, therefore, appears to grant forgiveness to Jesus' opponents. The sting is in the second half. The spirit of holiness is a metaphor for God in action. Nowhere is the action of God to be seen more vigorously and obviously than in Jesus' exorcisms. The accusation that he cast out demons by the power of the devil is an unforgivable sin. What Jesus seems to concede in the first part of the saying is, thus, quite removed in the second part. This polemic, like the content of the saying, accordingly provides an excellent setting in this dispute over Jesus' exorcisms. Jesus effectively invokes the power of God to consign to hell the scribes from Jerusalem who had attributed his ministry of exorcism to the devil. A prophet who did this could expect death in Jerusalem.

Our oldest sources contain a massive amount of further evidence of Jesus' attacks on Jewish observances, which cannot be discussed in detail here. For example, Mark reports another serious dispute with the "Pharisees and some of the scribes who came from Jerusalem" (Mark 7:1). They asked why Jesus' disciples did not walk according to the tradition of the elders, but ate bread with profane hands (cf. Mark 7:5). This is a typical orthodox expansion of purity law, and in calling it "the tradition of the elders" these orthodox Jews openly recognized that this behavior is not according to biblical regulation.

Jesus' reply was quite explosive. He retorted with a quotation from Isaiah 29:13 and accused these orthodox Jews of replacing the commandment of God with their own tradition, citing the central command to honor one's father and mother (Exod 20:12//Deut 5:16). This reply is another prophetic criticism of a central Jewish observance, and Jesus' declaration that they did other things of the same kind further indicates his drastic rejection of their basic ideas of how to keep the Law.[14]

Another large quantity of this material is found in Matthew 23, with significant parallels in Luke 11.[15] Scribes and Pharisees are again the major targets. Topics covered include a major Jewish concern, tithing (Matt 23:23//Luke 11:42). This is a biblical requirement, but Jesus criticized scribes and Pharisees whose expanded halakhah to tithing included mint, dill, and cumin, but whom he accused of ignoring central points of the Law, justice, mercy, and trust. This is the same prophetic attack on the way the Law was being observed as I have noted in other material. Of more direct relevance to Jesus' fate is his criticism of scribes and Pharisees who built the tombs of the prophets and declared that they would not have participated in killing them (Matt 23:29-31, uncomprehendingly edited at Luke 11:47-48). Jesus accused them of being the lineal descendants of those who murdered prophets; on account of their opposition to John the Baptist and to Jesus himself.

The final action against Jesus followed the cleansing of the Temple. Mark places this the day after the Triumphal Entry, another overtly prophetic act that showed Jesus as the leader of a significant religious movement. Mark's account of the Cleansing of the Temple was translated from an Aramaic source, which may reasonably be translated into English as follows:[16]

> And they came to Jerusalem, and he went to the temple, and began to throw out those who sold and those who bought in the temple. And he overturned the tables of the moneychangers and the chairs of those who sold the doves. [16]And he did not allow anyone to carry a vessel through the temple. [17]And he was teaching, and he said, "Is it not written 'My house shall be called a house of prayer for all the nations'[Isa 56:7]? And you have made it 'a brigands' cave' [Jer 7:11]." [18]And the chief priests and the scribes heard, and sought how they might destroy him (Mark 11:15-18).

This was intended to make the whole extended Herodian temple a house of prayer. The buying, selling, and changing of money was done in what we often call the "Court of the Gentiles," the outermost court, into which "everyone, even foreigners, was allowed to enter" (Josephus, *Ag.Ap.* 103). Money had to be changed for payment of the temple tax, and for the purchase of sacrifices and perhaps for other things. Jesus clearly objected to the temple being used for these purposes.

This act was quintessentially prophetic. It was a deliberate and vigorous attack on the way in which major Jewish observances, commanded in the Torah, were being kept. The nature of this event as a major prophetic attack on Jewish observances was underlined by the texts on which Jesus preached, Isaiah 56 and Jeremiah 7. Isaiah 56 addresses the acceptance of people who hold fast to the covenant. To make the point quite clear, they include even foreigners and eunuchs. Keeping the Sabbath is particularly specified, so these are people who were, or were becoming, observant. Isaiah 56:6-7 is concerned with foreigners, and Isaiah 56:7 is concerned entirely with their acceptance in the temple:

> [6]And the foreigners who join themselves to YHWH to serve him and to love the name of YHWH and to be his servants, everyone who keeps the Sabbath and does not profane it, and those who hold fast to my covenant, [I] will bring them to my holy mountain and make them joyful in my

house of prayer, their burnt offerings and their sacrifices shall be accepted on my altar, for my house shall be called a house of prayer for all peoples.

At the time of Jesus, everyone knew that the only part of the temple foreigners were allowed in was the Court of the Gentiles. Hence, if they are to be joyful "in my house of prayer," and this is to be "a house of prayer for all peoples," prayer, not trade, must be the function of the Court of the Gentiles. As well as praying in the outer court, foreigners who joined themselves to YHWH would have their sacrifices accepted. It follows that there is no question of an attack on the sacrificial system as such. The Isaiah passage goes on to complain about the leaders of Israel. At Isaiah 56:11, her "shepherds" have no understanding, they have turned each one to their own "profit," and the term בצע clearly indicates that their profit has been unjustly and violently gained. This is one point of contact with Jeremiah 7.

The text of Jeremiah 7 vigorously criticizes Jews who worship in the temple, but who commit various sins, including theft, idolatry, and murder. They would be allowed to dwell in the land if they repented. Otherwise, "I will do to the house over which my name is called, in which you trust, and to the place which I gave to you and to your fathers, as I did to Shiloh" (Jer 7:14). Everyone knew that God had destroyed Shiloh. Accordingly, exposition of Jer 7:14 could form the kind of conditional threat to the temple that might lead even genuine eyewitnesses to disagree about what Jesus said he would do and what he predicted. In this context, Jeremiah refers to the temple as "this house over which my name is called," a central point of contact between the two texts expounded. He labels it מערת פריצים, "a brigands' cave" (Jer 7:11). Jesus' use of this expression is a highly picturesque application of prophetic scripture to the Royal Portico. We must infer that the merchants were taking money from the poor—and in accordance with the Law. Poor people had to pay the temple tax, just like rich people, and moneychangers always sell money for more than its face value, to make a profit. Rich priests, however, did not pay the temple tax, and a number of judgments by scribes would increase the money that people had to pay, poor people included. The most dramatic decision was that the temple tax should be paid every year, rather than once in a lifetime. This decision is not an inevitable interpretation of Exodus 30:11-16 with Nehemiah 10:32, and it is contradicted by one of the Dead Sea scrolls, which preserves the older halakhah:

[Concer]ning [the ransom]: the money of valuation which a man gives as ransom for himself, half [a shekel], one t[ime] will he give it all his days (4Q 159 1 6–7).

The annual offering gave the temple far more money than it might be thought to need, and at half a shekel per person, it was burden only to the poor. Pigeons or doves were sacrificed by poor people, sometimes when richer people would sacrifice a larger animal (e.g., Lev 12:6-8). Consequently, it would have been obvious to everyone that doves were especially important for the sacrifices of poor people.

There is also evidence of the massive wealth of the temple and of the chief priests, who could legally extract tithes from the poor. This gives another level of meaning to the use of the scriptural polemic, "brigands' cave." Brigands hoarded their spoils, which authorities regarded as ill-gotten, in their caves. The merchants and moneychangers were essential in this system that accepted such massive quantities of money that it could be used for plating parts of the temple with gold, while some of the poor went hungry and naked.

Given this scenario, we can see that Jesus' criticism of the financial and trading arrangements in the temple is entirely consistent with his other prophetic attacks on Jewish observances. His action was a threat to the power of the chief priests and their scribes. Opposition was, there-fore, to be expected, and an attempt by chief priests and scribes to have him killed is an entirely logical outcome. This consequence is first men-tioned in the most appropriate place: immediately after the Cleansing of the Temple (Mark 11:18). From a practical point of view, however, for them to take immediate action would have been difficult, lest they pro-voke a bloody riot. Mark reports on them very precisely, just two days before Passover:

> And the chief priests and scribes were seeking how they might seize him by stealth, and kill him, for they said, "Not in the festival crowd (μὴ ἐν τῇ ἑορτῇ for בחגא לא), in case there is a riot of the people" (Mark 14:1-2).

Moreover, Jesus continued to cause opposition by his prophetic teaching in the temple. A delegation of chief priests, scribes, and elders came to ask him by what authority he acted in the temple (Mark 11:27-28). Jesus recalled the prophetic ministry of John the Baptist, asking whether his baptism was "from heaven or of men" (Mark 11:30). Mark's account of their difficulty over this question gives us the vital informa-tion that lots of people thought that John was truly a prophet but that the chief priests, scribes, and elders had not believed in him (Mark

11:31-32). Moreover, we should accept the full implication of the power of Jesus' charismatic action and preaching in the first place and the present tense of this delegation's question: "By what authority do you do these things?" (Mark 11:28), not "By what authority did you act yesterday?" We must infer that the moneychangers were changing money outside the temple, that doves were being sold outside the temple, and that no one was allowed to carry vessels through the temple. This practical display of power subverted the authority of the chief priests and their scribes.

Jesus went further. In a vigorous reworking of the prophetic criticism of Israel in Isaiah 5, he presented parabolically the rejection of the prophets sent by God to Israel (Mark 12:1-12). He then presented one final messenger, a "beloved son" as a symbol of himself as God's final, most important, and much beloved messenger to make the last call to all Israel to return to the Lord. This messenger was killed, a parabolic presentation of Jesus' forthcoming death. The vineyard, the symbol of Israel from Isaiah 5, would then be given to others, a parabolic representation of the coming of the kingdom, when the Twelve would judge the twelve tribes of Israel (Matt 19:28//Luke 22:30). Jesus ended with Psalm 118:22-23, part of one of the Hallel psalms set for Passover:

> The stone which the builders rejected has become the head of the corner: this has happened from the Lord, and it is amazing in our eyes.

We must remember that the building of the temple was by no means complete. By this stage, the chief priests and scribes were effectively in charge and could reasonably be seen as בניא, "the builders," standing in front of Jesus and continuing their rejection of him. The Aramaic זוייתא, "corner," is used in later Aramaic with reference to the temple as a whole (e.g. PRK 231:14), so ראש דזוייתא would soon be in charge of the temple as a whole. No wonder they sought to seize him, for the institutional leaders of Israel could hardly fail to realize that this parable was told against them and foretold the triumph of the man who already controlled the Court of the Gentiles, and some other aspects of the halakhah for offerings.

I do not repeat here the story of Jesus' betrayal and death. I note only that after his Jewish examination, he was beaten by his Jewish tormentors as a prophet (Mark 14:65, with Matt 26:68//Luke 22:64). To get him crucified by Pilate, they had to present him as an insurgent, the leader of a movement that was a threat to the peace. But they did not forget the prophetic nature of his ministry.

I conclude, therefore, that the conflicts during Jesus' ministry can be fully understood only if we recognize that he belonged to the prophetic form of Jewish identity. It is this which powered his vigorous and fearless attacks on scribes and Pharisees who belonged to the orthodox form of Jewish identity and on the institutional leaders of Israel. Jesus expected these conflicts to be terminal, and he deliberately cleansed the temple in the knowledge that this would lead to his death, which he interpreted elsewhere (Mark 10:45; 14:24). The presentation of his story in the Diaspora was inevitable. It did not require an Early High Christology, and, together with other factors, it led eventually to the separation of Rebecca's children. But that is another story.

Chapter 8

Pauline Exegesis and the Incarnate Christ

David B. Capes

We are not accustomed to thinking of Paul as an incarnational theologian.[1] Among the New Testament writers that place belongs to John, the traditional author of the Fourth Gospel and the Johannine letters. The elegant prose of the gospel prologue (John 1:1-18) leaves little doubt that the community of the beloved disciple believed that "the Word" (*Logos*) had existed from the beginning, was the agent of creation, and had "become flesh" in Jesus (v. 14) to reveal God and his glory. Some have concluded that the doctrine of the incarnation[2] originated in the Johannine community late in the first century A.D.[3] Accordingly, these interpreters have concluded that the earlier Christian communities may have held Jesus to be a prophet, Messiah, and the Son of God (in the messianic sense) but certainly not the preexistent and incarnate Son of God (in the divine sense). However, others find preexistence attributed to Jesus earlier in the first century. Simon Gathercole, for example, argues *"that preexistence [C]hristology is already widespread among various individuals and in various different communities around the Mediterranean well before A.D. 70."*[4] Gordon Fee traces the incarnation back even further, arguing that Paul not only asserts but assumes the preexistence of Christ in his letters.[5] Likewise, Larry Hurtado concurs with a growing majority of scholars who find preexistence and incarnation attested in Paul's letters.[6] The nature of the statements themselves indicates that these christological convictions were widely held, common currency in the Pauline mission. Never do we find Paul *arguing for* the preexistence of Christ; always we find him *arguing from* it toward some ethical, ecclesial, or theological point.

In order to account for this phenomenon, Hurtado argues against looking to Hellenistic religion. Instead, he believes that the apocalyptic and sapiential traditions within Second Temple Judaism provided the rich soil from which these convictions about Jesus grew and developed. He writes:

> [A]ttributing preexistence to Jesus proceeds from the conviction that he is the eschatological agent of redemption. Convinced as early believers were that Jesus has been sent from God, and that final salvation is to be realized through Jesus, it was, in the logic of Jewish apocalyptic, only a small and very natural step to hold that he was also in some way "there" with and in God from before the creation of the world.[7]

To put it another way, eschatology preceded protology in ascribing preexistence to Jesus. Furthermore, there is little doubt that early Christians like Paul mined the language and concepts associated with divine Wisdom to fashion christological formulas, confessions, and hymns to express the transcendent glory they saw in the face of Jesus. In some texts Wisdom is personified, present from the beginning with God, an agent of creation (e.g., Prov 8:22–31; Sir 1:4; 24:9; Wis 9:9; Philo *Quaest. in Gen.* 4.97; 4Q185; 11QPs^a 26:9–15). In other texts, Wisdom is identified with the commandments and God's eternal Torah (e.g., Sir 15:1; 17:11; 19:20; 21:11: 24.23, 32; Bar 3:9–4:4; 4Q525). Those who submit their lives to Lady Wisdom and the Torah will experience "the good life," which God has promised to his covenant people. Occasionally, Wisdom is even described as "the image of God" (e.g., Wis 7:26; Philo *Leg. All.* 1.43; cf. Col 1:15). It is widely affirmed that the language of Wisdom played an early and important role in helping Christians fashion appropriate ways to express their conviction that the risen, exalted Jesus held transcendent, pretemporal status.

In this essay I will examine Paul's christological exegesis of scripture in Romans 9:30–10:13. This passage is not listed among those texts typically cited as evidence that the apostle held to the divine preexistence and incarnation of Jesus.[8] However I will argue that Romans 9:30–10:13, properly interpreted, depends upon and reflects these convictions. My focus here will be on how Paul reads and expands the meaning of scripture by a hermeneutical process that is thoroughly Christocentric.

"The Stone of Stumbling"

In Romans 9–11 Paul laments the status of unbelieving Jews and its resultant disjuncture with Jewish and Gentile believers now included in the people of God. He attempts to justify this astonishing situation by frequent appeals to God's plan revealed in scripture.[9] Pivotal to his discussion is Romans 9:30–10:13 which describes why Israel had not yet attained God's righteousness revealed in Christ.[10] Paul's discourse follows carefully along the path of scriptural exegesis in allusions and comments on the Law (Lev 18:5; Deut 9:4; 30:12-14) and the Prophets (Isa 8:14; 28:16; Joel 3:5).[11]

Paul's first scriptural echo in the focal passage is found in Romans 9:33. It is precipitated by his previous remarks on the state of unbelieving Israel vis-à-vis God's saving righteousness now revealed in Christ. He puts forth what is for him a disturbing observation, namely, that Gentiles, who have not been pursuing righteousness,[12] are, nevertheless, obtaining it through faith. On the other hand, Israel, who has pursued "the law of righteousness," has failed to keep the Law altogether. The reason, he suggests, is because Israel does not pursue righteousness through faith; instead, she pursues it through works (9:32).[13] Many of his countrymen, he claims, are stumbling over "the stone of stumbling."

The stone remark in 9:32 is prompted by the stone references in Isa 8:14 and 28:16. He introduces the scripture with a standard introductory formula, καθὼς γέγραπται ("just as it is written"). Such formulae are typical when Paul is engaging in explicit citations. He quotes:

Ἰδοὺ τίθημι ἐν Σιὼν λίθον προσκόμματος καὶ πέτραν σκανδάλου
Καὶ ὁ πιστεύων ἐπ᾽ αὐτῷ οὐ καταισχυνθήσεται

(Behold, I lay in Zion a stone of stumbling and a rock of offense,
And the one who believe on it [or "him"] will not be shamed.)

Utilizing an exegetical method known to Hillel and other first century biblical exegetes as *gezera shawa*,[14] Paul blends the scriptural images around the key word "stone." For him these texts from the prophets illuminate his current situation.

Isaiah 8 and 28 not only contain the same keyword ("stone"), but they also derive from a similar context. In Isaiah 8, the prophet utters judgment upon Israel during the threat of the Assyrian crisis. Apparently, many leaders were putting their trust in political alliances to protect them from their northern enemies. Unknown to them, however, was God's plan to use Assyria as his instrument to punish his recalcitrant people (8:5-10). In what seems to be a personal word to the prophet, God warns Isaiah not to fear foreign powers; instead, he should fear YHWH. His oracle claims that YHWH will be a "stone of stumbling" and "a rock

of offense" to both houses of Israel. For those who would rather trust in
political treaties rather than YHWH, Isaiah warns: YHWH will be a trap
and a snare. A similar account in Isaiah 28 depicts God's judgment upon
the arrogant rulers in Jerusalem. They boast of their accomplishments
and brag that they have successfully negotiated a covenant with death
and the grave (28:14-15).[15] In this oracle, however, God promises to
respond to their prideful claims with judgment. He lays a stone in Zion
that establishes justice and righteousness, dissolving their covenants with
death and the grave (28:16-20). Although the referent for "stone" in this
passage is not entirely clear, it likely refers to God since Isaiah prophesies
a day when YHWH rises up like Mt. Perazim (28:21) to judge the
unrighteous and become a glorious crown on the head of the righteous
remnant (28:5-6).

The Paul returns to these oracles because the situation in Isaiah's day parallels his own. Just as Isaiah predicted judgment upon Israel in the eighth
century B.C., so now Paul understands that, at least for a time, God's
hand is moving against those in Israel who reject the righteousness that
comes by the faithfulness of Jesus, the Lord and Messiah (Rom 9:6-29;
11:7-32). Again, Isaiah's oracles condemn the leaders for establishing
political alliances with weak nations rather than putting faith in God's
deliverance. In the same way, Paul suggests that the current failure of his
countrymen to attain righteousness is due to their dependence upon
"works" (10:3). Finally, even though both Isaiah 8 and 28 threaten judgment, they also contain elements of hope. Paul's scriptural echo likewise
does not end with stumbling; it ends with the hope of (universal) salvation for those who trust in Christ (9:33d; Rom 10:11-13).

The question remains, however: Who or perhaps what is the "stone"
in Paul's exegesis? Some interpret the passage theocentrically; they take
the "stone" as referring to the Torah with faith directed toward God.[16]
This is possible, but it is not the likely interpretation. The most plausible referent, for several reasons, is Christ. First, early Christians frequently made christological use of these and other "stone" texts. Unless
there are compelling reasons to do otherwise, we should interpret these
"stone" passages christologically as well.[17] Second, in Romans 10:11,
Paul quotes Isaiah 28:16 again in a context where confession and faith
are christologically oriented. Since the apostle reads the passage christologically in 10:11, he probably does so a few verses earlier. Third, in a
parallel passage, 1 Corinthians 1:23, Paul relates that his preaching of the
crucified Messiah is "a stumbling block" (σκάνδαλον) to unbelieving
Jews. He uses the same word in his merged quotation (9:33) with the

phrase "rock of offense" (πέτραν σκανδάλου). Contextually, both passages have to do with how gospel proclamation creates offense to unbelieving Jews. Because this phrase varies from the LXX, which reads πέτρας πτώματι (8:14), it is plausible that Paul alters the text to express clearly his conviction that the preaching of the crucified Messiah is a "scandal" to unbelievers. The christological reading of "stone" is given even more weight if Jewish teachers were already using "stone" passages with messianic import.[18] If this is the case, Paul heightens the offense for inhospitable Jews by adapting these messianic "stone" passages as references to Jesus. Finally, we must note the overall context of Paul's argument.[19] For him unbelieving Israel is not attaining right standing before God because she fails to put faith in Jesus as Messiah and Lord. The Israelites have heard the message proclaimed by Paul and his coworkers (10:14-17); however, they are not obeying that message (10:18-21). Unbelieving Jews are not stumbling over the Torah but over Jesus as Messiah and Lord.

It should not be overlooked that Isaiah 8 clearly—and Isaiah 28 somewhat less clearly—names YHWH as "the stone of stumbling." If Paul is aware of this connection, as he seems to be of other salient factors in these texts, his application of these "stone" passages to Jesus carries significant christological implications. At the level of exegesis, he associates Christ with YHWH and posits him in an eschatological role that scripture reserves for God.[20] These convictions about the transcendent significance of Jesus as Messiah are consonant with the notion that Jesus is the preexistent, incarnate Christ.

Descent and Ascent of Christ

In Romans 10, Paul expands his argument regarding the relationship of Jews and Gentiles to his message. Although his coreligionists have a zeal for God, the apostle laments that it is misdirected. Ironically, while trying to establish and maintain their own righteousness, they are missing God's righteousness completely because they seek theirs through the works of the Law. What they have failed to learn from Israel's past is that the crux of the Law is now and has always been righteousness through faith.[21] If this has been unclear in the past, God has made this evident in Christ. For Paul saving righteousness is the righteousness of God constituted ultimately in God's act to reconcile the world through Christ (e.g., Rom 3:21-26).[22] To Paul's dismay, many fail to acknowledge that Christ is the *telos* ("end") of the Law (Rom 10:1-4) and that righteousness comes to all by faith.[23] This does not mean, of course, that the Law is finished; it means rather that the Law has achieved its goal. In and through the crucified and risen Christ, the ultimate purpose of the Law has been finally and completely realized (cf. Gal 3:21-29). This realization has enormous consequences for the persecutor-turned-apostle, not only for his understanding of the Law but for his understanding of the significance of Jesus.

Romans 10:5-13 provides scriptural warrant for Paul's contention that Christ is the *telos* of the Law and that God's righteousness extends to all who believe in him. The passage contains quotations and allusions from the Law and the Prophets that we will now consider. If Christ is the proper "end" of the Law, then we should expect to find his story anticipated and prefigured in earlier texts.

To make his argument, Paul mines the words of Moses (Lev 18:5) for a negative assessment of a righteousness derived from the Law. He quotes the same verse with similar intent in Galatians 3:12.[24] He writes (Rom 10:5): ὁ ποιήσας αὐτὰ ἄνθρωπος ζήσεται ἐν αὐτοῖς ("the person who does them [i.e., the commandments] will live by them"). He contrasts Moses, who speaks for the former order, and personifies the "Righteousness-from-faith," who speaks for the new.[25] Ironically, the "Righteousness-from-faith" echoes the message of Deuteronomy, a book well known as Moses' farewell address to Israel (9:4; 30:12-14).

Not all interpreters agree that Paul is quoting scripture in Romans 10:6–8; they opt instead to read these sayings as proverbial.[26] Nevertheless, (1) the frequency of Old Testament quotations in Romans 9–11, (2) the verbal affinity of Romans 10:6-8 with Deuteronomy 9:4 and 30:11-13, and (3) the τοῦτ᾿ ἔστιν formula, which is used elsewhere to express commentary on an explicit scriptural citation (e.g., Rom 9:7-8; Heb 7:5; 1 Pet 3:20; cf. Acts 2:16), indicate that Paul is engaging in explicit citation and commentary.[27]

The following lays out the texts of Deuteronomy, as quoted by Paul, and his commentary:

Text (10:6b; Deut 9:4):
μὴ εἴπῃς ἐν τῇ καρδίᾳ σου
(Do not say in your heart)

Text (10:6c; Deut 30:12):
τίς ἀναβήσεται εἰς τὸν οὐρανόν;
(Who will ascend into heaven?)

Commentary (10:6d):
τοῦτ᾽ ἔστιν Χριστὸν καταγαγεῖν·
(that is, to bring Christ down)

Text (10:7a; Deut 30:13):
τίς καταβήσεται εἰς τὴν ἄβυσσον
(Who will descend into the abyss?)

Commentary (10:7b):
τοῦτ᾽ ἔστιν Χριστὸν ἐκ νεκρῶν ἀναγαγεῖν
(that is, to bring Christ up from the dead)

Text (10:8b; Deut 30:14):
ἐγγύς σου τὸ ῥῆμά ἐστιν ἐν τῷ στόματί σου καὶ ἐν τῇ
καρδίᾳ σου
(the word is near you, in your mouth and in your heart)

Commentary (10:8c):
τοῦτ᾽ ἔστιν τὸ ῥῆμα τῆς πίστεως ὃ κηρύσσομεν
(that is, the word of faith which we [even now] preach)

Several factors should be noticed. First, Paul's quotations of Deuteronomy 9:4 and 30:14 are virtually identical to the Greek text found in the LXX. At the same time, his renderings of Deuteronomy 30:12 and 30:13 vary significantly. As we will suggest below, the variations may be due to the development of Deuteronomy 30:11-14 in the Wisdom tradition. It is also possible, however, that (a) Paul alters the text to conform with the story of Jesus or (b) the Greek textual tradition of Deut 30:11–14 is not fixed in his day. Second, each commentary Paul offers begins with the phrase τοῦτ᾽ ἔστιν ("that/ this is"; cf. Rom 9:7-8). The use of this phrase suggests that Paul interprets these texts in a manner similar to *pesher* exegesis at Qumran (cf. 1QpHab 5.6-8; 6.2-8; 7.3-5; 10.2-4; 12.2-10).[28] The driving conviction of this kind of exegesis is a sense of fulfillment, that is, that recent events have fulfilled a promise or prophecy made in scripture. This completion of prophecy corresponds well with Paul's conviction that in Christ the purpose of the Law has been fulfilled. Obviously then, Paul interprets Deuteronomy christologically. With each comment, he explains the essential meaning of scripture over against the larger story of Jesus as the Christ. So, for Paul, Christ is the climax of the covenant made with Moses and the content of his preached word of faith.[29]

To appreciate Paul's exegesis, we must explore the story behind Deuteronomy 9 and 30 and track its subsequent development in Jewish exegetical history. The phrase "do not say in your heart" (Rom 10:6) recalls Deuteronomy 9:4 (cf. Deut 8:17). As the Israelites prepare to enter the Promised Land, God warns them not to take credit for the coming victory. He will fight the battle and drive out the wicked before his people, but the victory will be his, totally and completely. Israel, therefore, should not presume on her own righteousness (Deut 9:6, NRSV): "Know, then, that the LORD your God is not giving you this good land to occupy because of your righteousness; for you are a stubborn people." As the account unfolds, Moses reminds Israel how she provoked God in the wilderness. The victory will not be won by the righteousness or the military prowess of Israel and her commanders. The coming victory will be God's act from beginning to end.

Paul's use of Deuteronomy 9:4 recalls not only the text but the context as well. Many of Paul's coreligionists are missing God's promises by relying on their own righteousness. The apostle revives the story of Deuteronomy to argue that no remnant of self-righteousness will bring a people into the divine promise; only God's act can establish saving righteousness. Thus Paul's intertextual echo of Deuteronomy 9:4 lays the foundation for recognizing God's act in Christ as establishing divine righteousness. That act is spelled out through the way the story of Jesus intersects with Israel's past, fresh from the pages of Deuteronomy.

In Deuteronomy 30, Moses prophesies restoration for the banished people of God who are scattered among the nations. Through the prophet, God promises to gather them to the land, to make them prosperous, to punish their enemies, and to circumcise their hearts. As a result, they will one day love God and observe his commandments. Specifically, commandments are the focus of Deuteronomy 30:11-14. God's commandments are not far off. They are not up in heaven so that someone would have to go up, retrieve them, bring them back, and proclaim them (30:12). Neither are they beyond the sea that someone would have to cross the sea, retrieve them, bring them back, and announce them (30:13). On the contrary, God has already brought the commandments near, "in your heart and in your mouth" (30:14). Since God has already given the commandments (at Sinai), no human effort is necessary or even relevant. From Deuteronomy 30, Paul learns that the covenant depends solely upon God's act.

In tradition history, Deuteronomy 30 proves an important text. Philo, for example, recalls this text and refers to it as a search for "the good" (τἀγαθὸν). "The good" is not far off, he writes, but it is near. There is no need to fly up to heaven or traverse the sea, for it resides near in the mouth (στόματι), heart (καρδία) and hands (χερσί). For the Alexandrian, these three aspects of the human constitution represent speech, thought, and action, respectively. When these live in harmony, there is happiness (*Som* 2.180; *Post* 84–85; *Praem* 80; *Mut* 236–37). Philo also appropriates Deuteronomy 30:11-14 as applicable to "virtue" (*Prob* 68) and a life transformed by repentance (*Virt* 183).

Other exegetes read Deuteronomy 30:11-14 and interpret it as referring to Wisdom. Perhaps the most compelling example is Bar 3:29-30:

τίς ἀνέβη εἰς τὸν οὐρανὸν καὶ ἔλαβεν αὐτὴν
    καὶ κατεβίβασεν αὐτὴν ἐκ τῶν νεφελῶν
τίς διέβη πέραν τῆς θαλάσσης καὶ εὗρεν αὐτὴν
    καὶ οἴσει αὐτὴν χρυσίου ἐκλεκτοῦ

(Who has gone up into heaven and taken her (Wisdom)
    and brought her down from the clouds?
Who has gone across the sea and found her
    and will buy her with precious gold?)

This passage echoes and elaborates Deuteronomy 30:11-14, passages originally referring to the commandments, and relates these lines to divine Wisdom. It underscores the inaccessibility of Wisdom through human effort (cf. Sir 7:23-24; Job 28:12-22), just as Deuteronomy 30:11-14 emphasizes the inaccessibility of the commandments without God's act to bring them near. Contextually Baruch 3:9–4:4 praises Wisdom and identifies it with Torah (cf. Wis 6:4-9; 9:9; Sir 24:23). Note particularly Baruch 4:1 (cf. Prov 1–9; Wis 7:27):

αὕτη ἡ βίβλος τῶν προσταγμάτων τοῦ θεοῦ
    καὶ ὁ νόμος ὁ ὑπάρχων εἰς τὸν αἰῶνα

(She [Wisdom] is the book of the commandments of God
    and the Law that abides forever.)

In other Wisdom texts, "heaven" and "abyss" signify the inaccessibility of Wisdom. Sirach 24:5 reads:

γῦρον οὐρανοῦ ἐκύκλωσα μόνη
    καὶ ἐν βάθει ἀβύσσων περιπάτησα

(I [Wisdom] encircled the vault of heaven alone
    and I walked in the depths of the abyss.)

Likewise, in Job 11:5-9, Zophar desires that God speak and reveal his Wisdom. He declares that the Wisdom, depths and limits of God, are as "high as the heavens" and "deeper than Sheol"; they are "longer than the earth" and "broader than the sea." Additionally, Job 28 describes the search by man for Wisdom in the depths of the sea (28:14) and in death (28:22). Though one may search for Wisdom, one does not find it in the land of the living (28:13). Only God's act establishes it (28:23-28). Again, Baruch 3:31-32 advocates that man cannot attain Wisdom; yet God has revealed it to Jacob and Israel (Bar 3:36-37; cf. Sir 24:8-12).

We find then that the sapiential tradition uses a variety of images to signify the inaccessibility of Wisdom: the height of heaven, the breadth of the sea, the span of the earth, and the depths of the abyss (and, therefore, death). These are used interchangeably to express the conviction that God's Wisdom is unavailable through human effort, and yet it is brought near by God's own, gracious act. Specifically, God has brought his Wisdom near to Israel in the Torah.[30]

In Romans 10:6-7, Paul appropriates Deuteronomy 30:11-14—both text and narrative context—and construes the phrases in vertical (heaven/abyss) rather than horizontal (heaven/across the sea) symbols.[31] His construal reflects insights from the Wisdom tradition that already signified the inaccessibility of Wisdom with this passage. Moreover, his echoes extend the meaning of this text christologically through the use of a commentary style similar to pesher. When Righteousness-from-faith speaks (Deut 30:12), "Who will ascend into heaven?" Paul explains, "that is, to bring Christ down" (Rom 10:6). Again as Righteousness-from-faith declares, "Who will descend into the abyss?" Paul comments, "that is, to bring Christ up from the dead" (Rom 10:7). His commentary expands these quotations beyond their original and developed referents of Torah and Wisdom to include Christ as well.[32] He reads these texts to suggest that Israel and the nations ultimately need the Messiah to establish righteousness, the Messiah who came down from heaven and came back from the dead. No one can attain this righteousness from below; in fact, there is no need because God has already brought it near by his gracious act in Christ.

At this hermeneutical juncture, the story of Jesus intersects with Israel's past and her own sacred story. Just as God brought to Israel the Torah in earlier times, in these last days God has brought to both Jew and Gentile the Messiah from heaven in order to redeem and save the world. That salvation, according to Paul, is apprehended through faith and not works of the Law. In this passage we see Paul engaging in a type of christological reflection that can be regarded as incarnational. He reads Deuteronomy 30:12 and extends its meaning to reflect the descent of the Messiah from heaven. The claim is made without explanation or qualification, which suggests it is an established element of Paul's gospel. Then, to complete the story, he interprets Deuteronomy 30:13 as portraying the resurrection of the Messiah from the dead. Thus both the incarnation and resurrection of Messiah Jesus are celebrated in Paul's intertextual play.[33] He thereby extends the coming and the role of the Messiah in surprising and new ways, ways which may not have been anticipated, ways which had clearly caused offense.

Not all, of course, agree that Paul's exegetical moves here refer to the incarnation. James D. G. Dunn, arguing that incarnational Christology emerges later in the first century, interprets 10:6 as bringing down the ascended, not the preexistent, heavenly Christ. The point of Paul's argument, he claims, is that Christ is distant and unavailable to humankind; at the same time, however, saving righteousness is near in the preaching of the gospel.[34] While some have supported Dunn's conclusions, I submit that (1) his conclusion regarding the current passage is unwarranted and (2) Romans 10:6-7 should be interpreted as incarnation/resurrection (descent/ascent) for the following reasons.

First, Paul's christological interpretation of Deuteronomy 30 underscores the nearness of Christ to his people not his distance. The analogy between Christ and the commandments is obvious. Just as God brought the commandments near for Israel many generations ago, so now, at the proper time (Gal 4:4), he brings the Messiah down and makes him available to all by faith. The commandments of God are not regarded as distant. To the contrary, God has brought them close so they can be heard and obeyed. Similarly, it does not follow that Paul regards the risen Jesus as distant. His powerful, religious experiences and his understanding of the Spirit suggest that he considers the risen, heavenly Jesus available to all Christ-believers. Even while he was persecuting the church, Saul receives a "revelation" of Jesus (Gal 1:11-12). Afterward, as Christ's apostle, he has other visions and revelations of the Lord Jesus that defy his full cooperation and understanding (2 Cor 12:1-10).[35] He speaks of his own spiritual transformation as an experience of the glory of God in the face of Jesus (2 Cor 3:16–4:6).[36]

Based upon his experiences with the risen Christ, it is unlikely he would have seen the risen Jesus as distant and unavailable to him. Moreover, through the contingent circumstances of his letters, Paul speaks of the nearness of Christ to all his followers. In Romans 8:9-10, he writes that "the Spirit of God dwells in you [the Roman Christ-believers]." He refers to the same Spirit of God as the Spirit of Christ that is "in you." The phrase "in you" and corollary expressions imply that baptized believers are united and connected with Christ. Later in that same chapter, Paul celebrates the risen Jesus seated at the right hand, interceding for us (8:34), and yet confesses that nothing in heaven or earth can separate the faithful from the love of God, which is in Christ Jesus. In Colossians 1:27 the apostle describes the heavenly mystery, now revealed, as "Christ in you, the hope of glory." These and other passages indicate that Paul does not consider the risen Christ as distant and unavailable to his followers. This does not mean, of course, that Paul's eschatology is fully realized; he longs for and encourages his churches to pray for the second advent of Christ to complete what he started (e.g., 1 Cor 16:22; Phil 1:6; 3:20-21).[37] Still, longing for the parousia does not mean he considers the Lord Jesus absent and unavailable.

Second, while Paul's commentary in Romans 10:6-8 contains no explicit reference to Christ as Wisdom, Wisdom Christology, nevertheless, underwrites his whole discussion. Paul's statement that Christ is the *telos* of the Law reflects this linkage. Since Jewish exegetical tradition had already related Torah with Wisdom and portrayed them as eternal agents of God's plan, the connection between Torah and Christ in 10:4-7 echoes divine Wisdom as well.[38] Paul's christological use of Deuteronomy 30:11-14, a text already well-traveled in reference to Wisdom, also confirms this. By identifying Christ as Torah-Wisdom that comes from heaven, he appears to attribute preexistence to him. Preexistence, of course, is a prerequisite for incarnational thinking. Paul takes what is implicit here regarding Christ and Wisdom and makes it explicit in 1 Corinthians 1:24, 30 where he states that Christ is "the Power and the Wisdom of God."[39]

Third, by interpreting Romans 10:6 as a reference to the incarnation, the order of the clauses (a) bringing Christ down from heaven and (b) bringing Christ up from the abyss corresponds to both the narrative order of Deuteronomy and the chronological order of Jesus' life. To interpret bringing Christ down from where the Risen One is after the ascension violates the narrative structure of Paul's essential story.[40] Despite the various, contingent issues facing Paul and his churches, Paul's theology exhibits a coherent, narrative shape. At the heart of that narrative are two intersecting stories: (a) the story of Israel and (b) the story of Jesus. While not completely parallel, they are related. From scripture, Paul learns that God brought the commandments near to his covenant people; no one had to traverse heaven or sea to bring them near. Likewise, he discovers that God has brought the Messiah down from heaven and up from the dead in order to demonstrate his righteousness. The catalyst for this discovery may well have been the Christophany and various other revelations informed and hermeneutically shaped through scriptural reflection. For Paul, now that the Messiah has come, the only appropriate response from Jews and Gentiles is faith. As Michael Gorman has argued, his essential story—including Christ's preexistence, life, death, and resurrection—forms a type of "master story," which finds expression in various places throughout his letters.[41]

This leads to our final point. To read Romans 10:6-8 in reference to the incarnation and resurrection takes seriously other Pauline texts that reflect a descent/ascent motif. Take, for example, 2 Corinthians 8:9. In this passage, Paul construes the descent motif metaphorically as wealth: "[T]hough he [Jesus] was rich yet for your sake he became poor." The nadir of Jesus' impoverishment was, indeed, the cross. Of that there can be no doubt. But in what way could the crucified one be described as "rich" before becoming poor? As we consider other, relevant texts,[42] that Paul had in mind Jesus' preincarnate, heavenly existence is likely. The description of Jesus as "rich" before he became "poor" parallels the movement of "bringing down [to earth the heavenly] Christ" (Rom 10:6).[43]

Another important passage in this regard is Philippians 2:6–11, a remarkable hymn Paul incorporates into his letter to make Jesus the lordly example of humility and self-giving.[44] Despite some detractors,[45] most scholars interpret the Philippian hymn against the backdrop of a descent/ascent narrative that begins in Christ's preexistence ("in the form of God"), continues with his incarnation ("emptied himself"; "taking the form of a slave"; "born in human likeness"; "found in human form") and culminates in his cross and exaltation. The language of the hymn is widely regarded as incarnational. As Gordon Fee has argued, a nonincarnational reading disregards the grammar and the content of the passage.[46] If the Christ had to become human, what was he before?[47] Although the nearest antecedents to this kind of transcendent language are personifications of Wisdom and Torah, this does not mean that Paul employs the language about Jesus' preexistence in the same way. Wright writes: "[What we have in the hymn is] no mere personification, then, but a person, a conscious individual entity, is envisaged. . . . The one thus exalted is to be identified as an individual entity existing, equal to God the Father, prior to his human birth."[48]

Another passage that may have some relevance is 1 Corinthians 15:47-49. In this passage, Paul contrasts the first Adam as the man "from earth" with the second Adam as the "man from heaven."[49] This does not require, of course, that the second Adam existed as "man" in his pretemporal, heavenly existence any more than the first Adam existed as "man" while he was still in the dust (Gen 2:7). The issue here for Paul has to do with how the believers' identity is determined vis-à-vis Adam and Christ. Since flesh and blood cannot inherit the kingdom of God, it takes the transformation into the image of the man from heaven to make one fit for the kingdom to come.

To read Romans 10:6 as incarnation as proposed here (1) satisfies the logic of the argument, namely, God's act brings Christ near in the incarnation; (2) gives full weight to Paul's Wisdom-Torah-Christ Christology; (3) fits the narrative structure of Deuteronomy 30:11-14; (4) fits the chronological framework: (a) incarnation and (b) resurrection; and (5) parallels the descent/ascent motif found elsewhere in Paul and the rest of the New Testament.[50]

Paul draws together these thoughts with a final quotation from Deuteronomy 30:14 (Rom 10:8). He prefaces it with the phrase: "but what does it [scripture] say?" Quoting nearly verbatim from the LXX, he writes: ἐγγύς σου τὸ ῥῆμά ἐστιν ἐν τῷ στόματί σου καὶ ἐν τῇ καρδίᾳ σου ("the word is near you, in your mouth and in your heart"). Utilizing a technique similar to *pesher*, he interprets this text as referring to "the word of faith that we are preaching." Yet again his commentary correlates closely with the original context of Deuteronomy 30:11-14, which also contains an element of proclamation: "[W]ho shall go up for us to heaven and get it [the commandments] and *cause us to hear it* that we may do it?" (italics added, Deut 30:12). The proclamation of the commandments previously contained in heaven is a prerequisite to covenant obedience. Likewise, the proclamation of the gospel of Christ—the one who has come down from heaven and come up from the dead—is necessary for Jew and Gentile to embrace the obedience of faith (Rom 10:14-17).

Calling Upon the Name

In Romans 10:9-13, Paul elaborates on the content of "the word of faith" in terms of Jesus' Lordship and resurrection, two potent Pauline themes. Moreover, he comments further on Deuteronomy 30:14 and moves the phrases "in your mouth" and "in your heart" in a christological direction.

He writes (10:9): "If you confess with your mouth (ἐὰν ὁμολογήσῃς ἐν τῷ στόματί σου) 'Jesus is Lord' and believe in your heart (καὶ πιστεύσῃς ἐν τῇ καρδίᾳ σου) that God raised him from the dead, you will be saved."

As is well known, the confession "Jesus is Lord" is fixed within early Christian circles.[51] Paul uses it here and elsewhere (1 Cor 12:3; 2 Cor 4:5; Phil 2:11; Col 2:6; 3:24), linking it carefully to his preaching and the appropriate response of faith. In each case, the affirmation is something "said" or "confessed." Since it is prevalent in Paul's correspondences in the middle of the first century, we may rightly conclude that it emerges "from the earliest stratum of Christian conviction."[52]

Parallel to the confession of Jesus' Lordship is faith in the resurrection (10:9). As Paul returns to his theme and advocates a faith-righteousness, he reverses the order of the verbs in 10:10 to form a chiastic pattern (ὁμολογήσῃς . . . πιστεύσῃς . . . πιστεύεται . . . ὁμολογεῖται; confess . . . believe . . . believe . . . confess). Faith, he writes, leads to righteousness; confession of faith leads to salvation. Although the two statements are elaborative parallelisms, the keyword here continues to be "faith." This is confirmed by Paul's citation of Isaiah 28:16 in 10:11, which also contains the word "faith."

Once again Paul recycles scriptural materials to support the maxim that faith has always been what leads to righteousness. He introduces the quotation with the formula λέγει γὰρ ἡ γραφή (for the scripture says), returning to the same passage he quoted previously in 9:33 (Isa 28:16). This time, however, he adds πᾶς (everyone) as his own interpretive gloss to emphasize the universality of the gospel.[53] He writes (10:11): πᾶς ὁ πιστεύων ἐπ᾽ αὐτῷ οὐ καταισχυνθήσεται (everyone who believes on him will not be put to shame). Paul's use of the future tense in this quotation differs from what we find in the LXX. This may reflect fluidity in the scriptural tradition or a deliberate alteration to accommodate his eschatological outlook. Paul exploits the ambiguity of the phrase ἐπ᾽ αὐτῷ (on it/him) as he again construes faith as christologically oriented.[54] Interpreted, Paul indicates that those who "faith" Christ will not suffer shame in the eschaton; conversely, those who depend on works-righteousness will.

In 10:12 Paul expounds on the universality implicit in the "everyone" of v. 11. He states: "[F]or there is no distinction between Jew and Greek, for the same Lord is Lord over all, granting riches to all those who call upon him" (cf. Rom 1:16-17; 3:22, 29; Gal 3:2). Such a conviction must be understood against Paul's own uniquely Jewish story. Throughout his life, he had believed that distinctions do exist between Jews and non-Jews. He had grown up with the firm assurance that Israel was not like the other nations (see, e.g., Rom 2:17, 25; 3:1-2; 9:4-5; Phil 3:2-7). Now, due to God's act in Christ, Paul not only reads scripture differently; he looks at the world differently. In the new creation, there is no distinction; the same Lord is Lord of all.

At this point in his argument, Paul retrieves the *kyrios* predicate referenced earlier in the christological confession (10:9). The phrase "the same Lord is Lord of all" refers to Jesus[55] whom Paul describes as bestowing riches upon "all who call upon him."[56] This passage is reminiscent of the 2 Corinthians 8:9 discussed earlier: "[F]or you know the grace of our Lord Jesus Christ: although he was rich, he became poor for you, so that you through his poverty might become rich." The narrative structure of wealth to poverty is consistent with our focal passage that exegetically portrays the coming down of the Christ from heaven. Both 2 Corinthians 8:9 and Romans 10:12 suggest that his becoming poor/coming down has a greater purpose: the bestowal of riches upon "all who call upon him."

This last phrase provides the verbal link between 10:12 and 10:13. Jews and Gentiles alike are now able to "call upon the name of the Lord" and receive riches, especially salvation. The Greek word ἐπικαλέω ("to call upon") is used commonly in Greek texts to refer to the invocation of a god.[57] In the Septuanint, it occurs with similar meaning as petitioners call upon YHWH.[58] Carl Davis concludes that "calling upon the name of the Lord" in the Hebrew tradition refers to "a religious act which characterized and even determined God's people."[59] Its use in the New Testament is restricted to calling upon Jesus (Rom 10:12-13; 1 Cor 1:2; Acts 2:21; 9:14, 21; 22:16; 2 Tim 2:22). Hurtado is correct to argue that this phrase is evidence of a pattern of religious devotion in which Jesus is the recipient of prayer, worship, and praise.[60] Since this pattern is observable in the earliest writings of the Christian movement, it is likely that devotion to Christ rose early among the first believing communities. In 1 Corinthians 1:2, Paul describes Christ-believers everywhere as "those who call upon the name of our Lord Jesus Christ." This cultic act set Christ-believers apart from their pagan and Jewish countrymen. In Acts, Luke writes that Saul's persecution in Jerusalem and Damascus is directed against "those who call upon the name" of the Lord Jesus (9:14, 21). This passage suggests a possible motive for his attacks against the church. Christ devotion among his Jewish coreligionists may have provided the impetus for his campaign to wreak havoc against the first communities of Christ-believers in Palestine and beyond.

The phrase "all those who call upon him" (10:12) emerges in Paul's discourse because of its prominent place in scripture. In 10:13 Paul quotes Joel 2:32 (LXX, 3:5): πᾶς γὰρ ὃς ἂν ἐπικαλέσηται τὸ ὄνομα κυρίου σωθήσεται (for "everyone who calls upon the name of the Lord will be saved"). The apostle discovers in Joel the scriptural warrant for the kind of universal gospel he is preaching. The quotation aptly summarizes his discourse from 10:9-12, for it contains elements of universality, *kyrios*-Christology, soteriology, and invocation. Paul interprets it to teach the inclusion of believing Gentiles along with believing Jews. Without any hesitation, he affirms what scripture has prophesied, namely, that any Jew or Gentile who calls upon the name of the Lord Jesus will be saved.

The phrase "will be saved" in 10:13 stands parallel to "will not be put to shame" in 10:11 (quoting Isa 28:16: οὐ καταισχυνθήσεται). A similar negation of eschatological shame for the righteous occurs in the context of Paul's scriptural echo in Romans 10:13 (Joel 2:32). The context of Joel's oracle is instructive. After God's judgment comes at the hand of the northern army (Joel 2:20), the prophet foresees a day when God will drive out Israel's enemies and bring peace and prosperity to the elect. In that day, Joel writes, God's people will realize that YHWH dealt marvelously with them, and they will never again be put to shame (οὐ μὴ καταισχυνθῶσιν; 2:27). Isaiah (28:16) utilizes a similar phrase as he envisages Israel's vindication from her enemies. In that day, the prophet remarks, those who believe will not be put to shame (οὐ μὴ καταισχυνθῇ).

These textual echoes resonate in Paul's scriptural memory, so much so that the apostle retrieves their message and gathers them to amplify his own prophetic voice. Paul stands in agreement with the canonical preachers who looked down the corridors of history past Israel's shame to a day of salvation for God's people. One significant difference, however, is evident in Paul's quotation. He omits two words: καὶ ἔσται (and it will be). While the prophet and his Greek translators await that day, Paul believes that it has already dawned in the new age inaugurated by Jesus. For him God's act of bringing Christ down from heaven and up from the dead has already established the new covenant community, united by faith and destined for salvation at the end of the age.[61]

The confluence of these notions, namely, faith, calling upon the Lord, the reversal of shame, and salvation in the *eschaton*, flow together in Paul's quotation of Joel 2:32: "[F]or 'everyone who calls upon the name of the Lord will be saved.'" The divine name YHWH stands in the original oracle (Joel 3:5; translated into English as LORD in most modern translations). Paul quotes this text and applies both the eschatological role and the name of God to Jesus.[62] Several factors demonstrate this. First, whereas the bulk of Romans 9–11 is theocentric, this portion of Paul's discourse is decidedly Christocentric as this essay has attempted to show. The story of Jesus from the incarnation to the resurrection forms the substructure of the passage and provides an interpretive key to unlocking Israel's past, present, and future. Second, clear references to the resurrection in 10:6-7 and 10:9 suggest that the *kyrios* in 10:13 refers to Christ. As other Pauline passages indicate, the apostle understands that the title *kyrios* belongs to Jesus as a result of the resurrection (e.g., Rom 1:3-4; 14:8-9; Phil 2:9-11). Third, the relationship of these verses to eschatological salvation also intimates that Paul applies this YHWH text to Jesus.[63] It is his custom to relate salvation ultimately to the eschaton as evidenced by the future tense verbs: σωθήσῃ (10:9), καταισχυνθήσεται (10:11), and σωθήσεται (10:13). Generally, he associates his thoughts about final things to the person of Christ via the *kyrios* predicate.[64]

Finally, further evidence that Jesus relates this YHWH text in Romans 10:13 to the Lord Jesus is found in the christological confession in 10:9. He characterizes his preaching and the appropriate response of faith with the confession "Jesus is Lord" (κύριον Ἰησοῦν). He then proceeds to quote Joel 2:32, a text that contains the *kyrios* predicate for the divine name. Since Paul understands Jesus to be the Lord-*kyrios* of the confession, he also means for his readers to take him as the Lord-*kyrios* of Joel 2:32 as well. Had he employed it as a patrological reference in the quotation, he would have confused his audience. So, in light of the Christocentric focus of Romans 9:30–10:13, the emphasis upon the resurrection, the relationship of this passage to Paul's eschatology, and the confession "Jesus is Lord," there can be little doubt that Paul refers this YHWH text to the Lord Jesus Christ.

Concluding Remarks

Standing behind Paul's use of scripture in Romans 9:30–10:13 is his conviction that Christ is the climax of the covenant (10:4). As N. T. Wright notes, through scriptural exegesis, Paul expresses *"the essentially Jewish story now redrawn around Jesus."*[65] The apostle to the Gentiles offers a new reading of his Bible because he finds in Christ the resolution of Israel's unresolved story. At the same time, he discovers the scriptural warrant for the situation at hand, namely, Israel's unbelief. From Israel's past, he recounts God's gift of the land and commandments (Deuteronomy) to discredit any attempt to establish self-righteousness. He remembers God's past judgments against disobedience (Isaiah), which provide some insight into the plight of those disobedient to the gospel in his day. He recalls the promised reversal of Israel's shame and expresses his still unresolved hope in the *eschaton*, a hope now reckoned in universal terms and reconfigured exegetically around Jesus.

As Israel's story intersects with Jesus', Paul interprets scripture as depicting (a) the descent of Christ from heaven and (b) the ascent of Christ by resurrection from the dead. Although Romans 10:6–8 is not often cited as evidence of incarnational thinking on Paul's part, this passage, properly interpreted, exhibits his belief that the Messiah existed in heaven prior to his earthly journey that led ultimately to the cross and resurrection. This does not, of course, proffer a fully developed doctrine of incarnation; but it does provide the raw materials and the hermeneutical impulse for further incarnational thinking. The descent and ascent of Christ are framed by other scriptural texts in which Paul describes Jesus as "the stumbling stone" and "Lord." In both cases the original context identifies YHWH as the "stone of stumbling" (Isaiah 8 and 28) and the Lord upon whom the faithful must call (Joel 2).

Paul's application of these texts to Jesus has significant christological implications. At the level of exegesis, he brings Christ and God into such close connection that the lines of distinction blur. He suggests that Christ existed in heaven prior to coming down to manifest saving righteousness. He posits Christ in roles reserved in scripture only for God. He quotes texts containing the holy, ineffable name of God and applies them to Jesus. Though some insist that Paul never identifies Christ with God in any substantial manner,[66] this study calls that conclusion into question. Through comments on Israel's sacred texts, Paul attributes to Christ a preexistent, heavenly status, divine functions, and even the divine name, thus associating him essentially with the YHWH.

Chapter 9

Christophany as a Sign of "the End"

Carey C. Newman

The apostle Paul is often considered the second most important figure in the history of Christianity, and in some quarters his popularity begins to rival and even obscure the portrait of Jesus, the "founder" of Christianity. Such an appraisal of Paul is not without justification. Born in Tarsus, a free Roman city, during the first century C.E., Paul was trained in Jerusalem as a Jewish Pharisee. After converting from Judaism to Christianity, he undertook an ambitious mission to spread his new found faith throughout the known world—from Palestine in the east to Spain in the west.

Paul's missionary strategy was quite simple. He and his trained coworkers would travel to the capital city of a Roman province and preach in the local synagogue. He would remain in the area until a congregation (comprised of both Jews and Greeks) was established. After moving on to another mission opportunity, Paul would continue communication with his fledgling churches through letters. Paul's letters—literary substitutes for his apostolic presence—are the primary source material for his life and thought but also for the character and shape of earliest Christianity. Because of the influence of his life and letters, Paul has earned the title the "second founder" of Christianity.[1]

Paul's celebrated life as a Christian apostle and his literary deposit enshrined in the New Testament depend directly upon Christ's dramatic appearance to him on the road to Damascus. Though it forever changed his life—and thus the history of Christianity—the Christophany remains shrouded in mystery. Viewing the conversion against the proper linguistic, formal, and religious matrix helps resolve some of the questions. Paul's conversion draws upon three tributaries—theophanies, prophetic calls, and apocalyptic throne visions. Akin to the mighty arrivals of Yahweh to or from his holy mountain, Christ came from heaven to convert Paul. Just as the prophets of old were confronted by Yahweh and sent to preach, Paul was confronted by the risen Jesus and commissioned to evangelize the nations. Similar to the throne visions contained in Jewish apocalypses, his mystical experience of the crucified Christ disclosed to him eschatological information about God's purpose for the world.[2]

Despite some agreement as to the historical background, scholars have come to very different conclusions about how to understand the Christophany. The approaches to the Christophany are almost as numerous as those who write on the great apostle. The options include denying that Paul's letters contain numerous and/or significant references to the Christophany;[3] ignoring the Christophany in lieu of Hellenistic[4] or Rabbinic backgrounds;[5] transforming the Christophany into a decision for authentic existence;[6] reducing the Christophany to a commission to extend Judaism to the gentiles;[7] revaluing the Christophany for psychological and/or sociological insights into Paul's life in his community;[8] and plundering the Christophany as a content-filled religious experience which serves as a catalyst for Paul's theology.[9]

The diversity of approaches embraced by scholars not only reflects different ways of reading Paul's epistles, but graphically highlights the enigmatic character of the Christophany itself. In this essay, by appropriating literary theories developed by Jacques Lacan, Peter Brooks, and Marianna Torgovnick, I want to investigate how the Christophany functions as a pure signifier within the Pauline corpus.[10] As a pure signifier, the Christophany does not refer "to individual signifieds but rather to other signifiers."[11] Approaching the Christophany as a signifier with metonymic and metaphoric potential enables us to move away from a concern with the historical event (subjective hallucination and/or objective appearance) and toward unearthing the paradigmatic relationships between the Christophany and other signs in the Pauline letters. Through such a semiotic reading of the Christophany, the normal black holes and cul-de-sacs of misunderstanding associated with this area of Pauline study can be avoided and, it is hoped, the significance of a powerful sign can be uncovered.

Three necessary caveats need to be noted, though. First, the focus here is solely upon references in the Pauline letters; Acts is not employed as a source, for all too often Luke's three-fold telling of Paul's conversion overshadows the true significance of the Christophany in Paul's writings.

The shape of the Christophany in Paul should not be blurred by looking through the lens ground by Luke.

Second, it must be admitted that Paul never uses the word "Christophany." He does, however, employ a whole range of technical constructions to refer to this event. However, as Kim points out, Paul does employ technical constructions to refer to his conversion, and they include the following: "having seen Jesus as Lord" (1 Cor 9:1); "he appeared to me also" (1 Cor 15:8); "to reveal his Son in/to me" (Gal 1:16; cf. Eph 3:5); "[a revelation of] the covenant in Glory" (2 Cor 3:8, 9; cf. 3:18, 4:4, 6); "a revelation of Jesus Christ" (Gal 1:12); "knowledge of Christ Jesus my Lord" (Phil. 3:8); "receive mercy" (2 Cor 4:1; cf. 1 Tim 1:13, 16); "receive authority" (2 Cor 10:8, 13:10); "received/given grace" (Rom 1:5, 15:15; 1 Cor 3:10, 15:10; Gal 1:9; Eph 3:2, 7, 8; Col 1:25; cf. 1 Tim 1:14); "sent me to preach Christ" (1 Cor 1:17); "entrusted" (1 Cor 9:17; Col 1:25; 1 Thess 2:4).[12] According to how one reckons Paul's letters, there may be as many as twenty-nine semantic echoes of the Christophany.

A third caveat concerns the narrative power latent within the Pauline corpus. Traditionally, Paul's letters, in terms of both form and function, have been construed against the grid of Greco-Roman epistles, epistles which relate to highly specific and contingent social contexts.[13] Recent interpreters, however, have accentuated the narrative worlds that both inform and depend upon Paul's letters. There are at least four such narrative worlds. First, as Richard Hays argues, a "narrative substructure" lies beneath Paul's letters.[14] This story Paul applies to specific and highly contingent situations. Paul's autobiography constitutes a second narrative world. Paul has his own story and retells it for apologetic and/or ethical reasons.[15] Third, the letters themselves evoke a narrative of continual conflict and reconciliation, misunderstanding and instruction, rebellion and correction between Paul and his churches. The relationship among Paul, the letters (the literary substitute for his apostolic presence), and the churches evinces essential narrative features of causality and time.[16] Finally, Paul's theology was shaped in conversation with the story of Israel. The narrative which Paul preached and applied can be understood only against the narrative horizon generated by the Jewish scriptures. Paul's storytelling is nested in yet a larger story.[17] Given that his letters, though rightfully classified as epistles, do evoke such narrative worlds, it is my contention that the Christophany is an important sign within Paul's narrative worlds. The Christophany wields such power because, for Paul, it is the end.

In his "Seminar on the Purloined Letter," Jacques Lacan performs a structural, psychoanalytic analysis of the well-known Edgar Allan Poe text, "The Purloined Letter." Specifically, Lacan highlights the necessary signifying chain enacted by the loss and/or gain of the "purloined" letter. He selects Poe's work because the story is particularly helpful (and susceptible) in demonstrating the way in which the positions of "subjects" are structured by the "itinerary of a signifier."

Lacan divides Poe's tale into two scenes (a primal scene and its repetition) in which the letter is stolen, and three sets of glances (those of the King and the police, the Queen and the Minister, and the Minister and Dupin). Lacan asks, What is common to both scenes and all three glances? His answer: the letter—it is the letter, either its possession or nonpossession, which structures the scenes; the itinerary of the letter determines the sequence of the plot; the letter's displacement determines the subject positions of the various characters in the story. The letter is, therefore, the "true *subject* of the tale: since it can be diverted, it must have a course *which is proper to it*, the trait by which its incidence as signifier is affirmed."[18]

Lacan relates the determination of the signifying chain to Freud's notion of drives. He argues that it is the "specific law of that chain which governs those psychoanalytic effects that are decisive for the subject":

> If what Freud discovered and rediscovers with a perpetually increasing sense of shock has a meaning it is that the displacement of the signifier determines the subjects in their acts, in their destiny, in their refusals, in their blindnesses, in their end and in their fate, their innate gifts and social acquisitions notwithstanding, without regard for character of sex, and that, willingly or not, everything that might be considered the stuff of psychology, kit and caboodle, will follow the path of the signifier.[19]

Lacan underscores the power of a signifier: falling in possession of the letter is, in fact, to be possessed by the letter. The true subject of the narrative is the letter, a letter whose contents are never disclosed.

Lacan's analysis of Poe, I argue, is helpful for understanding the consequences of possession or nonpossession of the Christophany in the Pauline corpus. In appropriating Lacan, I want to emphasize Paul's Saussurian side rather than his Freudian. Although I think Paul is susceptible to such an analysis,[20] my concern is with the structuring role the Christophany plays in Paul's letters.

There can be little doubt that the Christophany, as a signifier, configured much about Paul as a signified. In and through the Christophany, Paul received his authority to engage in ministry. In and through the Christophany, God appointed Paul to the office of apostle, minister, and servant. Paul argues that his own apostolic worthiness and freedom are derived from the Christophany. In and through the Christophany, God commissioned Paul's prophetic mission to the nations. In and through the Christophany, God entrusted Paul with the stewardship of the divine plan, the mystery hidden from ages past, the gospel which Paul preaches. The Christophany, as signifier, determined much about Paul, the signified. The issue at hand, however, is the way in which the Christophany, as signifier, determined subject positions in Paul's letters.

The story of Paul's relationship with the Galatian church illustrates the semiotic power inherent in the Christophany. The narrative world generated by Galatians, as Daniel Patte points out, indicates the conflagration of conflicting systems of convictions—those of Paul, of the Galatians, and of various brands of "Judaizers," all of which revolve around conversions past, present, and hoped-for.[21] Another system of convictions was threatening to displace the convictional system (i.e., the gospel) Paul had preached and the Galatians had accepted—such a displacement Paul could not tolerate.

> For I would have you know, brethren, that the gospel which was preached by me is not man's gospel. For I did not receive it from man nor was I taught it, but it came through a revelation of Jesus Christ. For you have heard of my former life in Judaism, how I persecuted the church of God violently and tried to destroy it; and I advanced in Judaism beyond many of my own age among my people, so extremely zealous was I for the traditions of my fathers. But when he who had set me apart before I was born and had called me through his grace, was pleased to reveal his Son to me, in order that I might preach him among the Gentiles. . . . (Gal. 1:11-16)

The Galatian letter echoes a primal scene in which Paul preached the gospel and the Galatians gladly received and believed his message. In the next scene, trouble-makers (1:7; 5:10, 12) arrive and instigate something of a defection from Paul's preaching. Through the preaching of a "different gospel" (1:6), the trouble-makers subvert Paul's gospel and thus his apostolic control. In the third scene, that in which Paul writes the letter, he counters the trouble-makers by means of repetition—repetition of the event by which he first received his gospel and commission, that is, his Christophany, and repetition of the events by which the Galatian community was first constituted, that is, the preaching of the (authentic) gospel and their conversion.

In Galatians 1 Paul retraces the steps leading to his own revelatory independence. The gospel that he preaches was not "a man's gospel" (v. 11); neither did he "receive it from a man" (v. 12a); nor was Paul "taught it" (v. 12b). His gospel came "through an apocalypse of Jesus Christ" (v. 12c). The syntactical relationship between "an apocalypse" and "Jesus Christ" should be construed as a genitive of means, referring to the method by which Paul received his gospel and, therefore, the antithesis to the other (inappropriate) revelatory events ("to receive"; "to be taught"). Further, as a revelatory event, "an apocalypse of Jesus Christ" is a homologation for the "gospel" of verse eleven.

As Paul's cryptic autobiographical comments indicate, the "apocalypse of Jesus Christ" enacted a series of dramatic convictional and relational revaluations. Paul, by birth, was "in possession of" Judaism (v. 13), a construction with double signifying force. Judaism's possession of Paul and Paul's possession of Judaism empowered his life: he was driven onward and upward, excelling beyond his contemporaries ("and I advanced in Judaism beyond many of my own age among my people," v. 14). The possession of Judaism also drove Paul to persecute those who compromised Jewish monotheism; he "persecuted the church of God violently and tried to destroy it" (v. 13). The signifier for Paul's former life was the "traditions of the fathers" (v. 14).

Despite being in the grip of such power, Paul's life gave way when (v. 15) he fell into the possession of the Christophany: God "was pleased to reveal his Son in/to me" (v. 16a). The Christophany reconfigured his relationship to traditional Judaism and the emplottment of his life. In the possession of Judaism, Paul had automatically persecuted Christianity—because it was not Judaism. In the possession of the Christophany, he necessarily stood over against traditional Jewish construals—because they were not Christianity—and unleashed a powerful reappraisal of the nations, those who stood outside the boundaries of traditional Judaism. Through imposition and repetition of his Christophany, Paul sought communal relations with those formerly excluded (v. 16a).

Moreover, the Christophany, as a sign, determined Paul's relationship to those in Jerusalem (1:18–2:21). The attempts of the trouble-makers to wrest the reins of control away from Paul rested (apparently) upon the power of Judaism in general and the Jewish-Christian community in Jerusalem in particular. Its position was at one and the same time a denial of Paul's authority and a repudiation of his reconstruing of Jewish tradition. Through illegitimate claims, the trouble-makers sought to divert the proper path of the signifying chain enacted by Paul's

Christophany. His possession of the Christophany determined his response and conferred upon him the authority of narrative voice.

The true subject, therefore, in the narrative world of relationships generated by Galatians is not the apostle himself; the true subject is the Christophany, the "apocalypse of Jesus Christ" (v. 12b = "to reveal his Son in/to me," v. 16a). The possession (or nonpossession) of the Christophany configured the relationships. The Christophany enacted a series of profound relational transformations, a series of revaluations and reassignations. The Christophany, as a signifier, determined the subject positions of Paul, his congregations and his opponents.

The Christophany also determined Paul's own narrative about himself, his autobiography, and his narrative construction of the Christian life. Here three ideas from Peter Brooks's highly suggestive book *Reading for the Plot* prove instructive.

Brooks moves beyond the structuralist's synchronic definition of plot as simply metaphor to speak about temporal sequence, or metonymy. Brooks notes that the beginning and end of a narrative stand in a metaphorical "same-but-different" relationship; plot, however, encompasses the "metonymic process" of transformation.[22] Plot is the linking of metaphor. Narrative is, therefore, constituted by the emplottment of metonymy—that is, syntactic sequencing invests plot with paradigmatic, metaphorical power.

Besides highlighting a dynamic notion of plot, Brooks also points to the structuring power wielded by the end a story. Narrative plotting enacts an enchained desire for and drive toward the end, for locked within the narrative is a nearly obsessive desire for the end, be it syntactic, ethical, or cosmological:

> The very possibility of meaning plotted through sequence and through time depends on the anticipated structuring force of the ending: the interminable would be the meaningless, and the lack of ending would jeopardize the beginning. We read incidents of narration as "promises and annunciations" of final coherence: the metaphor reached through the chain of metonymies: across the bulk of the as yet unread middle pages, the end calls to the beginning, transforms and enhances it.[23]

Brooks then links narrative ends with the human ends, with death. According to Brooks, life is lived retrospectively, for death and death alone confers meaning upon life. One must live one's own obituary. But life resists death and seeks to conquer it. Through repetition in life, a mastery of death is sought. Repetition seeks to assert control over what must in fact be submitted to: the end, death. This effort is suggestive for narrative's grammatical and metaphorical march toward the end: just as life repetitively drives toward death, so also does narrative.

Between the beginning and the end lies the middle of life. Into the middle is introduced any number of detours, or, alternatives to death. There is an appropriate path toward the end, and the subplot of a narrative (and thus of life) is the possibility, through repetitive variations of a primal scene, to offer an improper end, or an unnatural death. Subplots, therefore, offer solutions that differ from the proper end. The textual energy produced by a narrative resides in the possibility of premature or inappropriate discharge. The possibility of short-circuiting the proper drive toward the end fills narrative (and thus life) with tension and a sense of the fantastic. According to Brooks,

> We emerge from reading *Beyond the Pleasure Principle* with a dynamic model which effectively structures ends (deaths, quiescence, non-narratability) against beginnings (Eros, stimulation into tension, the desire of narrative) in a manner that necessitates the middle as detour, as struggle toward the end under the compulsion of imposed delay, as arabesque in the dilatory space of the text.[24]

Brooks's comments on plot, endings, and Freud are highly suggestive for reading Paul. Again, I do not so much want to emphasize the psychoanalytic issues as I do the narratological.

The Christophany, as end (i.e., as death/resurrection) determines Paul's own narrative about himself, his autobiography, and his narrative construction of the Christian life. Philippians 3 opens with a warning about the "dogs" (v. 2a), "evil workers" (v. 2b), "those who mutilate the flesh" (v. 2c). Paul then antithetically situates himself as one of the true "circumcision" (v. 3a), one who truly worships and serves (v. 3b). To validate his claims, Paul narrates his life story. He begins by chronicling the shape of his former life in Judaism: "circumcised on the eighth day, of the people of Israel, of the tribe of Benjamin, a Hebrew born of Hebrews; as to law, a Pharisee; as to zeal, a persecutor of the church; as to righteousness under the law, blameless" (vv. 4–6).

Paul's narrative, however, took an unexpected turn. Paul underwent transvaluation: what was "gain" (v. 7), Judaism, became "loss" (vv. 7, 8); what was despised and persecuted, Christ/Christianity, became valuable.[25] Why? Why such a reappraisal? "Because of Christ" (v. 7)—more particularly, "because of the surpassing worth of the knowledge of Christ" (v. 8). In both verses the preposition *dia* + the accusative should be rendered as the (ultimate, eschatological) ground or cause of transformation.[26] The construction, the "surpassing worth of the knowledge Christ" is the semantic equivalent of "through an apocalypse of Jesus Christ" (Gal 1:12) and "to reveal his Son in/to me" (Gal 1:16), all of which are technical references to the Christophany. Paul assigns apocalyptic potency to this "knowledge of Christ": it is a knowledge of "surpassing" (v. 8) value. The signifying power of his Christophany, the "knowledge of Christ," rests upon its eschatological character as end-of-time resurrection (cf. 1 Cor 12:31; 2 Cor 4:7, 17; 9:14; Eph 1:9; 2:7; 3:19).

The Christophany empowered Paul to narrate his life story because Christophany forms an end, the eschatological end. Knowing the end confers voice upon Paul: he can speak because he knows, and he knows because he possesses the end, the Christophany. Ironically and paradoxically, though typically treated as the beginning of Paul's apostolic life, the Christophany is, in fact, the end. He can narrate his own life story because his life had already reached an end or death/resurrection: in the Christophany Paul died (to the old life), and his formalized autobiography is an attempt to bind the energy released by his experience of resurrection (cf. Rom 6:1-4; Eph 2:4-7; Col 2:12). Paul's former life in Judaism and life in Christ(ianity) are similar and yet dramatically different. As the power of transformation, the Christophany is thus imbued with a textual status: the Christophany is the plot-producing change.

Though Paul had already experienced his own death, and thus was able to narrate (to live), Paul continued seeking death/resurrection. Paul repeated the end/beginning metamorphosis over and over; he was driven to further eschatological knowledge ("that I may know him and the power of his resurrection," v. 10a) and suffering and death ("and may share his sufferings, becoming like him in his death," v. 10b-c). Indeed, only by being repeatedly coconformed into the death of Jesus did Paul envision life and the mastery of death through resurrection ("becoming like him in his death, that if possible I may attain the resurrection from the dead," vv. 10c-11). Paul again releases the "power" (v. 10a) of Christophany, not only by rehearsing the effect of the Christophany, transvaluation, but by formalizing Christophany into a continuing middle of dying and rising. By repeating his end, the Christophany, Paul mastered his life and thereby relentlessly pursued completion ("but I press on to make it my own," vv. 12, 14). The end toward which Paul obsessively drove was none other than his initial calling ("forgetting what lies behind and straining forward to what lies ahead, I press on toward the goal for the prize of the upward call of God in Christ Jesus,"

v. 13b-14). That which effects the transformation from "call" to "goal" is none other than the repetition of the event which first initiated his Christian narration—the Christophany. Paul repeatedly seeks to lay hold of Christ in the identical way he was laid hold of by Christ (v. 12). Paul's own end is his beginning, and his beginning is his end.

Paul then offers his own narrative as a paradigm for all Christians. He invites all desiring completion, the "mature" (v. 15; cf. 1 Cor 2:7), to participate in his story, to reenact death/resurrection (i.e., Christophany), to become coimitators ("join in imitating me, and mark those who so live as you have an example in us," v. 17). He warns, however, of a dangerous detour, an improper death, which is a subplot to the Christian narration of transformation into Christ. Those who set their mind on earthly things, whose "desire" is shame, are traveling to a completely different end, to "destruction" (v. 19). Ironically, those whose life narrative conforms to this ominous subplot are enemies of the only authentic death, which is found in Jesus: they "live as enemies of the cross of Christ" (v. 18). The proper and natural end, to which repetition leads, is identification with Jesus; it is he "who will change our lowly body to be like his body of Glory" (v. 21)— an eschatological transformation into a Christophanic end. Paul, therefore, connects his beginning, Christophany, with his end, the final transformation into Glory. We are left only to state Paul's conviction: as a revelation of final Glory, the Christophany inaugurates the process of transformation into Glory to which repeated Christophanic experiences necessarily lead.

Normally, some grand apocalypse is thought of as the end of the narrative world generated by the Jewish scriptures: prophetic, apocalyptic eschatology foreshadows the appropriateness of such a conclusion, and early Jewish and Christian apocalypses attempt to complete the linkage successfully. Paul's Christophany also provides a sense of closure. The strategies of closure as enumerated by Marianna Torgovnick are helpful in demonstrating how the Christophany, as end, provides closure.

Torgovnick begins by defining "closure" as the process by which an adequate and appropriate conclusion is reached. Her concern is the relationship of the ending, the last definable unit, to the beginning and the middle of a narrative. Dissatisfied with previously incomplete, inflexible, and polemical approaches to closure, she introduces a new vocabulary for evaluating closure.

Torgovnick identifies two strategies for relating an ending to the beginning and middle: circularity and parallelism. Circularity occurs when the ending—through language, situation, and the grouping of characters—clearly recalls and controls the beginning. Parallelism occurs "when language, situation, or the grouping of characters refers not just to the beginning of the work but to a series of points in the text."[27] An ending successfully provides a sense of closure through circularity and parallelism. When an ending omits the necessary information for circularity or parallelism or introduces a new, tangential topic or seeks to link the ending with another narrative, the pattern of closure can be said to be incomplete or open.

Torgovnick goes on to discuss other terminology used in evaluating these strategies: such terms include "overview" and "close-up" (measuring the distance of the ending from the middle); "complementariness," "incongruence and confrontation" (measuring the relationship between the author and the reader); and "self-awareness and self-deception" (measuring the relationship of the author to his own ideas). My present concern, however, is how Christophany, as end, provides a sense of closure.

In 2 Corinthians 3:4–4:6, Paul repeatedly echoes his Christophany. In 3:5 he claims his apostolic "competence is from God"—a phrase which, as Kim notes, parallels other references to his Christophany (25–29). He goes on in 3:6 to state emphatically that it was God who "called" him—a direct reference to his Christophany (cf. 1 Cor 15:9; *Georgi* 231–34). By describing conversion as a "turning to the Lord," Paul contextually identifies Jesus as "Lord"[28] and points to his own self-discovery in the Christophany. Initial and repeated acts of transformation into the image of God occur by "beholding the glory of the Lord" (3:18), reflecting, as Segal argues, his own mystic encounter with Glory.[29] When the apostle reports that the light shined into his own heart, giving the "knowledge of the Glory of God in the face of Jesus" (4:6), Paul is interpreting his Christophany.[30] Clearly, 2 Corinthians 3:4–4:6 echoes Paul's Christophany. Of particular note are the circular connections between Christophany, as end, and Genesis, as beginning.

There are three strong terminological connections between Genesis 1 and 2 Corinthians 4. Both Genesis 1 and 2 Corinthians 4 share the terminology of light and darkness: "light": Gen 1:3, 2 Cor 4:4, 6; "shine": 2 Cor 4:6 [twice]; "darkness": Gen 1:1, 4, 5; 2 Cor 4:6). In both Genesis and 2 Corinthians 4, God speaks the creative activity into process ("God said": Gen 1:3; "For it is God who said": 2 Cor 4:6). And in both Genesis 1 and 2 Corinthians, God's image is borne by an earthly man ("Then God said, 'Let us make man according to our image and likeness'": Gen 1:26, 27; "Christ, who is the image of God," 2 Cor 4:4). Based upon his detection of just one of these strong echoes, this is an "allusion [that] can hardly be missed."[31]

Paul's Christophanic dance with Genesis provides a sense of closure. Genesis begins with the story of creation: how God spoke light into existence, how God separated light from the darkness, and how God named light and darkness. Now, in and through Christophany, God has effected a second creation, and again light has conquered darkness. In Genesis God spoke and created order into being. God in the Christophany unleashes the creative power once again, causing a light to shine into Paul's heart. Finally, as Adam was the first man created in the image of God, Paul's Christophany was a revelation of Jesus as the image of God. Through circularity, Paul intertextually situates the Christophany as a second, creative act of God.

But Paul in 2 Corinthians 3 also employs parallelism to provide closure. Paul interprets his Christophany as a revelation of God's Glory in Jesus. While Paul recognizes that Moses' reception of the law was attended and thus legitimized through/by God's Glory (vv. 7, 8, 9, 11), Paul counters that a revelation of God's Glory also attended and thus legitimized his stewardship of the gospel (vv. 8, 9, 11). The Sinai revelation of Glory to Moses and the Christophanic revelation of Glory to Paul are thus comparable: in both, the revelation of Glory legitimizes authority and message. The Glory which legitimizes Paul's apostleship, however, is a surpassing, final, eschatological Glory—it will not pass away.

By comparing and contrasting the two revelations of Glory, Paul legitimizes his apostolic authority, establishes the eschatological superiority of his gospel and vindicates his life of apostolic suffering. The Christophany, as a revelation of final, eschatological enables him to appropriate the legitimizing power inherent in the Sinai Glory tradition. Here Paul aligns himself with the long, exegetical tradition stemming from Exodus 24 and 34.

Within the Christophany resides also a sense of incompletion and openness. Not only does Paul, through circularity and parallelism, link the Christophany with the beginning, but he also links the Christophany with the parousia (the second coming of Christ). There is yet a story to unfold; the Christophany, as end of the beginning, is also the beginning of the end—the beginning of closure, the inaugural sign of the end.

I also hope that this investigation has highlighted the way in which the Christophany functions as a signifier within Paul's letters. As I have attempted to demonstrate, in the narrative world generated by Paul's letters, the possession (or nonpossession) of the Christophany determines the subject positions among Paul, his congregations, and his opponents. Indeed, the Christophany acts as "intersubjective sign," a pivot around which all of his human relationships turn. The Christophany also enables Paul's narration of his own story; in fact, his autobiography presupposes that he has experienced the end, death/resurrection, in the Christophany. Further, in the middle of his narration, the time between Christophany and parousia, Paul seeks a mastery of death through reenactment and repetition of Christophany—dying so that he might rise. He patterns the plot line of the Christian life in accordance with the narration of his own story—Christophany—and acknowledges the threat of experiencing an unnatural death or end. Moreover, through circularity and parallelism, the Christophany provides a sense of closure to the story of the entire Bible. The Christophany wields such narrative power because it is a signifier of the end.

Chapter 10

When Did the Understanding of Jesus' Death as an Atoning Sacrifice First Emerge?

James D. G. Dunn

In his valuable study of *The Genesis of Christology*,[1] Petr Pokorny follows a well marked path in sketching the emergence of atonement theology in earliest Christianity. He notes the several "older formulaic expressions which articulate the meaning of the death of Jesus";[2] he sees in them indication of influence from the Septuagint version of Isaiah 53:10-12, and, consequently, counts them "as reflection on the events of Easter on the part of Greek-speaking Jewish Christians." Nevertheless, he adds that "in their intention, however, they may reach back to the time before Easter and reflect the self-understanding of Jesus indirectly."[3]

This is a briefer and more nuanced conclusion than that reached by Martin Hengel in his classic study of *The Atonement*, whose subtitle indicates that he was asking more or less the same question as that posed in our title.[4] After a much fuller examination of the data, Hengel concludes that "there is nothing from a historical or tradition-historical point of view which stands in the way of deriving it (the soteriological interpretation of the death of Jesus) from the earliest (Aramaic-speaking) community," and he goes on to press behind to Jesus' own representation of his own death in the light of Isaiah 53.[5]

The discrepancy between Hengel and Pokorny may not be very great, but there is, nonetheless, a tension: on the one hand, the agreed probability that Paul was echoing confessions of the Greek-speaking Christians; on the other, the differing degrees of confidence about the possibility of tracing the thought back to the Aramaic-speaking Jerusalem believers or even to Jesus himself. This tension seems to me reason enough to justify a fresh look at the question.

Three areas require attention: the formulaic expressions drawn upon or alluded to in our earliest sources (Paul's letters); the problem of what may and may not be deduced from the Synoptic tradition regarding Jesus' own understanding of the matter; and third, the often neglected evidence provided by the account in Acts of the earliest Christian community in Jerusalem.

The pre-Pauline Formulae

This section need not detain us long. By far the most significant passage here is 1 Corinthians 15:3b. Paul states that the message he received (ὃ καὶ παρέλεβον), that is, no doubt, at the time of his conversion, contained as its first article "that Christ died for our sins in accordance with the scriptures." The fuller formula is well structured and evidently the product of some careful, agreed, and mature consensus.[6] Since Paul's conversion dates to within two or three years of Jesus' death, we can date this already settled conviction regarding Jesus' death to within a year or two of Christianity's own emergence.

That early formula attests that Jesus' death was already valued positively because it dealt with "our sins." In a religious tradition for which it was axiomatic that sins required atonement by sacrifice, a formulation like this can only mean that Jesus' death was already being understood in sacrificial terms. The same implication can be drawn from the final phrase, "in accordance with the scriptures." It is true that the scriptures provided various precedents or models on which an understanding of Jesus' death as having a positive outcome could be based—covenant sacrifice or Passover sacrifice (neither properly described as "for sins"), righteous sufferer or martyr. But the "for our sins" pushes the allusion firmly towards the scriptural regulations for sin offering and Day of Atonement, or to other models insofar as they absorbed or merged with sacrificial imagery.[7] An allusion specifically to Isaiah 53 is neither obvious nor necessary for the sacrificial allusion to be loud and clear.[8]

The understanding of Jesus' death as sacrifice is evidently an article of faith that Paul took over wholeheartedly.[9] It is obvious from the way he refers to the theme that the understanding was widely shared and little disputed in early Christian circles.[10] For instance, he frequently draws on other earlier formulae, whose wide acceptance and resonance he evidently could take for granted.[11] Furthermore, Paul never found it necessary to expound in any detail his own belief in Jesus' death as atoning sacrifice.[12] Paul, it would appear then, did not regard the teaching on

Jesus' death "for our sins" as distinctively his own, nor did he see any need much to elaborate it. In short, more than in any other matter of earliest Christian doctrine, we can read a consensus in early Christian theology about Jesus' death from Paul's writings.

If, then, 1 Corinthians 15:3b was the first teaching Paul received regarding the salvific effect of Jesus' death, and perhaps became the root of his own teaching on the subject, to clarify, as much as possible, when and how this teaching was first formulated is important. We can assume that Paul received the formula in Damascus or possibly Antioch (Gal 1:17; Acts 11:25-26). In either case, the implication from Acts is that the welcoming Christians were Hellenists who had been driven out of Jerusalem by persecution (Acts 8:1-3; 9:1-2; 11:19-20). Were they responsible for the formulation that Paul received?

The formula itself provides two indications of its origin. First, it attests knowledge of Jesus' burial[13] as well as his death and resurrection, and it gives pride of place to Cephas and the Twelve in its list of witnesses of the resurrected Jesus. This information suggests an origin in Jerusalem itself where, again according to Acts, Peter and the Twelve formed the acknowledged leadership in the earliest days. Second, there has been a long-running debate over whether an Aramaic version can be discerned under the Greek formulation– the key issues being the lack of a Semitic equivalent to "according to the scriptures," and whether anarthrous *Christos* could be a translation from Aramaic.[14] Although we should not forget that an Aramaic form could be rendered faithfully in Greek without being a literal translation of the Aramaic, we might expect a credal formula to be more rigid. Even so, Acts attests the presence of Hellenist converts in Jerusalem from very early days, that is, presumably, Diaspora Jews who had settled in Jerusalem but who spoke only Greek—hence Hellenists, Greek-speakers.[15] In other words, it is entirely plausible to envisage the confessional formula being composed by and for Greek-speaking converts, but already in Jerusalem and still very early.

In sum, then, the answer provided to our question by this initial probe into pre-Pauline formulae enables us to trace belief in Jesus' death as atoning sacrifice to the earliest days of the Jerusalem Church, though the earliest traceable formula suggests that the formula was coined by Greek-speaking believers. Should we, therefore, deduce as a further corollary that the belief itself was first formulated by the Christian Hellenists? It is time to turn to our second body of evidence, namely, what the Synoptic tradition may reveal about Jesus' beliefs regarding his own death.

Can We Say What Jesus Believed Regarding His Death?

Most probably Jesus anticipated the strong likelihood of his suffering a violent death. The issue has been discussed thoroughly in early studies and requires no fresh discussion.[16] Jesus would have been well aware of the proverbial fate of Israel's prophets and the tradition that the righteous could expect to suffer and often to die unjustly. He would hardly have been unaware of what had happened to his predecessor and mentor, John the Baptist. He would know full well that serious charges had been made against him—of sorcery (Mark 3:22-26 pars.) and possibly of being a rebellious son[17]—crimes punishable by stoning (Deut 21:21; *m. Sanh.* 7.4). According to Matthew 23:37 and Luke 13:34, Jesus himself may have reckoned with the possibility of being stoned. And according to Mark 14:8, he may have anticipated the likelihood of burial without anointing, that is, a criminal's burial. Arguably, the fact that such premonitions were not realized (he was not stoned, and he probably was given a proper burial) indicates that Jesus was remembered as so surmising, despite the fact that a different outcome transpired.[18] And whatever had gone before, Jesus could hardly have undertaken the symbolic action in the temple (whatever it was) without being fully aware that he was throwing down a gauntlet to the temple authorities, especially if he had also spoken provocatively about the temple's destruction and replacement.[19] Nor is it likely that he was at all surprised by his subsequent arrest or by the accusations brought against him. Jesus would have been extraordinarily naïve to not see where such actions and opposition were likely to end.

Therefore, we can go on to question whether Jesus was remembered as speaking of his death and of giving the possibility some significance. In particular, did he speak of it in sacrificial terms or in terms that would explain the subsequent confession of his death as "for our sins," whether in substance or in "intention"? (Pokorny). That is to say, can we answer the title's question by affirming that it was with Jesus himself that the understanding of his death as an atoning sacrifice first emerged? Three motifs in the Synoptic tradition call for attention at this point.

First, passages with allusions to Isaiah 53 have been found. Can we confidently deduce that Jesus saw his death in terms of the suffering servant, as one on whom the Lord had laid "the iniquity of us all," "an offering for sin"? (Isa 53:5-6, 8, 10-12). Strongly affirmative answers were characteristic of earlier generations of scholarship,[20] but in the second half of the twentieth century, a more negative answer quickly became dominant across a wide spectrum of scholarship.[21] The difficulty in returning an affirmative answer lies in the character of the evidence.

The only explicit quotation from Isaiah 53 in the Synoptic tradition is to be found in Luke 22:37—"And he was counted among the lawless" (Isa 53:12). The quotation belongs to an obviously ancient context: the mysterious "two swords" saying (Luke 22:38) would probably be embarrassing in many circles (hence its absence from Mark and Matthew?). But the quotation itself is framed by characteristic Lukan language.[22] The passage does seem to disrupt the context, where verse 38 follows directly from verse 36.[23] And it fits with Luke's use elsewhere of the servant image as part of a humiliation-exaltation motif (rather than in terms of vicarious suffering).[24] Thus, the possibility of tracing the quotation itself back to Jesus with any confidence is problematic.

The problems with Mark 10:45 are different but leave the significance of the text for our question equally unclear. Jeremias finds a clear echo, but Hooker notes that the allusion is not obvious and has to be worked over before it becomes clear.[25] More significant from a tradition-history perspective is the fact that Luke seems to know a different version of the teaching, which climaxes in the saying, including a version of the conclusion which lacks any of the elements on which the allusion to Isaiah 53 depends.[26] Even if we can trace the idea of his death as a ransom back to Jesus, the more plausible echoes are of Psalm 49:7-8[27] and Isa 43:3-4,[28] which work with different imagery than that of the atoning sacrifice.

The other passage most frequently cited is Mark 14:24: "This is my blood of the covenant, which is poured out on behalf of many." The suggested allusion in this case is to Isaiah 53:12 ("he poured out his life to death"), though the imagery is not sacrificial.[29] Jeremias makes much of the reference to "(the) many," since a five-fold reference to "(the) many," is a striking feature of Isa 52:13-53:12.[30] But the parallel Lukan/ Pauline version contains no reference to "(the) many," and Paul's version does not even talk of the blood "poured out" (Luke 22:20; 1 Cor 11:25). Since it is more than likely that the Lukan/ Pauline version of the cup-word is older than that of Mark/Matthew,[31] the plausibility of tracing the thought back to Jesus himself is, again, problematic.

All told, then, the case for seeing an allusion to the Servant of Isaiah in the earliest Jesus tradition—thus, also to Jesus' own assessment of his anticipated death in sacrificial and atoning categories—is not very strong.

The alternative (if that is the best way to put it), strongly suggested in both versions, is that Jesus spoke of his anticipated death in terms of a *covenant sacrifice*, rather than a sin offering. The precedent here would be Exodus 24:8: "Moses took the blood and dashed it on the people, and said, 'See the blood of the covenant that the Lord has made with you. . . .' "[32] This collates with the possibility that Jesus saw the group around him (the twelve!) as somehow constituting the renewal of God's covenant with Israel,[33] or spoke with a view to the establishment of the new covenant promised in Jeremiah 31:31-34.[34] Jesus may well have gone the more willingly to his death because he saw it as the sacrifice that would bring into effect that long-promised covenant.[35]

Another possibility, for which I have argued elsewhere,[36] is that Jesus foresaw his death as a suffering of the eschatological tribulation. This possibility emerges from Jesus' remembered talk of his death as a baptism (Mark 10:38 pars.). His words, I argue, were an echo of John the Baptist's anticipation of one to come who would baptize *others* in "fire(y spirit)" (Matt 3:11 pars.), the Baptist using his own distinctive practice (baptism) as an image of the eschatological tribulation. Jesus was thus remembered as affirming the Baptist's expectation—from where else could this specific metaphor have come?—but as indicating that he *himself*, rather than dispensing the judgment, would have to endure it.[37]

This possibility brings us quite close to Schweitzer's infamous scenario: that Jesus not only expected the final tribulation to happen imminently, but by the time he reached (set off for?) Jerusalem, he had also concluded that he himself would have to endure the same tribulation.[38] But the question for us is whether such an expectation can be characterized in terms of atoning sacrifice. Was this a suffering on his behalf only? Or in solidarity with others? Or somehow on their behalf only? The fact that the tradition of Jesus expecting his disciples also to suffer[39] confuses the issue further. More immediately appealing is the image of Christ as the forerunner and leader going ahead of his people to open up the way for them, as in Hebrews 2:10 and 6:20.

Third, the suggestion has recently been strongly promoted that Jesus, in coming to Jerusalem, intended nothing less than to replace the Jerusalem cult itself. This is achieved by the bold correlation of Jesus' word and action in regard to the temple, with his words and actions at the last supper. Gerd Theissen and Annette Merz argue that Jesus intended the latter (the Last Supper) to replace the former (the temple). Jesus intended to confront not just the leaders of Israel, but the whole temple and cult as such. His word and action in the temple declared the end of the temple.[40] His words and actions in the upper room declared the beginning of the temple cult's replacement, bread instead of a sacrificial animal, a new covenant without sacrifice.[41] Bruce Chilton presses the case more strongly still: "body" and "blood" are sacrificial terminology and indicate that Jesus' meals themselves were being understood as sacrifices, indeed, as better sacrifices than those offered in Caiaphas's corrupt temple. In other words, Jesus was setting up an alternative cult; wine and bread replaced sacrifice in the temple.[42]

The conjunctions of thought here are indeed intriguing. But the significance of Jesus' action in the temple is a matter of unresolved dispute. Was it so clearly an action symbolizing the temple's destruction, as E. P. Sanders insists?[43] Some sort of protest, against assumed or real abuse, seems more likely implied. Or some sort of "purifying" as part of Mount Zion's role to receive the eschatological pilgrimage of the nations.[44] Mark 11:17, in fact, quotes one of the principal expressions of the hope for the final conversion of the nations (Isa 56:7), a passage which includes the expectation that the burnt offerings and sacrifices of these foreigners will be accepted on the temple altar.[45]

As for the word that Jesus was accused of speaking against the temple, it certainly envisaged the destruction of the temple; but the accusation was regarded as false in the earliest Synoptic tradition (Mark 14:58 par.). And even if, as is likely, Jesus was remembered as saying something on the subject,[46] it is not clear what he may have envisaged to replace the destroyed temple: a new temple, in accord with an important strand of Jewish expectation?[47] A community that would replace the temple, somewhat as Qumran thought of itself as a temple community?[48] Either way, the difficulty of correlating the temple word with the temple action and the dismissal of the former as a legitimate charge against Jesus leaves the relevance of both word and action to our particular inquiry unclear.

Moreover, in the conjunction between temple cult and Last Supper, the juxtaposition presented is between sacrifice and supper (the Lord's Supper, the Eucharist) rather than of Jesus' death as sacrifice. Would a protest against the cult of sacrifice so readily have been transposed into or prompted the thought of Jesus' own death as such a sacrifice? The setting of temple cult and Last Supper in such antithesis is much too contrived, especially when it sets in shadow the more immediate link between Last Supper and Jesus' death. Any thought of Jesus' death as sacrifice depends on the language used in relation to his death at the Last Supper, not on an artificial juxtaposition of Jesus', at best ambiguous, action in the temple with his almost equally enigmatic utterance at the root of the words of institution.

Where does this leave us? We can be confident that Jesus anticipated his death. Thus, behind the various traditions that recall Jesus' reflections on his death is a memory of Jesus having tried to make sense to his disciples of what was likely to happen to him. Of the traditions most relevant to our particular question, we can conclude that Jesus probably spoke of his death as a means of (re-)establishing Israel's (new) covenant with God, or as a suffering of the eschatological woes predicted most recently by the Baptist. That he saw his death as replacing the temple cult seems to press the evidence too hard; an important element within the Synoptic tradition looked rather for the (rebuilt) temple to be the goal for the eschatological pilgrimage of the nations. And while the possibility can hardly be excluded that Jesus was influenced in his sense of destiny by Isaiah 53, the evidence is too contested (or our methodology does not allow us to recognize its validity). In short, that Jesus was the first to understand his death in terms of atoning sacrifice cannot be demonstrated with any confidence. And his intention, so far as it has been preserved in the Jesus tradition, works more clearly with other images in regard to his death than that of atoning sacrifice as such.

The Testimony of Acts

There is something of a puzzle here. Clearly, Jesus was understood to have died "for our sins" from very early on. There are also texts within the synoptic tradition that portray Jesus as envisaging his death in sacrificial terms, his blood poured out for many, for the forgiveness of their sins. Yet, at the same time, there is an awkward gap between the events surrounding Jesus' death and the earliest formulae evidenced in the Pauline letters, a gap which such evidence as we have in the Acts of the earliest Jerusalem church seems to leave empty. The gap seems to mark a discontinuity in the evidence and poses the question of our title more sharply.

The sharpness of the issue is inescapable. For if the first Christians believed Jesus' death to be an atoning sacrifice—and remembered Jesus as instructing them so to believe—then that belief must have deeply affected their attitude toward the regular sin offerings and annual Day of Atonement rituals of the Jerusalem temple. If Jesus' death was an effective sin offering, indeed *the* effective sin offering, then the unavoidable conclusion was that the temple atonement ritual had thereby been rendered unnecessary and passé, that Jesus' death had wholly replaced the temple cult as a way of dealing with sin. The conclusions to be drawn by Hebrews in due course (Heb 10:1-10) would already have been drawn at the very dawn of the Christian movement. To continue to attend the temple and to depend on its ritual would be to deny the validity of the gospel and the effectiveness of Jesus' death "for sins," would be tantamount to apostasy, as, again, the text of Hebrews was soon to point out (6:4-8; 10:26-31).

But it is precisely this conclusion which, according to Acts, the first Christians did not draw. According to Luke, the first Jerusalem Christians *did* continue to attend the temple. Peter and John were going[49] to the temple "at the hour of prayer, the ninth hour" (Acts 3:1), that is, the hour at which the afternoon Tamid sacrifice was offered (Josephus, *Ant.* 14.65; Dan. 9:21). This sacrifice of a male lamb, twice a day, was probably not thought of as atoning.[50] But it was evidently regarded as essential for the continuing welfare of Israel, including the Diaspora.[51] The first Christians' continued association with this integral part of the temple cult cannot but raise the question whether the understanding of Jesus' death as the final sacrifice had yet taken hold in the thought and consequent practice of his first followers. Some argue that for Luke the temple was a place of preaching and prayer only, and no longer a place of sacrifice.[52] But there is no hint of a concern to preach in 2:46, and to preach in effect against the cult at the time of the evening sacrifice would assuredly have aroused great hostility (and differently directed) than is envisaged in chapters 3–4. If the purpose was to pray privately, the ninth hour was precisely the time for public prayer; anyone going to the temple at that time was thereby publicly associating himself with that prayer.[53] Anyone who still prized the temple as "the house of God," but who thought of its sacrificial ritual as obsolete, would have gone to the Temple at any other time to preach or for his devotions.[54] This line of reflection argues decisively against the possibility that Jesus intended to establish a new cult in place of the temple. For in that case his closest disciples, as represented here by Peter and John, must have wholly misunderstood his intention in the matter.[55]

That the implications of Acts 3:1 are not at odds with Luke's own understanding of the situation in Jerusalem is confirmed by his later account of the Jerusalem Church. According to Luke's account, James, leader of the Jerusalem church, told Paul that myriads of Jews had come to faith, "and all are zealots for the law" (21:20). No one living in Jerusalem could be so described who did not avail himself of the temple cult. It is impossible that there were "zealots for the law" in Jerusalem who did not observe the temple cult, and almost as impossible that they could have tolerated any fellow-believing Jews who discounted or dismissed the temple cult so central to the Law.

This is also the implication of the sequel in which Paul himself participated in the temple rituals (21:23-24, 26). At James's suggestion, Paul joined with four men who were under a vow; he purified himself with them and paid their expenses, in order that they might shave their heads. The circumstances envisaged are presumably those covered by the legislation in Numbers 6:9-12, where a Nazirite's "separation" has been defiled by contact with a corpse; the defilement required a seven-day purification and the shaving of the previously uncut hair; and on the eighth day the offering of two turtle doves or young pigeons, the one as a sin offering, the other as a burnt offering in atonement for his sin. It is unclear whether Paul counted himself as similarly "under a vow" (cf. Acts 18:18), or as unclean and required to offer sacrifice for himself. Some sort of compromise was evidently involved; but to what extent would it have constituted a departure from what he himself believed? (cf. 1 Cor 9:20-21).[56] In any case, Paul accompanied those who observed the cult, including the offering of sacrifice for sin. And even if Paul was acting out of character, the action is portrayed as very much in character with the faith and practice of the Jerusalem community itself. Is it possible that such a community also believed that Jesus' death was an atoning sacrifice to end all sacrifices? Do we have to believe that the majority of the Jerusalem believers had already relapsed into traditional Judaism? Or is it simpler to deduce that the understanding of Jesus' death as an atoning sacrifice had never been clearly expounded within the church of Jerusalem itself?[57]

The line of deduction could be countered by detecting features of Luke's own theology rather than a historical account. For one thing, Luke seems to avoid or to play down any idea of Jesus' death as an atonement for sins in his account of the earliest preaching.[58] And since F. C. Baur, a recurring claim is that Luke attempted to reconcile diverging strands of Christianity by, *inter alia*, rejudaizing Paul. If this supposition is true, Luke's account of the earliest period of Christianity cannot be expected to provide any historical data that would bridge the gap between Jesus' death and the early confessions of Jesus' death as "for our sins."

On the other hand, there are indications elsewhere that Luke's account of the Jerusalem community's continued participation in the temple cult is, indeed, firmly rooted in historical memory.

(1) The very fact that Jerusalem was and remained the mother church of Christianity from the beginning is significant. Since Jerusalem itself existed primarily for the temple and to serve the temple cult, the only reason why Galileans would relocate in Jerusalem would be the desirability of living close to the temple.[59] Even if this move resulted only because they expected the climactic events of the age to take place there, temple and Zion were inextricable concepts in such an expectation.

(2) Those who opposed Paul's Gentile mission so vigorously on behalf of the Law were unlikely to abstract the temple cult so central to the Torah from their zeal for the Law. The fact that the temple cult does not feature in the disputes of Paul speaks against this, though since the disputes took place in the Diaspora, loyalty to the temple cult may not have been a practical issue anyway.

(3) Hebrews does, however, attest that the tangibility of the temple cult proved a strong attraction to many Gentile Christians. If *all* Christians had renounced the temple cult— including those living in Jerusalem and Judea—then it is hardly likely that Gentile believers would have been so attracted to it as part of their faith in Christ. Such Gentiles would surely have by-passed the Christian sect entirely and embraced Judaism itself.

(4) Finally, it is worth recalling that the Jesus tradition contains a saying which suggests continued recourse to the provisions of the temple cult: "If you are offering your gift at the altar, and there remember that your brother has something against you, leave your gift there before the altar and go; first be reconciled to your brother, and then come and offer your gift" (Matt 5:23-24). The term "gift" (δῶρόν), of course, need not signify a sacrifice as such, but the phrase used here, "bring an offering, offer a gift," is more or less a technical term for participation in the temple sacrificial cult, as its regular use in Leviticus makes clear.[60] The point is that this instruction was remembered as part of Jesus' teaching. Had Jesus turned his face against the temple sacrificial system, it is hardly likely that such a saying would have been preserved. Those who took it seriously as practical advice for their daily living presumably continued to observe the cult to which it referred. Were they then misguided? Had they relapsed into traditional Jewish observance despite Jesus' teaching, or despite a deduction drawn from the death of Jesus from earliest days? Or is Matthew 5:23-24 simply further attestation to the fact that the understanding of Jesus' death as atoning sacrifice had not yet emerged among those who treasured the saying?

A Plausible Scenario?

There is one other strand of evidence provided by Acts—that concerning Stephen and the Hellenists (Acts 6–7). Luke's account suggests the
emergence of a group within the earliest Jerusalem community whose
attitude to the temple was more conducive to a belief that Jesus' death
had marked the end of the temple cult. There are three significant
points.

(1) As already noted, the Hellenists ("Greek-speakers") were proba-
    bly so described because they spoke only Greek. That is, unlike
    most Jerusalem Jews who could communicate, at least to some
    extent, in both Aramaic and Greek,[61] the Hellenists spoke only
    Greek.[62] Their ignorance of Aramaic indicates an origin in the
    Diaspora and implies a return to Jerusalem, presumably to be
    near the temple. But the mention of a synagogue used by the
    Hellenists (6:9) probably also implies that their regular prayers
    and Torah reading took place in Greek-speaking assemblies.
    Nevertheless, significant numbers of them became members of
    the new sect of the Nazarene.

(2) If Stephen was at all representative of the Hellenist believers, the
    accusation against him is significant: he spoke against "this holy
    place [the temple] and the Law" claiming that Jesus would
    destroy this place and change the customs delivered by Moses
    (6:13-14). Apparently, Stephen was heard as taking up the word
    of/attributed to Jesus (Mark 14:58 par.; John 2:19) in terms
    explicitly negative against the temple. His turning to "the way"
    of Jesus, in other words, was in part also a turning away from
    Judaism's central institution, the very institution that presum-
    ably had drawn his Hellenist seniors back to Jerusalem.

(3) The speech attributed to Stephen climaxes in a dismissal of the
    temple as a house "made with hands" (7:48). Since "the thing
    made with hands" was Hellenistic Judaism's way of characteriz-
    ing idolatry,[63] such a description of the temple would have been
    heard by Greek-speakers as an outright condemnation of the
    temple and its cult. Of course, no one thinks (or should think)
    of the speeches in Acts as historical transcripts. But since Luke
    elsewhere seems well disposed to the temple,[64] quite likely he
    has drawn on good sources for this representation of Stephen's
    (or Christian Hellenists') view of the temple.

Much of this conclusion is unavoidably speculative. And in Acts 6–7
nothing is said explicitly about the temple sacrificial cult, and nothing at

all about Jesus' death as rendering that cult unnecessary. Nevertheless, what begins to emerge is a context in which the thought of Jesus' death as an atoning sacrifice could have emerged as part of or even the reason for the hostility to the temple suggested by Luke's account of the Hellenist believers.[65] The point is, of course, that it was evidently just these Hellenist believers who were driven from Jerusalem and scattered northwards taking the gospel to Damascus and Antioch, where Paul first learned the confession of Jesus' death as "for our sins."

In sum, the Hellenists do seem to bridge the gap indicated by Acts between Jesus' own talk of his death and the first Christian confession of that death as an atoning sacrifice. The understanding of Jesus' death in soteriological terms does not seem to have been grasped or articulated within the earliest Jerusalem community. This is not to accuse Peter and James and John of abandoning or ignoring a clear teaching of Jesus himself on the subject. For Jesus' teaching, even as still remembered in the Synoptic tradition, is itself not clear on the subject. But neither is it to accuse Hellenists like Stephen of a radical departure from or overturning of Jesus' relevant teaching. Jesus had showed himself critical of the temple's functioning. And he was remembered as interpreting his anticipated death in eschatological terms, perhaps as instituting afresh God's covenant with his people, or perhaps as opening the way through the tribulation to come. So even if he himself had not spoken of his death in sacrificial imagery, it was hardly a departure from his teaching to interpret it as a sacrifice to end all sacrifices, an atonement that rendered any other atonement superfluous.

As Pokorny so well appreciated,[66] and the work of Larry Hurtado and Alan Segal in their different ways confirm,[67] the resurrection of Jesus was the "decisive impulse" that lies behind and which integrates the different christological emphases in the NT. But this need not mean that all expressions of Easter faith were formulated at or in the immediate aftermath of the first Easter. In this case, there are indications both that the understanding of Jesus' death as atoning sacrifice did not emerge immediately and that it did so within a year or two of the Easter event, most probably within the circles of the Hellenist believers in Jerusalem—ironically, as part of their understanding of the gospel, which began to create the tensions that subsequently strained so severely the relations between Paul and the Jerusalem church!

Chapter 11

Discarding the Seamless Robe
The High Priesthood of Jesus in John's Gospel

Helen K. Bond

As the Johannine Jesus hangs on the cross, the Roman soldiers divide up his clothing (John 19:23-24). The scene is well known from the Synoptic Gospels (Mark 15:24 and pars.), but John adds a unique feature: Jesus' tunic (χιτών), he says, was "seamless" (ἄραθος), woven from the top throughout (ἐκ τῶν ἄνωθεν ὑφαντὸς δι᾽ ὅλου). The symbolism behind this detail has been debated from earliest times, with recent commentators tending to favor either the view that the tunic represents Christian unity or that it signifies the self-giving son.[1] In this essay, however, I shall argue first that it is more likely that the tunic represents high priestly garb; second, that high priestly Christology is not as alien to the Fourth Gospel as many have supposed; and third, that there is a specific point in the history of the Fourth Gospel's community that would make such symbolism not only plausible but highly relevant and meaningful.

Discussing Johannine Christology in his "Big Book" (*Lord Jesus Christ: Devotion to Jesus in Earliest Christianity*), my highly respected Edinburgh colleague Larry Hurtado notes that views of Jesus were shaped by "opposition and controversy."[2] I hope that this essay will go a small way toward underlining the truth of this observation.

John 19:23-24 in Context

John's crucifixion narrative, with its series of five tightly knit scenes, is distinctive in several ways. Most striking is its air of "pervading calm":[3] distracting or unpleasant details known from the Synoptics have been eliminated—Simon of Cyrene, the mocking bystanders, the derisory criminals, the cry of abandonment, the portents at Jesus' death, and the sympathetic centurion. What comes across most clearly in John's account is Jesus' majesty. The debate over the *titulus* and Pilate's irony only underline what the audience knows to be true: Jesus is the shepherd-king who willingly lays down his life for his sheep (19:17-22). Elevated to the cross, Jesus assumes his kingly throne; he is symbolically "lifted up" that the whole world might see his divine glory; and he dies in the knowledge that his work of redemption is complete (19:28-30). Jesus' death is undoubtedly the supreme moment of divine revelation, but it also has sacrificial overtones: Jesus dies as the paschal lamb (19:14, 31-33; Exod 12:46; Num 9:12)[4] for the forgiveness of sins (John 1:29). Yet even as Jesus dies on the cross, death clearly is not the end but the beginning of the community of believers: his mother and the beloved disciple represent the new community (19:25-27), and the truth of the gospel will be proclaimed by his followers (19:35).

Although his presentation of this scene is distinctive, John shares with the other evangelists an interest in showing that everything was in accordance with scripture. He makes this explicit four times (19:24, 28, 36, and 37), quoting directly from the scriptures in each case.[5] The first, and lengthiest, of these scriptural citations occurs in the passage concerning the seamless robe. When the soldiers crucified Jesus, John notes, they took his garments (τὰ ἱμάτια) and divided them into four parts, one for each soldier.[6] Since the tunic was without seam, however, they decided not to tear it but to cast lots for it. In this way, both lines of Psalm 22 (LXX: 21):19 were fulfilled: "[T]hey parted my garments (τὰ ἱμάτια) among them, and for my clothing (τὸν ἱματισμόν) they cast lots" (19:24). While each Synoptic Gospel alludes to the Psalm, only John cites it here.[7]

One obvious first question is whether there is any symbolism at all in the details surrounding the tunic, or are they simply part of a literary-theological device to ensure that both parts of Psalm 22:19 should be fulfilled? That is, are we told that the tunic was seamless and woven *only* to necessitate the drawing of lots? This belief has been argued by a number of commentators,[8] yet three features suggest that there is more to the story than scriptural fulfilment alone. First, the Greek syntax in verse 23 relating to the robe is rather labored. It would have been enough had John simply noted that the robe was "seamless"; his details regarding the weave and construction of the garment suggest something significant about it. Second, the evangelist often exhibits an interest in clothing and frequently endows it with symbolic significance: the grave clothes of Lazarus are symbolically untied as confirmation of his resurrection

(11:44); grave clothes appear once again at Jesus' own resurrection, this time neatly rolled up (20:6-7); in 13:4 Jesus symbolically lays aside his garments and girds himself with a towel as a sign of his humility and love for his disciples; and in 19:2, 5 Jesus is clothed with a crown of thorns and a purple robe (ἱμάτιον πορφυροῦν) as a sign of his majesty.[9] Third, in a tightly constructed and highly theological scene, set in a gospel that delights in double-meaning and symbolism, not to suspect a deeper meaning here is difficult. As R. E. Brown maintains, the tunic is "the centre of the theological symbolism in the episode."[10]

But what is being symbolized? I shall discuss three suggestions: first, that the robe represents the unity of believers; second, that it highlights the self-giving of the Son; and third, that it evokes the tunic of the Jewish high priest.

The Unity of Believers

Throughout the history of the Church, the most common way to interpret the seamless robe was to see it as a symbol of Christian unity. This was argued clearly by Cyprian in the mid-third century[11] and, as already noted, is still prevalent today.[12] On first consideration, this view has much to recommend it. Unity is certainly a concern of the fourth evangelist (quite possibly in reaction to divisions that he already sensed were beginning to beset his church). In 10:16, Jesus speaks of the ingathering of his "other sheep," "so that there will be one flock, one shepherd"; in 11:52 Caiaphas prophesies that Jesus' death would "gather together the scattered children of God," and the prayer of chapter 17 ends with a clear plea for unity (17:20-23).[13] It would, therefore, be entirely appropriate to find some reference to unity at the climactic moment of this narrative.

Yet, as R. Schnackenburg notes, these early passages do not require that a reference to unity be found at this point.[14] Other themes associated with Jesus' death are absent: Jesus' death represents the defeat of the "ruler of this world" (12:31; 16:11, 33), for instance, but this is not directly alluded to in the crucifixion scene. The most serious problem with this reading, however, is that the robe lies *discarded*, and although it remains intact, it is finally in the possession of one of Jesus' executioners.[15] T. L. Brodie (following Augustine)[16] tries to make something of the universalism of the four soldiers (four representing the corners of the earth) and the fact that they are Gentile (suggesting that John has the universal church in mind here),[17] but we still have the problem that these men are Jesus' executioners. The Greek syntax at 24c-25 (οἱ μὲν . . . δε) suggests that John sees a contrast between the callous behavior of the soldiers and the faithful women at the cross:[18] we are a long way from Mark's sympathetic centurion (Mark 15:39). If the robe symbolizes church unity, why is it discarded? Why does it end up in enemy hands?

The Seamless Robe as the Self-Giving of the Son

Sensing this difficulty, Schnackenburg, followed by an increasing number of recent commentators, links the seamless robe to the footwashing scene in 13:1-20. Just as Jesus earlier laid aside his garments (τὰ ἱμάτια, 13:4) and humbled himself, so here Jesus has his most intimate garment (his χιτών) taken from him. Jesus suffers utter degradation, though the fact that the tunic is not destroyed shows that he remains under God's care.[19]

On a general level, there are certainly many important connections between these two scenes: the foot washing anticipates the cleansing brought about by Jesus' death; both concern the self-abasement of Christ; and both express the paradox of the humbled Lord. Yet the parallels remain on a general level: the seamlessness and the weave of the robe are incidental to this reading (all that is required is a reason why the soldiers should refrain from tearing it), and the crucial element—that Jesus lays aside his garment or has it taken from him—is not even mentioned. The stress is on the *fate* of the robe, not its removal. Furthermore, although χιτών does tend to mean an "undergarment," its use in the Septuagint is much wider than this: it is used of Joseph's long robe (Gen 37:3, 23, 31, 32, 33), for a "rich robe" (Isa 3:24), and for Andronicus' purple robe (2 Macc 4:38). The use of χιτών, then, does not necessarily lend connotations of debasement and humility to the scene. But what of our third interpretation: that the tunic represents that worn by the Jewish high priest?

The Seamless Robe as Symbol of the High Priest

Initially, the link between Jesus' χιτών and the high priestly vestments is not an obvious one, at least not to most modern interpreters.[20] It is important, however, to appreciate the profound significance of these vestments to first-century Jews. The dazzling robes, which were only worn on ceremonial occasions in the temple, were commonly believed to be the clothes of Adam.[21] Exodus 28:2, 40 speaks of the "glory and beauty" of the robes, while Ben Sira, too, wrote of the glory and majesty of the high priest in his vestments and compared the officiating high priest to divine wisdom.[22] The author of the *Letter to Aristeas* speaks of his "astonishment and indescribable wonder" at the sight of the robed high priest and "the holy quality which pertains to each detail" (*Let. Aris.* 99). Such was the power of the vestments that, first, Herod and then the Roman governors sought to keep them under their own control in the Antonia Fortress. (They were picked up seven days prior to festivals to allow for their purification.) When the robes were restored to Jewish custody in 37 C.E., the Syrian legate responsible was welcomed into Jerusalem amid jubilant scenes.[23] Furthermore, there are many examples of Greek-speaking Second Temple Jews subjecting the various components of the vestments to allegorical and theological speculation: this appropriation had begun, to some extent, in the Exodus texts themselves (particularly in the longer account of Exod 28:1-39) and is apparent in Wis 18:24 and Sirach—all of which were presumably known to John. Other examples can be found in the *Testament of Levi* 8:2, Philo,[24] and Josephus (*Ant.* 3.172); and even after the temple's destruction, rabbis continued to ponder the significance of the garments.[25] The idea of using high priestly robes in a symbolic, theological manner, then, would not strike Jewish readers as extraordinary.

John 19:24 contains several indications that the evangelist has priestly garments in mind. Most important, perhaps, is the note that the χιτών was "woven from the top throughout." It is surely significant that every one of the eleven uses of the adjective "woven" (ὑφαντός) in the Septuagint refers to priestly garments;[26] out of its four uses in Josephus, two refer to drapes in the sanctuary (which Josephus simply calls "the woven things," or "the fabrics").[27] This evidence, added to the fact that the woven nature of priestly robes was still commented on in rabbinic times,[28] makes it likely that John's audience would understand that the woven χιτών was not simply any undergarment, but one worn by a priest. The seamlessness of the garment, too, adds to its priestly origins. *B. Zebahim* 88b (commenting on Exod 28:32) notes that "the priestly garments were not sewn," a view echoed by *b. Yoma* 72b (commenting on Exod 31:10) and by Josephus who tells us that at least one of the high priestly garments was seamless (see below). Finally, the fact that the garment was not torn may echo the injunction of Leviticus 21.10 against tearing the high priestly robes.[29] Taken together, these arguments do suggest that John's Jewish readers might well interpret the χιτών as a priestly garment.

But does the evangelist have a particular robe in mind here? The high priest wore eight ceremonial garments, four of which were unique to him: the long violet robe of the ephod (the מְעִיל); the ephod itself (which seems to have been a shorter waistcoat or apron); a breastplate, which was attached to the ephod; and a headdress.[30] Taking their cue from the *seamlessness* of the robe, several commentators have linked the χιτών with the long violet robe of the ephod, which Josephus (who was himself a serving temple priest) refers to as a χιτών made from one long woven piece of cloth (*Ant.* 3.159–61). This identification, however, is not without its difficulties. First, Josephus, though undoubtedly correct, is the only ancient writer to testify to the seamlessness of this particular robe.[31] And second, although the robe could be referred to as a χιτών, it was by no means always referred to as such. Contemporary writers used a wide variety of terms: ὑποδύτης,[32] ποδήρης χιτών or simply ποδήρης,[33] or the more general στολή[34]—with ποδήρης (meaning a full-length robe) emerging as the clearly preferred term.

Another possibility, however, is that John intends his readers to think of the χιτών worn by the high priest on the Day of Atonement (Lev 16:4). This was the plain, linen tunic worn by the high priest in order to enter the Holy of Holies on this one special day; when he had finished in the sanctuary, the high priest removed his χιτών, bathed, put on his ceremonial vestments—the robes of glory—and offered sacrifice at the altar for Israel's sin (Lev 16:23-26).[35] This identification of the χιτών has the advantage that the evangelist uses exactly the same word as Leviticus 16:4: the Psalm used ἱματισμός, but John deliberately chose to refer to the garment instead as a χιτών; anyone familiar with the Septuagint or temple cult would hear the connection. That this χιτών could be the object of theological speculation as much as the ceremonial vestments is shown by Philo's comparison of this plain robe (which, he suggests, was truly glorious and honored by the father) with the precious vestments honored by humans.[36]

Admittedly, this robe (which was the same as that worn by ordinary priests) is never explicitly said to be seamless by any extant ancient author, but we should perhaps not be too prosaic in our search for a precise priestly robe. The ancient sources are full of slight discrepancies in their descriptions of high priestly vestments; communities that had only the rather patchy descriptions of Exodus and their own eyes to depend upon might well have developed their own images and interpretations of the robes (some of which may have conformed to historical fact, and some of which doubtlessly did not).[37] How many practicing Christians would be able to describe their priest's weekly vestments (and their manufacture) in detail, let alone his or her ceremonial ones? What is important is that the constellation of ideas and images in 19:24 evokes high priestly robes.

Furthermore, the discarding of the χιτών according to this interpretation is not a problem. John may want to show that as Jesus dies on the cross, the woven, seamless χιτών of the high priest lies redundant and discarded: it is Jesus, and no longer an earthly Jewish high priest, who takes away the sins of the world (1:29; 6:51; 13:8-10; 19:34).[38] God's people are about to be reconstituted around the person of Jesus, and the role and functions once reserved for the high priest—intercession, sacrifice, reconciliation, cleansing, and forgiveness from sin—are now fulfilled and superseded by Jesus himself. (Recorded after the fall of the temple, the fact that the robe ends up in Roman hands may well be a reflection on historical events, as we shall see in the last section of this chapter). Finally, although De la Potterie is correct that no Church father associated the robe with the high priesthood,[39] some of John's earliest interpreters, even if not commenting directly on the χιτών, are quite explicit in their use of high priestly imagery. Both 1 John 2:1 and Revelation 1:13, both probably slightly later than the gospel and showing some connection to it,[40] are explicit in their presentation of Jesus as high priest, a presentation which would be curious if no grounds for it whatsoever were in the gospel itself.

If this is the correct reading of the significance of the χιτών, we should expect it to find some corroboration in the wider context of the Fourth Gospel. One of the most common reasons why the identification of the χιτών with high priestly clothing is often rejected by scholars is that elsewhere John appears to have little interest in the high priesthood.[41] Lindars speaks for many when he claims that the theme of Jesus as high priest "receives no attention by John."[42] This, to some extent, is true: John has more exalted claims to make regarding Jesus—he is the divine word, Wisdom, even God himself (1:1; 20:28)—and there is no speculation on the high priesthood in the manner of Hebrews.[43] I would not wish to claim that John has a strongly developed, high priestly Christology, rather that his treatment of the high priesthood links with his treatment of other Jewish feasts and institutions. To those links I shall now turn.

The Temple and its Cult

A striking feature of John's gospel is that its very structure is linked to Jewish cultic observance. While Mark arranged his material so that the first half of the gospel described the Galilean ministry and the second half Jesus' journey to and time in Jerusalem, the Johannine Jesus travels continually between Galilee and Jerusalem, visiting the holy city whenever he can.[44]

Jesus' first trip to Jerusalem in John comes as early as 2:13-22. It is worth spending a few moments looking at this because, rather like the first of the signs in 2:1-11, this first Jerusalem visit is programmatic for what will follow. Jesus' first (and only) act on this occasion is to enter the temple, drive out the animal sellers, overturn the tables of the money-changers, and forbid the transformation of his father's house into a market. This is the same incident which occurs at the end of Jesus' ministry in the other gospels (Mark 11:15-19 and pars.), and which leads directly to his arrest. But John has reset it in Jesus' first visit to Jerusalem, and he follows it with a discussion between Jesus and "the Jews" who ask him for a sign. "Destroy this temple," Jesus says, "and in three days I will raise it up again" (2:19). Characteristically, "the Jews" misunderstand, declaring that it has taken forty-six years to build the temple, so how could Jesus possibly claim to rebuild it in such a short time? (2:20). But the Johannine narrator gives the true meaning of his words: "[T]he temple he was speaking of," he says, "was the temple of his body" (2:21). No one seems to have understood him at the time but later, after the resurrection and thoughtful perusal of their scriptures, the disciples realized what he had meant (2:22).

But what precisely does the Johannine Jesus mean here? Unlike other early Christian thinkers, John's Jesus does not declare that *the Church* or *the community of believers* now represents the temple, rather they represent his own *body*. It is the same body, or flesh, in which the glorious divine Word is said to have tabernacled in 1:14. However given the fact that for John there is a close connection between Jesus and believers—such that the latter abide in the Son—and the fact that the temple is naturally a place where people gather, we perhaps should not press this distinction too far.[45] The central question seems to revolve around worship: in the light of the revelation brought by Jesus, how is God to be worshipped? And the answer for this evangelist is clearly that the entire system of traditional Jewish worship, with its feasts and cultic activities centred in the Jerusalem temple, has been fulfilled (and, therefore, superseded) by Christ. His revelation and glorification on the cross have inaugurated a new age, an age of universal holiness where sacrifice and the temple are rendered unnecessary.[46] Heaven and earth meet not in the temple, but in Jesus' person (1:51). In his discussion with the Samaritan woman in 4:22, Jesus makes it clear that true worship is not in Jerusalem or on Mount Gerizim, but "in spirit and in truth." As Schnackenburg notes, "the Johannine Church sees itself as the worshipping community in which this eschatological 'adoration in the spirit and the truth' made possible by Jesus Christ is reali[z]ed, because the community is united with the person of Christ who is himself the true 'temple.' "[47]

And this fundamental point is underlined time and time again throughout the rest of the gospel: Jesus is the one who embodies the real meaning of the Sabbath (chap. 5), the real meaning of the Passover (chap. 6), Tabernacles (chaps. 7–10), and Dedication (chaps. 10–12).[48] Noticeably, although Jesus dutifully makes his way to Jerusalem and even to the temple itself, there is never any suggestion that he intends to worship there. In fact, quite the opposite: his teaching in the temple creates divisions and threatens to disturb events. John always carefully notes that these are feasts "of the Jews," thereby driving a wedge between Jesus and the cultic festivities. As Talbert notes, "Jesus participates in Jewish worship only in order to show he fulfils and supersedes it,"[49] and, as Motyer has shown, by 11:55-57 Jesus himself in Bethany seems almost to have replaced Jerusalem as the focus of pilgrimage: people in the temple inquire as to his whereabouts.[50] But Jesus, for this evangelist, supersedes not only the feasts, but other Jewish institutions as well: he transforms the water of Jewish purification into good wine (2:1-11); he contrasts the bread of his body (presumably the Eucharist) with the manna given by Moses in the wilderness (6:25-65); he claims priority and superiority over Abraham (8:58); and most dramatically of all, he will die as the new paschal lamb (19:14). John's narrative strategy, then, is quite clear, as are his reasons for beginning Jesus' Jerusalem ministry with the dramatic incident in the temple: Jewish worship—in all its forms and manifestations—has now been superseded by Christ.

But what can be said of the high priest? Given its immense importance, not to have any mention of the high priesthood in this context, it seems to me, would be worthy of note. In fact, however, John has a much greater interest in the high priesthood than any other evangelist. The problems raised by the author's predilection for grouping all Jesus' opponents together under the term οἱ Ἰουδαῖοι have tended to blind commentators to the fact that Caiaphas and his father-in-law Annas play a much more prominent role in this gospel than in any other; indeed, in the short trial scene of 18:19-24, John seems deliberately to contrast Jesus and the high priest, presumably to show the former's superiority.[51] Moreover, alone of the evangelists, John seems to subscribe to the popular Jewish belief that high priests were occasionally granted the gift of prophecy (11:51), a belief which betrays some residual respect for the office.[52] Furthermore, in 17:19 Jesus behaves as the high priest, as he both consecrates the sacrifice (himself) and intercedes with the father.[53] That Jesus' exaltation on the cross should render the earthly high priest of the Jews redundant would not be out of place at all in John's overall theology. In the same way that Jesus transcends and supersedes the temple, so he transcends and renders redundant the earthly high priest; everything that Jewish Christians once looked to the high priest to achieve is now accomplished to the full in Christ.

The Historical Location of the Idea of Jesus as "Replacement High Priest"

One final question is at what stage did these ideas permeate John's thinking? Were they part of the earliest traditions, perhaps inspired by Jesus himself? Or were they a much later development, linked conceivably with the destruction of the temple and its cult in 70 C.E.? A number of factors need to be taken into account here. First, in the discussion of the temple in chapter 2, John makes it quite clear that Jesus' disciples did not understand the significance of his words at the time; it was only after the resurrection and a process of sifting through the scriptures that the full implications dawned on them. This suggests at least some distance from the ministry of Jesus himself. But how long? It is clear from Paul's letters from the 50s that he found it perfectly possible to think of groups of Gentile Christians or even individuals in terms of a new temple (1 Cor 3:16-17; 6:19; 2 Cor 6:16), and could refer to the leaders of the Jerusalem church as "pillars" (Gal 2:9), a metaphor which fits well with the image of Christians as a spiritualized temple. Possibly, then, the Johannine community's understanding of the body of Christ—and indeed of itself—as a replacement temple may be relatively early.

However J. Klawans has recently argued persuasively that Paul's use of temple imagery is metaphorical, that he is extending the sanctity of cultic activity to the Christian community rather than replacing and rejecting it.[54] Furthermore, the tremendous interest displayed by John both in the temple and its annual cycle of feasts suggests that observance of these elements is not in the community's distant past but is still part of their communal memory, indeed, still forms a large part of their disputes with the Jewish synagogue.[55] Perhaps they, like other Jewish Christian groups, continued to worship in the temple and to hold it dear, at least as long as it was possible for them to do so.[56] If the gospel took on its formative shape in Syria or Palestine, as is often suggested, then it would have been quite possible for John's Jewish-Christian group to have been regular attendees at the Jerusalem temple.[57]

The event which would have brought this accord to an end was the fall of the temple and the cessation of cultic activity in 70 C.E.[58] The traditions which made up the Fourth Gospel would undoubtedly have undergone a radical revision at this time as stories from the group's past were adapted to changing conditions.[59] Speculation on the catastrophic events of 70 C.E. might well have caused major dissent between Johannine Christians and their Jewish "neighbors."[60] Although we regard 70 C.E. as the end of an era and tend to assume that Jews of the period saw it in the same way, it was by no means clear to most people that the temple would not be built again, and most seem to have longed for the day when a new temple would rise from the ashes of the old. Perhaps it was at this period, particularly as relations between Jewish Christians and other Jews became ever more strained, that Johannine Christians began to realize that they could do without the temple. As far as they were concerned, Jesus had fulfilled and superseded everything they once held sacred: they had their own spiritual temple and their own high priest, true worship was no longer to be found in a sacred place, but among those who chose to abide in the body of Jesus Christ.

In its final form,[61] the death of Jesus in John's gospel is a highly complex interweaving of several themes: predominantly it is the supreme moment of revelation; the ultimate display of Jesus' divine glory; the first part of Jesus' departure to the father; and a manifestation of the divine will. But it also has clear sacrificial overtones as Jesus dies as both the victim and the presiding priest; fulfilling and superseding the role of both the paschal lamb and the high priest in Jewish tradition. Jesus' priesthood is not a major theme in John's gospel, rather it takes its place in a long series of Johannine reappropriations of Jewish feasts and institutions. Like so much else in this gospel, the implications of the woven, seamless tunic are not spelled out in detail but are left to the reader to interpret. If the rabbis could speculate on the high priestly robes long after the destruction of the temple, there is no reason why John should not do so within a decade or two of the events of 70 C.E. For Johannine

Christians, the old high priesthood is at an end, brought to a sorry demise by Roman troops, but this end is of little concern: everything they once expected from the high priest—intercession, sacrifice, reconciliation, cleansing, and forgiveness from sin—is now accomplished completely through Christ.

Chapter 12

Remembering and Revelation
The Historic and Glorified Jesus in the Gospel of John

Larry W. Hurtado

In a recent book, *Lord Jesus Christ* (2003), I noted that one of the features common to all four of the intracanonical gospels is that they situate Jesus explicitly and rather fully within a time, place, and culture.[1] This is all the more remarkable in light of the interesting and well-known differences among them in some other matters, and also in comparison with the rather unlocalized way that Jesus is depicted in extracanonical "Jesus books" such as the *Gospel of Thomas* and the *Gospel of Philip*.[2] That is, all four intracanonical Jesus books concur broadly in emphasizing that the risen and glorified Jesus is to be identified as the historic figure who first appeared in Galilee, and whose career was framed by the prophet-ministry of John (the Baptizer) and by Jesus' execution in Jerusalem at the hands of the Roman governor, Pilate. By contrast, from the *Gospel of Thomas*, for example, one would scarcely suspect that Jesus was a Jew, where he may have operated, or any specific timeframe for him, to say nothing of anything more specific about him in historical terms.

All four intracanonical accounts, however, are rich in geographical references (e.g., Lake Galilee, Capernaum, Nazareth, Bethsaida, Caesarea Philippi, the Decapolis, Samaria, Jericho, Bethlehem, Bethany, Emmaus, the Jordan River, Tyre and Sidon, and Jerusalem), and references to the religious and cultural setting, including religious parties (e.g., Pharisees, Sadducees, Herodians), issues about observance of Jewish religious law (e.g., Sabbath, food laws, divorce and remarriage, skin diseases, oaths, tithing, and taxation), festivals such as Passover, issues of belief such as resurrection. We also get information on governing structures and personalities (e.g., Herod the Great, Herod Antipas, Caiaphas, and the

Roman governor Pilate). There are references to local occupations such as fishing, farming, tax gathering, and shepherding. Indeed, it seems to me that this emphasis that the Lord and Christ of Christian devotion is to be linked to, and defined with reference to, the historic figure of Jesus may also have been a major impetus for these texts, and an important factor in shaping their genre as narrative books about him.[3]

Also notable is the use of Semitic words and expressions in these Greek texts.[4] The most familiar instances are echoed in one or more of the four gospels, such as "Hosanna" (Mark 11:9-10; Matt. 21:9; John 12:13), "Gehenna" (Mark 9:43-47; Matt. 10:28; 23:15, 33; Luke 12:5), "Rabbi" and "Rabbouni" (e.g., Matt. 23:7-8; John 1:38; 20:16), and the famous cry of Jesus on the cross reported in varying forms by Mark (15:34) and Matthew (27:46). It is very interesting that the use of such Semitic loanwords seems particularly frequent in GMark and GJohn.[5]

With more direct reference to the literary nature of GJohn, we might note particularly that, although this gospel is readily distinguishable from any of the Synoptics in various specific matters—in the ordering of events, selection of material, vocabulary, characters, and key themes— nevertheless, this distinctive account can be likened to the Synoptics in its emphatic placement of Jesus in a historically specific setting, and with lots of local color.[6] To underscore the point, although GJohn is very well known for its uniquely explicit presentation of an exalted view of Jesus, the text in its own way also emphatically identifies the incarnate Logos and the risen/gloried Lord fully with reference to the historic Jesus.[7]

The author's concern, however, was obviously not that typical of modern "historical Jesus" scholars.[8] He was not aiming to *separate* or even to distinguish the historic figure from the glorified recipient of Christian devotion, or to offer what can be made of Jesus historically apart from what he became in Christian faith. Instead, the author's emphasis was on the direct *identity* and *continuity* of the earthly and the risen Jesus. The author's reason for giving his account of the ministry of Jesus was entirely *theological*, not to serve some academic, modern inter- est in historical exactitude, but to shape and nurture the faith of the intended readers. This is, I believe, reasonably well known and uncon- troversial among informed readers of GJohn.

In this discussion, consequently, I focus on three features of GJohn, elaborating on some more fleeting observations registered in *Lord Jesus Christ*. I contend that these features are all unique to GJohn, and yet they also reflect the commonality of the intracanonical gospels by linking the earthly and risen/gloried Jesus. First, in GJohn there is actually a sharper

and more explicit distinction between the perceptions of Jesus' true significance in the earthly (pre-Easter) and post-resurrection periods than is
projected in the Synoptics. Second, GJohn also emphasizes distinctively
and rather clearly the agency of the Holy Spirit/Paraclete in specifically
communicating the fuller post-resurrection grasp of Jesus' significance.
Finally, GJohn uses a distinctive terminology to refer to the revelatory
work of the Spirit and the major cognitive developments represented in
the greater realization of Jesus' true glory that is reserved for the post-resurrection situation.

Pre-Resurrection and Post-Resurrection Knowledge

The first point that I want to address is how GJohn actually makes an
explicit and emphatic distinction between the understanding of Jesus'
significance in the pre-resurrection and the post-resurrection situations.[9]
This distinction is particularly interesting in light of the clear concern in
GJohn to link the situation of Jesus' ministry and the life-setting of the
intended readers. This latter emphasis is well recognized, and for many
of us may be especially associated with the classic work by J. Louis
Martyn, who argued cogently that GJohn presents a "two-level drama,"
the account of Jesus intended also to speak directly to the later issues and
situation of the readers.[10]

To cite one example, it is widely accepted that the unique GJohn references to Jesus' followers being excluded from the Jewish *synagogē* (9:22;
16:1; and cf. 12:42-43) most likely reflect experiences that actually happened to Jewish Christians sometime subsequently to the time of Jesus'
ministry.[11] In GJohn, however, references to these experiences are
intended to help orient and strengthen believers who have suffered this
treatment, and/or who fear something similar for themselves, whether
from fellow Jews or, in the case of Gentile believers, from other social circles. Moreover, as Martyn further argued, GJohn also has Jesus debating
with Jewish leaders over his true significance, articulating his own status
in the supernal categories that must actually derive from and more
directly represent the christological rhetoric of those Christians whose
faith is reflected in the text (e.g., 5:19-47; 6:25-59).[12] Indeed, throughout
GJohn, the explicit claims of the "post-Easter" period are the main matters under debate in the many controversies that mark the text. That is,
the Jewish rejection of Jesus is put very much in terms of the sort of critical rhetoric that was more likely directed against the christological claims
and devotional practices of Johannine Christians (e.g., 5:18; 19:7).

Moreover, GJohn programmatically (and uniquely among the intra-canonical gospels) frames the account of Jesus' earthly activities with the pre-mundane setting of the prologue, repeated references to Jesus' descent from heaven, and his imminent return and glorification by the Father. In short, in a manner easily distinguishable from the Synoptics, Jesus ministry is very explicitly presented in terms of his transcendent stature and significance. GJohn 1:14 will serve to illustrate this, as perhaps *the* interpretive statement of what the ensuing account conveys: "We have seen his glory, the glory as the unique son from the Father, full of grace and truth."[13]

Yet this same account also repeatedly presents the immediate cognitive effects of Jesus' ministry, including his explicit assertions of his divine origins and significance, as misunderstanding and the failure to perceive aright or fully who he really is. To be sure, GJohn typically portrays the responses of Jesus' opponents as *culpable* misunderstanding and failure (e.g., 6:39-47; 8:42-47; 12:37-43). It is not simply an intellectual deficiency in these hearers, and in GJohn certainly not a lack of clarity on Jesus' part! Instead, Jesus' critics and opponents *willfully* choose darkness instead of the light.

But there is not simply a critique of Jesus' opponents. For even Jesus' disciples are presented as falling considerably short of the full truth of his person. True, among them only Judas is pictured as directly under the influence of Satan (6:70-71; 13:2, 27). Although the cognitive failures of others are treated much more benignly, these disciples, too, seem unable to realize adequately what the author and intended readers perceive clearly. For instance, Jesus' disciples mistake the meaning of his reference to nourishment (4:31-34); some complain that his teaching is difficult to accept, failing to understand that his words are "spirit and life" (6:60-66); and others cannot grasp his reference to giving spiritual freedom to those who believe in him (8:31-33). His disciples are also pictured as obtuse in reaction to Jesus' statements about Lazarus (11:7-16). In the farewell-discourse material (chs. 13–17), the frequent questions and other comments of Jesus' disciples further illustrate their well-meaning confusion and dim perception. We might note, for example, Peter's reaction to Jesus' foot-washing (13:6-11); Peter's puzzlement over Jesus' reference to his imminent departure (13:36-38); Philip's request to be shown the Father (14:8-9); the further puzzlement about Jesus' departure (16:16-18); and Jesus' response to their overconfident claim to understand and believe (16:29-33).

Also, of course, in a couple of significant scenes, there is a specific contrast between the level of the disciples' understanding before and after

Jesus' resurrection. I shall return to these passages later in this discussion, to focus on the author's use of "remembering" language in them. At this point, I simply note briefly the chronological distinction between levels of understanding. In 2:18-22, the disciples seem to be implicitly included among those who mistake Jesus' reference to raising up the temple; only after Jesus' resurrection, do they perceive the true meaning.[14] Likewise, in 12:12-16 there is a similar contrast; the disciples did not really understand the contextual events "at first" (τò πρῶτον), but after Jesus was "glorified," they perceived them as fulfillment of prophecy.

Several times in the "farewell discourse" material, Jesus explicitly contrasts the limited understanding of his disciples in the setting of his earthly presence with the greater understanding to come after his departure. In 14:25-26 (another passage to which I return shortly), for instance, there is a distinction between the things that Jesus says then and the full truth that will come via the *Parakletos* (Spirit of Truth) whose activity is directly tied to Jesus' departure from the earthly sphere through his death and resurrection (16:7). Likewise in 16:12, Jesus refers to "many things" that he wished to communicate but that could not then be borne by his disciples, and Jesus promises a future revelation of "all the truth," again set after his departure. I take the distinction in 16:25 between Jesus' use of "parables" (ἐν παροιμίαις) and a future hour when all will be openly declared as yet another Johannine reference to the different levels of understanding available in pre-resurrection and post-resurrection settings.[15] For, although in this same scene the disciples claim to see clearly (16:29-30), Jesus' response casts doubt on this claim, warning that, in fact, they will yet forsake him (vv. 31-32).

On the other hand, we should not exaggerate the matter. The contrast in GJohn between the time of Jesus' earthly ministry and the post-resurrection period is not one of complete ignorance and understanding, or of deliberate secrecy and subsequent forthrightness. So, for instance, Ron Cameron's characterization of GJohn as distinguishing between "the incomprehensible ministry of the earthly Jesus and the post-resurrection period of understanding the work and words of Jesus" must be judged an exaggeration that oversimplifies the more nuanced tension in GJohn.[16] The unbelief of Jesus' audience results from their rank refusal to accept what is plainly shown them in Jesus' works and words. The problem was not an incomprehensible Jesus but that some of the Israelites loved darkness rather than light (3:19). And the result of Jesus' ministry was not total incomprehension and unbelief. For in GJohn, Jesus' disciples do respond favorably and commendably. They certainly have much more to learn, particularly involving a much larger grasp of Jesus' person and significance. Still, there is a clear distinction in GJohn between their faith (limited though it is in cognitive depth) and the unbelief of those who accuse Jesus of blasphemy or simply do not know what to make of him. As Schnackenburg noted, several times in GJohn, Jesus is pictured speaking openly (παρρησία) and to the general public (7:25-31; 10:22-26; 18:19-21).[17] To repeat the point for emphasis, in distinction from the limited understanding of him among his disciples, those who completely misconstrue and oppose him are portrayed as doing so willfully and in disobedience to God.

Although the comprehension of Jesus' disciples falls considerably short of the full realization of his status that comes only after his resurrection, they do have a relatively positive view of him that is sharply contrasted with Jesus' opponents. For example, although Jesus' response to Nathaniel's acclamation indicates that it does not adequately capture Jesus' full significance (1:49-51), nevertheless, it is true, so far as it goes. In GJohn, Jesus is the rightful king of Israel, and Son of God in a far more profound sense than Nathaniel realizes. Also, in the structurally crucial prayer in GJohn 17, Jesus refers to his disciples in very positive terms, as, for example, those to whom he has given revelation and who, therefore, believe that he has come from God (17:6-8); and those who are, therefore, distinguished from "the world" (17:14-16); the ones for whose sake Jesus now sanctifies himself (17:19) and through whom others will come to believe (17:20).

Even if one grants the comparatively positive treatment of Jesus' disciples, nevertheless, there is a real discrepancy in GJohn between what people were able to perceive about Jesus prior to his death and resurrection and afterward. Unlike those contemporaries of Jesus even most positively inclined, the author and his intended readers—standing this side of Jesus' resurrection—see with minds illumined to see his fuller glory. It is a distinction in degree or depth, but it is still a major difference. Although GJohn can rightly be characterized as programmatically presenting the earthly ministry of Jesus in light of what believers subsequently came to perceive as his full significance, the author also actually underscores the comparatively limited grasp of Jesus' person that characterized the time of his ministry. Indeed, the rather blatant presentation of Jesus' exalted significance in GJohn actually makes all the more explicit the contrast with the level of understanding of him attained by his followers during his ministry.[18]

The Agent of Post-Resurrection Comprehension

I turn now to discuss the way that GJohn explicitly indicates how the fuller and more adequate grasp of Jesus' significance characteristic of the post-resurrection period was made possible. There are two factors to note. First, Jesus had to complete his work, including particularly his death, and be resurrected and glorified, which also involved him departing from earthly activity and presence with his followers. That is, although GJohn presents Jesus as the incarnate and human expression of the pre-mundane divine Logos through whom the world was made (1:1-3), the author also clearly attributes great significance to Jesus' ministry, death, and resurrection/exaltation as further revelations of Jesus' person. He also provides the crucial content and bases for the proper confession of him as divine Son and Lord. In GJohn, in other words, a fully adequate confession of Jesus requires that it be shaped crucially by these events. For this reason, I suggest, GJohn is a *narrative* about Jesus. GJohn is known classically for its propositional statements of faith (e.g., 1:1-18; 20:31), but these christological propositions take their *specific content* and have their *basis* in the *actions and events* that form the substance of this essentially *narrative* text.

However, GJohn uniquely emphasizes a second factor as the crucial agency through which the fuller grasp of Jesus' significance was made possible after Jesus' resurrection: the Spirit/Paraclete.[19] Although respectable scholars have made other suggestions, for example, that the Paraclete is the implied author and/or an unnamed teacher/prophet figure, I consider the textual evidence rather clear that the reference is to the divine Spirit (a.k.a., Holy Spirit, and Spirit of Truth).[20] Granted, there are also references in the Synoptics to the Spirit providing the impetus and content of Christian witness. In Mark 13:9-11, part of the discourse directly predictive of and for the post-resurrection period, Jesus is pictured as warning that his followers subsequently will face arraignment "because of me." He instructs them to "say whatever is given you at that time, for it is not you who speak, but the Holy Spirit" (v. 11). In a Lukan parallel to these words (12:11-12), the Holy Spirit "will teach you at that very hour what you ought to say," and the Matthew parallel in 10:19-20 promises "the Spirit of your Father [will speak] through you."[21]

GJohn, however, more frequently and more explicitly links the impartation of the Spirit among Jesus' followers to Jesus' resurrection, and also more fully elaborates the work of the Spirit in conveying to Jesus' followers a greater understanding of his significance than was theirs prior to his resurrection. In the unique statement in 7:39, the author both explains Jesus' contextual saying about "rivers of living water" as predicting the work of the Spirit and links the reception of the Spirit among Jesus' followers to him being "glorified." In another passage unique to GJohn, the risen Jesus breathes upon his disciples and bestows the Holy Spirit (20:21-22).

But, obviously, the unique and large body of material comprising the Johannine "farewell discourse" has the most explicit treatment of the cognitive work of the Spirit in the post-resurrection setting. This material is frequently worked over by scholars, of course, and I do not intend to do much more here than to highlight a couple of matters.[22] My main point is the central role of the Spirit/Paraclete in conveying christological truth subsequent to Jesus' departure from the earthly scene.

Let us quickly review the key sayings, beginning with 14:15-17. We should note the reference to "the Spirit of truth" (v. 17), which I take to reflect the projected role of the Spirit in teaching and conveying deeper insight, more explicitly and fully brought out in subsequent sayings. Also noteworthy is the promised bestowal of the Spirit here presented in response to Jesus' request to the Father, which reflects a clear link between Jesus and the Spirit.

In 14:25-26, there is more explicit reference to the cognitive work of the Spirit, who "will teach you everything, and remind you of all that I have said to you" (v. 26).[23] There is a distinction here between the things that Jesus speaks/has spoken in the time of his earthly presence (ταῦτα, v. 25) and the fuller revelation (πάντα, v. 26) that the Holy Spirit will deliver. The specific content or focus of the Spirit's teaching is not spelled out in these verses, but in the larger context of the farewell section in GJohn it should be obvious that this teaching concerns the person of Jesus. From 14:1-7 onward, the high and unique significance of Jesus is the clear central theme. He is "the way, and the truth, and the life," and access to God is mediated entirely through him (esp. vv. 6-7). Still closer to this Paraclete saying, in 14:18-21 Jesus promises a future revelation of himself to his followers, which seems here rather clearly placed after his death/departure from the earthly sphere. So, surely, the reference to the Spirit's work of reminding Jesus' followers of all that he has said to them (v. 14:26) must mean particularly sayings that concern him. Note also that the Spirit is to be sent by God "in my name," which further links the Spirit to Jesus.[24] In the final section of this paper, I shall return to the use of terms of "reminding" and "remembering." At this point, I want to draw attention to the clear emphasis on the agency of the Spirit in effecting a greater understanding of Jesus' person and significance than was conveyed and apprehended during his earthly ministry.

In a third passage, 15:26-27, there is an interesting balance between two emphases. On the one hand, Jesus will send the Spirit-Paraclete and, on the other, the provenance of this Spirit is "with the Father" (παρὰ τοῦ πατρός, twice in v. 26). Another interesting feature of this passage is that this "Spirit of *truth*" (or "*true* Spirit") will "testify" specifically about Jesus (v. 26b). This statement confirms our earlier surmise that the greater truth that the Spirit is to reveal will have to do specifically with Jesus. This positive testimony to Jesus will contradict and correct the unjustified negativity toward Jesus portrayed in 15:18-25, and it also will implicitly inform and empower the testimony of Jesus' followers (v. 27). That is, in 15:26-27, the future revelatory work of the Spirit is to shape their greater christological claims and witness. I suggest that GJohn is itself intended by the author as a paradigmatic presentation of these claims and this witness, as a forthright declaration of Jesus' glorious significance, through which his earthly ministry is retrospectively portrayed. That is, GJohn is supposed to be taken as the product of the Spirit-Paraclete's testimony. It is common for scholars to judge that GJohn is to be understood as reflecting the work of the Paraclete; I wish to urge further that the author of GJohn always *intended* his readers to know this.

The post-resurrection cognitive and forensic work of the Spirit-Paraclete is still more fully expressed, and more precisely targeted, in 16:5-15. There are two main emphases here. First, in vv. 5-11, the Spirit's testimony to Jesus is set over against the unbelief in Jesus that is characteristic of "the world," and which is here *the* sin (v. 9). Because the Spirit is promised exclusively to Jesus' followers (e.g., 14:15–17) and his revelatory work is directed to them (e.g., 14:25-26), we must infer that the demonstration of the error of the world is likewise directed to believers, and then through them to the world, as believers are enabled to echo the Spirit's witness to unbelievers (15:27), in arraignment/persecution and other settings.[25]

Second, in 16:12-15, the final reference to the Spirit-Paraclete in the farewell discourse material, we have the most explicit statement of the cognitive content of what he is to convey.[26] We noted briefly earlier the contrast in vv. 12-13 between the comparatively limited teaching conveyed (and capable of being apprehended) in Jesus' earthly ministry and fuller truth (about Jesus' person) into which the Spirit will lead believers after Jesus' departure. We now should also note that the cognitive focus of the Spirit's work is not on the Spirit, but consists in declaring "the things to come" (τὰ ἐρχόμενα, v. 13) and in glorifying Jesus (v. 14). There is some uncertainty among commentators about what "the things to come" are, and whether they are distinguishable from the more explicitly christological content of the Spirit's teaching in v. 14. Settling the matter is not crucial here, and to imagine that I could do so would be presumptuous.[27] To focus on the dominant emphasis of these verses is sufficient for the present purpose. That emphasis shows that *the Spirit's work relates directly to Jesus' historic ministry and words* and extends and conveys some of the "many things" that could not be conveyed in the pre-resurrection setting. And I repeat that these "many things" to be revealed seem particularly to do with Jesus' glorious significance.

What else can we make of 16:14-15 than to take these verses as ascribing to the Spirit a post-resurrection role of leading Jesus' followers into a deeper, fuller apprehension of who Jesus really is? Despite the (understandable) theological anxiety among some commentators about the idea of a further revelation beyond Jesus, we must do justice to the forthright declaration here.[28] As Haenchen put it, John 16:13 rather clearly implies "that what the spirit [*sic*] will teach will go beyond the message of the earthly Jesus," for, as we have noted already, in GJohn "in spite of continuity, there exists a distinction between the earthly Jesus and the post-Easter spirit, and the real message [I take this to mean the full truth of Jesus' person] is first proclaimed by the spirit."[29] Of course, in GJohn the reality of the crucial event of Jesus' resurrection is first revealed by Jesus himself, through his appearances and interaction first with Mary Magdalene, in 20:17-18, and then the other disciples, 20:19-29. Further, in GJohn, the Spirit is explicitly imparted as a consequence of Jesus' resurrection and by the risen Jesus himself (20:22-23).

Nevertheless, I contend that, corresponding to the genuine distinction that we have noted in GJohn between the levels of truth about Jesus' person conveyed and perceived during his earthly ministry and in the post-resurrection situation, GJohn also clearly ascribes a significantly further and fuller revelation of Jesus' person to the agency of the Spirit.[30] Moreover, as indicated in 15:26-27, the witness of Jesus' followers as well will be prompted and informed by the post-resurrection testimony of the Spirit about Jesus.

Unquestionably, the *kerygma* reflected in GJohn and arising from this fuller revelatory work of the Paraclete concerns *Jesus*, and, as I have already proposed, the whole *genre* of GJohn manifests the strong emphasis that the Jesus whom believers confess and proclaim is none other than the historic figure who lived and died at a specific time in Roman Judea. So, certainly, in GJohn there is no prospect of a revelation beyond Jesus. Any fuller, further revelation can only be about him. But the point I emphasize here is that GJohn also candidly indicates, perhaps most explicitly in 16:12-15, that the content of believers' confession and proclamation is to be crucially informed by the revelatory work of the Spirit-Paraclete that will come in the aftermath of Jesus' departure.[31]

In GJohn the Spirit has a particularly explicit *cognitive* role. The Spirit will "glorify" Jesus (16:14), which I take to mean that the Spirit will powerfully convey to believers the previously unimagined glory that Jesus has from and with the Father. Of course, much more frequently, GJohn refers to the Father glorifying Jesus (8:54; 13:31-32; 14:13; 17:1, 5). So, as the immediate context indicates, the Spirit glorifies Jesus *to believers* precisely by declaring to them what the Spirit "receives" from Jesus (ἐκ τοῦ ἐμοῦ λαμβάνει, v. 15). And what the Spirit declares will be glorious indeed, for it involves a disclosure of all that Jesus shares of that which pertains to the Father (πάντα ὅσα ἔχει ὁ πατὴρ ἐμά ἐστιν, v. 15).

We may ask what form(s) the revelatory work of the Spirit-Paraclete is to take. Here, too, there are differences of opinion among scholars (and a good deal of ducking the issue too!). Schnackenburg prefers to see these references to the Spirit-Paraclete's activity as reflecting "a community which is guided and instructed by the Spirit, but which in fact also receives this teaching from those who are qualified to teach and called to proclaim the message."[32] To be sure, as anyone who has acquaintance with modern form of charismatic religious group will know, a strong experiential appreciation of the Spirit's powers can go well in hand with strong leadership by particular individuals seen as especially gifted. But Schnackenburg's statement seems to me to project a bit too uncritically a traditional Roman Catholic outlook upon the "Johannine" Christians.[33]

I contend that the way to take the sayings about the Spirit-Paraclete "guiding," "teaching," "speaking," "testifying," and "proclaiming" is that they reflect charismatic utterances and insights, that is, prophetic oracles and such phenomena.[34] Certainly, other evidence of first-century Christianity suggests such experiences were apparently characteristically welcome, sought, and even expected.[35] For example, Paul's extended discussion of such things in 1 Corinthians 12–14 includes his almost off-hand reference to "revelation" and "a tongue" with its "interpretation" as regular and expected parts of the worship gathering (14:6). Much closer to GJohn, the author of 1 John warns readers to judge carefully among

prophets, which presupposes a religious setting in which such phenomena are frequent (4:1-3). So, I think that we should take GJohn's references to the work of the Spirit-Paraclete as reflecting religious
experiences of the writer and intended readers, who have direct acquaintance with insights that were disclosed in prophetic oracles and other
experiences of apprehension of truth that struck recipients as divine revelations.[36] The latter include what David Aune has called "charismatic
exegesis" of biblical (OT) texts, finding in them previously unrecognized
disclosures and confirmations of Jesus' status and role in God's plan.[37]

In addition, we should probably allow for a similar "charismatic exegesis" of sayings of Jesus, experiences in which the Spirit-Paraclete
revealed an understanding of their greater and fuller import.[38] These
understandings would be consistent with, and, indeed, would help
explain, the findings of other scholars that in the Johannine form of
Jesus' sayings we can often perceive a core-saying that echoes or resembles sayings reported in the Synoptics.[39] GJohn is certainly a textual/lit-
erary product that, in some sense, reflects a process of authoring and
editing; but it also reflects a lively experiential "micro-culture" of inspiration and revelation, in which new insights came with forceful effects,
and often occurred in circumstances that included prayerful and expec-
tant pondering of scripture and traditional sayings of Jesus.

These new insights and revelations focused particularly on Jesus and
involved the sweeping and startling claims advanced in GJohn. They
were taken to be bestowed by the Spirit-Paraclete, the agent of a fuller
revelation of Jesus than he was able to communicate in his earthly ministry. GJohn reflects a candid recognition of such new truths, or at least
a depth of truth that went noticeably beyond what Jesus had taught in
his pre-resurrection activity. Yet, to underscore the point again, the
GJohn insists that Spirit-Paraclete's revelations concerned *Jesus* and were
actually the fuller disclosure of what he was all along. To be sure, GJohn
presents Jesus as "glorified" in his death and resurrection and exalted to
heavenly status. Yet, according to GJohn, this really involves God giving
to Jesus the glory that he had with God before the creation (e.g., 17:5).

In short, the Spirit-Paraclete's revelations included the realization
that, though not disclosed and certainly not grasped during his earthly
activity, the historic Jesus was the unique human embodiment of the
divine Word, the transcendent Son, whose intimate relationship with the
Father transcends all time (e.g., 8:58). From this perspective, the author
felt it was perfectly understandable and correct to tell the Jesus-story with
the benefit of this realization and even to ascribe to the historic Jesus say-

ings that reflect these greater insights into Jesus' person and the Spirit-utterances through which they were first manifested. Indeed, I propose that the author knew very well that the historic Jesus had not actually said many of the sayings that he utters in GJohn, particularly those that reflect the exalted christological claims about Jesus' pre-existence and divine significance, and yet the author felt free to put these words on Jesus' lips. In doing so, the author believed that he was simply reflecting the true and ultimate significance of Jesus. For the author, these articulations of Jesus' divine status—although revealed by the Paraclete subsequent to Jesus—expressed truths that had always been valid.[40]

In GJohn, moreover, the Spirit-Paraclete not only delivers a new and deeper dimension to Jesus' person, the Spirit actually gives continuing voice to Jesus in the post-resurrection setting. In the farewell discourse material, along with promises that the Spirit will come in Jesus' name and testify about him, are promises that Jesus himself will come again to his followers and reveal himself to them after his departure (14:18-21, 27). Other first-century texts show that early Christians also witnessed oracles spoken under the inspiration of the Spirit as coming from the risen/exalted Jesus.[41] This is, of course, precisely how the author of Revelation presents his material.[42] While "in the Spirit" (1:10), the author has visions and auditions of the risen Jesus (e.g., 1:12-20), and the messages to the seven churches are to be taken as direct utterances from the glorified Jesus, delivered through the Spirit.[43] Therefore, the new insights about Jesus' person that were communicated by the Spirit—for example, in prophetic oracles and other charismatic-type phenomena—were also additional teaching from Jesus. This is another reason why the author of GJohn felt free to ascribe these revelations to Jesus. In the author's mind, this may be technically anachronistic, but on a more profound level it is actually a fully legitimate rendition of the historic Jesus inspired directly by the risen Jesus himself, expressing a full truth about him conveyed through the agency of the Spirit.

Reminding and Remembering

The final aim in this paper is to explore the use of terms for reminding and remembering in GJohn to refer to the cognitive work and effects involved in a full apprehension of Jesus' person.[44] Three closely-related Greek words used in GJohn require our attention: μιμνήσκομαι, μνημονεύω, and ὑπομιμνήσκω.[45] Each is used quite a number of times as well in other New Testament writings, each overwhelmingly used with the ordinary connotations of remembering something or someone.[46] I want to trace here, however, the special use of these terms in GJohn and consider what they represented for the author.

We begin with the passage where GJohn alone among the four gospels ascribes to Jesus a promise that the Spirit-Paraclete will come to "teach you everything and *remind* [ὑπομνήσει] you of all the things that I said to you" (14:26). For Bultmann and Brown, this is a case of synonymous parallelism, the two actions interpreting each other.[47] Schnackenburg's view appears somewhat similar, describing the action of reminding as "very closely related" to the teaching function of the Spirit, whereas Haenchen saw a "tension between the two statements," reflecting a potentially problematic relationship between "the new experience of the spirit [*sic*] and the old tradition," the reference to the Spirit's reminding of Jesus' words intended to eliminate "the danger that the experience of the spirit will turn out to be a subjective dream."[48] But whether the two activities of the Spirit in 14:26 are to be taken as synonymous or as complementary makes little difference for my discussion. Either way, this verse promises a post-resurrection, full disclosure of truth by the Spirit that is closely linked with "reminding" Jesus' followers of his pre-resurrection teaching.

Earlier, we noted briefly the references to specific instances in which the disciples "remember" some saying or event in the post-resurrection setting. Granted, in 2:17, the remembering (ἐμνήσθησαν) of the line from Psalm 69:10 (LXX 68:10) is not explicitly set in a post-resurrection circumstance, and so one may question whether it should be included in a list of such references.[49] I take verse 17 as referring to a post-resurrection reading of the Psalm, the author here giving an instance of what he refers to in verse 22; but my analysis does not depend upon this question, and so I move on to the remaining texts.[50]

Undeniably, in 2:22, GJohn refers to a post-resurrection setting in which Jesus' disciples remembered (ἐμνήσθησαν) Jesus' saying about him raising "this temple" (v. 19), their remembrance also involving belief in "the scripture [passage] and the word that Jesus spoke." The remembering and the believing recognition of the import of the scripture passage and Jesus' saying seem here to be so closely connected that they really comprise one cognitive development. Clearly, the remembering posited in this passage involved more than recollection; it also included a new perception that Jesus' actions are prefigured in, and interpreted by, scripture, and also a new understanding of Jesus' pre-resurrection sayings and actions in light of his resurrection.

In 12:16, we have a further instance where "remembering" is used to designate a specifically post-resurrection cognition that contrasts sharply with a pre-resurrection lack of perception. In the immediately preceding verses (12-15), GJohn recounts Jesus' entry into Jerusalem and how a great crowd met him jubilantly, the author using scripture passages to signal the larger significance of these events. Then, he tells us that, whereas in the first setting (τὸ πρῶτον) the disciples did not grasp these things (ταῦτα οὐκ ἔγνωσαν), after Jesus was "glorified" they "remembered" (ἐμνήσθησαν) his actions and that they were prophesied in scripture (ταῦτα ἦν ἐπ᾽ αὐτῷ γεγραμμένα). Clearly, the more precise nature of the cognitive events here involves much more than a simple recollection. What the author seems to designate by "remembered" is actually a new perception of what the narrated events really represented as parts of a divinely intended drama. This significant cognitive development involved a creative appropriation of biblical passages, along with a radically sharpened view of who Jesus is and what this fateful entry into Jerusalem represented in God's purposes and plan.

It is, I think, not accidental that the two passages in which GJohn explicitly identifies instances of this post-resurrection memory occur where they occur; in the narrative about the temple-incident and in the scene where Jesus enters Jerusalem for the fateful, final time. The Johannine temple-incident functions to foreshadow Jesus' death and resurrection, as 2:19 makes explicit, and 12:12-19 marks Jesus' movement to the setting of his looming suffering and glorification. In short, the two scenes where GJohn refers to post-resurrection remembrance seem, in this sense, to form an inclusio, bracketing a particular body of narrative material that concerns Jesus' ministry prior to the passion-resurrection narratives.

Surely, in light of these other Johannine uses of the terms for reminding and remembering, we should also take Jesus' admonition in 15:20 to "remember the word which I said to you" as intended by the author to designate the same post-resurrection cognitive phenomena.[51] Here Jesus is pictured as exhorting, and thus as *advocating and authorizing*, the developments in belief that GJohn explicitly ascribes to the work of the Spirit-Paraclete in the post-resurrection setting.

Likewise, in 16:4, Jesus expresses the hope that in a future setting his disciples might "remember" (μνημονεύητε) the things (ταῦτα) that he has said. Curiously, however, immediately following this statement, Jesus refers to things that he did *not* say while he was (physically present) with his disciples (v. 4b). He then promises the advent of the Spirit-Paraclete, whose advocacy of Jesus to disciples—against the unbelief of the world—we have already noted. Consequently, I take the remembering urged by Jesus in verse 4a to be another reference to the post-resurrection cognitive developments more unambiguously referred to in the other passages that we have just considered.[52]

In sum, in GJohn we have several instances where verbs for "to remind" and "to remember" are used with a technical meaning, indeed a meaning that seems peculiar to GJohn. I propose that the author of GJohn chose these terms and invested them with this technical meaning precisely to express his *dialectical* view of the Spirit-Paraclete's revelatory work. On the one hand, this work consists in a significantly fuller measure of truth than was disclosed during Jesus' earthly ministry. On the other hand, the author insists, this fuller revelation will simply be all about Jesus, pointing back to him with the aim of showing forth his true/full glory, and his full participation with "the Father" (esp. 16:14-15). That is, the new revelations from the Spirit-Paraclete simply bring forth a fuller disclosure of what was true of Jesus all along, and what his earthly activities actually portended.

Precisely to hold together these two emphases, GJohn ingeniously uses the terms that we have noted here. To speak of the Spirit as "reminding" disciples of Jesus' words and actions and to portray the disciples as "remembering" the import of these things and also how scripture actually predicts and confirms Jesus as the human embodiment of God's name and glory—indeed the one whose glory Isaiah saw and about whom he prophesied (12:37-41)—these all represent a profound theological position. The author's concern was to emphasize that the revelations that shaped his faith and Christology are entirely truths about *the historic figure, Jesus,* and they serve simply to unfold more completely his true import and significance.

In other early Christian writings also, we have terms of reminding and remembering used with technical meaning, and a brief comparison with a couple of these texts actually helps us to appreciate more clearly the distinctive emphasis in GJohn. In the "Hymn of the Pearl,"which forms part of the *Acts of Thomas*, a figure who leaves his luxurious home and in disguise goes "down to Egypt" to retrieve "the one pearl" forgets his royal status and his mission.[53] In response to a message from his royal parents, however, he awakens from his sleep of forgetfulness and "remember[s] that I [am] a son of kings" (καὶ ὑπεμνήσθην παρα–χρῆμα ὅτι βασιλέων εἰμὶ υἷος) and recalls his mission to fetch the pearl (111:56-57). In its present context, this obviously seems to reflect a view of redemption as discovery of one's divine provenance and destiny, discovery portrayed here as a remembering

This narrative fits perfectly with the "gnostic" idea that the elect are divine by origin and nature, and only need to be reawakened to their true identities and significance.[54] But this is clearly very different from GJohn's special use of reminding/remembering terms, which has to do entirely with believers having a full grasp of the full divine glory of *Jesus*. Indeed, I see no relationship between GJohn and the Hymn of the Pearl in this matter. Instead, the latter may reflect the Socratic/Platonic notion that teaching involves helping students to bring to remembrance what they, in fact, already knew but have forgotten.

To note yet another contrasting instance of early Christian use of remembering, Ron Cameron drew attention to *The Apocryphon of James*.[55] In this text, however, we have a use of the idea of remembering Jesus' words, which is much closer to the topos that we have examined in GJohn. Early in *Ap.Jas.* (2.9-15), the twelve disciples of Jesus are portrayed as "all sitting together and recalling what the Savior had said to each one of them, whether in secret or openly, and [putting it] in books."[56] Cameron rightly notes that here we have a specifically post-resurrection scene where remembering goes on among the disciples. Moreover, Cameron also discusses explicitly the use of remembering/reminding language in GJohn, noting similarities and differences in comparison with *Ap.Jas.*[57] But I want to register disagreement here on a few points.

First, I am not sure that Cameron is correct in claiming that in GJohn the "hermeneutical turning point" is located in the farewell discourses.[58] As indicated in the preceding analysis of relevant passages, contra Cameron, I do not think that the disciples' statement in 16:29 is to be taken as the author's indication that the full secret of Jesus' person was unveiled to the disciples in this setting. Cameron's contrast between GJohn and *Ap.Jas.* seems to me flawed. As I have argued, in GJohn the full realization of Jesus' transcendent glory comes after his resurrection and through the agency of the Spirit-Paraclete. In this conclusion, GJohn and *Ap.Jas.* actually agree.

The decisive difference between the two texts is that *Ap.Jas.* shows little interest in linking the post-resurrection disclosures of Jesus with his pre-resurrection activity and teaching, whereas GJohn *emphasizes* the link between the revelatory activity of the Spirit-Paraclete and the historic ministry/teachings of Jesus. Indeed, in *Ap.Jas.* 8.1-10, Jesus appears to treat as second-class those for whom his pre-resurrection teaching ("parables") was sufficient, in contrast with which the disciples (and intended readers) are urged to go on to the more secretive truth revealed in this text.[59]

Moreover, in *Ap. Jas.*, unlike GJohn, the reference to the post-resurrection revelation and reinterpretation of Jesus as "remembering" is not really a major motif. It does not appear again in *Ap. Jas.* after this early scene. But in GJohn, I contend, the cognitive work of the Spirit-Paraclete is more prominently portrayed as a reminding/remembering, and precisely to indicate that the new truths that the Spirit revealed after Jesus' death and resurrection had to do with the historic figure, and simply unpacked more fully the significance of who he is and what he did. In GJohn, although what believers know of Jesus is heavily shaped by the post-resurrection work of the Spirit-Paraclete, the cognitive import of the further truth that the Spirit has revealed should help them *to appreciate more fully that the ministry, death, and resurrection of Jesus* comprise the embodied manifestation of the glory and name of God. Indeed, as others have noted, GJohn is probably to be taken as a formal literary expression of what it means to view the historic Jesus in light of the post-resurrection revelatory work of the Spirit-Paraclete.[60] That is, GJohn is intended to be understood as a direct product of the very operation of the Paraclete that is portrayed in this text.

Conclusion

I end this essay simply by reiterating briefly my main theses and the implication for our view of GJohn. First, GJohn distinctively emphasizes the contrast between the cognitive possibilities in the pre-resurrection and post-resurrection situations, indicating more explicitly than in the Synoptic Gospels, that in his earthly ministry Jesus did not reveal all that came later to be known of his divine significance. Second, GJohn distinctively also gives an explicit explanation of the agency of the greater apprehension of Jesus' significance that came in the post-resurrection setting: the Spirit-Paraclete, who will speak of Jesus and unfold more fully his glory. Finally, GJohn uses a distinctive terminology to describe this work of the Paraclete, the language of reminding and remembering that is intended to signify the strong Johannine emphasis that the new truths about Jesus revealed by the Spirit in the post-resurrection time are actually disclosures of what was true of the Jesus of Galilee and Judea all along.

In this very real sense, to take what Clement of Alexandria is famously reported to have written, GJohn is intended to be "*a spiritual gospel*," presenting in a skillful literary form the historical figure of Jesus with a radical transparency toward what the author accepts and offers as his true divine status and significance, *as revealed by the Spirit-Paraclete*.[61] To make the point clear, the author was, I propose, perfectly aware that much of what he put into the mouth of Jesus was never spoken by Jesus in his earthly life, and, indeed, the author gives readers rather clear indication of this also. But this deliberate anachronism was prompted by the profound conviction that the post-resurrection views of Jesus ascribed to him were simply revelations of what had always been true of him. Moreover, in this tactic, the author also emphasized that genuine revelations given by the Spirit were to have the effect of directing believers back to the historical figure of Jesus as the nonnegotiable center of their faith. But, GJohn insists, through the work of the Spirit, the full glory of Jesus is rightly to be seen as part of the historical truth of his person.

Chapter 13

Jesus
"The One Who Sees God"

Marianne Meye Thompson

Rudolf Bultmann was one of the most influential commentators on the Gospel of John in the last century. Although many of his interpretations of the gospel have now been abandoned, their influence lingers on in some quarters. One place in which that influence has been felt has been in the tendency to elevate hearing over seeing as the preferred way of coming to faith in Jesus. In his treatment of the Gospel of John in his *Theology of the New Testament*, Bultmann included a chapter entitled simply "Faith," with its first subsection called "Faith as the Hearing of the Word."[1] Noticeably missing is any equally prominent role given to seeing because, as is probably well known, Bultmann denigrated faith based on signs or seeing as superficial and needing external crutches, as Jesus' rebuke to Thomas exemplifies. Bultmann writes:

> As the miracle is a concession to the weakness of man, so is the appearance of the Risen Jesus a concession to the weakness of the disciples. Fundamentally they ought not to need it! Fundamentally it ought not to be the sight of the Risen Lord that first moves the disciples to believe "the word that Jesus spoke," for this word alone should have the power to convince them.[2]

At least some ancient writers saw matters differently. Oft-quoted is Heraclitus' dictum "Eyes are surer witnesses than ears."[3] This sentiment was echoed by ancient Greek historians. For example, Polybius comments, "Nature has given us two instruments, as it were, by the aid of which we inform ourselves and inquire about everything. These are hearing and sight, and of the two sight is much more veracious according to Heraclitus. The eyes are more accurate witnesses than the ears, he says"

(*Histories* 12.27.1; cf. 4.2.1–2).[4] In a similar vein, Herodotus recounts the tale of the ill-fated Candaules' desire to convince his guard, Gyges, of the beauty of his wife, and so arranges that he should see her undressed because, "You do not believe what I tell you of the beauty of my wife; men trust their ears less than their eyes" (*Histories* 1.8). The general and commander Thucydides comments on the Athenians' reluctance "to speak about matters quite remote, whose only witnesses are the stories men hear rather than the eyes of those who will hear them told" (*Wars* 1.73.2). While Dio Chrysostom echoes the sentiment, he also notes the greater difficulty of convincing the eyes: "The popular saying that the eyes are more trustworthy than the ears is perhaps true, yet they are much harder to convince and demand much greater clearness; for while the eye agrees exactly with what it sees, it is not impossible to excite and cheat the ear" (12.71). Finally, in his handbook, *How to Write History,* Lucian refers to the dictum of Heraclitus but goes on to mock those historians who made false claims about what they had seen, or who "neither see what is worth looking at, nor, if they did see it, have they the ability to give it suitable expression" (29).[5] Claims to seeing could be falsified, and the possibility of seeing without understanding remains.

The Jewish author Philo quotes Heraclitus's pronouncement (*Drunkenness*, 82). He speaks of "the more certain testimony of sight," and notes that "hearing stands second in estimation and below sight, and the recipient of teaching is always second to him with whom realities present their forms clear to his vision and not through the medium of instruction" (*Confusion*, 57, 148; cf. *Abraham*, 57, 61). Similarly, he contrasts Ishmael and Israel in terms of hearing and seeing, to the detriment of the former:

> "Ishmael" means "hearkening to God." Hearing takes the second place, yielding the first to sight, and sight is the portion of Israel, the son free-born and first-born; for "seeing God" is the translation of "Israel." It is possible to hear the false and take it for true, because hearing is deceptive, but sight, by which we discern what really is, is devoid of falseness. (*Flight*, 208)

A similar juxtaposition of hearing and sight occurs in the Gospel of John. For example, in John 6, Jesus states that everyone who "has heard and learned from the Father" comes to him, thus making it plain that they have been "taught by God" (6:45). This affirmation, however, is quickly modified by the assertion that no one "has *seen* the Father except the one who is from God; he has seen the Father" (6:46). Hence, there is a distinction between hearing and seeing God, and between the many who have heard from the Father and the one who has seen the Father (1:18; 5:38–39; 6:46; 8:38).[6] This contrast between the way in which Jesus apprehends God and the way in which all others—including those who believe in Jesus—apprehend God provides another aspect of John's distinctive christological portrait. Indeed, John's presentation of Jesus   as the sole eyewitness of God is yet another piece of John's high Christology.

In order to flesh this thesis out a bit, I would like first to review briefly the evidence for the importance and primacy of seeing in the Gospel of John. Even as ancient Greek historians prized the knowledge gained by or from eyewitnesses, so in the Gospel of John seeing is deemed a superior way of knowing because it implies being in the presence of the one who is seen. In the Gospel of John, because Jesus—and he alone—has been in the presence of the Father, he has seen the Father. Hence, Jesus' status and role as eyewitness of the Father underscore his unique origin from and preexistence with God.

Second, I will look at some biblical and Jewish traditions that indicate the impossibility of seeing God, or the secondary ways in which human beings may behold God in the manifestation of his glory or name, or in other forms. It is at this point particularly that the work of our honorees can be taken into account. Both Larry Hurtado and Alan Segal have emphasized the ways in which New Testament Christology develops the idea of Jesus as the embodied glory, name, or image of God.[7] According to both John and Paul, those who see Jesus see the enfleshed glory of God. Indeed, this aspect of Johannine—and also Pauline—Christology suggests the unique status accorded to Jesus and shows some of the theological imagery appropriated by the early Church in the development of its Christology. By contrast, in the Fourth Gospel, Jesus is not said to see the glory or form of God, but rather to have seen the Father. Jesus, having had direct access to and sight of God, apprehends God differently than do all others, thus underscoring Jesus' unique status and relationship to God.

The Primacy of Seeing in the Gospel of John

As already noted, one of the legacies bequeathed by Bultmann to Johannine studies was the evaluation of hearing as superior to seeing as a way of knowing God or apprehending the truth. One might attribute Bultmann's assessment of the superiority of hearing to his Lutheranism— for Martin Luther preferred the Gospel of John to all others as giving more of the words of Jesus—or, to his form-critical study of the trans-mission of the words of Jesus. But one might add as well that recent stud-ies of both Judaism and early Christianity have taken into greater account the developing mystical tradition, and the role of visions and human experience, in explaining the growth and evolution of both of these movements. Not only has the study of apocalyptic, mystical, hekahlot, and other Jewish texts revised the way that early Judaism—including developing rabbinic Judaism—has been characterized, but such study has led to a reevaluation of aspects of early Christianity as well. When one turns to the Gospel of John, therefore, it is not particu-larly surprising, as it may have been to Bultmann, to discover the posi-tive role that seeing plays in grasping God's revelation. Elsewhere, I have set out a case for the primacy of seeing in John, but here I wish to high-light three aspects of the gospel's emphasis on what one sees that point to Jesus' uniqueness—both in manifesting the glory of God and in being the unique one who sees God—because he has been in God's presence and, indeed, is God.[8] Those who see Jesus see the manifestation of the glory of God; but Jesus himself sees God directly.

At the outset, we note that while the words "seeing" and "sight" refer to physical observation or perception in John, they are also used metaphorically. "Sight" sometimes refers not merely to observation of an object or person, but to the insight to perceive or understand the signif-icance or truth about a person or thing that is seen.[9] But the double-layered significance of "seeing" should not be construed so as to deny its primary simple sense of (physical) seeing. In his exploration of the emer-gence of devotion to Jesus in earliest Christianity, Larry Hurtado shows how the biblical traditions of the revelation of God's glory, and particu-larly those found in Isaiah 40–66, were appropriated in the Gospel of John.[10] As Hurtado notes, in biblical thought, God's glory indicates that which is seen; it refers to a *visual* phenomenon, and, hence, can be described as appearing, shown, revealed, and seen. John's use of this glory theme is signaled early on in the prologue: "The Word was made flesh, and we beheld his glory" (1:14). Throughout John, one sees the glory of Jesus in the account of Jesus narrated in the gospel, including his signs, his teaching, and his death. Like Isaiah, which links the "glory of the Lord" with the "light" that God reveals, so John speaks of the "light" and "glory" that can be seen through and in Jesus (1:4–5; 1:14; 8:12; 9:5). "The Johannine treatment of Jesus amounts to him being the one in whom God's glory is manifested, the unique human embodiment of God's glory on earth. . . . Not only is [Jesus] associated with the glory of

God, he is the glory of God *manifest*."[11] To be in his presence, to see him, is to behold the embodied glory of God.

Second, then, whereas those who see Jesus have seen the embodied glory of God, Jesus himself has seen God; he has been in the presence of God. The link between "presence" and "seeing" features early in John, when the prologue of the gospel indicates that the Word was *with* God. That affirmation lays the foundation for the subsequent claims that Jesus, the Incarnate Word, has *seen* the Father (5:37-38; 6:46; 8:38). His heavenly origins, his preexistent presence with the Father, authorize the revelation that he brings: he speaks of what he has seen (3:12–13, 31–32; 8:38). Jesus' subsequent exaltation and return to the Father mean that he is once again in God's presence and, hence, again sees God (1:18; 17:5, 11, 13). The linking of seeing with presence is particularly noticeable in the Farewell Discourses, where Jesus' riddles about his departure are couched in terms of the possibility or impossibility of seeing him. Thus Jesus tells his disciples that while the time is coming when they will not see him (16:10), after "a little while" they will see him again (16:16; cf. 16:17-18). That this paradox refers initially to Jesus' death construed as departure or absence, and to his presence in the resurrection appearances, is suggested by Jesus' own words: "Truly, truly, I say to you, you will weep and lament, but the world will rejoice; you will be sorrowful, but your sorrow will turn into joy" (16:20; see 14:19). When absent, he cannot be seen; but when with them, they will see him and rejoice.

Indeed, the witness to the resurrected Lord is repeatedly framed in terms of someone's having seen him, so that they may testify that they have been in the presence of the risen Lord. Thus Mary Magdalene tells the others, "I have seen the Lord" (20:18). When the risen Jesus appears to the disciples gathered in the upper room, John writes that "they were glad when they saw the Lord" (20:20). The ten, in turn, report to Thomas, who had been absent from their company: "We have seen the Lord" (20:24). In all three cases, the witnesses to the resurrection not only attest that Jesus lives, but they also claim to have seen him and been with him, thus foreshadowing the future hope of being with him permanently (cf. 1 John 3:2). In the present, they bear witness to what they know, to the manifestation of his glory and to his resurrection, and what they know comes from having been in the presence of Jesus, the incarnate and resurrected one. John will use this association of seeing and presence to press the superiority of Jesus' knowledge of God: since Jesus alone has been in God's presence, and has seen God, he knows God and can make God truly known.

A third instance of the primacy of seeing—and of its importance for grasping the identity of Jesus and of comprehending the truth of the revelation through him—can be found in John's quotation of Isaiah 6:9–10. It is striking that all four gospels—and also the book of Acts—quote the text from Isaiah to explain the lack of response to Jesus and to Paul. But while in the Synoptic Gospels the quotation from Isaiah accounts for the failure to hear and respond to the parables, and in Acts to the preaching of Paul, John has used the text from Isaiah so as to cast the prophetic rebuke not as a failure to *hear* but rather as a failure to *see*. Isaiah's word of judgment reads as follows:

> And he said, "Go, and say to this people:
> 'Hear and hear, but do not understand;
> see and see, but do not perceive.'
> Make the heart of this people fat,
> and their ears heavy,
> and shut their eyes;
> lest they see with their eyes,
> and hear with their ears,
> and understand with their hearts,
> and turn and be healed."

In this passage, Isaiah essentially equates hearing and seeing as means of knowing or apprehending the truth.[12] All three Synoptic Gospels quote some form, even if shortened, of this passage (Matt 13:14-15; Mark 4:12; Luke 8:10). But even in abbreviated form, the Synoptic Gospels maintain the parallelism between hearing and seeing. While John quotes Isaiah 53:1 ("Who has believed what we have heard? And to whom has the arm of the LORD been revealed?"; John 12:38), he follows with a shortened form of the quotation from Isaiah 6: "He has blinded their eyes and hardened their heart, lest they should see with their eyes and perceive with their heart, and turn for me to heal them" (John 12:40). He adds the editorial remark, "Isaiah said this because he saw his glory and spoke of him" (12:41). John eliminates the references to "hearing" in his citation of Isaiah 6:9-10, thus highlighting the failure of Jesus' contemporaries to see the glory of Jesus—something that Isaiah had not missed. As the climactic summary of Jesus' public ministry, John's use of the passage from Isaiah emphasizes the significance and primacy of seeing and the judgment that falls on those who have failed to see God's glory in Jesus (similarly, 6:36, 40).

In sum, then, in the Gospel of John, Jesus is both the one in whom the glory of God is manifest—and so may be seen—and the one who himself sees God directly. As the one sent by God, Jesus mediates the vision of God ("he who sees me sees him who sent me," 12:45). As the Son of the Father, Jesus is also the unique eyewitness of God the Father.[13] He is the one—and the only one—who sees and hence knows God (1:18; 5:37-38; 6:45-46; 8:38). If he is the manifestation of God's glory, its unique embodiment, he also sees God in a way that transcends the way in which any other individual has ever seen God. Jesus does not see the glory, likeness, or form of God; rather, he has been with God and so has seen God.[14] The claim that Jesus has seen God thus underscores the uniqueness of Jesus' status and identity. A brief look at some of the biblical and Jewish traditions about human inability to see God directly will emphasize the point further.

"No One Has Ever Seen God"

We turn to a brief sampling of several texts from the Old Testament and Judaism that suggest the possibility—or impossibility—of seeing God. The point here is to be suggestive, rather than exhaustive, of biblical and Jewish traditions especially that spoke, on the one hand, of the hiddenness or inaccessibility of God, but, on the other hand, of the revelation or visible manifestations of God. And, indeed, precisely this tension exists between certain texts and even within the same text: the claims that one can see God or one has seen God are persistently qualified in one way or another. Furthermore, we might also note that the biblical point of view is not that God is invisible but that God is hidden from human sight. If God cannot be seen, it is not because God is invisible, but because God hides himself or because "no one can see God and live." The possibility of seeing God always remains; but it is qualified in numerous ways, due, perhaps, to the character and nature of God, to the virtue or status of the particular individual, or to the variety of ways in which "seeing" can be understood.

Biblical Passages on "Seeing God"

We turn, first, to a brief look at various OT passages in which someone is said to have seen God face to face. In Genesis 32:30, Jacob is described as having seen God "face to face" (MT 32:31: פָּנִים אֶל־פָּנִים; LXX 32:31 πρόσωπον πρὸς πρόσωπον) and Moses is said to have spoken with God "face to face" on more than one occasion (Exod 33:11; LXX ἐνώπιος ἐνωπίῳ; Deut 34:10 πρόσωπον κατὰ πρόσωπον).

Indeed, God is a God who is seen "face to face" (Num 14:14 בְּעַיִן עַיִן;
LXX ὀφθαλμοῖς κατ᾽ ὀφθαλμούς; Deut 5:4 בְּפָנִים פָּנִים; LXX
πρόσωπον κατὰ πρόσωπον). So also the seventy elders of Israel "saw
the God of Israel" (Exod 24:9-11). And yet, a few verses later, the text
appears to qualify this somewhat unguarded assertion when it states that
"the appearance of the glory of the LORD was like a devouring fire on
the top of the mountain in the sight of the people of Israel" (Exod
24:17). The statement corrects the earlier assertion that the elders of
Israel "saw the God of Israel;" rather, the elders of Israel actually saw the
appearance of the glory of the Lord. This is in keeping with the later
account of Moses' request to see the glory of God (33:18), to which God
replies that "no one shall see me and live" (33:20; 33:23). Moses sees a
manifestation of the glory of God, but he does not behold God directly.

Similarly, the book of Deuteronomy recounts Moses' encounter
with God at Sinai as follows: "Then the LORD spoke to you out of the
midst of the fire; you heard the sound of words, but saw no form; there
was only a voice" (Deut 4:12; cf. 5:4-5). Echoes of this passage are in the
Gospel of John where, as noted earlier, the possibility of being taught by
God is subtly contrasted with seeing God (6:46), but where it is also said
that Jesus' contemporaries have neither heard the voice nor seen the form
of God (5:37).[15] One could also note the accounts in Isaiah 6 and
Ezekiel 1—texts which were taken up into merkabah mysticism—in
which visions of God are said to be visions of his glory (Isa 6) or of "the
likeness of the glory of the Lord" (Ezek 1:28). As Alan Segal notes, this
description of seeing God safeguards the divine dignity by speaking of
seeing the likeness (*demuth*), form (*tavnith*), or image (*tselem*) of God,
rather than the actual being of God.[16] Thus, while Moses saw God's *glory*
(Exod 33:20-23), Ezekiel saw "the likeness of the glory of the Lord." And
neither Moses nor Ezekiel saw God directly. In sum, while there are passages in the Old Testament that speak of seeing God "face to face," there
are also denials and qualifications of the same possibility. Either the
vision of the holy God is deemed fatal to mortal humankind or it is
explained in terms of a vision of the manifestation of God, rather than a
face to face encounter.

Targumic Interpretations of Seeing God

The Targums moved toward readings of these texts that made it clear
that human beings did not and cannot see God face to face. The biblical

texts alluded to above are translated or interpreted so as to read that what was seen was the glory of God or the glory of God's presence. Certainly God was not seen "face to face." Jacob, for example, does not see God "face to face" (Gen 32:30), but sees either an angel or the angels of the Lord (so *Targum Onqelos, Ps. Jonathan*, and *Neofiti*). Or, again, the elders of Israel see "the Glory of the Lord" rather than God himself (Exod 24:10).[17] God tells Moses that he may not see "the face of My Presence" (Exod 33:20). While the biblical text denies Moses a vision of God "face to face," even so the Targum still strives to avoid the anthropomorphism in speaking of God's face and renders instead "the face of My Presence."[18] *Onqelos* simply substitutes "presence" for "face" (e.g., Exod 33:14, 15). At Numbers 14:14, *Onqelos* renders the description of God as one who is known "face to face" as follows: "The inhabitants of the land have already heard that You are the Lord, whose Shekhina rests among this people, who with their own eyes have seen the Shekhina of Your Glory, O Lord." What is seen is not God, but God's Shekhina or, in other Targums, the glory of the Shekhina.[19] In the *Isaiah Targum*, Isaiah's vision is presented not with the directness of the biblical text—"I saw the Lord sitting upon a throne"—but again with the somewhat indirect assertion—"I saw the glory of the LORD resting upon a throne." However, in John's gospel, Jesus is both the embodied glory of God and the one who has seen God "face to face." This privilege, then, sets him apart from all others, including Moses and Jacob, with whom Jesus is also contrasted in the Gospel of John. Jesus' vision of God is different in that it is not mediated or indirect. Whereas others see the glory of God, Jesus is in the presence of God; he has seen the Father.

Philo and the Vision of God

Particularly interesting at this point are Philo's repeated references to the possibility of "seeing God."[20] Philo distinguishes the sight of the eyes from the sight of the mind, and it is with the sight of the mind that one may see God, for "what belongs to the mind can be apprehended only by the mental powers" (*Names* 6; cf. 3–4; *Abraham* 57–58). Philo also qualifies the ways in which God can be seen. For example, at times Philo asserts that it is possible to see the manifestations of God's power (*Names* 15; cf. *Dreams* 1.64–67), perhaps "an image of the one who is" (*Moses* 1.66), or some manifestation in the perceptible realm (*Confusion* 95–97; cf. *Dreams* 1.65). In any case, seeing God "according to his essence"

(κατὰ τὸ εἶναι) is impossible for "he is not apprehensible even by the
mind, save in the fact that He is" (*Unchangeableness* 62; cf. *Dreams*
1.229–30; *Names* 8).

Philo further lodges the possibility of seeing God within the character or virtue of the one who sees God (e.g., *Embassy* 4–6). In a striking
passage that again contrasts seeing and hearing as ways of knowing, Philo
speaks of those who have knowledge of the One who is Maker and
Father of all as "sons of God." Those who are not fit to be thought of as
"sons of God" may be "sons of Israel," that is, sons of "the one who sees
[God]."[21] They are hearers, because "hearing stands second in estimation
and below sight" (*Confusion* 148). Philo's account is particularly striking
because the contrast between the "sons of Israel" and the "sons of God"
is a contrast between those who hear and those who see, with the latter
holding the higher status. Philo goes even further when he asserts that
one may see "*that* He is, not *what* He is . . . [for] to God alone is it permitted to apprehend God" (*Rewards* 40; 43–44). Similarly, Philo states
that in response to Moses' plea to see God, God replies, "The request
cannot fitly be granted to any that are brought into being by creation . .
. the apprehension of me is something more than human nature, yea
even the whole heaven and universe will be able to contain" (*Special Laws*
1.43–44). In short, like is known by like.[22]

Here Philo's description of Moses' encounter with God on Sinai is
relevant. In commenting on the designation of Moses as "god" (Exod
7:1), Philo writes that Moses was "named God and king of the whole
nation, and entered . . . into the darkness where God was. . . . Thus he
beheld what is hidden from the sight of mortal nature . . . " because he
himself was "a piece of work beautiful and godlike" (*Moses* 1.158–59; cf.
Posterity 28–29; *Giants* 47–49; *Questions and Answers on Exodus* 2.46).[23]
Moses sees God, having himself been made "godlike." Moses' ascent to
Mt. Sinai in Philo is essentially interpreted as a mystical vision or mystic
ascent to heaven. At least some rabbinic interpretation denied this possibility. We read, for example, in the *Mekhilta*, "Neither Moses nor Elijah
ever went up to heaven, nor did the Glory ever come down to earth."[24]
This passage apparently denies, as does also the Gospel of John, the possibility of ascent to heaven ("No one has ascended into heaven, except the
one who descended from heaven," 3:13) and of a mystical vision of God
attained through it. John agrees that "no one has ever seen God" or ever
"ascended into heaven"—with the exception of the Son, that very "Glory"
who came down to earth. Jesus is both the incarnate Glory of God and
the one who has seen God, not via mystical ascent but "in the beginning,"

when the Word was with God. Since like is known by like, the one who was with God, and was God, has known God and can make God known.

In the Fourth Gospel, then, Jesus is the Son of God who sees God, in contrast to the children of God who may see the embodied glory of God in that Son (1:14), and who may hear the one who has seen God. Jesus is the incarnation of the Word who was with the Father. Even though Jesus can say that "the one who has seen me has seen the Father," that vision of God is still mediated rather than direct. According to John, the Son—and only the Son—has, indeed, seen the Father and has seen him without intermediaries of any kind. In John, Jesus' distinctive and immediate knowledge of God—his face to face vision of God—is explained by his origins: only the one who is "from God" (1:1; 1:18; 8:58), who has been "in the bosom of the Father" (1:18), in the presence of God, has seen God (6:46), can in turn make God known. Jesus' unique vision of God distinguishes him not only from his contemporaries, who are said never to have seen God (1:18; 5:37-38; 6:45-46), but also from his disciples, who see the Father in the Son, rather than seeing him directly as the Son does (12:45; 14:8-9). And inasmuch as "like is known by like," the implication is that Jesus apprehends God because he himself partakes in God's divine identity.

Jesus, the One Who Sees God

Whatever one makes of the Gospel of John, it stakes its claim to credibility on one whom it describes as an eyewitness, namely, the beloved disciple, who had a particular personal memory of Jesus (19:35; 21:24-25). While the story of Jesus can be told in other ways, the Fourth Gospel claims that this particular way of telling the story of Jesus' life and ministry has the authority of the witness who was the disciple loved by Jesus. The accountability of later interpreters to the testimony of "eyewitnesses to the word of life" is pointedly illustrated in Irenaeus' letter to Florinus, in which he asserts that as an eyewitness of the apostles, Polycarp would have recoiled in horror at Florinus' Gnostic account of their teaching.[25] If the gospel account cannot simply be equated with or reduced to reports of what the eyewitnesses saw, the testimony of those eyewitnesses, nevertheless, serves to authorize that account. The Beloved Disciple was with and in the presence of Jesus and, therefore, has seen him, knows him, and can testify to him.[26]

Similarly, Jesus' knowledge of God is guaranteed by the fact that he has been with the Father. When the gospel speaks of Jesus as having been

with the Father, it has in mind the Son's preexistence with the Father.
Jesus is, therefore, authorized to speak and testify to what he has seen,
and his testimony is trustworthy since, as we noted, seeing is a way of
knowing superior to that of hearing. John reflects, albeit not directly, the
dictum of Heraclitus followed by ancient historians, that "eyes are surer
witnesses than ears." Not surprisingly, in the Gospel of John, seeing,
understood as both "sight" and "insight," has primacy as a way of knowing God. The one who sees God has a distinct or unique status. Indeed,
in biblical tradition there is something of a tension in the accounts of the
possibility of human beings' seeing God: while sometimes people are said
to see God face to face, more consistently the OT affirms the possibility
of seeing only the glory of God, or of seeing God in an indirect manner.
The Targums underscore the indirect character of seeing God. Philo also
notes the superior spiritual status of the one who attains to a vision of
God, that is, one who apprehends God in a mystic vision, as did Moses.
Someone such as Moses may attain a mystic vision of God; but, on the
whole, one sees the manifestations of God's powers or perceives him
indirectly, not "according to his essence."

Many of the qualifications found in both the OT and later Jewish
traditions apply to the Johannine understanding of seeing God. In the
Gospel of John, one sees the glory of God manifested in the person of
Jesus; but no human being directly sees God. In fact, the gospel makes
it clear that "no one has ever seen God" (1:18; 5:37; 6:46). Even the
vision of the Father in the Son remains a mediated vision. But the Son
has seen the Father. These Johannine assertions single Jesus out as the
one who knows God uniquely, because he has been with God and seen
God and, indeed, because he himself is the incarnate Word of God. To
be sure, he also hears the Father, but he has not only heard; he has seen.
Jesus is the unique eyewitness to God, whose testimony is, therefore,
trustworthy.

Chapter 14

The Lamb (Not the Man) on the Divine Throne

Charles A. Gieschen

The climatic scene of the Book of Revelation is the introduction and worship of the Lamb during the divine throne scene that culminates in the universal worship of *both* "the one who is seated upon the throne and the lamb" (Rev 5:5-14).[1] Many scholars have noted the startling reversal of expectations between the introduction of Christ as "the Lion of tribe of Judah, the Root of David" (5:5) and his subsequent appearance as "a lamb standing as one who had been slaughtered" (5:6). Richard Bauckham, for example, makes this emphatic statement: "The key to John's vision of the slaughtered Lamb (5:6) is to recognize the contrast between what he hears (5:5) and what he sees (5:6)."[2]

Without discounting the remarkable contrast between these messianic titles that are heard—especially "the *Lion* of the tribe of Judah"—and the Lamb who is then seen, one purpose of this study is to demonstrate that the primary reason the image of the slaughtered-yet-standing lamb is so jarring is because those who are reading or hearing this apocalypse expect that they will soon see the very impressive "likeness of a son of man" on the throne, who was seen by John earlier in his visionary experience (1:12–3:21).[3] The real shock, then, is seeing *a lamb* on the throne instead of *the man*.

Furthermore, although scholars have offered several reasons for this visionary experience of Christ as the lamb, most have not emphasized that this unexpected depiction of Christ also has high congruence with the experience of Christ in the paschal feast of Eucharistic worship.[4] The first words of the Book of Revelation explicitly identify the visionary experience that follows as the "apocalypse of Jesus Christ" (Ἀποκάλυψις Ἰησοῦ Χριστοῦ). Previous scholarship on the Christology of Revelation has confirmed that two primary depictions of Jesus are prevalent in several scenes of this apocalypse: he appears as either the glorious man or the exalted lamb, with the later portrait being dominant.[5]

In addition to explaining why the depiction of Christ as a lamb is so unexpected, this study will also demonstrate that *lamb Christology*, especially the central scene in Revelation 5, functions in a complementary manner with the *angelomorphic Christology* found in other scenes in order to present Jesus Christ *both* as the visible form of YHWH who appeared to prophets in the past and as the flesh and blood man who has conquered Satan through his faithful witness and sacrificial death.[6] To express this in other words, the glorified man scenes provide the reader/hearer with a Christology that depicts the risen Christ in continuity with previous theophanies of YHWH, while the exalted lamb scenes provide a Christology that accents Jesus' humanity, atoning sacrificial death, resurrection victory, and authoritative status as universal ruler.

The Man on the Divine Throne

Theophanic traditions in the Hebrew Bible testify that YHWH appeared to the patriarchs and prophets on various occasions in the form of *a man*.[7] Several of these are experiences where YHWH appears as a man on earth; a prominent example is YHWH and two angels appearing to Abram at the Oaks of Mamre in Genesis 18. In a few literary traditions, however, select individuals see YHWH enthroned in the heavenly realm. Such traditions are also present in the noncanonical apocalyptic literature of Second Temple Judaism.[8] Although the textual evidence is by no means uniform, YHWH is depicted in some of these texts as *a man* sitting on the divine throne, even though his visible form is sometimes identified as "the Glory of YHWH." The prominent examples of these appearances of YHWH enthroned will be presented below in order to substantiate that the Book of Revelation is, indeed, striking because it does *not* follow this dominant pattern of presenting the form of YHWH as a man seated upon the divine throne.

Because the theophany at Sinai in Exodus 24:9-11 does not describe in any manner the actual appearance of YHWH on the throne, the call of Isaiah is the foundational text for the theophanic pattern of YHWH appearing as a man seated upon the divine throne: "I saw the Lord [וָאֶרְאֶה] sitting upon a throne, high and lifted up; and the train of his robe filled the temple" (Isa 6:1). The prophet's reply in text of Isaiah reflects both the amazement and fear of seeing the tangible form of

YHWH: "Woe is me . . . for my eyes have seen the King, YHWH Sabaoth [יהוה צבאות]" (Isa 6:5b). Although no explicit reference in this vision is to YHWH appearing as a man, such a form is implicit from the description that he was wearing a long "robe" as well as the characterization of him "sitting upon a throne" (Isa 6:1).

In the opening scene in Ezekiel's visionary experience, the prophet beholds the elaborate chariot throne and the Glory of YHWH seated upon it. Its importance, both in influencing and interpreting later apocalyptic literature—including the Christology of Revelation—can hardly be overstated.[9] The scene concludes with this description of the figure on the throne:

> [Ezek 1.26] And above the expanse over their heads there was something like a throne, in appearance like sapphire; and seated above the likeness of a throne was *the likeness as the appearance of a man* [MT: אדם דמות כמראה; LXX: ὁμοίωμα ὡς εἶδος ἀνθρώπου]. [27] Upward from what appeared like the loins I saw something like gleaming amber, something that looked like fire enclosed all around; and downward from what looked like the loins I saw something that looked like fire, and there was a splendor all around. [28] Like the bow in a cloud on a raining day, so was the appearance of the brightness round about. Such was the appearance of the likeness of the Glory of YHWH.

Although the prophet expresses the difficulty of describing this theophany by stating that he saw the "*likeness* of a throne" and the "*likeness* as the appearance of a man," nevertheless, this chapter gives much more detail than Isaiah or subsequent throne theophanies, including a specific description of YHWH's visible form as *a man*. The labeling of this theophany as "the appearance of the likeness of the Glory of YHWH" also connects it with the strong "Glory" theophanic tradition of the Exodus.

The theophanic pattern of YHWH appearing in the form of a man is both continued and complicated by the prominent vision of Daniel 7:9-14. It is complicated because two man-like figures appear in this vision, "the Ancient of Days" and the "one as a son of man."[10] Even though the latter is explicitly described with the term "man," the former has the man-like characteristics of wearing clothing and having hair:

> [Dan 7:9] As I looked, thrones were placed and one who was ancient of days took his seat; his raiment was white as snow, and the hair of his head like pure wool; his throne was fiery flames, its wheels were burning fire. [10] A stream of fire issued and came forth from before him; a thousand thousands served him, and ten thousand times ten thousand stood before

him; the court sat in judgment, and the books were opened. [11] I looked then because of the sound of the great words which the horn was speaking. And as I looked, the beast was slain, and its body destroyed and given over to be burned with fire. [12] As for the rest of the beasts, their dominion was taken away, but their lives were prolonged for a season and a time. [13] I saw in the night visions, and behold, with the clouds of heaven there came one like a son of man, and he came to the Ancient of Days and was presented before him. [14] And to him was given dominion and glory and kingdom, that all peoples, nations, and languages should serve him; his dominion is an everlasting dominion, which shall not pass away, and his kingdom one that shall not be destroyed.

In light of prior theophanic traditions, especially the likeness of a man on the divine throne in Ezekiel 1, one is left with this question: Which of these two should be understood to be the man-like form of YHWH? It appears rather obvious that the Ancient of Days would be understood to be the Glory of YHWH seen by Ezekiel because he is an enthroned man-like figure, yet the one like a son of man arrives and is given universal dominion fitting only for one who is YHWH. Furthermore, the explanation of the vision states that "the Ancient of Days *came*, and judgment was given" (7:22). This detail and the difficult possibility of *two* man-like divine figures may have influenced the LXX rendering of Daniel 7:13 that indicates one figure "came as a son of man, as [the] ancient of days he has come" (ἰδοὺ ἐπὶ τῶν νεφελῶν τοῦ οὐρανοῦ ὡς υἱὸς ἀνθρώπου ἤρχετο καὶ ὡς παλαιὸς ἡμερῶν παρῆν).[11]

One of the earliest throne theophanies in noncanonical Second Temple Jewish apocalyptic literature is found in an impressive divine throne scene described in *1 Enoch* 14 (c. second century B.C.E.):

[14:18] And I observed and saw inside it a lofty throne—its appearance was like crystal and its wheels like the shining sun; and the voice of the cherubim; and from beneath the throne were issuing streams of flaming fire. It was difficult to look at it. [20] And the Great Glory was sitting upon it— as for his gown, which was shining more brightly than the sun, it was whiter than any snow. [21] None of the angels was able to come in and see the face of the Excellent and the Glorious One, and no one of the flesh can see him—[22] the flaming fire was round about him, and a great fire stood before him. No one could come near unto him from among those that surrounded the tens of millions that stood before him. [23] He needed no council, but the most holy ones who are near to him neither go far away at night nor move away from him.

Although the textual tradition of *1 Enoch* is very complicated, influence upon this theophanic description from Ezekiel 1 is unmistakable (enthroned "Glory" language) and from Daniel 7 is probable (appearance "whiter than any snow" and "surrounded the tens of millions that stood before him"). The restraint shown in describing the appearance of the Great Glory, however, is quite apparent. The influence of Daniel 7 is especially visible in *1 Enoch* 37–71, which dates to the first century C.E., and probably is even pre-Christian.[12] In these chapters of *1 Enoch*, however, the Son of Man is not on a separate throne as in Daniel, but is seated upon the one divine throne in order to execute eschatological judgment on behalf of the Lord of the Spirits.[13] In addition to an elaborate focus on the Son of Man as the preexistent man-like form of YHWH with little actual description of the Lord of the Spirits, this portion of *1 Enoch* concludes with the revelation of the man Enoch as the Son of Man and his enthronement.

The restraint in describing any physical appearance of YHWH in the theophany of Exodus 24:8-11 has already been noted. Even though Exodus 24:2 acknowledges that the theophany that Moses experienced was more extensive than what was revealed to the elders in 24:8-11, the subsequent description of Moses' interaction with YHWH does not fill in many details. The interaction between YHWH and Moses in Exodus 33:18-23 affirms the limits of what Moses saw; yet YHWH appears to have the form of a man when he allows his backside to be seen by Moses (Exod 33:23). Ezekiel the Tragedian, a second-century B.C.E. Jewish playwright in Alexandria, takes some liberty with the Exodus traditions—probably inspired by Ezekiel 1—in composing a dream vision that Moses had prior to his call at the burning bush, a vision that prepares him for his post-Exodus theophany at Sinai. In this dream vision, Moses sees YHWH as a man seated upon a cosmic-sized divine throne. Notice these lines of his play *Exagoge*:

> [68] On Sinai's peak I saw what seemed a throne
> [69] so great in size it touched the clouds of heaven.
> [70] Upon it sat a man of noble mien,
> [71] becrowned, and with a scepter in one hand
> [72] while with the other he did beckon me [Moses].

This pattern of God appearing as a man on the divine throne is reinforced in an even more radical manner a few lines later when this man-like form of YHWH descends from his throne while beckoning Moses to ascend and be seated upon it (*Exagoge* 74–81).[14]

Christ as the Man on Patmos

Indisputably, the author of the Book of Revelation was very familiar with the basic pattern of these literary traditions that have YHWH appearing as a man on the divine throne. This conclusion is founded upon his use of specific language from some of the theophanies discussed previously as he records the opening scene of his own visionary experience where Christ appears as a glorified man on the island of Patmos (1:8-20). Although this is not a scene of Christ enthroned in heaven, it shows that the author understood the Christ who appeared before him to be none other than the visible form of YHWH enthroned as seen by earlier prophets such as Isaiah, Ezekiel, and Daniel. The text of Revelation states:

> [1:12] And I turned to see the voice that was speaking with me. And after I had turned, I saw seven golden lampstands; [13] and in the middle of the lampstands the likeness of a son of man, who was clothed in a long flowing robe, and tied across his chest with a golden girdle/sash. [14] And his head and his hair were white like white wool, like snow; and his eyes were like a flame of fire; [15] and his feet were like burnished bronze, when it has been caused to glow in a furnace, and his voice was like the sound of many waters. [16] And in his right hand he held seven stars; and out of his mouth came a sharp two-edged sword; and his face was like the sun shining in its power.

In this description are several verbal allusions to earlier theophanic texts. First, and of primary importance, Christ is described as "[the] likeness [of a] son of man" (ὅμοιον υἱὸν ἀνθρώπου), an unmistakable allusion to Daniel 7:13 (LXX: ὡς υἱὸς ἀνθρώπου). Although Daniel 7:13 is clearly in view because of the "son of man" language, it must be recognized that by means of the author's use of ὁμοίωμα he also intends readers/hearers to see Christ as the Glory of YHWH in Ezekiel 1:26-28 who is "the *likeness* in appearance of a *man*" (LXX: ὁμοίωμα ὡς εἶδος ἀνθρώπου). One other detail links the description of Christ here with the Glory of Ezekiel. The description "and his voice was as a voice of many waters" in Revelation 1:15b is the sound coming from the four living creatures of the throne of the Glory in Ezekiel 1:24 (καὶ ἤκουον τὴν φωνὴν τῶν πτερύγων αὐτῶν ἐν τῷ πορεύεσθαι αὐτὰ ὡς φωνὴν ὕδατος πολλοῦ) as well as the sound of the voice of the Glory in Ezekiel 43:2 (MT, but not LXX). The description of the head of the "as a son of man" also alludes to Daniel 7: "and his head and hair were white as wool, white as snow" (ἡ δὲ κεφαλὴ αὐτοῦ καὶ αἱ τρίχες λευκαὶ ὡς ἔριον λευκόν ὡς χιών). This description, however, is not of "a son of man" in

Daniel 7:13, but of "the Ancient of Days" in Daniel 7.9 who has hair like white wool (LXX: τὸ τρίχωμα τῆς κεφαλῆς αὐτοῦ ὡσεὶ ἔριον λευκόν), while the rest of his appearance was "white as snow."[15] This detail in the description is very significant because it demonstrates some type of identification of the "likeness of a son of man" with the Ancient of Days. Either it is identifying them as distinct figures who are both divine and eternal, or it is presenting Christ as the Ancient of Days who came in the latter days as the likeness of a son of man.

Two details in the description of Christ in Revelation 1 allude to the text of Isaiah. In describing the apparel of the "likeness of a son of man" as "being clothed in a long flowing robe" (ἐνδεδυμένον ποδήρη) in Revelation 1:13b, the author links his vision of Christ with the theophany of Isaiah where YHWH's "skirt" fills the temple (Isa 6:1; MT: ושוליו מלאים את־ההיכל).[16] The description "and a sharp two-edged sword was coming out of his mouth" (καὶ ἐκ τοῦ στόματος αὐτοῦ ῥομφαία δίστομος ὀξεῖα ἐκπορευομένη) in Revelation 1:16b alludes primarily to Isaiah 49:2 where the Suffering Servant states that YHWH made his mouth like a "sharp sword" (καὶ ἔθηκεν τὸ στόμα μου ὡσεὶ μάχαιραν ὀξεῖαν).[17]

Another piece of the physical apparel of Christ in Revelation 1, as well as the description of his eyes and feet, draws especially on the appearance of the glorious being in Daniel 10. The description "and tied around the chest with a golden girdle/sash" (καὶ περιεζωσμένον πρὸς τοῖς μαστοῖς ζώνην χρυσᾶν) in Revelation 1:13c alludes to Daniel 10:5 (LXX καὶ τὴν ὀσφὺν περιεζωσμένος βυσσίνῳ; but Theod. περιεζωσμένον ἐν χρυσίνῳ). The description "and his eyes were like flaming fire" (καὶ οἱ ὀφθαλμοὶ αὐτοῦ ὡς φλὸξ πυρός) in Revelation 1:14b reflects Daniel 10:6 where the eyes of the glorious one are described as "torches of fire" (καὶ οἱ ὀφθαλμοὶ αὐτοῦ ὡσεὶ λαμπάδες πυρός). The description "and his feet were the likeness of burnished bronze, as having been fired in a furnace" (καὶ οἱ πόδες αὐτοῦ ὅμοιοι χαλκολιβάνῳ ὡς ἐν καμίνῳ πεπυρωμένης) in Revelation 1:15a reflects Daniel 10:6 where the arms and feet of the glorious being are described in a very similar manner (LXX καὶ πλήρης ὁ οἶκος τῆς δόξης αὐτοῦ). The three possible identifications of this figure in Daniel 10 are: Gabriel; the "one as a son of man"; or an unnamed exalted angel. The author of Revelation's use of the specific language of Daniel 10 in recording his vision of Christ (1:13c, 1:14b, and 1:15a) indicates that he probably identified the figure of Daniel 10 with the "one as a son of man" in Daniel 7:13, and understood this figure to be the Glory of YHWH.[18]

Christ is depicted in Revelation 1, therefore, as the Glory of YHWH, the visible manifestation of YHWH, who showed himself at times to the prophets in the likeness of a "man" or "son of man." This identification is clear from the allusions in this pericope to the "man" in Ezekiel and Daniel. Furthermore, the white hair of the Ancient of Days in Daniel 7 is seen in Revelation 1 on Christ. This shows that he is identified with YHWH in this scene and in the overall understanding of the author of Revelation. Even more, this scene may reflect an interpretation of Daniel 7 that identifies the Ancient of Days with the likeness of a son of man. Although the divine throne is not present in Revelation 1, this scene depicts a continuity of YHWH's revelation and presence between the earlier prophets of Israel and the "prophet" John.

Christ as the Lamb on the Divine Throne

The appearance of Christ in Revelation 1, as well as the reinforcement of this appearance through the restatement or addition of various characteristics of Christ at the start of each of the seven letters in Revelation 2–3, nurtures the expectation that when Christ is seen again, he will appear as this glorious man-like form of YHWH. This expectation is strengthened further by the setting of Revelation 4–5, which is the divine throne room. In light of the texts discussed previously, one would expect to see the man-like form of YHWH in this apocalypse, of all places, upon the divine throne in this scene. The vision of the throne in Revelation 4 depicts "the one who sits upon the throne" being present and worshipped as "our Lord and God" (4:11), and yet no man-like form is seen on the throne in this chapter, only a brilliance shining from the area of the throne that resembled precious stones and a rainbow (4:3).

It is noteworthy that Revelation does not describe "the one who sits upon the throne" in Revelation 4 with the title or characteristics of the Ancient of Days of Daniel 7 or the Glory of YHWH in Ezekiel 1. Furthermore, the expectation of seeing the man-like form of YHWH who is distinct from "the one who sits upon the throne" is also encouraged by the powerful messianic tone of the announcement that the one worthy to open the scroll is "the Lion of the tribe of Judah, the Root of David" (Rev 5:5).[19]

This paradoxical pattern of not being able to see YHWH and yet being able to see him as a man enthroned is not only present in Jewish apocalyptic literature as presented previously, but also in some early

Christian apocalypses such as the *Ascension of Isaiah*.[20] In this apocalypse, "the Great Glory" (i.e., the Father) is acknowledged as present on the divine throne, yet Isaiah is unable actually to see the Great Glory (*Ascen. Isa.* 9:37; 10:2; see *1En.* 14:21). "The Beloved," who is the Son standing at the side of the Great Glory with the Angel of the Holy Spirit on the other side, is visible as the man-like form of YHWH.[21] Although there is a hierarchy of glorious persons within the trinitarian theology of the *Ascension of Isaiah*, nevertheless, the Beloved is the primary *visible* Glory figure in this document (e.g., *Ascen. Isa.* 9:27–31). This document follows the pattern seen in the literature examined previously, but clearly identifies the visible form of YHWH as Christ.

Instead of seeing the expected "likeness as a son of man" on the throne in Revelation 5, this surprising sight is unveiled: "And I saw, in the middle of the throne and the four living creatures and in the middle of the twenty four elders, a lamb who was standing even though he had been slaughtered, who has seven horns and seven eyes that are the spirits of God who were sent to all of the earth" (5:6). As stated previously, the surprise here is *not* that the reader or hearer expects to see a lion and then sees a lamb, but that one expects to see the man-like form of YHWH, and instead sees a slaughtered lamb, standing enthroned as ruler of the cosmos. It is, therefore, not helpful to characterize this as a rhetorical reversal (i.e., promising a lion and then presenting a lamb), but rather as a redefinition of messianic expectations: John understands the promised Lion is the slaughtered-yet-standing lamb.[22] Richard Bauckham explains this redefinition process:

> The two messianic titles evoke a strongly militaristic and nationalistic image of the Messiah of David as conqueror of the nations, destroying the enemies of God's people (cf., e.g., 1QSb 5:20-29). But this image is reinterpreted by what John sees: the Lamb whose sacrificial death (5:6) has redeemed people from all nations (5:9-10). By juxtaposing the two contrasting images, John has forged a new symbol of conquest by sacrificial death. The messianic hopes evoked in 5:5 are not repudiated: Jesus really is the expected Messiah of David (22:16). But insofar as the latter was associated with military violence and narrow nationalism, it is reinterpreted by the image of the Lamb. The Messiah has certainly won a victory, but he has done so by sacrifice and for the benefit of people from all nations (5:9). Thus the means by which the Davidic Messiah has won his victory is explained by the image of the Lamb, while the significance of the image of the Lamb is now seen to lie in the fact that his sacrificial death was a victory over evil.[23]

The reversal that the reader and hearers experience, therefore, is seeing the *lamb* on the throne instead of the (son of) *man*. The significance of this scene for the Christology of this apocalypse is difficult to overstate. It introduces the lamb Christology that dominates the presentation of Christ in this apocalypse.[24] The importance of this scene for the Christology of the book of Revelation is reinforced by the fact that the Lamb appears in the midst of the throne (ἐν μέσῳ τοῦ θρόνου), not separated from it (5:6 and 7:17; cf. 3:21 and 22:1, 3).[25] As seen in the examples of apocalyptic literature examined previously, the depiction of the divine throne is the central scene of these texts, and there is no more important figure(s) in these scenes than the one(s) upon the throne. To see the lamb in the middle of the throne is a visual way of expressing the identification of Christ within the mystery of the one God of Israel. The veneration of the lamb, moreover, is another way through which this scene depicts Christ within the mystery of the one God, because to worship anyone other than YHWH is idolatry.[26] The veneration of the lamb follows—and even expands—the pattern established in the worship of "the one who sits on the throne."[27] This parallel worship climaxes in this scene when both are worshipped together: "To him who sits on the throne and to the lamb be blessing and honor and glory and might forever and ever" (5:13).

Although the depiction of the throne room in Revelation 4–5 is by far the dominant scene of this apocalypse for lamb Christology, the lamb appears again in two other scenes. First, in describing the eschatological bliss of the saints at the end of Revelation 7, the author again identifies the lamb within the mystery of God through references to the divine throne:

> [15] Therefore they are before *the throne of God*, and serve him day and night in his temple; and *the one who sits upon the throne* will shelter them with his presence. [16] They shall hunger no more, neither thirst any more; the sun shall not strike them, nor any scorching heat. [17] For *the lamb in the midst of the throne* will be their shepherd, and he will guide them to springs of living water; and God will wipe away every tear from their eyes.

It is too often assumed that the referent of "God" in these verses is "the one who sits on the throne" described in Revelation 4 (i.e., the Father). It is noteworthy that both "the one who sits upon the throne" (7:15) and "the lamb in the midst of the throne" (7:17) occupy "the throne *of God.*" *Both* have shepherding functions ("shelter" in 7:15 and "guiding them to springs" in 7:17). From the structure of these verses, one is left with the impression that the referent of "God" in "God will wipe away every tear from their eyes" (7:17) is *both* "the one who sits upon the throne" (7:15) and "the lamb in the midst of the throne" (7:17).[28]

The other scene that features the lamb occurs when the 144,000 are gathered with the lamb on Mount Zion (Rev 14:1-5). Two details are especially significant. First, the 144,000 have the lamb's "name and his Father's name written on their foreheads" (14:1). This detail recalls the scene where the saints are sealed with the Divine Name (7:1-8). It communicates that the lamb and the one seated upon the throne share the same Divine Name, YHWH.[29] Second, although the lamb is not explicitly mentioned as being on the throne here, the text does note that the 144,000 "sing a new song *before the throne and before the four living creatures and before the elders*" (14:3). The implication is that the lamb standing in the midst of the throne is the object of this worship.

In order to understand the Christology being communicated by these appearances of Christ as a lamb in the book of Revelation, it is important first to explore the tradition-history background for this lamb imagery. Most discussions of the tradition-history of this lamb imagery focus on one of three possible traditions, or a combination of the three: *the Passover lamb* of Exodus 12 and subsequent annual Passover observances; *the atonement lambs* that are discussed in Leviticus 16, and are the basis for the image of the servant who is the sin-bearing, sacrificial lamb in Isaiah 53; and *the eschatological warrior lamb* that is found in some apocalyptic literature (e.g., *1 En* 89). Which of these three traditions is central in the lamb Christology of Revelation[30] is still debated considerably. As will be seen in the discussion that follows, it is best to see all three traditions contributing to the portrait of the lamb in Revelation, with the Passover lamb traditions being dominant.

The importance of the eschatological warrior lamb tradition for understanding the lamb in Revelation is advocated, for example, by Timo Eskola: "It is obvious that the Lamb appearing here is the apocalyptic ram, a figure known from Jewish sources."[31] The seven horns (e.g., Dan 7:8, Zech 1:18-21, and *1 En* 90:9) and seven eyes (e.g., Zech 4:10) of the lamb certainly help one to see the lamb of Revelation within the wider apocalyptic tradition visible in Daniel's varied use of animal imagery as well as in the so-called Animal Apocalypse of *1 Enoch* 83–90. To illustrate, *1 Enoch* 89:45 states this about David: "So the Lord of the sheep sent the sheep another sheep [David] and promoted him to become a ram [Samuel's anointing of David] and lead the sheep in place of that sheep

which had abandoned his own glory [Saul]." Later in the Animal
Apocalypse, Judas Maccabeus is depicted as a ram that will smash the ani-
mals oppressing the sheep (*1 En* 90:9). Although this eschatological warrior ram tradition probably exercised some influence upon the depiction
of the lamb of Revelation (e.g., 6:16; 17:14), the slaughtered-yet-standing
lamb scenes of Revelation are not primarily militaristic, even though some
other christological scenes are (e.g., Christ as the eschatological conqueror
who is riding the white horse in 19:11-16).

Most scholars have emphasized the importance of traditions concerning either Passover or the Day of Atonement for interpreting the
lamb imagery in Revelation. One of the primary reasons for seeing these
traditions as more central to the christological lamb in Revelation is the
repeated emphasis on the blood of this lamb: Christ is the lamb who has
been "slaughtered" but now stands (5:6; 13:8), who "has loosed us from
our sins by his blood" (1:5; cf. 5:9), in whose blood the saints have
washed their robes and made them white (7:14), and by whose blood the
faithful conquer (12:11). Although mention of blood "loosing sins" (1:5)
or "purchasing people" (5:9) could indicate that atonement traditions
form much of the background of this lamb Christology, it must be
remembered that there is recurring Exodus imagery in Revelation, and
there is considerable sacrifice and blood associated with the Passover.[32]
Furthermore, a melding of Passover and atonement traditions is visible
in other early Christian texts since *Christ's death at Passover* was interpreted as *an atoning sacrifice*.[33] While recognizing that atonement traditions are part of the portrait, Pierre Prigent notes the value of
emphasizing the Passover background for the presentation of Christ as a
lamb in Revelation:

> It is in this way that one can best explain the emphasis on the blood of this
> Lamb and the effect of his sacrifice, which guarantees mankind's redemp-
> tion (Rev 5:9), as of old during the first Passover, when Israel was ransomed
> from the land of slavery. When we recall the eschatological notion in the
> Passover celebrations, we can more readily accept the possibility of identi-
> fying Jesus with the lamb of the eschatological Passover whose blood will
> guarantee definitive and perfect redemption, that is, one that is worldwide
> (Rev 5:9).[34]

In light of the evidence presented (see section 1) and the appearance
of Christ in Revelation 1–3, the crucial question of this study is finally
addressed: Why *this lamb* instead of *the man*? The answer is rather complex and multifaceted. A fundamental—yet sometimes overlooked—rea-

son for the presence of a lamb instead of the man in the dominant scene of Revelation is found not primarily in the author's exegetical use of traditions in writing this apocalypse but in an actual mystical vision that is the experiential basis for his literary work (e.g., Rev 1:1-2, 10-11; 4:1-2; 17:1-3; 21:9-10). In other words, the distinction of his depiction of the throne room scene from previous accounts affirms that he wrote about what *he saw* in his visionary experience rather than what his readers would have *expected him to see* in such an experience.[35] Many other details in his writing show continuity with previous literary traditions, but *not* the physical appearance of the one in the midst of the throne.

Although actual visionary experience of the lamb can explain its presence in Revelation, this does not explain why the author allowed the lamb Christology to dominate this apocalypse as it does. The reasons lamb Christology is given prominence in the final literary product center around what the author was trying to communicate about Christ (especially about his incarnation, humanity, and death) and the Christian life (especially about "faithful witness," even unto death). Larry Hurtado expresses this point with great clarity: "The designation of Jesus as the Lamb reflects the author's emphasis on Jesus' sacrificial death as the key event that both secured the redemption of the elect and also serves as the model for their own commitment (e.g., 1:5–6; 5:9-10)."[36]

Of these two, the former reason is more important, as Richard Bauckham states: "It is the central role which the death of Jesus played in the Christian understanding of redemption which accounts for the centrality of the Lamb to Revelation's use of the new exodus motif."[37] The lamb scenes communicate that the exalted and reigning Christ is none other than the faithful one who was sacrificed on the cross and rose victorious. The atoning death of a fully human and divine Jesus as the continuing source of cosmic victory over Satan occupies center-stage in this vision. Furthermore, this imagery of the slaughtered lamb who was a faithful witness to death resonates with Christians who are experiencing some persecution, even death, and feel like "sheep to be slaughtered" (Rom 8:36).[38] The portrait of the slaughtered-yet-standing lamb who conquered by means of his own death encourages the faithful to conquer also through his death.[39]

Another reason for the prominence of this lamb imagery is that the lamb stands in stark contrast with the (first) beast, the form that Satan (the dragon) takes in order to deceive the nations (Rev 13:1-18).[40] Even as there is a contrast in Revelation between the two cities (Babylon and the New Jerusalem) that are two women (the Harlot of Babylon and the

Bride of Christ), there is also a major contrast depicted between *the lamb* as the visible face of the true God who is the object of true worship and *the beast* as the visible face of a false god who is the object of false worship. These contrasting images, in turn, help the hearer of the apocalypse to see that outward appearances can be deceptive; the powerful and impressive beast is conquered through the sacrifice of the pitiful and lowly lamb.

Finally, even though visionary experience is a difficult phenomenon to explain, actual experiences in the life of the author and his audience may help us understand the presence of lamb Christology in this visionary experience and resulting literary document. Although not widely acknowledged by scholars, another reason for the author's visionary experience of Christ as this lamb and his audience's understanding of this christological image was their frequent mystical experience of Christ as the lamb in the Eucharist.[41] Stated succinctly, this lamb Christology is consistent with the way early worshippers saw Christ in the Eucharist. Although it is often the historical Exodus from Egypt that comes to mind when we hear the term "Passover," it is vital that the annual festival, which centered on the Passover *meal* and recounted the whole Exodus and wilderness deliverance, also be kept in mind when interpreting this imagery in Revelation. First-century Jews remembered the Passover deliverance and anticipated the eschatological deliverance in the Passover *meal* where they ate an unblemished *lamb*. This depiction of Christ as the Passover lamb in the heavenly sanctuary would help Christians to see that he is one and the same as the Christ whose flesh they ate and whose blood they drank when they celebrated the Christian Passover each Lord's Day on earth.[42]

Christ as the Man in Other Scenes

The fact that Christ does not appear as the man-like form of YHWH when he is seen in the midst of the throne does *not* mean that these traditions are marginal or unimportant in the Christology of Revelation. Although the lamb imagery is featured in the central and most important christological scene of Revelation, nevertheless, the spotlight is given over to Christ as the man-like form of YHWH on several occasions. In addition to Revelation 1–3, which was discussed previously, at least three other scenes can be described as examples of angelomorphic Christology, or appearances of Christ as the man-like form of YHWH (14:14-16, 19:11-16, and 10:1-11). These scenes reinforce the impact of the opening appearance of Christ; they communicate that the risen Jesus is the visible form of YHWH who has been active throughout history, and who will bring the world to both judgment and restoration. This additional evidence of Christ as the man-like form of YHWH will be reviewed briefly here in order to demonstrate the author's extensive awareness of these traditions and their important role in the Christology portrayed in this apocalypse.[43]

The scene that has a direct verbal link to Christ as he was described in the opening scene (Rev 1:12-16) is the brief appearance of the "likeness of a son of man" (ὅμοιον υἱὸν ἀνθρώπου) as the eschatological reaper seated on a white cloud in Revelation 14:14-16. Even though Joel 3:13 (MT 4:13) is the primary background for this harvest scene, the theophanic imagery of being seated on a cloud and wearing a crown in 14:14, joined with the designation "likeness of a son of man," recalls the judgment scene of Daniel 7:13 (cf. Rev 1:7). Although the detail of being "seated on" the cloud(s) is not present in Daniel, an amalgamation of the traditions in Daniel 7 with Psalm 110 is found in the passion narratives of the Synoptic Gospels: "You will see the Son of Man seated at the right hand of the Power and *coming on the clouds of heaven*" (Mark 16:62; Matt 26:64; cf. Luke 22:69). Understood in light of Revelation 1, this scene communicates that Christ is the man-like form of YHWH who will bring eschatological judgment upon the earth.

The most extensive portrait of Christ as the man-like form of YHWH after the opening scene of Revelation 1–3 is found near the end of the apocalypse in Christ's appearance as the conquering warrior riding the white horse (19:11-16). Although the characteristics of riding a white horse, having many crowns, and being followed by the armies of heaven are all indicators of his divine status, the description of this warrior's "eyes like blazing fire" (19:12) explicitly connects him with the opening vision of Christ (1:14) and with the glorious man in Daniel (Dan 10:6). Another theophanic characteristic of this depiction of Christ is his unknown "name"; this name is certainly the Divine Name, the Tetragrammaton, which he shares with the Father.[44] The ancient theophanic roots of this christological scene are understood most clearly by seeing the relationship of this description to that given YHWH in Isaiah 63:1-6.[45] Here Christ is the eschatological warrior, none other than the man-like form of YHWH who both protected and punished Israel after the Exodus (cf. Isa 63:7-14).

Although some scholars have identified the Mighty Angel in Revelation 10 as a created angel, this is very probably another vivid

example of Christ depicted as the man-like form of YHWH.[46] The theophanic characteristic of the rainbow in 10:1 points back to the throne
room in 4:3 and points to this "mighty angel" as the Glory of YHWH
seen by Ezekiel (Ezek 1:26-28; cf. *Apoc. Ab.* 11:3). The theophanic characteristic of being "robed in a cloud" (10:1) resonates with theophanic
Exodus traditions as well as the description of Christ seated upon a cloud
in 14:14. The face of this angel "like the sun" links this description with
that given Christ in the opening scene (Rev 1:16). The opened scroll
imagery connects this angel with Christ as the lamb who opened the
seven seals of the scroll (Rev 6:1, 2, 5, 7, 9, 12; 8:1). Once again, Christ
is depicted as the man-like form of YHWH.

In addition to these three instances of angelomorphic Christology,
two other scenes may be depicting Christ as the man-like form of
YHWH. First, the "angel" who ascends "from the rising of the sun, with
the Seal of the Living God" and commands the sealing of the saints (7:2-
3) may be understood to be Christ. This figure appears to be a depiction
of the angelomorphic Glory, since the Glory was to return from the East
(Ezek 43:1-2) and he bears the seal, which is the Divine Name (Exod
23:21; cf. Exod 28:36).[47] The identification of the Son of Man/Glory as
the Risen Christ in Revelation 1 makes a christological identification of
this angel possible. Second, the angel who binds Satan in Revelation
20:1–2 may also be identified as Christ based upon his authority symbolized by his possession of "the key of the bottomless pit" (cf. 1:18) and
binding action against Satan (cf. Matt 12:29). It is clear from these
scenes, especially those where the figure is unambiguously Christ, that
traditions about the man-like form of YHWH play a significant role in
several scenes of Revelation as well as in its overall christological portrait.

The Relationship between the Christological Scenes

I have presented evidence of the centrality of lamb Christology and the
significant presence of angelomorphic Christology in the book of
Revelation, as well as the background and function of this imagery. The
lamb Christology offers a substantial redefinition of the theophanic traditions surrounding the (son of) man on the divine throne found in earlier apocalyptic literature. One question remains to be addressed: What
is the relationship between these christological traditions as they were
experienced in a vision as well as expressed in a textual form?

These two different christological traditions, visible in the various
scenes of this vision, function in a complementary—rather than compet-

tetive—manner. Absence of one would affect how we understand the other image; they function together to communicate the reality of Christ in a manner that could not happen if only one tradition were used. For example, even though the divine identity of the lamb is apparent from characteristics found in Revelation 5 (e.g., position on the throne, seven horns, and receiving worship), the scenes where Christ appears as the man-like form of YHWH give much more historical depth and breath to Christ's divine identity in this apocalypse. Conversely, it would be difficult to communicate the ongoing significance of the humanity and death of Jesus through only scenes where Christ appeared as the glorious man-like form of YHWH. This apocalypse communicates that the appearance of the form of YHWH upon the throne in the heavenly sanctuary that is the focus of faithful worship has changed due to the sacrificial death of Jesus. As Christopher Rowland has stated: "The secret of the heart of God and proximity to God's own person is rooted in the sacrificial death of the lamb. The character of God is revealed in this."[48]

The book of Revelation unveils the visible form of YHWH, the one eternal God of Israel, to be none other than Jesus who was crucified and rose on the third day. The Christology of Revelation communicates that the death and resurrection of Jesus have transformed the image of YHWH on the divine throne for eternity. The man *previously seen* on the divine throne by the prophets is henceforth the slaughtered-yet-standing lamb *now seen* on the same throne by the prophet John, and by those hearing this apocalypse in Eucharistic worship and then participating in the paschal feast.

PART III

STUDIES IN COMMUNITY

Chapter 15

The Promise of the Spirit of Life
in the Book of Ezekiel

John R. Levison

Ezekiel 36–37, with its promise of a new heart and spirit and the famed vision of the valley of dry bones, appears to have exercised extensive influence upon the development of early Christian pneumatology. F. W. Horn, for example, recognizes the importance of Ezekiel 36–37 as a foreground to Pauline pneumatology: "insofern es sich hier explizit um den Geist Gottes als Gabe an die endzeitliche Gemeinde handelt, die mit dieser Gabe zu einem neuen Handeln befähigt wird . . . Übereinstimmend mit den ntl. Aussagen ist jedoch, dass die Gabe des Geistes, für Ez zukünftige Gabe, hier als gegenwärtige Grösse functional endzeitliches Verhalten eröffnet."[1] M. V. Hubbard similarly connects Ezekiel and Paul: "Like Ezekiel before him, Paul perceived the chief significance of the eschatological Spirit to lie in its ability to produce *life*."[2] J. D. G. Dunn, therefore, is hardly alone in observing that the ubiquitous phrase, "give the spirit," and its variations may ultimately have been derived from "Ezek. 37:6, 14, part of Ezekiel's so powerfully evocative vision of spiritual renewal."[3]

This unique volume, which honors the achievements of scholars who have emerged from disparate Jewish and Christian traditions to discover a meeting-point in which Judaism and Christianity share so much in common, provides an exceptional opportunity to observe and examine one important dimension of the early Christian appropriation of Jewish scripture.[4] Viewed from the perspective of much of Pauline scholarship, Ezekiel's vision of a "new creation" becomes single-dimensional. It becomes an eschatological gift of the spirit that has the ability to produce life, an evocative, though fairly flat, vision of spiritual renewal. This appropriation of Ezekiel focuses principally upon Ezekiel 36–37, eclipsing related texts from Ezekiel that are of no less importance. For example, even in an otherwise detailed recent analysis of the Hebrew scriptures, F. Philip analyzes the notion of a "new heart and spirit" in Ezekiel 36–37 without comparing it to related texts in Ezekiel 11 and 18.[5] What can be lost in such a construal of Ezekiel are the textures of his visions, the painstaking way in which Ezekiel's visions of the spirit were metamorphosed, as historical realities pressed upon him and his people.[6] The contribution of this study is to recapture those textures within Ezekiel's vision of a new creation that have been lost due to the unintentional and subtle tendency to isolate individual scriptural texts on the basis of their presumed relevance for Pauline theology.

What emerges in the powerfully positive visions of Ezekiel 36–37 is the end of a long process that encompasses as well Ezekiel 11:17, 21 and 18:31-32. Taken together, these visions convey the distinct impression that the process of revitalization is not a simple one; the life-giving procedure takes its time. A central thrust of this essay is to say just this, that the spiritual renewal that is envisaged in the writings of Ezekiel is a protracted process, one far more protracted than a reading of Pauline literature would suggest. It is possible to track the way in which Ezekiel's own take on the action of spiritual renewal shifted in the course of a few debilitating decades. As the situation in Jerusalem deteriorated with successive deportations during that first and fateful decade of the sixth century B.C.E., Ezekiel adapted his view of renewal by the spirit. His earliest oracles of restoration are less trenchant and more optimistic. Later, however, Ezekiel receives an oracle to preach to a disheartened Israel, and here his conceptions of the spirit begin their metamorphosis. Only in these subsequent oracles does Ezekiel grapple with the protracted process that is required to lead Israel from its old ways, from its familiar, faulty worship to a new way of life in the land of Israel. Yet this place is still not the end of the road; the truest end is a valley of very many, very dry bones. Here, in the valley of the shadow of death, Ezekiel reckons with the discontinuity that surely must divide the ghastly present from a splendid future.

A New Heart and Spirit

Human Initiative

As the Babylonian noose tightened around Israel's neck, some Israelites naturally, and probably justifiably, raised the question of responsibility.

This probing was encapsulated in a proverb, "The parents have eaten sour grapes, and the children's teeth are set on edge" (18:2).[7] Ezekiel's older contemporary, Jeremiah, quotes this maxim in order to dispel the shadow of death. God has broken down and destroyed; God will build and plant. No one will any longer quote this maxim, and people will die for their own sins. The shadow of death, therefore, will be dispelled by a new covenant that God will initiate: God will write Torah on Israel's hearts, and Israel will no longer even need teachers (31:27-34). In short, the dawn of a new day will eclipse the days of destruction; it will be a day that occurs at God's initiative, with God's provision, through the inscription of God's Torah on human hearts.

Ezekiel attends to this maxim far more elaborately than Jeremiah. He demonstrates at length, with many case studies, what Jeremiah dispenses in a few words, that each individual's sin or obedience determines his or her destiny. This lengthy response to the maxim concludes climactically with a divine challenge:

> Therefore I will judge you, O house of Israel, all of you according to your ways, says the Lord GOD. Repent and turn from all your transgressions; otherwise iniquity will be your ruin. Cast away from you all the transgressions that you have committed against me, and make [for] yourselves a new heart and a new spirit! Why will you die, O house of Israel? For I have no pleasure in the death of anyone, says the Lord GOD. Turn, then, and live. (Ezek 18:30-32)

The perspective of this oracle is extraordinary: Ezekiel commands the people to *make for themselves* a new heart and spirit. These are realities that the Israelites can bring about themselves, a condition they can ensure. This claim is remarkable, prompted by the maxim about sour grapes, that individuals have it under their own control, not only to repent, but even to develop in themselves a new heart and a new spirit. It is similar to the Deuteronomic command to circumcise the foreskin of the heart, but Ezekiel's oracle goes far beyond this. He expects individual Israelites to do more than snip the foreskin; they have the capacity and responsibility to create for themselves a new heart and a new spirit.

Jeremiah's and Ezekiel's responses to the maxim about sour grapes form a striking contrast. Though each Israelite is said to die for his or her sins, in Jeremiah's vision of the future God exercises the initiative entirely. *God* will establish a new covenant. *God* will put Torah within Israel. *God* will write Torah on human hearts. Ezekiel grasps the other end of the stick; it is left to individual Israelites to repent, to throw away their sins, and to make *for themselves* a new heart and a new spirit.

Ezekiel expects Israel to manufacture its own liberation through repentance, by making a new heart and a new spirit.[8]

Divine and Human Initiative

This vision of human initiative also contrasts with Ezekiel's oracles at the eastern gate, in which he presumes that *God* will place the new heart and new spirit within. These oracles are prompted by an ever-growing consciousness of the horrendous state of the temple and its worship. In a series of visions, Ezekiel sees successively the sins that are committed in the temple's inner chambers, and he watches as the cherubim, symbols of the glory of God, withdraw from the temple's inner sanctum, finally to fly away altogether (Ezek 8:1–11:25). During this period of growing awareness, just prior to the final departure of the cherubim from the temple's east gate, Ezekiel, in a further vision, observes twenty-five leaders of Israel gathered together. The spirit explains that these elders mislead the people, so Ezekiel prophesies against them, during which time, his friend, Pelatiah, dies. Ezekiel reacts to Pelatiah's death by falling on his face and crying out, "Ah, LORD God! will you make a full end of the remnant of Israel?" (Ezek 11:13). In response, Ezekiel receives a divine word in which he learns that the leaders are unfaithful because they presume that the land is theirs, that those in exile have forfeited their right to the land. Consequently, Ezekiel receives the command to offer two oracles. In the first, God explains that God is a sanctuary to those who are scattered (11:16). The second oracle, which is longer, promises a fresh gathering of Israelite exiles and a new heart and spirit within:

> Therefore say: Thus says the Lord GOD: I will gather you from the peoples, and assemble you out of the countries where you have been scattered, and I will give you the land of Israel. When they come there, they will remove from it all its detestable things and all its abominations. I will give them one heart, and put a new spirit within them; I will remove the heart of stone from their flesh and give them a heart of flesh, so that they may follow my statutes and keep my ordinances and obey them. Then they shall be my people, and I will be their God. But as for those whose heart goes after their detestable things and their abominations, I will bring their deeds upon their own heads, says the Lord GOD. (Ezek 11:17-21)

Despite what he has observed in his vision of temple irregularities, Ezekiel's optimism is not yet extinguished, perhaps because he is giving hope in this particular oracle, not to the inhabitants of Jerusalem, but to those in exile who now have nothing to do with the temple. Ezekiel promises that God, who is now a temporary sanctuary for the faithful exiles, will gather these faithful and falsely accused exiles in their homeland. This will prompt them to put away idols and other stumbling-blocks. Once they have taken this step of removing the causes of sin, God will give to the restored exiles a heart of flesh and a new spirit to enable them to be fully God's people. The only pessimistic tone in Ezekiel's prophecy has to do with those who refuse to receive such a heart and allow their hearts to continue to embrace idolatry.

Divine Initiative

Despite a fundamental difference about the roles of divine and human initiative, Ezekiel's oracles at the eastern gate (11:14-21) and his response to the maxim about sour grapes (18:30-32) share a perspective that is absent during the period following the catastrophe of 587 B.C.E. According to each of the earlier oracles, Israelites are capable of putting away their sins and setting aside their idols. In the oracle from the eastern gate, the gift of a new heart and spirit is contingent upon repentance. Human responsibility, though, lies even more at the center of the oracle delivered in response to the maxim about sour grapes. In this oracle, Israelites must do more than set aside their sins; they must also cultivate for themselves a new heart and a new spirit.

It is absolutely essential to grasp the role of initiative in the oracles that precede the devastation of Jerusalem in order to appreciate the contrast of these with Ezekiel's later oracles and his vision of the valley of dry bones. Neither of the earlier oracles of a new spirit reflects the concomitant experiences of divine anger and human desolation that come in the wake of the annihilation of Jerusalem in 587 B.C.E. Thus far, the deportations have been partial, leaving many still in Jerusalem—those who are so sufficiently well-situated as to denigrate their brothers and sisters who are exiled in Babylon (11:1-4). During this period prior to the devastation of Jerusalem, Ezekiel's oracles assume that individual Israelites can repent, can cast away their transgressions, and, as a consequence, can obtain a new heart and spirit, either as a gift of God or entirely of their own doing.

The situation in which Ezekiel introduces a new heart and spirit a third time is altogether different. Now the Israelites are in the throes of grief, which they utter in the triadic threnody, "Our bones are dried up, and our hope is lost; we are cut off completely" (37:11). Now Ezekiel, too, reckons with the harsh reality that Israel is unable to catalyze its own liberation from exile. In its third iteration, lying under the surface of this promise for Israel's future, is the darker side of Israel's past, the irredeemable aspect of Israel's character that rules out human initiative:

> Thus says the Lord GOD: It is not for your sake, O house of Israel, that I am about to act, but for the sake of my holy name, which you have profaned among the nations to which you came. I will sanctify my great name, which has been profaned among the nations, and which you have profaned among them; and the nations shall know that I am the LORD, says the Lord GOD, when through you I display my holiness before their eyes. I will take you from the nations, and gather you from all the countries, and bring you into your own land. I will sprinkle clean water upon you, and you shall be clean from all your uncleannesses, and from all your idols I will cleanse you. A new heart I will give you, and a new spirit I will put within you; and I will remove from your body the heart of stone and give you a heart of flesh. I will put my spirit within you, and make you follow my statutes and be careful to observe my ordinances. Then you shall live in the land that I gave to your ancestors; and you shall be my people, and I will be your God. (Ezek 36:22-28)

This promise has not emerged from thin air but out of Ezekiel's fidelity to the tradition of Deuteronomy:

> When all these things have happened to you, the blessings and the curses that I have set before you, if you call them to mind among all the nations where the LORD your God has driven you, and return to the LORD your God, and you and your children obey him with all your heart and with all your soul, just as I am commanding you today, then the LORD your God will restore your fortunes and have compassion on you, gathering you again from all the peoples among whom the LORD your God has scattered you. Even if you are exiled to the ends of the world, from there the LORD your God will gather you, and from there he will bring you back. The LORD your God will bring you into the land that your ancestors possessed, and you will possess it; he will make you more prosperous and numerous than your ancestors. (Deut 30:1-5)

Although Ezekiel is faithful to this tradition, the dire situation brought about by the fall of Jerusalem propels him to transpose this tradition into a higher key. While Deuteronomy 30 promises restoration without cleansing, the dire situation of Israel in protracted exile evokes from Ezekiel a more radical solution of purification: "I will sprinkle clean water upon you, and you shall be *clean* from all your uncleannesses, and from all your idols I will *make you clean*" (Ezek 36:25).

It is not possible, from Ezekiel's point of view in the aftermath of 587 B.C.E., to gather Israel in the land, for this will be a collection of Israelites with the same tendency toward idolatry, the same sort of people whose actions led to the fall of Jerusalem. Gathering them without cleansing (Deut 30:1-5) them would simply not be enough to remove the kernel of disloyalty that lay at the heart of exiled Israel. Nor is circumcision of the heart (30:6) adequate; an entirely new heart and spirit are required by the extent of Israel's fall.[9] Nor can Israel be asked to repent (Ezek 11:14–21), as they failed to do so even as the Babylonian armies deported and decimated them for more than a decade. Nor is it possible any longer to expect that Israel can make for themselves a new heart and a new spirit (18:30-32); Israel no longer has the life in them to cultivate a new heart and a new spirit. Israel has been eclipsed by the shadow of death.

Variations on a Theme

The canonical book of Ezekiel offers no less than three perspectives on the promise of a new spirit within.

(1) In response to the proverb in which Israelites lay the blame at their parents' feet, Ezekiel lays singular responsibility for recreation squarely at his hearers' feet when he tells them to make for themselves a new heart and a new spirit.
(2) In the context of a vision in which the glory departs in stages from the tainted temple, he links divine and human initiative. God will give a new heart and a new spirit when Israel takes care of itself, when the nation puts pollutants aside.
(3) When there is, in the wake of 587 B.C.E., not a trace of hope left, Ezekiel lays responsibility wholly at the feet of God. God will cleanse Israel. God will bring Israel back to life in a series of remarkable acts that entails bones clanking, sinews growing, flesh overlaying, and inbreathing by a convergence of the winds—the spirits—at the four corners of the earth.

In none of these, we should be careful to observe, is the gift of the spirit simply a product of divine eschatological initiative. In one instance, Israelites are themselves responsible. In another, Israelites are responsible for removing pollutants in order to receive a new heart and spirit. In the third, the process is no instant transformation, no spontaneous combustion. The process of recreation is a protracted one, and Israel should not expect their tears to be turned to joy overnight. None of these texts ought to be read in isolation from one another; the unique emphases must not be amalgamated into a single vision.

Spirit in a Valley of Very Many, Very Dry Bones

Spirit and the Valley of the Shadow of Death

Ezekiel can hardly be characterized as reticent about his alleged experiences of the spirit. He claims frequently to have been transported by the spirit—though whether in vision or body is never entirely clear—to meet the exiles in Babylon (3:14-15), back to Jerusalem to the temple's inner court (8:3), then to its east gate (11:1) to watch the disheartening departure of the cherubim, and back again to the exiles (11:24). Following the catastrophe, he returns once more in a vision to a meticulously restored and glory-laden temple whose reality is still in the offing (43:5). The spirit leads Ezekiel's imagination full circle from the departure of God's glory from the temple, scarred by idolatrous graffiti and vile priests, to the return of God's glory to an ideal temple. This transport, physical or otherwise, between the exiled in Babylon and the temple in Jerusalem is a mysterious journey of hope, a hope measured not in vague visions of the future. Rather, it is gauged in cubits and handbreadths, measurements intended to press the possibility of restoration into the psyche of exiled Israel, measurements for each wall, precise and deliriously mundane except to those whose deadened imaginations begin to track with the vision, with the restatement of the measurements of each of the four walls, with the precision of an exiled priest whom an angel, holding a linen cord and measuring reed in his hand, has ordered, "Son of *adam*, look closely and listen attentively, and set your mind upon all that I shall show you . . ." (40:3-4). The spirit leads ultimately to the transport of imagination, fueling the dreams of a nation.

Yet, between the departure of glory and its reappearance lies a vast wasteland that is emblematized by a vision that encapsulates the protracted nature of restoring a dead nation to life. Fundamental to this vision is the overpowering reality of death that must be overcome, a horrible reality which Ezekiel captures as he describes the unthinkable: the spirit transports him, of priestly stock, to the land of the dead, to a valley where the bones lie brittle and bleached by the sun and sands of time:

> The hand of the LORD came upon me, and he brought me out by the spirit of the LORD and set me down in the middle of a valley; it was full

of bones. He led me all around them; there were very many lying in the valley, and they were very dry. (Ezek 37:1-2)

In the echo of this valley of death, Ezekiel gives ear to Israel's triadic and tragic lament: "Our bones are dried up, and our hope is lost; we are cut off completely" (37:11). Immediately, Ezekiel measures the death around him: very many bones and very dry bones. This is death to the core. Even Ezekiel, with his fertile imagination, which had depicted in detail the siege of Jerusalem on a brick, which had led him to climb through a wall in exile, which had conjured parables and allegories and erotic depictions of Israel's sordid dalliances with other nations—even with this imagination, Ezekiel cannot answer, "Yes," to God's question, "Son of *adam*, can these bones live?" (37:3). Life in such a valley of death is inconceivable even within the boundless imagination of Ezekiel.

And yet, in this valley of death the spirit has deposited him. In this valley, among these very many, very dry bones, the spirit will accomplish its most astounding act of vivification. In this valley, Ezekiel discovers hope, hope that resides in the presence and the power of the spirit:

> Then he said to me, "Prophesy to these bones, and say to them: O dry bones, hear the word of the LORD. Thus says the Lord GOD to these bones: I will cause *spirit* to enter you, and you shall live. I will lay sinews on you, and will cause flesh to come upon you, and cover you with skin, and put *spirit* in you, and you shall live; and you shall know that I am the LORD." (Ezek 37:4-6)[10]

With these words, Ezekiel peers beyond the cusp of death to a world with bones clattering, fresh sinews laid on the bones like a linen tablecloth, flesh layered on the sinews, and skin covering the flesh. Notwithstanding the vividness of this vision and the promise of the spirit, there is still "no spirit in them" (37:8). For these are not just the bones of those who died naturally, but the bones of those who were "slain," those who died under the curse of Deuteronomy, who have become an object of horror to all the kingdoms of the earth. "Your corpses shall be food for every bird of the air and animal of the earth, and there shall be no one to frighten them away" (Deut 28:25-26). These bones cannot, therefore, easily return to life. They cannot be raised as they had been, in the throes of sin and the pangs of disloyalty to God. Their dismemberment is due to disloyalty, and they cannot be brought back simply by being layered with sinews, flesh, and skin.

Ezekiel's ponderous repetition underscores the theme of this vision, that the spirit brings life to a dead nation in stages, each of which is punctuated by the promise or the presence of life brought about by the spirit within.

> I will cause *spirit* to enter you, and *you shall live*. (37:5)

> I will lay sinews on you, and will cause flesh to come upon you, and cover you with skin, and put *spirit* in you, and *you shall live*. (37:6)

> So I prophesied as I had been commanded; and as I prophesied, suddenly there was a noise, a rattling, and the bones came together, bone to its bone. I looked, and there were sinews on them, and flesh had come upon them, and skin had covered them; but there was no *spirit* in them. (37:7–8)

> Then he said to me, "Prophesy to the breath, prophesy, mortal, and say to the *spirit:* Thus says the Lord GOD: Come from the four winds, O *spirit*, and breathe into these slain, that *they may live*." I prophesied as he commanded me, and the *spirit* came into them, *and they lived*, and stood on their feet, a vast multitude. (Ezek 37:9-10)

This sequence, with its prediction of the spirit within followed by reconnection of bones and restoration of bodies followed by the perception that there is still no life, no spirit, followed still by the inbreathing of spirit, amply expresses the realization of how difficult the transition to a new national existence can be. Life-giving takes place in phases, from prediction to partial reality to complete fulfilment.

The Spirit and a New Eden

Israel's story-telling begins in Eden. Ezekiel's vision for recreation returns to Eden. In a renewed promise of the spirit after the final deportation of Israel's leaders to Babylon (Ezek 36:26-27), Ezekiel includes, quite understandably, the promise that the land will be restored:[11]

> Thus says the Lord GOD: On the day that I cleanse you from all your iniquities, I will cause the towns to be inhabited, and the waste places shall be rebuilt. The land that was desolate shall be tilled, instead of being the desolation that it was in the sight of all who passed by. And they will say, "This land that was desolate has become like the garden of Eden; and the waste and desolate and ruined towns are now inhabited and fortified." (Ezek 36:34-35)

This promise is rich with the imagery of Eden. The verb Ezekiel adopts to depict the inbreathing of Israel occurs earlier in the story of the first human's being inbreathed by God (Gen 2:7). Yet other reminiscences of

Eden are promised. The land will be tilled, as in Genesis 2:15. Those who pass by will take note of how the former wasteland is now like a garden of Eden. Even the ensuing vision of dry bones may contain a reminiscence of creation in Genesis 2:23. Ezekiel describes the initial connection of the bones with the words, "bone to its bone" (Ezek 37:7)—words that are familiar from the creation of woman, whom Adam recognizes as "bone of my bone." Though the resemblance is not exact, it is, nonetheless, evocative, for this expression appears now in a context that is rife with reminiscence: a new spirit enters Israel—which has been reconnected, bone to its bone—and brings them to life so that eventually they may again till their homeland and transform it into a region like the garden of Eden.

Ezekiel still clings to this extraordinary vision of the transformation of Israel's homeland into a pristine, Edenic state, despite three deportations to Babylon, devastation of the temple, forfeiture of land, capture of king. Such imagery, of course, is common in the book of Ezekiel. Ezekiel makes rich play of the story of Adam and Eve in his mock lamentation for the king of Tyre, whom Ezekiel describes as if he were Adam in the garden of Eden prior to a plummet into arrogance and violence:

> You were in Eden, the garden of God; every precious stone was your covering. . . . You were blameless in your ways from the day that you were created . . . I cast you as a profane thing from the mountain of God, and the guardian cherub drove you out. . . . (Ezek 28:13-16)

Ezekiel is himself addressed by the divine being as "son of *adam*" (2:1), a phrase that, even if it means merely "mortal," conjures up memories of the first *adam*, especially in its earliest occurrences. When he is first addressed in this way, Ezekiel, like the first *adam*, receives a spirit that sets him on his feet (Ezek 2:1-2; Gen 2:17). As a son of *adam*, moreover, Ezekiel accepts the divine charge to act as a sentinel or watchman for Israel: "Son of *adam*, I have made you a sentinel for the house of Israel. . . . I say to the wicked, 'You shall surely die,' and . . . give them no warning . . ." (Ezek 3:18). It is incumbent upon Ezekiel to repeat the words, "You shall surely die." With this warning, which occurs first and famously in Genesis 2:17, God makes clear the consequences for eating from the tree of the knowledge of good and evil.[12]

Ezekiel is never, ever prosaic. As a consequence, his perspective on Israel's recreation is no mere reiteration of the creation story. Salient among his innovations is the entrance of the spirit into a reconnected community. There is no single inbreathing into Adam's nostrils, but the spirit speeds its way from around the world, even as the exiles will be gathered from around the world to receive the spirit and to be restored to a land that they will till until it resembles Eden. This is a breathtaking vision that begins at the beginning of time and concludes in the certain future, when life comes full circle, when Israel receives the spirit within, when bone connects to bone, when the homeland is tilled and Eden restored. Eden comes around and recreation occurs, but only in the throes of grief. The grieving exiles hear the promise of a new heart and a new spirit. The survivors of catastrophe, the living dead in the valley of the shadow of death, will receive the spirit and begin, haltingly perhaps, life afresh.

Conclusion

Arguably the most dramatic vision in an altogether dramatic book is Ezekiel's tramping the valley of very many, very dry bones. The force of this vision notwithstanding, it must not eclipse other dimensions of the spirit in the book of Ezekiel. This vision, and the oracle which it fulfills (36–37), followed the Babylonian devastation of Jerusalem. In that period, so little was left to the Israelites that hope lay only in divine initiative, in the promise of divine cleansing, in the expectation of revitalization by the rushing of the spirit afresh into a vast gathering of reconnected bones, in the dream of tilling the land once again until it would become nothing less than a new Garden of Eden. When hope was still alive, in the wake of partial deportations but not yet in the face of a final national collapse, the thrust of the new spirit lay elsewhere. When it retained the note of promise to beleaguered exiles and rebuke to the arrogant inhabitants of Jerusalem, the promise of a new spirit was bound to the responsibility of returned exiles who would have to remove anything detestable in their homeland (11:17-21). For those who complained that God's ways were unfair, for those who claimed that their teeth were set on edge by the sour grapes their parents had eaten, Ezekiel had another message. Individual Israelites must turn from evil and make for themselves a new heart and a new spirit. They must not wait passively for a promise to be fulfilled. They must not pine away for a pristine future. They must not remain docile because they expect to receive a gift of life. On the contrary, they have a responsibility, right here and right now, to produce a new heart and a new spirit. "Why will you die," asks Ezekiel. "Turn, then, and live" (Ezek 18:31-32). To the plaintiffs who put God in the dock over the issue of fairness, then, the so-called promise of the eschatological spirit had the character of command. In brief, the promise of a new spirit offers no simple, spontaneous hope of recreation.

Even in Ezekiel 37, much lies underneath the surface in the folds of Ezekiel's vision. In this, the final vision of recreation in the valley of very many, very dry bones, recreation is a process that transpires in stages. First comes the promise of the spirit, then the promise of sinews, flesh and skin with spirit within. The fulfillment is not linear, not singular in its simplicity. Fulfillment begins with rattling bones that come together, covered with sinews and flesh and skin, though without the spirit within. These bodies are still empty of life. The spirit must be called, commanded, to the reconstituted body. There can, in other words, be the form of the body without spirit pulsing and moving within. At that stage of recreation, there is still no life. The third of the oracles of the new spirit within communicates, therefore, what the three do together: the process of recreation is powerful but protracted.[13]

If this study has an implication for Pauline scholarship, it is this: the Pauline conception of a "new creation" may be grounded in an even richer understanding of the spirit than what is offered by Ezekiel 37. Certain allusions to Ezekiel 37 in Paul's letters, in fact, are few—the clearest occurs in 1 Thessalonians 4:8, in which Paul concerns himself with sexual purity. In the absence of identifiable allusions to Ezekiel 37 in Paul's discussions of "new creation," Pauline scholars would do well to explore and incorporate the fullest complement of texts about the gifts of the spirit in the Ezekiel corpus and to embrace the complexity that underlies early Christian pneumatology.

Chapter 16

Sadducees, Zakokites,
and the Wisdom of Ben Sira

Jonathan Klawans

Instead of evincing a willful heresy to the tradition of the fathers, the Sadducean position actually reflected the converse. The Sadducees knew that when the Bible is interpreted literally there is scant evidence for any afterlife worth living.[1]—Alan Segal

Sadducees and Zadokites: What We Do and Do Not Know

The scholar who seeks a fuller understanding of the ancient Jewish Sadducees faces a number of challenges. Our source material is not extensive, and what we have is purely external: no *verifiably* Sadducean literature exists. Moreover, we can name surprisingly few Sadducees, and we know precious little about those rare figures—like the high priest Ananus—who are explicitly identified as Sadducees in our sources.[2] We are only slightly more fortunate when it comes to Sadducean doctrines. Josephus, to be sure, discusses their basic beliefs as compared to the Pharisees and Essenes in the well-known passages from *Antiquities* (13.171–73; 18.11–25) and *Jewish War* (2.119–66).[3] Further information can be derived from the New Testament (e.g., Acts 23:6-8). But our evidence remains less helpful than it might at first seem. Josephus's descriptions of Sadducean doctrines are largely negative: Pharisees affirm immortality; Sadducees deny it (*War* 2.165). The Pharisees observe unwritten legal traditions; the Sadducees reject these (*Ant.* 18.16). The Essenes affirm the power of fate; the Sadducees deny fate, too (*War* 2.163).[4] The meager information to be culled from the New Testament also serves to itemize the beliefs that the Sadducees reject (Matt 22:23; Mark 12:18; Luke 20:27; Acts 23:6-8).

Our sources are not only grammatically negative; they are substantially negative as well. According to our self-proclaimed Pharisaic historian, the Sadducees were boorish and rude (*War* 2.166).[5] It does not help matters that the Sadducees, according to Acts, appear to be at the wrong places at the wrong times (Acts 4:1, 5:17, 23:6–8).[6] Adding insult to injury, the rabbinic sources—at least as traditionally preserved[7]—also display hostility toward the Sadducees (e.g., *Sifre Numbers* §112; *b. Baba Bathra* 115b). The antagonism, unfortunately, does not end there. Jewish scholarship, since the days of *Wissenschaft des Judentums*, has endeavored, with some success, to rehabilitate the reputation of the Pharisees. Yet in many cases, the reevaluation of the Pharisees has come at the expense of the Sadducees. If not boorish and rude, they are hardly to be liked; their theology does not stand on principle, reflecting purely their social, aristocratic position. Louis Finkelstein, for instance, spoke blatantly of the "self-serving" views of the Sadducees, while the Pharisees inherited the mantle of the prophetic tradition.[8] More recently, Martin Goodman asserted that Sadducaism "embodies a smug self-congratulation about the status quo that only the rich could accept."[9]

But scholarship on the Sadducees can be more than unduly negative. It can also be unduly creative. Facing the relative absence of evidence, a number of scholarly myths regarding the Sadducees have surfaced. Perhaps the most significant of these is the claim that Sadducees were particularly committed to—and perhaps even named for—the line of descent from the priest Zadok who served both David and Solomon (2 Sam 8:17; 1 Kgs 1:8, 24-48, 2:35).[10] Prominent in scholarship since the days of Abraham Geiger (1810–1874),[11] this theory was adopted in some influential reference works[12] and continues to surface in overviews of ancient Judaism.[13] The theory played a particularly important role in the standard formulations of the Essene Hypothesis of Qumran origins.[14] Needless to say, centralizing Zadokite descent also plays an important role in recent works tracing the development of "Zadokite" (as opposed to "Enochic") Judaism.[15]

And yet, much about this hypothetical association of Sadducees with Zadokites remains unsubstantiated.[16] As far as the name "Sadducees" is concerned, it is important to remember that not a single ancient Jewish source associates this term with the Zadokite high priestly line. Those rabbinic (and Karaite) sources that do seek to explain the origins of the Sadducees' name all point to some later, nonpriestly figure named

"Zadok," who purportedly played some role in propagating what were to become characteristic Sadducean views, such as the rejection of life after death.[17] The early Christian "heresiologist" Epiphanius goes one step further than the Jewish sources by suggesting that the Zadok for whom the Sadducees might be named was a priest—but he, too, stops well short of explicitly pointing to the Zadok of David and Solomon's day.[18] Finally, the *Damascus Document* speaks of "Sons of Zadok" (e.g., III, 21–IV, 4) as well as an individual historical figure named "Zadok" (V, 5). While it remains entirely unclear who this Zadok was or when he lived, we can safely eliminate the priest of David and Solomon's day.[19] According to CD, David's sins were forgiven him because the law was hidden in his day, and not revealed until much later when Zadok appeared (V, 2–6). None of these sources, of course, is historical, and the only source listed above that reliably preserves perspectives from the Second Temple period (the *Damascus Document*) betrays no explicit connection with Sadducees. Still, the survey is sufficient to question the wisdom of assuming that the name "Sadducee" is to be associated with the Zadok of 2 Samuel and 1 Kings. The bulk of these sources would suggest—for what it is worth—that the eponymous founder Zadok lived much later, and was significant for his perspectives or achievements, not for his offspring.[20]

Indeed, there is also good reason to question whether the issue of Zadokite descent was as important to ancient Jews generally (or Sadducees specifically) as scholars assume. Not a single ancient Jewish source states that disputes over the genealogical descent of the high priesthood played any significant role in fomenting sectarian disputes among Second Temple period Jews. Geiger's creative theories seemed finally to find firm textual support when the *Rule of the Community* first appeared, with its references to the leadership of the sons of Zadok (1QS V, 2, 9; cf. 1QSa I, 2, 24; II, 3). Yet subsequent discoveries—including especially the Cave 4 manuscripts of the *Rule of the Community*, which lack specific mention of Zadokites—have raised serious questions regarding the centrality of Zadokite descent to the Qumran sect, at least with respect to the purported origins of the group in the early Maccabean era.[21] It is equally important to ask how precisely a presumably celibate sect could give great importance over any length of time to a priestly line of descent.[22] This leads us back to the *Damascus Document*, where the explicit discussion of Zadokites involves a decidedly nonliteral interpretation of Ezekiel 44:15: the reference to sons of Zadok is understood as a metaphor for the "chosen of Israel, called by the name, who will stand at the end of days" (CD V, 3–4).[23] Interestingly, even 1QS speaks repeatedly of the Sons of Righteousness (*b'nei zedeq*; 1QS III, 2, 22, cf. IX, 14). Whether the seemingly literal passages should be read in light of the clearly metaphorical ones remains unclear.

But even if, at some point, the sectarians assigned leadership positions to the sons of Zadok (in the plural), how can we easily extrapolate from this the notion that the ideal form of leadership in their mind was a *single* Zadokite *high* priest? Indeed *all* of our sources concerning Zadokites—and there are not all that many—speak of a *group* of Zadokite priests serving in the temple (e.g., Ezek 40:46, 43:19, 44:15, 48:11; Sir 51:12i[Heb]), or serving in some capacity at Qumran (e.g., 1QS V, 2, 9; 1QSa I, 2, 24; II, 3; 1QSb III, 22). Over against these sources are a greater number that assert the legitimacy of all the sons of Aaron to serve either at the temple (e.g., Pss 115:10, 12, 118:3, 135:19; 1 Chr 23:32–24:6; 2 Chr 13:10, 26:18, 35:14; Tob 1:7; Sir 45:6-24, 50:13, 16; Josephus, *Ant.* 20.225–26)[24] or in some capacity for the Qumran community (e.g., 1QS V, 21, IX, 7; 1QM VII, 10, XVII, 12; 4QMMT B 16–17, 79; 11QT XXXIV, 13).[25] Why is it that we lack even a single Second Temple period source that explicitly de-legitimizes non-Zadokite holders of the high priestly office?[26] It has recently been claimed that the general acceptance by ancient Jews of the Hasmonean line as legitimate may be explained in part because the Hasmoneans were in fact Zadokites.[27] This possibility is intriguing, and, of course, it is true that no source—including even the *Habakkuk Pesher* with its concern for the "wicked priest"—explicitly denies that this was the case. But no source explicitly affirms that the Maccabees were Zadokites either. There is, therefore, an even more intriguing possibility, one that equally fits the evidence (or, lack thereof): The Hasmoneans, and those priests who followed them in the Herodian Period,[28] were not descended from Solomon's priest Zadok, and no one—Sadducees included—cared a great deal about this particular issue. For most Jews, therefore—as for the authors of 1 and 2 Maccabees and Josephus—the Zadokites' displacement by the Hasmoneans was likely understood as an outcome well deserved, resulting from the sinful behavior described in these three sources. From what we are told about the Sadducees' aristocratic and priestly affiliations (e.g., *Ant.* 13.298; Acts 4:1), we have no reason to think that the Sadducees disagreed with other Jews on this matter.

The Sadducees and Wisdom: What We May Still Learn

Unless a truly Sadducean library should turn up, we can never hope to have more sources. Still, I think some progress can be made toward a better understanding of the sources we do have, and in the process a few matters regarding the ancient Sadducees might be clarified. It is striking that so much of the discussion of the Sadducees is based on speculation concerning their name and priestly affiliation, while comparatively little is spent on exploring the possible scriptural background of Sadducean Judaism. If one were to ask, quite simply, where one might look to explore the origins of a group that is commonly characterized as aristocratic, cosmopolitan, and conservative—all the while believing in freedom of choice, earthly justice, and the finality of death—one obvious candidate presents itself: the wisdom tradition of ancient Israel, as evidenced especially (but not exclusively) in the Wisdom of Ben Sira.

Although the question has not, to my knowledge, been put quite that way, a number of scholars have suggested in some fashion that there might be some connection between the Sadducees and the wisdom tradition. Long ago, Kaufman Kohler suggested that Ecclesiastes was composed by a Sadducee.[29] We have already had occasion to mention those who view Sirach as a Zadokite work; more pertinent to the present concern is the fact that some scholars have explicitly compared Ben Sira's theology with that of the Sadducees.[30] Among others, Alan Segal has noted the affinities between Ben Sira and the Sadducees in both *Rebecca's Children* and *Life after Death*.[31] Indeed, it was my recent reading of the latter that motivated me to reconsider this connection more deeply; it is likely that my reading of the former many years ago set the stage for my taking the connection seriously now.

Yet asserting some connection between the wisdom tradition and the later Sadducees is hardly commonplace. Most surveys of the Sadducees—excepting those mentioned above among some others, to be sure—say little or nothing about the wisdom tradition, and the converse is true for discussions of the wisdom tradition,[32] even those that seek to identify the heirs of wisdom among later Second Temple period groups or texts, such as apocalyptic literature, Gnostic sources, or Q.[33]

Of course, perhaps the most obvious divide between the Sadducees and the wisdom tradition is a chronological one. Proverbs, Job, and Ecclesiastes were likely composed by the Persian or during the early Hellenistic era; Sirach was likely composed before the Maccabean era.[34]

Only Wisdom of Solomon among the clearly identified wisdom documents takes us into the era of the Sadducees, but this document—with its fervent belief in immortality—can hardly be Sadducean and is likely a product of the Hellenistic Diaspora. Sirach, by contrast, circulated in Hebrew in the land of Israel at least until 73 C.E.—and thus could easily have been revered by and had influence over the Sadducees. Other extant wisdom works—such as Baruch 3:9–4:4—are of unknown date, but could easily stem from the late Second Temple period. Still other various wisdom works—both canonical and noncanonical—circulated in Judea as well, as evidenced by the Qumran finds.[35] We, therefore, easily find that the chronological barriers to reconsidering the relationship between the Sadducees and the wisdom tradition break down.

Another wedge can be driven between the Sadducees and the biblical wisdom tradition by recalling the claim that the Sadducees canonized only the Pentateuch.[36] This view is likely mistaken—stemming possibly from the Church Fathers' misunderstanding of Josephus (*Ant.* 18.297).[37] But even if it were correct (as seems unlikely) this hardly militates against reconsidering the connection between the Sadducees and the wisdom tradition, precisely because the greatest similarities are between them and the generally noncanonical Sirach. Another motivation for separating the wisdom tradition from the Sadducees is the claim—typically applied to Proverbs, Job, and Ecclesiastes (sans the pious epilogue)—that the wisdom tradition exhibits little concern with either the Mosaic covenant or the priestly cult.[38] But if that is true as far as these books go, the melding of wisdom with priestly and/or Mosaic concerns is evident in various Psalms (e.g., Pss 1, 34, 37, 73), Tobit 4:3-21, Sirach (e.g., 24:1-29), Wisdom of Solomon, and, of course, the epilogue to Ecclesiastes (12:12-14). Indeed, much of the discussion about the relationship between certain documents (e.g., Pss 34 and 37) and the wisdom tradition revolves around the question of whether a work that is rooted in the covenant and cult can be considered wisdom at all.[39] Of course, by the time of the Sadducees, the sustained effort aimed at integrating wisdom with Torah was long underway, as evidenced, once again, by the literature just mentioned, along with the appearance of wisdom documents at Qumran (where cult and covenant were surely taken seriously), and the canonization of Proverbs, Job, and Ecclesiastes in the third section of the Jewish Bible, alongside Torah and Prophets. Regardless of how noncultic and noncovenantal wisdom may have been in an earlier era, this cannot preclude the possibility that the synthesis espoused by Ben Sira and others had an influence on later Second Temple period Jewish sects such as the Sadducees.

A fourth impediment to the linkage between the Sadducees and wisdom is that Josephus makes no such connection. As we will see below, subtle connections do emerge from Josephus's description of the Sadducees. As for the lack of explicit discussions of wisdom concerns in Josephus's description of the Sadducees, we should just keep in mind that Josephus does not make much of the wisdom tradition anywhere in his oeuvre. The sage Jesus Ben Sira goes unmentioned, as do the books typically attributed to the wisdom tradition.[40] Even in his discussion of Solomon (*Ant.* 8.1–211)—which surely does highlight the monarch's legendary wisdom—Josephus does not discuss the books of Proverbs or Ecclesiastes, or make any mention of their purported Solomonic authorship.[41] Indeed, if we had to rely entirely on Josephus, we would have no reason to think that Second Temple Jewish wisdom literature existed. The fact that he makes no explicit mention of wisdom with regard to Sadducees, therefore, becomes the kind of absence of evidence that yields nothing but an argument from silence.

A fifth impediment to establishing links between the Sadducees and the wisdom tradition has less to do with our sources and more to do with ourselves. It seems, simply, that scholarship has not been interested in making such a connection. Perhaps there is insufficient overlap in the interests of those who work in the realms of wisdom literature and ancient Jewish sects. Perhaps the hypothesis of the wisdom-apocalyptic connection has absorbed whatever energy there is for exploring echoes of wisdom in late Second Temple Judaism.[42] Perhaps scholars are too focused on the wisdom tradition as a singular, skeptical, phenomenon to entertain the possibility that there could be more than one heir to the tradition.[43] Or perhaps scholars are insufficiently interested in the possibility that Ben Sira's synthesis spoke to post-Maccabean Second Temple period priests and aristocrats. Of course it is also possible that I am entirely incorrect in taking this connection seriously. If so, I hope that scholarship can at least learn from this mistake.

The sections that follow seek to establish that the connection between the wisdom tradition and the Sadducees is worth taking seriously. Without much difficulty, we can find within the wisdom tradition—and principally within the Wisdom of Ben Sira—precise analogues to practically every perspective that Josephus attributes to the Sadducees. As we proceed with this demonstration, we will also find the opportunity to go some steps further, venturing to clarify some of Josephus's more ambiguous statements with what we find more clearly articulated in wisdom texts. Of course, venturing to fill in the gaps left in Josephus's testimony is a perilous business; speculative gap-filling was precisely what was criticized above with regard to the Zadokites. But below, the gap-filling will proceed in a more disciplined fashion. In what follows we will restrain ourselves to working with demonstrable thematic parallels between the wisdom tradition and Josephus's descriptions of the Sadducees. Moreover, in the conclusion we will carefully distinguish between well-established parallels and more inferential ones. Having already stated that Josephus's descriptions are in need of fuller nuance, it is worth considering whether what we find in Sirach can possibly allow us to better understand some of the doctrines ascribed to the Sadducees all too briefly by Josephus.

What the Wise Aristocrats Deny

That Ben Sira does not affirm any of the distinctly Pharisaic notions as described by Josephus should be obvious to any careful reader. There is no beatific immortality of the soul—and certainly no resurrection of the dead (*Ant.* 18.16; cf. Sir 14:12-19, 38:16-23). There is no authoritative body of oral tradition passed down through the generations (*Ant.* 13.297–98; cf. Sir 24:23-33, 38:34–39:11). And there is no effort at fusing fate with free will: human beings are entirely responsible for their behavior and destiny (see below). These observations in and of themselves cannot, of course, translate into the assertion that Sirach is a Sadducean work. Even if such an assertion were not wildly anachronistic, it would still be methodologically unsound: the absence of Pharisaism is not the definition of Sadducaism.

But there is more to this claim than what the wisdom book lacks. Sirach is a cosmopolitan, aristocratic work—characteristics that are common to both the later Sadducees and the earlier wisdom tradition. What is more, Ben Sira at times expresses his disdain for the foolish, sluggish, or unruly in ways that are downright snobbish (e.g., 21:12–22:10, 22:13–15)—could this be, perhaps, the kind of attitude that Josephus had in mind when he referred to the Sadducees as boorish (*War* 2.166)? Indeed, with regard to the nature of the Sadducees, Josephus also tells us that it is their nature to dispute with their teachers of wisdom (*Ant.* 18.16)[44]—is Josephus's reference to the Sadducees' teachers' wisdom here a hint that should be followed?

The Finality of Death, and the Underworldly Afterlife of Sheol

Turning to what we can say positively about the Sadducees, we find further reason to think in the direction that Josephus points us in *Antiquities* 18.16. As just noted, Josephus tells us that the Sadducees reject the characteristically Pharisaic beliefs in immortality of the soul (*Ant.* 18.16) and postmortem punishments for the wicked and rewards for the righteous (*War* 2.165). In other words, they believe in the finality of death.

This, of course, is precisely what we find in the wisdom tradition of ancient Israel. The Wisdom of Ben Sira preserves a number of reflections on death. Death awaits all (14:17; 17:30; 38:22; 41:1-4), is final (10:10-11; 38:21; 41:4), and is not particularly worth looking forward to (7:17; 10:11; 14:11-19). On a few occasions, Ben Sira speaks of bodily decomposition as the punishment for sinners (7:17, 10:11, 21:9). But presumably, Ben Sira is not suggesting that the wicked suffer after death in a particularly distinct way; the point seems to be, rather, that the sinners will slip to their deaths early (21:9), or after some well-deserved earthly suffering (11:25-28). Everyone's end is in Sheol, where there will be no pleasure (14:16), no praise for God (17:27-28), and no argument (41:4; cf. Eccl 9:10). The only ways around mortality are to be survived by progeny (Sir 30:4–5; 40:19, 44:12–13) and to be remembered for righteousness by subsequent generations (41:11-13; 44:14-15). Yet Ben Sira hardly denies afterlife in all its forms. The nonbeatific, nondualistic afterlife that characterizes those few biblical passages that do speak of Sheol (e.g., 1 Sam 28; Job 7:9-10, 17:13-16; Eccl 9:10)[45] is precisely what Ben Sira affirms (esp. 14:12-19 and 41:1-4, both extant largely in Hebrew).

With good reason, we can surmise that the Sadducees—with their reverence for scripture and their conservative theology—would have held similar views, including a belief in Sheol.[46] In order to be fully understood, the Sadducean denial of immortality needs to be translated into a number of distinct affirmative statements. First, the Sadducees affirm—precisely as Josephus puts it—that the soul and body *perish together* (*Ant.* 18.16; cf. Bar 3:19). This is not an absolute denial of all forms of immortality—what they deny (*War* 2.165) is that the soul could persist after death apart from the body. The Sadducees affirm—in line with the general biblical record—that human life consists of an inseparable amalgam of what others (including Josephus) will refer to separately as body and soul.⁴⁷ For the Sadducees, death is a unitary experience: body and soul (which Sadducees would not separate) together descend to Hades (= Sheol).

Josephus also tells us that the Sadducees denied that either rewards or punishments await the deceased in Hades (*War* 2.165). Once again, it is important to pay careful attention to precisely what is and is not denied. The Sadducees' rejection of rewards and punishments in the underworld does not need to mean—and most likely does not mean—that they rejected belief in an underworld altogether. The Sadducees' approach to death is unitary in this second way, too. They would likely affirm that Sheol is the "democracy of death,"⁴⁸ where the wicked and righteous reside together, for eternity, in a shady afterlife—precisely what we find in Sirach (38:21-24), and indeed in much of the wisdom tradition (e.g., Job 17:13-16; Eccl 9:10-11).

Wealth and Earthly Justice

Having considered two important parallels between Josephus's Sadducees and the wisdom tradition—that both affirm the finality of death and that the same destiny awaits the righteous and wicked alike—we turn now to the corollary of this second notion: the belief in earthly justice. Josephus intimates as much when he tells us (*Ant.* 13.173) that the Sadducees believe "we ourselves are responsible for our well-being, while we suffer misfortune through our own thoughtlessness" (ἀβουλία; cf. Prov [LXX] 14:17, Bar 3:28). Apparently, Josephus is telling us that the Sadducees believe that the righteous and wicked are punished in this world. This, of course, is a perspective that is commonly expressed in the wisdom tradition (e.g., Prov 10:27-31; Sir 16:1-23, 39:28-31, 40:12-17).

Josephus does not give us any further indication as to how precisely this earthly justice was meted out. Because of their aristocratic status, it is commonly inferred (as already noted above) that the Sadducees would have viewed their wealth as a sign of divine approval. There is, to be sure, some confirmation of this view in the wisdom tradition: wealth is one of the ways in which the righteous wise could be rewarded in this world (e.g., Prov 11:18, 24-26; 13:4; Job 1:1-10, 42:10-17; Sir 29:1-13, 31:8-11), and with some reason we can assume that wealthy Sadducees may have viewed their wealth as a gift bestowed by God (cf. Eccl 5:18). But even a cursory reading of the wisdom tradition should caution against the supposition that the Sadducees—or other ancient Jews for that matter—would have viewed current wealth as an assured or irrevocable reward for righteousness. One thread running throughout the wisdom tradition is the recognition that the current state of affairs by no means reflects God's final judgment: fortunes can change suddenly and rapidly (e.g., Prov 13:11; Eccl 4:14; 5:12-13; 9:12; Sir 11:4-6, 27-38, 18:25-28, 22:23-26). Moreover, to whatever degree wealth is one way in which God may choose to bestow blessings on the righteous, there are certainly many other methods as well including illness (Sir 38:9-15, see also 30:14-17), natural disasters (39:28-31), mental anguish (40:1-10), and a premature (21:10) or painful (11:27-29) death. Because God views discipline as a value, at times, the righteous are tested with suffering, such as disease or poverty (Prov 3:12; Job 1:13–2:10; Sir 2:1; 4:17; 44:20). Precisely because of the complexities involved, the wisdom texts across the board deny that humans can know at any given time their status in God's eyes (Prov 20:9; Eccl 3:11; Sir 5:4–6; 7:5).

The claim that the Sadducees viewed their wealth as a positive sign of God's favor is—like the Zadokite hypothesis—an unjustified inference. In this case, the juxtaposition of Josephus's Sadducees with the wisdom tradition reminds us that even a rich person can be made miserable by illness, anguish, or other sufferings, and life brings constant surprises. Surely the Sadducees knew this, just as Ben Sira did. There is, therefore, no basis for asserting that the Sadducees would, as a matter of course, see their wealth as a God-given reward for unquestionable merit.

Free Will and Human Responsibility

Josephus states that the Sadducees deny fate a role in determining human affairs (*Ant.* 13.173; *War* 2.164). In these passages, Josephus also translates this denial into the positive assertion that the Sadducees believe in free will. Josephus sets up a direct opposition between the Sadducees and the Essenes, for the latter assert that fate is the mistress of all (*Ant.* 13.172, 18.18). The Pharisees, for their part, hold that both fate and freewill play a role in governing human affairs (*Ant.* 13.172, 18.13; *War* 2.162-63).

The benefits of comparing Ben Sira in particular with Josephus's Sadducees can best be seen by juxtaposing the evidence just cited with Sirach 15:11-20:[49]

(11) Say not, "It was God's doing that I fell away";
         for what he hates, he does not do.

(12) Say not, "It was he who led me astray";
      for he has no need of the sinful.

(13) Abominable wickedness the Lord hates;
      he does not let it befall those who fear him.

(14) It was he from the first, when he created humankind,
      who made them subject to their own free choice.

(15) If you choose, you can keep his commandment
      fidelity is the doing of his will.

(16) There are poured out before you fire and water;
      to whichever you choose you can stretch forth your hands.

(17) Before each person are life and death;
      whichever one chooses will be given him.

(18) For great is the wisdom of the Lord;
      he is mighty in power and sees everything;

(19) The eyes of God see his handiwork
      and he knows every person's action.

(20) He has not commanded anyone to be wicked
      nor will he be lenient with liars.

What we find in this passage is the clear combination of three related, but separable, ideas: the freedom of choice (esp. vv. 14–17), the denial that anyone could be destined to do evil (vv. 11–12, 20) and God's absolute opposition to evil (vv. 13, 20). This combination of ideas is strikingly similar to Josephus's assertion that the Sadducees "do away with Fate altogether, and remove God beyond not merely the commission, but the very sight of evil. They maintain that man has the free choice of good and evil . . ." (*War* 2.164–65).

Once again, the similarity of the two passages allows us better to build on Josephus's descriptions by translating Sadducean beliefs into positive statements and by identifying various scriptural parallels to these views, especially from within the wisdom literature. Not only do the Sadducees deny fate, they affirm freedom of choice (cf. Prov 1:1–8:29).[50] Moreover, their denial of fate and their affirmation of human freedom are both related to the declaration that God is wholly good. He detests evil and participates not in its propagation (cf. e.g., Prov 6:16-19; 11:1, 20; 12:22; 15:9, 26; 16:5; 17:15). Responsibility for evil, therefore, lies purely with human beings. Divine justice, therefore, comes as a deserved punishment to those who freely choose to perform evil deeds. According to the Sadducean view—and before that, according to Sirach—those who believe that some people are predestined to be wicked have fundamentally misunderstood the inherent and immutable goodness of God. Presumably even the Pharisees—in their efforts to balance fate and free will, in order to allow for God's knowledge of the future—give too much credence to fate, and end up ascribing too much evil to God. For the Sadducees, presumably, evil comes not from above, but *exclusively* from poor human decisions. The polemic nature of Ben Sira's statements here—note the repeated "do not say"—serves, in turn, as a striking confirmation that Second Temple period Jews were, indeed, disputing over precisely those issues that, according to Josephus, characterized the differences among Pharisees, Sadducees, and Essenes.

Two problems arise when comparing Sirach 15 with Josephus's description of the Sadducees. The first stems from the one clear contrast between them: Ben Sira asserts, along with earlier wisdom traditions, that God sees all and knows when evil is committed (Prov 15:3; Job 34:21-22). Josephus, by contrast, implies that God is removed in some fashion from even seeing evil (*War* 2.164). Indeed, it is precisely with regard to this extreme statement by Josephus that some have asserted that Sadducaism must have amounted to atheism in practice, if not quite in theory: their God was without concern for human morality.[51] However, the truth of Josephus's description as it stands is difficult to accept: if God were removed from the sight of evil, would he not also be removed from the sight of any good? Would not that mean (against *Ant.* 13.173) that there would be no form of even earthly justice? So how do we explain this contradiction? Two possibilities present themselves: the stronger one is that Josephus (or his source) is exaggerating the matter, for polemical or simply rhetorical purposes.[52] Another possibility is that Josephus's comments were influenced by or developed from the biblical idea of God hiding his face from his people, in the event that they choose not to follow God's ways (e.g., Deut 31:17, 18; 32:20; cf. Isa 29:2).[53] Although I find the latter idea tantalizing, I have not been able to find any clear textual linkage between Josephus's description of the Sadducees' beliefs and the biblical notion of God hiding his face. This brings us back to the possibility that Josephus or his sources are exaggerating the Sadducean view in this case.[54]

The second challenge to a comparison between the wisdom book and Josephus's Sadducees comes from another passage in Sirach (33:7-15):[55]

> (7) Why is one day more important than another,
>   when the same sun lights up every day of the year?
> (8) By the Lord's knowledge they are kept distinct;
>   among them he designates seasons and feasts.
> (9) Some he exalts and sanctifies,
>   and others he lists as ordinary days.

(10) So, too, all people are of clay,
     for from earth humankind was formed;
(11) Yet in the fullness of his understanding the Lord makes people unlike:
     in different paths he has them walk.
(12) Some he blesses and makes great,
     some he sanctifies and draws to himself.
    Others he curses and brings low,
     and expels them from their place.
(13) Like clay in the hand of a potter,
     to be molded according to his pleasure,
    So are people in the hands of their Maker,
     to be requited according as he judges them.
(14) As evil contrast with good, and death with life,
     so are sinners in contrast with the just;
(15) See now all the works of the Most High:
     they come in pairs, the one the opposite of the other.

At first reading, the passage has a deterministic sound to it (cf. also 42:24). According to some interpreters, this passage can even be compared to the "Treatise of the Two Spirits" from the *Rule of the Community*.[56] The appearance, therefore, of an ostensibly deterministic passage such as this within the same work as another emphasizing free choice (15:11-20) leads some interpreters to see in Sirach a precursor to the fusion of fate and free will seen in Josephus's description of the Pharisees as well as in some passages of rabbinic literature (e.g., *m. Abot* 3.15).[57]

The resolution of this difficulty is to be found in a careful re-reading of Sirach 33, which demonstrates that determinism is far from the sage's mind here. The juxtaposition of holy and profane days (vv. 7-9) with holy and cursed people (vv. 10-12) is not meant to suggest that God has determined in advance the actions of individual sinners. The juxtaposition, rather, serves to explain the nature of divine election: just as the Sabbath is holy among days, so, too, the Jewish people are holy among peoples. There is, of course, a deterministic element to the idea of divine election; people cannot choose to be born as Jews or Gentiles. But whatever element of determinism there is in such a notion, this passage hardly articulates ideas that the Sadducees would have rejected. Surely they, too, believed that God had chosen Abraham and established a covenant that continues to separate the Jewish people from the other nations. Once again, we find that Josephus's brief statements must be qualified, and that the wisdom tradition helps us do so. What Josephus likely means when he says that Sadducees denied fate is something along what we find in Sirach 15: God has not destined anyone to sin, and each individual chooses to be righteous or wicked. The Saducean view is unlikely to have involved a denial of divine election, and thus nothing we find in Sirach 33 militates against comparing (without identifying) the positions articulated in the wisdom book with the views attributed to the Sadducees by Josephus.

Conclusion

The foregoing analysis has identified a number of clear parallels between Josephus's description of the Sadducees and the Wisdom of Ben Sira. Both hold that death is final, that divine justice is earthly, that human beings exercise the free choice to do good or evil, and that no one is fated to do evil. In addition to these clear parallels, it seems reasonable to infer that the Sadducees would have also agreed with Wisdom of Ben Sira to the effect that the righteous and wicked persist after death together, unhappily, in Sheol. While wealth at times may be a divine blessing, it is not a clear sign of God's pleasure with a person. Divine justice is not immediate; life brings too many surprises (including illness, natural disasters, and other rapid changes in fortune) for anyone to be certain that God's will is reflected in the current economic realities. It is also likely that the Saducean denial of fate is related to the desire to remove God from evil: the assertion of free choice not only preserves God's justice (by deeming human punishment to be truly deserved) but also God's righteousness (God is wholly good and detests all evil). The belief in free choice, however, is slightly tempered by the generally agreed notion of divine election; like practically all Jews in their day, the Sadducees along with Ben Sira asserted that God separated Israel from the nations as a holy people, just as the Sabbath is designated as a holy day.

I would argue, therefore, that there is very good reason for further serious consideration by scholars of the possible connections between the Sadducees and the wisdom tradition. Those who have recognized the connection—Alan Segal among them—are, indeed, on the right path. The possibility that the Sadducees' views rest more on principle than on their social standing is an important corrective to the tendency blindly to identify certain theological positions with an unthinking aristocracy. Moreover, the close affinity between the views of the Sadducees and the wisdom tradition presents us with an intriguing alternative to the problematic hypothesis connecting Sadducees with Zadokites. If we are to seek a putative ancestor for a late Second Temple period Jewish sect among figures from the early First Temple Israelite period—an exercise that may be entirely unjustified, in any case—we can, with some good reason, assert that the true founding father of the Sadducees was not Zadok the priest, but his boss, the putative founder of the wisdom tradition as a whole, Israel's sage-king Solomon.

Chapter 17

On the Changing Significance of the Sacred

Rachel Elior

"Sacred geography" has been a characteristic of religious creativity in diverse cultures from antiquity to the present. The term refers to the singling out of a particular place, to the exclusion of others, in mythological, cultic, or literary contexts linked to divine revelation or appearance of an angel, election, unique sanctity, and an etiological story whose importance transcends the boundaries of time and space.[1] This sacred geography, which is tied to mythological recollections and the crystallization of a unique national-religious identity,[2] is not confined to terrestrial realms and actual spaces. On occasion, it has cosmic and cosmographic dimensions. It bases the uniqueness of the sacred terrestrial place in its connection to its cosmic, mythic, or celestial counterpart, situated beyond time and space. And it grounds its premises in sacred writings derived from a heavenly source.[3]

Because of the importance and centrality of sacred sites—where heaven and earth touch and the divine appears on earth—and because of their links to supernal worlds, cosmic contexts, and terrestrial force-centers—their locations and names are not always the subject of universal agreement within their traditions, which evolve and change over the years. In some instances, the changing traditions regarding sacred sites appear to reflect not chance variation over the course of time but altered hegemonic structures or deliberate changes in the foci of identity and memory. Changing forms of literary expression that recast the myth and use novel imagery to portray the past can emphasize certain dimensions of the story and downplay others in the interest of expunging them from historical memory. Not infrequently, these changes reflect various stages of polemic and dispute over the sacred traditions and their terrestrial representations in changing historical circumstances.

In the Jewish culture of antiquity, the sacred place—that is, the place
associated with God's dwelling, divine or angelic revelation, covenant
and temple, cultic sacrifice, and the *aqedah*—was identified with two
mountains: Mount Moriah and Mount Zion. The relationship between
the two is far from clear. No mountainn today bears the name "Mount
Moriah"; that mountain is usually referred to as the "Temple Mount."[4]
The only circles today in which the Temple Mount is referred to as
"Mount Moriah" are those associated with *Makhon ha-Miqdash* and
Ne'emane Har Habayit, groups that want to return to the mountain and
build the Third Temple.[5] Meanwhile, the biblical-period sources
throughout the first millennium B.C.E. speak not of the Mount Zion
that is known to us today as the site of David's Tomb[6] and the Dormition
Abbey. They refer, rather, to the mountain that is today called the
"Temple Mount." During the first millennium B.C.E., that mountain
was the subject of diverse traditions and was known as *sela ẕiyyon* (Rock
of Zion), *har ṯsiyyon* (Mountain of Zion), or *har haqodesh* (the Holy
Mountain or the Mountain of the Holy.)[7] In the study that follows,
which pertains only to antiquity and aspects of late antiquity, I attempt
to show that the changes in the name of the sacred place and in the
memories associated with it are connected to a dispute among various
groups over the essential nature of the sacred place, the sacred time, and
the sacred memory.[8]

Sacred Geography in Second Chronicles

The biblical book Second Chronicles[9] tells that King Solomon built his
Temple on Mount Moriah: "Then Solomon began to build the house of
the Lord at Jerusalem in mount Moriah where [the Lord] appeared unto
David his father; for which provision had been made in the Place of
David, in the threshing-floor of Ornan the Jebusite."[10] The tradition
about the appearance of an angel of God in the threshing floor of Ornan
the Jebusite during the time of David, and the divine response to the sacrifice David brought there (2 Sam 24:18-25; 1 Chr 21:15-16, 18-30;
22:1) cannot, on its face, account for Mount Moriah as the name used
in Chronicles for the site of the Temple.

The book of Genesis, of course, mentions "the Land of Moriah" in
connection with a mountain, an altar, a burnt offering, and an angel's
revelation to Abraham. It is the site of the offering known in Jewish tradition as the *aqedah*: "And He said: 'Take your son, your favored one,
Isaac, whom you love, and go to the land of Moriah, and offer him there

as a burnt offering on one of the mountains that I will point out to you"
(Gen 22:2). LXX omits any reference to the Land of Moriah: "[A]nd go
into the high land, and offer him there for a whole burnt offering."[11] The
omission is prominent as well in the parallel account in *Jubilees* 18:2:
"[G]o into the high land [*erets ramah*] and offer him up on one of the
mountains that I will make known to you."

In calling the site of the altar in early monarchic times—associated
with the appearance to David of an angel of God (2 Sam 24:16-18,
25)—by the name of the site of the offering and angel's appearance in
patriarchal times, the Chronicler may have meant to invest Solomon's
Temple on Mount Moriah with the sacred memory of the site of the
aqedah in the Land of Moriah. He may have intended likewise to associate the site with the recollection of a founding moment in the life of
the nation and an eternal covenant between God and His people. On the
other hand, it is possible that the reference to the Land of Moriah was
inserted into MT's account of the *aqedah* in Genesis (as noted, it is lacking in the pre-Common-Era versions) in order to tie the site of the
Temple and altar in Chronicles to the site of the *aqedah* and the altar of
burnt offering in Genesis.

The alternative tradition that identifies Mount Zion as the holy
mountain and dwelling place of God is much more widely attested.
Mount Moriah, as noted, is referred to only once in the context of
"God's house," and that reference appears in Chronicles, a late composition, in an allusion to the binding of Isaac on the altar of burnt offerings.
Mount Zion, in contrast, is referred to frequently, in traditions that predate the composition of Chronicles by hundreds of years.[12] Moreover, we
know of second-century-B.C.E. traditions that explicitly identify Mount
Zion as the site of the *aqedah* and conclude the account with a verse
echoing the one in Genesis but making a significant change: "And
Abraham called that place 'the Lord has seen,' so that it is said 'in the
mountain the Lord has seen.' It is Mount Zion" (*Jub.* 18:13). These traditions also see Mount Zion as "the navel of the earth" and the sacred
dwelling-place of the deity (*Jub.* 8:19); the place where God was revealed
to Abraham (*Jub.* 18:14-16); and as the place where the angel of the presence appeared at the time of the *aqedah*. Beyond that, the tradition
recorded in the Dead Sea Scrolls emphatically ties "the rock of Zion" to
"the House of the Lord, the God of Israel," Mount Zion to the Temple,
and Zion to "the community of the children of righteousness," as we
shall see below.

Sacred Geography in the Prophets and Psalms

In the early prophetic books and in Psalms, Mount Zion is referred to dozens of times as the holy mountain in Jerusalem or as the place selected by God to be sanctified as His dwelling: "from the Lord of Hosts, who dwells on Mount Zion" (Isa 8:18); or "At the place where the name of the Lord of Hosts abides, at Mount Zion" (Isa 18:7; cf. Isa 24:23; Mic 4:7; Isa 31:4; Ps 132:13-14). It is explicitly referred to as the place of eternal blessing—"like the dew of Hermon that falls upon the mountains of Zion. There the Lord ordained blessing, everlasting life" (Ps 133:3; cf. Ps 134:3) —and as the site of divine revelation: (Ps 50:2). Of course, Zion was not limited in biblical memory to the holy site. It became transformed into a synonym for the City of David and a cognomen of Jerusalem. Still, "Mount Zion," for the most part, is a synonym for the holy mountain, the place where the divine and the terrestrial touch.[13]

During the time of King Hezekiah and the Assyrian King Sennacherib, Isaiah's prophecies of destruction portray Mount Zion as a place fraught with meaning,[14] and the site is similarly treated in the prophecies of consolation associated with the redemption or the return to Zion.[15] It is mentioned as the site of God's sovereignty and his holy mountain in various prophecies that clearly convey the identity between the holy mountain and Mount Zion;[16] "And you shall know that I the Lord your God dwell in Zion, my holy mount";[17] "Blow a horn in Zion, sound an alarm on my holy mount."[18]

Interestingly, not one of the preexilic references to Mount Zion limits God's place to a particular building. Instead, they all relate God's dwelling place to the entire mountain, known as "Mount Zion" or "My holy mountain," and make no mention of the Temple.[19]

Texts composed after the destruction of Solomon's Temple in 586 B.C.E. refer to the dirge imagery in Lamentations, which was used repeatedly in rabbinic literature and *midrash* to convey the intensity of the disaster: "Because of Mountain Zion, which lies desolate, jackals prowl over it."[20] The image is connected to Third Isaiah's description of the contrast between the source of life and the wasteland: "Your holy cities have become a desert: Zion has become a desert, Jerusalem a desolation. Our holy Temple, our pride, where our fathers praised you, has been consumed by fire; and all that was dear to us is ruined" (Isa 64:9-10).

The history of desolation and consolation in regard to the second temple on Mount Zion is further attested at the end of the second and during the first century B.C.E. in the books of Maccabees, where the temple on Mount Zion is mentioned as the focus of the Maccabean revolt: "'Behold, our enemies are crushed; let us go up to cleanse the sanctuary and dedicate it.' So all the army assembled and they went up to Mount Zion. And they saw the sanctuary desolate, the altar profaned, and the gates burned" (1 Macc 4:26-40, esp. vss. 36, 37, 38; cf. 5:54; 7:33).

The post-Second-Temple liturgical tradition expressed painfully the profound connection between God's sacred dwelling place and its various names related to Zion.[21] But even much earlier traditions, composed while the Second Temple was still in all its glory, contain striking associations between Mount Zion and the sacred site. These expand the biblical tradition, suggest an alternative recollection to that known from rabbinic traditions, and clarify the nature of the sanctity associated with it.

Sacred Geography and Qumran

A further set of references to God's dwelling place appears in the multifaceted priestly literature found in the Qumran scrolls—written and preserved in Hebrew and Aramaic during the final centuries B.C.E. by the "the priests of the House of Zadok and the keepers of their covenant"[22]—and in the translations of *Enoch, Jubilees*, and the *Testament of the Twelve Patriarchs*, known before their Hebrew and Aramaic originals were discovered. In these texts, God's heavenly dwelling place, seemingly above Mount Zion, is described as a celestial garden, an expansive source of life encompassing mountains, trees of life, running water, fragrant trees, and holy angels. It is described as well as a house whose expanse extends beyond the boundaries of time and space and that encompasses the chariot and cherubim. The garden is linked to the place from which life flows and to the source of eternal blessing, a sacred expanse where the divine is present and on which death holds no grip, a place subject to no earthly temporal flaws and where the holy angels serve in eternal order.

Jubilees briefly defines the garden and describes its sacred character in association to the sanctuary: "And he knew that the garden of Eden was the holy of holies and the dwelling of the Lord" (8:18); ". . . the garden of Eden because it is more holy than any land. And every tree which is planted in it is holy" (3:12).[23] It also applies the purity restrictions to this garden that are associated with the sanctity of the Temple (3:9-13).

The Thanksgiving Scroll describes the mystery within the sacred garden: "a watered garden, a plantation of cypress, pine and cedar for Thy glory, trees of life beside a mysterious fountain."[24] This sacred garden, which reflects the eternity of life and the link between eternity and righteousness, is also called "the Garden of Eden," "the Garden of Righteousness," "the Eternal Plantation," and "the Garden of Truth [pardes qushta]."[25] The garden that contains "trees of life" and the "fountain of life," which transcend bounds of time and space, is thus tied to the place beyond time that contains the chariot and holy cherubim.[26] It is also tied to eternal time, reflected in the quarterly and annual natural cycles observed by the angels and known as the "chariots of heaven,"[27] and to weekly cycles known as the "times of the Lord," the "times of righteousness," and the "times of freedom."

The Temple ("house") is connected to a sacred and pure place, situated beyond the boundaries of time and space. The divine is present there, and death has no dominion over it. It exists in both the celestial and terrestrial expanses. In both the "garden" and the "house," the divine presence is tied to the "holy cherubim," the "vision of the cherubim," the "fiery cherubim," or the "chariot of the cherubim," termed the "image of the throne-chariot" or the "firmament of the cherubim." The mystical-liturgical world of the celestial chariot is described in "Songs of the Sabbath Sacrifice," which describe the sacred place and the cycles of sanctified time in 4Q405 20–21–22, lines 6-14, and the following passage.

> The cherubim bless the image of the throne-chariot above the firmament, [and] they praise [the majes]ty of the luminous firmament beneath His seat of glory. When the wheels advance, angels of holiness come and go. From between His glorious wheels, there is as it were a fiery vision of most holy spirits. . . . The whispered voice of blessing accompanies the roar of their advance, and they praise the Holy One on their way of return.[29]

The chariot or the cherubim represent the sacred, eternal, divine source of life and the hidden divine presence; they are to be found in the Garden of Eden, in which grow "trees of life," "holy trees," and fragrant trees,[30] and their sacred representation is to be found in the holy of holies in the Temple on Mount Zion.

Situated at the summit of the holy mountain, the Temple is maintained in a strict state of purity that safeguards eternal life and distances it from death. This is necessary because the divine is present within the Temple, linked both to the chariot of the cherubim—which corresponds to the cherubim in the Garden of Eden, to the "trees of life in the fountain of secrets" and to "the fountain of life"[31]—and to the liturgical cycles, which perpetuate the visible and audible cycles of time during which the creatures of the chariot and the holy angels sing praises, as described in *Hymns for the Sabbath Sacrifice*.

The terrestrial Temple is the center for maintaining the sacred cycle of life and for preserving eternal, cyclical time, connected to the weekly and quarterly cultic cycles maintained by the assigned groups of priests who bring the fixed sacrifices and burn incense on a fixed cycle corresponding to the cycles of song described in the Psalms Scroll.[32] The celestial sanctuary—containing cherubim, chariot, holy angels, trees of life, and fragrant incense trees, cultic and liturgical cycles—and the terrestrial sanctuary, with its cherubim, chariot, incense-burning priests, and cultic and liturgical cycles, are experienced, on the one hand, as the Garden of Eden, the "garden of truth," the "garden of righteousness," and the world of the celestial chariot, and, on the other hand, as the Temple, "My holy mountain" the "holy of holies," the place of the cherubim (Exod 25; 1 Kgs 6:23-27; 2 Chr 3:10-14). These two sacred venues are linked by various cosmographic, mythic, mystic, and liturgical traditions.[33]

The sacred place in its terrestrial context is dramatically described at the beginning of the book of *Jubilees*, where it is explicitly linked to Mount Zion. After the giving of the Torah, as Moses stands on Mount Sinai, God's mountain in the desert, God depicts for him the future when the Temple will be created on Mount Zion, God's Mountain in Jerusalem, whose sanctity is given three-fold mention: "And I shall build my *sanctuary* (*miqdash*) in their midst, and I shall dwell with them. And I shall be their God and they will be my people truly and rightly . . . until my *sanctuary* is built in their midst forever and ever. And the Lord will appear in the sight of all. And everyone will know that I am the God of Israel and the father of all the children of Jacob and king upon Mount Zion forever and ever. And Zion and Jerusalem will be holy . . . until the *sanctuary of the* LORD is created in Jerusalem upon *Mount Zion*."[34]

Jubilees provides a priestly retelling of biblical history from creation to the encounter at Sinai; it presents that history as a course of forty-nine "jubilees," each forty-nine years in duration (cf. Lev 25:10). According to its account, Mount Zion is one of the four places in which God dwells. These places are described to Moses, as he stands on Mount Sinai, in the words of an angel of the presence (*mal'akh hapanim*). Two of the dwelling places are visible and present in the human realm, one in the present and one in the future; two are invisible and are to be found in the divine, cosmic realm: "For the LORD has four (sacred) places upon the earth: the garden of Eden and the mountain of the East and this mountain which you are upon today, Mount Sinai, and Mount Zion, which will be sanctified in the new creation for the sanctification of the earth."[35]

The sacred place, in both its heavenly and its earthly contexts, encompasses three mountains, a garden with trees of life, a house of crystal and meteoric stone, and cherubim. Its celestial/terrestrial context— referred to in *1 Enoch* as "the holy mountain" and "the center [lit., navel] of the earth"[36] and in *Jubilees* as "Mount Zion in the midst of the navel of the earth"[37]—establishes its cosmic character as the place where space comes into existence and heaven and earth touch. In *1 Enoch*, the protagonist, the founder of the priestly dynasty, describes his vision of the cosmic Temple linked to the tradition of the chariot and the appearance of the cherubim: "a great house which was built of white marble . . . the ceiling like the path of the stars and lightnings between which (stood) fiery cherubim."[38] Enoch's account also describes a divine throne and a throne of glory as part of the world of the chariot,[39] and the sacred space is described as a mountainous expanse filled with sweet-smelling trees, fragrant plants, and precious stones, inhabited by angels and cherubim.[40] In *Jubilees*, the place is called "the Garden of Eden."[41] It is referred to in *1 Enoch* as "the garden of truth," "the garden of righteousness," or the "garden of life."[42] The place is connected to the beginning of time, the underpinnings of space, and the source of eternal life. It is a place that challenges the boundaries of life and death, breaching the limits of time and space that are fixed in the world of ephemeral beings. In the words of the author of *2 Enoch*, "the Garden of Eden, it is between the ephemeral and the nonephemeral."[43]

The Garden of Eden is the place of God's habitation and the source of life, uniting life and eternity, space and time, sanctity, righteousness, and memory, testimony and knowledge. Its name (*gan eden*) is associated with witness and testimony (*ed, edut*); with time and epochs (*idan, idanim, a'dei-ad*); with delicacy, fragrance, and rejuvenation (*eden, ednah*). It is associated with supertemporal eternity, the eternal cycles of life and their sacred succession, linked to fertility, bounty, life and rejuvenation, holiness and purity, written memory and testimony. It underlies the spatial dimension, for it is the source of space and its bounty. Yet it partakes of the metaspatial, for the laws of reality that bind those who are subject to time and place do not apply in this invisible domain, which is free from the bounds of time. This place sometimes referred to in Aramaic as *pardes qushta*,[44] equivalent to the Hebrew *gan tsedeq* (garden of righteousness) or *gan ha'emet* (garden of truth).

The Septuagint, written in Alexandria during the third century B.C.E., translates "Garden of Eden" in Genesis as *paradisos*, known in English as "Paradise."[45] On occasion, the sacred place is called "a foundation of the Building of Holiness, and eternal Plantation throughout all ages to come,"[46] for it is the domain of the Tree of Life, the Trees of Life, the holy trees, and the fragrant trees linked to the incense, whose source is in the Garden of Eden.[47] The sacred place is the domain of cherubim and angels, the "fiery cherubim" and "voice of the cherubim" mentioned in Enoch's vision of the chariot,[48] in Ezekiel's vision of the chariot as described in the Qumran version,[49] and in Sirach 49:8.[50] The chariot of the cherubim in the supernal world is described in Songs of the Sabbath Sacrifice, where it is linked to the cherubim that Moses was shown on the Mount (Exod 25:17-20), to the chariot of the cherubim that David was shown in the vision described in the plan for the Temple,[51] to the cherubim in Solomon's Temple (1 Kgs 6:23-28; 2 Chr 3: 10-13), and to the "heavenly chariots" in *1 Enoch* 75:3.

In the priestly "chariot" tradition, the cherubim, the chariot, and the holy angels represent the mystery and eternity of life connected to the expanses of space and cycles of time and to the source from which they flow. They are the visual representation of the sacred divine domain from which all life flows, a domain protected by strict bounds of purity, which make the visible representation of the sacred practically invisible. They are tied as well to the eternal cycles of visible natural time, which are marked and preserved by the sacred companies of priests (cf. 1 Chr 24), marking the audible cycles of Sabbaths and appointed times in the Temple. The holy angels are appointed over the celestial cycles of time, as described in *Sefer Mahalakh ha-Me'orot* (*1 Enoch* 72–82) and in *Jubilees*. They also serve as the eternal witnesses and scribes who maintain the tablets and books that establish memory, as described in *Enoch*, *Jubilees*, and the *Testaments of the Twelve Patriarchs*. The *Community Rule* presents the parallel role of angels and priests as eternal witnesses of sacred memory: "God has given them to His chosen ones as an everlasting possession, and has caused them to inherit the lot of the Holy Ones. He has joined their assembly to the Sons of Heaven to be a Council of the Community, a foundation of the Building of Holiness, and eternal Plantation throughout all ages to come."[52]

The priestly cosmographic tradition in the Dead Sea Scrolls, in *Enoch*, and in *Jubilees*—tied to the chariot tradition, the Enoch literature, the Garden of Eden, the Holy of Holies, Mount Zion, and the Temple—deals with the dwelling place of the sacred. It identifies a sacred, celestial/terrestrial place with its terrestrial representation. The former is suspended beyond the limits of time and space, while the latter crosses the boundaries of time and space and is bound up with the interconnected places of divine revelation: "And he knew that the Garden of Eden was the holy of holies and the dwelling of the Lord. And Mount Sinai [was] in the midst of the desert and Mount Zion [was] in the midst of the navel of the earth. The three of these were created as holy places, one facing the other" (*Jub.* 8:19).

The three sacred quarters—the Garden of Eden, Mount Sinai, and Mount Zion—correspond to the foci of the priestly myth and to its seven protagonists, who transcend the boundaries of heaven and earth: Enoch and Melchizedek (Garden of Eden); Moses and Aaron (Mount Sinai); and Abraham, Isaac, and David (Mount Zion). The Garden of Eden, as noted, is God's eternal heavenly dwelling place. It is the heavenly "Holy of Holies," "God's habitation," the place of the cherubim and angels, "the Plantation of Eternity," the source of the sacred fragrant trees, and the abode of the man who attained immortality, since Enoch son of Jared, the founder of the priesthood was assumed into heaven (Gen 5:21-24; *Jub.* 4:23). Enoch was the first to master reading, writing, and counting and to burn incense in the heavenly Temple. It was he who established the priestly ritual when he brought the calendar of Sabbaths and seasons from heaven to earth.[53]

In describing the vision of Enoch's ascension heavenward, *1 Enoch* tells that Enoch reached "the navel of the earth": "And from there I went into the center [the navel] of the earth and saw a blessed place shaded with branches . . . and there I saw a holy mountain; underneath the mountain in the direction of the east, there was a stream. . . . And I saw in a second direction (another) mountain which was higher than (the former). Between them was a deep and narrow valley."[54] Some believe that the foregoing vision is referring to a place whose topography corresponds to that of Jerusalem in the Second Temple period[55] where, according to *Jubilees*, "Mount Zion is within the center [navel] of the earth."

In addition to Enoch, another individual of crucial importance in priestly myth resided in the Garden of Eden—Melchizedek the King of Shalem, the son of Enoch's great grandson. According to the tradition recorded in *2 Enoch*, Melchizedek was taken to the Garden of Eden before the flood and "kept there" so as to transmit to Abraham and his descendants the ancient priestly tradition going back to Enoch.[56]

Mount Sinai is associated with God's revelation outside the borders of the Holy Land and with the eternal covenant between God and His people. The covenant was entered into in the wilderness, when they were given the divine Law—an eternal, written Law transcending boundaries of time and space and establishing sanctity within the human world. In an introductory passage, *1 Enoch* states that "the God of the universe . . . will march upon Mount Sinai and appear in his camp emerging from heaven with a mighty power" (1:3-4).[57] In *1 Enoch* and in *Jubilees*, the divine Law is tied to the sevenfold cycles of sacred time made known at Sinai, called "the times of the Lord" and the "times of liberty," and to the fourfold cycles of nature, called the "chariots in heaven."[58] Both cycles kept by angels and priests, guide the sevenfold cycle of rest, freedom, and liberty in relation to the fourfold eternal cycles of nature.

In biblical tradition and Jubilees, Mount Sinai is associated with the figure of Moses—the man of God and founder of prophecy, who brought the Law from the heavens—and with the memory of Israel's coming into being as it emerged from slavery to freedom. According to *Jubilees*, Mount Sinai is associated as well with the angels. God's seven festivals and the cycles of time based on the number seven,[59] made known to Moses at Sinai, had been observed by angels and by the Patriarchs for forty-nine jubilees before then, from creation until the revelation at Sinai.[60]

Mount Zion is God's dwelling place within his Land. It is the sacred mountain chosen by God for that purpose. In the priestly and prophetic tradition, it is also the site of the Holy of Holies within the Temple, to be found on "Mount Zion in the midst of the navel of the earth."[61] That tradition associates the first divine revelation at the site with Abraham and Isaac, in the episode of Isaac's binding. The second revelation there is tied to David and the establishment of the monarchy in Zion and Jerusalem from the time David conquered the "Rock of Zion," as we shall see.

The site is associated as well with "the place of Aronah," mentioned as the site from which Enoch was transported heavenward in order to learn the tradition of the sacred calendar and as the site to which he returned in order to teach his sons, the priests, what he had learned from the angels. The place of Aravna/Aronah is the name of the site of the angelic revelation to David, where the Temple will be built on Mount Zion (2 Sam 24:16-25; 1 Chr 21:15, 18-30). Moreover, the mystical priestly tradition attributes to David, "the sweet singer of Israel," the sacred songs sung by the priests in the Temple as well as the psalms in praise of Zion sung by the Levites, linked to preservation of the cycles of sacred time and the bounds of the sacred place.[62]

Transformation of Sacred Space
in early Judaism and Christianity

The priestly tradition draws interesting connections among sacred place, sacred time, and sacred memory, in both celestial and terrestrial contexts; it departs noticeably form the traditional formulation. This priestly tradition has a subversive element, tied to an implicit and explicit conflict over the annual calendar. It is no coincidence that biblical figures are linked to the Garden of Eden, Mount Sinai, and Mount Zion. These three sacred places of the priestly myth are presented in contexts that are controversial with respect to calculating the festivals associated with them and are even linked to places where the angel of the presence speaks with the protagonists of the biblical story. This tradition regarding God's revelation on sacred mountains connected to covenants, to places concealed from the eye, to the revelation of angels, and to sanctity and eternity is alluded to in the words of Ezekiel ben Buzi the priest, who prophesies obscurely about the mountain of God, the holy mountain of God, the Garden of Eden, the cherub, and the Temple: "in Eden, the garden of God . . . [you were] on God's holy mountain . . . among stones of fire . . . from the mountain of God . . . shielding cherub from among the stones of fire . . . your sanctuaries."[63]

In *Jubilees*, which begins with the sanctity of Mount Zion as the future site of the temple (1:27-29), the angel of the presence describes for Moses the deeds of his predecessor who merited assumption into heaven—Enoch son of Jared, of the seventh generation of man. He does so as Moses stands on Mount Sinai on a Monday, the sixteenth day of the third month, following the giving of the Torah the day before, at the midpoint of the third month, that is, Sunday, 15 Sivan, in contrast to the rabbinic tradition that the Torah was given on 6 Sivan.

The chapter of Genesis that begins, "This is the record of Adam's line" tells that "Enoch walked with God; then he was no more, for God took him" (Gen 5:24). That heavenly taking is interpreted in Jubilees to mean that he reached the Garden of Eden: "And he was taken from among the children of men, and we led him to the Garden of Eden for greatness and honor. And behold, he is there, writing. . ." (*Jub*. 4:23). Enoch was taken to heaven at a sacred time in the priestly calendar, the first day of the first month[64]—the day on which Levi was born and the day on which the desert tabernacle was erected (Exod 40: 2). It is the first day of the year in the biblical calendar and in that of the Dead Sea Scrolls—the 364-day calendar, beginning on Wednesday, the first day of

the first month. That day, which is the vernal equinox in the Enochic tradition of the calendar, had been a matter of controversy from the time
that the Seleucid rulers replaced the biblical-priestly solar calendar with
the imperial lunar calendar.[65]

Enoch's elevation into the Garden of Eden is recounted in both
books of Enoch, in Jubilees, and in the Genesis Apocryphon, where he
learns, from the angel of the presence, the underpinnings of knowledge;
reading, writing, and arithmetic; the priestly tradition and the calcula-
tion of the calendar; the written annals; the covenant and the ritual
cycles. In addition, he offers incense in the celestial Temple on the
mountain of the south/east. (*Jub.* 4:17-25).[66]

Dwelling in the Garden of Eden on the mountain of the south/east
and having attained eternal life, Enoch, the founder of the priesthood,
disports himself as a high priest in the celestial temple. According to the
angel of the presence who describes his activities, Enoch "offered the
incense which is acceptable before the Lord in the evening at the holy
place on Mount Qater [Qater from *Qetoret*, incense in Hebrew]" (*Jub.*
4:25). The only other person to enter the Garden of Eden did so four
generations later—Enoch's great-great-grandson, Melchizedek, the
founder of future priesthood.[67] As Moses stands on Mount Sinai, the
angel of the presence recounts for him, over the course of fifty chapters
of the book of *Jubilees*, the unfolding of history from Creation to the revelation at Sinai (*Jub.* 1:27, 29, etc.). In so doing, he mentions, as already
noted, four sacred places tied to God's dwelling place: "For the Lord has
four (sacred) places upon the earth: the garden of Eden and the mountain of the East [sun-rise] and this mountain which you are upon today,
Mount Sinai, and Mount Zion, which will be sanctified in the new creation for the sanctification of the earth."[68]

Moses stands on Mount Sinai, the mountain of God,[69] on the sixteenth day of the third month, the day after the Shavuot festival according to the priestly calendar of Sabbaths (*Jub.* 1:1-3), at the place where
the historic covenant had been entered into between God and the children of Israel on the preceding day—the fifteenth day of the third
month, the festival of Shavuot. It is also the place where God speaks to
Moses,[70] gives him the tablets on which the written Law is inscribed, and
informs him that He will reign on Mount Zion forever (*Jub.* 1:1-28).

As noted, the prophetic and poetic literature of the First Temple
period refers to Mount Zion as God's terrestrial dwelling place. As a
general rule, however, it is not associated explicitly with the Temple itself.
Rather, it is tied to the sacred area called Mount Zion or "My holy

mountain."[71] In *Jubilees*, on the other hand, Mount Zion is the future site of the Temple, emphatically described to Moses by the angel of the presence who records God words (*Jub.* 1:26-28).[72]

Even more, it is a site of great importance in the sacred historical-geographical past, a site on which a unique national identity is grounded: Mount Zion is the mountain on which, seven generations earlier, Isaac was bound by his father and then rescued by the angel of the presence.[73] The story of the *aqedah*—which took place, according to *Jubilees*, on Mount Zion—links Abraham and Isaac to Mount Zion, the place where the sacrifice was offered, and to the angel of the presence, who is revealed at the time of the Passover festival, at the middle of the first month, and who rescues Isaac at the very place where the Temple is to be built (*Jub.* 18:9–19; 1:28). The story of Isaac's binding is a foundational story in the battle between life and death and in the promise of everlasting progeny. It is the place where the angel of the presence, acting at God's command, rescues Isaac from the death to which he had been sentenced by the prince Mastema.[74]

Not only is Mount Zion connected to sacred space, it is tied to sacred time, too—the time of Isaac's binding, according to *Jubilees*. That time, bound up in testing, in sacrifice at the altar, and in covenant, falls at the middle of the first month on the biblical calendar, that is, the festival of Passover (*Jub.* 17:15-17, 18:1-19).[75]

Jubilees, written within priestly circles during the second century B.C.E., presents an alternative to the familiar biblical account of the origins of the date of Passover festival. It describes "the feast of the Lord" as a seven-day festival at the middle of the first month. It begins on the twelfth of the month, and the day of the *aqedah* is three days thereafter, on the fourteenth (corresponding to the biblical paschal festival) or the fifteenth (corresponding to the biblical feast of unleavened bread). The account advances the institution of the seven days of the memorial festival that correspond to the date of Passover to the time of Abraham and Isaac. The narrative connects it to Mount Zion and the binding of Isaac in the book of Genesis rather than to the time of Moses in the book of Exodus, after hundreds of years of Egyptian slavery.

Jubilees thus explicitly associates a sacred site tied to Mount Zion, called "the place of God's mountain," with a burnt offering and the binding of Isaac. Likewise, it associates a sacred time called "the feast of the Lord" with the time of the Passover holiday and the lamb offered as a sacrifice. It thereby calls to mind another tradition—later than that of *Jubilees*—that uses that place, that time, and the story of a human sacrificial offering as the background for a founding story. I refer, of course, to the crucifixion of Jesus, "the lamb of God," at the paschal festival, in the midst of the first month, connected to Mount Zion.

Within the Christian tradition, there is a significant departure as well as an intertwining of several traditions regarding the burnt offering, the lamb, the binding of Isaac, the Passover, and Mount Zion. Using a typological mode of interpretation that regards past events as a mirror reflecting the future, the Christians identified Jesus as "the bound lamb" on Mount Zion and as the paschal sacrifice—that is, they identified the crucified one as the lamb given as a burnt offering instead of Isaac, and they set the fifteenth of Nisan as the time of the crucifixion.[76] The biblical Passover, at the midpoint of the first month, is regarded in Jubilees as the time of Isaac's binding. In Christian tradition, it becomes a prefiguring of the crucifixion at Passover, and Jesus corresponds allegorically to both Isaac and to the bound lamb, *agnus dei*, the lamb of God. According to the legends about Isaac's binding, Isaac was sacrificed, died, taken up to the Garden of Eden, and returned when he was healed.[77] Similarly, Jesus, once crucified, entered the celestial Temple or the Garden of Eden, and his terrestrial symbol, the lamb, stood opposite the Garden of Eden on Mount Zion: "Then I looked, and there was the Lamb, standing on Mount Zion!" (Rev 14:1).

In some verses in the Epistle to the Hebrews, Mount Zion is removed from terrestrial geography and transformed into part of the sacred Christian tradition: "But you have come to Mount Zion and to the city of the living God, the heavenly Jerusalem, and to innumerable angels in festal gathering, and to the assembly of the firstborn who are enrolled in heaven . . . and to Jesus, the mediator of a new covenant (Heb 12:22-23). In Christian tradition, Mount Zion, the sacred place, becomes the place where the Holy Spirit descended on the apostles on Pentecost, as described in Acts 2: 1-4. In the fourth-century *Book of Travels* by the Spanish-Christian pilgrim Agaria, who went to Jerusalem and described the holy places: "Mount Zion is situated to the south...[there the Lord dined with his disciples] and there he sent the Holy Spirit upon the disciples"; "the other side of Mount Zion . . . for there, as the Lord had previously promised, they were filled with the Holy Spirit."[78]

Some writers describe the relationship between the Jewish and Christian traditions during the first centuries of the Common Era as one of mutual rejection and mutual acceptance: "[Judaism's] historical formation [took] shape through the rejection of the alternative offered by Christianity to the crisis of the Destruction of the Second Temple. The confrontation with Christianity lies at the very heart of Midrashic and Talmudic Judaism, which deal intensively with a renewed self-definition of who is a Jew and what is Judaism, as part of determining the reverse definition—namely, who is not a Jew. . . . Self-definition is an extensive and open process, one based not solely on automatic denial, but also on absorbing new religious ideas, ceremonies, and symbols from the outside."[79]

An example of this sort of process is provided by the transformations in the tradition of the sacred place that is the object of our inquiry here. "The name Mount Zion, known to all contemporary Jews as the name of Jerusalem's upper city, is Christian (or Jewish-Christian) in its origin. It is always used to annul the sanctity of the Temple Mount following the destruction of the Temple and to transfer it to an alternative mountain— the mountain on which is located the traditional burial place of King David, the prototype of Jesus."[80] Nevertheless, the Jews used, and to this day still use, the name "Mount Zion," evidently oblivious to the absurdity of doing so, even though the name "Mount Zion" at the outset was the name of the Temple Mount itself. They adopted the Christian nomenclature because their conflict with Christianity was not solely a matter of rejection but also of absorption and assimilation of traditions, names, rituals, and symbols.[81]

Quite likely this dialectic of appropriation and rejection characterized the Jewish Christian relationship during the rabbinic period in the first centuries of the Common Era. However, one must never disregard the Christian tradition's adoption of Jewish elements and the complex question of fragmentation within the old religion in the centuries preceding the growth of Christianity.

The pre-Christian priestly tradition expressly identified the Temple's location with Mount Zion, as stated in Jubilees, written while the Temple was still standing. The site, however, had been defiled—in the view of the Hasmonean regime's opponents and of those who sided with the House of Zadok—to the point that the priests of the House of Zadok and their allies abandoned the Temple. Their separatist stance is documented in the scroll known as *Miqzat ma`asei ha-torah* (*MMT*) and in other scrolls that do battle over the sacred time and sacred place associated in their minds with Mount Zion.[82] The author of *Jubilees* describes the Temple on Mount Zion as the Temple of the future. Other writers in his camp—with respect to the battle over the sacred time and sacred place—preferred to imagine celestial sanctuaries in which holy angels served, as depicted in Songs of the Sabbath Sacrifice and the Scroll of Blessings associated with the tradition of the chariot described earlier.

In the view of the scrolls' writers, the desecration of the Temple resulted in large part from the changes in the sacred, biblical, and priestly calendar that had been followed in the Temple until 175 B.C.E. In that year, Antiochus IV, who called himself "Theos Epiphanes," imposed the Seleucid lunar calendar on Jerusalem, displaced Honyo ben Simeon, the last of the Zadokite high priests to serve in the Temple in accordance with the biblical scheme of high priesthood, and appointed Hellenizing high priests who acquired their priesthood by purchase or force. They were replaced by the Hasmonean priests improperly appointed from 152 B.C.E. and onward by the heirs of Antiochus IV—Alexander Balas and Demetrius II—who also imposed the Seleucid lunar calendar. The Hasmonean priests served in the sanctuary until the end of their dynasty in 37 B.C.E. The author of the Psalms of Solomon—an adherent of the biblical-priestly arrangements and a harsh opponent of the Hasmoneans, whom he describes as having "acted according to their uncleanness, just as their ancestors; they defiled Jerusalem and the things that had been consecrated to the name of God"[83]—bitingly depicts the takeover of the government by force of arms:

> Lord, you chose David to be king over Israel and swore to him about his descendants forever, that his kingdom should not fail before you. But because of our sins, sinners rose up against us, they set upon us and drove us out. Those to whom you did not (make the) promise, they took away (from us) by force; and they did not glorify your honorable name. With pomp they set up a monarchy because of their arrogance; they despoiled the throne of David with arrogant shouting.[84]

The future he hopes for is symbolized by the verse "Sound in Zion the signal trumpet of the sanctuary; announce in Jerusalem the voice of one bringing good news."[85] He is alluding to the priests who sound the horns (Josh 6:9; 7:4-16), to the words of the prophet Joel: "Blow the trumpet in Zion; sound the alarm on my holy mountain! Let all the inhabitants of the Land tremble, for the day of the Lord is coming, it is near" (Joel 2:1), and to the psalms recited in the Temple, in which the priests sounded trumpets and horns and Levites sang (Ps 47:7; 81:4; 150:3).

In contrast to the chaotic reality of the expulsions and displacements depicted in the Psalms of Solomon, the proper state of affairs is reflected in the words of the priest Joshua Ben Sira, who wrote during the second decade of the second century B.C.E., before the Antiochian revolution, about the Zadokite priests serving in Zion: "Give thanks to him who makes a horn to sprout for the house of David, for his steadfast love endures forever. Give thanks to him who has chosen the sons of Zadok to be priests, for his steadfast love endures forever."[86] Earlier, Ben Sira had written, "In the holy tent I ministered before him, and so I was established in Zion. Thus in the beloved city he gave me a resting place, and in Jerusalem was my domain."[87]

A later priestly tradition, known as *2 Enoch*, dating to the early part of the first century C.E., identified the "place of Aronah" (connected to the foundation of the Temple in David's time)[88] with the "navel of the earth" and Mount Zion, "the dwelling of the holy." It also linked it to the priestly dynasty that began with Enoch, the founder of the priesthood, who was taken to heaven from the place of Arona, later to be identified with Mount Zion. The priesthood was renewed in the days of Abraham with Melchizedek, the priest of priests forever, also connected to Mount Zion: "His abode has been established in Salem, his dwelling place in Zion" (Ps 76:3); "And King Melchizedek of Salem . . . he was priest of God Most High" (Gen 14:18); "The Lord has sworn and will not change his mind, you are a priest forever according to the order of Melchizedek" (Ps 110:4); *2 Enoch* proclaims that "Melchizedek will be the priest to all holy priests, and I will establish him so that he will be the head of the priests of the future. . . . And behold, Melchizedek will be the head of the 13 priests who existed before. . . . He, Melchizedek, will be priest and king in the place of Akhuzan,[89] that is to say, in the center of the earth, where Adam was created."[90]

This tradition continues with a statement that connects past with future, celestial holy site with terrestrial: "The Lord said to Michael, 'Go down onto the earth to Nir the priest [Melchizedek's father] and take my child Melchizedek, who is with him, and place him in the paradise of Eden for preservation.'"[91] It continues, "I will place him in the paradise of Eden, and there he will be forever,"[92] and concludes with the renewal of the priesthood in the city of Salem, through Melchizedek's descendants.

The preceding Qumran "Melchizedek Scroll" describes "the Sons of [Light] and the men of the lot of Mel[chi]zedek"[93] and says "It is the time for the year of grace of Melchizedek and his armies, the nation of the holy ones of God."[94] Melchizedek is referred to in Qumran as "Melchizedek the priest in the assembly of God . . . who "announces salvation, saying to Zion 'your God is king.'"[95] He is referred to in

Qumran as "the chief of the princes of the wonderful [priesthoods] of Melchizedek,"[96] which asserts that "Zion is the congregation of all the sons of justice, those who establish the covenant . . . and your God is Melchizedek who will free them from the hand of Belial."[97] Bridging the mythological, antediluvian, priestly past and the priestly future at the end of days, Melchizedek plays an important part in the priestly tradition of the Dead Sea Scrolls, which we see also in the Christian tradition when the Epistle to the Hebrews associates Jesus with Melchizedek.

Another unknown priestly text found at Qumran, known as "Joshua's apocryphon," describes a link between the "rock of Zion" and the Tabernacle and the House of the Lord. It emphasizes the connection between the sacred place and the House of David—who conquered Jerusalem and initiated the building of the Temple—as well as the connection between the House of David and the House of Zadok—the priests who served there:

> We could not come to Zion to place there the Tent of Meeting and the Ark of the Covenant until the end of times. For behold, a son is born to Jesse, son of Perez, son of Judah, son of Jacob, and he will capture the rock of Zion and expel from there all Amorites, from Jerusalem to the sea; and he will set his heart on building the Temple for the Lord God of Israel. He will prepare gold and silver, copper and iron, and will import cedar wood and cypress from Lebanon; and his small child will build it, and Zadok the priest will be the first to serve there; he of the descendants of Phineas and of Aaron; and he will be pleasing all the days of his life and be blessed with all from the heavenly dwelling; for he will be a friend of the Lord, securely dwelling in Jerusalem for all days, and He will dwell with him forever.[98]

In a prophetic tradition ascribed to Joshua and pertaining to the construction of the Temple of David and the beginning of the Zadokite priesthood, this priestly tradition considers the fate of the Tent of Meeting and the Ark of the Covenant. They were supposed to reside in Zion upon the Israelites' entrance into the Promised Land, but Joshua sees in his vision that the conquest of the Rock of Zion will be completed only in King David's time and that the House of the Lord will be built on it only in the time of David's younger son, Solomon. He also foresees that Zadok will serve there as first among the priestly descendants of Levi through the line of Phineas and that his descendants—thereafter called Zadokites—will serve in Jerusalem forever.

This vision seems to have been written by Zadokite priests after they had been displaced from the Temple by the Hasmoneans, but it preserves the term "Rock of Zion" (*sela tsiyyon*), unique in the priestly tradition and not mentioned in scripture. The expression "foundation stone" (*even shetiyyah*) (*m. Yoma* 5:2), known in later traditions and related to the huge rock at the base of the Temple Mount, may be a later incarnation of this unique term. In any event, Joshua's vision intertwines David and the Rock of Zion with Jerusalem and the House of God, and it even sees continuity between the Tent of Meeting and the House of God and its associated priestly dynasty.

The Zadokite priesthood is associated with the Tent of Meeting, the Temple, Jerusalem, Mount Zion, and the Rock of Zion, as noted earlier. An additional statement that establishes continuity between the Tent of Meeting and the Temple appears in *MMT*, where the Zadokite priests say that "we consider the Sanctuary [miqdash, the Temple] as the tent of meeting."[99]

A text entitled *Divrei ha-me'orot* ("The Words of the Heavenly Luminaries") includes an instructive passage on Zion the holy city and the house of God's glory. The passage appears to have been written around the time the House of David—which had entered into a covenant with the Zadokite priests—was divested of the monarchy. The monarchy was then improperly transferred to the Hasmoneans, who had forcibly assumed both priesthood and kingship:

> Thy dwelling place . . . a resting-place in Jerusalem, the city which Thou hast chosen from all the earth that Thy Name might remain there for ever . . . Thou hast chosen the tribe of Judah and hast established Thy Covenant with David that he might be as a princely shepherd over Thy people and sit before Thee on the throne of Israel for ever. . . . Thou who hast sanctified Thyself in the midst of Thy people Israel . . . , that they might glorify Thy people, and Zion Thy holy city and the House of Thy majesty. And there was neither adversary nor misfortune, but peace and blessing.[100]

The rabbinic tradition in these matters stands in contrast to the priestly tradition. The priestly tradition assigns critical importance to "Zion My holy mountain," "Mount Zion, the navel of the earth," "the Rock of Zion," and "the place of Aronah." Rabbinic tradition transformed "Mount Zion" to *har habyit* (the mountain of the house) and did so after a time when there was no longer a house. The "Temple Mount," was addressed in this fashion after its destruction. The rabbinic tradition suppressed Mount Zion's name and discarded the tradition regarding Enoch and Melchizedek, who were dwellers in Eden and associated with Mount Zion, Salem, and the place of Aronah. It declined to maintain the tradition of the place of Aronah as the sacred place of the altar of the sacrifice and of the angelic revelation in the time of David (2 Sam 24:16-25; 1 Chr 21:15-28; 22:1), the place where the temple was built in the days of Solomon (2 Chr 3:1), the place from which Enoch and Melchizedek were taken to paradise[101] in order for Enoch to study the priestly calendar, the priestly ritual, and the priestly written memory[102] and for Melchizedek to keep the priestly dynasty and to impart it to Abraham.[103]

Rabbinic tradition exchanged the priestly calendar, commencing in the spring, and moved the place of Isaac's binding from Mount Zion to the Land of Moriah and its time from the first month to the seventh— the month associated with the New Year festival (Rosh Hashanah), a holiday not mentioned in the Torah or the Scrolls and instituted with this name by the rabbis in *m. Rosh HaShanah*.[104]

What accounts for these far-reaching changes in sacred times, sacred places, and sacred memories? Were they made by the rabbis only vis à vis Christianity, which transferred Mount Zion to a new place (today's Mount Zion) and tied it to the "Lamb of God" and to the ancient time of the *aqedah*, at Passover? Or were they made also vis à vis the ancient priestly tradition, which had maintained its hegemony for hundreds of years, from the time of Moses and Aaron through the First-Temple Zadokite priestly dynasty down to the governmental changes of the Hasmonean period? Those governmental changes were intertwined with the replacement of the biblical solar calendar by the Seleucid lunar calendar (Dan 7:25) and the ascendancy of a new priestly dynasty lacking biblical legitimacy. That dynasty, the Hasmoneans, came to power during the second century B.C.E. under Seleucid patronage and usurped both the high priesthood and the monarchy. It remained in power until 37 B.C.E., disrupting the ancient order of Zadokite priesthood and other aspects of the biblical world.

The struggle by the ancient Zadokite priesthood to retain its standing during the Hasmonean and early rabbinic periods is actually the struggle between Sadducees and Pharisees. The Sadducees are "the Zadokite priests and their allies," whose writings appear in the Dead Sea Scrolls. As the source of their authority, they look to the biblical tradition assigning the high priesthood to Aaron's descendants in a direct line to the end of the biblical canon,[105] and to traditions related to angels, the calendar, the world of the celestial chariot, and the Temple on Mount Zion. The Pharisees, who interpreted the Torah through the use of sovereign human power and ancestral tradition, shaped a social order distinct from the biblical priestly way of life and the ancient priestly calendar—the calendar that had begun in the first month (Nisan) on a Wednesday and was based on a fixed, solar year, reckoned in advance, having 364 days divided into 52 weeks. That calendar was preserved by squads of priests and angels connected to the sacred place called "Mount Zion" on earth and the "Garden of Eden" in the heavens, a place whose guardians saw time as a sacred, eternal, divine element not subject to human dominion.

For the Pharisees and the rabbis, in contrast, time is based on a new social order, headed by sages who reckon according to a new lunar calendar, beginning in the seventh month (Tishri). That calendar neither fixes in advance the number of days in a year or any particular month, nor does it states the number of weeks in a year. Time is given over to human dominion and is based on ad hoc determinations related to the appearance of the new moon, unrelated to any specific celestial or terrestrial sites.[106] As noted, the priestly calendar maintained by the Zadokites was connected to Enoch son of Jared, who had been taken up to heaven from the Place of Aronah, on Mount Zion, on the first of Nisan. The Pharisee calendar, which began on the first of Tishri, was not linked to a particular place or a particular person and lacked all support in biblical tradition, which continued consistently counts Nisan as the first month (cf. Exod 12:2).

Did the sages move the binding of Isaac from Passover to the seventh month because the Christians identified Passover with the crucifixion and Jesus' ascent to heaven? Did these considerations lead them to move, as well, the site of the *aqedah* from Mount Zion, where the Lamb of God was "standing" (Rev 14:1-3; cf. Heb 12:22), to the Land of Moriah, which had no other claimants? Or were the changes the result of old disputes between Sadducees and Pharisees: Did the year begin at the first month of Passover or at Rosh Hashanah on the seventh month? Is the sacred place to be identified with Mount Zion or Mount Moriah, with the eternal dwelling place of the sacred tied to the chariot tradition or with the destroyed Temple Mount? Did the *aqedah* take place during the first month or the seventh? Was leadership to be vested in Zadokite priests (Sadducees) or in Pharisees? Was the calendar an eternal reckoning of precalculated, sacred time brought down from heaven by Enoch son of Jared or a variable reckoning based on human time, reckoned in accord with tractate *Rosh ha-Shanah*?

The Sadducees and the Pharisees represent two opposing traditions regarding sacred space, sacred time, sacred memory, and sacred service.

Each group encompassed a range of voices, not necessarily uniform, as well as texts written in various circles from various viewpoints, reflecting different memories. Early Christianity adopted some of the concepts of the Zadokite priestly tradition related to Mount Zion as a place tied to the *aqedah* and the crucifixion, to Passover and the revelation of angels, and to the sacred place of ascent to heaven. These appropriations may well have brought about the displacement of that tradition from the central stream of the rabbinic tradition.

Christians likewise associated some of the ancient priestly tradition's heroes—the immortal Enoch and Melchizedek, who breached the boundaries of time and space and dwelled in the holy of holies, the Garden of Eden—with Jesus, who came to be regarded by the new tradition as immortal. This, too may, have led to the rejection of the priestly tradition involving the heavenly sanctuary and the chariot, the Garden of Eden and the Garden of Truth, which encompassed all of the foregoing. It is certainly logical to infer that the dispute between Sadducees and Pharisees over the time of the Festival of Shavuot—the central festival in the priestly covenant tradition as reflected in Jubilees and in the Rule of the Community—led to the sages' rejection of the Shavuot tradition associated with the chariot and with the renewal of covenant. And it may be inferred as well that the new place assumed by Shavuot in the Christian tradition, as Pentecost—the time when the Holy Spirit descended on the Apostles (Acts 2)— contributed to its displacement from the rabbinic tradition. That Mount Zion was consecrated by the nascent Christian tradition is already evident in Hebrews 12:22-24.

The rabbis, for their part, did not mention the name "Shavuot" (they called it Azeret) and did not write a tract on Shavuot. They forbade study of the account of the chariot (*t. Ḥag.* 2:1) and disallowed use of Ezekiel's vision of the chariot as the prophetic reading for Shavuot (*m. Meg.* 4:8). They, thereby, declined to direct attention to the world of the sacred, the world of the cherubim and the chariot, or to the concealed sanctuaries where one may find cherubim and angels in a sacred celestial expanse called the "Garden of Eden" or the chariot where Enoch son of Jared is situated—a heavenly expanse whose earthly embodiment is called "Zion" and "the sacred dwelling place": "[T]he Garden of Eden was the holy of holies and the dwelling of the Lord. And Mount Sinai [was] in the midst of the desert and Mount Zion [was] in the midst of the navel of the earth. The three of these were created as holy places, one facing the other" (*Jub.* 8:19). The Psalms scroll from Qumran says of this place, where heaven and earth commingle: "I will remember you, O Zion, for a blessing; with all my might I love you. . . . Be exalted and increase, O Zion; Praise the Most High, your Redeemer! May my soul rejoice in your glory";[107] "Like the dew of Hermon that falls onto Mount Zion, for there the Lord directed the eternal blessing; peace be upon Israel."[108]

In contrast to the priests and prophets who excelled in their praise for Mount Zion and in the mythic and mystical dimensions associated with it, the sages neutralized the priestly-mystical chariot tradition and denigrated its hero. In their version of events, Enoch son of Jared— Metatron, the celestial High Priest (*Num. Rab.* sec. 12), the hero that was taken to heaven from Mount Zion—was displaced from his celestial dwelling in the Garden of Truth and struck with sixty pulses of fire (see *B. Hag.* 15b). The hero of the priestly solar calendar is also spoken of disparagingly in *Tg. Onq.* on Genesis 5:24 and in *Gen. Rab.* sec. 25; his eternal righteous life in paradise, in the priestly tradition, was exchanged with punishment, humiliation, and death, in the rabbinic tradition.

In opposing the tradition of the chariot, the sages suppressed the sacred historical status of Mount Zion as the eternal holy mountain of the priestly tradition. This tradition is described in *Jubilees* (4:26), in the priest Joshua ben Sira's book (Sir 24:10-11), and in the accounts of the "navel of the earth" in *1* and *2 Enoch*. The sages transformed the desolate Mount Zion, on which the Temple no longer stood, into *har habayit* ("the mountain of the house"), though no house now stood there. They eliminated the word "sanctuary" or "temple" from its name. They listed the cultic recollections associated with the lost Temple, which had been on Mount Zion, but they did so in past tense, associated with the tradition of the destruction, in accord with the verse "because of Mount Zion, which is desolate; jackals prowl over it" (Lam 5:28).

Moreover, the sages declined to participate in the mystical consciousness that transcends the bounds of terrestrial time and space. They forbade directing attention to the heavenly counterpart of the Temple, situated in the Garden of Eden, in the world of the divine chariot of the cherubim. Even though, the celestial temple continued to operate in the world of the chariot and of the angels, and it continued to figure in the ramified Enoch literature and in the poetic world of the *heikhalot* and *merkavah* literature that developed in parallel to the Mishnah and the Talmud,[109] the sages shied away from involvement with it.

Concluding Remarks

Consideration of the priestly Enoch literature in its entirety and of its associations with Mount Zion, the navel of the earth, is beyond the scope of this article. However, it appears to reflect a set of alternative memories to those that coalesced in rabbinic thought. The latter, which gained hegemony within the Jewish world following the destruction of the Temple, blurred the biblical vision of the sacred Mount Zion and the associated mystical-priestly memory related to the chariot, the Garden of Eden, the navel of the earth, the *aqedah*, Enoch, Melchizedek, the place of Arona on Mount Zion as the place of the heavenly ascent, and the place where the calendar was brought from heaven to earth. The alternative memories embodied in the rejected priestly-mystical literature serve to link the tradition of the chariot, the Garden of Eden, Mount Zion, the place of Aronah, and the priestly tradition with, on the one hand, the *hekhalot* literature and, on the other, Christian literature.

The various groups generated endless arabesques associated with Mount Zion as the dwelling of the sacred and with the traditions regarding a priestly cult of incense and altars of sacrifice. These ideas were associated with the Garden of Eden, Enoch son of Jared, his great-grandson Melchizedek, the *aqedah* and the navel of the earth, with the Lamb and Mount Zion, and with David, the Rock of Zion, and Zion as "the assembly of all sons of righteousness." Their development, begun during the years before and after the start of the Christian era, continued throughout the first and second millennia C.E. along the various paths of mystical creativity, recalling through written memories what had ceased to exist in a physical sense.

Chapter 18

Vespasian, Nerva, Jesus, and the *Fiscus Judaicus*

Paul Foster

There can be little doubt that by 65 C.E. politically, militarily, and socially Vespasian appeared to have little in the way of prospects to reignite his formerly illustrious career. This shining star that had risen through the ranks during the reign of Claudius was remembered for his successful campaign when his forces had conquered the remote and uncivilized isle known as "Britannia."[1] He had then distinguished himself administratively as proconsul of Egypt.[2] Next, he had become politically active in Rome and a confidant of Nero. However, this proximity to Nero was to prove Vespasian's undoing. As Suetonius tells the incident, Vespasian's crime was failure to show the same degree of delight as the self-adoring Nero did in relation to his musical talents:

> In consequence he not only lost the imperial favour but was dismissed from Court, and fled to a small out-of-the-way township, where he hid in terror of his life.

Vespasian's fear was well founded, as was his decision to avoid the spotlight of the imperial capital and to settle in a rural Italian village. In many ways, Vespasian was lucky to escape with his life from the maniacal Nero. After the dismissal of Vespasian, while still in Greece Nero became convinced of a plot against him. Whether this was real or imagined is impossible to say. The consequence was that the legates of the upper and lower Rhine armies were summoned to Greece and forced to suicide, as was Corbulo, general of the Syrian legions. The fate of Corbulo is not unrelated to that of Vespasian. Nero's decision to remove some of his most experienced generals meant that there was a shortage of military tacticians in whom the legions had confidence.

The Introduction of the *Fiscus Judaicus*

Shortly after Corbulo's suicide, rebellion broke out in Jerusalem in reaction to the excesses of Florus, the procurator of Judaea. In November 66, Cestius Gallus, the newly appointed governor of Syria, led the legions southward in an attempt to quell the uprising. The campaign was a disaster. Roman forces were heavily defeated in Galilee, and Cestius died a short time afterwards.[3] Moreover, the Jewish rebels had tasted victory, which strengthened their resolve against Roman forces. Despite apparent perception, Vespasian's career was far from ended, and he was recalled to command the campaign against the Jewish uprising.

The campaign waged by Vespasian was not easy, nor were the rebels beaten into quick submission. In fact, while attempting to capture Gamala, Vespasian was cut off from his troops and almost lost his life.[4] Despite such setbacks, the Roman campaign moved on with an irresistible force. With Galilee subdued and most of Judea restored to Roman control, Vespasian regrouped his troops at Caesarea in preparation for the assault on Jerusalem.[5] As preparations were being made, news arrived of Nero's death. From harsh experience, Vespasian had learned not to act without the imperial imprimatur. Josephus relates how the campaign was delayed while political events unfolded in Rome:

> Vespasian, therefore, when the news first came, deferred his expedition against Jerusalem, anxiously waiting to see upon whom the empire would devolve after Nero's death; nor when he subsequently heard that Galba was emperor would he undertake anything, until he received further instructions from him concerning the war.[6]

Events moved quickly in Rome. During his reign of less than seven months, Galba alienated many of the influential Roman citizens and made his position untenable by sentencing a number of senators and knights to death without trial. As Suetonius comments, "Thus he outraged almost all classes at Rome; but the most virulent hatred of him was found in the army."[7] On January 15, 69, the emperor was assassinated in the Forum. Galba's death plunged Rome into civil war. Being the principal political figure in Rome, Otho, the instigator of the assassination, was quickly elected to the purple.[8] However, there was a ready challenger to Otho's claim. Vitellius, backed by the Rhine armies, marched on Rome in an attempt to press his claims. After Otho's forces were defeated on the south bank of the river Po, he committed suicide in the hope that he could save the imperial capital and his relatives from the horror of further bloodshed.[9] Vitellius's claim to the imperial throne was poor, his power base was weak, and his tyrannical actions alienated him from the population of Rome. He had Vespasian's brother Sabinus and his Flavian relatives killed, his troops looted Rome, and many buildings were destroyed by fire. Vespasian, the military strategist, then made his move. Rather than march directly on the capital, Vespasian, the former proconsul of Egypt, marched to Alexandria. His administrative knowledge made him aware of the importance of the wheat that was shipped from Egypt to the imperial capital. He cut off the food supply from Africa and with the allegiance of the Danubian armies, who had been loyal to Otho, he cut off the supply routes to the north of the capital. Vespasian had been a master of siege tactics; he used them with great effect against Vitellius. In the not too distant future, they would be used by his armies against Jerusalem, too. Soon, news of Vitellius's assassination reached Vespasian, who then quickly reached the capital. Much of Rome was in ruin, morale was low, and the people were wary of another harsh emperor.

Reading the mood of the populace, Vespasian commenced a rebuilding program.[10] Suetonius recalls that Vespasian, in a highly symbolic action, "personally inaugurated the restoration of the burned Capitol by collecting the first basketful of rubble and carrying it away on his shoulders."[11] From his own funds, he paid for the reconstruction of the aqueduct. He inaugurated several building programs, including the Colosseum.[12] Moreover, he sought to reform the justice system by clearing the waiting list of lawsuits, many of which had been left undecided because of the interruptions to normal government.[13]

Vespasian also had an unfinished rebellion to deal with in Judea, which he left to the charge of his son Titus. It is often asserted that Vespasian's unrelenting siege of Jerusalem and the annihilation of the inhabitants of the city were due to his desire to have a triumph at the beginning of his reign. In part this reasoning can be attributed to Suetonius's comment that "with such a mighty reputation—he had now been decreed a triumph over the Jews."[14] The explanation, however, is probably due to more pragmatic factors. Vespasian's Rome needed an injection of capital funding, and the easiest source of revenue was to be gained through booty. While despoiling the temple supplied the immediate solution to Rome's cash crisis, there was also a need for an ongoing source of revenue. Again, the Jews offered Vespasian the solution to his financial problems.

Figure 18.1: Sestertius of Titus, 80–81 C.E.

Struck 71 C.E. (Triton V. 1915)
FRONT: head of Vespasian. REVERSE: inscription IVDEA CAPTA with palm tree
flanked by standing male and seated female captive, recalling the triumph
Titus celebrated ten years earlier.

The *Fiscus Judaicus* and Winning Roman Hearts and Minds

The conceptual origin of the temple tax is usually seen as stemming back to the census described in Exodus 30:11-16. According to the divine oracle received by Moses, every Israelite male over the age of twenty was to pay half a shekel towards the construction of the sanctuary. In the post-exilic period, a similar practice was apparently introduced.[15] The description of the tax in Nehemiah 10:32, however, varies from the prescription in Exodus regarding the amount to be contributed to the temple. According to Nehemiah, the levy was to be one-third of a shekel. Later still, in the first century C.E. and prior to the destruction of the temple, Philo describes the collection of the temple tax among Diaspora Jews (*Spec. Laws* 1.78). Moreover, the rabbinic tractate *m. Seqal.*, probably dating from the early third century C.E. in its final form, discusses, possibly somewhat anachronistically, the rules pertaining to the collection of the tax.[16] Yet it consistently refers to the tax as "the shekel dues" or "the shekel." This reference should not be understood as a doubling of the rate payable, but rather as a generic term for the levy. This likelihood is supported in *m. Seqal.* 2.4, where the rabbis discuss the different units of currency that have been used to pay the tax, and as Danby points out, these amounts are equal in value to half a shekel.[17]

After the destruction of the Jerusalem temple, a major shift occurred in both the collection and purpose of the tax. Whereas previously the tax had only been levied from free Jewish males between the ages of twenty and fifty, under Vespasian those liable to pay were increased. There was no longer an upper limit on the age at which men ceased paying the tax,[18] and it was also expanded to include women up to sixty-two and children over three. Goodman suggests that Vespasian's imposition of the *fiscus Judaicus* was part of a deliberate strategy to degrade the Jewish state, culture, and religion:

> This tax, the *fiscus Judaicus,* symbolized the deliberate destruction not just of the free Jewish state but of the religion and society of Judaea before A.D. 66. No thought of repairing the Temple was to be entertained and it is highly unlikely (though not impossible) that any sort of sacrificial cult was revived on the ruined site.[19]

While Goodman's description may be correct in describing the consequences of Vespasian's fiscal policy towards the Jews, whether his motives have been accurately portrayed is doubtful. Having been elevated to the position of emperor shortly before the capitulation of Jerusalem, Vespasian found the imperial capital in a state of ruin, the morale was low, and people were reticent about the prospect of yet another military figure as emperor. The new emperor was not unaware that the stability of the empire and, consequently, his own premiership were dependent upon being able to portray life in the capital as having returned to normal. Apart from economic stability, Vespasian showed an awareness of symbolic actions as representations of the return of *pax romana.* Apart from the restoration of the burned Capitol, he promised to replace the 3,000 bronze tablets that had stood in the Capitol, which recorded senatorial decrees and other significant records of Roman history.[20] Such projects designed to restore public confidence required vast sums of money. Suetonius records that, at his accession, Vespasian stated that 40,000 million sesterces was the amount required to put the country on its feet again.[21] Such an immediate and large-scale injection of capital into the imperial treasury meant that the required prosperity in Rome could only be achieved by increasing the tax burden, mainly upon the provinces.

Undercutting Goodman's claim that the *fiscus Judaicus* was instituted to bring about the deliberate destruction of the Jewish state are the other tax reforms introduced by Vespasian. Suetonius notes that the emperor's fiscal policy resulted in higher taxes, and that he engaged in dubious financial ventures. Yet contrary to some opinions, Suetonius absolves Vespasian of the charge of avarice, and while acknowledging the morally ambiguous methods employed in his money raising, he, nevertheless, declares that the emperor used the income to ensure political stability and social benefit. As Suetonius states:

Figure 18.2 Relief on the Titus Arch depicting the Spoils of Jerusalem

The scene depicts the triumphal procession with the booty from the temple at Jerusalem—
the sacred Menorah, the Table of the Shewbread shown at an angle, and the silver
trumpets which called the Jews to Rosh Hashanah. Placards in the background explain
the spoils or the victories Titus won.

> Not content with restoring the duties remitted by Galba he levied new and
> heavier ones; increased, and sometimes doubled, the tribute due from the
> provinces; and openly engaged in business dealings which would have dis-
> graced even a private citizen. . . . Certainly he spent his income to the best
> possible advantage, however questionable its sources.[22]

Levick catalogues a number of the fiscal reforms that Vespasian
introduced after becoming emperor. He reclaimed public property and
used it for financial gain; he increased the rate of existing taxes; money
was collected from those using unallocated land in the colonies; in
Africa, provincial boundaries were altered so that the cinnabar mines
would fall under the jurisdiction of an imperial legate and, thus, be subject to taxation; he reintroduced some taxes abolished by Galba; and
with these reforms, he instigated the *fiscus Judaicus*.[23] Although this levy
had an obvious socio-religious focus, to view it as an ancient exercise in
ethnic cleansing is incorrect. Rather, it represented only a single part of
an overall economic strategy to bring prosperity and financial stability to
the people of Rome, and, hence, to protect Vespasian's own position.
Admittedly, the Jews were an easy target for the new emperor, and he

showed all the willingness of a cunning pragmatist in exploiting their marginalized position. Obviously, the tax was intended both as a punishment and deterrent for the Jews because of their rebellion. However, the important observation made by Griffin needs to be recalled: "Though the imposition of a tax on the Jews had a punitive origin, it also implied the legality of their practices."[24] Nonetheless, in order to portray himself as the bringer of peace and the benefactor of the citizens, Vespasian introduced a harsh regime of taxation, especially on those in the provinces and colonies.

Nerva and Tax Relief, but for Whom?

Details concerning the ongoing implementation and collection of the *fiscus Judaicus* are scant. In fact, chronologically the next reference in the classical sources is in connection with the harsh treatment meted out by Domitian in collecting the tax. In a well-known story, Suetonius relates how Domitian employed invasive techniques to establish whether a person was liable to pay the levy. He recounts:

> Domitian's agents collected the tax on Jews with a peculiar lack of mercy; and took proceedings not only against those who kept their Jewish origins a secret in order to avoid the tax, but against those who lived as Jews without professing Judaism. As a boy, I once remember attending a crowded Court where an imperial agent had a ninety year old man inspected to establish whether or not he had been circumcised.[25]

Once again, however, to see Domitian as singling out the Jews is a mistake.[26] The rapacious nature of Domitian's reign was a consequence of his lavish excesses in holding games and erecting monuments. Pliny rails against him as "that despoiler and executioner of the best men."[27] Yet the largest single contributing factor to Domitian's financial problems was his increase in military expenditure. This point is noted by Griffin. She states, "It was, however, an act of liberality, not of mere abstinence, that contrasts most strongly with Vespasian's frugality —the rise in army pay, regarded by both Suetonius and Dio as the prime cause of Domitian's financial shortfall."[28] Whereas Vespasian had introduced various taxes to restore imperial economic stability, Domitian required all the revenue he could glean simply to maintain his ostentatious spending program. The oppressive revenue-raising methods employed by Domitian were also aimed at non-Jews. Pliny draws a contrast between the Domitianic financial practices, which placed excessive burdens on private citizens, and the relief enjoyed under Trajan.[29] Similarly, Nerva's liberality in regard to financing the public aqueducts from his own revenue rather than extracting the money from private citizens is noted by Frontinus.[30] This practice implicitly appears to be in contrast with Domitian's reign.

Nerva's reign forms a marked contrast with the repression and fear that had been the hallmarks of his predecessor's period in office. Cruelty and rapacity were replaced by liberality and frugality. Reform of Roman fiscal policy was a priority.[31] Within the sphere of tax collection, relief was provided in many areas, including inheritance tax.[32] Evidence for the reform of the *fiscus Judaicus* in Nerva's reign is derived from a numismatic inscription. A series of coin issues under Nerva carried the legend *Fisci Iudaici Calumnia Sublata*, "relief from the abuses of the Jewish tax."

Figure 18.3

Reverse of Brass Coin of Nerva, Bearing Inscription "Fisci Iudaici Calumnia Sublata."[33]

What precisely constituted this *calumnia* is debated.[34] Thompson, however, makes a compelling case that:

> Domitian's innovation amounted to a systematic attempt to levy the tax on apostates from Judaism, and on other circumcised men who were not Roman citizens: people who had not previously been liable, but were regarded as *Iudaei* by Domitian's administration.[35]

While the inclusion of circumcised non-Jewish non-Roman citizens may be extending the category beyond the support of the evidence, the main point that apostate or nonpracticing Jews were subject to the tax is persuasive. This point also aligns with the incident recounted by Suetonius: the nonagenarian was unrecognizable as a Jew apart from the physical mark he had received in his infancy.

Thus, while Domitian's oppressive fiscal policy blurred the distinctions between self-declared and nonpracticing Jews, Nerva's removal of the *calumnia* did more than simply to revert the situation to that which existed during the reigns of Vespasian and Titus. At the instigation of the *fiscus*, as Goodman notes:

> Jews paid the tax because of their religion, but they were defined as Jews by their ethnic origin. It was simply assumed that all ethnic Jews subscribed to the national cult . . . . The assumption that ethnic origin presupposed religious practices is entirely in accordance with standard pagan use of the Greek term Ἰουδαῖος, Latin *Judaeus*, before A.D. 70. This assumption is not very surprising, since it was also the standard found in Philo and Josephus.[36]

From this observation, Goodman argues that Nerva's relief for nonpracticing Jews from payment of the tax redefined the basis of Jewish identity. The benefit for those who continued paying the tax was the freedom to practice their religious rites being protected by the state as a *religio licta*. Thus, it is suggested that, "[t]he (presumably unintended) side-effects of this new Roman criterion for Jewish identity—a Jew was anybody who volunteered to pay the *fiscus Judaicus* to the Roman state—were considerable, not least in a new awareness of the notion of a proselyte."[37]

In this vein Goodman argues that Nerva's removal of the *calumnia* had the inadvertent effect of reformulating Jewish identity no longer in terms of ethnic origin, but rather based upon three factors: practice, profession, and payment of the tax. Practice alone, however, was not enough for a Gentile to be considered as a convert to Judaism. Epictetus, in a discourse dating from the early second century during the reign of Trajan, makes this distinction: "Whenever we see a man halting between two faiths, we are in the habit of saying, 'He is not a Jew, he is only acting the part'. But when he adopts the attitude of mind of the man who has been baptized and has made his choice, then he both is a Jew in fact and is called one."[38] Thus, adoption of Jewish practices alone did not constitute identification as a Jew. Rather, profession was required. In the public arena, the payment of the *fiscus* not only was a declaration of Jewishness, but also came with the incentive of acting as a type of license that allowed the payee to practice the Jewish faith without fear of persecution. There is, however, the potential that too much can be attributed to the Jewish tax as the key factor in reformulating Jewish identity. Alongside the changes that the tax introduced in recognizing individuals as Jews, it must also be remembered that the destruction of the temple altered the very fabric of what it meant to be Jewish. No longer was religious identity centred upon the temple and participation in the great pilgrimage festivals,[39] rather a new identity was formulated from inside the matrix of Judaism. Temple was replaced by synagogue as the central religious locale, and scripture replaced sacrifice as an offering to God.[40]

Jesus and the Jewish Tax: A Temporal Anachronism?

The crucifixion of Jesus occurred under the prefecture of Pontius Pilate, during the reign of Tiberius, approximately forty years before the destruction of Jerusalem and the introduction the *fiscus Judaicus*.[41] It may, therefore, be asked: What relevance is contained in a story about Jesus for understanding the Jewish tax that was introduced four decades after his death? New Testament scholars, however, have long been aware that the records of Jesus' ministry that are contained in the gospels—while concerned with the life and sayings of Jesus himself—also seek to tell such stories in a manner that is relevant to the religious, social, and pastoral concerns of the communities for which the individual evangelists were writing. Although there have recently been some dissenting voices concerning the validity of utilizing gospel texts as windows into the social world of the communities of the evangelists,[42] the majority of scholars still advocate the use of this methodology.[43]

One such story that betrays signs of being told for its relevance to community concerns is contained in Matthew 17:24-27. This pericope describes an incident ostensibly set within the life of the historical Jesus. While in Capernaum, Peter is approached by the collectors of the didrachma tax and asked if his teacher pays the levy. Unequivocally, Peter answers in the affirmative, and then returns to the house where Jesus is staying. Before Peter has a chance to mention the topic, Jesus anticipates him and introduces a general discussion concerning the payment of tax. He implies that both he and his followers are not obliged to make the payment (contrary to Peter's assumption), but, nonetheless, he advises that they do so in order to avoid causing offence. Peter is then commanded to go to the sea to catch a fish, and he will find a stater in its mouth, a coin equal to four drachmas, the amount required to pay the tax for both Jesus and himself. Although only the command is recorded and not Peter's actual performance of this action, the reader is not meant to doubt that the miracle happened just as Jesus promised.

This text provides a number of clues that suggest the presence of redactional activity. Based primarily on Matthean stylistic traits,

Kilpatrick suggests that this pericope, which he sees as a composite of traditional and redactional elements, reveals the reworking of the editorial hand through distinctively Matthean vocabulary.[44] Moreover, the prominence of Peter in this story reflects a widespread tendency in the first gospel to heighten both the authority and significance of Peter.[45] Also, the folkloric quality[46] of the miracle suggests a common element added to the story, probably as a reflection of pastoral concerns. Having these redactional elements now identified, an investigation of the pastoral purpose Matthew intended for his community through the retelling of this story is appropriate.

Matthew's gospel was most likely written at some time during the reign of Domitian, and almost certainly while Roman officials were engaged in the collection of the *fiscus Judaicus*. While the incident in Matthew 17:24-27 is seen as having a pre-gospel history prior to 70 C.E. and, in that context, is addressing the issue of the payment of the temple tax, most scholars argue that when the story is taken up into the Matthean narrative, it ceases to deal with the question of taxes and instead its concerns are spiritualized.[47] Most commonly the pericope is seen in its present context as presenting teachings about the exercise of Christian freedom, or behaving so as not to cause offence (cf. 18:1-14). Carter notes an inherent difficulty with interpreting this story as advice from Jesus not to cause offence to the Jewish religious leaders who instigated the collection of the temple tax:

> If this is the temple tax and its collectors are the agents of the religious leaders, why is Jesus now concerned not to aggravate them? He has scandalized them (cf. 13:57) since ch[apter] 8, and warned his disciples that they will do the same and pay a price for it (10:17-18). He knows that the leaders are "scandalized" at him (15:12), intend to kill him (12:14-15), and he says so publicly (16:21-22). . . . The narrative context, then destroys the claim that 17:24-27 exhorts a disciple not to scandalize the religious leaders or their agents.[48]

However, to see this story functioning on two levels is possible. The first is the pre-gospel level, when it was recalled because of the instruction it offered about the temple tax; secondly, it is also preserved in the Matthean narrative because of the strategy it suggested in regard to the *fiscus Judaicus*.

It should be noted that as the pericope stands, it contains no reference to the temple or Jewish officials. If it ever had explicit connections with the Jewish context and temple cult, these have been stripped away.

Admittedly, neither are there any explicitly Roman links, however, there could be significant reasons for the evangelist veiling his political advice to the community for whom he was writing. It has already been argued, contrary to certain scholarly opinion, that the introduction of the tax under Vespasian was not concerned with some form of Roman ethnic cleansing directed towards the Jews. He needed to demonstrate that he could restore social stability and bring economic prosperity to the capital. In fact, payment of the tax almost granted a license to practice the Jewish religion without fear of persecution.[49] Similarly, Domitian's attitude toward the Jews was not designed to be harsh for its own sake. Instead, his goal was to exact as much revenue as possible from any person who had the slightest connection with Judaism. The Matthean community is recognized by New Testament scholars as being the most Jewish in character of all the groups for whom the canonical gospels were written.[50] Almost certainly in his zeal to raise revenue, Domitian instructed his collectors to target the Jewish-Christians who were members of the Matthean group. Garland suggests that:

> [I]t is unwise to conclude that Jewish or Gentile Christians were liable [to taxation] from the beginning since the evidence indicates that those who were obligated to pay were those who wished to observe the customs of the fathers—to practice Judaism. This would not have included Christians.[51]

The evidence from Suetonius undermines this argument. It is precisely the fact that a person who can in no way be identified as a Jew apart from the mark of circumcision—and the humiliating verification of this mark—which Suetonius recalls as the excesses of the tax collection.[52] While there is no evidence by which it can be demonstrated either way that the Matthean community maintained the practice of circumcision, it is likely that the male Jewish-Christian members had been circumcised in their childhood. Although the degree of separation between the Matthean community and formative Judaism is much debated,[53] no doubt they were more readily identified with Judaism than non-practicing Jews. The reading of the Jewish scriptures remained central; meeting regularly was part of their community life. Their worship centered on a messianic figure. The Roman tax collectors were not interested in the niceties of theological distinctions. The more they raised, the more they profited personally. Matthew's group surely would have been a target of revenue collection.

Perhaps community members felt aggrieved at being forced to pay the *fiscus*. The Matthean Jesus, in fact, agrees with them; nonetheless, he counsels compliance although they in fact know that their status as "sons" (Matt 17:26) exempts them from this requirement. Bauckham maintains that this argument must mean that the temple tax is under discussion, since only in respect to a tax, which God himself in effect levies, can he exempt his "sons" from the duty of payment.[54] However, the logic appears to be faulty. Since the Matthean community acknowledged the sovereignty of God over the whole world, they were exempt, at least theoretically, from all temporal requirements.[55] The advice to comply with the payment is both subversive and politically astute at the same time.

Obviously, compliance with payment of the tax was a politically shrewd decision in that it gave the Matthean community a certain degree of freedom in their religious practices.[56] Shrewdness, however, does not always comport with religious principles; Matthew had to demonstrate to community members that payment of the *fiscus* was not only astute, but was also a demonstration of the community's faith. The miraculous procuring of the coin demonstrates not only "God's sovereignty over creation, but also over the tax."[57] In this way, the very act of obedience to taxation can also be interpreted as a subversive action that actually declares to community members the sovereignty of God.

While such a strategy was possible during the reign of Domitian, such a practice may not have been possible after the reforms introduced by Nerva. The community was no longer forced into compliance, and no longer could they inadvertently benefit from the status of "Jew," which was forced upon them by tax collectors. While no documents exist for the Matthean community apart from the gospel,[58] relief from paying the tax, apparently, would not have been a blessing. It is not surprising that during the reign of Trajan, Christians became more visible and that Pliny the Younger sought imperial guidance concerning the attitude of the state towards Christians.[59] Therefore Nerva's reforms of the *fiscus Judaicus* not only introduced changed perceptions about Jewish identity, but perhaps contributed to creating a firmer boundary between Jews and Christians and perhaps made Christians more identifiable as a separate religious group within the empire.

The End of the *Fiscus Judaicus*

Many scholars have drawn the erroneous conclusion that the reform instituted by Nerva, as witnessed in the legend on his coinage, in fact denotes the abolition of the Jewish tax. Beare simply states such a conclusion: "this [the *fiscus Judaicus*] was collected through the reigns of the

Flavian Emperors (Vespasian, Titus, Domitian), but was abolished by
Nerva (97–98)."[60] Not only does such an interpretation misunderstand
the meaning of the inscription *Fisci Iudaici Calumnia Sublata*, but, more
important, it fails to take account of later evidence for the ongoing collection of the tax. Numerous ostraca discovered at Edfu in Egypt document the receipt of payment of the Jewish tax during the reign of Trajan
(98–117 C.E.). Often the receipts show that the *fiscus Judaicus* was paid
in conjunction with other dues, such as the *laographia*. A typical inscription on one of the ostrakon reads:

> Meious, son of Thedetos, in respect of the Jewish tax for the nineteenth
> year of our lord Trajan Optimus Caesar, four drachmai. Year 19,
> Pharmouthi 25.[61]

Such inscriptions provide evidence that the *fiscus Judaicus* was collected
throughout the Trajanic period, that is for the nineteen years following
the death of Nerva, which occurred in 98 C.E.

There is, however, more striking evidence from a later period. As late
as the first half of the third century, Origin refers to the ongoing collection of the *fiscus*.[62] Describing the privileges enjoyed by the ethnarch,
Origin mentions the fact that the Jews pay the half-shekel to the imperial authorities:

> Now, for instance, that the Romans rule, and the Jews pay the half-shekel
> to them, how great power by the concession of Caesar the ethnarch has; so
> that we, who have had experience of it, know that he differs in little from
> a true king.[63]

Although the reference from Origin does not provide a *terminus* for the
Jewish tax, it conclusively shows that it was still being collected as much
as one hundred and fifty years later than many scholars acknowledge.[64]

While certainty about the date of cessation of the *fiscus Judaicus* is
not possible, an infrequently cited letter from Julian to the community
of Jews[65] may, perhaps, give some clues. It must immediately be acknowledged that its references are opaque. While the tax that is mentioned may
plausibly be the levy originally instituted by Vespasian, it is not impossible that another toll might be under discussion. If it is in fact the case
that Julian is referring to the *fiscus Judaicus*, then it appears likely that the
tax was finally abolished during his reign (360–363 C.E.).[66] The text is
worth citing at length, both to illustrate the ambiguities it contains and
also to discern Julian's possible motivations for abolishing the tax in
question:

In times past, by far the most burdensome thing in the yoke of your slavery has been the fact that you were subjected to unauthorised ordinances and had to contribute an untold amount of money to the accounts of the treasury. Of this I used to see many instances with my own eyes, and I have learned of more, by finding the records which are preserved against you. Moreover, when a tax was about to be levied on you again I prevented it, and compelled the impiety of such obloquy to cease here; and I threw into the fire the records against you that were stored in my desks; so that it is no longer possible for anyone to aim at you such a reproach of impiety. My brother Constantius of honored memory was not so much responsible for these wrongs of yours as were the men who used to frequent his table, barbarians in mind godless in soul. These I seized with my own hands and put them to death by thrusting them into the pit, that not even any memory of their destruction might linger amongst us. And since I wish that you should prosper yet more, I have admonished my brother Iulus, your most venerable patriarch, that the levy which is said to exist among you should be prohibited, and no one is any longer to have the power to oppress the masses of your people by such exactions; so that everywhere, during my reign, you may have security of mind, and in the enjoyment of peace may offer more fervid prayers for my reign to the Most High God, the Creator, who has deigned to crown me with his own immaculate right hand.[67]

Although the tax in question is not directly named as the *fiscus Judaicus* there are a number of points in the letter that suggest this identification. Both the tax referred to here and the *fiscus Judaicus* raised vast amounts of money for the treasury,[68] they both had been in force for a long period of time,[69] they were levied on a regular basis,[70] moreover, both were burdensome and could be described as a yoke of slavery.[71] Obviously, these similarities are not strong enough to make such an identification secure, but it is, nonetheless, highly suggestive.

According to Julian, his explicit motivations in abolishing the tax were twofold: (1) to create economic stability among the Jews and (2) to enjoy the benefits that would accrue to his reign by having the Jews offer up prayers for him "to the Most High God."[72] Other reasons, however, may be adduced for Julian's decision to prevent a tax being levied from the Jews and to write to them directly about this matter. Implicit in the letter is the concern about the reputation of his cousin Constantius, who was emperor prior to Julian.[73] This concern, no doubt, also benefited Julian by promoting the integrity and honor of the Constantinian dynasty. A second undeclared concern may have been a desire to undermine the newfound status of Christianity within the empire. Julian's personal commitment to paganism is well known, and it had the unfortunate consequence of earning him the epitaph "the apostate." He actively disparaged Christianity and promoted a return to the ancestral pagan religious cults of the empire. In his tractate *Against the Galilaeans*,[74] Julian's main purpose is to demonstrate that, contrary to Christian claims, the Hebrew scriptures do not support the idea that their teachings are a development of Judaism. By strengthening the Jews financial position and removing the notion of their subservience as a vanquished people, Julian was seeking to undermine a key claim advanced by Christians in the Patristic period: namely, that the destruction of Jerusalem and the subjugation of the Jewish nation was God's punishment upon them for rejecting his Messiah. Not only did Julian seek to undercut this argument by restoring Jewish prosperity, he also wished to resettle Jews in Jerusalem:

> [W]hen I have successfully concluded the war with Persia, I may rebuild by my own efforts the sacred city of Jerusalem, which for so many years you have longed to see inhabited, and may bring settlers there, and, together with you, may glorify the Most High God therein.[75]

Due to Julian's brief reign, his promise never materialized.[76] Nevertheless, it illustrates his positive attitude towards Judaism, which is in marked contrast to the hostility displayed toward Christianity.

If the speculation is, indeed, correct—that the levy that Julian abolished was the *fiscus Judaicus*—then, like its introduction, the abolition of the tax was not conceived as an end in itself, but rather because it could be used to influence the attitudes of people within the empire. The specific mindset that Julian sought to overturn was the claim that Christianity was a universal religion that worshipped the true God, in opposition to the pantheon of pagan deities. Moreover, it claimed that this one true God had forsaken the Jewish people, since they had crucified his messianic envoy, and consequently had brought about the destruction of their cult. The reestablishment of Jerusalem, the reconstitution of the Jewish cult and the removal of the implied servitude under the burden of taxation were all key ways in which Julian envisaged attacking Christian claims.

Concluding Remarks

In as much as sources from antiquity allow comment on the purpose of the *fiscus Judaicus*, it is possible to see that while its primary purpose was to raise revenue, this appears often to be linked with producing attitudinal changes in the minds of various groups of imperial subjects. Initially, Vespasian introduced the tax to fund his rebuilding of Rome.[77] This was not, however, independent of the image he sought to portray in relation to his administration.

While the destruction of the temple may have caused new considerations to develop in regard to how one practiced Judaism, the reforms of Nerva may have inadvertently resulted in a fresh response to the question of who was Jewish. To attribute the reformulation of Jewish identity to this factor alone would be incorrect. Nonetheless, it was an important contributing cause to the way in which Jewishness was perceived by both Jews and non-Jews. Not only was profession of the Jewish faith (along with payment of the tax) the way in which one was granted certain immunity from civic cults and participation in court cases on the sabbath,[78] but nonpayment of the tax was allowed by those who were ethnically Jewish but chose to give up their Jewish practices.

The reforms introduced by Nerva may have had the reverse effect on the boundary between Jews and Christians, in effect making it less permeable. Domitian's harsh exaction of the tax from everybody who could loosely be classed as Jewish might, perhaps, have worked to the benefit of Jewish Christian groups such as Matthew's community. In effect, the nonvoluntary nature of the tax prior to Nerva meant that, while one was not choosing the label "Jew," one might claim that payment of the tax represented a quietistic attitude towards government, but it also allowed the practice of religious freedom. Perhaps early followers of Jesus might even have been thankful that they had been labelled "Jews," even if they would not label themselves as such. The Matthean story functioned as a shrewd pastoral and political strategy. Any concerns group members may have had about not confessing their faith in Jesus—by hiding behind a veneer of Jewishness—are abolished. Jesus himself, who supported the principle of nonpayment, counsels the pragmatic path of compliance with the fiscal levy. Moreover, as Carter notes, the miraculous provision of the coin transforms this strategy from one of weak subservience to that of radical subversion.[79]

If identifying the end of the *fiscus Judaicus* with the Jewish tax that Julian abolished during his brief reign is correct, then once again the desire to alter perceptions of the population of the Roman Empire comes to the fore. Julian's letter to the community of Jews[80] should not be seen solely as a benevolent act. Rather it should be seen as part of his wider program to rejuvenate pagan cults and to subvert Christianity.[81] The leniency shown toward Jews was not an indicator of Julian's personal attraction to the Jewish faith. Rather, he was just as capable of scoffing at Jewish beliefs as Christian beliefs.[82] Instead, the reempowerment of Jews was part of a strategy to undercut Christian claims, especially by negating the claim that God's favor had been transferred from Jews to Christians and that this had been powerfully exhibited in the destruction of the temple. Thus, through all of its major phases, the *fiscus Judaicus* was not just about raising revenue. It was also used to introduce attitudinal change in the empire.

Chapter 19

Paul's Religious Experience
in the Eyes of Jewish Scholars

Alan F. Segal

Larry W. Hurtado is one of the most brilliant and quick-thinking scholars I have ever met. These characteristics are usually mutually exclusive, and so to find them together is something of a rarity. I have constantly appreciated both his observations and the amazing speed with which he is able to understand the implications of an argument. No doubt he remembers exactly our first meeting. But I only remember that we sat together on a bus ride during the Canadian Society of Biblical Studies meeting at part of the Canadian Learneds. It was the beginning of, for me, a very fertile and important intellectual friendship.

One of the most important parts of that relationship has been his encouragement to investigate the importance of religious experience in the ancient world and, in particular, in Christianity. Most recently I was very touched when he dedicated *How on Earth Did Jesus Become a God? Historical Questions about Earliest Devotion to Jesus* to me.[1] That book, at core, reflects a series of essays that he gave in Israel at the Ben Gurion University of the Negev, inaugurating the Deichmann Program for Jewish and Christian Literature of the Hellenistic-Roman Era, a most unusual and high honor, which he richly deserves. In this series of essays, he provides an essay on the scholarly perception of religious experience in the NT. In this essay, I would like to supplement his perceptions by discussing a similar topic in Jewish appreciations of the apostle Paul.

Jews of the modern period have almost universally reacted to the early history of Christianity by separating Jesus and Paul as two very different kinds of Jews with two different effects on Jewish and Christian history. In Jewish eyes, Jesus is almost always viewed as an ordinary Jew, perhaps of extraordinary talents as a teacher and thinker, who lived his life prophetically as a Jew and who, like many others of his day, was martyred for his beliefs. Paul, on the other hand, has as often been seen as the real founder of Christianity and an apostate who misunderstood that Jesus' message was entirely comprehensible within Judaism.[2] Few Jews mention religious experience within the life of Jesus. Almost no Jews mention Paul's visionary religious experience as an important issue in his life. Probably this portrait has been maintained as much by the pulpit rabbinate, who need to mediate between their congregants and the pervasive Christian culture of the United States. On the whole, most Christians would be surprised to learn that ordinary Jews have not read any of the New Testament. And modern Jews do not easily discuss religious experience at all, preferring instead to discuss religion as prayer, service, and ethics.

Many Jews who entered academia in the nineteenth, twentieth, and twenty-first centuries developed a small but significant body of literature on the apostle Paul from an intellectual, Jewish perspective. Starting in the middle to latter part of the twentieth century and the beginning of the twenty-first century, Jews have entered the study of Hellenistic Judaism in greater numbers. A few have even been trained in New Testament studies, holding positions in New Testament at American universities and seminaries, and giving an expert interpretation of Paul's writings. All assume that new perceptions about Paul will be gained by reading him over against, as well as in consonance with, his Jewish environment. All assume that Paul's career exemplifies a growing difference between Jewish law and the Gentile converts to Christianity. All the Jewish critics identify with liberal Christian scholarship. Most (but not all) attempt to locate Paul's distinct error, which led to the separation between Judaism and Christianity. Many (but not all) see Paul within the context of Hellenistic Judaism rather than Pharisaic Judaism.

No doubt Paul has been significantly used by Jewish scholars to mediate issues of Jewish identity. Perhaps, this alone explains the lack of interest in Paul's religious experience. The earlier writers tend to use Paul as a symbol for their own particular theoretical understanding of Judaism and Christianity. The more recent Jewish commentators, as one might suspect, are better understood as proponents of one or another school of NT criticism rather than representing a distinctively Jewish school of historiography. However, this does not mean that the use of Paul as a symbol of Jewish identity issues has disappeared in the modern period. Reading the early treatments of Paul, one is struck by how much they tell us about the predicament of modern Jewish life and how little they tell us about Paul. Of the most recent discussants, one is struck about how professional they are.

The complete modern history of Jewish commentary on Paul has been amply and most ably recorded by Stefan Meissner, in his dissertation, "Die Heimholung des Ketzers: Studien zur jüdischen Auseinandersetzung mit Paulus."[3] This most helpful book deserves to be translated into other languages. There are also a number of significant monographs and articles in English. Primary among them is Nancy Fuchs-Kreimer's as yet unpublished dissertation, "'The Essential Heresy': Paul's View of the Law According to Jewish Writers, 1886–1986," although it obviously does not cover the most significant new writers on Paul and should do so before it is published.[4] Donald Hagner published a review article on Jewish writers on Paul called "Paul in Modern Jewish Thought."[5] His subsequent book, *The Jewish Reclamation of Jesus: An Analysis and Critique of the Modern Jewish Study of Jesus*,[6] presents material on a closely associated subject. Jonathan D. Brumberg-Kraus has published an interesting ideological critique of the work of Jewish NT scholars to date.[7] Daniel Langton, of the Centre for Jewish Studies at the University of Manchester in England, has graciously made available to me two long review articles that will appear in the *Journal for the Study of the New Testament*. They are "The Myth of the 'Traditional View of Paul' and the Role of the Apostle in Modern Jewish-Christian Polemics," and "Modern Jewish Identity and the Apostle Paul: Pauline Studies as an Intra-Jewish Ideological Battleground." He has followed up on Brumberg-Kraus's observations with a very searching programmatic article on the agendas of Jewish scholars studying NT and Paul. Pamela Eisenberg has reflected on these issues in quite a different way in her essay, "Following in the Footnotes of the Apostle Paul," in an essay in *Identity and Politics of Scholars in the Study of Religion*.[8] She feels, almost in polar opposition to Brumberg-Kraus, that there are no ideological agendas common to contemporary Jewish writers on the NT. Our job will be to decide between these polar positions.

Since the subject has already received comprehensive treatment, this article will only underline some of the principal themes of the history of Jewish scholarship on Paul and extend the study beyond 1996, when Meissner's book was published. It will make no attempt to cover the earlier period at all. Instead, I will emphasize some aspects of the writing of Klausner, Rubenstein, Schoeps, and Samuel Sandmel because they continue to influence contemporary Pauline scholarship written by Jews. I will then consider Segal (myself), Boyarin, and Mark Nanos, who have

all written at least one book on Paul. Finally, I will consider the main
question about whether ideology still mostly describes Jewish scholarship
on Paul. Throughout this essay, I will discuss each scholar's interest in
religious experience.

Joseph G. Klausner (1874–1958)

Joseph Klausner was born near Vilna but brought up as a Zionist in
Odessa in the Ukraine. Even in his earliest years, he evinced a strong
interest in Hebrew. He took a degree in Semitic languages at Heidelberg.
He eventually was invited to a position at Odessa after the Russian
Revolution. However, following the Bolshevik Revolution, he emigrated
to Israel, settling in Jerusalem and beginning a long academic career as
chair of Hebrew literature. Because of his secular views, he was not
appointed to his preferred position, chair in Jewish Literature at the
Hebrew University, until 1944, when he was seventy.

Besides his other accomplishments, he wrote two widely read books
on the beginnings of Christianity: *Jesus of Nazareth* (1922) and *From Jesus
to Paul* (1939), of which the latter largely concerned Paul. These two
books are the first books written on the subject of Christianity in modern
Hebrew. They also reflect Klausner's strong Zionism. For Klausner, Jesus
was a Jew who exemplifies the best and most prophetic qualities of
Judaism. Klausner speaks of Jesus' messianic self-consciousness and places
it within prophetic Judaism. Though he may have harbored some tendencies to separate himself from the rest of the Jewish community, he lived
and died a Jew born on the mainland of Jewish life. Klausner's Jesus of
Nazareth was widely accepted and praised in Christian circles. Though he
began the research of both books at the same time, his book on Paul,
From Jesus to Paul, was published some fifteen years later. In this book, he
describes Paul as a Diaspora Jew who did not understand Judaism in the
same way as a Jew born in the motherland. In some sense, it was Paul's
diaspora Judaism that allowed him to subsume his new Christian faith
into a more universal religion, but at the same time it was a religion that
was cut off from the living soil of Palestinian Judaism. Klausner relies on
other scholarship to link Paul's Christianity with the mystery cults of Late
Antiquity. Thus, any religious experience that Paul may have had came
from his contact with Hellenistic mysteries and not with Palestinian
Judaism. Without Jesus there would have been no Paul, but without Paul
there would have been no Christianity as we know it today. In some way
then, Jesus and Paul represent native Judaism and its less authentic

Diaspora Judaism. According to Klausner, Paul's ideas came to predominate in Christianity because of its universal, Diaspora character.

David Flusser (1917–1998)

David Flusser was an accomplished comparative religionist and historian of Second Temple Judaism. For Flusser, Jesus was also a Jew with a messianic self-consciousness who hid his messianic pretensions until such time as he could be revealed as the Messiah of Israel. Instead, however, he fell into the hands of the Romans and was never able to reveal his "messianic secret." This would imply that Jesus' private religious life was the only way in which his messianic identity could have been known. For Flusser, Jesus' messianic self-consciousness is his religious life. But he could not announce it until the Kingdom of God arrived, so it remained entirely private, only guessed at within his own community. For Flusser, though, Judaism and Christianity were not two fully different religions but two analogous responses to the social and political forces of Roman occupation in the Second Temple period. They both represented a new sensitivity to "divine justice as manifested in the world."[9]

Flusser sees Paul's dualism and various other aspects of his writings as due to sectarian Palestinian Judaism—the Dead Sea Scroll community and the Pharisees—as well as stoicism. So he does not subscribe to the Diaspora/homeland dichotomy that so pervaded Klausner's writing. He also disputes the dichotomy between grace and law that characterizes Lutheran scholarship on Paul. In this way, Flusser represents a more professionally trained scholar of late antiquity with fewer ideological leanings than Klausner. The greater part of Flusser's work is concerned with the Second Temple period, with Christian and Jewish writings intertwined for historiographic purposes. Klausner, on the other hand, certainly published significant works on the subject but had a more occasional interest.

Richard Rubenstein (1924–)

Richard Rubenstein's work almost represents the converse of Klausner, even as it was formulated in Diaspora Judaism. Richard Rubenstein is a Freudian interpreter of history and a death-of-God theologian. He was born in New York City and ordained at the Jewish Theological Seminary in 1952. After some congregational work, he settled into an academic position at the University of Florida, where he remained until his retirement, publishing on a number of issues concerning Judaism and

European history. After his retirement from the University of Florida, Rubenstein served as President of Fairfield University and now lives in retirement in Connecticut. His *After Auschwitz* (1966) was an enormously influential book for post-Holocaust Jewish theology and the death-of-God theological movement. In it, he maintained that God really did die at Auschwitz because the concept of a just God was no longer viable after the Holocaust. Religion might continue to have a role in human life, he went on to argue, because it organized human action in moral ways and tended to provide comfort to people in times of stress.

Rubenstein's approach to Paul, in his book *My Brother Paul*, is thoroughly psychoanalytic. He calls him his brother because he sees in Paul some of the same psychoanalytic dynamics that informed his own development. He sees Paul as a person who was able to conquer the self-effacing powerlessness of the rabbis and will himself, as well as his nascent Christian movement, toward political power.

To understand what this means in Rubenstein's life, one has to refer to his dissertation, which became the book *The Religious Imagination*,[10] and to his autobiography, *Power Struggle*. In *The Religious Imagination*, Rubenstein shows that the dynamic of rabbinic literature, and particularly the Midrash, was a fantasy of power by a group of people who essentially had no power in the world. The fantasy that God cared about rabbinic deliberations and that the history of the world depended on their moral behavior was the compensatory process which made a life of powerlessness possible. Just a few years later, in his autobiography, Rubenstein relates the story of how the lack of power had impinged on his life. He was wrongly accused of fighting by a policeman and his father. Powerless to change the situation, he completely acquiesced to the policeman's story. This, Rubenstein tells us, is one of the critical moments of his life. To see the close relationship between Rubenstein's own life and his analysis of Paul is entirely fair because for Rubenstein all history is psychohistory. Every historian is similarly working out the issues of his own life with his historiography. Nevertheless, it is hard to miss the way in which Paul becomes a symbol of psychological health for Rubenstein, but at the same time he is also a path out of Jewish identity.

Hans Joachim Schoeps (1909–1980)

H. J. Schoeps reflects a new, more *wissenschaftlicher* Jewish approach to the study of Paul in a European context. He was born in South Berlin to Prussian Jewish parents who later died in the Holocaust. Schoeps excelled in religious topics in school and attended university in "the science of comparative religion" (*vergleichenden Religionswissenschaft*). He was thoroughly acculturated to German society and an avid supporter of German nationality. He could, like most German Jews, distinguish between his cultural heritage and those of the Ostjueden, the much less sophisticated "Eastern European Jews." In his early years, he wrote on the "post-Jewish situation."

According to Daniel Langton, Schoeps was, in effect, converted back to Judaism by a Jewish friend and by the theology of the Protestant Neoconservative Karl Barth. Like most German reformers, Schoeps believed that his Judaism was based on the Sinaitic covenant rather than on a Jewish race.

Unfortunately, the Nazi party disagreed. Schoeps emigrated to Sweden in 1938, returning to Germany only after the war, where he taught religion and intellectual history at Erlangen, specializing in the history of early Christianity. He produced a major study of Paul, *Paulus: Die Theologie des Apostels im Lichte der juedischen Religionsgeschichte* (1959), which was translated quickly into English as *Paul: The Theology of the Apostle in the Light of Jewish Religious History* (1961). So Schoeps represents one of the first professionally trained Jewish NT scholars in Germany and certainly the most important professionally trained, early Jewish interpreter on Paul.

For Schoeps, Paul demonstrates characteristically rabbinic thinking, with some Hellenism nuances in his writing. As a pupil of Gamaliel in Jerusalem, he had direct access to the nascent, rabbinic movement. But he was unusual in his interest in eschatological apocalypticism and a personal messiah. Schoeps also believes that Paul's writings had been distorted by the Christian Church so that he appears more Hellenistic than he actually was. The key for Schoeps in understanding Paul's theology is to set him in his proper context. For him, as for W. D. Davies afterwards, Paul was a rabbinic Jew for whom the Messiah had come. Thus, the Law would be justly ended in the new messianic age. Schoeps and Davies did not see, however, how difficult it would be to find evidence in first-century Jewish sources that the Law would be ended in the messianic age. In any event, Schoeps was a fully functioning NT critic, living in the professional community of NT critics in Germany when it was the world capital of NT criticism.

Schoeps established himself as a cultural critic, too, when he criticized the failure of Jews throughout the centuries to distinguish adequately between the literal and a deeper understanding of Judaism. Langton, again, is a very good critic of Schoeps' position:

> If we understand the matter rightly, 1900 years ago, he [Saul] posed a question which tradition did not adequately answer as a Pharisaic theologian. We know the problem only in its Pauline setting, and so must translate it back into Judaic terms. It would then run somewhat as follows. If here and now the law as a whole does not seem "fulfillable," does not the fact perhaps suggest that the law is not an exhaustive expression of the will of God? [Should] the fulfilling of the law of Moses be understood literally and completely as a fulfilling of the will of God [?]. (Schoeps, *Paul*, 280)[13]

For Schoeps this error in Judaism was remediated in modern times with the thought of Hermann Cohen and Martin Buber, who can distinguish the commandment within the Law. So Schoeps, more or less, uses Paul as a cultural critic to point out what is necessary in his mind to keep Judaism a major force in modern history.

Samuel Sandmel (1911–1979)

Samuel Sandmel was born in Dayton, Ohio. He does not fit the characteristic profile of the midwestern American Jew who came to the United States in the nineteenth century with the failure of the liberal reforms in Germany. Instead, his family had fled Eastern Europe in the late nineteenth century in advance of the pogroms. He went to public school in Ohio and trained as a rabbi, obtaining ordination in 1937. As was traditional for Reform rabbis then, Sandmel served as a chaplain and was stationed in the Pacific in the navy during the Second World War years (1942–1946). He later attended Yale, where he studied under E. A. Goodenough and received a graduate degree in New Testament studies. He is, therefore, an example of the very few Jewish-American scholars of his generation to write on Paul and who trained in a New Testament program. Sandmel also worked as a rabbi for the Hillel Foundation (1939–1949) and so shouldered special responsibilities to Jewish college youth as well as represented Judaism to the university community. This combination of roles was hardly unique at the time, as many Christian Bible teachers in secular universities also served as chaplains.

Sandmel then became a professor of Bible and Hellenistic Literature at Hebrew Union College, the Reform Jewish Seminary of America (1952–1978), in Cincinnati Ohio. He was sometimes called "the Colonel" by his students because of his resemblance to a "Kentucky

Colonel" and his southern accent. Sandmel wrote extensively on the literature and history of the Judaism of Late Antiquity. His introduction to Philo Judaeus is still used in classrooms.[14] He also wrote *A Jewish Understanding of the New Testament* (1956) and *We Jews and Jesus* (1965) and *Anti-Semitism in the New Testament* (1978). As the titles suggest, these works both have academic concerns and also figure in the Jewish-Christian dialogue literature.

His work on Paul, *The Genius of Paul: A Study in History* (1958), was widely respected the world over. Frank Young said of the book in a brief private note to Sandmel: "You abandoned yourself to the possibility that St. Paul was a man of integrity, and whatever arguments could be raised over your definitions of his terms, you let him be a man with integrity. You showed your own in doing it."[15]

For Sandmel, Paul must be understood as different from Philo, his other great first-century interest. Paul rather should be seen in his early life within the milieu of the apocalyptic world, which the apostle made christological. This perception, not unique to Sandmel but the result of his own participation in the scholarly community of the NT and Late Antiquity, has been the basis of most subsequent understandings of Paul among scholars, except now Boyarin. Boyarin (whom we discuss later in this essay) mostly disagrees with the following statement of Sandmel, which talks about Paul's universalism (a theme particularly important for Boyarin, too): "Paul felt that his version of Judaism was for all humanity, yet Paul was no thoroughgoing universalist. His universalism did lead him to deny any difference between Jew and Greek, so long as both are in Christ."[16] As the title implies, Sandmel thought of Paul as a religious genius who was able to take the truths of Judaism to the Hellenistic world. So Paul was also part of the Hellenistic world. For Sandmel that meant no disrespect:

> To call Paul a Hellenistic Jew is not to put a value judgment on the nature of his Jewish fidelity but is only to state a fact. The Hellenistic world into which Paul was born, we know now, was one of many religious expressions and of earnest philosophical disputations. . . . There is no reason to be skeptical of his statement that in his study of Judaism he had surpassed his fellow students of his own age. Nor should there be doubt that he had achieved a skilful knowledge of Judaism. His statement that he had learned the traditions of his fathers is to be accepted—but the context of those Graeco-Jewish "traditions" is not to be confused with that which later centuries recorded as the product of the Jewish schools in Palestine and Babylonia. (16–17)

For Sandmel, part of Paul's genius is being able to package Judaism and make it understandable to a Hellenistic Jewish audience. This assessment, combined with Sandmel's prior recognition of Paul's conversion and his mystical apocalyptic context—which is handled in a more intellectually rigorous way than previous Jewish scholarship on Paul—comprises another important chapter in twentieth-century, Jewish NT scholarship.

Nowhere does Sandmel say that to translate Judaism into the Hellenistic world was an error. In fact, he goes out of his way to show that it was not. Yet, Sandmel also makes clear that this is a "road not taken" in Jewish history; so there is a hint of a backhanded compliment in his description of Paul with the term "genius." Paul was a genius, but his genius was in merchandising Judaism to the Gentile world. And merchandising also means simplifying and diluting. Part of this must surely come from his role as a rabbi and explicator of Judaism in his pastoral setting. Implicitly, for Sandmel—and for Boyarin too more explicitly—moving Judaism into the Hellenistic world promotes a kind of error, subtle though it might be: "His idiosyncratic involvement became expanded into a kind of universal and philosophic approach, and when his Epistles became canonized into scripture, that philosophical matrix came to be considered by orthodox Christians as revelation itself. But not everyone is built as was Paul."

Alan F. Segal (1945–)

I was raised as a Reform Jew in Worcester, Massachusetts. An English teacher's advice made me an early fan of the then unknown Joseph Campbell, whose work convinced me to go into English literature and, later, the field of comparative religion. Since then, I have maintained a "new history of religions approach" to the study of Judaism and Christianity. Unlike Campbell who was a Jungian and personally unfriendly to Judaism and Christianity, I made Jewish and Christian origins my linguistic focus and studied social science extensively. My perspective on religions is that they are all true in some way, but they are not all identical (even though I was also brought up as an active member of a Reform Jewish congregation). Although an English major at Amherst College, I also pursued a minor in religion and another in psychology. This dual track expanded into a fuller interest in sociology and anthropology in graduate work. After earning an M.A. in Near Eastern and Judaism studies from Brandeis University, with major interests in Bible and

Medieval Jewish philosophy, and a degree from Hebrew Union College-Jewish Institute of Religion (part of the Reform Jewish Seminary system in North America), I enrolled for doctoral work at Yale (1970–1974, degree in 1975). I should add that I never made a conscious decision not to become a rabbi. Teaching opportunities that came up at Princeton (1974–1978), a Guggenheim Fellowship in Israel (1977–1978), and a tenured offer from the University of Toronto (1978–1980) made finishing the rabbinic program impractical. Since 1980, I have been teaching at Barnard College and Columbia University, with a cross appointment at Union Theological Seminary. Upon arriving in New York City, my family joined a Conservative Jewish synagogue, where we worship, but my own theology remains much closer to Reform Judaism.

My dissertation was on rabbinic reports about "Two Powers in Heaven," which allowed me to discuss and compare both Jewish and Christian religious traditions. It was an unusual topic made more unusual when Yale assigned two dissertation directors to supervise the research: Nils A. Dahl (NT studies) and Judah Goldin (Judaic studies). My dissertation became my first book, published in 1977.

I have team-taught NT courses but usually teach Bible and Judaism for the Barnard-Columbia graduate and undergraduate student body. My second book, *Rebecca's Children*,[19] used social science to discuss the parting of Judaism and Christianity. My next book, *Paul the Convert: The Apostolate and Apostasy of Saul of Tarsus*,[20] took Paul's conversion and his continuing Jewish identity as its main subject. Another book, *Life After Death: A History of the Afterlife in Western Religion*,[21] contains a significant chapter on Paul. My entire publishing career has been devoted to works in the comparison of religion, with emphasis on Judaism and Christianity but with occasional forays into Islam and Eastern religions.

Paul the Convert takes as its premise that Paul was, indeed, a convert if one uses convert in a modern, social scientific way, even though he converted to what he considered another variety of Judaism and never in any way thought he had left Judaism. I use social science extensively to help define what conversion likely meant in Paul's society and history. Paul's conversion was an ecstatic one, based on visions and revelations that he received from the risen Christ. He was never a disciple of Jesus, and no evidence exists that he ever met him. Paul's revelations show us that Jewish mysticism, which we first meet in its merkabah form, was already alive and well in the first century C.E., when it coexisted with apocalypticism. Paul is the only confessional Jewish mystic in the first millennium and a half of Jewish mysticism. I take mysticism to be an extraordinarily important part of Western religious life, though certainly not the essence in and of itself. Paul's ecstasy shows us how spiritual experience existed in Judaism, how it helped innovate Judaism, and, therefore, how it helps us understand early Christianity. To me, conversion is the primary experience that characterizes all of Paul's subsequent work—that he came from Pharisaic Judaism, experienced visions of the risen Christ, and spent the rest of his life working out what the visions of Christ meant religiously, socially, and politically.

In Galatians, for example, Paul conceived a theory of how the Law could be limited. But the social circumstances made this change necessary. Paul preaches to the Galatians that the Jews of their neighborhood are actually too lax, not too strict, in their practice of the Law. As an ex-Pharisee, Paul warns the Church at Galatia that they must not allow themselves to be circumcised because the result will be they will have to become Jews entirely. And the Galatian Jews and Jewish Christians are not themselves good examples of what good Jews should be. Instead, people who want to be Jews should prepare to be as pious as Paul himself was, which is virtually impossible for Galatian Gentiles.

In my view, the alleged contradictions some interpreters find in Paul are not contradictions at all; they only seem to be so to those who have already adopted the notion that he advocates for Grace over Law. Instead, Paul's position is less ideological and more legally based, trying to apply his principles to specific situations. His basic principle is that none of the laws must be done for salvation, though following the ethical parts of the Law is necessary even for those in Christ. The special laws of Judaism, the so-called works of the law, are not necessary for salvation so Gentiles and Jews could discard them when necessary. Paul himself did not follow the special laws of Judaism when he was preaching in Gentile contexts; but he seems to return to them whenever he was in a Jewish community.

Paul also recommends doing observing some of the laws for church unity. He attends the first church council and agrees to the Apostolic decrees (Acts 15), at least when there are Jews and Gentiles present in the Christian community. Although he believes that the special laws have no particular soteriological value, he now must convince his converts that accommodating to the scruples of the Jewish Christians has value for the Church. The Apostolic Decrees contain no ruling about circumcision. One might assume that Paul himself succeeds in having it deleted from consideration. What was decided at the first church council in Jerusalem and what he preaches to both his radical and conservative Christian readers is this: they do not need to observe the special laws of Judaism, but they should accommodate the wishes of the weak when they are present in the community so that church unity and peace will be maintained. Paul is not Luther. He is a Christian rabbi constantly trying to adapt his thought to the exigencies of communal life. For example, his statements about food observances suggest his ideological position—a radical solution that no food laws mean anything. Yet, if fellow Christians are upset by this lack of piety, then even the strong may, in fact, observe them. This seems impossible to readers who hold unerringly to the notion that Paul believes that only faith and never Law brings salvation. But that is a later imposition on Paul's text. Paul does believe that faith saves, but he sees no problem with observing law while church unity is imperiled. He even might observe Jewish Law for the purposes of ethnic identification. If Paul had had a son from a Jewish mother, he might well have circumcised him, since the son would have been a Jew as well.

Paul's view on these issues made him the perfect candidate for "apostle to the Gentiles." Yet, whether Paul is an apostle or an apostate depends entirely on the perspective of the observers in Paul's time. Some Jews certainly called Paul an "apostate" (some of those were Christians, too), and yet he was, in his own estimation, always a Jew and always true to the legal traditions of his heritage. And he believed that God would save all of Israel in his own mysterious way. A number of scholars have been confused about what I wrote on that matter in *Paul the Convert*, so now let me clarify. What I think is that although Paul was accused in his own day of being an apostate, he did not accept that term. He showed no sign of having thought he had left either Judaism or the Jewish people. This is quite independent from Paul's identity as a Pharisee, which he must have left behind, of necessity.

One of the most interesting and least accepted aspects of this version of Paul's life is in my interpretation of Romans 7. I have argued and continue to think that in Romans 7 Paul is talking about himself, itself a minority opinion; but further, I conclude that he is talking about himself after his conversion, which is a minority within a minority position (though some important ancient and modern exegetes have opted for the same position). For Paul, observing the Law reveals the fact and nature of sin even as the power of sin exploits the Law to bring death. This seems to be a postconversion observation about sin and the Law that Paul reaches.

Paul could also have already understood rabbinic notions of "universalism" through the Noachide commandments. This universal law provided for the salvation of Gentiles without conversion to Judaism. Thus, for Paul, the true issue separating Gentile from Jewish Christians was not the means to salvation but how the two different communities making up the early Church could have sat down easily for lunch and what the menu would be. This was the matter that most distracted Paul.

In *Life After Death*, I develop a larger theme of how notions of the afterlife affect conceptions of the self in Western communities. Originally planned only as a contribution to the Anchor Bible Reference Library, the book has become a general history of afterlife in the West. The chapter on Paul attempts to make the case that Paul's ambiguous and ambivalent description of the *soma pneumatikon* (1 Cor 15:44; sometimes translated "spiritual body") bespeaks a more mystical and spiritual resurrection body of Christ and the believer (not flesh and blood). In later gospel writings, this notion was deliberately refashioned into the actual physical body of Christ. As the first Christian writer, Paul's ambiguity and attempt to connect the body with astral mysticism in 1 Corinthians 15 should be more widely acknowledged in Christian scholarship. The distinction between Paul's mystical Christ and the gospels' literal Christ is very much like the differences in description between apocalypticism and mysticism in general.

Daniel Boyarin (1946–)

Daniel Boyarin describes himself as an Orthodox Jew. His doctoral work was done at the Conservative Jewish Seminary, The Jewish Theological Seminary (JTS) of America, rather than Yeshiva University so he has combined deep immersion in Judaism with acute and critical education about it. At JTS he studied Talmud with S. Lieberman and D. Weiss-Halivni, two of the foremost Talmudists of the twentieth century, among other scholars, and developed an especially keen interest in Aramaic philology, even traveling weekly to Yale for Franz Rosenthal's famous seminar on the subject (where we met for the first time). After achieving his doctorate, he emigrated to Israel, where he served in various capacities at Ben Gurion University and the Hebrew University. His most important appointment came at the religiously sponsored Bar Ilan University in its prestigious Talmud department. He taught there for more than a decade. When the opportunity to return to the United States as a chaired professor in Judaica at the University of California at Berkeley came up, he accepted it. From that position he has had an important role as a teacher of bright graduate students who combine traditional Jewish learning with modern methodology.

Although his teaching responsibilities have been fully within Judaica, he has never taught a standard NT or early Church course. In his book on Paul, Boyarin relates the difficulties he had with contemporary Israeli society, which is a significant issue both in his scholarship and in his life. He describes himself as a "[T]almudist and post-modern Jewish cultural critic."[22] This is not a modest claim, and the juxtaposition of the two together would make him virtually unique, a hybridized scholar as he would style himself. But let us not forget that previous Jewish scholars looking at Paul have also been Talmudists, and at least one, H. J. Schoeps, can lay claim to being a cultural critic (though Klausner was certainly a Zionistic cultural critic without ever claiming the title). At least one other Jewish intellectual, namely Jacob Taubes, had also claimed the title of cultural critic in his philosophical discussions of Paul.

This is how Boyarin lays claim to the title: since his return to the United States, Boyarin developed strong interests in postmodern studies. In his *Carnal Israel*,[23] Boyarin put those tools to work in showing the gender issues implicit in rabbinic literature. It was a book that both amazed and scandalized some of the academic community, coming together with equally fascinating books on sexuality in Judaism by David Biale (*Eros and the Jews*)[24] and Howard Eilberg-Schwartz (*God's Phallus*).[25] The three scholars had, it turned out, been meeting together as a study group to discuss these issues and the three books, which reflected their meetings, established them as a postmodern school on Jewish gender studies, in addition to their earliest well-respected scholarship. As a postmodern scholar, Boyarin discusses the issue in personal and scholarly terms together, an interest which he continues in his controversial work *Unheroic Conduct*,[26] which explores the sexual character of the modern Jewish male.

His major work on Paul is *A Radical Jew: Paul and the Politics of Identity*. The ambiguity of whether Boyarin or Paul is the radical mentioned in the title is deliberate. He shows throughout the book that the two issues are deeply intertwined. Paul is a sounding board for his own issues of radicalization after living in Israel and being unhappy with the treatment of Arabs in the occupied territories. He gained inspiration for his critique of Judaism from Paul. This is a deliberate personalization of Boyarin's hitherto more disinterested scholarship, which he lays to postmodern theory and the conclusion that none of us ever escape our own biases. So rather than hide them, Boyarin makes them as explicit as possible. In a way, Boyarin is following the theoretical path already tread by Rubenstein, who stressed that the only way humanity could be saved was through saving itself in Freudian therapy. The only history was, therefore, personal history, hopelessly biased by personal experience. Historiography, like therapy, allows the historian to get perspective on his or her personal experience. For Rubenstein, the personal path to salvation was the triumph of the therapeutic in his own writing. For Boyarin, it is the triumph of the hermeneutic that saves from meaninglessness.

According to Boyarin, Paul should be regarded as a radical reformer and cultural critic of Jewish society, but not an unalloyed, positive force in Jewish life. He ignores Paul both as a religiously Jewish mystic and a significant Pharisee. Instead, he critiques a Paul who is expert in Greek philosophy, which might entail some mystical experience, as Platonists might practice a mystical life. But Boyarin ignores these aspects of Paul's personality because they are irrelevant to the cultural critique (of modern times?) which he wishes to develop. Paul's insight was to erase the national borders between Jew and Gentile in Christianity: "Paul was motivated by the Hellenistic desire for the One, which among other things produced an ideal of a universal human essence, beyond difference and hierarchy" (9).[27] "My claim is that there is ample evidence throughout the corpus that what is being affirmed is the spiritual sense—the universal Law of Christ, of love, of faith—and what is being denied is the carnal sense—the Jewish law of circumcision, kashruth, and the Sabbath" (188).[28] But Boyarin himself resists this temptation to unify humanity and opts for continued hybridism as a Jew no longer in Israel, which is too mired in particularity, but in Diaspora as an Orthodox Jew continuing to practice the law.

Boyarin believes Paul to represent Hellenistic Jewish life. This is quite in line with Klausner and earlier Jewish views of Paul. Indeed, one wonders whether Boyarin first encountered Paul in a serious way from reading Klausner because he adopts Klausner's critique of Paul's Judaism but then opts for Judaism in Diaspora rather than in Israel as the corrective itself. It is almost as if Boyarin is Klausner turned on his head in the same way that Marx is Hegel turned on his head. Boyarin's view also coheres with Susan Handelman's thesis in her book, *The Slayers of Moses*.[29] So while he professes great admiration for Paul, it is a Hellenistic Paul whom he likes, who makes the lives of Hellenistic Jews easier. In this respect, his book also resembles Samuel Sandmel's *The Genius of Paul*.

Boyarin describes Paul as having given up the rabbinic world of differentiation and hierarchy, using Platonism to solve the challenge of universalism for Judaism. For Boyarin, Paul's view is summed up in Galatians 3:28: "There is neither Jew nor Greek, slave nor free, male nor female, for you are all one in Christ Jesus." This view has negative consequences for ethnicity, obviously, because it requires the end of the Jewish people. It also has negative consequences for gender for the same reasons: it requires the subjugation of women to the ideal of men. It also might mean the end of slavery, which seems to me to be an unalloyed good. But none of these outcomes will be realized literally until the eschaton. At most, they are created through liturgy in anticipation of the presence of Christ, which is a powerful didactic image. In spite of his protestations—that this is a compliment to Paul and an appreciation of him—it is hard to take Boyarin's admiration seriously. Indeed, why should a scholar care whether Paul is admirable or not, as long as he can explain something important about him? Boyarin is also critical of rabbinic Judaism for its ethnic differentiations, parochial cultural values, and gender prejudices. The one way out of this double bind is to become a Jew in Diaspora where the mixture of culture assures that the positive aspects of both values can be preserved.

In his last chapter, which I find the most interesting part of the book, Boyarin speaks quite frankly of his early excitement about emigrating to the state of Israel and his later disillusion with it. Clearly, the categories that he finds to describe this journey are from his earlier work on Paul—or more exactly the categories that he adduces from Paul were taken from his time in Israel and his justification for leaving it. It makes for a fascinating read.

But does Boyarin actually give us a portrait of the biblical Paul? Boyarin would answer, I suppose, "Who could ever know that?" Objective history is not possible. So the best one can ask for is consistent history, relevant to the modern world and personal biography. Boyarin's book is both consistent and relevant to his personal biography. But what if one can show Paul to be a very different person from the one Boyarin describes from the ancient sources? For one thing, Paul never claims to be a Greek philosopher, much less a Platonist. He does not write like a Platonist. His Greek is serviceable but not very atticized or educated or aristocratic.

The most important term in this argument and his most important term for Boyarin's argument, *Logos*, is not a Platonic term. It is sometimes a term used by Stoics, and it is used by Philo in place of the more technically Platonist term *nous*. Boyarin does not speculate on this anomaly, only suggesting that Paul uses the term like Philo and that this represents a Jewish Hellenism. But Paul never does use the term *Logos* in the sense that Philo does. When Paul uses the term *Logos*, he always means "the Word" in the sense of scripture and never "the Word" with the sense of a preexistent form of God. When he discusses the *Logos* of the cross (not the Christ), which is rare, he means the life, lessons, and paradigm that Christ reveals. Meeks describes this usage as defining "a story to think with." So where is Paul's Platonic dualism? Paul may be a dualist, but he is not a Platonic dualist. He does not contrast body and soul like a Platonist, rather flesh and spirit, which is a more traditional Jewish anthropology. To be sure, Jewish wisdom tradition has a respectable place in Paul's writings, but that tradition could not easily be characterized with the term *Logos* as if his use were similar to Philo's. Paul seems much more like an apocalyptic dualist—expressed as flesh and spirit, now and then, this age and the next—and, yes, famously as neither slave nor free, neither Jewish nor Gentile, neither male nor female. Paul does not even explain himself as a Hellenized Jew but as a Pharisee–indeed, a quite zealous one. This is how he tells his story and establishes his identity. He never even mentions where he was born. It is Luke who supplies the city of Tarsus as Paul's birthplace, and so it remains a bit dubious.

So the question arises, Does Boyarin give us a true picture of Paul as he appears in his letters? Or does he create a new Paul, the Jewish social critic who shares some of Boyarin's political perspectives? I think the latter. He truly has returned to the previous situation in the Jewish appreciation of Paul: Paul becomes a symbol of Jewish identity politics and not a subject for historical analysis. The fact is that Paul's religious life, together with his visions and revelations, is almost entirely ignored by Boyarin.

Boyarin has been heavily criticized for his particular portrait of Paul, though praised for making his book an interesting read. In the end, Boyarin is probably to be blamed for his quick study. He published his results much too soon in his process of research. Although he can claim considerable expertise in Jewish texts of the Talmudic period, he was still a neophyte in Pauline studies.

By 2004, Boyarin was no longer a neophyte in Christian studies, but he is still a quick study. He has published a very enviable sum of three more, very original books since *The Radical Jew*: (a) a significant and very controversial book on martyrdom, *Dying for God: Martyrdom and the Making of Christianity and Judaism*;[32] (b) *Unheroic Conduct*, and (c)

Boyarin's most recent book, *Borderlines: The Partition of Judaeo-Christianity*.[33] As with all of Boyarin's books, Borderlines really begins in the present so the term "partition" is carefully chosen, showing his disagreement with the Partition of Palestine in 1948. This book, he explicitly says, took him longer than any other. But it was a labor of love. Boyarin admits at the outset that although he is comfortable with his Orthodox Judaism, he has always been fascinated and in love with the Christian tradition. In this book, which was, nevertheless, published quickly, Boyarin sums up some of his assertions in his two previous books. He suggests that Judaism and Christianity remained together for a long time (not in itself an innovation, though Boyarin brings the unity down to the fourth century or later, which is notable). This partition was a result of both rabbinic intolerance and Christian prejudice.

In *Borderlines*, Boyarin adds the dimension of history that he has explored in *Dying for God*, to his work on Paul and the split between Judaism and Christianity. In *Borderlines*, he traces the entire history of the Jewish-Christian split. The primary interest for our study of Jewish portraits of Paul is Boyarin's extension of the term *Logos*. Now no longer the province of Paul, it becomes the name for the whole series of intermediations all over the Hellenistic Jewish world.

Now this is a bold stroke. Having been deeply criticized for his previous misapplication of the philosophical terminology of *Logos*, Boyarin decides to turn the critique of his interpretation of *Logos* in Paul into a virtue by extending that term to describe the entire world of Jewish mediation and, thus, obviate the whole earlier problem. Of course, this is possible only if the original, technical meaning of the term in Hellenistic philosophy is ignored. It will become very confusing to have two different meanings of the term, one referring to the technical *Logos* in philosophy and the other referring to Boyarin's personal term for mediation. It has to be understood as an etic term, one that is imposed on the entire historical situation in place of the more traditional terminology—Jewish intermediation, two powers systems, and so forth—of which *Logos* was a very specific philosophical variety.

Boyarin criticizes most past scholarship for having assumed that Judaism and Christianity separated before they actually did. Yet, like Susan Landesman, he describes a real dualism between rabbinic Judaism, on the one hand, and the Hellenistic kinds of Judaism (the *Logos*-centered kind), on the other. This is a return to the older view that the two were separate and different, a great deal like Klausner's distinction. But will it convince the academic community? Only time will tell.

Mark D. Nanos (1954–)

Mark D. Nanos is the youngest Jewish writer on Paul to be considered here. Although he received his doctorate less than a decade ago, he has already amassed a large portfolio of major writings on Paul. Nanos was, for a good part of his life, a successful business man who owned and managed a marketing and advertising company in Kansas City. He was brought up in a largely nonpracticing Jewish and Christian home but one in which the intermarriage caused tensions with both larger families. So he has, with some justification, been able to call himself both a "Jew" and a "Christian," or at least a Jew with deep sympathies for the Christian community. In addition, he is no novice in the study of identity politics, since his own home was a board in which these issues were constantly arrayed.

Over the years, he has developed a strong interest in early Christian/Jewish relations. In pursuing this goal, he produced a manuscript, which impressed both Krister Stendahl and me. Both of us recommended to Fortress Press that it be published. As a result, Nanos published his first book, *The Mystery of Romans: The Jewish Context of Paul's Letter* (1996) before he actually began his graduate studies. These, he completed at the University of St. Andrews in Scotland, in record time (2000). Afterward he published his Ph.D. dissertation, *The Irony of Galatians* (2002), and edited a book of essays on Galatians entitled *The Galatians Debate*.[35]

Nanos is neither a cultural critic nor a post-modern scholar. Like his NT teachers, Nanos is properly a NT scholar, trying to figure out the puzzle of Paul's seemingly contradictory statements on Jews and Judaism. Nanos is the first Jewish scholar to offer commentary not merely on Paul generally but to publish separate volumes on individual Pauline letters (Galatians and Romans). This further advances the professionalization of Jewish scholarship on Paul. In an indirect way, Nanos has also championed the reevaluation of Acts, in which Paul appears as a Torah-true Jew. But Nanos goes further than either of his mentors, believing that the actual Paul, the Paul of the letters, is equally Torah true and remains so his entire life. This is a daring hypothesis, given the predominance of the notion of Paul's critique of Torah in Pauline studies. Other than Pinchas Lapide in his book with Stuhlmacher,[36] Nanos is unique in making the argument that Paul observed Torah as a matter of faith and conscience, even after his conversion. Furthermore, Nanos argues significantly that Paul's communities are Jewish communities and those to whom he wrote in Romans and

Galatians were subgroups within the large non-Christ-believing Jewish communities in those places.

That Paul remained Law-observant throughout his life is possible, and it certainly should be investigated in detail. But several passages make this conclusion difficult: Paul says that he behaves as a Gentile when he is with Gentiles and as a Jew when he is with Jews (1 Cor. 9:20-22). He cannot be a Pharisee and do this, and, of course, Paul tells us he is a former Pharisee. But, having given up Pharisaism, can he be an ordinary, Hellenistic Jew, who might be more pious in one situation and less in another? It is possible, in my view, and Nanos discovers some evidence for this behavior in the ancient world. But the answer is not yet clear.

Nanos believes that Paul's opponents in Galatia were Jewish (rather than Jewish Christian). I believe that this is possible; still this does not rule out the possibility that some Jewish-Christians were insisting that Gentile believers be initiated into the way by circumcising them into Judaism as well. The text, it seems to me, allows for either or both interpretations. But Nanos goes further, showing that the letters of Paul are essentially a Jewish correspondence.[37] This is quite in line with my own notion that the Pauline letters are correspondences that evidence Jewish historiography as well as vice-versa. But Nanos takes these observations further than I am willing to do now. To say that there were Jews and Gentiles in the Christian community at Galatia and the various churches in Rome is one thing. It is another to claim that they were entirely and only Jewish. If this can be established, it will take time.

The big payoff involves what Paul thinks is the fate of Jews and Christians, which is the issue he raises in Romans 9–11. Will Jews be saved as Jews or will God eventually superintend their conversion to Christianity? Gager, Gaston, and, in a way, Stendahl think that Jews might have reason to enter salvation as themselves without conversion. In my perspective, I think Paul expected that God would eventually convert all to faith in Christ. But on this matter, the apostle is voicing a private opinion because he did not have the guidance of a revelation on which to base his belief. He argues strongly that God has constantly moved in surprising and unexpected ways to fulfill promises. In the end there can be no triumphalism.

Concluding Remarks

No one can write objective history. But that biases are inevitable is not necessarily bad; nor is the reason necessarily ideological. Scholars write out of a certain time or place where certain questions are alive and others are not. They all have personal histories, training, and predispositions.

The discovery of bias is not original to postmodernism. It is one of the first lessons of a modern historian, and technical training is needed to control for it, especially in anthropology and history of religions. But the question is, Is scholarship possible at all? Is doing history impossible or only very, very hard? If it is extremely difficult but possible, one should try to make all one's assumptions conscious, work as hard as possible to write dispassionately, control for every personal prejudice, and hope to move the field forward by a little with each perception. Objectivity may be impossible, but dispassionate study is an attainable goal if a book survives the process of peer review over the decades. What one finds is very much dependent on the questions one asks, and each generation brings a new set of questions to the study of history. Thus, one can say that the job of history is never over.

But, if doing history is actually impossible, then why not write about oneself and turn every historical question into a memoir and an exercise in ideology? After all, it is easier to interest a sympathetic readership with ideology than more disinterested scholarship. In his memoir, Boyarin identifies himself with Paul as a radical but differs with him over the solution to the problem of Jewish identity. And he takes a position that is hardly popular in the general community but has a great deal of sympathy in the academic community. At this point in the history of the New Testament discipline and also Jewish historiography, I think one must allow that either path is possible, though they may demand different skills and be directed at different audiences and toward entirely different purposes. These observations seem to argue against hybridization and for defining one's task clearly and without confusion. Fortunately, people are sensitive readers and can live with a great deal of ambiguity.

Jewish scholars of Paul have concentrated far more on the politics of Paul's identity within the first-century Jewish community and less on Paul's spiritual and religious experience. So the Brumberg hypothesis has some cogency. One wonders whether the reason for the importance of the issue can be laid at the foot of Jewish identity politics. The lack of emphasis on Paul's internal religious dimension as a human being is certainly characteristic of some of this scholarship, but one should also admit that it is characteristic of Pauline studies generally. Perhaps that is the same as saying that Paul still figures in Christian (Protestant, Catholic, established vs. free church, etc.) identity politics as well.

The most important point to make is that Jewish interpreters of Paul have an enormous range of possibilities available to them today—from social criticism in the Jewish community to technical study of NT and everything in between. I can only hope, with Larry Hurtado, that they turn to the task of understanding the nature of religious experience in all its dimensions.

Chapter 20

Liturgy and Communal Identity
Hellenistic Synagogal Prayer 5
and the Character of Early Syrian Christianity

Troy A. Miller

Geographical specificity has become a staple of investigations of formative traditions for early Christianity. Certainly since Bauer's *Orthodoxy and Heresy*, describing the development of early Christianity in monolithic terms has waned, hence the more recent response to employ pluralities when talking about Christianity (and Judaism) in this period.[1] One such region that has sustained interest in these discussions is Syria. While some have noted the Jewish character of early Christianity in Syria, even relatively late, there still remain some who cling to and argue for other primary shaping traditions. Helmut Koester contends that the cradle into which Syrian Christianity was born was neither primarily Hellenistic nor Jewish; he firmly asserts Gnosticism as the primary formative tradition for early Syrian Christianity. In a section entitled, "Syria, The Country of Origin of Christian Gnosticism," Koester states that,

> In the course of our discussion of the development of early Christianity in Syria, it has been necessary to refer repeatedly to Gnosticism. Gnostic concepts, terms, myths, hymns, and sayings traditions have been mentioned on several occasions. Not to do so would make the history of early Syrian Christianity and its literature an impenetrable puzzle.[2]

For Koester, Gnosticism is the interpretive key that unlocks our understanding of early Syrian Christianity.

As a means of showing appreciation for and honoring the work and careers of two scholars, Larry Hurtado and Alan Segal, who have contributed so significantly to our understanding of the Jewish character of early Christianity, the present volume represents a fitting place to further examine such trajectories, in this case in Syria.[3] In this essay, I will examine *Hellenistic Synagogal Prayer 5* (*HSP5*), a piece of synagogal liturgy embedded in the *Apostolic Constitutions*, as a test case for Koester's view on the relationship of Gnosticism to the birth of early Syrian Christianity.[4] I will argue, (1) contra Koester (and others), that *HSP5* testifies to Judaism being the primary shaping influence for early Syrian Christianity, and (2) *HSP5* bears witness to these early Syrian Christian tradents *intentional* location of their Christian identity *within* Judaism.[5]

The Jewish Matrix of *HSP5*

Readily apparent in even a cursory reading of *HSP5* is the evidence of redactional activity. While scholars may debate how many distinct layers may be evident in the text of the Prayer, most have recognized—at the very least—the addition of some distinctly Christian elements. As Goodenough notes,

> The general method of the Christian redactor is obvious and clumsy enough. There is no attempt to alter the fundamental Judaism of the prayers by any method other than the crudest sort of casual insertion of references to Christ or bits of Christian creed.[6]

When these readily identifiable Christian elements are set aside, we see the Prayer in an early (the earliest?) form. At the very least, even if we do not or cannot have certainty on the original form of *HSP5*, this step of setting aside the Christian interpolations does allow us a view, front-and-center, of the distinctly Jewish content and character of the Prayer. In the sections below, I will identify several distinctly Jewish traditions, practices, and themes that are evident in *HSP5* in an effort to exemplify its Jewish origin.[7]

The Seven Benedictions for Sabbaths and Festivals

The six uncontested *Hellenistic Synagogal Prayers* (*Apos. Con.* 7.33–38) mirror the first six of the Seven Benedictions.[8] The Seven Benedictions consist of the first three and the last three of the Eighteen Benedictions for daily recitation, and the middle benediction is related specifically to the Sabbath or a specific festival. *HSP5* has two prominent parallels with the fourth of the Seven Benedictions for Sabbaths and festivals. The first parallel is with the fourth benediction for Sabbaths. The benediction states,

> Thou hast sanctified the seventh day unto Thy name, marking the end of the creation of heaven and earth; Thou didst bless it above all seasons. . . .

Our God and God of our fathers, accept our rest. Sanctify us through Thy commandments, and grant our portion in Thy Torah. Give us abundantly of Thy goodness and make us rejoice in Thy salvation. Purify our hearts to serve Thee in truth. In Thy loving favor, O Lord our God, grant that Thy holy Sabbath be our joyous heritage, and may Israel who sanctifies Thy name, rest thereon. Blessed art Thou, O Lord, who hallowest the Sabbath.[9]

The parallels between *HSP5* (in *Apos. Con.* 7.36.1) and this Benediction can be seen in (1) the Sabbath being their common subject—the "Seventh day" in the benediction and "Sabbath day" in *HSP5*; (2) the Sabbath marking the end of creation and being for the purpose of the remembrance of creation; and (3) the two-fold human response to the Sabbath as rest, as God rested from creation, and reading of and dedication to Torah. The two liturgical pieces share a common focus on and an expressed reverence for the Sabbath.

The second parallel comes in the common focus between *HSP5* and the fourth benediction for festivals or holy days, where the latter reads,

And Thou hast given us in love, O Lord Our God, holidays for gladness, festivals and seasons for rejoicing. Thou hast granted us [space left for special interpolated references and readings for the individual festival]. Our God and God of our fathers, may our remembrance and the remembrance of our forefathers come before Thee. Remember the Messiah of the house of David, Thy servant, and Jerusalem, Thy holy city, and all Thy people, the house of Israel. Grant us deliverance and wellbeing, loving-kindness, life and peace on this day of [space left to insert name of the specific festival]. Remember us this day, O Lord Our God, for our good, and be mindful of us for a life of blessing. With Thy promise of salvation and mercy, deliver us and be gracious unto us, have compassion upon us and save us. Unto Thee do we lift our eyes for Thou art a gracious and merciful God and King. O Lord Our God, bestow upon us the blessing of Thy festivals for life and peace, for joy and gladness, even as Thou hast graciously promised to bless us. Sanctify us through Thy commandments, and grant our portion in Thy Torah; give us abundantly of Thy goodness and make us rejoice in Thy salvation. Purify our hearts to serve Thee in truth. In Thy loving favor, O Lord our God, let us inherit with joy and gladness Thy holy festivals; and may Israel who sanctifies Thy name, rejoice in Thee. Blessed art Thou, O Lord, who hallowest Israel and the seasons.[10]

The Benediction and the Prayer share the common focus on festivals as (1) consistently being a gift for rejoicing and gladness—the Benediction notes that God has given them "holidays for gladness, festivals and seasons for rejoicing," and the Prayer recounts that God "appointed festivals for the gladdening of our souls" (*Apos. Con.* 7.36.1); and (2) remembrance being their assigned purpose, in connection with the "fathers." The Prayer does the latter as it reads, "For you, O Lord, have led out from the land of Egypt even our fathers" (*Apos. Con.* 7.36.3), and then by briefly narrating, in succession, the historical events underlying the Passover, the Exodus and wilderness events, and the giving of the Law at Sinai. Like the Sabbath parallel, the Benediction and Prayer share a common understanding of the origin and purpose of the festivals.

On the significance of the parallels between the Seven Benedictions for Sabbaths and Festivals and the *Hellenistic Synagogal Prayers,* for the latter's Jewish character, Simon observes that,

> In the general arrangement of the petitions, in their content and style, and in the choice and groupings of the biblical quotations, the prayers in the *Apostolic Constitutions* are so very similar to those of the Jewish liturgy that there can be no possible doubt about their Jewish connections.[11]

Fiensy further notes that these connections are compelling because (1) the prayers are grouped together, not scattered, within the Apostolic Constitutions; (2) the compiler of the Apostolic Constitutions used the prayer collection in a succession of three distinct sources—*Didascalia* (books 1–6), the *Didache* (7.1–32), and the *Hellenistic Synagogal Prayers*; and (3) the Prayers correspond, both in general content and order, to these Seven Benedictions.[12] In all, these parallels between the fourth of the Seven Benedictions for Sabbaths and festivals and *HSP5* wed the two documents tightly together within a distinctly Jewish liturgical substructure.

The Three Main Jewish Festivals

A second stream of Jewish liturgical tradition evident in *HSP5* is the narrative remembrance of the festivals themselves, specifically Passover, Sukkot, and Pentecost. This tripartite festival structure is evident in *HSP5* through the successive narration of the historical events related to each of these (*Apos. Con.* 7.36.3–4), which are temporal markers for these Jewish festivals.

The Prayer narratively invokes the first of these festivals, Passover, through several literary allusions. First, the words of the Prayer generally highlight God's providential act of deliverance of the Israelites from Egypt with the words, "For you, O Lord, have led out from the land of Egypt even our fathers" (*Apos. Con.* 7.36.3). The Prayer's reference to the

Passover is enumerated further as it highlights the Israelites condition of slavery while in Egypt. It reads, God "rescued them [fathers] out of an iron furnace, and out of clay and making bricks" (*Apos. Con.* 7.36.3). The "iron furnace" and the making of "bricks" are stock images of Passover remembrances; they are vivid reminders of the toil and strife endured by the Israelites while enslaved under the Egyptians.[13] These elements of *HSP5* are pointers back to and are markers that liturgically reinvoke these events and Jewish tradition.[14]

The next events invoked in this section of the Prayer are the Exodus and wilderness stories, which underlie Sukkoth. The Prayer recounts that God "redeemed them [fathers] out of Pharaoh's hand, and the hand of those under him. And you [God] led them through the sea as through dry land, and you bore with their manners in the wilderness with manifold goodness" (*Apos. Con.* 7.36.3). Similar to the literary allusions made to the Passover, *HSP5* does likewise with the Exodus and wilderness accounts. The mention of "Pharaoh's hand" is a staple in descriptions of the Exodus tradition, specifically as a symbol of the power of Pharaoh's enforced bondage of the Israelites. Deuteronomy 7:8b exemplifies this tradition: "The LORD has brought you out with a mighty hand, and redeemed you from the house of slavery, from the hand of Pharaoh king of Egypt."[15] The other prominent allusion in the Prayer to the Exodus occurs in describing God leading out the captives and bringing them through "the sea as through dry land" (*Apos. Con.* 7.36.3). This aspect of the tradition originates in the Exodus story (Exod 14:21-22, 29) and is recounted in similar language in other later texts, such as Psalms 66:6: "He [God] turned the sea into dry land; they passed through the river [or waters] on foot. There we rejoiced in him" (see also Neh 9:11). Finally, an invocation of the wilderness experiences of the Israelites rounds out this section of the Prayer: "And you bore with their manners in the wilderness with merciful goodness" (*Apos. Con.* 7.36.3). It draws on Jewish tradition again, this time stemming from Deuteronomy 1:31, further solidifying *HSP5*'s liturgical emphasis on the remembrance of the festivals.

The third event narrated in this section of the Prayer is Sinai, with the giving of the Law, which underlies Pentecost. The Prayer reads, "You gave to them a Law, ten oracles uttered by your voice, and engraved by your hand" (*Apos. Con.* 7.36.4). Yet again, this recounting is directly connected to Jewish tradition, not only in its general focus but also linguistically. The liturgical remembrance of God's actions at Sinai further encases the Prayer in Jewish festal traditions.

Though there are no early instances of these three events being brought together in a single narrative, each of them is firmly embedded in the fabric of early Israelite identity, and even more so for Jews of the Second Temple period. Possibly the earliest instance where these events are gathered in one account is in Nehemiah 9:9-15a, which reads,

> And you saw the distress of our ancestors in Egypt and heard their cry at the Red Sea. You performed signs and wonders against Pharaoh and all his servants and all the people of his land, for you knew that they acted insolently against our ancestors . . . you divided the sea on dry land, but you threw their pursuers into the depths, like a stone into mighty waters. Moreover, you led them by day with a pillar of cloud, and by night with a pillar of fire, to give them light on the way in which they should go. You came down also upon Mount Sinai, and spoke with them from heaven, and gave them right ordinances and true laws, good statutes and commandments, and you made known your holy Sabbath to them and gave them commandments and statutes and a law through your servant Moses. For their hunger you gave them bread from heaven. . . ."

It is apparent that *HSP5*, as a writing that also has these events in focus—namely the Passover and Exodus while in Egypt, the subsequent experience in the wilderness, and the reception of the Law at Sinai—is an inheritor of, or at least shares in, this tradition evident in Nehemiah. While this still does not allow us to affix the date of the Prayer firmly, it does allow us to locate these festal traditions, with a greater amount of certainty, within Second Temple Judaism.

Parallels with Philonic Thought

Also evident within the Jewish traditions of *HSP5* are several parallels with Philonic thought. Though an argument for a direct line of influence from Philo to this Prayer is untenable (because it would be from silence), it is more readily acceptable that, based on the parallels that will be noted below, there are other distinct (Diaspora?) Jewish influences embedded within *HSP5*—parallels that become evident through a comparison with themes and emphases in Philo.[16] The first evidence of this type of parallel is the discussion of the "true Israel" being the one "who sees God" (*Apos. Con.* 7.36.2). Philo maintains a unique position for sight over hearing in the nature of human encounter with God. He recounts, in one instance, that "hearing stands second in estimation and below sight" (*Confusion* 148). Elsewhere, he identifies "seeing God" as definitive of "Israel." In a programmatic statement on this topic, Philo states,

> Hearing takes the second place, yielding the first to sight, and sight is the portion of Israel, the son free-born and first-born; for "seeing God" is the translation of "Israel." It is possible to hear the false and take it for true, because hearing is deceptive, but sight, by which we discern what really is, is devoid of falseness. (*Flight* 208)[17]

In all, Philo asserts both a singular position for the one who "sees God," Israel, and a necessarily lesser status for all who only hear.[18] The compiler and/or community behind *HSP5*, by borrowing this language, has employed what is likely an emerging Jewish tradition, one that asserts uniqueness in identity not in contrast to outsiders, but in contrast to other Jews. It is an act of self-definition within Judaism.

Another parallel between *HSP5* and Philonic thought is the references to the number seven. The Prayer cites the number seven as something that causes joy; that indicates a holy cycle of days, weeks, months, and years; and that acts as a sign by which no man can claim ignorance of its appearance (*Apos. Con.* 7.36.4–5). The number seven in the Prayer assumes a quality that much exceeds an ordinary ordinal. Likewise, in Philonic thought, the number seven also gains a very high status through his use of allegory. In allegorizing the number seven, Philo states that, "nature takes delight in the number seven" and that "what nature produces in the atmosphere, she effects mainly by the influence of figures dominated by seven" (*Alleg. Interp.* 1.8–9). He also identifies seven as a unique sign of specific cycles of months and years for things, such as (1) pregnancy, when he notes: "Who does not know that seven months' infants come to the birth, while those that have taken a longer time, remaining in the womb eight months, are as a rule still-born?" (*Alleg. Interp.* 1.9–10); and (2) the cycle of human maturity being in a series of seven year segments, from a "reasoning being" in the first seven years, to "complete consummation" in the second seven years, and in the third seven years the human reaches "the end of growth" and is in his "prime" (*Alleg. Interp.* 1.10). More generally, he also states that, "the power of the number seven reaches also to the most beneficent of the arts" (*Alleg. Interp.* 1.13–14).

Philo's relentless use of allegory in connection with the number seven often makes the number seem as (or more) significant as the thing he is describing. The references to the number seven in *HSP5* are not allegorized to the same degree as they are in the thought of Philo. However, the connection between the two certainly appears to be from the same Jewish tradition. Van der Horst notes that, "This unexpected emphasis on the importance of the number seven is totally atypical of the compiler." Therefore, he argues that this emphasis on the number seven belongs to an earlier Jewish version of the Prayer and not to the hand of the compiler.[19] This is yet another example of the Jewish character of *HSP5*.

The Prayer's overt Jewish character, as reflected in its parallels with the fourth of the Seven Benedictions for Sabbaths and festivals, the three main Jewish festivals, and its connections with Philonic thought, strongly commend not only the Jewish character of the prayer but also likely a Jewish community originally standing behind it. Also, the fact that this all is encased in a piece of liturgy should not be overlooked. Liturgy helps form communal identity and defines community boundaries. Jewish liturgy means a Jewish community with a Jewish vision. Turning back to Koester's thesis—that Gnosticism was the primary force that shaped early Syrian Christianity—it finds no support in this liturgical text. The abundant evidence of exclusively Jewish streams of tradition evident in *HSP5* overwhelms his thesis.[20] The Prayer seems to be an overlooked piece in his "impenetrable puzzle" of Syrian Christianity.[21]

While the character of the Prayer is clearly evident as Jewish, not Gnostic, based on the incorporated traditions and parallels in thought and practice, the question of the Christian community's (or at lest compiler's) stance toward the Judaism evident in this piece of liturgy remains. Below I will examine the Christian additions or interpolations evident in *HSP5* in an effort to see what they may tell us about this stance.[22]

The Christian Additions to *HSP5*

While the overt Jewish character and content of *HSP5* is striking, and largely uncontested in scholarly works, interpretations of the significance of the Christian additions to the Prayer for the community from which it emerged have been more varied. The final compiler of the Prayer has not veiled the Christian additions; the bulk of them are interpolations inserted in mass. Therefore, the effort to identify exactly what sections or phrases in *HSP5* have been inserted by the Christian redactor is rather simple. However, once the discussion shifts to what these added elements collectively convey about the Christian community that they reflect (and the compiler who inserted them)—concerning its relationship to Judaism there—opinions diverge. Some see in these Christian additions a discontinuity with its Jewish predecessors. Stephen Wilson, in examining patterns of early Christian worship, sees examples of "ritual and liturgical practices that are thought to depend on Jewish precedents but that at the same time evince a tendency toward deliberate distancing from Judaism."[23] He argues that the works surveyed in this chapter (all of which focus on liturgy and worship), including *HSP5*, reveal instances "where evidence of Jewish influence goes hand in hand with a conscious distancing from, or even hostility toward Judaism."[24] In contrast to Wilson, I will argue in a later part of the essay that the Christian additions to *HSP5* are conscious attempts by these early Syrian Christian tradents not to distance themselves from Judaism, but rather intentionally to place their recounting of Christianity specifically within the aforementioned Jewish framework and traditions.

Christ and Wisdom Traditions in HSP5

The first two examples of Christian additions to the Prayer both reflect an intentional effort by the compiler to connect the Christ, Jesus, to Jewish wisdom traditions. The first addition is a prepositional phrase that is inserted in a section on creation: "You created (the) cosmos through Christ" (*Apos. Con.* 7.36.1). Charlesworth, in his listing of the types of Christian additions to pseudepigrapha, notes this as an example of the most minor type of interpolation that can be made by a Christian redactor but as still having a significant intention and function.[25] He states,

> In these simple interpolations, the Christian scribe has confessed his identity by clarifying the *means* by which one should—indeed must—according to him, interpret the previous actions of God (especially in creation), the means by which prayers and hymns are to be addressed to the Almighty, and the means by which the individual can hope for the future. These short prepositional phrases stick out as Christian interpolations because they are grammatically loosely related to the context, are intrusive to the flow of thought, and singularly exhibit the Christian perspective.[26]

Here a clear assertion is made concerning Christ as the means through which the LORD created. Evidence for the personification of Wisdom is abundant. Proverbs 8:22–31 describes Wisdom as God's companion, architect, and master workman in the act of creation. *Wisdom* 10:1–12:11 also extols wisdom by eulogizing its legacy within God's acts of salvation history. While it is unclear whether or not "through Christ" may have replaced another phrase, such as "through Wisdom" or "in [Your] Wisdom," in a previous (i.e., pre-Christian additions) form of the Prayer, the connection of Jesus with Jewish wisdom traditions in order to

identify the Christ as the agent of God in the creative process is quite
apparent and striking.[27]

The second evidence of Christian additions related to Jewish wisdom traditions is found in a "liturgical confession."[28] The Prayer narrates
a series of events in the life of Jesus—birth, incarnation, baptism, suffering, death, and resurrection (*Apos. Con.* 7.36.2), which function to
delimit the interpretation of the surrounding material, in this case
Wisdom. The preceding lines to this interpolation read, "and you
appointed festivals for the gladdening of our souls, so that we may come
into remembrance of the Wisdom created by you" (*Apos. Con.* 7.36.1).
Then, in a clear-cut effort to place Jesus into this tradition, the christological confession is inserted. Although the name "Jesus" is never articulated in the Prayer, the compiler again exclusively delimits the
understanding of and, in a liturgical document, praise for Wisdom to the
Christ, Jesus. The clearest sign of this wholesale transition is, as van der
Horst observes in referring to this section of Christian additions, "that
the participles and pronouns in the Greek, although referring back to
Σοφία, are now in the masculine form because the compiler identifies
Wisdom with Jesus Christ."[29]

The replacement of "wisdom" with "Christ," linguistically and/or
conceptually, in *HSP5* is evidence of what most scholars have cited as
"clumsy" redaction.[30] The implicit claim being made is that the
Christian compiler understood all too well the implications of inserting
this new Christian content into the Prayer. It is thought to be an act of
polemic and replacement. I am proposing a different reading, namely
that the substitution of Christ for Wisdom is an expression of these early
Jewish Christian tradents' beliefs about Jesus, and, therefore, reflects an
intentional effort to articulate them within a Jewish matrix. While the
veneration of Jesus in the Prayer seems to go beyond what may be typical (and monotheistically allowable) for personified attributes in Jewish
tradition, and thus seems to be an example of Hurtado's argument about
the Christian "mutation" of Jewish monotheistic traditions as related to
the worship of Jesus, it still reflects a continuity with Judaism by encasing the beliefs about Jesus within Jewish wisdom traditions.[31]

Sabbath and Sunday Celebration in HSP5

Another critical issue in the interpretation of the Christian additions to
HSP5 centers on the Lord's Day and its relationship to Sabbath celebration for the community behind the Prayer. The phrase the "Lord's Day"

occurs in two sections within the Prayer. The first identifies it as the day for celebrating the "resurrection festival" (7.36.2). This interesting description places Easter within the annual cycle of Jewish festal celebrations, which is a direct extension of the Prayer's thanksgiving for the festivals noted above (*Apos. Con.* 7.36.1). The internal logic for the inclusion of this addition to the annual festal celebrations is not to nullify the remembrance of these other festivals. It is rather to add the "resurrection festival" to it, with its celebration being on the Lord's Day, thus extending the Jewish structure and character present in *HSP5*. Just as the Prayer declares that the Sabbath is for the "remembrance of this [creation]" (*Apos. Con.* 7.36.1), the Lord's day offers a chance to remember and celebrate not only the resurrection, but also the very life of Jesus, which is recounted in the immediately preceding liturgical confession in *Apos. Con.* 7.36.2.

The other two occurrences of the "Lord's Day" lie within the final section of the Prayer and are part of an excursus on how it "surpasses" the Sabbath (*Apos. Con.* 7.36.6). Ironically, these occurrences come directly after a lengthy extolling of the Sabbath as "a rest from creation, a completion of the cosmos, a seeking out of the laws, thankful praise to God on behalf of those things which he has freely given" (*Apos. Con.* 7.36.5). The pressing question for these and really all of the references to the Lord's Day in *HSP5* is, how are the "Sabbath" and the "Lord's Day" being construed, and what does that imply about the worship practices of the community behind the Prayer?

Most scholars cite these sections on the Sabbath and the Lord's Day as evidence of radical discontinuity. Fiensy holds that the section on the Lord's Day "stands in tension with the rest of the prayer."[32] Likewise, Simon observes that "the text ends with another tacked-on piece of Christology. It asserts the superiority of Sunday to all other festival days. In doing so, it breaks the unity of the passage and makes nonsense of it."[33] Wilson, in line with Fiensy and Simon, reinvokes the clumsy redaction language, noting that,

> The editor then rather clumsily inserts praise for the superiority of the Lord's Day, which for the Christian has taken the place of the Sabbath. The Christian feast is not only different from, but preferable to the Jewish.[34]

The contention of each of these assertions is that not only is the Lord's Day different from—or even superior to—the Sabbath, but also that the former is distinctly out of place in the prayer by breaking its (Jewish) continuity. Though unstated, informing this assumption appears to be the notion that Judaism and Christianity were both already fully self-conscious, entirely distinctive, and separate religions, thus largely removing the possibility of early Christian participation in both Sabbath and the Lord's Day. However, ancient evidence suggests this possibility should not be ruled out too quickly.

Evidence for early Christian participation in both Sabbath and Sunday can be found in various places. Eusebius, within book 3 of his *Ecclesiastical History*, cites two unique groups called "Ebionites." While he pejoratively describes the first of these groups as having a deficient Christology, he says of the second that

> they observed the Sabbath and the other Jewish customs, as did the former; yet on the other hand, each Lord's day they celebrated rites similar to ours, in memory of the Saviour's resurrection (*Hist. eccl.* 3.27.2).[35]

Ignatius also provides a snapshot of this phenomenon when he criticizes those who profess to follow Christ but continue to "live in accordance with Judaism" (Ign. *Magn.* 8.1). Later in the letter, he continues: "If, then, those who had lived in antiquated practices came to newness of hope, no longer keeping the Sabbath but living in accordance with the Lord's day . . . how can we possibly live without him?" (Ign. *Magn.* 9.1–2). Similar to Eusebius, Ignatius, in bringing criticism against a Christian group who maintains Jewish practices, incidentally offers testimony of a Christian group continuing their Sabbath observance alongside their celebration of the Lord's Day—in Ignatius' understanding, wrongly so!

These references open the possibility of mutual observance of both the Lord's Day and Sabbath within the same community. However, the Prayer plainly asserts that the Lord's Day "surpasses" (Fiensy and Darnell's translation of προέχουσα) the Sabbath. The translation of προέχω, consequently, becomes a crucial point of interpretation in addressing this issue. In the NT and early Christian literature, προέχω simply means "to surpass" or "to excel" without necessarily meaning "to replace."[36] For example, the term is also found in *Herm. Mand.* 12.2 within a passage discussing the "evil desires" that put men to death. In response, the author states that "above all" [πάντων προέχουσα] is the desire for someone else's wife or husband, and for the extravagance of wealth. . . ." Here, the sins of desiring another's spouse or desiring great wealth are not replacing other sins; but rather asserting that they, above all others, will lead a person to death. While a number of scholars have used this term as a primary means for asserting supersession of the Lord's

Day over the Sabbath, they have mistakenly interpreted the latter as an exclusive *replacement* for the former.[37] The Lord's Day "surpasses" the Sabbath in *HSP5*, but it is not a substitution for or replacement of the Jewish day of worship. It is the day that "by its magnitude covered over every other good deed" (*Apos. Con.* 7.36.6). Van der Horst, in his commentary on *Apostolic Constitutions* 7.36.6, notes that

> there is not the slightest doubt that these two paragraphs were appended by the Christian compiler to demonstrate that, even though his community kept the Sabbath—with which he fully agreed—still Sunday is to be regarded as superior to the Sabbath.[38]

This section of Christian additions and emphases, then, should not be understood as an effort by these early Christians to distance themselves from Judaism but as an intentional act to remain within it.

"True Israel" and Christian Identity in HSP5

A final segment of Christian additions relates to the notion of being the "true Israel." *HSP5* reads: "For by him [Jesus] you brought the gentiles to yourself, for a treasured people, the true Israel, the friend of God who sees God" (*Apos. Con.* 7.36.2). At first glance, the employment of "true Israel" language sparks thoughts of Christian supersessionism. It appears that these Christians are usurping Israel's heritage as God's elect by taking the unique identity language of Israel, found in Deuteronomy 7:6 and elsewhere in Jewish tradition, and applying it to the Gentiles. Yet one must remember that internal diversification within Judaism in the Second Temple period is common, not only later with the flourishing of Jewish groups and sects, but even as far back as the return from exile. Additionally, the "true Israel" language, especially as seen in Philo, is a distinction asserted within Judaism—that is, among Jewish groups.[39] Therefore, reemploying the notion of the "true Israel" by no means represents an effort to distance themselves from Judaism; it is rather an extension of a Jewish practice, the reference to the Gentiles not withstanding. In line with Philo's use of this phrase and concept, these Christians are redefining (by expansion) who is part of God's elect.

In summary, the Christian additions to *HSP5* reflect a conscious attempt by these early Syrian Christian tradents (1) to articulate their beliefs about the Christ, Jesus, by way of Jewish wisdom traditions; (2) to relate their understanding of the Lord's Day within and as a part of the Jewish festal traditions; and (3) to express their own unique identity by means of traditional Jewish identity rhetoric, distinctive from other Jewish groups. Absent from the Prayer is any tangible evidence of "deliberate distancing" from or "hostility toward" Judaism that Wilson asserts to be part of a larger pattern of Christian worship (including *HSP5*) in its relationship with Judaism. Clearly, *HSP5* is not only a prayer that can be characterized as Jewish, but the details of this liturgy show a Christian group well at home within and seeking to maintain connection to these overt Jewish traditions, themes, and practices. Wilson's thesis, then, is overruled, at least with respect to *HSP5*.

Observations and Implications

The primary observations and implications that emerge from this study include the following:

(1) some previous conclusions about the character of early Syrian Christianity must be reassessed (including Koester's), namely those that undervalue—or do not value at all—the significance of Jewish formative traditions in Syria;

(2) abstract notions of what is normatively Christian and Jewish must not be anachronistically read into early Christian texts and communities; they must be able to communicate their own brand of Christianity, however common or unique it may appear; and

(3) the Jewish character of Christianity in Syria seems to have lasted longer than in some other regions and, inasmuch HSP5 is characteristic of Syrian Christianity, we see an example of an interesting Christology, wherein Jesus, as the Christ, continues to be understood in strictly Jewish terms (i.e., "wisdom," "festivals," and "Philonic thought") even up through the second to fourth centuries C.E.[40]

In all, *HSP5*, in some functions and emphases, clearly matches up with other early Christian texts and communities, but the Prayer also provides a vantage point from which to observe some new—or at least not common—features of early Christian identity formation in light of Judaism.

Chapter 21

Anger, Reconciliation, and Friendship in Matthew 5:21-26

John T. Fitzgerald

As is generally recognized,[1] Matt 5:21-26 is formed from three separate and originally independent blocks of material: 5:21-22, 5:23-24, and 5:25-26.[2] In 5:21-22 the Matthean Jesus inveighs against anger towards one's brother (πᾶς ὁ ὀργιζόμενος τῷ ἀδελφῷ), not merely when it leads to homicide (οὐ φονεύσεις) as prohibited by the Torah (Exod 20:13 = 20:15 LXX; Deut 5:17 = 5:18 LXX)[3] but even when it is expressed in demeaning and insulting words (ῥακά = "airhead"; μωρέ = "moron").[4] In 5:23-24 he makes reconciliation with one's brother the necessary preliminary to sacrifice,[5] and in 5:25-26 he advises swift action to prevent an opponent from taking judicial action that would lead to imprisonment for debts (see also 18:30). In terms of source analysis, the first two units are unique to Matthew and derive from his special sayings material (M), and the third is either taken from Q or is an independent variant of the logion that stood in Q (see Luke 12:57-59).[6]

Anger as a Greco-Roman Topos

That Matthew has Jesus begin this section of the Sermon on the Mount by dealing with the subject of anger is not at all surprising.[7] The emotions or passions (πάθη) had been widely discussed throughout the ancient Mediterranean world for several centuries. In Greek philosophical circles the first systematic discussions of the emotions had begun in Plato's Academy, and they were continued after his death by both Xenocrates and Aristotle. The former may have written the first *On Emotions* (Περὶ παθῶν), though that distinction may belong to Aristotle (Diogenes Laertius 4.12; 5.23-24). In any case, the emotions commanded the attention of a broad spectrum of thinkers throughout

359

the Greek and Roman periods, with particular attention given to the emotion of anger. In fact, the philosophical discussions of anger were so numerous that Cicero could say to his brother Quintus, "I won't take it upon myself here to expound to you what philosophers are apt to say on the subject of irascibility, for I don't want to take too long, and you can easily find it in many books" (*Quint. fratr.* 1.1.37, trans. Shackleton Bailey, LCL).[8] This emphasis upon anger reflects the widespread perception that it was the most dangerous of all the emotions, leading not only to acts of homicide but also to various lesser forms of assault, especially within the family, both nuclear and extended (see, for example, Plato, *Leg.* 866d–869e). Indeed, anger was the most common reason for domestic violence in the ancient world (and that remains true for the modern world), and Greco-Roman tractates on anger are replete with examples of violence within the household.[9]

Thoughtful people throughout the ancient Mediterranean world gave great attention to the πάθη because they recognized that the emotions were inextricably linked to proper conduct. From both a theoretical and a practical standpoint, to speak of virtue without giving due attention to the emotions was as impossible as it was inconceivable. Understanding the nature of the emotions was viewed as the basis of all ethical philosophy.[10] Consequently, for most people, the philosopher-physician Galen was only stating the obvious when he argued that "the doctrine of the virtues follows necessarily from the doctrine of the emotions" (*On the Doctrines of Hippocrates and Plato* 5.6.1). Particular emotions were often linked to specific virtues or characteristics. The emotion of anger was associated with various virtues, but for our purposes in this essay, the most important was that of πραότης/πραΰτης. From at least the time of Aristotle, that virtue was often viewed as the opposite of anger. In his *Rhetoric*, Aristotle affirms that "becoming angry (τὸ ὀργίζεσθαι) is the opposite of becoming mild (τῷ πραΰνεσθαι), and anger (ὀργὴ) of mildness (πραότητι)," and he defines "making mild (πραΰνσις) as the quieting and appeasing of anger (ὀργῆς)" (*Rhet.* 2.3.1–2, trans. Freese, LCL). Centuries later, Ignatius of Antioch was still making that same inverse correlation between anger and mildness, advising the Christ-believers in Ephesus to "be mild in the face of their [adversaries'] angry outbursts (πρὸς τὰς ὀργὰς αὐτῶν ὑμεῖς πραεῖς)" (*Eph.* 10.2).

From this perspective, the discussion of anger in Matthew 5:21-22 should be viewed as thematically picking up the beatitude of Matthew 5:5, μακάριοι οἱ πραεῖς ("Blessed are the meek"). As is well known, that beatitude is formed on the basis of Psalm 37:11 (= 36:11 LXX) and its promise that "the meek will inherit the earth." But it is less often noted that the πραεῖς in this psalm are those who have accepted the admonition "Cease (παῦσαι) from anger (ὀργῆς) and forsake (ἐγκατάλιπε) rage (θυμόν); do not be vexed (μὴ παραζήλου) so as to act wickedly (πονηρεύεσθαι)" (Ps 36:8 LXX = 37:8 MT). As is evident from this linkage, the πραεῖς who inherit the earth are those who wait on the Lord and do not succumb to anger. They stand in vivid contrast to those who act wickedly (οἱ πονηρευόμενοι) because of anger and thus will be utterly destroyed (Ps 36:9 LXX = 37:9 MT). Because anger leads to wrongdoing and thus makes one "liable to judgment" and to even more dire fates (Matt 5:22), the Matthean Jesus begins the "antitheses section" of the Sermon (Matt 5:21-48) by discussing the dangerous consequences of anger.

This first unit (5:21-22) of Matt 5:21-26 is linked to the second unit (5:23-24) both thematically and logically. Thematically, both units are concerned with social relations with one's "brother," with a two-fold reference to "the brother" occurring in both the first (5:22) and the second (5:23-24) unit. Logically, the two units are linked by οὖν (5:23, "therefore"), which Matthew has added in order to link these originally separate sayings.[11] By redactionally joining these two units, Matthew wishes to show that the angry person not only risks severe personal punishment (judgment [τῇ κρίσει], council [τῷ συνεδρίῳ], and hell fire [τὴν γέενναν τοῦ πυρός]) for his antisocial behavior (5:22), but also alienates his brother (ὁ ἀδελφός σου ἔχει τι κατὰ σοῦ, "your brother has something against you") at the same time (5:23-24).

That is, as a separate and independent unit of material, 5:21-22 is concerned only with the potentially dire *personal* consequences of anger; the adverse *social* consequences of anger receive no attention whatsoever. Matthew corrects that problem or limitation by adding 5:23-24, which emphasizes the importance of reconciling one's brother and thus terminating the social strife. As a separate and independent unit of material, 5:23-24 is silent as to the reason for the brother's alienation, but by joining this unit to 5:21-22, Matthew has supplied the basis for the fraternal discord, namely, anger. One brother has been alienated by the other's angry words. In short, the brother who "has something against you" (5:23) is now none other than the brother with whom one has been angry and to whom one has spoken words of abuse and contempt (5:22).[12] Victims of one's anger must be reconciled before offering one's gift to God (5:23-24).[13]

Reconciliation and Friendship as Matthean Priorities

The third unit of material (5:25-26) not only continues the second unit's social concern for reconciliation[14] but also concludes by emphasizing, like the first unit, the potentially adverse personal consequences involved, namely, imprisonment (φυλακὴν). In this case, however, the prospect of punishment is not for showing anger (as in the first unit), but for failing to reconcile a hostile opponent.[15]

Matthew's concern for reconciliation may be highlighted by comparing his version of this third unit with Luke's, which has the counsel δὸς ἐργασίαν ἀπηλλάχθαι ἀπ᾽ αὐτοῦ (12:58).[16] There is some evidence that might suggest that the passive voice of the verb ἀπαλλάσσω can be used in the sense of "to be reconciled,"[17] so it is perhaps possible to translate the Lukan directive with "try hard to be reconciled to him" (NIV).[18] But ἀπαλλάσσω is not the usual word for reconciliation, and the lexical support for this meaning is, at best, meager. Luke's version is much more plausibly translated "make an effort to get rid of him" (middle)[19] or "do your best to be rid of him" (passive).[20] In short, settling the opponent's claim and being released from any obligation to him is the chief concern in Luke's form of this saying. There is absolutely no interest in any kind of ongoing relationship with the opponent once the debt has been discharged.[21] Two grammatical observations undergird this point. First, the correlative formulation with ἀπό (ἀπηλλάχθαι ἀπ᾽) makes it emphatic that the Lukan Jesus is stressing *separation from*, not reconciliation with, the opponent.[22] If Luke had wanted to indicate reconciliation with the adversary, he surely would have used a verb such as συναλλάσσω (as he does at Acts 7:26).[23] Second, the tense of the infinitive ἀπηλλάχθαι is perfect; the point is "get free from and stay free of your opponent." Reconciliation, on the other hand, has precisely the opposite goal, namely, overcoming and ending separation, not perpetuating it.[24]

Matthew's version of this saying has two distinctive features that set it apart from Luke's version and merit comment. First, rather than using a form of ἀπαλλάσσω or διαλλάσσω (as in 5:24), Matthew has Jesus say ἴσθι εὐνοῶν (5:25).[25] The term εὐνοέω belongs to the *topos* on friendship (φιλία), where it and its cognates (such as εὔνοος and εὔνοια) not only are used to describe the traits of a good friend (φίλος) but also function as synonyms of φίλος and φιλία.[26] Thus εὔνοια and φιλία are sometimes interchangeable terms not only in the Middle Stoa and Middle Platonism but also in Philo and Josephus.[27] Even for

Aristotle, who sought to distinguish between these two sets of terms, εὔνοια marks the beginning of friendship, which then grows through association (*Eth. eud.* 7.7.1–3; *Eth. nic.* 8.2.3–4; 9.5.1–4).[28]

The close connection between εὔνοια and φιλία is especially important for understanding the import of Matthew's ἴσθι εὐνοῶν, which is best translated "be friendly with" (TEV) or "make friends with."[29] The emphasis is on establishing friendship, or to be more precise, on restoring an amicable relationship, not settling a debt. Imprisonment and the full repayment of all debts are the dire consequence for the failure to (re)establish a friendship[30] with one's adversary (ἀντίδικος).

Second, the location of the key term also reveals Matthew's emphasis on friendship. The word ἀπηλλάχθαι in Luke 12:58 occurs in the middle of the saying, where it is combined with the Latinism "make an effort" (δὸς ἐργασίαν = *da operam*). Matthew, by contrast, emphasizes the restoration to friendship by placing ἴσθι εὐνοῶν at the beginning of the unit (5:25).[31]

Ancient readers, who would have recognized the close connection between "be reconciled" (Matt 5:24) and "be friendly, make friends" (Matt 5:25), would have readily understood that the third unit was continuing the concern of the second unit.[32] Indeed, one of the primary meanings of "reconciliation" (διαλλαγή) is "the restoration of friendship." That this is the case has long been recognized by lexicographers. For example, the fifth-century C.E. lexicographer Hesychius of Alexandria gives φιλία ("friendship") as one of the two meanings of καταλλαγή, the Pauline noun for "reconciliation" (Rom 5:11; 11:15; 2 Cor 5:18). In a similar way, he defines ἀδιάλλακτος ("irreconcilable") as "not to be made a friend of" (ἀφιλίωτος) and gives "to make a friend" (φίλον ποιῆσαι) as the meaning of the verb ἀποκαταλλάξαι, the deutero-Pauline verb for "to reconcile" (Eph 2:16; Col 1:20, 22). These definitions were hardly innovations on the part of Hesychius. On the contrary, he was simply giving expression to meanings that had been self-evident and axiomatic for centuries in the Greek-speaking world. Modern lexicographers usually agree that this is the case and typically define both διαλλάσσειν and καταλλάσσειν as "to change from enmity to friendship."[33] On this point Ceslas Spicq is unequivocal: "For pagans and Christians alike, *reconciliation* is the action of reestablishing friendship between two persons who are on bad terms, to replace hostility with peaceful relations."[34] This same understanding is reflected in texts that were written by Greek-speaking Jewish authors. Philo, for instance, in discussing Genesis' account of Joseph's reconciliation with

his brothers, says that "his brethren will make with him covenants of reconciliation (καταλλακτηρίους), changing their hatred [μῖσος] to
friendship (φιλίαν), their ill-will (κακόνουν) to good-will (εὔνοιαν)"
(*Somn.* 2.108, trans. Colson and Whitaker, LCL).[35]

When the Matthean Jesus, therefore, follows up his command "be
reconciled" (διαλλάγηθι) with the directive "be friendly" (ἴσθι
εὐνοῶν), his first readers would immediately have seen the two instructions as parallels. Like "the brother who has something against you"
(Matt 5:23), the ἀντίδικος is someone who must be reconciled, and
that reconciliation and the concomitant restoration of an amicable relationship are depicted as a matter of urgency. The action necessary to
achieve this goal is to be undertaken "quickly" (ταχύ), without any
delay. The idea of a speedy reconciliation is well attested in both Greek
and Jewish sources,[36] and it is motivated here by Jesus' graphic depiction
of what will happen if his counsel is ignored. Of course, full-fledged
friendships are not established "quickly," for trust is only established over
a long period of time. But the inception of that process can take place
quickly, and that is why Matthew has Jesus use εὐνοέω, since it points
to the good will and friendly disposition that calms rage (ὀργιζόμενος:
Matt 5:22) and ultimately culminates in true friendship. In short,
εὔνοια can only begin when ὀργή ceases.[37] That is also why the appeal
"be reconciled" often means concretely "be angry no longer."[38]

In terms of ancient law, the course of action advised by the Matthean
Jesus belongs to the realm of out-of-court dispute settlements. This procedure, which was less formal than private lawsuits carried out before a
judge (called a κριτής in Matt 5:25), was extremely common throughout the ancient Mediterranean world, and its popularity as a means of
resolving conflict is seen in New Comedy, where private arbitrations and
mediated reconciliations are the most common form of dispute settlement.[39] The whole process reflected what Adele Scafuro has called an
"ideology of friendship," with the arbitrators or mediators usually being
either friends or relatives of the disputants, and the goal of the endeavor
understood as the establishment of friendly relations between the hostile
parties.[40]

This goal is reflected in two typical elements of these reconciliation
agreements. First, there was an "amnesia clause" in which previous mis-
deeds were to be forgotten, not retained in the memory so that they
could form grounds for a new reproach. In addition to such grants of
amnesty and promises "to forgive and forget" in regard to past injuries,
a disputant might grant certain concessions to the person who was seek-

ing reconciliation, or he could even eliminate reparations altogether. These actions were typically taken in order to facilitate the reconciliation.[41] "In disputes over money," for example, "a creditor or other potential plaintiff might grant a release (*aphesis*) to the debtor or potential defendant upon payment of an agreed upon sum of money; a mutual settlement, i.e., a meeting of the terms demanded by the creditor or potential plaintiff (*apallagē*), might also end the dispute."[42]

Second, as part of the reconciliation agreement, the disputants pledged to regard each other henceforth as friends and to treat each other accordingly. This intention is particularly clear in those cases where the compensation paid by one disputant to another is characterized as a "gift."[43] Gift-giving was central to ancient friendship, and the application of the language of gifts to the terms of reconciliation indicates the desire of all parties to resolve the conflict in a way that not only reconciled alienated friends but also laid a foundation for the future preservation of that friendship. They knew that "the success of non-binding out-of-court settlements would depend on the preservation of goodwill between the participants" and that was best achieved by using "language that pays heed to the values of friendship, to mending disturbed relationships and to maintaining restored ones, to the giving of gifts rather than the paying of forced penalties."[44]

Both of these elements—amnesia in regard to the past and a pledge of friendship in regard to the future—are present in Apollodorus's speech *Against Neaera* (= Ps.-Demosthenes, *Or.* 59), which gives the terms of a private arbitration agreement that had been prompted by the intervention of their friends (*Neaer.* 45). A man by the name of Phrynion had brought suit against an old family foe named Stephanus because the latter had taken away from him Neaera, a "deluxe prostitute"[45] and courtesan (ἑταίρα) with whom both men were enamored. The arbitrators succeeded in reconciling the two men, with the terms of the reconciliation being that each man was to enjoy Neaera's company an equal number of days each month (*Neaer.* 47). As far as the relationship of the two men themselves was concerned, "from then on, they were to be friends to one another and were not to remember past injuries (ἐκ τοῦ λοιποῦ χρόνου φίλους εἶναι ἀλλήλοις καὶ μὴ μνησικακεῖν)" (*Neaer.* 46).

This same idea of friendship as a consequence of an out-of-court settlement appears also in Demosthenes, *Pro Phorm.* [*Or.* 36].16, where the arbitrators persuaded Phormio "to give as a gift" (δοῦναι δωρειὰν) to Apollodorus the 3,000 drachmas and other items that he was demanding as compensation and thus "have him as a friend (φίλον) rather than as an enemy (ἐχθρὸν) because of this." A variant of this basic idea appears in Hyperides' *Against Athenogenes* 5, where a woman named Antigone, acting as a mediator in a dispute between Epicrates and Athenogenes, "reconciled" (διή[λλ]αξε) the two men, and exhorted them "in the future to treat each other well (τ]οῦ λοιποῦ εὖ ποιεῖν ἀλλήλους)."[46]

Therefore, in advising his disciples to seek reconciliation and to make friends of foes, Jesus is commending a course of action that was often an assumed or explicit part of the out-of-court settlement of disputes, especially when the disputants had once been friends. In Matthew 5:25, the individual to be conciliated is twice designated the ἀντίδικος. This term can indicate one's judicial opponent, but it also (and more fundamentally) signifies one's "enemy." As such, it is a virtual synonym for ἐχθρός, the standard antonym of φίλος.[47] The ἀντίδικος is precisely the kind of person at whom anger is usually directed. Sirach, for example, calls upon God to act in this way: "Rouse your rage (θυμὸν) and pour out your wrath (ὀργήν), destroy the adversary (ἀντίδικον) and wipe out the enemy (ἐχθρόν)" (Sir 36:6). Obviously, the attitude of the Matthean Jesus to human adversaries stands in radical contrast to the desire to see one's foes annihilated.

Of particular interest is the fact that the Epicurean philosopher Philodemus uses the term ἀντίδικος in his discussion of anger (*Ira* col. 31.12 Indelli), applying it to anyone, including members of one's own family, who encourages individuals in their display of anger and thereby discourages them from living in accordance with Epicurean principles.

> [Nothing is reliable] except canonic argument;[48] on the contrary, everyone is your opponent (ἀντίδικος)—those on the one hand who are non-philosophers[49] egging you on in every conceivable way, parents and all your relatives for the most part even rejoicing over you as being manly (ἐπάνδροις) (when you show anger), and of the philosophers, some talking rubbish in their "consolations," and some even strengthening your anger by their advocating it, for I dismiss orators and poets and all such trash (col. 31.11-24 Indelli).[50]

Matthew's use of the term in a pericope concerned with anger and its consequences is thus neither surprising nor unprecedented. But Philodemus and the Matthean Jesus have two quite different concerns and thus give radically different counsels in regard to the ἀντίδικος. In the case of Philodemus, the ἀντίδικος is not only the non-Epicurean or the family member who confuses anger with courage[51] but also fellow Epicureans and members of other philosophical schools who either are inept in their harangues against anger or, worse, explicitly endorse anger. Such opponents are to be rejected and ridiculed, not reconciled. In Matthew 5:25, by contrast, the ἀντίδικος is contextually not some ancient loan shark from whom one has borrowed money and who now must be repaid. He is rather an estranged "brother" (5:22-24) with whom the individual has had financial dealings. As a result of conflict, he now "has something against" his former friend and is taking the latter to court.[52] That money is involved in this dispute should come as no surprise, for ancient friendship normally involved financial considerations.[53] But while money is involved, the real issue is the dissolution of friendship owing to anger. The urgent task in regard to such a person is reconciliation and restoration to friendship. As Hans Dieter Betz notes, "By gaining control over that anger and by changing it into friendliness, they will find that they have no reason to go to court and can part as friends rather than foes."[54]

Two Different Rationales for Action

The actions advised in the second and third units are based on completely different considerations. In the second unit, the rationale is theological and similar to what one finds in rabbinic discussions of Yom Kippur (the Day of Atonement). The most important early text is the Mishnaic tractate *Yoma*:

> If a man said, . . . "I will sin and the Day of Atonement will effect atonement," then the Day of Atonement effects no atonement. For transgressions that are between man and God the Day of Atonement effects atonement, but for transgressions that are between a man and his fellow the Day of Atonement effects atonement only if he has appeased his fellow. This did R. Eleazar b. Azariah expound: *From all your sins shall ye be clean before the Lord*—for transgressions that are between man and God the Day of Atonement effects atonement; but for transgressions that are between a man and his fellow the Day of Atonement effects atonement only if he has appeased his fellow. (*m. Yoma* 8.9)[55]

In this text, it is explicit that there is atonement for transgressions against one's fellow if and only if an individual has succeeded in conciliating the estranged person. That means that the reconciliation of one's foes is the essential prerequisite for forgiveness from God for wrongs done to others. Both logically and temporally, therefore, transgressors must go first to those whom they have wronged before seeking atonement from God on Yom Kippur. This principle proved to be highly

influential in Jewish tradition and contributed to the modern idea that
the month of Elul is not only a time of repentance in preparation for the
High Holy Days of Rosh Hashanah and Yom Kippur but also "a time for
reconciliation with enemies."[56] Especially important in this regard is
Erev Yom Kippur, "The Day before Yom Kippur," since it is "almost the
last chance to ask the forgiveness of people one has hurt."[57]
Consequently, especially on this day one should apologize and seek forgiveness from relatives, friends, and others for any wrongdoings done to
them. Conversely, it is incumbent on those who seek forgiveness to grant
it to others at whose hands they have suffered. Erev Yom Kippur is thus
not only an appropriate occasion "for giving restitution to those we have
wronged" but also for "forgiving those who have hurt us."[58]

Although Jesus' instructions to his disciples in the Sermon on the
Mount are not linked to Yom Kippur, his teaching is consonant with this
scribal tradition.[59] In Matthew 5:23-24, Jesus' followers are to be reconciled with their brother "first" (πρῶτον), and only "then" (τότε) bring
their gifts to the altar.[60] Here the transgressors are in view, seeking the
reconciliation of enemies. In the Lord's Prayer, the situation is reversed,
and they are the ones who are called upon to grant forgiveness. "And forgive us our debts, as we also *have forgiven* (ἀφήκαμεν) our debtors"
(6:12).[61] The prayer presupposes that the one asking for forgiveness from
God has already extended that same forgiveness to others.

Furthermore, there is biblical precedent for the idea that an essential
prerequisite for approaching the altar is making things right with the
person that one has wronged. One clear example of this idea is Leviticus
5:20-26 MT (= 6:1-7 NRSV), which deals with reparation offerings.[62]
The envisioned situation is one in which someone has trespassed against
God by wronging another person: "When any of you sin and commit a
trespass against the LORD by deceiving a neighbor in a matter of a
deposit or a pledge, or by robbery, or if you have defrauded a neighbor,
or have found something lost and lied about it . . ." (6:2-3 NRSV = 5:21-
22 MT). In this circumstance, the Torah stipulates that restitution to
human beings must precede the reparation offering to Yahweh.[63] "When
you have sinned and realize your guilt, and would restore what you took
by robbery or by fraud or the deposit that was committed to you, or the
lost thing that you found, or anything else about which you have sworn
falsely, you shall repay the principal amount and shall add one-fifth to it.
You shall pay it to its owner when you realize your guilt" (6:4-5 NRSV
= 5:23-24 MT).[64] It is only then, when restitution to one's neighbor has
been fully made along with the added penalty of twenty percent, that the

transgressor brings an unblemished ram or its equivalent as a reparation (guilt) offering (6:6 NRSV = 5:25 MT), and "the priest shall make atonement on your behalf before the LORD, and you shall be forgiven" (6:7 NRSV = 5:26 MT).[65]

Whereas the second unit of Matthew 5:21-26 is thus highly theological and draws on an established biblical principle, the action advised by Jesus in the third unit is based purely on utilitarian considerations. It is the need to avoid imprisonment that provides the impetus to friendship (5:25-26). While theologically one may wince at this kind of counsel, friendship based on utilitarian concerns was the most common kind of ancient friendship (Aristotle, *Eth. eud.* 7.2.14), and there is reason to believe that many early Christians thought of friendship in this way, though others had a more elevated conception.[66] People of different financial levels usually had this kind of friendship (Aristotle, *Eth. nic.* 8.8.6), so it is not surprising that one finds the Matthean Jesus giving utilitarian advice to a debtor. That is, it is likely that the initial friendship between these two parties had been based on need, and thus it is natural for Jesus to make use of that understanding when he offers counsel. In any case, the saying here belongs to the tradition of ancient sapiential admonitions, which were often grounded in utility.[67]

It should be recalled that Jesus elsewhere gives utilitarian considerations as the basis for action. One especially clear example is the action of the younger son in Jesus' so-called "parable of the prodigal son" (Luke 15:11-32). Once the younger son "came to himself" (Luke 15:17), he realized that even his father's hired hands were far better off than he was and thus decided to return home. "The story presents his repentant attitude as springing not from remorse but from his desire for food to sustain himself."[68] When he gets home, he uses "religious language" to affirm that he has sinned, but the preceding part of the parable makes abundantly clear that the real motivating factor in his "conversion" was not his sense of religious or moral failure in regard to God and his father, but his desperate, needy situation. In a similar way, in Matthew 5:25-26 it is the fervent desire and pressing need of the debtor to avoid imprisonment, not a yearning for reconciliation and friendship, that is the key motivation. At the same time, one should note that other sayings in the Sermon on the Mount and the Gospel of Matthew as a whole provide a check against the idea that one's relationship with others should be based on purely utilitarian considerations (e.g., 5:43-48).

Conclusion

Finally, though there are some dissenting views, the *communis opinio* is that Matthew is responsible for linking the third unit to the second, and the preceding discussion lends support to this view.[69] Matthew's redactional activity indicates that he recognized the close connection between reconciliation and friendship. In connecting these two themes with the *topos* on anger, he is not unique but is following a longstanding moralist tradition in which anger and angry words are discussed as dangers to friendship and in conjunction with the need for reconciliation when the bonds of friendship have been broken.[70] This connection is present in both the Hellenistic moralists (for example, Philodemus, *Ira*, and Seneca, *Ira*) and Jewish writers (for instance, Sir 22:19-22). As Sirach said, "The one who reviles a friend destroys friendship" (22:20); but "If you should open your mouth against a friend, don't despair, for reconciliation (διαλλαγή) is possible" (22:22). That is a sentiment with which Matthew clearly agreed.

Notes

Chapter 1

1 All the standard works on Christology assume this language to some extent. Cf. Wilhelm Bousset, *Kyrios Christos: Geschichte des Christusglaubens von den Anfangen des Christentums bis Irenaeus* (FRLANT 21; Göttingen: Vandenhoeck & Ruprecht, 1913; rev. ed., 1921); Oscar Cullmann, *Die Christologie des Neuen Testaments* (Tübingen: Mohr Siebeck, 1957); J. N. D. Kelly, *Early Christian Doctrines* (London: Continuum, 5th ed., 1977, repr. 2003; first published by A&C Black, 1958); Richard N. Longenecker, *The Christology of Early Jewish Christianity* (Studies in Biblical Theology 2:17; Naperville: Alec R. Allenson, 1970); Martin Hengel, *The Son of God: The Origin of Christology and the History of Jewish-Hellenistic Religion* (Philadelphia: Fortress, 1976); James Dunn, *Christology in the Making: A New Testament Inquiry into the Origins of the Doctrine of the Incarnation* (Philadelphia: Westminster, 1980); Donald Juel, *Messianic Exegesis: Christological Interpretation of the Old Testament in Early Christianity* (Philadelphia: Fortress, 1988); Maurice Casey, *From Jewish Prophet to Gentile God: The Origins and Development of New Testament Christology* (Louisville: Westminster John Knox, 1991); Raymond E. Brown, *An Introduction to New Testament Christology* (New York: Paulist Press, 1994); Jarl Fossum, *The Image of the Invisible God: Essays on the Influence of Jewish Mysticism on Early Christology* (ed. Jarl Fossum; NTOA 30; Göttingen: Vandenhoeck & Ruprecht, 1995); Crispin H. T. Fletcher-Louis, *Luke-Acts: Angels, Christology and Soteriology* (WUNT 2/94; Tübingen: Mohr Siebeck, 1997); Richard Bauckham, *God Crucified: Monotheism and Christology in the New Testament* (Grand Rapids: Eerdmans, 1998); Charles A. Gieschen, *Angelomorphic Christology: Antecedents and Early Evidence* (AGJU 42; Leiden: Brill, 1998); Frank

Matera, *New Testament Christology* (Louisville: Westminster John Knox Press, 1999); Larry W. Hurtado, *Lord Jesus Christ: Devotion to Jesus in Earliest Christianity* (Grand Rapids: Eerdmans, 2003); Hurtado, *How on Earth Did Jesus Become God? Historical Questions about Earliest Devotion to Jesus* (Grand Rapids: Eerdmans, 2005); Simon J. Gathercole, *The Pre-existent Son: Recovering the Christologies of Matthew, Mark, and Luke* (Grand Rapids: Eerdmans, 2006).

2   See especially, Alan Segal, *Two Powers in Heaven: Early Rabbinic Reports about Christianity and Gnosticism* (SJLA 25; Leiden: Brill, 1977); Larry W. Hurtado, *One God, One Lord: Early Christian Devotion and Ancient Jewish Monotheism* (Philadelphia: Fortress, 1988); Hurtado, *Lord Jesus Christ*; Hurtado, *How on Earth*. Also foundational to this discussion are the works of Jarl Fossum. See Jarl Fossum, *The Name of God and the Angel of the Lord* (WUNT 36; Tübingen: Mohr Siebeck, 1985); Fossum, *Image of the Invisible God*. Important recent works that argue for "early high Christology" include, Gieschen, *Angelomorphic Christology*; Bauckman, *God Crucified*; Timo Eskola, *Messiah and the Throne: Jewish Merkavah Mysticism and Early Christian Exaltation Discourse* (WUNT 2/142; Tübingen: Mohr Siebeck, 2001).

3   A. D. DeConick, *Recovering the Original Gospel of Thomas: A History of the Gospel and Its Growth* (LNTS 286; London: T&T Clark, 2005).

4   The literature on social memory studies is vast, but those which I have found most applicable to my work on early Christianity include M. Halbwachs, *On Collective Memory* (trans. L. A. Coser; Chicago: University of Chicago Press, 1992 [1925]); M. Halbwachs, *The Collective Memory* (trans. F. Ditter and V. Ditter; New York: Harper & Row, 1980 [1950]); P. Berger and T. Luckmann, *The Social Construction of Reality: A Treatise in the Sociology of Knowledge* (New York: Doubleday, 1966); B. Lewis, *History: Remembered, Recovered, Invented* (Princeton: Princeton University Press, 1975); F. Zonabend, *The Enduring Memory: Time and History in a French Village* (trans. A. Forster; Manchester: Manchester University Press, 1984); R. Rosenzweig and D. Thelen, *The Presence of the Past: Popular Uses of History in American Life* (New York: Columbia University Press, 1988); J. Bodnar, *Remaking America: Public Memory, Commemoration, and Patriotism in the Twentieth Century* (Princeton: Princeton University Press, 1992); J. Assman, *Das kulturelle Gedächtnis: Schrift, Erinnerung und politische Identität in frühen Hochkulturen* (München: D. H. Beck, 1992); R. Terdiman, *Present Past: Modernity and the Memory Crisis* (Ithaca: Cornell University Press, 1993); B. Zelizer, "Reading the Past Against the Grain: The Shape of Memory Studies," *CSMC* 12 (1995): 214–39; Y. Zerubavel, *Recovered Roots: Collective Memory and the Making of Israeli National Tradition* (Chicago: University of Chicago Press, 1997); B. Swartz, Abraham *Lincoln and the Forge of National Memory* (Chicago: University of Chicago Press, 2000).

5   On the connection between religious experience and hermeneutics, see my article, "What Is Early Jewish and Christian Mysticism?" in *Paradise Now: Essays on Early Jewish and Christian Mysticism* (ed. April D. DeConick; Symposium 11; Atlanta: Society of Biblical Literature, 2006), 5–8. The literature on the centrality of religious experience in the theological and practical development of early Christianity is beginning to be acknowledged in the Academy. See especially, Larry W. Hurtado, "Religious Experience and Religious Innovation in the New Testament," *JR* 80 (2000): 183–205. The classic works include Hermann Gunkel, *Die Wirkungen des heiligen Geistes nach der populären Anschauung der apostolischen Zeit und der Lehre des Apostels Paulus* (Göttingen: Vandenhoeck & Ruprecht, 1888), which has now been translated into English as *The Influence of the Holy Spirit: The Popular View of the Apostolic Age and the Teaching of the Apostle Paul* (trans. by R. A. Harrisville and P. A. Quanbeck; Philadelphia: Fortress, 1979); H. B. Swete, *The Holy Spirit in the New Testament* (London: Macmillian, 1909); Adolf Deissmann, *Paul: A Study in Social and Religious History* (1911; English trans., 1927; repr., New York: Harper, 1957); P. Gardner, *The Religious Experience of St. Paul* (London: Williams & Norgate, 1911); Rodney Stark, "A Taxonomy of Religious Experience," *Journal for the Scientific Study of Religion* 5 (1965): 97–116. More recently, see James D. G. Dunn, *Jesus and the Spirit: A Study of the Religious and Charismatic Experience of Jesus and the First Christians as Reflected in the New Testament* (London: SCM Press, 1975); Luke T. Johnson, *Religious Experience in Earliest Christianity: A Missing Dimension in New Testament Studies* (Minneapolis: Fortress, 1998).

6   The work of Alan Segal on the topic of resurrection has been comprehensive. See his book, *Life after Death: A History of the Afterlife in Western Religion* (New York: Doubleday, 2004). See now also Dale C. Allison, *Resurrecting Jesus: The Earliest Christian Tradition and Its Interpreters* (London: T&T Clark, 2005).

7   The recent books that have been most helpful to me on this topic are Segal, *Life after Death*, 285–321, 351–96; and Arthur J. Drodge and James D. Tabor, *A Noble Death: Suicide and Martyrdom Among Christians and Jews in Antiquity* (San Francisco: Harper, 1992). The classic study is W. H. C. Frend, *Martyrdom and Persecution in the Early Church: A Study of a Conflict from the Maccabees to Donatus* (Garden City, N.Y.: Anchor Books, 1967).

8   See especially Burton Mack, *A Myth of Innocence: Mark and Christian Origins* (Philadelphia: Fortress, 1988).

9   H. M. Teeple, *The Mosaic Eschatological Prophet* (Philadelphia: Society of Biblical Literature, 1957); Longenecker, *The Christology of Early Jewish Christianity*, 32–38.

10 Fossum, *The Name of God*, 83–84, 87–94, 111–12.

11 Hurtado, *One God, One Lord*, 51–70.

12 David Capes, *Old Testament Yahweh Texts in Paul's Christology* (WUNT 2/47; Tübingen: Mohr Siebeck, 1992).

13 Christopher Rowland, "The Vision of the Risen Christ in Rev i.13ff: The Debt of an Early Christology to an Aspect of Jewish Angelology," *JTS* 31 (1980): 1–11; Christopher Rowland, *The Open Heaven* (London: SPCK, 1982), 94–113; Fossum, "Kyrios Jesus as the Angel of the Lord in Jude 5–7," *NTS* 33 (1987): esp. 23–37; Rowland, *Name of God*; Rowland, *Image of the Invisible God*; Jarl Fossum, "Glory," in *Dictionary of Deities and Demons in the Bible* (eds. Karel van der Toorn et al.; Leiden: Brill, 1996), 348–52; Carey Newman, *Paul's Glory-Christology: Tradition and Rhetoric* (NovTSup 69; Leiden: Brill, 1992).

14 See especially the synthetic work of Charles Gieschen, *Angelomorphic Christology*, particularly 6, 51–69, and 349–51; cf. Bauckman, *God Crucified*; Eskola, *Messiah and the Throne*.

15 Jarl Fossum, "Jewish-Christian Christology and Jewish Mysticism," *VC* 37 (1983): 266–70; Fossum, *The Name of God and the Angel of the Lord*, 269–70, 284; cf. M. Bockmuehl, "'The Form of God' (Phil. 2:6): Variations on a Theme in Jewish Mysticism," *JTS* 48 (1997): 1–23; R. Martin, *Carmen Christi: Philippians ii.5-11 in Recent Interpretation and in the Setting of Early Christian Worship* (SNTSMS 4; Cambridge: Cambridge University Press, 1967); J. T. Sanders, *New Testament Christological Hymns: Their Historical Religious Background* (SNTSMS 15: Cambridge: Cambridge University Press, 1971), 58–74.

16 Hengel, *The Son of God*.

17 Gieschen, *Angelomorphic Christology*, 114–19.

18 Gieschen, *Angelomorphic Christology*, 119–20.

19 Fossum, "Jewish-Christian Christology," 26–71; Charles Gieschen, "The Seven Pillars of the World: Ideal Figure Lists in the Christology of the Pseudo-Clementines," *JSP* 12 (1994): 67–82; Gieschen, *Angelomorphic Christology*, 201–13.

20 O. Skarsaune, *The Proof from Prophecy. A Study of Justin Marytr's Proof-Text Tradition: Text-Type, Provenance, Theological Profile* (SupNovT 56; Leiden: Brill, 1987), 409–23; D. Trakatellis, *The Pre-existence of Christ in the Writings of Justin Martyr* (HDR 6; Missoula: Scholars Press, 1976); B. Kominiak, *The Theophanies of the Old Testament in the Writings of St. Justin* (Washington: The Catholic University of America Press, 1948).

21 J. Rendel Harris, "The Origins of the Prologue to St. John's Gospel," *Expositor* 8.12 (1916): 147–60, 161–70, 314–20, 388–400; Rudolph Bultmann, "Der religionsgeschichtliche Hintergrund des Prologs zum Johannes-Evangelium," in *Eucharisterion: Festschrift für Hermann Gunkel* (ed. H. Schmidt; FRLANT 37.2; Göttingen: Vandenhoeck & Ruprecht, 1923), 3–26; Dunn, *Christology in the Making*, 168–76; James Dunn, "Let John Be John: A Gospel for Its Time," in *Das Evangelium und die*

Evangelium: Vorträge vom Tübinger Symposium 1982 (ed. P. Stuhlmacher; WUNT 28; Tübingen: Mohr Siebeck, 1983), 337.

22   C. H. Dodd, *The Interpretation of the Fourth Gospel* (Cambridge: Cambridge UniversityPress, 1953), 275.

23   Jarl Fossum, "In the Beginning Was the Name: Onomanology as the Key to Johannine Christianity," in *The Image of the Invisible God: Essays on the Influence of Jewish Mysticism on Early Christology* (ed. Jarl Fossum; NTOA 30; Göttingen: Vandenhoeck & Ruprecht, 1995), 109–33.

24   I think that John Ashton is correct in his opinion that Jewish angelology goes a long way to explain the perplexing Christology in John's gospel. See John Ashton, "Bridging Ambiguities," in *Studying John: Approaches to the Fourth Gospel* (ed. John Ashton; Oxford: Clarendon, 1994), 71–89.

25   April D. DeConick, *Voices of the Mystics: Early Christian Discourse in the Gospels of John and Thomas and Other Ancient Christian Literature* (JSNTS 157; Sheffield: Sheffield Academic, 2001), 117–21.

26   Fossum, "Glory," 1486–98.

27   There are some scholars who do not think the Gospel of John reflects sacramental imagery. I find this position naïve and have discussed it at length in *Visions of the Mystics*, 128–31. On mysticism in the Gospel of Thomas, see particularly my book, *Seek to See Him: Ascent and Vision Mysticism in the Gospel of Thomas* (VCSup 33; Leiden: Brill, 1996).

Chapter 2

1   An earlier version of this essay was published in *Studies in Religion/ Sciences Religieuses*, vol. 35, no. 2, 2006. We wish to thank the editorial staff of this journal for granting permission to allow its contents to be represented.

2   A. D. Nock, *Conversion* (London: Oxford University Press, 1933), 7.

3   Krister Stendahl, *Paul among the Jews and Gentiles* (Philadelphia: Fortress, 1976).

4   John Gager, *The Origins of Anti-Semitism* (New York: Oxford University Press, 1983), 209–11; Gager, *Reinventing Paul* (New York: Oxford University Press, 2004); Alan Segal, *Paul the Convert: The Apostolate and Apostasy of Saul the Pharisee* (New Haven: Yale University Press, 1990).

5   Paula Fredriksen, "Paul and Augustine: Conversion Narratives, Orthodox Traditions, and the Retrospective Self," *JTS* 37 (1986): 3–34.

6   Some English translations strive to create wiggle-room here by translating *ethnê* as "heathen," but this simply imports back into the mid-first century the Gentile/pagan distinction, using the idea of pagan but not the word.

7   John Gager, "Some Notes on Paul's Conversion," *NTS* 27 (1981), 697–704; John Gager, "Paul, the Apostle of Judaism," in *Jesus, Judaism, and Christian Anti-Judaism* (eds. Paula Fredriksen and Adele Reinhartz;

Louisville: Westminster John Knox, 2002), 64. For precisely this reason, Gager (2002) insists that the words "Christian" and "Christianity" must not be used for this first generation: "There was no Christianity as such in Paul's time." This conviction does not, alas, prevent him from the no less anachronistic use of the term "convert" of Paul, but that usage is driven by Gager's perduring attachment to the psychological model of "transvaluation experiences." See also Gager (1981), and frequently thereafter.

8 This list of identifiers is, of course, a paraphrase of Romans 15.

9 For obvious reasons, *homoglôssa* cannot indicate "Jewishness" for Paul in the way that it could indicate "Greekness" for Herodotos.

10 Paula Fredriksen, "What 'Parting of the Ways?'" in *The Ways That Never Parted* (eds. A. Becker and A. Y. Reed; TSAJ 95; Tübingen: Mohr Siebeck, 2003), 44–45.

11 L. I. Levine, *The Ancient Synagogue: The First 1000 Years* (New Haven: Yale University Press, 2000), 271–75; 350; 480–82. The Aphrodisias inscription has recently been redated to the fourth ad fifth centuries. This newer date opens to the intriguing possibility that (some of) these Gentile benefactors may have been Christian. For the later date, see A. Chaniotis, "The Jews of Aphrodisias: New Evidence and Old Problems," *Scripta Classica Israelica* 21 (2002): 209–42.

12 S. J. D. Cohen, *Beginnings of Jewishness* (Berkeley: University of California Press, 1999), 125–39, 156–74.

13 Paula Fredriksen, "Judaism, the Circumcision of Gentiles, and Apocalyptic Hope: Another Look at Galatians 1 and 2," *JTS* 42 (1991): 544–48.

14 Paula Fredriksen, "Judaism."

15 Mary Beard, "Priesthood in the Roman Republic," in *Pagan Priests* (eds. M. Beard and J. North; Ithaca: Cornell University Press, 1990), 38 and n. 55.

16 N. T. Wright, *Jesus and the Victory of God* (Minneapolis: Fortress, 1996), 398–403; 405–28. Wright sees Jesus' program as essentially motivated by "anti-nationalism."

17 James D. G. Dunn, *The Partings of the Ways* (Philadelphia: Trinity Press International, 1991), 124–39.

18 W. H. C. Frend, *Martyrdom and Persecution in the Early Church* (Oxford: Basil Blackwell, 1965), 220, 429; M. Simon, *Verus Israel* (London: Littman Library of Jewish Civilization, 1996 [1948]), 115.

19 T. D. Barnes, "Legislation against the Christians," *JRS* 58 (1968), 32–50; Fergus Millar, "The Imperial Cult and the Persecutions," in *Le Culte Des Souverains Dans L'empire Romain* (Entretiens Hardt 19; Geneva: Vandoeuvres, 1973), 145–75.

20 A. Linder, *The Jews in Imperial Roman Legislation* (Detroit: Wayne State University Press, 1987); Miriam Pucci ben Zeev, *Jewish Rights in the Roman World* (Tübingen: Mohr Siebeck, 1998).

21 B. Isaac, *The Invention of Racism in Classical Antiquity* (Princeton: Princeton University Press, 2004).

22   K. M. Coleman, "Fatal Charades: Roman Executions Staged as Mythologi-
     cal Enactments," *JRS* 80 (1990): 44–73; D. S. Potter, "Martyrdom as
     Spectacle," in *Theatre and Society in the Classical World* (ed. R. Scodel; Ann
     Arbor: University of Michigan Press, 1993), 58–88.

23   Shortly before Decius attempted to mandate universal homage to the
     gods of Rome, Origen claimed that "few, whose number could easily be
     counted, have died occasionally for the sake of the Christian religion," *c.
     Celsum* 3.8.

24   J. B. Rives, "The Decree of Decius and the Religion of the Empire," *JRS*
     89 (1999): 135–54.

25   E.g., Eusebius's story of the Gentile Christian who contemplated conver-
     sion to Judaism in order to avoid such harassment (*Hist. eccl.* 6.12.1).

26   On this last point, most recently, see Isaac, *Invention of Racism*, 447.

27   Roman respect for foreign deities informed their practice of *evocatio deo-
     rum*, promising cult to those gods in exchange for their support when
     Roman armies went up against those gods' humans. Recently, J. S.
     Kloppenburg has argued that Josephus and the Gospel of Mark preserve
     traces of evidence suggesting that Titus performed such a ritual when
     conquering Jerusalem, see "*Evocatio Deorum* and the Date of Mark," *JBL*
     124 (2005): 419–50.

28   Bauckham, *God Crucified*; Hurtado, *Lord Jesus Christ*; L. T. Stucken-
     bruck and Wendy E. S. North, eds., *Early Jewish and Christian
     Monotheism* (JSNT Suppl. 263; London: T&T Clark, 2004).

29   If by *archontes tou aiônes toutou* Paul meant astral powers (1 Cor 2:8),
     then these lesser gods had crucified the son of Israel's god.

30   P. Athanassiadi and M. Frede, eds., *Pagan Monotheism* (Oxford: Oxford
     University Press, 1999).

31   Annette Reed, "The Trickery of the Fallen Angels and the Demonic
     Mimesis of the Divine: Aetiology and Polemics in the Writings of Justin
     Martyr," *JECS* 12 (2004): 141–71.

32   G. W. Bowersock, "Polytheism and Monotheism in Arabia and the Three
     Palestines," in *Dumbarton Oaks Papers* (1997), 1–10; Paula Fredriksen,
     "Christians in the Roman Empire in the First Three Centuries A.D.," in
     Companion to the Roman Empire (ed. David Potter; Oxford: Blackwell,
     2006), 587–606. Hence the confusion of those Gentile Christians
     named in the canons of the Council of Elvira c. 303, who continued to
     function in public as flamines in the imperial cult, processing and spon-
     soring gladiatorial matches (see nos. 2, 3, 4). The problem was not the
     divinity of the emperor, but, c. 303, the emperor's religious allegiances.
     Once Constantine sponsored the church, the cult of the (Christian)
     emperor, minus blood offerings, continued.

33   Fredriksen, "What 'Parting of the Ways?' " 35–63.

34   E. Gruen, *Heritage and Hellenism* (Cambridge, Mass.: Harvard
     University Press, 2002).

Chapter 3

1   Hurtado, *One God, One Lord*; Segal, *Two Powers in Heaven*.

2   Among recent contributions, see especially Stuckenbruck and North, *Early Jewish and Christian Monotheism*.

3   William Horbury, "Jewish and Christian Monotheism in the Herodian Age," in Stuckenbruck and North, *Early Jewish*, 16–44.

4   Horbury, "Jewish," 17.

5   E.g. Peter Hayman, "Monotheism—A Misused Word in Jewish Studies?" *JJS* 412 (1991): 1–15; Michael Mach, "Concepts of Jewish Monotheism during the Hellenistic Period," in *The Jewish Roots of Christological Monotheism: Papers from the St. Andrews Conference on the Historical Origins of the Worship of Jesus* (eds. C. C. Newman, J. R. Davila, and G. S. Lewis; SJSJ 63; Leiden: Brill, 1999), 21–42.

6   In the ancient world such a god is always grammatically "he."

7   See Martin L. West, "Towards Monotheism," in *Pagan Monotheism in Late Antiquity* (eds. Polymnia Athanassiadi and Michael Frede; Oxford: Clarendon, 1999), 21–40 (here 21–29).

8   This is not to deny that steps toward a stronger definition of the unique-ness of God can be found in pagan monotheism, especially that of the philosophers; cf. Michael Frede, "Monotheism and Pagan Philosophy in Later Antiquity," in Athanassiadi and Frede, *Pagan Monotheism*, 41–67.

9   I borrow the terms "gradient" and "binary" from David H. Aaron, *Biblical Ambiguities: Metaphors, Semantics, and Divine Imagery* (Leiden: Brill, 2001) without meaning to agree with all the uses to which he puts these terms.

10 Richard Bauckham, "The Throne of God and the Worship of Jesus," in Newman, Davila, and Lewis, *The Jewish Roots*, 43–69 (here 45–48).

11 I exclude Daniel from this count and include it in early Jewish literature simply because it so clearly belongs chronologically with the latter.

12 Gen 14:18, 19, 20, 21; Num 24:10; Deut 32:8; 2 Sam 22:14; Ps 7:18(17); 9:3(2); 21:8(7); 46:5(4); 47:3(2); 50:14; 57:3(2); 73:11; 77:11(10); 78: 17, 35, 56; 82:6; 83:19(18); 87:5; 91:1, 9; 92:2(1); 97:9; 107:11; Isa 14:14; Lam 3:35, 38. For conjectural emendations that, if accepted, would supply a few other instances, see Hans-Jürgen Zobel, "עֶלְיוֹן, *'elyôn*," *TDOT* 11.121–39 (here 122-23); Baruch A. Levine, *Numbers 21–36* (AB 4A; New York: Doubleday, 2000), 188, 193–94 (Num 24:3).

13 The Enoch literature collected in *1 Enoch* accounts for only seventeen of these occurrences. There is, therefore, no substance at all to Margaret Barker's claim that the use in *1 Enoch* is evidence of continuity between the Enoch literature and the Elyon cult of the First Temple (Barker, *The Older Testament: The Survival of Themes from the Ancient Royal Cult in*

Sectarian Judaism and Early Christianity [London: SPCK, 1987], 246). The occurrences in *1 Enoch* are part of a much broader phenomenon.

14 Even here the other uses are ancillary to the two occurrences in the liturgical blessing of Gen 14:19-20.

15 Major works of Palestinian Judaism that do not use it include 1 Maccabees and the *Psalms of Solomon*.

16 Martin Hengel, *Judaism and Hellenism* (trans. J. Bowden; London: SCM Press, 1974), 298, misleadingly states that "the designation 'Hypsistos' . . . appears particularly often in the early evidence from the Diaspora." The evidence he cites from R. Marcus (200–201, n. 265) consists of only twelve passages in Diaspora literature (the references to *Sib.Or.* 1 and fragm. 1, *Ezekiel the Tragedian*, Philo the Epic Poet, Wisdom, 2 Maccabees, 3 Maccabees, given in my list), besides some inscriptional evidence.

17 Zobel, "עֶלְיוֹן," 126.

18 Translation from Henry Chadwick, *Origen: Contra Celsum* (Cambridge: Cambridge University Press, 1965), 297; cf. also *C. Cels.* 1.24; 8.69.

19 For the textual issues, see P. Sanders, *The Provenance of Deuteronomy 32* (Oudtestamentliche Studiën 37; Leiden: Brill, 1996), 154–60.

20 The text is fragmentary: אל, אלים, and אלהים are all possible.

21 E.g. Mark S. Smith, *The Early History of God: Yahweh and the Other Deities in Ancient Israel* (San Francisco: Harper & Row, 1987), 7–8; Robert Kahl Gnuse, *No Other Gods: Emergent Monotheism in Israel* (JSOTSup 241; Sheffield: Sheffield Academic, 1997), 182.

22 Note also that "created" (קנה) in 32:6 is typically El/Elyon language (cf. Gen 14:19, 22), but has YHWH as its subject: see John Day, *Yahweh and the Gods and Goddesses of Canaan* (JSOTSup 265; Sheffield: Sheffield Academic, 2000), 20. For other features of El attributed to YHWH in Deut 32:6-7, see Smith, *The Early History*, 11.

23 Margaret Barker, *The Great Angel* (London: SPCK, 1992), 6.

24 Barker, *The Great Angel*, 6–7, can only read Job 1–2 and Ps 29:1 in this way because she reads them in the light of her interpretation of Deut 32:8-9. Contrast, e.g., Day, *Yahweh*, 22.

25 NRSV. This verse is not extant in Hebrew.

26 Translation from O. S. Wintermute, "Jubilees," in *The Old Testament Pseudepigrapha* (ed. James H. Charlesworth; vol. 2; London: Darton, Longman & Todd, 1985), 34–142 (here 87).

27 Translation from Wintermute, "Jubilees," 88.

28 This is part of an allegorical exegesis of Deut 32:7-9, quoted in *Post.* 89. Translation by F. H. Colson and G. H. Whitaker in LCL.

29 Translation by F. H. Colson and G. H. Whitaker in LCL.

30 Eusebius, *Dem. Evang.* 4.9, quoted in Barker, *The Great Angel*, 192. It should be noted that Eusebius's theology was rather closer to Arius than to Nicene trinitarianism and could appropriately be called "ditheistic."

31 Segal, *Two Powers in Heaven*.

32 Horbury, "Jewish," 19.

33 On the uniqueness of YHWH in Deuteronomy, see Richard Bauckham, "Biblical Theology and the Problems of Monotheism," in *Out of Egypt: Biblical Theology and Biblical Interpretation* (eds. Craig Bartholomew, Mary Healy, Karl Möller, and Robin Parry; Scripture and Hermeneutics Series; Milton Keynes: Paternoster, 2004), 188–96, where I take issue to some extent with Nathan MacDonald, *Deuteronomy and the Meaning of "Monotheism"* (FAT 2/1; Tübingen: Mohr Siebeck, 2003).

34 For these usages in the Hebrew Bible, see Zobel, "עֶלְיוֹן," 126–27. Robert C. T. Hayward, "El Elyon and the Divine Names in Ben Sira," in *Ben Sira's God* (ed. Renate Egger-Wenzel; BZAW 321; Berlin: de Gruyter, 2002), 180–98, provides a detailed study of Ben Sira's usage. A particular usage that does not fit obviously within these three fields is "the law of the Most High": Sir 9:15; 19:17; 23:23; 41:8; 42:2; 44:20; 49:4; 4Q525 2:24; 11Q5 18:14; cf. (using terms equivalent to "law") Ps 78:56; 107:11; 2 Bar 77:4; 82:6; *Jub.* 21:23; *1 Enoch* 99:10; *SibOr* 3:580, 719. On this usage in *Ben Sira*, see Hayward, "El Elyon," 185–87.

35 Is 46:4(5); Sir 50:7; Tob 1:4; 2 Bar 80:3; Philo, *Flacc.* 46; *Leg. Gai.* 278. Cf. *Ps-Eupolemus* 1:5.

36 Sir 7:9; 34:23; 35:8, 12; 50:14, 15; 1QapGen 10:17-18; 21:2, 20; Tob 4:11; Cairo Geniza *TLevi* (Bodl. d 16); 1 Esd 6:30(31); Philo, *Leg. Gai.* 157, 317.

37 Ps 7:18(17); 9:3(2); 50:14; 92:2(1); Dan 4:31(34); Sir 17:27; 47:8; 50:17; *Jub.* 16:27; 20:9; 4Q242 1–3 5; Ps 154:3, 10; 11Q5 22:15; 4Q291 1 3; 1 Esd 9:46. Cf. vows: Ps 50:14.

38 Sir 50:21; *Jub.* 22:11, 13, 19; 25:11; 36:16; 1QapGen 22:16; 11Q14 1 2:4, 7; Jdt 13:18.

39 Ps 57:3(2); Sir 35:21; 39:5; 46:5; 47:5; 50:19; 2 Bar 64:8; 71:2; *Jub* 12:19; 13:16, 29; 22:6; 25:11; *1 Enoch* 9:3; 4Q242 1–3 3; 3 Macc 6:2. Prayers made away from the Temple might well be associated with the Temple, being offered to the God who makes himself accessible to his people in the Temple, and as assisted by the sacrifices and incense offerings in the Temple.

40 Gen 14:18; *Jub.* 32:1; 1QapGen 22:15; *TMos* 6:1; Cairo Geniza *TLevi* (Bodl. b 5–6); Philo, *Leg. All.* 3:82; Josephus, *Ant.* 16:163.

41 Pss 47:3(2); 83:19(18); 97:9 ("over all the earth"); Sir 50:15 ("king of all"); Dan 4:14(17), 21(24), 22(25), 29(32), 31(34); 5:18, 21 ("sovereign over all human kingdoms"); *Jub.* 22:27 ("God of all," "Creator of all"); 1QapGen 20:12-13 (Lord and Master of everything and rule all the kings of the earth); 22:21 ("Lord of heaven and earth"); 4Q491 15:6–7 ("over all the nations"); 4Q550c 3:1 ("governs the whole earth"); Philo, *Plant.* 58–59 ("the universal Ruler, to whom sovereignty over all pertains"); Philo, *Post.* 89–92 ("the All-sovereign Ruler"); 3 Macc 6:2 ("governing all creation"); Philo the Epic poet 3 ("Lord of all"); *Ps-Aeschylus*

("power over all"). For other uses of "Most High" that clearly connote universal lordship, see Sir 41:4; 1 Esd 2:2(3); *SibOr* 3:718 ("he alone is sovereign").

42 Ps 82:8; 2 Bar 13:8; *Jub.* 39:6; *1 Enoch* 9:3; 10:1; 97:2; 100:4; 1QapGen 20:12–13, 16; *TMos* 10:7; *SibOr* 1:179; 3:519, 718.

43 Gen 14:19-20; Dan 3:26, 32(4:2); 4:14(17), 21(24), 22(25), 29(32), 31(34); 5:18, 21; 2 Bar 80:3; 4Q242 1–3 3, 5, 6; Philo, *Leg. Gai.* 157, 317; 1 Esd 2:2(3); 6:30(31); 8:19, 21; *SibOr* 3:519, 574, 580, 719; *SibOr* 1:179, 200; Ezekiel Tragedian 239; 3 Macc 7:9; 2 Macc 3:31; Josephus, *Ant.* 16:163; *Ps-Aeschylus*. Acts 16:17 is a New Testament instance of this usage.

44 Gen 14:22; Dan 4:14(17), 21(24), 22(25), 29(32); 5:18, 21; 4Q550c 3:1; Philo, *Flacc.* 46; *Leg. Gai.* 278; *SibOr* 3:519, 574, 580, 719; *SibOr* 1:179, 200; Wis 5:15; 6:3; *Ps-Aeschylus*. The Sibylline Oracles are ascribed to the pagan prophetess, the Sybil, and addressed (ostensibly at least) to Gentiles. Wisdom is ostensibly addressed by Solomon to Gentile rulers.

45 Note also that the emperor Julian gave the Jews permission to rebuild the temple of the Most High God (τοῦ ὑψίστου θεοῦ): Stephen Mitchell, "The Cult of Theos Hypsistos between Pagans, Jews and Christians," in Athanassiadi and Frede, *Pagan Monotheism*, 81–148; here 111 n. 82.

46 Hebrew Bible: "God of heaven" used by Gentiles: 2 Chron 26; 23; Ezra 1:2; 6:9, 10; 7:12, 21, 23; (Rev 11:13; 16:11 also conform to this usage); used by Jews addressing Gentiles: Ezra 5:11, 12; Neh 2:20; Dan 2:44; Jon 1:9; also used in Neh 1:4, 5; 2:4; Ps 136:26; Dan 2:18, 19. Postbiblical Jewish literature: Tob 7:12; 8:15; Jdt 11:17 (Jew addressing Gentile); 3 Macc 6:28 (Gentile speaking); *Jub.* 12:4 (Abraham to his pagan father); 20:7; 22:19 (in parallel with "God Most High"); cf. also "Lord of heaven" in Tob 6:18; 7:11, 16; 10:13; 1QapGen 12:17; Cairo Geniza *TLevi* (Bodleian b 6); *1 Enoch* 106:11; "Lord God of heaven" in Jdt 6:19.

47 5:41, 56; 6:38, 55, 57; 8:20, 24, 36, 63; 9:29; 14:2. This presumably represents אדני (not as substitute for YHWH). Ezra also uses it in addressing the angel.

48 3:4; 5:23, 38; 6:11; 7:17, 45, 58; 12:7; 13:51. Perhaps this represents יהוה אדני in the original Hebrew.

49 The fifth instance is 9:45. On this title in *4 Ezra*, see Michael E. Stone, *4 Ezra* (Hermeneia; Minneapolis: Fortress, 199), 175. The original Hebrew may have been גבור (as in 1Q19 2:5) or אדיר (as in 1QM 19:1).

50 Cf. Stone, *4 Ezra*, 57; Jacob M. Myers, *I and II Esdras* (AB 42; New York: Doubleday, 1974), 121 ("No particular significance can be attached to these terms").

51 This title is also common in the *Apocalypse of Abraham*, along with "the Eternal One." Probably in this work these two titles represent אל and יהוה, respectively (cf. the combined name Yahoel in 17:13).

52 6:8; 7:1; 13:2, 4. It is used by Gentiles in 7:1. The Oxyrhynchus frag-
    ment preserves the Greek in 13:2 (ἰσχυροῦ θεοῦ).

53 For the possibility that at Qumran אל was sometimes a substitute for
    יהוה, see Sean M. McDonough, *YHWH at Patmos: Rev. 1:4 in Its
    Hellenistic and Early Jewish Setting* (WUNT 2/107; Tübingen: Mohr
    Siebeck, 1999), 69–70. According to Arthur Marmorstein, *The Old
    Rabbinic Doctrine of God* (Oxford: Oxford University Press, 1927; 2nd
    ed.; Farnborough: Gregg, 1969), 67–68, early rabbinic literature avoids
    both אל and אלוהים.

54 This is the only instance of בני עליון in the Hebrew Bible. For postbib-
    lical Jewish literature, see Sir 4:10; 4Q246 2:1.

55 That Psalm 47 calls on the gods to worship their ruler, the Most High
    (Tryggve N. D. Mettinger, *In Search of God: The Meaning and Message of
    the Divine Names* [trans. Frederick H. Cryer; Philadelphia: Fortress,
    1988], 122), is not at all apparent in the text of the psalm itself.

56 W. Randall Garr, *In His Own Image and Likeness: Humanity, Divinity,
    and Monotheism* (Culture and History of the Ancient Near East 15;
    Leiden: Brill, 2003), 211 n. 49.

57 See Bauckham, "Biblical Theology," 206–17.

58 Bauckham, "The Throne," 52–53.

59 Isa 6:1; *1 Enoch* 14:18; *2 Enoch* 20:3J; Ps-Philo, *Bib. Ant.* 12:8.

60 *ApAbr* 19:4; *2 Enoch* 20–22; *QuEzra* A21.

61 Ps 8:1; 57:5, 11; 108:5; 113:4; cf. Isa 66:1; *1 Enoch* 84:2; Ps-Orpheus B
    33–34.

62 God as sole Ruler of all things: e.g., Dan 4:34–35; Bel 5; Add Est
    13:9–11, 16:18, 21; 3 Macc 2:2-3; 6:2; Wis 12:13; Sir 18:1–3; *SibOr*
    3:10; 19; *SibOr* fragm. 1:7, 15, 17, 35; *1 Enoch* 9:5; 84:3; *2 Bar* 54:13;
    2 Enoch 33:7; 1QH 18:8–10; Josephus, *Ant.* 1.155–56.

63 Bauckham, *God Crucified*, 9–13.

64 It is worth noting that Celsus, the pagan critic of Christianity, seems to
    know of the use of ὕψιστος by Jews (apud Origen, *C. Cels.* 1.24; 2.74).
    Since he also knows of the Jews' use of Adonai and Sabaoth (1.24), there
    may be some value in his evidence.

65 Gen 14:22-23: Philo, *Ebr.* 105; *Leg. All.* 3:24, 82; Num 24:16: Philo,
    Mut. 202; Deut 32:8-9: Philo, *Post.* 89; *Plant.* 59; *Congr.* 58.

66 We have no evidence that עליון or an Aramaic equivalent was used in
    non-Jewish cults in the Near East at this time. Philo of Byblos (64–141
    C.E.) writes (ap. Eusebius, *Praep. Evang.* 1.10.14–15) that he found in the
    Phoenician historian Sanchunyaton (c. 1300 B.C.E.) the divine name
    "Elioun," which he translates as ὕψιστος. This is not evidence for the use
    of the name in the late Second Temple period. The Zeus Olympios to
    whom worship in the Jerusalem Temple was dedicated (2 Macc 6:2) by
    the Hellenizing faction at the beginning of the crisis under Antiochus
    Epiphanes seems to have been identified with the Semitic "Lord of

heaven" (*Ba'al Shamem*), but there is no evidence that he was called "the Most High" (עליון). It would seem unlikely that the book of Daniel would have adopted the latter title so prominently if he had been. Hengel, *Judaism*, 297–99, associates too much evidence too indiscriminately.

67   C. H. Dodd, *The Bible and the Greeks* (London: Hodder & Stoughton, 1935), 12.

68   Dodd, *The Bible*, 12.

69   Deut 4:35, 39; 32:39; 1 Sam 2:2; 2 Sam 7:22; 1 Kgs 8:60; 1 Chron 17:20; Isa 44:6; 45:5, 6, 14 (*bis*), 18, 21 (*bis*), 22; 46:9; Joel 2:27; cf. 2 Sam 22:32 = Ps 18:32; Isa 64:4; Wis 12:13; Jdt 8:20; 9:14; Bel 41; Sir 18:2; 24:24; 36:5; 1QH 15:32; 18:9; 20:11, 31; 1Q35 1:6; 4Q377 frag. 1r 2:8; 4Q504 [4QDibHama] frag. 1–2 5:9; *2 Enoch* 33:8; 36:1; 47:3; *SibOr* 3:629, 760; 8:377; *ApAbr* 19:3–4; *Ps-Orpheus* 16; Philo, *Opif.* 23, 46; *Leg. All.* 3.4.

70   Mitchell, "The Cult"; Paul R. Trebilco, *Jewish Communities in Asia Minor* (SNTSMS 69; Cambridge: Cambridge University Press, 1991), 128–40; Irina Levinskaya, *The Book of Acts in Its Diaspora Setting*, vol. 5 of *The Book of Acts in Its First Century Setting* (Grand Rapids: Eerdmans/Carlisle: Paternoster, 1996), chs. 5–6; W. Horbury and D. Noy, *Jewish Inscriptions of Graeco-Roman Egypt* (Cambridge: Cambridge University Press, 1992), 200–201.

71   James R. Davila, *The Provenance of the Pseudepigrapha: Jewish, Christian, Other?* (JSJSup 105; Leiden: Brill, 2005), makes an important case for greater methodological rigor and caution in judging works in the category of "Old Testament Pseudepigrapha" to be (non-Christian) Jewish works. In particular, he shows that this cannot be assumed just because a work lacks obvious Christian features. I share his doubts about *Joseph and Asenath* (190–95) and the *Testament of Abraham* (199–207), but I remain convinced that *Sibylline Oracles* book 3 (181–86) and the Wisdom of Solomon (219–25) are so probably non-Christian Jewish that scholars are justified in citing them as such. On the other hand, Davila is right to reject the case recently made by Rivka Nir, *The Destruction of Jerusalem and the Idea of Redemption in the Syriac Apocalypse of Baruch* (SBLEJL 20; Atlanta: SBL, 2003) for considering *2 Baruch* a Christian work. On *Joseph and Asenath*, see also Ross Shephard Kraemer, *When Asenath Met Joseph* (New York: Oxford University Press, 1998), and my review in *JTS* 51 (2000): 226–28. Dale C. Allison in his excellent work, *Testament of Abraham* (CEJL; Berlin: de Gruyer, 2003), is clear that the texts of both recensions of this work as we have them have many Christian elements, but still thinks a non-Christian Jewish Ur-text underlying both "overwhelmingly probable" (28–29). Even this judgment, however, makes the work unusable for our purposes, since there is no way of knowing whether the occurrences of "Most High" belong to the Ur-text. David Satran, *Biblical Prophets in Byzantine*

Palestine: Reassessing "The Lives of the Prophets" (SVTP 11; Leiden: Brill, 1995) shows that in its present form *The Lives of the Prophets* dates from the early Byzantine period. It undoubtedly contains early Jewish material but cannot provide reliable evidence for our present purposes. *The Testaments of the Twelve Patriarchs*, as Marinus de Jonge has long and extensively argued (most recently in *Pseudepigrapha of the Old Testament as Part of Christian Literature: The Case of the Testaments of the Twelve Patriarchs and the Greek Life of Adam and Eve* [SVTP 18; Leiden: Brill, 2003]), is similarly a Christian composition with Jewish sources that cannot be confidently delimited. (The strongest case for a substantial Jewish source is in the case of the *Testament of Levi*, owing to the existence of related Levi material in the Dead Sea Scrolls and Geniza fragments and some of the occurrences of "the Most High" plausibly belong to it, but the point cannot be pressed here.) The Prayer of Manasseh may well be Jewish, but a strong case has yet to be made. On the other hand, even though the Ladder of Jacob is one of the least studied of the Old Testament *Pseudepigrapha* included in recent collections, I think the case for regarding chapters 1–6 as Jewish is strong (see James Kugel, "The Ladder of Jacob," *HTR* 88 [1995]: 209–27), especially now that a Hebrew version of the prayer in chapter 2 has been identified (Reimund Leicht, "Qedushah and Prayer to Helios: A New Hebrew Version of an Apocryphal Prayer of Jacob," *JSQ* 6 [1999]: 140–76).

72 In all cases "the Most High" (*altissimus*). In the following notes, no attention is drawn to Hebrew texts that have only the simple עליון or Greek texts that have only the simple ὕψιστος, but for other texts, variations (such as "the Most High God") are noted, as are the terms used in Aramaic texts.

73 Forty-seven is the number of occurrences in the Greek text (though in four of these cases there are variant readings without ὕψιστος). The title occurs twenty times in the (incomplete) Geniza and Masada Hebrew texts, not always corresponding to the usage in the Greek. Alexander A. Di Lella, in Patrick W. Skehan and Alexander A. Di Lella, *The Wisdom of Ben Sira* (AB 39; New York: Doubleday, 1987), 182, speaks of "the fluidity of the divine names in the book and its translations."

74 "The Lord Most High": *2 Bar* 6:6; "the Most High": *2 Bar* 13:8; 17:1; 24:2; 25:1; 54:17; 56:1; 64:8; 67:3, 7; 69:2; 70:7; 71:2; 76:1; 77:4, 21; 80:1, 3; 81:4; 82:2, 6; 83:1; 85:8, 12.

75 "The Most High": *Jub.* 16:18; "the Most High God": *Jub.* 12:19; 20:9; 22:13, 23; 25:3, 11; 32:1; "God Most High": 13:16, 29; 16:27; 21:22, 23. 25; 22:6, 19, 27; 25:21; 27:15; "the Lord Most High": *Jub.* 22:11; 36:16; 39:6; "the Lord God Most High": *Jub.* 21:20.

76 *1 Enoch* 9:3; 10:1; 46:7; 60:1, 22; 62:7; 77:1; 94:8; 97:2; 98:7, 11; 99:3, 10; 100:4; 101:1, 6, 9 (all "the Most High").

77   "The Most High" (עליא): Dan 4:14(17), 21(24), 22(25), 29(32), 31(34); 7:25; "God Most High" (אלהא עליא): Dan 3:26, 32 (4:2); 5:18, 21; "the Most High" (עליונין): Dan 7:18, 22, 25, 27. For the plural form עליונין as referring to God, against other suggestions, see John J. Collins, *Daniel* (Hermeneia; Minneapolis: Fortress, 1993), 312.

78   "The Most High" (עליא): 1QapGen 2:4; 10:18; "God Most High" (אל עליון): 1QapGen 12:17; 20:12, 16; 21:2, 20; 22:15, 16, 21.

79   "God Most High" (אלהא עליא): 4Q242 1–3 2, 3, 5, 6.

80   11Q14 1 2 4, 7 (= 4Q285 1 3); 4Q491 15 7; 4Q492 1 13.

81   Tob 1:4 (AB), 13 (AB, S); 4:11 (AB). These verses are not extant in the Qumran fragments of Tobit.

82   "The Most High" (עליון): 26:1, 3; "God Most High" (אלהים עליון): 26:4.

83   Both "the Most High God" (*summus Deus*).

84   Both "God Most High" (אל עליון).

85   The occurrence at 7:1 belongs to the later Christian addition to the book.

86   "The Most High" (העליון).

87   "The Most High" (עליון).

88   Aramaic עליא.

89   "God Most High" (אל עליון).

90   It is a question whether עליונין should be read as a true plural ("highest ones") or as referring to God, as in Dan 7:18, 22, 25, 27.

91   Apud Eusebius, *Praep. Evang.* 9.17.5. Pseudo-Eupolemus is widely thought to have been a Samaritan author.

92   "The Most High" (ὁ ὕψιστος: Philo, *Post.* 89; *Plant.* 59; *Congr.* 58; *Mut. Nom.* 202; "the Most High God" (ὁ ὕψιστος θεός): Philo, *Leg. all.* 3.24, 82 [*tris*]; *Ebr.* 105; *Flacc.* 46; *Leg. Gai.* 157, 278, 317.

93   "The Lord Most High" (κύριος ὁ ὕψιστος): 1 Esd 2:2(3); "the Most High God" (ὁ θεός ὁ ὕψιστος): 1 Esd 6:30(31); 8:19, 21; "the Lord God Most High" (ὁ κύριος θεός ὕψιστος): 1 Esd 9:46. It is possible that the Greek 1 Esdras originated in Palestine (see Martin Hengel, *The "Hellenization" of Judaea in the First Century after Christ* [trans. John Bowden; London: SCM Press/Philadelphia: Trinity Press International, 1989], 25), but most scholars see it as a product of the Diaspora.

94   "The Most High" (ὕψιστος): SibOr 3:519, 574, 580; "God Most High" (ὕψιστος θεός): SibOr 3:719.

95   "The Most High God" (ὕψιστος θεός): SibOr 1:179; "The Most High" (ὕψιστος): SibOr 1:200.

96   "The Most High" (ὕψιστος): 3 Macc 6:2; "God Most High" (θεός ὕψιστος): 3 Macc 7:9.

97   2 Maccabees is an epitome of a much longer work by Jason of Cyrene, who, though from the Diaspora, lived in Palestine, but 2 Maccabees

probably reached its present form, with the two epistles prefaced in chapter 1, in Egypt.

98 Apud Eusebius, *Praep. Evang.* 9.24.1. On this passage, see Carl R. Holladay, *Fragments from Hellenistic Jewish Authors*, vol. 2: *Poets* (Atlanta: Scholars Press, 1989), 267–68, arguing correctly that the reference is to God.

99 "The Most High God" (ὕψιστος θεός).

100 Apud Clement of Alexandria, *Strom.* 5.14.131.3.

101 "The Most High": *JosAsen* 8:9; 11:7, 9, 17; 14:8; 15:7 (*bis*), 8, 12 (4 times); 16:14 (*bis*), 16; 18:9; 21:4, 21; 22:13; 25:6; "God the Most High": *JosAsen* 8:2; 9:1; 15:7 (*tris*); 18:9; 19:5, 8; 21:15; 22:8,13; 23:10; "the Lord God Most High": *JosAsen* 15:7; 17:6; 21:6.

102 "The Most High": *TAbr* A9:1, 2, 3, 8; 15:13; 16:1, 6; "God the Most High": *TAbr* A14:9; 15:11; 16:9 (also B13:6; 14:7).

103 This apocalypse, of which we know just one fragment, quoted by Clement of Alexandria, *Strom.* 5.11.77, is probably not the same work as the Apocalypse of Zephaniah extant in Coptic. The fragment is too short to allow any confidence as to its Jewish or Christian provenance, though its resemblance to Merkavah literature suggests the former is more likely.

104 *TSim* 2:5; 6:7; *TLevi* 3:10; 4:1, 2; 5:1; 16:3; 18:7; *TGad* 3:1; 5:4; *TAsh* 2:6; 5:4; *TJos* 1:4, 6; 9:3; *TBenj* 4:5; 9:2.

105 These passages have no parallels in the other versions of the *Life of Adam and Eve* (Greek, Armenian, Georgian, Slavonic): see Gary A. Anderson and Michael E. Stone, eds. *A Synopsis of the Books of Adam and Eve* (SBLEJL 05; Atlanta: Scholars Press, 1994).

Chapter 4

It is a pleasure to offer this study to my friends and colleagues, Alan Segal and Larry Hurtado. I have learned much from each of them. I first met Alan Segal at a conference at Brown University in 1984, and I am grateful to Larry Hurtado for his hospitality when I visited Edinburgh in 1998 and 2007. This essay more directly addresses Hurtado's work. His two scholarly books, *One God, One Lord*, and *Lord Jesus Christ*, and his more popular *How on Earth* have stimulated much thought, conversation, and publication on the part of biblical scholars. His articulation of bold hypotheses and his energetic elaboration and defense of them have contributed much to the field by evoking responses and further work, both from scholars who agree and from those who disagree with him. In this essay, I would like to clarify some points, raise some questions, and make some suggestions as a way of furthering the discussion.

1 Bousset, *Kyrios Christos*; ET *Kyrios Christos: A History of the Belief in Christ from the Beginnings of Christianity to Irenaeus* (trans. John E. Steely; Nashville: Abingdon, 1970). The ET is cited here.

2   Hurtado, *How on Earth*, 25–55.

3   Hurtado *How on Earth*, 25. Hurtado does not object to such an approach on theoretical grounds, but attempts to refute it on historical grounds, i.e., if the worship of Jesus originated early, there is no need to posit an evolutionary development culminating in such worship.

4   On the significant degree of Hellenization and Romanization of Jerusalem in the first century CE, see Mark A. Chancey, *Greco-Roman Culture and the Galilee of Jesus* (SNTSMS 134; Cambridge, UK: Cambridge University Press, 2005), 78–79, 96–98, 129–30, 148, n. 140, 182–83. On "religious pluralism" in Colossae, see Clinton E. Arnold, *The Colossian Syncretism: The Interface between Christianity and Folk Belief at Colossae* (WUNT 2.77; Tübingen: Mohr Siebeck, 1995), 380.

5   See, e.g., Hengel with Markschies, *The "Hellenization" of Judaea*.

6   According to Ralph Marcus, "some measure of assimilation" was unavoidable on the part of "the Jews in the Diaspora"; "Divine Names and Attributes in Hellenistic Jewish Literature," *Proceedings of the American Academy for Jewish Research* (1931–1932): 43–120; quotation from 44.

7   See the criticism by Todd E. Klutz of the social and cultural theories of Ruth Benedikt and A. R. Radcliffe-Brown in Klutz, "Re-Reading 1 Corinthians after 'Rethinking Gnosticism,'" *JSNT* 26.2 (2003): 193–216, esp. 205–6.

8   William Horbury, *Jewish Messianism and the Cult of Christ* (London: SCM Press, 1998), 68–77.

9   Horbury, *Jewish Messianism*, 68.

10   Horbury, *Jewish Messianism*, 69.

11   Horbury, *Jewish Messianism*, 77.

12   1 Cor 1:2; Acts 9:14, 21; Bousset, *Kyrios Christos*, 130; Hurtado, *How on Earth*, 25, 28, 173.

13   Hans Conzelmann, *1 Corinthians* (Hermeneia; Philadelphia: Fortress, 1975), 23.

14   Hans Conzelmann, *1 Corinthians*, 23 and n. 38.

15   Bousset, *Kyrios Christos*, 131.

16   On this distinction, see the next section below.

17   Horbury, *Jewish Messianism*, 70.

18   Mark 9:38; Matt 7:22; Bousset, *Kyrios Christos,* 131, 134.

19   Acts 2:38; 3:6; 16:18; Hurtado, *How on Earth*, 135, 157. Lars Hartman speaks of "heavenly power" as well as of "divine power"; "*Into the Name of the Lord Jesus": Baptism in the Early Church,* (Studies of the New Testament and Its World; Edinburgh: T&T Clark, 1997), 47–48.

20   Consider, for example, the contexts of the baptisms of John the Baptist, those attributed to Peter in Acts 2:37-42 and those to which Paul refers

in 1 Cor 1:14-15. Consider also the contexts of the healings and exorcisms carried out by the followers of Jesus as they are described in Acts.

21   Richard Bauckham rejects the distinction between "'functional' Christology" and "'ontic' (or ontological) Christology" because it is based on the premise that "first-century Jewish monotheists could attribute divine 'functions' to Jesus without difficulty," but not "divine 'nature'" (*God Crucified,* 41–42). He constructs a concept of the unique identity of the God of Israel by way of analogy with human personal identity (7–8). He then tries to show that the "exalted Jesus participates in God's unique sovereignty over all things" (28–29) and that the "pre-existent Christ participates in God's unique activity of creation" (35–40). Like Hurtado's "binitarianism," Bauckham's argument that Jesus Christ participates in God's unique identity seems to impose later, creedal concerns on texts of the New Testament. See the discussion in the section "Jesus as Son of God in the Gospel According to John" below, especially the paragraph related to n. 89.

22   This interpretation is based on my judgment that οὐχ ἁρπαγμὸν ἡγήσατο τὸ εἶναι ἴσα θεῷ in Phil 2:6 should be translated "did not consider equality with God something to be seized." Hurtado argues that the passage should be translated "did not consider equality with God something to be exploited." He thus concludes that the passage implies that Christ, before becoming human, was already equal to God (*How on Earth,* 97–100). On these and other issues related to the interpretation of Phil 2:6-11, see Adela Yarbro Collins, "Psalms, Phil. 2:6-11, and the Origins of Christology," *Biblical Interpretation* 11 (2003): 361–72. Even if Roy Hoover is right that "τὸ εἶναι ἴσα θεῷ represents a status that belonged to the preexistent Christ, it can be argued that this Greek phrase does not mean equal in a binitarian sense (see the discussion below in the section "Equality with God"); Hoover, "The Harpagmos Enigma: A Philological Solution," *HTR* 64 (1971): 95–119; quotation from 118.

23   Hurtado, *How on Earth,* 157.

24   Hurtado, *How on Earth,* 93.

25   Erhard S. Gerstenberger, *Psalms,* part 2 and *Lamentations* (FOTL 15; Grand Rapids: Eerdmans, 2001), 194; Hans-Joachim Kraus, *Psalms 60–150: A Commentary* (Minneapolis: Augsburg Fortress, 1989; trans. from 5th German ed., 1978), 257; Frank-Lothar Hossfeld and Erich Zenger, *Psalms 2: A Commentary on Psalms 51–100* (Hermeneia; Minneapolis: Fortress, 2005), 469.

26   A comment of Philo is interesting in this regard: "Now the name denoting the kind and gracious power is 'God,' and that denoting the kingly ruling power is 'Lord'"(χαριστικῆς μὲν οὖν δυνάμεως θεός, βασιλικῆς δὲ κύριος ὄνομα); *Somn.* 1.163; text and trans. from LCL.

27   Hurtado, *How on Earth,* 111.

28 The lack of attention to the category "Messiah" in *One God, One Lord* is somewhat rectified in *Lord Jesus Christ*, 98–101, 289–90, 358–62. In *How on Earth*, however, the role of Messiah is consistently subordinated to Jesus' divine sonship and other categories.

29 Gal 1:15–16; cf. 1:23.

30 Hurtado, *How on Earth*, 170.

31 Hurtado, *How on Earth*, 170.

32 Hurtado, *How on Earth*, 169. Cf. the discussion of Torrey Seland's work.

33 Hurtado, *How on Earth*, 175.

34 See Adela Yarbro Collins, "The Charge of Blasphemy in Mark 14.64," *JSNT* 26 (2004): 379–401.

35 Hurtado discusses 1 Cor 12:3 at *How on Earth*, 175, and Gal 3:13 at 176.

36 Hurtado, *How on Earth*, 176. Note that in both the Hebrew and the Greek of these passages, it is a false prophet that is spoken of, not a false teacher.

37 Hurtado, *How on Earth*, 177.

38 Hurtado, *How on Earth*, 177–78.

39 Cf. John 11:45-53.

40 Cf. Paula Fredriksen, "Judaism, the Circumcision of Gentiles, and Apocalyptic Hope: Another Look at Galatians 1 and 2," *JTS* NS 42 (1991): 532–64, esp. 556.

41 Pss 2:7; 89:26–27; 2 Sam 7:14. See also Ps 109:3c Septuagint and 4QFlorilegium (4Q174) col. 1, lines 10–12, where 2 Sam 7:14 is interpreted as a reference to the "branch of David," i.e., to the Messiah of Israel.

42 John J. Collins, "The King as Son of God," in John J. Collins and Adela Yarbro Collins, *Messiah and Son of God: Early Christologies in Light of Biblical and Jewish Traditions* (Grand Rapids: Eerdmans, forthcoming).

43 See especially Ps 109:3 LXX.

44 4Q246 2:1. The referent of the phrase "son of God" here is disputed. See John J. Collins, *The Scepter and the Star: The Messiahs of the Dead Sea Scrolls and Other Ancient Literature* (ABRL; New York: Doubleday, 1995), 154–64; see also Adela Yarbro Collins, "Mark and His Readers: The Son of God among Jews," *HTR* 92 (1999): 393–408.

45 1QSa (1Q28a) 2:11–12.

46 Cf. the expression "the sons of God" in Gen 6:2, 4.

47 Collins, *The Scepter and the Star*, 165.

48 Origen, *Cels.* 8.14; translation from ANF, 4. 644. Cf. the translation in Horbury, *Jewish Messianism*, 110. Horbury interprets this comment by Celsus as mocking the usage as inflatory (114).

49 Plutarch, *De laude* 12 (543 D-E); Greek phrase and translation from LCL. According to Horbury, Scott inferred that Plutarch's remark was critical of the contemporary imperial cult (*Jewish Messianism and the Cult of Christ*, 184, n. 39).

50   Gal 3:25-26.

51   Rom 8:14-17.

52   Rom 8:23.

53   1 Thess 4:15-17; 1 Cor 15:20-23, 50-57.

54   Although the Greek term used here is εἰκών, translated "image" in Gen
     1:26–27 LXX and 2 Cor 4:4, its usage and sense here are different; see
     BDAG, s.v. 3.

55   Rom 8:29.

56   This translation takes the preposition ἐκ here as expressing the effective
     cause; see BDAG, s.v. 3.d.

57   Text from Rahlfs; translation by author.

58   *1 Enoch* 62:7; cf. 48:2-3; translation (slightly modified) from George W.
     E. Nickelsburg and James C. VanderKam, *1 Enoch: A New Translation*
     (Minneapolis: Fortress, 2004), 80. The "Son of Man" is called the
     "Messiah" or "Anointed" in 48:10 and 52:4. He is also called the
     "Chosen One" (e.g., 39:6) and the "Righteous One" (38:2).

59   1 Cor 8:5-6; 2 Cor 4:3-4. For discussion see Adela Yarbro Collins, "Jesus
     as Messiah and Son of God in the Letters of Paul," in Collins and
     Collins, *Messiah and Son of God*.

60   Hurtado, *Lord Jesus Christ*, 119–22.

61   Horbury, *Jewish Messianism and the Cult of Christ*, 113. See also the dis-
     cussion of the views of Fossum and Rowland in Hurtado, *One God, One
     Lord*, 85–90.

62   Acts 2:29-36. The terms "Leader and Savior" (ἀρχηγός καὶ σωτήρ),
     associated with the exaltation of Christ in Acts 5:31, are synonymous
     with "Messiah (of Israel)."

63   Hurtado, *How on Earth*, 95.

64   Bousset, *Kyrios Christos*, 138–43; cf. Horbury, *Jewish Messianism*, 114,
     195, n. 16.

65   Joseph A. Fitzmyer, "The Semitic Background of the New Testament
     Kyrios-Title," in *A Wandering Aramean: Collected Aramaic Essays* (SBL
     Monograph Series 25; Missoula, Mont.: Scholars Press, 1979); reprinted
     with same pagination in Fitzmyer, *The Semitic Background of the New
     Testament* (Biblical Resource Series; Grand Rapids: Eerdmans/ Livonia,
     Mich.: Dove Booksellers, 1997), 117 and n. 26. Fitzmyer notes that "the
     kyrios-title has regal connotations" in Mark 12:36 and parallels; he also
     points out that "the entire tradition of the royal character of Yahweh in
     the OT would seem to be associated with the kyrios-title" (Fitzmyer, *The
     Semitic Background*, 131–32).

66   *1 Enoch* 48:2-3, 6; translation (slightly modified) from Nickelsburg and
     VanderKam, *1 Enoch*, 62.

67   Hurtado, *How on Earth*, 26, 50, 91–92.

68   Hurtado, *How on Earth*, 50.

69 See the discussion above in the opening paragraphs of this chapter. Note also that Isaiah 45 begins with a presentation of Cyrus as messiah (the Lord's anointed).

70 See n. 22 above.

71 Cassius Dio 51.20.1; text and translation from Horbury, *Jewish Messianism*, 114. See also the LCL translation: "that his name should be included in their hymns equally with those of the gods."

72 E. Badian, "Alexander the Great between Two Thrones and Heaven: Variations on an Old Theme," in *Subject and Ruler: The Cult of the Ruling Power in Classical Antiquity* (Journal of Roman Archaeology Supplementary Series 17, ed. Alastair Small; Ann Arbor: Journal of Roman Archaeology, 1996), 11–26; cited by Horbury, *Jewish Messianism*, 183, n. 29. Badian states that, for the Greeks, "the king was ἰσόθεος, which was far from divine" ("Alexander the Great," 22).

73 Hurtado, *How on Earth*, 18.

74 Hurtado, *How on Earth*, 19.

75 On the decisive influence of the speeches of divine Wisdom on the discourses of Jesus in John, see Raymond E. Brown, *The Gospel According to John* (2 vols.; AB 29; Garden City, N.Y.: Doubleday, 1966–1970), 1:lxi.

76 On the "naive docetism" of John, see Ernst Käsemann, *Jesu letzter Wille nach Johannes 17* (Tübingen: Mohr Siebeck, 1966); ET *Testament of Jesus: A Study of the Gospel of John in the Light of Chapter 17* (trans. Gerhard Krodel; Philadelphia: Fortress, 1968).

77 See the discussion above in section "Equality with God." For a binitarian interpretation, see Hurtado, *How on Earth*, 52.

78 See the discussion of Celsus and especially Plutarch above in the section "Was the Messiah Believed to Be Divine?" The same issues arise in the interpretation of John 10:31-33; cf. Hurtado, *How on Earth*, 52.

79 John 8:57-59.

80 Ernst Haenchen, *John 2: A Commentary on the Gospel of John Chapters 7–21* (Hermeneia; Philadelphia: Fortress, 1984; German ed. 1980), 30.

81 See the discussion in Brown, *John,* app. 4 (1:533–38).

82 Brown, *John*, 1:535.

83 Six times in Deutero-Isaiah; Hos 13:4; Joel 2:27; see Brown, *John,* 1:536.

84 Brown, *John*, 1:536–37.

85 Brown, *John*, 1:367.

86 Hurtado, *Lord Jesus Christ*, 372; emphasis original.

87 Hurtado, *Lord Jesus Christ*, 385.

88 See, e.g., Hurtado, *How on Earth*, 1–2.

89 John 1:41; 4:25-26; 11:27; 20:31.

90 John 1:14; cf. 1:18; 3:16, 18.

91 John 5:19, 26-27, 30; 8:28b, 29b; 17:2a.

92 See especially Hurtado, *One God, One Lord*, chs.1–4.

93 See the discussion above in the section "The Preexistence of the Messiah."

94 For an analogous critique of the use of the term "binitarian" in relation to New Testament texts, see Paul A. Rainbow, "Jewish Monotheism as the Matrix for New Testament Christology: A Review Article," *NovT* 33 (1991): 78–91, esp. 90–91.

95 On the Monarchian controversy, see Henry Chadwick, *The Early Church* (Harmondsworth/Baltimore, Md.: Penguin Books, 1967), 85–90. On the Arian controversy, see Chadwick, 133–51.

Chapter 5

1   Segal, *Life after Death.*

2   Hurtado, *Lord Jesus Christ.*

3   Although he does not press precisely this point, Joseph Fitzmyer's analysis of the pre-Pauline formula in Rom 1:3-4 emphasizes the fact that "Son" governs both the affirmation about Jesus as "Son of David" in the human sphere and "Son of God" in the power of the resurrection. Therefore, an inchoate form of preexistence finds expression at an early stage.   See Joseph A. Fitzmyer, *Romans: A New Translation with Introduction and Commentary* (AB 33; New York: Doubleday, 1993), 233.

4   Dunn, *Christology in the Making,* 35.

5   Fitzmyer, *Romans,* 236.

6   Fitzmyer, *Romans,* 235–36.

7   Fitzmyer, *Romans,* 235.

8   Friedrich Schliermacher, *The Christian Faith* (eds. H. R. MacKintosh and J. S. Stewart; Edinburgh: T&T Clark, n.d.; 2nd German edition 1830), 422.

9   Schliermacher, *Christian Faith,* 418.

10 See Kenan B. Osborne, *The Resurrection of Jesus. New Considerations for Its Theological Interpretation* (Mahwah, N.J.: Paulist Press, 1997), 13, 116–29. Osborne points out that subsequent church statements about resurrection have been quite modest, often repeating biblical phrases or asserting that Jesus' risen body is the same as that he had in life (23).

11 Hurtado insists upon religious experiences that early Christians credited as revelation as the key element in the reconfiguration of monotheistic faith that underlies early high Christology (*Lord Jesus Christ,* 64–65). That suggests a more limited set of experiences than the broad range of ecstatic or Spirit-infused experience characteristic of early Christianity.

12 Larry W. Hurtado, "Pre-70 CE Jewish Opposition to Christ-Devotion," *JTS* NS 50 (1999): 35–58.

13 Hurtado, "Jewish Opposition," 51.

14 William Horbury, "Larry Hurtado, *Lord Jesus Christ: Devotion to Jesus in Earliest Christianity*," *JTS* NS 56 (2005): 531–39.

15 Such associations might be said to venerate a deified founder as Horbury intimates in suggesting that Hurtado has not dealt adequately with Bousset on Christ cult and piety ("Hurtado," 539). However Hurtado's insistence on the origins of Christology as constrained within the parameters of Jewish monotheism rules out that interpretation (Hurtado, *Lord Jesus Christ*, 3, 35). Along with other scholars like Fitzmyer (*Romans*, 112–13), the first-century evidence that "Lord" was used of God in Jewish Aramaic sufficiently counters Bousset's view that Greco-Roman influences are responsible for that designation (Hurtado, *Lord Jesus Christ*, 20–21).

16 Hurtado, *Lord Jesus Christ*, 29, 35, 50.

17 Horbury, "Hurtado," 535–37.

18 Hurtado does not sever the link between Jesus as Messiah and devotion to Jesus as Lord. He agrees with the consensus view that Jesus was crucified as a messianic pretender, a claimant to the royal line of David (*Lord Jesus Christ*, 54–57). But Hurtado introduces a methodological caveat against presuming that Jesus' own aims or the context of his message exhausts the effects of his life (55).

19 Horbury, "Hurtado," 538.

20 Segal, *Life after Death*, 404.

21 Not surprisingly, Dunn chides Hurtado for inadequate use of Segal's work on Paul. See James D. G. Dunn, "When Was Jesus First Worshipped? In Dialogue with Larry Hurtado's *Lord, Jesus Christ: Devotion to Jesus in Earliest Christianity*," *Exp. Tim.* 116 (2005): 194.

22 Fitzmyer, *Romans*, 111–16.

23 Fitzmyer, *Romans*, 111–12. Fitzmyer considers Christology subordinate to Paul's main emphasis on soteriology. He describes Paul's theology in Romans as articulating a "christological soteriology" (111).

24 N. T. Wright, *The Resurrection of the Son of God* (Grand Rapids: Eerdmans, 2003), 24–27. Also note Hurtado's insistence that there is no precedent for the idea of the Messiah being appointed through resurrection after a shameful death (*Lord Jesus Christ*, 105).

25 Hurtado, *Lord Jesus Christ*, 73.

26 Hurtado, *Lord Jesus Christ*, 72.

27 See Wright's presentation of the Jewish view of resurrection as an event that only ensues after an intermediate period during which those raised are among the dead. It is not equivalent to "life after death" or separation of an immortal soul (*Resurrection*, 31, 203). Thus, he insists that resurrection is not a transition to being "in heaven" (204)—contrary to the view of most twentieth-century Christians.

28 Hurtado, *Lord Jesus Christ*, 100.

29 Wright, *Resurrection*, 320.

30 For detailed analyses of 1 Cor 15, see Wright, *Resurrection*, 277–395; M. C. de Boer, *The Defeat of Death: Apocalyptic Eschatology in 1 Corinthians 15 and Romans 5* (JSNT Supp. 22; Sheffield: JSOT, 1988), 93–139; A.

Thiselton, *The First Epistle to the Corinthians* (NIGTC; Grand Rapids: Eerdmans, 2000), 1169–306.

31 Roger Beck, *The Religion of the Mithras Cult in the Roman Empire: Mysteries of the Unconquered Sun* (Oxford: Oxford University Press, 2006), 2–4.

32 Beck, *Mithras*, 5.

33 Segal, *Life after Death*, 389.

34 Dale B. Martin, *The Corinthian Body* (New Haven: Yale University Press, 1995), 120–21.

35 Abraham J. Malherbe, *The Letters to the Thessalonians* (AB 32B; New York: Doubleday, 2000), 263–81. Malherbe presumes that Paul had provided some instruction about the resurrection of the faithful (262). Paul's lack of interest in such topics as the intermediate state of the dead should be attributed to the influence of the genre of letters of consolation on this section of the letter (281).

36 Gregory E. Sterling, "Wisdom among the Perfect: Creation Traditions in Alexandrian Judaism and Corinthian Christianity," *NovT* 37 (1995): 355–84.

37 Sterling, "Wisdom," 360–67; Martin, *Body*, 113–25. Martin presumes that the views that Paul rejects belong to the wealthier, elite members of the Corinthian community, since he considers resurrection of the body a view more popular among the lower classes.

38 De Boer, *Defeat*, 138–39.

39 For a detailed discussion, see Gerard P. Luttikhuizen, *Gnostic Revisions of Genesis Stories and Early Jesus Traditions* (NHMS 58; Leiden: Brill, 2006), 44–71.

40 For discussion of Gnostic Christology, see Hurtado (*Lord Jesus Christ*, 523–48).

41 For a discussion of soteriology in the classic Gnostic representation of mythological transformation of Genesis traditions, see Karen King, *The Secret Revelation of John* (Cambridge, Mass.: Harvard University Press, 2006), 134–41.

42 King, *Secret Revelation*, 172. Her attempt to provide the Gnostic author some purchase in this world by treating this alienation as social criticism of violence and injustice seems more an appeal to contemporary sentiments about the authentic function of religion than an accurate reflection of the second century.

43 Elaine Pagels, "Exegesis of Genesis 1 in the Gospels of Thomas and John," *JBL* 118 (1999): 477–96; April D. DeConick, *Recovering the Original Gospel of Thomas. A History of the Gospel and Its Growth* (London: T&T Clark, 2005), 74–76; 213–17. The crucifixion is transformed into a model of the soul's victory over the passions whose power is associated with embodiment (DeConick, *Recovering*, 217).

44 As Thiselton rightly insists (*1 Corinthians*, 1227).

45 Thiselton, *1 Corinthians*, 1226.

46 Thiselton, *1 Corinthians*, 1283–84.

47 Segal makes an important observation that although the risen Christ, the Lord of Glory, is the object of worship (2 Cor 3:18ff; Phil 3:10), the key religious experience of Christ for Paul is an identification with the death of Christ on the cross (*Life after Death*, 417–20).

Chapter 6

Larry Hurtado was my Ph.D. student at Case Western Reserve University. He was one of those rare graduate students for whom a mentor simply opens the door to scholarship and the student does the rest. His high native intelligence, his eagerness to learn, and his sincerity and dedication were obvious from the beginning, and his dissertation was patently publishable. With some revision and refined argumentation, it appeared as *Text-Critical Methodology and the Pre-Caesarean Text: Codex W in the Gospel of Mark* (Studies and Documents 43; Grand Rapids: Eerdmans, 1981), and it is recognized as having altered forever our understanding of the presumed Caesarean text. My acquaintance with Alan Segal has been more casual, but with no less respect as a distinguished scholar of Judaisms and early Christianities, and I am pleased to join in celebrating the influential careers of two accomplished scholars and fine human beings.

1 For example, see Bruce M. Metzger and Bart D. Ehrman, *The Text of the New Testament: Its Transmission, Corruption, and Restoration* (4th ed.; New York: Oxford University Press, 2005), 50–51, though a cautionary footnote points to the "relatively fragmentary" nature of most papyri (51 n. 80). Also in E. J. Epp, "Textual Criticism," in *The New Testament and Its Modern Interpreters* (eds. E. J. Epp and G. W. MacRae; Philadelphia: Fortress/Atlanta: Scholars Press, 1989), 91; repr. as "Decision Points in Past, Present, and Future New Testament Textual Criticism," in E. J. Epp and Gordon D. Fee, *Studies in the Theory and Method of New Testament Textual Criticism* (SD 45; Grand Rapids: Eerdmans, 1993), 31–32; and in Epp, *Perspectives on New Testament Textual Criticism: Collected Essays, 1962–2004* (NovTSup 116; Leiden: Brill, 2005), 258–60; and in my "Textual Criticism in the Exegesis of the New Testament, with an Excursus on Canon," in *Handbook to Exegesis of the New Testament* (ed. Stanley E. Porter; NTTS 25; Leiden: Brill, 1997), 52–53; repr. in Epp, *Perspectives*, 469–70.

2 For recent understanding of the term "original text," see the author's "The Multivalence of the Term 'Original Text' in New Testament Textual Criticism," *HTR* 92 (1999): 245–81; repr. in Epp, *Perspectives*, 551–93.

3 Kurt Aland, with Michael Welte, *Beate Köster, and Klaus Junack, Kurzgefasste Liste der griechischen Handschriften des Neuen Testaments* (2nd ed; ANTF 1; Berlin: de Gruyter, 1994) serves as the major source for the

data here and in the following charts, supplemented in *Bericht der Hermann Kunst-Stiftung zur Förderung der neutestamentlichen Text-forschung für die Jahre 1995 bis 1998* (Münster/Westfalen: Hermann Kunst Stiftung, 1998) 14–18; and Aland et al., *1998 bis 2003* (2003), 74–80; and with past and current updates on the Institut's website: http://www.uni-muenster.de/NTTextforschung/. See also K. Aland, ed., *Repertorium der griechischen christlichen Papyri, I: Biblische Papyri, Altes Testament, Neues Testament, Varia, Apokryphen* (Berlin/New York: de Gruyter, 1976) 215–360, for detailed descriptions of the papyri through P88. Valuable data (when updated) is found also in Kurt Aland and Barbara Aland, *The Text of the New Testament: An Introduction to the Critical Editions and to the Theory and Practice of Modern Textual Criticism* (2nd ed.; trans. Erroll F. Rhodes; Grand Rapids: Eerdmans/Leiden: Brill, 1989), 81–170.

4   Though of no great consequence, this was not done, e.g., in Metzger and Ehrman, *The Text of the New Testament*, 50, where only the raw numbers occur.

5   For the source of the latest update, see n. 3, above.

6   Four are subtracted if P4 is considered part of P64+67; on the case for a single manuscript, see T. C. Skeat, "The Oldest Manuscript of the Four Gospels," *NTS* 43 (1997): esp. 1–9; Graham Stanton, "The Fourfold Gospel," *NTS* 43 (1997): 327–28.

7   The forty majuscules not counted include thrity-nine that are parts of other manuscripts or otherwise removed from the official list, but also 0212, a Diatessaron manuscript no longer counted as a New Testament manuscript. Exact copies of manuscripts also are no longer counted, namely, majuscules D$^{p\ abs\ 1\ and\ abs\ 2}$ and also minuscules 9^{abs}, 30^{abs}, 96^{abs}, 205^{abs}, 1909^{abs}, 1929^{abs}, 1983^{abs}, 2036^{abs}.

8   The total number of different papyri is 114 if P4 is part of P64+67 (see n. 6, above).

9   The other nineteenth-century minuscule is 1777, though a copy of the twelfth-century 1160, namely 1160abs, has an 1888 date, but exact copies generally are not counted among the manuscripts (see n. 7, above). Ten other eighteenth-century lectionaries are extant, four of them dated, and all on paper (*ll* 423, 508, 713, 733, 992, 1361, 1463, 1466, 1796, and 2381).

10   The seven papyri of non-Egyptian provenance are P11+14 (Sinai in the Negev, 6th c.); P59, P60, P61 ('Auja el Hafir = Nessana in the Negev, 7th, but P61 ca. 700); P68 (Sinai, 7th?); and P83 and P84 (Khirbet Mird = Hyrcania near the Dead Sea in Judaea, 6th).

11   One papyrus (P118, with portions of Romans 15 and 16) and one majuscule (0305, with four verses of Matthew 20) remain undated; therefore, in some discussions or charts where dates are relevant, these

two manuscripts may not be included, and counts of papyri or majuscules may vary by one or two numbers.

12 Bruce M. Metzger, "Explicit References in the Works of Origen to Variant Readings in New Testament Manuscripts," in *Biblical and Patristic Studies in Memory of Robert Pierce Casey* (eds. J. Neville Birdsall and Robert W. Thomson; Freiburg: Herder, 1963), 81–91; repr. in Metzger, *Historical and Literary Studies: Pagan, Jewish, and Christian* (NTTS 8; Leiden: Brill, 1968), 90–101.

13 See Epp, "The New Testament Papyrus Manuscripts in Historical Perspective," in *To Touch the Text: Studies in Honor of Joseph A. Fitzmyer* (eds. M. P. Horgan and P. J. Kobelski; New York: Crossroad, 1989), 274–77; repr. in Epp, *Perspectives*, 325–28.

14 This was done by Ernst von Dobschütz in his 1923 revision of Eberhard Nestle's *Einführung in das Griechischen Neuen Testament*; for discussion and references, see Epp, "The New Testament Papyrus Manuscripts," 277–78; repr. in Epp, *Perspectives*, 328–29.

15 Dated manuscripts are more frequent among the minuscules, with two in the 9th c.; four in the 10th and 10th/11th; thirteen in the 11th; and, e.g., thirty-one in the 16th; twenty-three in the 17th; seven in the 18th; and three out of the four nineteenth-century minuscules.

16 For details, see Epp, "Issues in New Testament Textual Criticism: Moving from the Nineteenth Century to the Twenty-First Century," in *Rethinking New Testament Textual Criticism* (ed. David Alan Black; Grand Rapids: Baker Academic, 2002), 61–64; repr. in Epp, *Perspectives*, 682–85.

17 The seven non-Egyptian New Testament papyri are P11+14 (Sinai, 6th), P59 and P60 ('Auja el Hafir = Nessana, 7th), P61 (Nessana, ca. 700), P68 (Sinai, 7th ?), and P83 and P84 (Khirbet Mird, 6th).

18 Aland and Aland, *Text*, 55, 70.

19 Harry Y. Gamble, *Books and Readers in the Early Church: A History of Early Christian Texts* (New Haven: Yale University Press, 1995), 120–22; 158–59.

20 For the latest critique of previous lists of "complete" New Testament manuscripts, see Daryl Schmidt, "The Greek New Testament as a Codex," in *The Canon Debate: On the Origins and Formation of the Bible* (ed. Lee M. McDonald and James A. Sanders; Peabody, Mass.: Hendrickson, 2002), 469–84, esp. 469–72. Helpful also is J. Keith Elliott, *A Survey of Manuscripts Used in Editions of the Greek New Testament* (NovTSup 57; Leiden: Brill, 1987), who marks complete manuscripts with a "C." Though Vaticanus (B, 4th) often is listed as complete, it lacks the Pastoral Epistles, Philemon, and the Apocalypse of John, and ends with Heb 9:14. A further issue arises in cases such as ℵ and A (and others), where nonbiblical books are included: What conception of "canon" is implicit? I arrived at fifty-three complete New

Testaments by using Schmidt, "Greek New Testament as a Codex," 479–84, where he lists fifty-eight minuscules and two majuscules (‭א‬ and A), to which I add Codex C, for a total of sixty-one; I subtract the four-composite manuscripts (made up of various manuscripts: 180, 209, 517, 1668) and four apparently lacking one or more entire books (218, 498, 1352, 1384 [perhaps also 2201]), but I ignore the "lost" manuscripts (241, 339, 1785, 2554?). This leaves fifty-three likely complete New Testament manuscripts.

21   The listed combinations include only continuous-text manuscripts—those containing the running text of one writing or of two or more writings in one of the several conventional sequences. Lectionaries, of course, are not continuous-text manuscripts, but contain selected portions for reading in church services.

22   This table employs the sources cited in n. 3, above. For an earlier tabulation (now requiring updating), see Aland and Aland, *Text*, 78–79; cf. my "Issues in the Interrelation of New Testament Textual Criticism and Canon," in McDonald and Sanders, *The Canon Debate*, 487; repr. in Epp, *Perspectives*, 597–98.

23   The eighth-century palimpsest majuscule 0168 contains gospel material, but its specific contents and size are unknown.

24   P45 has portions of all four gospels and of Acts; P53 contains fragments of Matthew and of Acts.

25   The exact content of 0168 is unknown (see n. 23, above), so it is not included here. Papyri and majuscules at this time totaled 315.

26   P6 and P2 (below) are included because they have portions of two different books, though in each case one writing is in Greek and the other in Coptic.

27   Actually, the four gospels with Acts are not a common grouping, though the four gospel unit becomes the most common of all: see Aland and Aland, *Text*, 78–79, 83.

28   On P46, for the complex problem and analysis, see Epp, "Issues in . . . Textual Criticism and Canon," 495–502; repr. in Epp, *Perspectives*, 609–19.

29   For discussion of P72, see Epp, "Issues in . . . Textual Criticism and Canon," 491–93; repr. in Epp, *Perspectives*, 603–5.

30   Aland and Aland, *Text*, 159–62.

31   Minuscules with 11–24 leaves number 47, peaking in the fourteenth century; those with 25–60 leaves amount to 82, with about twelve in the tenth and eleventh centuries, then rather evenly spread from the twelfth through the sixteenth (12 to 15 mss in each), with a few in the seventeenth and eighteenth centuries. Overall, nearly 260 minuscules have 60 or fewer leaves (about 10%), while the remaining 90% have 61 or more leaves.

32   Paper manuscripts of the New Testament are found from the twelfth into the nineteenth century and number roughly 1200 (minuscules and lectionaries, somewhat evenly divided).

33 I refer here to the work of Gordon D. Fee, which is summarized in my
    "The Papyrus Manuscripts of the New Testament," in *The Text of the
    New Testament in Contemporary Research: Essays on the Status Quaestionis*
    (ed. B. D. Ehrman and M. W. Holmes; SD 46; Grand Rapids:
    Eerdmans, 1995), 15–16; repr. in Epp, *Perspectives*, 429–30.

34 For a summary, see Epp, "Issues in New Testament Textual Criticism,"
    41–43; repr. in Epp, *Perspectives*, 663–65; and earlier, Epp, "The
    Significance of the Papyri for Determining the Nature of the New
    Testament Text in the Second Century: A Dynamic View of Textual
    Transmission," in *Gospel Traditions in the Second Century* (ed. William L.
    Petersen; Studies in Christianity and Judaism in Antiquity 3; Notre
    Dame: University of Notre Dame Press, 1989), 92–100; repr. in Epp,
    Perspectives, 367–77.

35 D. C. Parker, "A New Oxyrhynchus Papyrus of Revelation: P¹¹⁵ (P.Oxy.
    4499)," *NTS* 46 (2000): 159–74. The text-types in the Revelation are
    different than those in the rest of the New Testament.

36 The textual variants alluded to below can be found easily in Nestle-
    Aland²⁷ and/or in UBS⁴. Drawing only upon the nine earliest fragmen-
    tary manuscripts (see table 6.9), several examples will illustrate how they
    close the connection between the earliest known phase of New Testament
    textual transmission and the later, more ample phases.

    (1) P52 is supported by B in its word-order variation, while ℵ has one
    of two other sequences (John 18:33).

    (2) In John 18:36—19:7, P90 is supported by ℵ versus B in a sequence
    of words (18:36); by P66 ℵ B in a similar variant (18:39, and again in
    19:3); by ℵ versus B and versus P66, i.e., three differing readings (19:1);
    by P66 ℵ versus B (19:4); by B versus P66 and versus ℵ (18:38); by P66
    (19:6); by ℵ versus P66 B (again, 19:6); by P66 ℵ (19:7); and alone ver-
    sus P66 (19:6). Also, P90 is the only Greek witness for one of three dif-
    fering word sequences, standing against ℵ and P66 (19:4).

    (3) P32, in two variants in Titus 2:7, is supported first by F G 1881
    versus ℵ, and second by ℵ D F G 1881, etc.

    (4) P64+67 presents a similar array of agreement and disagreement with
    relevant witnesses, not only ℵ and B, but the early papyri P37 and P45.
    Nearly all possible combinations occur among these five manuscripts in
    some fifteen variation-units where P64+67 is extant, though the most
    common is support of P64+67 by ℵ and B (Matt 5:22, 25; 26:8, 23,
    28*bis*, 31). ℵ and B part company in Matt 3:15; 5:28; 26:20, 26.

    (5) P77 is supported by ℵ versus B (Matt 23:38). Finally, (6) 0189 is
    supported by P45 ℵ B D (Matt 5:17, 18); by ℵ B (5:8); by B (5:19); by
    B D (5:3); and by B versus D (5:16).

37 For more on the living text and related issues, see Epp, *Perspectives*,
    566–75; 674–82; 744–48.

Chapter 7

1 For detailed discussion, see P. M. Casey, *Aramaic Sources of Mark's Gospel* (MSSNTS 102; Cambridge: Cambridge University Press, 1998), 188–89.

2 For detailed discussion, see Casey, *Aramaic Sources*, 111–37; idem., *An Aramaic Approach to Q: Sources of the Gospels of Matthew and Luke* (MSS-NTS 122; Cambridge: Cambridge University Press, 2002), 115–21.

3 For detailed discussion, including a complete reconstruction of Mark's Aramaic source, see Casey, *Aramaic Sources*, 138–92.

4 For discussion of this perspective, including a response to some criticism, see P. Maurice Casey, *From Jewish Prophet to Gentile God* (Louisville: James Clarke/Westminster John Knox, 1991), 17–20, 61–64; *Aramaic Sources,* 145–50, 174, 191–92; *Aramaic Approach*, 64–104, esp. 65–70.

5 For full discussion, P. Maurice Casey, *The Solution of the Son of Man Problem* (London: T&T Clark International, forthcoming).

6 Casey, *Aramaic Sources*, 182–83.

7 Josephus has the more accurate account, but the wayward midrash of Mark 6:17-29 was put together on the basis of the known fact that Herod executed John the Baptist: see R. D. Aus, *Water into Wine and the Beheading of John the Baptist: Early Jewish-Christian Interpretation of Esther 1 in John 2:1-11 and Mark 6:17-29* (Atlanta: Scholars Press, 1988); J. G. Crossley, "History From the Margins: The Death of John the Baptist," in *Writing History, Constructing Religion* (eds. J. G. Crossley and C. Karner; London: Ashgate, 2005), 147–61.

8 For detailed discussion, including a reconstruction of Luke's Aramaic source, see Casey, *Aramaic Sources*, 188–89.

9 For detailed discussion, including reconstructions of "Q" and of the Aramaic sources of both Mark and Q, see Casey, *Aramaic Approach*, 146–84.

10 For detailed discussion, see Casey, *Aramaic Approach*, 167–73.

11 For detailed discussion, see Casey, *Aramaic Approach,* 176–77.

12 For detailed discussion, see Casey, *Aramaic Approach*, 177–82; and on the idiom itself, Casey, *Solution*, ch. 2.

13 For detailed discussion of this passage, see especially R. P. Booth, *Jesus and the Laws of Purity. Tradition and Legal History in Mark 7* (Sheffield: JSOT Press, 1986); J. G. Crossley, *The Date of Mark's Gospel. Insight from the Law in Earliest Christianity* (London: T&T Clark International, 2004), chs. 7.

14 For detailed discussion of Matt 23:23-36//Lk 11:39–51, including reconstruction of an original Aramaic source, see Casey, *Aramaic Approach*, ch. 3.

15 For detailed discussion, including reconstruction of Mark's Aramaic source, see P. M. Casey, "Culture and Historicity: The Cleansing of the Temple," *CBQ* 59 (1997): 306–32 (with bibliography).

Chapter 8

1   It is noteworthy that the popular *Dictionary of Paul and His Letters* (eds. Gerald F. Hawthorne, Ralph P. Martin, Daniel G. Reid; Downers Grove: InterVaristy Press, 1993) does not contain an entry for "incarnation." Note however, the references to the incarnation in Larry Hurtado, "Pre-existence," *DPL* 743–46.

2   Brian Daley, "Nature and the 'Mode of Union': Late Patristic Models for the Personal Unity of Christ," in *The Incarnation* (ed. Stephen T. Davis et al.; Oxford: Oxford University Press, 2002), 164–65, defines the incarnation as "the fundamental conviction of the Christian faith that in Jesus of Nazareth God's eternal, personally substantial Word `became flesh and dwelt among us.'" Note how the language of Gospel of John informs the definition.

3   Maurice Casey, *From Jewish Prophet to Gentile God: The Origins and Development of New Testament Christology* (Louisville: Westminster John Knox, 1991), 23–40; Dunn, *Christology in the Making,* 251–68; Jerome Murphy-O'Connor, "Christological Anthropology in Phil. 2, 6-11," *RevB* 831 (1976): 25–50.

4   Simon Gathercole, *The Pre-Existent Son: Recovering the Christologies of Matthew, Mark and Luke* (Grand Rapids: Eerdmans, 2006), 23, italics are the authors. See the review of research presented on pp. 1–21.

5   Gordon Fee, *Pauline Christology: An Exegetical-Theological Study* (Peabody, Mass.: Hendrickson, 2007), dedicates an entire chapter (12) to Christ as the preexistent, incarnate Savior. I am grateful to the staff at Hendrickson for providing me with a copy of the relevant pages of Fee's book several months before publication.

6   Hurtado, *Lord Jesus Christ,* see particularly pp. 118–26. Scholars often cite the following texts as reflecting preexistence in Paul's letters: 1 Cor 8:6; 10:4; 15:47; 2 Cor 8:9; Gal 4:4; Rom 8:3; and especially Phil 2:6-8.

7   Hurtado, *Lord Jesus Christ,* 124–25.

8   Note for example, that in Douglas McCready's recent monograph *He Came Down from Heaven: The Preexistence of Christ and the Christian Faith* (Downers Grove: InterVarsity, 2005), no treatment of Romans 9:30–10:13 is offered.

9   E. Earle Ellis, *Paul's Use of the Old Testament* (Grand Rapids: Baker, 1957), 160–70, lists twenty-six quotations and/or allusions to the OT in Romans 9–11.

10 Richard B. Hays, *Echoes of Scripture in the Letters of Paul* (New Haven and London: Yale University Press, 1989), 74–75, concludes—incorrectly to my mind—that Romans 9:30–10:21 is "parenthetical" to Paul's argument in Romans 9–11. If it is parenthetical, could it be eliminated without diminishing the argument? The answer is clearly no. The christological confession "Jesus Is Lord" and the word of faith preached by Paul were the

theological boundary-markers between Paul's Jewish-Gentiles churches and his countrymen now "cut off" from the Messiah (Rom 9:3). For Paul, God's righteousness is meaningless now apart from what Christ has done. He clearly presents divine righteousness as coming "through the faithfulness of Jesus Christ" (Rom 3:21-26). Rather than parenthetical, this portion of Paul's discourse is crucial to his argument.

11   Aspects of the following argument were published previously in David B. Capes, "YHWH and His Messiah: Pauline Exegesis and the Divine Christ," *Horizons in Biblical Theology* 16.2 (1994): 121–43.

12   The notion of "pursuing righteousness" may arise from the Wisdom tradition. See, e.g., Sir 27:8: "[I]f you pursue righteousness/ you will obtain it and wear it as a robe of glory." Also, Prov 15:9: "[T]he ways of the ungodly are an abomination to the Lord, but he loves those who pursue righteousness." Cf. 4Q295. Unless otherwise noted, the author is responsible for all translations.

13   Presumably, Paul means "the works of the law." Later copyists no doubt understood it so since they added the genitive νόμου following "works." See ℵ², D, Y, 𝔐.

14   Juel, *Messianic Exegesis*, 38–42; Michael Fishbane, *Biblical Interpretation in Ancient Israel* (Oxford: Clarendon, 1985), 248–89; Richard Longenecker, *Biblical Exegesis in the Apostolic Period* (Grand Rapids: Eerdmans, 1975), 207. Hillel's rules are set out in *t.Sanh.* 7.11.

15   R. E. Clements, *Isaiah 1–39* (NCBC; Grand Rapids: Eerdmans, 1980), 229. The satirical language refers to international treaties negotiated with Egypt.

16   Paul Meyer, "Romans 10:4 and the End of the Law," in *The Divine Helmsman: Studies on God's Control of Human Events Presented to Lou H. Silberman* (ed. A. Crenshaw, ed.; New York: KTAV, 1980), 64; see also C. K. Barrett, "Romans 9:30–10:21: Fall and Responsibility in Israel," in his *Essays on Paul* (Philadelphia: Westminster, 1982), 144.

17   For example, C. H. Dodd, *According to the Scriptures* (London: Nisbet, 1952); Jeremias, *TDNT*, 4:272–73. Isaiah 8:14 is quoted or alluded to in Matt 16:23; 21:42; Luke 2:34; 1 Pet 2:8; Isaiah 28:16 is quoted or alluded to in Matt 21:42; Luke 20:17; Eph 2:20; 2 Tim 2:19; 1 Pet 2:4, 6. Cf. Ps 118:22 with Matt 21:42; Acts 4:11; 1 Pet 2:4, 6–8.

18   See Jeremias, *TDNT*, 4:272–73. Käsemann, *Romans*, 278–79, follows Jeremias. Note that Josephus, *Antiquities* 10.210, knows of messianic connections to the stone passage in Dan 2:34ff.

19   E. P. Sanders, *Paul and Palestinian Judaism* (Philadelphia: Fortress, 1977), 37.

20   See L. Joseph Kreitzer, *Jesus and God in Paul's Eschatology* (Sheffield: Sheffield Academic, 1987), 112–29, who explores the eschatology of Jewish pseudepigraphical texts *(1 Enoch, Jubilees, 2 Enoch, 4 Ezra,* and *2 Baruch)* and its probable impact on Paul's thinking. He concludes that

Paul's writings exhibit a "conceptual ambiguity" regarding the eschatological roles of God and Christ. In some places there is "an outright substitution of christocentrism for theocentrism," which occurs with OT quotations and allusions. These "referential shifts" center primarily on the *kyrios*-title.

21 Hays, *Echoes*, 75.

22 Käsemann, *Romans*, 280–81.

23 See Sanders, *Paul*, 39.

24 There is a slight variation from Paul's quotation and the LXX. Since (1) the purpose of this essay is to analyze quotations and allusions that Paul uses christologically and (2) he does not so use Lev 18:5, it is noted only in passing. The fact that Paul uses Lev 18:5 with similar interest in Galatians 3 suggests that it had become or was becoming a part of his standard response to questions of Christ and the Law.

25 See James D. G. Dunn, " 'Righteousness from the Law' and 'Righteousness from Faith': Paul's Interpretation of Scripture in Rom 10:1-10), in *Tradition and Interpretation in the New Testament: Essays in Honor of E. Earle Ellis for His 60th Birthday* (eds. Gerald F. Hawthorne and Otto Betz; Grand Rapids: Eerdmans, 1987), 216–26.

26 For example, see W. Sanday and A. C. Headlam, *A Critical and Exegetical Commentary on the Epistle to the Romans* (ICC; New York: Charles Scribner's Sons, 1920), 289. Also Longnecker, *Biblical Exegesis*, 21, agrees but admits these lines are grounded in scripture.

27 See Jack Suggs, " 'The Word Is Near You': Rom 10:6-10 within the Purpose of the Letter," in *Christian History and Interpretation: Studies Presented to John Knox* (eds. W. R. Farmer, C. F. D. Moule, and R. R. Niebuhr; Cambridge: Cambridge University Press, 1967), 300–302.

28 For a helpful description of pesher, see G. J. Brooke, "Pesharim," in *Dictionary of New Testament Background* (eds. Craig A. Evans and Stanley Porter; Downers Grove: InterVarsity, 2000), 778–82. T. H. Lim, *Holy Scripture in Qumran Commentaries and Pauline Letters* (Oxford: Clarendon, 1997), cautions against the overuse of the term to include other kinds of biblical interpretation. I do stop short of calling what Paul does "*pesher*"; however, I do think that in its form and theological interests, it is similar or *pesher*-like. The categories employed by J. Carmignac, "Le Document de Qumrân sur Melkisédeq," *RevQ* 7, no. 31 (1969): 343–78, are helpful. He distinguishes between continuous (e.g., 1QpHab; 4QpNah) and thematic (e.g., 4QFlorilegium; 11QMelchizedek). Paul's interpretation of Deuteronomy would be similar to the thematic variety. Hays, *Echoes*, 79, defines *pesher* as "cryptically encoded allegory of the community's own history, apocalyptically interpreted."

29 N. T. Wright, *The Climax of the Covenant* (Philadelphia: Fortress, 1991), 231–57.

30 Suggs, " 'The Word,' " 308–9; Dunn, "Rom 10:1-10," 220.

31 Dunn, "Rom 10:1-10," 217, explains the variation of Paul's words from Deuteronomy in light of *Targum Neofiti*, which relates the story to Jonah's descent into the abyss of the sea. Cf. Philo, *Post* 84–85.

32 On the identification of Torah-Wisdom-Christ, see W. D. Davies, *Paul and Rabbinic Judaism: Some Rabbinic Elements in Pauline Theology* (4th ed.; Philadelphia: Fortress, 1980), 147–76. See also Suggs, " 'The Word is Near You,' " 302–4.

33 Cranfield, *Romans*, 2:525.

34 Dunn, *Christology in the Making*, 184–87; similarly, Käsemann, *Romans*, 290.

35 See James D. Tabor, *Things Unutterable: Paul's Ascent to Paradise in Its Greco-Roman, Judaic, and Early Christian Contexts* (Lanham, Md.: University Press of America, 1986).

36 Segal, *Paul the Convert*, 34–71. No one has done more than Alan Segal in elucidating the mystical aspects of Paul's religious experience and demonstrating how these experiences relate to other mystical traditions.

37 Cf. Hays, *Echoes*, 79; Barrett, "Rom 9:30–10:31," 148–89; Longenecker, *Christology*, 60.

38 Hays, *Echoes*, 80.

39 For other connections between Christ and Wisdom, see E. J. Schnabel, "Wisdom," in *Dictionary of Paul and His Letters* (Downers Grove: InterVarsity, 1993), 967–73.

40 N. T. Wright, *The New Testament and the People of God* (Philadelphia: Fortress, 1992), 403–9. Contra Dunn, *Christology in the Making*, 184–87. Otherwise, see Francis Watson, "Is There a Story in These Texts?" in *Narrative Dynamics in Paul: A Critical Assessment* (ed. B. W. Longenecker; Louisville: Westminster John Knox, 2002), 233ff.

41 Michael Gorman, *Cruciformity: Paul's Narrative Spirituality of the Cross* (Grand Rapids: Eerdmans, 2001), 82–94.

42 All the texts typically cited as referring to Christ's preexistence: Phil 2:6-11; Col 1:15-20; 2:9; 1 Cor 8:6; 10:4, 9; Rom 8:3; Gal 4:4. I would include Rom 10:6-8.

43 Hurtado, *Lord Jesus Christ*, 120; Gathercole, *The Pre-Existent Son*, 26; Fee, *Pauline Christology*, 504.

44 Larry W. Hurtado, "Jesus as Lordly Example in Philippians 2:5-11," in *From Jesus to Paul: Studies in Honor of Francis Wright Beare* (eds. Peter Richardson and J. C. Hurd; Waterloo, Ontario: Wilfrid Laurier University Press, 1984), 113–26.

45 Most notably Dunn, *Christology in the Making*, 114–21, who concludes that an Adam-Christology provides the conceptual framework for the hymn. The parallel between Adam and Christ suggests that Paul means for the language to be analogical and metaphorical. Accordingly, a preexistent reading of the hymn is unnecessary. Dunn (*The Theology of Paul the Apostle* [Grand Rapids: Eerdmans, 1998], 286) remarks that, other

than Heb 2:5-9, Phil 2:6-11 contains the "the fullest expression of Adam christology in the NT." Wright, *Climax*, 90–97, accepts that Adam-Christology is present in the hymn; however, for him its presence does not automatically exclude a preexistent reading.

46   Fee, *Pauline Christology*, 506–7.

47   Oscar Cullman, *The Christology of the New Testament* (Philadelphia: Westminster, 1959), 177, offers that Christ is "the pre-existent Heavenly Man, the pre-existent pure image of God, the God-man already in his pre-existence."

48   Wright, *Climax*, 97.

49   A similar tradition is reflected in John 3:13, which declares that the Son of Man descended from heaven. Otherwise, see Gordon Fee, *The First Epistle to the Corinthians* (NICNT; Grand Rapids: Eerdmans, 1987), 791–92; C. K. Barrett, *The First Epistle to the Corinthians* (HNTC; New York: Harper & Row, 1968), 375–76, who emphasizes that Jesus is the man who will come from heaven. This reading, however, is problematic if Paul is discussing the origin of the Adam and the Christ.

50   John 3:13; 6:62; 1 Pet 3:18-22; 1 Tim 3:16. See Longenecker, *The Christology of Early Jewish Christianity*, 58–62.

51   E.g., Oscar Cullmann, *The Earliest Christian Confessions*, (trans. J. K. S. Reid; London: Lutterworth Press, 1949), 28–29; Rudolph Bultmann, *Theology of the New Testament* (2 vols.; trans. Kendrick Grobel; New York: Charles Scribner's Sons, 1951–1955), 1:121–28; Leonhard Goppelt, *Theology of the New Testament* (2 vols.; trans. John Alsup; Grand Rapids: Eerdmans, 1982), 2:79–86.

52   Longenecker, *Christology*, 127; cf. Werner Kramer, *Christ, Lord, Son of God* (trans. Brian Hardy; Naperville, Ill: A. R. Allenson, 1966), 65.

53   See Jacques Dupont, "Le Seigneur de tous' (Ac 10:36; Rm 10:12): Arriére-fond scripturaire d'une formule christologique," in Hawthorne and Betz, *Tradition and Interpretation in the New Testament*, 229–30; Cranfield, *Romans*, 2:531.

54   Kreitzer, *Jesus and God*, 124; Cranfield, *Romans*, 2:531.

55   See Capes, *Yahweh Texts*, 116–22.

56   Cf. Rom 2:4; 9:23; Phil 4:19; also Eph 2:4, 7; 3:8.

57   K. L. Schmidt, "ἐπικαλέω," *TDNT*, 3:496–500.

58   E.g., Gen 13:4; 21:33; 26:26; Ps 78:6; 79:18: 104:1; 118:4: Isa 64:6: Jer 10:25; Zeph 3:9; Zech 13:9; and Joel 2:32.

59   C. J. Davis, *The Name and Way of the Lord: Old Testament Themes, New Testament Christology* (JSNTSup, 19; Sheffield: Sheffield Academic, 1996), 106.

60   Hurtado, *Lord Jesus Christ*, 143. Otherwise see Käsemann, *Romans*, 292, who denies that prayers were offered to Jesus in the early Christianity. He relates the word primarily to preaching and confession.

61 The variation may be due to textual fluidity during the period. However, given the context, it is more likely Paul's variation represents a theological statement.

62 Lucien Cerfaux, "<<Kyrios>> dans les citations pauliniennes de l'Ancien Testament," in *Recueil Lucien Cerfaux: Etudes d'exegese et d'histoire religieuse de Monseigneur Cerfaux* (vol. 1; Gemblux: J. Duculot, 1954), 179; Kreitzer, *Jesus and God,* 114, 124; Capes, *Yahweh Texts,* 116–23.

63 A YHWH text is a quotation of or an allusion to an Old Testament text that contains the divine name in the Hebrew Bible. In the Septuagint and in Paul, *kyrios* translates the divine name. See David B. Capes, "YHWH Texts and Monotheism in Paul's Christology," in Stuckebruck and North, *Early Jewish and Christian Monotheism,* 120–37.

64 E.g., 1 Thess 4:6; 5:2, 9; 2 Thess 2:8; 1 Cor 1:7-8; 4:4-5; 5:3-5; 11:32; 2 Cor 1:14. Capes, *Yahweh Texts,* 82–88.

65 Wright, *People of God ,* 78–79.

66 Robin Scroggs, *Christology in Paul and John* (Philadelphia: Fortress, 1988), 52.

Chapter 9

1 William Wrede, *Paul* (Boston: American Unitarian Association, 1908).

2 Newman, *Paul's Glory-Christology,* 79–156.

3 Günther Bornkamm, *Paul* (New York: Harper, 1971), 16–25.

4 Richard Reitzenstein, *Die hellenistischen Mysterienreligionen* (3rd ed.; Stuttgart: Teubner, 1927), 378–81; Bousset, *Kyrios Christos,* 169, 208.

5 Sanders, *Paul,* 434–35; Davies, *Paul and Rabbinic Judaism,* 36, 324.

6 Bultmann, *Theology of the New Testament,* 1:187–88; Hans Conzelmann, *An Outline of the Theology of the New Testament* (New York: Harper, 1969), 164.

7 Stendahl, *Paul Among Jews and Gentiles,* 7–22.

8 J. C. Gager, J. C. "Some Notes on Paul's Conversion," *New Testament Studies* 27 (1980/81): 697–704; Beverly R. Gaventa, *From Darkness to Light* (Philadelphia: Fortress, 1986); Paula Fredricksen, "Paul and Augustine: Conversion Narratives, Orthodox Traditions and the Retrospective Self," *Journal of Theological Studies* 37 (1986): 3–34; Segal, *Paul the Convert*; Hurtado, *Lord Jesus Christ.*

9 Otto Michel, "Die Entstehung der paulinische Christologie," *Zeitschrift für die neutestamentliche Wissenschaft* 28 (1929), 324–33; Joachim Jeremias, *Der Schlüssel zur Theologie des Apostles Paulus* (Stuttgart: Calwer, 1971); Seyoon Kim, *The Origin of Paul's Gospel* (2nd ed.; Tübingen: Mohr-Siebeck, 1984); Peter Stuhlmacher, *Reconciliation, Law, and Righteousness* (Philadelphia: Fortress, 1986).

10 Jacques Lacan, "Seminar on 'The Purloined Letter,'" *Yale French Studies* 48 (1972): 38–72; Peter Brooks, *Reading for the Plot* (New York: Vintage,

1984); Marianna Torgovnick, *Closure in the Novel* (Princeton: Princeton University Press, 1981).

11 John P. Muller and William J. Richardson, *The Purloined Poe: Lacan, Derrida, and Psychoanalytic Reading* (Baltimore: Johns Hopkins University Press, 1988), 53.

12 Kim, *Origin*, 3–31.

13 William G. Doty, *Letters in Primitive Christianity* (Philadelphia: Fortress, 1973), 21–48; David E. Aune, *The New Testament in Its Literary Environment* (Philadelphia: Fortress, 1987), 183–225.

14 Richard B. Hays, *The Faith of Jesus Christ* (Chicago: Scholars, 1983), 85–138.

15 George Lyons, *Pauline Autobiography* (Atlanta: Scholars, 1985), 123–69.

16 Norman R. Petersen, *Rediscovering Paul* (Philadelphia: Fortress, 1985), 43–88.

17 Wright, *The Climax of the Covenant*, 18–40, 231–57.

18 Lacan, "Seminar," 45.

19 Lacan, "Seminar," 40, 60.

20 Sidney Tarachow, "St. Paul and Early Christianity: A Psychoanalytic and Historical Study," *Psychoanalysis and the Social Sciences* 4 (1955): 223–81; Robin Scroggs, "The Heuristic Value of a Psychoanalytic Model in the Interpretation of Pauline Theology," *Zygon* 13 (1978): 136–57; Robert L. Moore, "Pauline Theology and the Return of the Repressed: Depth Psychology and Early Christian Thought," *Zygon* 13 (1978): 158–68.

21 Daniel Patte, *Paul's Faith and the Power of the Gospel* (Philadelphia: Fortress, 1983) 42–48.

22 Brooks, *Reading for the Plot*, 27.

23 Brooks, *Reading for the Plot*, 93–94.

24 Brooks, *Reading for the Plot*, 107–8.

25 Gager, "Notes," 697–704.

26 F. Blass, A. Debrunner, and Robert W. Funk, *A Greek Grammar of the New Testament and Other Christian Literature* (Chicago: University of Chicago Press, 1961), §222.

27 Torgovnick, *Closure*, 13

28 Capes, *Yahweh Texts*, 155–57.

29 Segal, *Paul the Convert*, 59–60.

30 Hurtado, *Lord Jesus Christ*, 113.

31 Hays, *Echoes*, 153.

Chapter 10

It is a particular and double pleasure to make this small offering to two friends and colleagues in whose company I have found such delight and benefit both in frutiful discussion and in enjoyable fellowship. A toast to two stalwarts of the EHCC from a slightly dissenting member.

1   P. Pokorny, *The Genesis of Christology: Foundations for a Theology of the New Testament* (1985; ET Edinburgh: T&T Clark, 1987), 68–72.

2   "Christ died for us" —Rom 5:6, 8; 14.15; 1 Cor 1:13; 8:11; 2 Cor 5:14; 1 Thess 5:9ff.; 1 Pet 2:21; 3:18; 1 John 3:16. Self-giving—Rom 4:25; 8.32; Gal 1:4; 2:20; 1 Tim 2.5–6.; Tit 2:14; John 3:16.

3   He refers back to his earlier discussion on Jesus' farewell meal (48–52); "[W]hen Jesus identified himself with the will of God, it is conceivable that he also placed his death in the service of his offer of salvation" (51).

4   M. Hengel, *The Atonement: A Study of the Origins of the Doctrine in the New Testament* (1980; ET London: SCM Press, 1981).

5   Hengel, *Atonement*, 64, 71–73.

6   To avoid unnecessary controversy, I refer here only to the formula extending through v. 5. For the debate about Paul's fuller version, see, e.g., G. Strecker, *Theologie des Neuen Testaments* (Berlin: de Gruyter, 1996), 80–81; W. Schrage, *1 Korinther* (EKK VII/4; Düsseldorf: Benziger, 2001), 53–54.

7   Most strikingly 4 Macc 17:22.

8   See the discussion with bibliography in Thiselton, *1 Corinthians*, 1190–92; and Schrage, *1 Korinther*, 32–34. Hengel, however, is convinced "that Isa 53 had an influence on the origin and shaping of the earliest kerygma" (*Atonement*, 59–60).

9   See my *Theology*, 207–23.

10 Hengel, *Atonement*, 54.

11 Rom 4:25; 5:6, 8; 8:32; 14:15; 1 Cor 8:11; 11:24; 2 Cor 5:14–15; Gal 1:4; 2:20; 1 Thess 5:10. Rom 4:25 might be enough to tip in favor of a conscious allusion in 1 Cor 15:3 to Isaiah 53 (Hengel, *Atonement*, 35–38); see further below n. 21.

12 Contrast Hebrews, particularly 9:1–10:18.

13 The tradition of Jesus' being buried is one of the oldest pieces of tradition we have (1 Cor 15:4—*hoti etaphê*), a point especially emphasized by M. Hengel, "Das Begräbnis Jesu bei Paulus," in *Auferstehung Resurrection* (eds. F. Avemarie and H. Lichtenberger; WUNT 135; Tübingen: Mohr Siebeck, 2001), 119–83 (here 121, 129–38, 175–76).

14 See Pokorny, *Genesis*, 64 n. 4; and Schrage's brief review (*1 Korinther*, 4:23–24).

15 See further below, pp. 180–81.

16 Particularly J. Jeremias, *New Testament Theology*. I: *The Proclamation of Jesus* (London: SCM Press, 1971), 277–86; V. Howard, "Did Jesus Speak about His Own Death?" *CBQ* 39 (1977): 515–27; J. Ådna, *Jesu Stellung zum Tempel: Die Tempelaktion und das Tempelwort als Ausdruck seiner messianischen Sendung* (WUNT; Tübingen: Mohr Siebeck, 2000), 412–19; P. Balla, "What Did Jesus Think about His Approaching Death?" in *Jesus, Mark and Q: The Teaching of Jesus and its Earliest Records*

(eds. M. Labahn and A. Schmidt; JSNTS 214; Sheffield: Sheffield Academic, 2001), 239–58. In what follows I draw on my *Jesus Remembered* (Grand Rapids: Eerdmans, 2003), 796–824.

17 Jeremias argues that the denigration of Jesus as "a glutton and a drunkard" (Matt 11:19; Luke 7:34) is derived from Deut 21:20 and "stigmatizes him on the strength of this connection as a 'refractory and rebellious son,' who deserved to be stoned." (*The Parables of Jesus* [1962; ET London: SCM Press, 1963], 160).

18 Jeremias, *Proclamation*, 284.

19 See further below.

20 In the twentieth century, the case was argued afresh particularly by H. W. Wolff, *Jesaja 53 im Urchristentum* (2nd ed.; Berlin: Evangelische, 1950); J. Jeremias, *"pais theou," TDNT* 5:712–17 = with W. Zimmerli, *The Servant of God* (1957; rev. ed.; London: SCM Press, 1965), 99–106; O. Cullmann, *The Christology of the New Testament* (trans. Shirley C. Guthrie and Charles A. M. Hall; London: SCM Press, 1959), 60–69; P. Stuhlmacher, "Der messianische Gottesknecht," *JBTh* 8, *Der Messias* (1993): 144–50; also *Biblische Theologie des Neuen Testaments*. 1: *Grundlegung von Jesus zu Paulus* (Göttingen: Vandenhoeck & Ruprecht, 1992), 124, 127–30.

21 In English-speaking scholarship, M. Hooker's *Jesus and the Servant* (London: SPCK, 1959) was foreshadowed by C. F. D. Moule, "From Defendant to Judge—and Deliverer" (1952), *The Phenomenon of the New Testament* (London: SCM Press, 1967), 82–99, and quickly supported by C. K. Barrett, "The Background of Mark 10:45," in *New Testament Essays: Studies in Memory of T. W. Manson* (ed. A. J. B. Higgins; Manchester: Manchester University Press, 1959), 1–18. Hooker now accepts that Rom 4:25 contains a clear echo of Isaiah 53, but remains convinced that a negative answer still has to be given to the question, "Did the Use of Isaiah 53 to Interpret His Mission Begin with Jesus?" in *Jesus and the Suffering Servant: Isaiah 53 and Christian Origins* (eds. W. H. Bellinger and W. R. Farmer; Harrisburg: Trinity Press International, 1998), 88–103. In German scholarship, the influence of H. E. Tödt, *The Son of Man in the Synoptic Tradition* (London: SCM Press, 1965), 158–61, 167–69, 202–11; and F. Hahn, *Christologische Hoheitstitel* (1963; 5th ed.; Göttingen: Vandenhoeck & Ruprecht, 1995), 54–66, proved decisive for most of the following generation.

22 J. Nolland, *Luke* (WBC 35; Dallas: Word, 1993) refers particularly to "what is written" and "must be fulfilled in me" (3:1076–77).

23 B. Lindars, *New Testament Apologetic* (London: SCM Press, 1961), 85. The rationale of 22:37 is fulfilment/completion (*telesthênai, telos*); as an explanation of 22:36, 38, it is rather contrived with so much having to be read in, and still leaving the intent of 22:36 unclear.

24 J. A. Fitzmyer, *The Gospel according to Luke: Introduction, Translation and Notes* (2 vols.; AB 28A; Garden City, N.Y.: Doubleday, 1981–1985), 1432.

25 The challenge of Hooker, *Servant,* 74–79, and Barrett, "Mark 10:45," in particular, was against the claim that linguistic connections could be demonstrated between Mark 10:45 and Isaiah 53; see now also V. Hampel, *Menschensohn und historischer Jesus: Ein Ratselwort als Schlussel zum messianischen Selbstverstandnis Jesu* (Neukirchen-Vluyn: Neukirchener, 1990), 317–25, and Casey, *Aramaic Sources,* 211–13 (particularly on *lutron*).

26 It is less likely that Luke omitted Mark 10:45b for soteriological reasons; he does not avoid "ransom" language elsewhere—Luke 1:68; 2:38; 24:21; Acts 7:35 (Fitzmyer, *Luke,* 28A:1212). More likely, he knew the variant tradition and used/reworked it in preference to Mark 10:35-45.

27 Hampel, *Menschensohn,* 328–31.

28 The parallel was first noted by W. Grimm, *Die Verkündigung Jesu und Deuterojesaja* (2nd ed.; Frankfurt, 1981), 239–68, and has proved influential (see Hampel, *Menschensohn,* 326–33, and those cited by him in n. 453, including Hengel, *Atonement,* 49–50; also Stuhlmacher, *Biblische Theologie,* 1:121).

29 "Die feste Wendung haima ekchein enthält also keine direkte Anspielung auf Jes 53:12" (R. Pesch, *Markusevangelium* [Freiburg: Herder, 1977], 2:359).

30 J. Jeremias, "*polloi,*" *TDNT* 6:537–38; 53:11c, 12a (with article), 52:14; 53:12e (without article); once as an adjective (52:15).

31 See further my *Unity and Diversity in the New Testament* (1977; 2nd ed.; London: SCM Press, 1990), 165–67, and those cited there in n. 23; R. F. O'Toole, "Last Supper," *ABD* 4:234–41 (here 237–39); G. Theissen and A. Merz, *The Historical Jesus: A Comprehensive Guide* (London: SCM Press, 1998), 420–23.

32 "The blood of the covenant" (Exod 24:8; cf. Zech 9:11) is echoed in "my blood of the covenant" (Matt 26:28; Mark 14:24), but the Paul/Luke version "is scarcely any less of an allusion to the covenantal sacrifice of Exod 24:3-8 than the Marcan formula" (Fitzmyer, *Luke,* 28A:1391).

33 The Qumran community saw itself as participants in the "new covenant" (CD 6.19; 8.21; 19.33–34; 20.12; 1QpHab 2.3–6; cf. 1QSb [1Q28b] 3.26; 5.21–23).

34 The point does not depend on the presence of the word "new" (i.e., "new covenant"; only in the Paul/Luke version), though if early tradents did introduce it, they would no doubt have claimed that they were simply making explicit what was implicit.

35 We should not, however, play covenant-sacrifice and atoning-sacrifice against each other, since there was a tendency to run the two together, evident in the Targums (Pesch, *Markusevangelium,* 2:359), as also in

description of the Passover lamb as a sacrifice (1 Cor 5:7) (Hengel, *Atonement*, 46, 53–54).

36   "The Birth of a Metaphor: Baptized in Spirit," *ExpTim* 89 (1977–1978): 134–38, 173–75, reprinted in my *The Christ and the Spirit*, vol. 2, *Pneumatology* (Grand Rapids: Eerdmans, 1998), 103–17 (here 107–12); also *Jesus Remembered*, 366–69, 802–4, 808–9.

37   Cf. B. F. Meyer, *The Aims of Jesus* (London: SCM Press, 1979), 213; G. R. Beasley-Murray, *Jesus and the Kingdom of God* (Grand Rapids: Eerdmans, 1986), 250–52; R. Leivestad, *Jesus in His Own Perspective* (Minneapolis: Augsburg, 1987), 103.

38   *The Quest of the Historical Jesus* (1906; 2nd ed.; London: SCM Press, 2000), 347–49. N. T. Wright argues similarly in *Jesus and the Victory of God* (London: SPCK, 1996), 577–84, 609–10.

39   E.g., Matt 5:11-12/Luke 6:22-23; Matt 10:16/Luke 10:3; Mark 8:34-37 pars.; Matt 10:24-25.

40   Cf. the earlier argument of F. Hahn, *The Worship of the Early Church* (1970; ET Philadelphia: Fortress, 1973), 23–30.

41   Theissen and Merz, *Historical Jesus*, 432–36; similarly Ådna concludes that the death of Jesus "replaces and supersedes the sacrificial cult in the Temple once for all as the atoning death for the many" (*Jesu Stellung* 419–30 [here 429]; see also his "Jesus' Symbolic Act in the Temple (Mark 11:15-17): The Replacement of the Sacrifical Cult by his Atoning Death," in *Gemeinde ohne Tempel* (eds. B. Ego et al.; WUNT 118; Tübingen: Mohr Siebeck, 1999), 461–75.

42   Chilton's much repeated thesis, particularly in *The Temple of Jesus: His Sacrificial Program within a Cultural History of Sacrifice* (University Park: Pennsylvania State University Press, 1992), 150–54; and *Rabbi Jesus: An Intimate Biography* (New York: Doubleday, 2000), 253–55.

43   In the debate about the significance of Jesus' act occasioned by Sanders, *Jesus and Judaism* (London: SCM Press, 1985), 61–71, see R. Bauckham, "Jesus' Demonstration in the Temple," in *Law and Religion* (ed. B. Lindars; Cambridge: James Clarke, 1988), 72–89; C. A. Evans in B. Chilton and C. A. Evans, eds., *Jesus in Context: Temple, Purity and Restoration* (Leiden: Brill, 1997), 395–439; H. D. Betz, "Jesus and the Purity of the Temple (Mark 11:15-18): A Comparative Religion Approach," *JBL* 116 (1997): 455–72; P. M. Casey, "Culture and Historicity: The Cleansing of the Temple," *CBQ* 59 (1997): 306–32; K. H. Tan, *The Zion Traditions and the Aims of Jesus* (SNTSMS 91; Cambridge: Cambridge University Press, 1997), 166–81; Ådna, *Jesu Stellung*, 335–76.

44   E.g., Isa 4:4; Mal 3:1-3; *Pss. Sol.* 17:30.

45   The hope that the nations would finally acknowledge Yahweh and proselytize is deeply rooted in the Isaiah prophecies (Isa 2:2-4; 45:20-23;

56:6-8; 66:19-20, 23). Even Pss. Sol. 17 looks for "the nations to come from the ends of the earth to see his glory" (17:31). See further J. Jeremias, *Jesus' Promise to the Nations* (London: SCM Press, 1958), 56–62; T. L. Donaldson, "Proselytes or 'Righteous Gentiles'? The Status of Gentiles in Eschatological Pilgrimage Patterns of Thought," *JSP* 7 (1990): 3–27.

46 Both in Mark (Mark 13:2; Matt 24:2; Luke 21:6) and in Q material (Matt 23:38; Luke 13:35); also John 2:19 and *Gos. Thom.* 71. C. A. Evans summarizes the various premonitions and prophecies of the destruction of the Temple in "Jesus and Predictions of the Destruction of the Herodian Temple," in *Jesus and his Contemporaries: Comparative Studies* (Leiden: Brill, 1995), 367–80.

47 Tob 14:5; *Jub.* 1:15-17, 29; *1 En.* 90:28-29; 91:13; 11Q19 (11QTemple) 29.2-10; *T. Benj.* 9.2; *Sib. Or.* 3.294. See Sanders, *Jesus and Judaism*, 77–87; and further Ådna, *Jesu Stellung*, 25–89.

48 See particularly CD 3.12–4.12; *4QFlor.* 1.1-7; and further B. Gärtner, *The Temple and the Community in Qumran and the New Testament* (SNTSMS 1; Cambridge: Cambridge University Press, 1965), chs. 2 and 3; G. Klinzing, *Die Umdeutung des Kultus in der Qumrangemeinde und im Neue Testament* (Göttingen: Vandenhoeck & Ruprecht, 1971), 2. Teil.

49 Acts 3:1 could be translated, "Peter and John used to go into the temple at the hour of prayer, the ninth hour" (cf. 2:46).

50 E. P. Sanders, *Judaism: Practice and Belief, 63 BCE–66 CE* (London: SCM Press, 1992), 104–5.

51 It was paid for by the temple tax, which flowed in from all male Jews including those living in the Diaspora. These twice daily sacrifices were or included offerings on behalf of the nation and of Caesar, and it was the decision to abandon "the customary offering for their rulers" that laid the foundation for the first Jewish revolt (Josephus, *War* 2.197, 409–10).

52 Hengel, *Atonement*, 57; G. Schneider, *Apostelgeschichte* (Freiburg: Herder, 1980), 288–89, 299; cited approvingly by R. Pesch, *Apostelgeschichte* (EKK; Zürich: Benziger, 1986), 137.

53 C. K. Barrett, *Acts* (ICC; Edinburgh: T&T Clark, 1994), 178; J. A. Fitzmyer, *Acts of the Apostles: A New Translation and Commentary* (AB 31; New York: Doubleday, 1998), makes the obvious deduction from 2:46 that they frequented the temple together and shared in its prayers, sacrifices, and services; "even though they had been baptized as followers of the risen Christ, they continued to be exemplary Jews, seeing no contradiction in this" (272).

54 It may be argued that much of the sacrificial cult was not concerned with atonement, so that an atoning significance could have been attributed to Jesus' death without affecting participation in the rest of the cult (cf. R. Bauckham, "The Parting of the Ways: What Happened and Why," *ST*

47 [1993]: 135–51 [here 150–51 n. 37]; A. J. M. Wedderburn, *A History of the First Christians* [London: T&T Clark, 2004], 206 n. 54). But would such a sharp disjunction within the sacrificial cult have occurred among Jesus' followers? Not according to Luke (see on 21:23-24, 26 below).

55 M. Bockmuehl, *This Jesus: Martyr, Lord, Messiah* (Edinburgh: T&T Clark, 1994) 75 and 201–2 n. 50; J. Klawans, "Interpreting the Last Supper: Sacrifice, Spiritualization and Anti-Sacrifice," *NTS* 48 (2002): 1–12 (here 9–10). Contrast Hengel, who thinks it "probable that from the beginning the Jewish Christians adopted a fundamentally detached attitude to the cult" (*Atonement*, 56), but who ignores the evidence of 2:46 and 3:1 completely at this point.

56 See the discussion in Barrett, *Acts*, 11–13; Fitzmyer, *Acts*, 694; S. E. Porter, *The Paul of Acts* (WUNT 115; Tübingen: Mohr Siebeck, 1999), 180–82.

57 Cf. Hurtado, *Lord Jesus Christ*: "It is reasonable to suppose that the particular emphasis upon Jesus' death as atoning for sins that we find developed in Paul may not have been made in the early Jewish Christian setting" (186).

58 See Acts 2:23-24; 3:14-15; 4:10; 5:30; 8:32-33; 10:39-40; 13:28-30; on Luke 22:37 see above at n. 23.

59 J. Becker, *Jesus of Nazareth* (Berlin: de Gruyter, 1998), observes that "If Jesus had predicted the destruction of the temple or had pronounced God's judgment on Jerusalem, the earliest post-Easter church would probably have established itself in Galilee rather than in Jerusalem" (334).

60 *BDAG* 267; W. D. Davies and D. C. Allison, *A Critical and Exegetical Commentary on the Gospel according to Saint Matthew* (3 vols.; ICC 26; Edinburgh: T&T Clark, 1988), 1:516–17.

61 Hengel, *The "Hellenization" of Judaea*.

62 M. Hengel, *Between Jesus and Paul* (London: SCM Press, 1983), 11; and Fitzmyer, *Acts*, 347, both follow C. F. D. Moule, "Once More, Who Were the Hellenists?" *ExpTim* 70 (1958–1959): 100–102, on this point. Bibliography in J. Jervell, *Apostelgeschichte* (KEK; Göttingen: Vandenhoeck & Ruprecht, 1998), 216 n. 609.

63 See the Septuagint of Lev 26:1, 30; Isa 2:18; 10:11; 16:12; 19:1; 21:9; 31:7; 46:6; Dan 5:4, 23; 6:27; Judith 8:18; Wis 14:8.

64 Note the inclusion formed by Luke 1:8-23 and 24:53; similarly, the life of the earliest Jerusalem community is bracketed between Acts 2:46 and 5:42.

65 Cf. Hengel, *Atonement*, 49.

66 *Genesis,* ch. 3. His conclusion on 73 is relevant: "[T]he statements about the awakening or resurrection of Jesus are the oldest component parts of the more detailed extant formulae. It was only where the message of the

resurrection, through the contrast with the death on the cross, was thrown into relief as the resurrection from the dead that it became necessary to interpret the ignominious death of Jesus."

67 I am thinking particularly of Segal's *Paul the Convert*; and Hurtado's *Lord Jesus Christ*.

Chapter 11

1   I would like to thank Professor Hans Barstad, Dr. John Lyons, and members of the Edinburgh Biblical Studies Seminar for their help and comments on earlier versions or aspects of this paper. For a survey of patristic interpretations, see M. Aubineau, "Dossier patristique sur Jean, XIX, 23–24: la tunique sans couture du Christ," in *Bible et les pères* (Paris: Presses Univ. de France, 1971), 9–50; post-Renaissance interpretations can be found in I. De la Potterie, "La tunique sans couture, symbole du Christ grand prêtre?" *Bib* 60 (1979): 255–69 and in the notes below.

2   (Grand Rapids: Eerdmans, 2003), 350.

3   B. Lindars, *The Gospel of John* (Grand Rapids: Eerdmans, 1971), 573.

4   The hyssop (19:29), which seems an unsuitable plant with which to lift a wet sponge, may be a reference to the twigs of hyssop used to sprinkle doors of homes during Passover (Exod 12:22), and so a further link with the feast.

5   For an analysis of each of these, see E. D. Freed, *Old Testament Quotations in the Gospel of John* (Leiden: Brill, 1965), 99–116; and more generally J. Beutler, "The Use of 'Scripture' in the Gospel of John," in *Exploring the Gospel of John in Honor of D. Moody Smith* (eds. R. Alan Culpepper and C. Clifton Black; Louisville: Westminster John Knox, 1996), 147–62.

6   In the following discussion, I am assuming—along with the majority of scholars—that Jesus is now back in his own clothes rather than the purple cloak and crown of thorns given to him by the soldiers (19:2, 5), though John does not make this explicit.

7   A number of texts of Matt 27:35 cite the psalm, though they are in the minority; see B. M. Metzger, *A Textual Commentary on the Greek New Testament* (Stuttgart: UBS, 1971), 69. On John's use of parallelism here (which has affinities with Matt 21:2-5), see C. K. Barrett, *The Gospel According to St John* (2nd ed.; London: SPCK, 1978), 150, 550.

8   See, for example, R. Bultmann, *The Gospel of John: A Commentary* (trans. by G. R. Beasley-Murray, general editor, R. W. N. Hoare, and J. K. Riches; Philadelphia: Westminster, 1971), 671; B. Lindars, *Gospel*, 578; A. T. Lincoln, *The Gospel According to John* (London: Continuum, 2005), 476. The earliest patristic discussions similarly focused primarily on prophetic fulfillment, see Aubineau, "Dossier Patristique," 10–15.

9   See also 21:7: Does Peter clothe himself because greeting Jesus is a reli-
    gious act? See C. K. Barrett, *Gospel*, 580–81. On clothing generally in the
    ancient world, see D. R. Edwards, "Dress and Ornamentation," ABD
    2:232–38.

10 Brown, *John*, 2:920.

11 *Unit. eccl.* 7. As the collection of Aubineau makes clear, however, these
    Church fathers reflected the controversies of their time and used the
    seamless robe as a metaphor for their own day; they were not specifically
    offering exegeses of John 19:24, "Dossier patristique," 20–26.

12 Of particular influence in establishing this view is I. De la Potterie, "La
    tunique sans couture" and "La tunique 'non divisé' de Jésus, Symbole de
    l'unité messianique" in *The New Testament Age: Essays in Honor of B.
    Reike* (ed. W. C. Weinrich; 2 vols.; Macon, Ga.: Mercer University Press,
    1984), 1:127–38. See also E. C. Hoskyns, *The Fourth Gospel* (2nd ed.,
    rev. F. N. Davey; London: Faber & Faber, 1950), 529; R. H. Lightfoot,
    St. John's Gospel: A Commentary (Oxford: Clarendon, 1956), 315; and C.
    K. Barrett, *Gospel*, 550–51.

13 21:11 should perhaps be included here, too.

14 R. Schnackenburg, *The Gospel according to St John* (3 vols.; trans. Cecily
    Hastings; New York: Seabury Press, 1980), 3:274.

15 This is also the objection of R. Bultmann, *Gospel*, 671, n 2; and C. S.
    Keener, *The Gospel of John: A Commentary* (Peabody, Mass.:
    Hendrickson, 2003), 1140.

16 *Ev. Jo.* 118.4.

17 T. L. Brodie, *The Gospel According to John: A Literary and Theological
    Commentary* (Oxford: Oxford University Press, 1993), 547.

18 So also Schnackenburg, *Gospel*, 3:273; Barrett, *Gospel*, 551; D. A.
    Carson, *The Gospel According to John* (Grand Rapids: Eerdmans, 1991),
    615; and Keener, *Gospel*, 1140.

19 Schnackenburg, *Gospel*, 3:274; G. R. Beasley Murray, *John* (Waco, Tex.:
    Word Books, 1987), 347–48; Carson, *Gospel*, 614–15.

20 This particular view enjoyed its heyday in the early twentieth century:
    see, for example, B. F. Westcott, *The Gospel According to John* (London:
    John Murray, 1989), 275; G. H. C. MacGregor, *The Gospel of John*
    (London: Hodder & Stoughton, 1928), 346; and A. Guilding, *The
    Fourth Gospel and Jewish Worship* (Oxford: Clarendon, 1960), 169–70. It
    is raised as a possibility and discussed by Barrett, *Gospel*, 550–51; Brown,
    John, 2:920–22 (and *The Death of the Messiah: From Gethsemane to the
    Grave. A Commentary on the Passion Narratives in the Four Gospels* [2
    vols.; New York: Doubleday, 1994], 2:958); and Keener, *Gospel*,
    1140–41, to name but a few, though all ultimately prefer another solu-
    tion or (in the case of Brown) prefer to remain undecided.

21 This may already be apparent in Sir 50.1 (Heb), see C. T. R. Hayward
    who also lists a number of rabbinic writings which testify to this tradi-

tion (*The Jewish Temple: A Non-Biblical Sourcebook* [London: Routledge, 1996], 45–47).

22 45:6-13 (Heb); 50:5-11 (Gk). See Hayward, *Jewish Temple*, 38–84.

23 See Josephus, *Ant.* 15.405; 18.90–95, 122–25; for discussion of the chronological problems raised by these texts, see H. K. Bond, *Caiaphas: Friend of Rome and Judge of Jesus?* (Louisville: Westminster John Knox, 2004), 84–87.

24 *Mos.* 2.117–35; *Flight* 110–12; *Spec. Laws* 1.84–85, 93–96; and *QE* 2.107–24. Philo's, as might be expected, is the fullest allegory; he sees the high priestly robe as a symbol of the cosmos. For fuller discussions of the high priest in Philo's writings, see E. R. Goodenough, *By Light, Light: The Mystic Gospel of Hellenistic Judaism* (Amsterdam: Philo Press, 1969); and J. Laporte, "The High Priest in Philo of Alexandria," *SPhilo* 3 (1991): 71–82.

25 *b. Zebahim* 88a–b and *y. Yoma* 72b. On this phenomenon generally, see M. D. Swartz, "The Semiotics of the High Priestly Vestments in Ancient Judaism" in *Sacrifice in Religious Experience* (ed. A. Baumgarten; Leiden: Brill, 2002), 57–80. E. R. Goodenough notes a similar development in other religious movements of the day, *By Light,* 119.

26 Exod 28:6, 32; 35:35; 36:10, 12, 15, 29, 34; 37:3, 5, 21. Is the preposition ἄνωθεν a reference to the divinely inspired nature of the priestly robes?

27 *Ant.* 3.108, 132. (The word is also used at *Ant.* 3.57 to refer to the rich fabrics won from the Amalekites and *War* 7.438 of a weaver named "Jonathan.")

28 See *b. Zebahim* 88a and *b. Yoma* 72b.

29 So Isidore of Seville, *Quaes. in Vet. Test. Lev.* 12:4. The Greek words used in each case, however, are different: Lev 21:10 uses διαρρήγνυμι while John has σχίζω. The latter word is usually used, both in John and the New Testament generally, for dissention among people; interestingly, though, it is also used by all three Synoptic writers for the tearing of the temple curtain (Mark 15:38 and parallels; Mark and Matthew also use the word ἄνωθεν nearby), a tradition unknown or omitted by John.

30 The vestments are described in Exod 28:2-39; 39:1-30, Lev 8:9-9, *Let. Aris.* 96–99, *T. Levi 8.2*, Philo, *Mos.* 2.109–16, Josephus, *Ant.* 3.159–78, and *m. Yoma* 7.5. There are also two pictorial representations of the vestments, one from a synagogue at Sepphoris, the other from Dura Europos (for details, see Swartz, "Semiotics," 63–64, n. 16). The Exodus texts add a ninth garment (an outer chequered coat) that disappears in later literature; perhaps this item had fallen out of use by the Second Temple period.

31 Exod 28:31-35 does not specifically say that this robe was seamless, though the brief description does not preclude the possibility. The priestly and aristocratic background of Josephus makes it highly likely that his information is historically reliable (as does the fact that he does

not try to make any theological point out of the seamlessness of the robe). See the discussion by C. Houtman, *Exodus* (3 vols.; Kampen: Kok Pharos, 1993–2000), 3:308.

32 Used by Exod 29:5 (ὑποδύτην ποδήρη), Philo, *Mos.* 2.109, 110, 117; *QE* 2.117.

33 Used by Exod 29:5; Wis 18:24; *T. Levi* 8.2; Philo, *Spec. Laws* 1.85, 93, 94, *Alleg. Interp.* 2.56; and Josephus, *War* 5.231.

34 Used by Philo, *QE* 2.117.

35 This robe is also cited by Barrett, *Gospel*, 550, though he ultimately rejects any link with high priestly vestments.

36 Philo, *QE* 2.107, also *Drunkenness,* 85–87.

37 De la Potterie, in my view, expects too high a level of precision among ancient witnesses and is, therefore, too quick to reject the link between the χιτών and high priestly vestments ("La tunique sans couture," esp. 259–66). The fact that there is no unanimity regarding the names of these garments, let alone their symbolic functions, should alert us to a certain fluidity in the tradition.

38 For discussion of these passages, see M. C. de Boer, *Johannine Perspectives on the Death of Jesus* (Kampen: Kok Pharos, 1996), 219–309, esp. 296–98. This theme is made much more explicit in the epistles, especially 1 John 1:7-9; 2:1-2, and 4:10.

39 De la Potterie, "La tunique sans couture," 256.

40 On the relationship of the gospel, 1 John, and Revelation, see Keener, *Gospel*, 122–39.

41 The connection is dismissed by, for example, Schnackenburg, *Gospel*, 3.274; Lincoln, *Gospel*, 476; and Carson, *Gospel*, 614.

42 Lindars, *Gospel*, 578.

43 Hebrews 2:17; 3:1; 4:14–5:10; 6:20–8:4; 9:11; 10:21; 13:11.

44 Although unlikely to be historical, the contention of Polycrates of Ephesus that "John wore the mitre" (Eusebius, *Hist. eccl.* 5.24) is an accurate reflection of the fourth evangelist's intense interest in the Jewish cultic year.

45 See also Brown, *John*, 1:141 who cites 1 Cor 12:12-27.

46 Zechariah 14:20-21 may have been influential here.

47 Schnackenburg, *Gospel*, 1:356.

48 S. Motyer, "The Fourth Gospel and the Salvation of Israel: An Appeal for a New Start" in *Anti-Judaism and the Fourth Gospel* (eds. R. Bieringer, D. Pollefeyt, and F. Vandecasteele-Vanneuville; Louisville: Westminster John Knox, 2001), 83–100, here 90–91.

49 C. H. Talbert, *Reading John: A Literary and Theological Commentary on the Fourth Gospel and the Johannine Epistles* (London: SPCK, 1992), 93.

50 Motyer, "Fourth Gospel," 90.

51 For a literary reading of 11:47-53 (the meeting of the council) and 18:19-24 (the hearing in front of Annas), in which I suggest that John deliber-

ately contrasts Jesus with the high priestly leaders, see Bond, *Caiaphas*, 131–38; see also J. P. Heil, "Jesus as the Unique High Priest in the Gospel of John," *CBQ* 57 (1995): 729–45; and B. Escaffre, "Pierre et Jesus dans la cour du grand prêtre (Jn 18, 12–27)," *RTL* 31 (2000): 43–67.

52   *Ant* 3.214–18; see also *m. Sotah* 33a, *m. Yoma* 53b. For discussion see Bond, *Caiaphas*, 172, n. 20.

53   The word ἁγιάζω used in this verse can be used of the sanctification of priests (Exod 28:41; 29:1, 22) and of sacrifices (Exod 28:38, Num 18:9). On the history of interpretation of John 17, see M. Edwards, *John* (Oxford: Blackwell, 2004), 156–62. While modern scholars are right to eschew the title "high priestly prayer" for the entire chapter, it would be unwise to ignore the clear intercessory tone of parts of it.

54   J. Klawans, *Purity, Sacrifice, and the Temple: Symbolism and Supersession- ism in the Study of Ancient Judaism* (Oxford: Oxford University Press, 2006), 218–21; also P. Fredriksen, *Jesus of Nazareth: King of the Jews* (New York: Vintage, 2000), 36–38.

55   Brown suggests that the antitemple passages come from a group (possi- bly Hellenists from Palestine) who joined the Johannine community at a relatively early stage, see *The Community of the Beloved Disciple* (New York: Paulist Press, 1979), 34–54. An early assimilation of such views, however, does not adequately explain why the evangelist should still be so preoccupied by Jewish cultic observance in the late first century.

56   See, for example, Matt 5:23-24; 23:21. Acts, too, allows traditional wor- ship for Jewish Christians as long as the temple stands: 3:1; 21:23-24; 22:17; 24:18.

57   Brown, *Community*, 39, 56–57; Schnackenburg, *Gospel*, 1:152; and G. M. Burge, "Situating John's Gospel in History" in *Jesus in Johannine Tradition* (eds. R. T. Fortna and T. Thatcher; Louisville: Westminster John Knox, 2001), 35–46.

58   Motyer also links the Fourth Gospel's interest in the temple and Jesus as the replacement of Jewish feasts with the fall of the temple, "Fourth Gospel."

59   On the development of oral traditions in response to present concerns, see J. Dewey, "The Gospel of John in its Oral-Written Media World" in Fortna and Thatcher, *Jesus in Johannine Tradition*, 239–52.

60   For a similar argument, see R. Bauckham, "The Parting of the Ways," 135–51.

61   It is highly likely that the gospel underwent several revisions before it reached its present state, though I am not so confident as some that these are recoverable. See discussions in Brown, *John*, 1:xxxiv–xxxix; Lindars, *Gospel*, 46–54; and J. Ashton, *Understanding the Fourth Gospel* (Oxford: Clarendon, 1991), 199–204. What is more interesting is that the evangelist or compositors of the gospel chose to leave different inter- pretations of Jesus side by side in the final product.

Chapter 12

1 An earlier form of this essay was given as a presentation at the 2005 SBL annual meeting, the "John, Jesus and History" program-unit, November 20, 2005. I am pleased to offer it now in tribute to my friend Alan Segal. In light of his informed and fair handling of matters of religious experience (e.g., his justifiably well-received book on Paul), I hope that this modest investigation will be an appropriate contribution to this volume honoring him.

2 To avoid confusion, when referring to the texts of gospels (as distinct from putative authors), I attach a capital "G". So, e.g., GMatthew = Gospel of Matthew, and GJohn = Gospel of John. For what it is worth, as someone interested in ancient manuscripts, in which the order of the four Gospels varies, I am not comfortable with "Fourth Gospel" for GJohn, e.g., in Codex W (and quite likely also in p^{45}, the order of the four Gospels is GMatthew, GJohn, GLuke, GMark).

3 I do not have space to explicate further this claim or to defend it. In *Lord Jesus Christ*, ch. 5 ("Jesus Books"), I have probed the historical significance of the narrative-gospel genre as a literary expression of devotion to Jesus.

4 Michael O. Wise, "Languages of Palestine," *DJG*, 434–44, points to some thirty instances of the use of Semitic loanwords in the intracanonical gospels, most of these involving Aramaic.

5 In addition to instances cited above, note, e.g., "Messiah" (John 1:41), "Cephas" (1:42), "Bethzatha" (5:2), "Gabbatha" (19:13), "Golgotha" (19:17).

6 As is known, especially among Johannine scholars, the classic study of this is C. H. Dodd, *Historical Tradition in the Fourth Gospel* (Cambridge: Cambridge University Press, 1976).

7 Note, e.g., how the risen "Jesus" who appears to the disciples in 20:19-29 is acclaimed also as "my Lord and my God" by Thomas in 20:28.

8 See, e.g., the balanced and discerning discussion by Marianne Meye Thompson, "The Historical Jesus and the Johannine Christ," in R. Alan Culpepper and Black, *Exploring the Gospel of John* (Louisville: Westminster John Knox, 1996), 21–42.

9 After forming this judgment, I was encouraged to find that the point had been registered previously by John Painter in his major paper, "The Interface of History and Theology in John: John and the Historical Jesus" (SBL Consultation on The Gospel of John and the Historical Jesus, November 2004), 31: "Of the four Gospels, only John explicitly makes clear the epistemological distance/difference between the time of Jesus' ministry and the post-resurrection period in which the Gospel was self-consciously written (see 2:22; 7:39; 12:16; 16:7, 13-16)."

10 J. Louis Martyn, *History and Theology in the Fourth Gospel* (rev. ed.; Nashville: Abingdon, 1979 [original ed., 1968]).

11   Martyn, *History and Theology*, esp. 37–62.

12   E.g., Martyn, *History and Theology*, 129.

13   For ὡς μονογενοῦς παρὰ πατρός, cf., e.g., the NRSV: "as of a father's only son" (although "the Father's only Son" is given in the marginal notes as an alternative).

14   It is likely, though somewhat less obvious, that in 2:17, also, the disciples' "remembering" of Ps 69:10 in connection with his clearing of the temple court is a cognition that is placed in the postresurrection period. The two incidents that I treat here will do, however, to make the point.

15   So also, e.g., Schnackenburg, *Gospel*, 3:161–62.

16   Ron Cameron, *Sayings Traditions in the Apocryphon of James* (HTS 34; Philadelphia: Fortress, 1984), 118–19, also 130.

17   Schnackenburg, *Gospel*, 3:162.

18   One could perhaps argue that GLuke in its own way also makes explicit such a contrast, especially in the scenes where the risen Jesus opens the disciples' eyes to the scriptures' manifold testimony to him and his glory (Luke 24:25-27, 31-32, 44-49), and even criticizes their prior understanding as "slow of heart to believe all that the prophets have declared" (24:25). But it seems to me that the contrast in GJohn is more frequently deployed.

19   Among earlier studies still very instructive, I mention Heinrich Schlier, "Zum Begriff des Geistes nach dem Johannesevangelium," in his collection of essays, *Besinnung auf das Neue Testament: Exegetische Aufsätze und Vortäge*, II (Freiburg: Herder, 1964), 264–71. More recently, there is the extensive discussion by Hans-Christian Kammler, "Jesus Christus und der Geistparaklet: Eine Studie zur johanneischen Verhältnisbestimmung von Pneumatologie und Christologie," in *Johannesstudien: Untersuchungen zur Theologie des vierten Evangeliums* (eds. Otfried Hofius and Hans-Christian Kammler; WUNT 88; Tübingen: J.C.B. Mohr [Paul Siebeck], 1996), 87–190, which includes interaction with a large body of scholarly publications. These and other studies, however, have foci different from mine in this essay.

20   See, e.g., the excursus in Schnackenburg, *Gospel*, 3:138–54, for a review of various issues and further bibliographical references.

21   Of course, the sayings in Luke 12:11-12 and Matt 10:19-20 may have been part of the "Q" collection. See now, e.g., James M. Robinson, Paul Hoffmann, John S. Kloppenborg, *The Critical Edition of Q* (Minneapolis: Fortress, 2000), 312–17. Cf. Luke 21:12-15, in the Lukan version of the eschatological discourse, Jesus promises that he "will give you words and a wisdom that none of your opponents will be able to withstand or contradict." The Matthean 24 parallel to Mark 13 has no equivalent saying.

22   From the classic essays by Hans Windisch onward (translated as a booklet, *The Spirit-Paraclete in the Fourth Gospel* [Philadelphia: Fortress, Facet

Books, 1968; German originals, 1927, 1933]), the references to the Paraclete have received considerable attention. E.g., Raymond E. Brown, "The Paraclete in the Fourth Gospel," *NTS* 13 (1966–1967): 113–32; George Johnston, *The Spirit-Paraclete in the Gospel of John* (SNTSMS, 12; Cambridge: Cambridge University Press, 1970); and now Tricia Gates Brown, *Spirit in the Writings of John: Johannine Pneumatology in Social-Scientific Perspective* (JSNTSup253; London: T&T Clark, 2003), esp. 170–234. The dominant questions, however, have often been the derivation of the term *Paraklētos* and the tradition/redactional history of the sayings. These matters do not concern us here. Kammler's recent study focuses more on the relationship between Jesus and the Spirit in GJohn, and he includes a close exegetical study of the particular sayings ("Jesus Christus und der Geist-Paraklet").

23 Barrett, *Gospel*, 467, notes the variant reading in D, ἂν εἴπω, instead of εἴπον, and judges that it "gives an entirely different meaning to the work of the Paraclete, who (according to this reading) receives fresh teaching from Jesus and transmits it to the church . . . contrary to the meaning of the passage as a whole." To be sure, the D variant does place the emphasis on the Spirit as agency of a continuing communication from Jesus. But this is not, in my view, totally at variance with how GJohn presents the Spirit's work. As to the text-critical question, however, I concur with the reading preferred, e.g., in the Nestle-Aland text here.

24 I suggest that ἐν τῷ ὀνόματί μου here alludes to the cultic practice of invoking Jesus by name, which we know characterized early Christian baptismal practice, exorcisim, and, perhaps most characteristically featured in the worship setting. See, e.g., Hurtado, *Lord Jesus Christ*, 140–44, and other bibliographical references cited there. I further contend that corporate worship was a characteristic setting for prophecy and other revelatory phenomena (e.g., 1 Cor 14:26), i.e., a setting in which the Spirit-Paraclete would be expected to bestow revelations of Jesus' glory.

25 "The Paraclete accuses and exposes the world and proves it guilty only by means of the community [of Jesus' followers], and the community also requires faith in the Paraclete and the support of the Paraclete in order to fulfil that task." Schnackenburg, *Gospel*, 3:132.

26 The masculine pronoun used of the Paraclete here I intend simply to reflect the personal quality that is implicitly attached to the Spirit-Paraclete in the farewell discourse material. As numerous commentators note, this personal quality even seems reflected in the grammar of this passage, in the masculine pronoun (ἐκεῖνος) used in apposition with the neuter τὸ πνεῦμα (v. 13).

27 I take τὰ ἐρχόμενα to refer primarily to eschatological/future events, which the Spirit reveals in prophetic oracles. So, to my mind, Rev.1:19,

where "things which are and things which are to be" reflects the sort of religious "micro-climate" in which revelations of religious truths and of future events are accepted matters of prophetic oracles. Cf. Schnackenburg, *Gospel* , 3:151.

28 E.g., Schnackenburg, *Gospel*, 3:132–37. He grants that "the Paraclete is not only [Jesus'] interpreter, but also his 'successor,' who will continue his revelation" (133), and that this involves "a more profound penetration into the content of revelation" (135). Yet he then insists that the Paraclete will not "proclaim anything with new content" (135). Similarly, Brown, *John*, 2:714–17, takes John 15:15 as excluding further revelations, and prefers to see 16:12-15 as promising "deeper understanding," judging it "unlikely that in Johannine thought there was any concept of further revelation after the ministry of Jesus, for Jesus is the revelation of the Father, the Word of God" (714).

29 Ernst Haenchen, *John 2: A Commentary on the Gospel of John, Chapters 7–21* (Hermeneia; Philadelphia: Fortress, 1984), 144.

30 So also Brown, *Spirit in the Writings of John*, 210, and others she cites (n. 56); and Kammler, "Jesus Christus und der Geistparaklet," e.g., 140.

31 In this sense I judge Haenchen right in stating: "In any case, the church, in fact, took the Easter message and not the preaching of Jesus of Nazareth as the basis of its own proclamation and teaching. And perhaps one may say that it is precisely the Fourth Gospel that confirms the church in that move" (*John 2*, 144).

32 Schnackenburg, *Gospel*, 3:152.

33 I use the scare-quotes here to indicate an open attitude toward exactly who the intended readers of GJohn were and what Christians might be reflected in the text. I am confident that GJohn reflects some early Christians, but I am not so sure that they comprised a totally distinct circle over against all other Christian groups of the time. Then as now, Christian groups can be distinguishable and distinctive without being separatist and sectarian. But the issue cannot be engaged adequately here.

34 As I have argued in previous publications, one does not have to accept the religious validity of such experiences to recognize their historical reality and efficacy in contributing to religious innovation. See esp. Hurtado, "Religious Experience," 183–205, which appears now also in my book, *How on Earth*, ch. 8. For a sympathetic treatment of such phenomena in the NT, see esp. Dunn, *Jesus and the Spirit*.

35 David E. Aune, *Prophecy in Early Christianity and the Ancient Mediterranean World* (Grand Rapids: Eerdmans, 1983).

36 It is curious, and reveals perhaps more about the scholars in question than about GJohn, that a good many include no treatment of such religious phenomena in accounting for the text. Even among those whose religious orientation is favourable to GJohn this is the case. See, e.g., Craig L. Blomberg, *The Historical Reliability of John's Gospel* (Downers

Grove: InterVarsity, 2001), esp. 17–67, where he offers an account of how GJohn came to have its distinctive qualities.

37   Aune, *Prophecy in Early Christianity*, 339–36; and idem., "Charismatic Exegesis in Early Judaism and Early Christianity," in *The Pseudepigrapha and Early Biblical Interpretation* (eds. James H. Charlesworth and Craig A. Evans; Sheffield: Sheffield Academic, 1993), 126–50.

38   Johannes Beutler, "The Use of 'Scripture' in the Gospel of John," in Culpepper and Black, *Exploring the Gospel of John*, 147–62, noted that the words of Jesus had "a comparable authority" to scripture for the author of GJohn (154), pointing to 2:22, where both are linked explicitly as the focus in postresurrection insights.

39   E.g., Dodd, *Historical Tradition*, 315–65.

40   In preparing this revised version of my essay, I was encouraged to discover a somewhat similar contention by Otfried Hofius, "'Unknown Sayings of Jesus'," in *The Gospel and the Gospels* (ed. Peter Stuhlmacher; Grand Rapids: Eerdmans, 1991 [German: 1983]), 359–60, n. 132 (336–60): "The sayings and discourses of Jesus contained in [GJohn] are in no way intended to be primarily understood as pronouncements of the earthly Jesus. . . . When the evangelist offers his witness to Christ in the form of sayings and discourses of Jesus, he thereby brings to expression the idea that the apostolic witness to Christ does not constitute a human value-judgment about Christ. The witness can only utter what the Lord who is present in the Spirit has disclosed to him. . . ." See a similar view in Franz Mussner, *The Historical Jesus in the Gospel of St. John* (trans. W. J. O'Hara; London: Burns & Oates, 1967 [German edition: 1965]), e.g., 52, 63.

41   Note, e.g., Acts 9:10-16, where the risen Jesus ("the Lord") speaks in a vision to Ananias. I take Paul's reference to a word from Jesus in 2 Cor 12:9 in light of the references in the context to frequent "visions and revelations of the Lord" (12:1, 7).

42   I cannot linger here over the question of how much Revelation reflects actual visions and how much it is simply a literary work. Even if strongly the latter, it reflects and was intended to commend itself to early Christian readiness to entertain such claims of prophetic revelation.

43   Each of the seven messages has an opening statement ascribing it to Jesus (2:1, 8, 12, 18; 3:1, 7, 14), and each concludes with a statement ascribing it to the Spirit (2:7, 11, 17, 29; 3:6, 13, 22).

44   See also Peter Stuhlmacher, "Spiritual Remembering: John 14:26," in *The Holy Spirit and Christian Origins: Essays in Honor of James D. G. Dunn* (eds. Graham N. Stanton, Bruce W. Longenecker, and Stephen C. Barton; Grand Rapids: Eerdmans, 2004), 55–68. Stuhlmacher's essay, however, differs from my own in being more concerned with the usefulness of the way GJohn handles Jesus tradition for historical Jesus investigation.

45 A fourth word, ἀναμιμνῄσκω, does not appear in GJohn, but is used in Mark (11:21; 14:72), and several other NT writings (1 Cor 4:17; 2 Cor 7:15; 2 Tim 1:6; Heb 10:32). In both Markan uses, it refers to Peter remembering a saying of Jesus (about Peter's betrayal of him, or Jesus' cursing of the fig tree) in light of subsequent events.

46 See, e.g., Otto Michel, "μιμνῄσκομαι, κτλ.," *TDNT* 4:675–83; K. H. Bartels, "Remember," *NIDNTT* 3:230–47. According to the *Computer Concordance to the Novum Testamentum Graece* (Berlin/New York: de Gruyter, 1985), μιμνῄσκομαι appears in the NT twenty-three times in all, μνημονεύω twenty-one times, ὑπομιμνῄσκω seven times, and ἀναμιμνῄσκω six times.

47 Brown, *John*, 2:651, agrees with Rudolf Bultmann, *Das Evangelium des Johannes* (Göttingen: Vandenhoeck & Ruprecht, 1941), 485; ET, *The Gospel of John: A Commentary* (trans. G. R. Beasley-Murray; Philadelphia: Westminster/Oxford: Basil Blackwell, 1971), 626 n. 6.

48 Cf. Schnackenburg, *Gospel*, 3:83; Haenchen, *John 2: A Commentary*, 128.

49 Cf. Brown, *John*, 1:115, who leaves the question open; Barrett, *Gospel*, 198, who sees this remembering as "at the time" of Jesus' action; and Bultmann, *The Gospel of John*, 124, who reads v. 17 in light of v. 22 and 12:16, taking their recall of the Psalm as a later (postresurrection) cognition.

50 If we take τῇ γραφῇ in v. 22 as Ps 69(68):10 (the only scripture passage cited in the larger context), then the christological understanding of it posited in v. 17 would be a postresurrection cognition.

51 In the immediate context (15:18-21), there are warnings and exhortations to Jesus' followers about being hated by the world for their faith in him, and being rejected by the world, just as Jesus was rejected. And, of course, only a few verses later we have one of the Spirit-Paraclete sayings that we have noted earlier in this essay (15:26-27).

52 So also, e.g., Brown, *John*, 2:702.

53 There is an English translation in Edgar Hennecke and Wilhelm Schneemelcher, *New Testament Apocrypha* (rev. ed.; trans. R. McL. Wilson; Louisville: Westminster John Knox/Cambridge: James Clarke, 1992), 380–85. For the Greek text of *Acts of Thomas*, see Maximilian Bonnet, *Acta Apostolorum Apocrypha: Acta Philippi et Acta Thomae accedunt Acta Barnabae* (reprint; Hildesheim/New York: Georg Olms Verlag, 1972 [1903]), 99–288. The "Hymn of the Pearl" forms chs. 108–13.

54 I write the word "gnostic" in scare-quotes in acknowledgment of the force of Michael Williams's argument about the dubious value of the term as a historical descriptor: *Rethinking "Gnosticism": An Argument for Dismantling a Dubious Category* (Princeton: Princeton University Press, 1996).

55 Ron Cameron, *Sayings Traditions in the Apocryphon of James* (Philadelphia: Fortress, 1984), esp. 91–124. Cf. also the incisive discus-

sion of this matter in Charles E. Hill, *The Johannine Corpus in the Early Church* (Oxford: Oxford University Press, 2004), 250–58.

56 I cite here from the translation of *Ap. Jas.* by Francis E. Williams in *The Nag Hammadi Library in English* (rev. ed.; ed. James M. Robinson; Leiden/New York: Brill, 1988), 29–37, here 30.

57 Cameron, *Sayings Traditions*, 116–24.

58 Cameron, *Sayings Traditions*, 119. Cameron rightly notes that it is significant that GJohn offers a "life" of the historic Jesus, and that *Ap. Jas.* does not. But he seems to me to miss the import of this.

59 I fear, thus, that Cameron (*Sayings Traditions*, 120) may overemphasize a supposedly intended continuity in *Ap.Jas.* with the teaching of the earthly Jesus.

60 E.g., Windisch, *The Spirit-Paraclete*, 12, GJohn is "the Gospel inspired by the Paraclete for the mature who have done away with their immaturity. . . ."

61 The expression appears in a passage purporting to give tradition about the gospels from Clement in Eusebius, *Hist. eccl.* 6.14.7.

Chapter 13

1 Bultmann, *Theology of the New Testament*, 2:70–74.

2 Bultmann, *The Gospel of John: A Commentary* (ET Philadelphia: Westminster, 1971), 696.

3 Cited in Hermann Diels, *Die Fragmente der Vorsokratiker, griechisch und deutsch* (3 vols.; ed. Walther Kranz; Zurich and Berlin: Weidmann, 1964), 22B frg. 101a; English translation given as, "The eyes are more exact witnesses than ears" in Kathleen Freeman, *Ancilla to the pre-Socratic Philosophers: A Complete Translation of the Fragments in Diels, Fragmente der Vorsokratiker* (repr.; Cambridge, Mass: Harvard University Press 1983), 131. To be sure, Heraclitus also claims, "Eyes and ears are poor witnesses for human beings having barbarian souls," cited in Diels-Kranz, 22B frg. 107. (I have standardized the spelling of Heraclitus throughout the essay.)

4 Unless otherwise noted, all English translations from classical literature are taken from the Loeb Classical Library.

5 For similar views in Josephus, see *Apion* 1.55; *Wars* 1.1, 3, 22.

6 Note also the possible contrast in John 8:38: "I speak of what I have seen with my Father, and you do what you have heard from your father."

7 See the discussion in Hurtado, *Lord Jesus Christ*, esp. 374–81; and Segal, *Paul the Convert*, 52–53. See also Bockmuehl, " 'The Form of God'," 8–11.

8 In my *The God of the Gospel of John* (Grand Rapids: Eerdmans, 2001), 110–17, I have argued this case at greater length.

9 See the remarks of Samuel Byrskog, *Story as History, History as Story: The Gospel Tradition in the Context of Ancient Oral History* (Boston: Brill, 2002), 146–76, on "The Eyewitness as Interpreter."

10 See the discussion in his *Lord Jesus Christ*, esp. 374–81.

11 Hurtado, *Lord Jesus Christ*, 380.

12 As does a similar word of judgment in Deut 29:2-4: "And Moses summoned all Israel and said to them: 'You have seen all that the LORD did before your eyes in the land of Egypt, to Pharaoh and to all his servants and to all his land, the great trials which your eyes saw, the signs, and those great wonders; but to this day the LORD has not given you a mind to understand, or eyes to see, or ears to hear.'"

13 See here also Andrew Lincoln, *Truth on Trial: The Lawsuit Motif in the Fourth Gospel* (Peabody, Mass.: Hendrickson, 2000), who comments that Jesus, as Son of Man, "is in effect the sole eyewitness of that which is above, the heavenly world," and that it is Jesus' heavenly origin that "qualifies him to be the chief witness in the trial between God and the world" (68, 71).

14 At this point, Hurtado (*Lord Jesus Christ*, 420–22) offers a further intriguing suggestion regarding the secessionists in 1 John. Noting that they may have taken the assertion that "no one has ever seen God" (1:18) to underscore God's transcendence and subsequent inaccessibility to human sense perception, Hurtado argues that they may have seen Jesus as a "mystical exemplar," whose heavenly origins and spiritual status they shared. Claims to have fellowship with God (1:6), to know God (2:4), to abide in God (2:6), and to be in the light (1:7) reflect mystical experiences of enlightenment attainable by those who shared Jesus' mystical experiences. Hurtado thus suggests how the Gospel's emphasis on Jesus' unique vision of God might have figured into the secessionists' christological deviations. One could further observe, as indeed Hurtado does, that in the book of Revelation, the faithful witness (*martyria*) of Jesus serves as an example to be imitated by his followers.

15 John uses the term εἶδος, whereas the LXX of Deut 4:12 uses ὁμοίωμα. As Markus Bockmuehl notes, "[T]he great mystical passages in the Bible and in later Judaism are almost exclusively visual in character" ("'The Form of God'," 14).

16 Segal, *Paul the Convert*, 52–53.

17 *Neofiti* has "they saw the Glory of the Shekinah of the Lord," and *Ps. Jon.* specifies that Nadab and Abihu of the seventy, apparently excluding Moses, "saw the glory of the God of Israel."

18 *Neofiti* asserts that what Moses will be allowed to see is "the Dibbera of the Glory of Shekinah," but what it is not possible for Moses to see is "the face of the Glory of my Shekinah."

19 *Tg. Ps.-Jon.* is nearly identical at this point. *Tg. Neofiti* has "[T]hey have heard that you are he, the Glory of whose Shekinah is in the midst of this people; that appearance to appearance, you have been revealed in your Memra, O Lord, and the cloud of the Glory of your Shekinah was upon them."

20 For discussions of Philo on "seeing God," see Ellen Birnbaum, *The Place of Judaism in Philo's Thought: Israel, Jews, and Proselytes* (Brown Judaic Studies 20; Studia Philonica Monographs 2; Atlanta: Scholars Press, 1996), 61–127; Markus Bockmuehl, *Revelation and Mystery in Ancient Judaism and Pauline Christianity* (WUNT 2.36; Tübingen: J.C.B. Mohr [Paul Siebeck], 1990), 69–75; Donald A. Hagner, "The Vision of God in Philo and John: A Comparative Study," *JETS* 14 (1971): 81–93; H. A. Wolfson, *Philo: Foundations of Religions Philosophy in Judaism, Christianity, and Islam* (vol. 2; Cambridge, Mass.: Harvard University Press, 1948), 1–11; Segal, *Paul the Convert*, 38–56.

21 Philo explained Israel etymologically as "the one who sees God." For a discussion of this etymology in Philo, see Birnbaum, *The Place of Judaism*, 70–77. While John does not refer to this etymology, note that Nathanael is called a "true Israelite" who will "see the heavens opened" (1:47–51).

22 See Talbert, *Reading John*, 98.

23 See Wayne Meeks, *The Prophet-King: Moses Traditions and the Johannine Christology* (Leiden: Brill, 1967), 122–31.

24 Attributed to R. Jose, *Mekhilta de Rabbi Ishmael* (trans. J. Z. Lautenbach; vol. 2; Philadelphia: Jewish Publication Society of America, 1976), 224.

25 Cited in Eusebius, *Hist. eccl.*. 5.20.6.

26 While the gospel asserts the Beloved Disciple was present at some of the events of Jesus' life, it does not imply that he "saw" them all. He has, however, been with and known Jesus; therefore, he may bear truthful testimony to him.

Chapter 14

1 Although my indebtedness to the scholarship of both Alan Segal and Larry Hurtado is apparent in the footnotes of my previous writing, with this essay I express my sincere thankfulness for their kind friendship since being introduced by Jarl Fossum in 1991. The subject matter and methodology of this article reflect, in a small manner, some of the interests of these esteemed "founding fathers" of the EHCC.

2 *The Theology of the Book of Revelation* (Cambridge: Cambridge University, 1993), 74.

3 The lion imagery echoes Numbers 23:24, Micah 5:8, and Genesis 49:9 (cf. *4 Ezra* 11:37–12:3). For a discussion of the religio-historical background for the depictions of Christ as a man in Revelation, see Gieschen, *Angelomorphic Christology*, 245–69.

4 Against those who understand apocalyptic literature as solely an exegetical process of creating an experience for the reader through the construction of a text, Alan Segal has encouraged scholars to consider how this literature reflects the actual visionary experiences of those writing, or of

those influencing the writing of these documents. My point here is similar. I will argue that the mystical experience of Christ as the Lamb in Eucharistic worship played a role in why John would have such a visionary experience as well as played a role in the ability of early hearers to understand the depiction of Christ as the Lamb; see also Charles A. Gieschen, "Sacramental Theology in the Book of Revelation," *CTQ* 67 (2003): 149–74.

5 The classic study of the Christology of Revelation is Traugott Holtz, *Die Christologie der Apokalypse des Johannes* (2nd ed.; TU 85; Berlin: Akademie-Verlag, 1971). Richard Bauckham has also done fine work on this topic; see *Theology of the Book of Revelation*, 54–108, and *The Climax of Prophecy: Studies on the Book of Revelation* (Edinburgh: T&T Clark, 1993), esp. 118–49 and 174–98. For a brief summary of scholarly approaches to the Christology of Revelation, see Loren T. Stuckenbruck, *Angel Veneration and Christology: A Study in Early Judaism and in the Christology of the Apocalypse of John* (WUNT II.70; Tübingen: Mohr Siebeck, 1995), 22–43.

6 For lamb Christology, see Loren L. Johns, *The Lamb Christology of the Apocalypse of John: An Investigation into Its Origins and Rhetorical Force* (WUNT II.167; Tübingen: Mohr Siebeck, 2003). Although various labels could be given to the glorified man traditions in Revelation, I have previously used "angelomorphic Christology" nomenclature, as have others. For example: Gieschen, *Angelomorphic Christology*, 245–60; Stuckenbruck, *Angel Veneration and Christology*, 271–72; Robert Gundry, "Angelomorphic Christology in the Book of Revelation," *SBLSP* 33 (1994); 662–78; and Peter R. Carrell, *Jesus and the Angels: Angelology and Christology of the Apocalypse of John* (SNTSMS 95; Cambridge: Cambridge University Press, 1997).

7 Find examples in Gieschen, *Angelomorphic Christology,* 51–123. In other theophanic traditions, YHWH appears in the form of fire or a cloud.

8 For the importance of enthronement in early expressions of Christology: Richard Bauckham, "The Throne of God and the Worship of Jesus," in Newman, Davila, and Lewis, *The Jewish Roots,* 43–69; Martin Hengel, "Sit at My Right Hand! The Enthronement of Christ at the Right Hand of God and Psalm 110:1," in *Studies in Early Christology* (London: T&T Clark, 1995) 119–225; and Timo Eskola, *Messiah and Throne: Jewish Merkabah Mysticism and Early Christian Exaltation Discourse* (WUNT II.142; Tübingen: Mohr Siebeck, 2001).

9 This point is made especially in the research of Christopher C. Rowland, "The Visions of God in Apocalyptic Literature," *JSJ* 31 (1979): 137–54; "The Vision of the Risen Christ in Rev. i.13ff.: The Debt of an Early Christology to an Aspect of Jewish Angelology," *JTS* 31 (1980): 1–11; and *The Open Heaven: A Study of Apocalyptic in Judaism and Early*

Christianity (New York: Crossroad, 1982). See also David J. Halperin, *The Faces of the Chariot: Early Jewish Reponses to Ezekiel's Vision* (TSAJ 16; Tübingen: Mohr Siebeck, 1988).

10 For the important debate within Judaism that spawned largely from Daniel 7, see Segal, *Two Powers in Heaven*.

11 Rowland, "Vision of the Risen Christ," 2–3.

12 See the most recent scholarly consensus in *Enoch and the Messiah Son of Man: Revisiting the Book of Parables* (ed. Gabriele Boccaccini; Grand Rapids: Eerdmans, 2007).

13 Darrell D. Hannah, "The Throne of His Glory: The Divine Throne and Heavenly Mediators in Revelation and the Similitudes of Enoch," *ZNW* 94 (2003): 68–96; see also Bauckham, "The Throne of God," 57–60.

14 See Pieter van der Horst, "Moses' Throne Vision in Ezekiel the Dramatist," *JJS* 34 (1983): 19–29. Although the divine throne is not mentioned, Ezekiel 1 also appears to have influenced the depiction of a deliverer in *Sibylline Oracles* 5.414–27 where "a blessed man came from the expanses of heaven" who is "the Glory of the eternal God, a form desired."

15 Peter Carrell's suggestion that the white hair is not necessarily a divine characteristic reflecting the appearance of the Ancient of Days in Daniel 7:9—but could be reflecting the kind of tradition found in the description of Noah in *1 Enoch* 106—is problematic; see *Jesus and the Angels*, 168–69. One has to consider what the author wants the reader to link this image with in order that it communicate the significance he intends. Daniel 7:9 is much more prominent and probable as the antecedent that gives this detail in Rev 1:14 profound significance.

16 The LXX has YHWH's "glory" filling the temple (καὶ πλήρης ὁ οἶκος τῆς δόξης αὐτοῦ).

17 Jan Fekkes III, *Isaiah and Prophetic Traditions in the Book of Revelation: Visionary Antecedents and Their Development* (JSNTSup 93; Sheffield: JSOT Press, 1994), 117–22. There is also an allusion here to Isa 11:4, a text that asserts the Messianic Branch will strike the earth with the "rod of his mouth" (MT, but not LXX).

18 This interpretation of "the man" in Daniel 10 that is visible through the use of Daniel 7 and 10 in Revelation 1 is not emphasized enough by scholars. A. Yarbro Collins, for example, notes that John considered "the risen Christ to be identified with Gabriel" through the use of Daniel 10 in Revelation 1; see *"The 'Son of Man' Tradition and the Book of Revelation," The Messiah* (ed. James H. Charlesworth; Philadelphia: Fortress, 1992), 558. This point also was not very clear in my analysis of Revelation 1 in *Angelomorphic Christology*, 246–49.

19 The image of "the Lion of the tribe of Judah" is almost certainly alluding to Gen 49:9, which is in the midst of the weighty messianic words of Jacob to Judah (Gen 49:8-12). "The Root of David" is alluding to Isa

11:1-10. Jesus identifies himself with a similar title in Rev 22:16 ("I am the root and descendent of David, the bright morning star"). See further Bauckham, *Climax of Prophecy*, 179–85.

20   Gieschen, *Angelomorphic Christology*, 229–44.

21   There is a hierarchy of glory within the three who are the deity, in this order: the Great Glory, the Beloved, and the Angel of the Holy Spirit (*Ascen. Isa.* 7:7–8; 9:27). Even though all three are worshiped as God, the latter two, in turn, worship the former (*Ascen. Isa.* 9:40).

22   For the "rhetorical reversal" analysis, see Johns, *Lamb Christology*, 150–205, esp. 170.

23   Bauckham, *Theology of Revelation*, 74. See also the provocative observations of G. B. Caird, *A Commentary on the Revelation of St. John the Divine* (New York: Harper & Row, 1966), 292–93.

24   The "lamb" title (τὸ ἀρνίον) occurs 28 times in Revelation, more than any other christological title; see Bauckham, *Climax of Prophecy*, 34–35. The background for the use of ἀρνίον in Revelation is a notoriously difficult question; see Johns, *Lamb Christology*, 22–39.

25   Darrell D. Hannah, "Of Cherubim and the Divine Throne: Rev 5.6 in Context," *NTS* 49 (2003): 528–42. For the significance of standing enthroned (Acts 7:56), see Gieschen, *Angelomorphic Christology*, 31.

26   Larry Hurtado has frequently stressed the importance of worship as a christological category; see *Lord Jesus Christ*.

27   The praise sung to the "one seated upon the throne" (4:15) corresponds closely to the praise sung to the Lamb (5:9-10).

28   In light of the saints directing worship "to God" (Rev. 7:11) and offering doxology "to God" (Rev 7:12), it is perhaps best to interpret Rev 7:10 in this manner: "Salvation belongs to our God, [namely] to the One who is sitting on the throne and to the Lamb" (cf. Rev 5:13).

29   For a complete argument supporting this assertion, see Charles A. Gieschen, "The Divine Name in Ante-Nicene Christology," *VC* 57 (2003): 131–34.

30   See Pierre Prigent, *Commentary on the Apocalypse of St. John* (Tübingen: Mohr Siebeck, 2001), 43–44 and 249–51.

31   *Messiah and the Throne*, 213.

32   Most commentaries note the recurrent Passover/Exodus imagery, so a few examples will suffice: the plagues of Egypt inform some the imagery in the cycles of seven (especially the bowls in Rev 16:1–21); the Exodus through the Red Sea stands behind the image of the saints besides the sea of glass (Rev 15:2); the "Song of Moses" sung after the Exodus is transformed into the song of the lamb (Rev 15:3–4); and the *Hallel* Psalms (113–18) used at Passover celebrations are prominent in Revelation 19.

33   For example, Paul calls Christ our "Mercy Seat sacrifice [ἱλαστήριον]" (Rom 3:25), but in another place writes "for Christ *our Passover* [τὸ πάσχα ἡμῶν] has been sacrificed" (1 Cor 5:7b). 1 Peter also combines

the unblemished lamb of Passover with the sacrifice and sin-bearing goats of Atonement: "Knowing that you were not redeemed with perishable things like silver or gold from your futile way of life inherited from your forefathers, but with *precious blood, as of a lamb unblemished and spotless, the blood of Christ*" (1 Pet 1:18-19), and "He himself *bore our sins in his body on the tree,* so that we die to sin and live to righteousness" (1 Pet 2:24-25). Another example is John's Gospel that combines a depiction of Jesus as the Passover Lamb with atonement imagery and language. John the Baptist announces him to be "the Lamb of God *who takes away* [ὁ αἴρων] *the sin of the world*" (John 1:29, 36). Jesus is then crucified on the Day of Preparation when all the lambs are slaughtered for the Passover Feast (John 19:14). John's quotation of Exod 12:46 at the close of his passion narrative identifies Jesus as the eschatological Passover sacrifice (John 19:36).

34 *Commentary on the Apocalypse of St. John,* 250.

35 Larry Hurtado makes a similar point about Revelation 4 not being merely adapted from Jewish apocalyptic tradition due to its unique content; see "Revelation 4–5 in Light of Jewish Apocalyptic Analogies," *JSNT* 25 (1985): 105–24.

36 *Lord Jesus Christ,* 592. One could argue, however, that Revelation presents Jesus' sacrificial death as having secured the redemption of all, even though only the elect will benefit (Rev 1:5 and 5:9).

37 *Theology of the Book of Revelation,* 71.

38 Although the extent of persecution within these churches is often debated in the commentaries, there is internal evidence that some persecution existed (e.g., Antipas in Rev 2:13); for external evidence, see Steven J. Friesen, *Imperial Cults and the Apocalypse of John* (Oxford: Oxford University Press, 2001).

39 Loren Johns overstates the rhetorical function of encouraging nonviolent "faithful witness," yet it is an important function of the book of Revelation; see *Lamb Christology,* 150–206.

40 Bauckham, *Climax of Prophecy,* 174–98.

41 For a broader discussion of this topic, see Gieschen, "Sacramental Theology in the Book of Revelation," 149–74.

42 It is, without doubt, this strong Passover theme in the Eucharist that led to use of the *Agnus Dei* ("Lamb of God" canticle) as part of the Eucharistic liturgy.

43 For further analysis of these scenes, see Gieschen, *Angelomorphic Christology,* 245–69.

44 See the research of Jarl E. Fossum in *The Name of God and the Angel of the Lord: Samaritan and Jewish Concepts of Intermediation and the Origin of Gnosticism* (WUNT I.36; Tübingen: Mohr Siebeck, 1985), and *The Image of the Invisible God: Essays on the Influence of Jewish Mysticism on Early Christology* (NTOA 30; Göttingen: Universitätsverlag Freiburg Schwiez/

Vandenhoeck & Ruprecht, 1995), esp. 111–16; see also Segal, *Two Powers in Heaven*, 212–13, and Gieschen, "Divine Name in Ante-Nicene Christology," 131–32.

45 Fekkes, *Isaiah and Prophetic Traditions*, 197–99.

46 Find argument in Gieschen, *Angelomorphic Christology*, 256–60.

47 Robert H. Gundry, "Angelomorphic Christology in Revelation," *SBLSP* 33 (1994): 662–78; and Margaret Barker, *The Revelation of Jesus Christ* (Edinburgh: T&T Clark, 2000), 159–63. There is also evidence of Jesus being "sealed" by the Father; see John 6:27 and other texts presented in Gieschen, "The Divine Name in Ante-Nicene Christology," 127–56.

48 *Revelation* (London: Epworth Press, 1993), 77.

Chapter 15

1 F. W. Horn, *Das Angeld des Geistes: Studien zur Paulinischen Pneumatologie* (Göttingen: Vandenhoeck & Ruprecht, 1992), 63–64.

2 Moyer V. Hubbard, *New Creation in Paul's Letters and Thought* (SNTSMS 119; Cambridge: Cambridge University Press, 2002), 120.

3 Dunn, *Theology*, 419.

4 See, for example, the Qumran hymns: 1QH 5.25; 1QH 8.19–20; 20.11–12; 1QH 21.14=4Q427; 4Q429 11.

5 Finny Philip, *The Origins of Pauline Pneumatology* (WUNT [2] 194; Tübingen: Mohr Siebeck, 2005), 36–50.

6 This is especially important in light of the recognition that, in the book of Ezekiel, a theme is introduced and then picked up later. For select examples: 3:16-21 is developed in 18:1-32 and 33:1-30; 5:11 is developed in 8:15-18; 37:26-28 is developed in 40-48.

7 Translations of the Bible are from the NRSV unless otherwise noted.

8 The compilation of the book of Ezekiel is more complicated than these questions suggest. Although the community that survived the devastation of 587 B.C.E. would have understood the implication that Israel failed to repent, the command itself suits the period prior to 587, when repentance was still a possibility. While K.-F. Pohlmann (*Der Prophet Hesekiel/Ezechiel Kapitel 1-19* [ATD 22.1; Göttingen: Vandenhoeck & Ruprecht, 1996], 274–75) regards Ezek 18:1-13 as the kernel of this chapter, which is then developed after 587 B.C.E., he still recognizes that the opportunity of repentance "vor der Katastrophe bis zuletzt die Möglichkeit der Umkehr für jeden einzelnen mit entsprechend positiven Folgen gegeben war" (274).

9 The promise of a new heart and spirit is also more radical than circumcision of the heart in Deuteronomy 30, which continues with the promise that "the LORD your God will circumcise your heart and the heart of your descendants, so that you will love the LORD your God with all your heart and with all your soul, in order that you may live" (30:6). In

Ezekiel's promise, circumcision of the heart is supplanted by a new heart and spirit altogether.

10   I have substituted "spirit" for "breath" (NRSV) to preserve the relationship to Ezek 36:25-27 and other such texts.

11   The theme of cleansing, a theme absent from the first two promises of a new spirit (11:14-21; 18:30-32), provides both a new dimension to the promise of a forgiven and spirit-filled people and a segue to the related topic of the restoration of the land.

12   Ezekiel is also commanded to eat what God offers to him (Ezek 2:8), which may provide an intriguing counterpoint to the illicit eating of the tree of the knowledge of good and evil.

13   I was prompted in my own reflections by a stirring essay on Revelation 21—another vision of recreation—by the Taiwanese author, C. S. Song. Song's reflections upon the significance of Rev 21:1–22:5 resonate with the interpretation I have offered, more prosaically, of Ezekiel's vision of new creation. He writes, "But the distance between Asia's exploited people and God's reign of justice and freedom, between the old heaven and the old earth and a new heaven and a new earth, is enormous. We cannot cover that distance with one giant leap. Nor can we reduce it by taking a shortcut. It takes all the tribulations, both personal and communal, for John the seer finally to envision that new heaven and earth. And he knows that the churches have to be tested and tried before they can be given glimpses of a new heaven and a new earth. It must be the same for Christians in Asia." And so must it have been for Israel. See J. R. Levison and P. Pope-Levison, *Return to Babel: Global Perspectives on the Bible* (Louisville: Westminster, 1999), 217.

Chapter 16

1   Segal, *Life after Death*, 377.

2   On Ananus b. Ananus the high priest (identified as a Sadducee in *Ant.* 20.199), see James C. VanderKam, *From Joshua to Caiaphas: High Priests after the Exile* (Minneapolis: Fortress, 2004), 476–82. The only other individual explicitly identified by Josephus as a Sadducee is an otherwise unknown Jonathan who persuaded John Hyrcanus to incline toward the Sadducees, against the Pharisees (*Ant.* 13.289–96); see discussion in VanderKam, *From Joshua to Caiaphas*, 297–304.

3   On the Sadducees according to Josephus, see Günther Baumbach, "The Sadducees in Josephus," in *Josephus, the Bible, and History* (eds. L. H. Feldman and G. Hata; Detroit: Wayne State University Press, 1989), 173–95. See also Anthony J. Saldarini, *Pharisees, Scribes and Sadducees in Palestinian Society: A Sociological Approach* (Wilmington, Del.: Michael Glazier, 1988), 107–33; and Günter Stemberger, *Jewish Contemporaries*

of Jesus: Pharisees, Sadducees, Essenes (trans. A. W. Mahnke; Minneapolis: Fortress, 1995), 5–20, 67–73.

4 *Ant.* 13.173 does discuss what the Sadducees affirm; we will return to this passage below.

5 On Josephus's anti-Saducean views, see Baumbach, "Sadducees," 175–78; compare Stemberger, *Jewish Contemporaries*, 5–20.

6 Going one step further than the New Testament, Jean Le Moyne blames the Sadducees for Jesus' death; see Le Moyne, *Les Sadducéens* (EBib; Paris: Librairie Lecoffre, 1972), 403–4.

7 For a brief survey of the rabbinic sources on the Sadducees, see Gary G. Porton, *ABD* 5:892–95; on the problems pertaining to the fluidity of the terms referring to Sadducees, Boethusians, sectarians, and Epicureans in rabbinic manuscripts, see Le Moyne, *Les Sadducéens*, 97–102.

8 Louis Finkelstein, *The Pharisees: The Sociological Background of their Faith* (3rd ed. with suppl.; 2 vols.; Philadelphia: Jewish Publication Society, 1962), 2:637, 753. For similar views, see also Salo Wittmayer Baron, *A Social and Religious History of the Jews* (16 vols.; New York: Columbia University Press, 1952–1983), 2:35–38; Marcel Simon, *Jewish Sects at the Time of Jesus* (Philadelphia: Fortress, 1967), 24; Victor Tcherikover, *Hellenistic Civilization and the Jews* (Philadelphia: Jewish Publication Society, 1959), 494 n. 44; and Solomon Zeitlin, *The Rise and Fall of the Judaean State: A Political, Social and Religious History of the Second Commonwealth* (3 vols.; Philadelphia: Jewish Publication Society, 1962–1978), 1:176–87.

9 Martin Goodman, *The Ruling Class of Judaea: The Origins of the Jewish Revolt against Rome A.D. 66–70* (Cambridge: Cambridge University Press, 1987), 79. See the important qualifications to such views introduced by Segal, *Life after Death*, 377. The Sadducees have had their defenders, of course; see in particular Sanders, *Judaism*, 337–39.

10 For a helpful (and creative) analysis of the biblical traditions concerning this figure, see Christian E. Hauer Jr., "Who Was Zadok?" *JBL* 82.1 (1963): 89–94.

11 Abraham Geiger, *Urschrift und Übersetzungen der Bibel, in ihrer Abhängigkeit von der innern Entwicklung des Judentum* (2nd ed.; Frankfurt am Main: Madda, 1928), 20–38.

12 E.g., Kaufman Kohler, "Sadducees," in *The Jewish Encyclopedia* (eds. Cyrus Adler et al.; 12 vols.; New York: Funk & Wagnall's, 1901–1906), 10: 630–33; Finkelstein, *Pharisees*, 1:80, 2:835; and Emil Schürer, *The History of the Jewish People in the Age of Jesus Christ* (4 vols.; rev. ed. Geza Vermes, et al.; Edinburgh: T&T Clark, 1973–1987), 2:405–7. See also— with some qualification—Rudolf Meyer, "Σαδδουκαῖος," *TDNT* 8:35–54, esp. 36–43; and Sanders, *Judaism*, 25–26.

13 E.g., Isaiah Gafni, "Historical Background," in *Jewish Writings of the Second Temple Period: Apocrypha, Pseudepigrapha, Qumran Sectarian Writings, Philo,*

Josephus (ed. Michael Stone; CRINT II.2; Assen: Van Gorcum, 1984), 12; and Lawrence H. Schiffman, *From Text to Tradition: A History of Second Temple and Rabbinic Judaism* (Hoboken, N.J.: Ktav, 1991), 108.

14 See, e.g., Frank Moore Cross, *The Ancient Library of Qumran* (3rd ed.; Minneapolis: Fortress, 1995), 100–110; Geza Vermes, *The Complete Dead Sea Scrolls in English* (New York: Allen Lane, 1997), 50–53, 63 n. 1.

15 Gabriele Boccaccini, *Roots of Rabbinic Judaism: An Intellectual History, From Ezekiel to Daniel* (Grand Rapids: Eerdmans, 2002), esp. 43–72.

16 Others have questioned the certitude of this identification already. See, e.g., Le Moyne, *Les Saducéens*, 63–67, 155–63; and more briefly, Porton, "Saducees," 892.

17 See *'Abot R. Nat.* A 5, B 10, ed. Solomon Schechter (Vienna: Ch. D. Lippe, 1887), 13a–b, cf. discussion in Le Moyne, *Les Sadducéens*, 113–17. For the Karaite sources, see Leon Nemoy, *Karaite Anthology: Excerpts from the Early Literature* (Yale Judaica Series; New Haven: Yale University Press, 1987), 50; and discussion in Le Moyne, *Les Sadducéens*, 137–41.

18 Epiphanius (*Pan.* 1.14) also puts greater weight on the simpler connection between the name "Sadducee" and the Hebrew word for righteousness (*zedeq*). See Frank Williams, trans., *The Panarion of Epiphanius of Salamis: Book I (Sects 1–46)* (NHS 35; Leiden: Brill, 1987), 36–37.

19 Louis Ginzberg already recognized this, and speculated that CD refers here to a priest in the days of Josiah. See Ginzberg, *An Unknown Jewish Sect* (New York: Jewish Theological Seminary, 1976), 21, 68; Ginzberg then goes further to identify this Zadok with the Teacher of Righteousness (211, 219–20).

20 It is presumably a coincidence—but a curious one, nonetheless—that the founder of the so-called fourth philosophy was (also?) a renegade Pharisee named Zadok (*Ant.* 18.4).

21 See Albert I. Baumgarten, "The Zadokite Priests at Qumran: A Reconsideration," *DSD* 4 (1997): 137–56; and Robert A. Kugler, "Priesthood at Qumran," in *The Dead Sea Scrolls after Fifty Years: A Comprehensive Assessment* (eds. P. W. Flint and J. C. VanderKam; 2 vols.; Leiden: Brill, 1999), 2:93–116, esp. 97–100.

22 It is possible, of course, that the group was not celibate; it is equally possible (if not more possible) that Zadokite descent was not taken literally. The real problem concerns those reconstructions—like Cross's and Vermes's—that presume both a celibate sect and a literal concern with Zadokite descent.

23 This understanding was suggested already by Ginzberg, *An Unknown Jewish Sect*, 15. For more on this passage, see Maxine Grossman, "Priesthood as Authority: Interpretive Competition in First-Century Judaism and Christianity," in *The Dead Sea Scrolls as Background to Postbiblical Judaism and Early Christianity: Papers from an International*

Conference at St. Andrews in 2001 (ed. J. R. Davila; Leiden: Brill, 2003), 117–31, esp. 126–28.

24 See Saul M. Olyan, "Ben Sira's Relationship to the Priesthood," *HTR* 80.3 (1987): 261–86, esp. 270–77, which argues that neither the figure Zadok nor Zadokite descent was of any particular interest to Ben Sira. Note especially 50:13, which refers to "all the sons of Aaron." On the reference to Zadokites in Sirach 51:12i (which is a subsequent addition to the book), see Olyan, "Ben Sira's Reliationship," 275–76; and Patrick W. Skehan and Alexander A. Di Lella, *The Wisdom of Ben Sira: A New Translation with Notes, Introduction and Commentary* (AB 39; New York: Doubleday, 1987), 568–71.

25 On 4QMMT in this regard, see Menahem Kister, "Studies in 4Miqsat Ma'aseh ha-Torah and Related Texts: Law, Theology, Language and Calendar" [Hebrew], *Tarbiz* 68.3 (1998–1999): 317–72, esp. 323, and nn. 20–21.

26 The closest our sources come to alluding to a problem of Zadokite descent in the Second Temple period is when Josephus notes that Onias was succeeded by Jacimus who "was indeed of the stock of Aaron, but not of the family of Onias" (*Ant.* 20.235; and note that Zadok goes unmentioned in *Ant.* 20.231). As Lester L. Grabbe (among others) has noted, it is not at all certain that Onias was a Zadokite; see *Judaic Religion in the Second Temple Period: Belief and Practice from the Exile to Yavneh* (London: Routledge, 2000), 145. Josephus does assert that all the first temple priests were descendants of Zadok (*Ant.* 10.151–54), and presumably the early Second Temple priests were likewise, perhaps down to the time of the Hasmoneans (*Ant.* 20.231–34). Yet Josephus—who does, to be sure, trace his own descent to the Hasmoneans (*Life* 1–2)— stops short of stating explicitly what so many have inferred: that the end of the Zadokite priesthood gave rise to a sectarian crisis among Jews. So there are two distinct levels of ambiguity here: (1) it is not known for certain that the Zadokite line continued down, unbroken, to Onias III; and (2) even if it did, that does not necessarily mean the breaking of the line caused a particular crisis.

27 Alison Schofield and James C. VanderKam, "Were the Hasmoneans Zadokites?" *JBL* 124 (2005): 73–87.

28 It has recently been argued—adding a third level of ambiguity to those listed in n. 26 above—that a number of the first-century high priests (such as those belonging to the house of Annas, including Joseph Caiaphas) were, in fact, Zadokites. See Helen K. Bond, *Caiaphas: Friend of Rome and Judge of Jesus?* (Louisville: Westminster John Knox, 2004), 24, 35, 149–53. Although she approaches the matter of Zadokite descent differently than I have, Bond's analysis confirms the larger claims being made here: that disputes concerning Zadokite descent were not of enor-

mous consequence to the history of late Second Temple Judaism, and that our sources say precious little about the matter.

29   Kohler, "Sadducees," 10:632; cf. Geiger, *Urschrift*, 131–32.

30   E.g., Meyer, *TDNT*, 8:49; compare also Boccaccini, *Roots of Rabbinic Judaism*, 134–50, read along with the chart on p. xii. Boccaccini sees Sirach as aligned with the Zadokite priesthood and (along with other works) leading toward later Sadducaism. Le Moyne, too, discusses Sirach in *Les Sadducéens*, 67–73, deeming it to be a pre-Sadducean work. William Horbury has suggested that Wisdom of Solomon in part serves to attribute to Israel's king views that are characteristically Pharisaic, thereby countering the fact that other wisdom works would support views that have come to be associated with the Sadducees. See "The Christian Use and the Jewish Origins of the Wisdom of Solomon," in *Wisdom in Ancient Israel: Essays in Honor of J. A. Emerton* (eds. J. Day, R. P. Gordon and H. G. M. Williamson; Cambridge: Cambridge University Press, 1995), 182–96, esp. 195–96.

31   Alan Segal, *Rebecca's Children: Judaism and Christianity in the Roman World* (Cambridge, Mass.: Harvard University Press, 1986), 46–47; and Segal, *Life after Death*, 254–55. Both passages discuss primarily Sirach 14:16-19. Compare the comments of Baumbach, "Sadducees," 175, with regard to Sirach 15:11-20, to be discussed below. Baumbach follows (and cites) Rudolf Leszynsky, *Die Sadduzäer* (Berlin: Mayer & Müller, 1912), 172–75; Leszynsky, notoriously, identified a large percentage of ancient Jewish works as Sadducean, including 1 Maccabees (175–76) and *Jubilees* (179–237) among others, so his judgment with regard to *Ben Sira* does not result from any specific interest in the wisdom tradition.

32   Sadducees remain unmentioned in two recent introductions to wisdom: James L. Crenshaw, *Old Testament Wisdom: An Introduction* (rev. and enl. ed.; Louisville: Westminster John Knox, 1998); and Roland E. Murphy, *The Tree of Life: An Exploration of Biblical Wisdom Literature* (3rd ed.; Grand Rapids: Eerdmans, 2002). The Sadducees are mentioned in passing (but tangentially) by Richard Horsley in *In Search of Wisdom: Essays in Memory of John G. Gammie* (ed. Leo G. Perdue, Bernard Brandon Scott, and William Johnston Wiseman; Louisville: Westminster John Knox, 1993), 223; and by John G. Snaith in Day, Gordon, and Williamson, *Wisdom in Ancient Israel*, 178.

33   Crenshaw, for instance, focuses on skepticism in his discussion of wisdom's legacies (*Old Testament Wisdom*, 184–204). The volume edited by Perdue, Scott, and Wiseman cited above contains essays on apocalyptic and the gospels (canonical and non-), including *Gospel of Thomas* and Q.

34   For general information on the wisdom tradition and ample bibliography, see Crenshaw, *Old Testament Wisdom*; and Murphy, *Tree of Life*.

35   On wisdom at Qumran, see Daniel J. Harrington, *Wisdom Texts from Qumran* (London: Routledge, 1996); and John Kampen, "The Diverse

Aspects of Wisdom at Qumran," in Flint and VanderKam, *The Dead Sea Scrolls after Fifty Years,* 1:211–43.

36 So, Epiphanius, *Pan.*, 1.14 and Hippolytus, *Haer.*, 9.24.

37 So already George Foote Moore, *Judaism: In the First Centuries of the Christian Era* (2 vols.; Cambridge, Mass.: Harvard University Press, 1927, 1930), 1:68. Not entirely unrelated is the narrower question of whether the Sadducees would have accepted Daniel (with its reference to immortality in 12:1-3) as canonical. For some brief comments on the issue, see Segal, *Life after Death,* 281.

38 See, e.g., Crenshaw, *Old Testament Wisdom,* 21, 197–201. Compare Boccaccini, *Roots of Rabbinic Judaism,* 103–11, who lists "sapiential Judiasm" among the opponents of what he calls "Zadokite Judaism." Boccaccini believes that a rapprochement between the two develops with works such as Tobit and Sirach (113–50; cf. the chart on xii).

39 On the issues surrounding the identification of wisdom Psalms, for example, see Crenshaw, *Old Testament Wisdom,* 171–75; and Murphy, *Tree of Life,* 103–4, 221, 270–73; and the literature cited in these works.

40 Josephus speaks of the wisdom books (presumably) only in a very general way in *Ag. Ap.* 1.40: "[T]he remaining four books contain hymns to God and precepts (ὑποθῆκαι) for everyday life" (cf. *Ant.* 7.166 and 8.126).

41 On Josephus's account of Solomon, see Louis H. Feldman, *Josephus's Interpretation of the Bible* (Hellenistic Culture and Society 27; Berkeley: University of California Press, 1998), 570–628; on Solomon's wisdom see esp. 579–98; cf. 97–106 on Josephus's general approach to praising the wisdom of biblical heroes. According to Feldman, Josephus's general goal is to counter calumnies (such as that offered by Apion—*Ag. Ap.* 2.135) to the effect that Jews never produced great wise men as did the Greeks.

42 On the wisdom-apocalyptic connection in modern scholarship, Lorenzo DiTommaso, "Apocalypses and Apocalypticism in Antiquity (Part II)," *CBR* 5.3 (2007): 367–432 (esp. 374–84). Saldarini, interestingly, considers Ben Sira (briefly) with regard to the scribes (*Pharisees, Scribes, and Sadducees,* 254–60).

43 The stark contrasts between Sirach and the Wisdom of Solomon (disagreeing, as they do, on issues that also separated Sadducees from Pharisees) should be enough to prove that the wisdom tradition had multiple heirs in the late Second Temple period.

44 On this understanding of this passage, see Baumbach, "Sadducees," 17; and Le Moyne, *Les Sadducéens,* 42. Contrast *Ant.* 18.16 with 18.12: the Pharisees accept the teachings of their teachers.

45 Segal, *Life after Death,* 120–70.

46 Cf. Le Moyne, *Les Sadducéens,* 40–41, following Leszynsky, *Die Sadduzäer,* 19.

47　Segal, *Life after Death*, 142–45.

48　For this term, and for an alternate survey of early Israel's attitude toward death, see George E. Mendenhall, "From Witchcraft to Justice: Death and Afterlife in the Old Testament," in *Death and Afterlife: Perspectives of World Religions* (ed. H. Obayashi; New York: Praeger, 1992), 67–81; term used on 69.

49　Translation largely follows Skehan, in Skehan and Dillela, *The Wisdom of Ben Sira*, 266–67, but NRSV has been consulted (and adopted at points for clarity). On this passage, see Skehan and Dillela, *The Wisdom of Ben Sira*, 81–83, 269–75.

50　Among other interpreters, Crenshaw (*Old Testament Wisdom*, 80–82) correctly emphasizes that freedom of choice is among the important messages of Proverbs 1–9, with its frequent juxtapositions of wisdom and folly, and Lady Wisdom with the seductive adulteress.

51　Baumbach, "Sadducees," 175; Meyer, *TDNT*, 8:46; and the literature cited in these works; note the critique of Stemberger, *Jewish Contemporaries*, 68–70; and cf. Le Moyne, *Les Sadducéens,* 38–39.

52　On the Sadducees' purported atheism, as related to Josephus's biases, see Baumbach, "Sadducees," 175; Stemberger (*Jewish Contemporaries,* 70) asserts that Josephus is simply mistaken.

53　This insight derives from an observation drawn by Ms. Sarah J. Chandonnet, who perspicaciously asked in class about Josephus's Sadducees upon reading (in Vermes's English translation) CD I, 3–4 and II, 8–9, which speak of God hiding his face from a sinful Israel.

54　On Josephus's anti-Sadducean views, see n. 5 above.

55　Again, translation follows Skehan in Skehan and Dillela, *The Wisdom of Ben Sira*, 393–94; see Skehan's notes and Dillela's discussion, 395–401.

56　Paul Winter, "Ben Sira and the Teaching of 'Two Ways,' " *VT* 5.3 (1955): 315–18.

57　So, e.g., Martin Hengel, *Judaism and Hellenism: Studies in Their Encounter in Palestine during the Early Hellenistic Period* (trans. John Bowden; 2 vols.; Minneapolis: Fortress, 1974), 1:141; Moshe Tzvi Segal, *Sefer Ben Sira ha-Shalem* (2d corrected and expanded ed.; Jerusalem: Mossad Bialik, 1958), 29. Compare Le Moyne, *Les Sadducéens*, 40 (and n. 11), who sees Ben Sira as continuing earlier biblical beliefs in his side-by-side juxtaposition of free will with determinism.

Chapter 17

1　Unless otherwise noted, quotations from *Jubilees* are taken from the translation by O. S. Wintermute in *The Old Testament Pseudepigrapha*, (ed. J. H. Charlesworth; New York: Doubleday, 1985), 35–142. Cf. J. C. VanderKam, *The Book of Jubilees* (CSCO 510–11; Leuven: Peeters 1989). Unless otherwise noted, quotations from *Enoch* are taken from the following translations: 1. (Ethiopic) *Enoch*, translated by E. Isaac, in Charlesworth, vol. 1, 5–90; 2. (Slavonic) *Enoch*, translated by F. I. Anderson, in Charlesworth, vol. 1, 91–222; 3. (Hebrew) *Enoch*, translated by P. Alexander, in Charlesworth, vol. 1, pp. 223–316. For *2 Enoch*, reference is provided as well to the Hebrew edition, in A. Kahana, *Hasefarim ha-hitsoniyyim* (Apocrypha and Pseudepigrapha) (Tel-Aviv: Kahana Masada, 1937). Translated from the Hebrew by J. Linsider. Except as otherwise noted, translations from original Hebrew and Aramaic sources are by the present translator. Except as otherwise noted, quotations from the Hebrew Bible are from the New Jewish Publication Society Tanakh (NJPS), copyright ©1985, 1999 by the Jewish Publication Society. Quotations from the Apocrypha and the New Testament are from the New Revised Standard Version Bible, copyright ©1989 by the Division of Christian Education of the National Council of the Churches of Christ in the U.S.A.

J. Z. Smith, *Map Is Not Territory: Studies in the History of Religions* (Leiden: Brill, 1978); idem, *Imagining Religion, from Babylon to Jonestown* (Chicago: University of Chicago Press, 1982); J. Scott and P. Simpson-Housely, eds., *Sacred Places and Profane Spaces: Essays in the Geographics of Judaism, Christianity and Islam* (New York: Greenwood Press, 1991).

2   On the connection between sacred spaces and the formation of nationalism, see B. R. O'Gorman Anderson, *Imagined Communities: Reflection on the Origin and Spread of Nationalism* (London and New York: Verso, 1991).

3   On cosmography in religious thought, cf. M. Eliade, *The Myth of the Eternal Return* (trans. from the French by W. R. Trask; New York: Pantheon Books, 1954), esp. 6–17. On the relationship between mountains and cosmic mountains on which heaven and earth commingle and on which the deity makes a terrestrial appearance, see R. E. Clements, *God and Temple* (Philadelphia: Fortress, 1965); R. J. Clifford, *The Cosmic Mountain in Canaan and the Old Testament* (Cambridge, Mass.: Harvard University Press, 1972).

4   *har habayit*; lit., "the mountain of the house [of the Lord]"; the familiar English designation "Temple Mount" is used in this article. See B. Mazar, *The Mountain of the Lord* (Garden City, N.Y.: Doubleday, 1975); C. T. R. Hayward, *The Jewish Temple* (London-New York: Routledge, 1996). Cf. also n. 8 below.

5   See Y. Shapira, *El giv`at halevonah* [To the hill of frankincense] (Yitshar: Agudat el Har Hamor, 1999); Shapira and Y. Pel'i, *El Har Hamor* [To the mountain of myrrh] (Yitshar: Agudat el Har Hamor, 1997); Y. Ezion, *Bein levanon le-levanon: Le-fesher qilelat ha-damim shel hitvardut ha-orqim* (Ofrah: published by the author, 1999). The *Targum on Song* 3:6 connects the Temple with "the mountain of myrrh . . . the hill of frankincense." The Samaritans identified Mount Moriah with Mount

Gerizim. The name "Temple Mount" reflects the vision of destruction described in Mic 3:12, dating from the time of King Hezekiah: "Assuredly because of you Zion shall be plowed as a field, and Jerusalem shall become heaps of ruins and the Temple Mount [*har habayit*] a shrine in the woods" (cf. Jer 26:18). It refers to the sacred mountain following the destruction; later, when the Jews no longer had the holy city within their reach (following the Bar-Kokhba rebellion), it provided a poignant description of what was lacking rather than what actually existed. The original source for the name was the prophetic usage *har beit adonai* (Isa 2:2), "the Mount of the Lord's house"; it was shortened after the destruction by its dissociation from God's name. cf. *b Git.* 56a; cf. *b. Ber.* 3a.

6   On David's tomb, whose identity as such developed first in Christian myth and was later adopted by the Jewish tradition, see: I. J. Yuval, *Two Nations in Your Womb: Perceptions of Jews and Christians in Late Antiquity and the Middle Ages* (trans. from the Hebrew by B. Harshav and J. Chipman; Berkeley: University of California Press, 2006), 23–24; and see below, text at n. 67.

7   Much has been written about Mount Zion in its various historical, literary, and archaeological contexts. See Y. Z. Eliav, *God's Mountain. The Temple Mount in Time, Place, and Memory* (Baltimore: Johns Hopkins University Press, 2005). In his introduction, Eliav maintains that only after the Temple had been destroyed by the Romans in 70 C.E. did the Temple Mount in Jerusalem become an important concept invested with religious significance. He notes that the term har habayit (Temple Mount) as a routine designation for the site of the no-longer-extant temple took shape only in the first century, though it is based on an ancient tradition (10). Eliav there also reviews the complex relationship between mountain and temple and discusses the various names used for Mount Moriah, Mount Zion, and the Temple Mount at various times. The book contains a thorough bibliography on each of these sites.

8   For background on the nature of the controversy over sacred time and sacred space within the Jewish world of the second and first centuries B.C.E., see R. Elior, *The Three Temples: On the Emergence of Jewish Mysticism* (trans. from the Hebrew by D. Louvish; Oxford: Littman Library of Jewish Civilization, 2004)

9   On Chronicles and the time of its composition in the fourth century B.C.E., see S. Japhet, *The Ideology of the Book of Chronicles and Its Place in Biblical Thought* (trans. A. Barber; Frankfurt-am-Main and New York: P. Lang, 1989); idem., *I and II Chronicles: A Commentary* (Louisville: Westminster John Knox, 1993); W. Riley, *King and Cultus in Chronicles: Worship and the Reinterpretation of History* (Sheffield: Sheffield Academic, 1993).

10   2 Chr 3:1. The translation is from the Old Jewish Publication Society version (OJPS) (Philadelphia: Jewish Publication Society of America, 1917),

which captures the sense of MT; NJPS translates in accord with the emendation next described. "The Lord" is bracketed in the English translation because the word does not appear in MT; LXX includes it. MT here appears corrupt and should be emended per LXX: "And Solomon began to build the house of the Lord in Jerusalem on Mount Moriah, where the Lord appeared to his father David, in the place which David had prepared in the threshing floor of Ornan the Jebusite" (*The Apostles Bible: A Modern English Translation of the Greek Septuagint*, ed. P. W. Esposito [http://www.apostlesbible.com]). Other ancient translations read "in the place which David had prepared in the threshing floor" or "the threshing floor of Aronah." See Y. Zackowitz, *David* (Jerusalem: Yad Yitshaq Ben-Zvi, 1995), 139. On the tradition regarding the altar built by David in the threshing floor of Ornan the Jebusite (or Arnia or Arona), see 2 Sam 24:18-25; 1 Chr 21:15, 18-30. No place at all is mentioned in the parallel tradition in 1 Kgs 6 regarding the construction of Solomon's Temple. Another interesting tradition on the "place of Aronah," connected to burnt offerings by the priestly dynasty of Enoch son of Jared, appears in *2 En.* 21 and 23 (Hebrew version). Corresponding to J. Charlesworth, Old Testament Pseudepigrapha edition of Second Enoch, chs. 69–71.

11   *The Apostle's Bible.*

12   See above, n. 9. Zion is mentioned hundreds of times in the Hebrew Bible, especially in the books of Isaiah, Jeremiah, Micah, Zechariah, Psalms, and Lamentations.

13   2 Sam 5:7; 1 Kgs 8:1; 1 Chr 11:5; 2 Chr 5:2; Isa 8:18.

14   2 Kgs 19:31 and parallel in Isa 37:32. Cf. J. D. Levenson, "The Jerusalem Temple in Devotional and Visionary Experience," in *Jewish Spirituality From the Bible through the Middle Ages*, (ed. A. Green; New York: Crossroad, 1986), 32–61, quote on 47.

15   Isa 35:10; cf. 51:11 and see 52:1, 7; 4:3-5.

16   Obad 1:21.

17   Joel 4:17; cf. 4:21—"And the Lord shall dwell in Zion"; 3:5—"for there shall be a remnant on Mount Zion and in Jerusalem, as the Lord promised."

18   Joel 2:1; cf. 3:5 and 4:16.

19   The cosmic mountain traditions that portray a high place where heaven and earth meet and the divine manifests itself on earth often note a correspondence between the mountain and a sanctuary (see Clifford and Clements, above, n. 3). The biblical traditions, however, make no such specific reference.

20   Lam 5:18; cf. Jer 26:18; *Lam. Rab.* 5:18 (Buber 80a); *Sifrei Devarim* 43 (Finkelstein, 95); *b. Mak.* 24b.

21   See, e.g., "[B]ring us to Zion Your city in song; to Jerusalem Your holy house in eternal joy"; "Have mercy, our God, on us and on Israel Your people; on Jerusalem Your city; on Zion, dwelling place of Your glory; on

Your sanctuary and Your habitation." (From the blessing after meals and the blessing Nahem, added to the standard prayers on the Ninth of Ab, the day commemorating the destruction of the first and second temples.)

22 On the meaning of this term, see *Community Rule* 1:19–21; 2:2–4; 5:1–3, 5, 8; *Damascus Document* 3:1, 4–21; 3:4; 5:5. (Except as otherwise noted, quotations from the Dead Sea Scrolls are taken from G. Vermes, *The Complete Dead Sea Scrolls in English* (New York: Penguin Books, 1997). On the significance of the tie between the Zadokite priests and the Sadducees, see Y. Sussman, "The History of Halakhah and the Dead Sea Scrolls: Preliminary Talmudic Observations on MMT," in *DJD X, Qumran Cave 4. V* (eds. E. Qimron and J. Strugnell; Oxford: Clarendon, 1994), 179–200. On the significance of this priestly context in the literary history of Jewish mysticism, see Elior, *The Three Temples*, 24–28.

23 The Qumran version of Jubilees states, "[for] the Garden of Eden is sacred and every young shoot which is in its midst is a consecrated thing," in *DJD XXXV, Qumran cave 4* (ed. J. Baumgarten; Oxford: Clarendon, 1999), 70. On the *Book of Jubilees*, see above, n. 1. For an up-to-date study of *Jubilees*, including a comprehensive bibliography, see M. Segal, "The Book of Jubilees" (Ph.D. diss, Hebrew University in Jerusalem, 2004); M. Albani, J. Frey, and A. Lange, eds., *Studies in the Book of Jubliees* (Tübingen: Mohr Siebeck, 1997).

24 Hymn 18 (formerly 14); Vermes, *The Complete Dead Sea Scrolls*, 278. The hymn includes a detailed account of the Garden of Eden. The citation above, which lists seven types of trees, alludes to Isa 41:9.

25 "Garden of Eden": see *Jub.* 8:29; cf. *2 En.* 5:3; "Garden of Righteousness": see *1 En.* 77:3; "Eternal Plantation": see *Thanksgiving Scroll*, Hymn 18 (formerly 14), Vermes, *Complete Dead Sea Scrolls*, 278 ("everlasting Plant"; "Fountain of Life": see Vermes, 279 ("well-spring of life"). On Garden of Truth, see below, n. 44. (In Licht's Hebrew edition, see Hymn 16, page 8, lines 6 and 12.)

26 *1 En.* 14:11; cf. C. Newsom, ed., *Songs of the Sabbath Sacrifice* (Atlanta: Scholars Press, 1985), 303. On the tradition of the chariot, see *Songs of the Sabbath*, 1–80; and cf. Elior, *The Three Temples*, 63–81.

27 *1 En.* 75:3-4.

28 See Newsom, *Song of the Sabbath Sacrifices*, 303–21 for the Hebrew text, discussion, and translation. Translation by the present author, based on the translations of D. Halperin, *The Faces of the Chariot* (Tubingen: J. C. B. Mohr, 1988), 52, 524–25; J. Strugnell, "The Angelic Liturgy at Qumran-4Q *Serek Sirot Olat hassabat,*" *Congress Volume*: Oxford, 1959 (VTSup 7; Leiden: Brill, 1959–1960), 318–45; and L. H. Schiffman, "Merkavah Speculation at Qumran: The 4QSerekh Shirot Olat Ha-Shabat," in *Mystics, Philosophers and Politics, Essays in Jewish Intellectual History in Honor of Alexander Altmann* (eds. J. Reinharz and D. Swetschinski; Durham, N.C.: Duke University Press, 1982), 15–47. The

unique poetic Hebrew syntax and mystical content makes this text particularly hard to translate; it can, therefore, be rendered in more than one way.

29 Vermes, *Complete Dead Sea Scrolls*, 328.

30 On holy trees and fragrant trees in the Garden of Eden, which are associated with the sacred tradition of Temple incense, see *1 En.* 24–32 and 17–18; cf. *2 En.* 5:1–4; *Jub.* 3:12, 27.

31 For both terms, see Hymn 18 (formerly 14), Vermes, *Complete Dead Sea Scrolls*, 278–79 ("mysterious fountain" and "well-spring of life"). (Hymn 16 in Licht.)

32 On the Psalms Scroll from Qumran and the cycle of songs associated with the cycle of sacrifices, see J. A. Sanders, "The Psalms Scroll of Qumran Cave 11(11QPs) col. xxvii:2–11," *DJD* IV (Oxford: Clarendon: 1965), 48, 91–93. Cf. Elior, *The Three Temple*, 50–55.

33 See Newsom, *Songs of the Sabbath Sacrifice* (above, n. 31), introduction; and cf. M Himmelfarb, "The Temple and the Garden of Eden in Ezekiel, The Book of Watchers and the Wisdom of Ben Sira," in *Sacred Places and Profane Spaces*, 63–78.

34 *Jub.* 1:17, 28-29 (emphasis supplied). Although Jerusalem is not mentioned in the Pentateuch itself, it is referred to explicitly (as in the quotation above) in *Jubilees'* retelling of the stories of Genesis and the first half of Exodus. The Dead Sea Scrolls version of *Jubilees* contains a slightly different reading from the one quoted above: "Until my sanctuary is built [among them for all the ages of eternity. The Lord will appear in the sight of] all; and [all] will know [that I am the God of Israel, father of all Jacob's [children], and king [on Mount Zion for all the ages of eternity; Then Zion and Jerusa]le[m will be holy]." (*DJD XIII, Qumran Cave 4, VIII: Parabiblical Texts* [part 1; eds. H. Attridge, J. VanderKam, et.al.; Oxford: Clarendon 1994], 11–12).

35 *Jub.* 4:26.

36 *1 En.* 26:1–3. On Enoch and his heavenly journey, cf. G. W. Nickelsburg, *1 Enoch: A Commentary on the Book of 1 Enoch Chapters 1-36; 81–108* (ed. K. Baltzer; Minneapolis: Fortress, 2001), 279–80; J. C. VanderKam, *Enoch and the Growth of Apocalyptic Tradition* (Catholic Biblical Quarterly, Monograph Series, 16; Washington, D.C.: Catholic Biblical Association of America, 1984); J. C. VanderKam, *Enoch: A Man for All Generations* (Columbia: University of South Carolina Press, 1995); J. L. Kugel, *Traditions of the Bible* (Cambridge, Mass.: Harvard University Press, 1998), 176–77; Elior, *The Three Temples*, 88–110.

37 *Jub.* 8:19. Cf. *2 En.* 71:35-36 in Charlesworth 23:45–46 in Kahana. On the meaning of the idea of "navel of the earth," see S. Terrien, "The Omphalos Myth and Hebrew Religion," *Vetus Testamentum* 20 (1970): 315–38.

38 *1 En.* 14:10-11.

39   *1 En.* 71:5-7; cf. *1 En.* 14:8-23 and 25:3; see also above, n. 24 and below, n. 47.

40   See *1 En.* 24-32 and 17-18; cf. *2 Enoch* 5:1-8.

41   *Jub.* 3:12, 3:27, 29; 4:23–26; 8:19.

42   See *1 En.* 24–36. For "garden of righteousness," see *1 En.* 77:3. On "garden of truth" see below, n. 44.

43   5:4 in Kahana; 8:4 in Charlesworth: "[P]aradise is in between the corruptible and the incorruptible."

44   4Q209, Frag. 23:9, E. J. C. Tigchelaar and F. Garcia Martinez, "209.4Q Astronomical Enoch ar," in *Qumran Cave 4 XXVI Discoveries in the Judaean Desert XXXVI* (eds. P. Alexander et al.; Oxford: Clarendon, 2001), 159. That is the name used for the Garden of Eden in the Aramaic *Enoch* found at Qumran. In the Hebrew translation, the Aramaic *pardes qushta* is rendered as *gan hatsedeq*; in English it is the "garden of righteousness" (Charlesworth, 1:56). In the Palestinian Aramaic translation of Genesis, the verse "Enoch walked with God" (5:22) is rendered *ufelah bequshta* ("[Enoch] served with righteousness").

45   See M. Zipor, *The Septuagint on Genesis* (Ramat-Gan: Bar Ilan University, 2006) (Hebrew), 81; J. A. L. Lee, *A Lexical Study of the Septuagint Version of the Pentateuch* (SCS 14; Chico: Scholars Press, 1983), 53–56.

46   *Community Rule* 11:8 (Vermes, *Complete Dead Sea Scrolls*, 115).

47   See *1 En.* 24:3-6; 29:2; 30:2-3; 31:1-2; 32:1-6; *2 En.* 5:1-4 in Kahana; 8:1-8 in Charlesworth; Elior, *The Three Temples*, 128, 180.

48   *1 En.* 14:8–25; for discussion on the vision see studies mentioned above, n. 36. "Voice of the cherubim" (v. 18) is per the translation in Charlesworth; the word rendered "voice" has been translated in other ways, including "vision."

49   "The vision which Ezek[iel] saw . . . a radiance of a chariot and four living creatures." Trans. per *DJD XXX, Qumran Cave 4 XXI: Parabiblical Texts,* Part 4 *Pseudo-prophetic Texts* (eds. D. Dimant and J. Strugnell; Oxford: Clarendon, 2001), 44. This Qumran version of Ezekiel, includes the word "chariot," which is missing in MT. See the MT Vision of the Chariot, Ezek. 1 and 10:9-19.

50   "It was Ezekiel who saw the vision of glory, which God showed him above the chariot of the cherubim."

51   "Gold for the pattern of the chariot . . . the cherubim," 1 Chr 28:18 (OJPS).

52   *Community Rule* 11:7-9 (Vermes, *Complete Dead Sea Scrolls*, 115). In my book *The Three Temples*, I consider the priestly chariot tradition at length.

53   See *1 En.* 1–36; *Jub.* 4:17-20. See also above, n. 36; cf. R. Elior, "You have chosen Enoch from among men," in *On Creation and Re-creation in Jewish Thought: Festschrift for Joseph Dan* (eds. R. Elior and P. Schäfer; Tubingen: Mohr Siebeck, 2005), 15–64 (Hebrew). *Jubilees* 4 considers

the biblical verse that is the point of departure for the Enoch tradition—
"Enoch walked with God; then he was no more, for God took him" (Gen
5:24) and, interpreting "walked" in a literal sense, states that Enoch spent
three hundred years with God's angels. The Qumran version of *Jubilees*
has the angel of the presence refer to "Enoch, after we taught him six
Jubilee of years. . . . And he wrote all the sky and the paths of their host
and the [mon]ths so that the righteous should not err (4Q227; *DJD*
XIII, 174); see Milik, *The Books of Enoch*, 12. The Septuagint renders
"And Enoch was well-pleasing to God, and was not found, for God
translated him" (*Apostles Bible*).

54   *1 En.* 26:2-3. On navel of the earth, see above, n. 37. Rabbinic midrash
preserves traditions about the holy mountain as the navel of the earth,
situated at the center of concentric circles of increasing holiness: "The
Land of Israel is situated at the center of the world, and Jerusalem at the
center of the Land of Israel, the Temple at the center of Jerusalem, the
sanctuary at the center of the Temple, and [the] ark at the center of the
sanctuary, and the foundation stone [*even ha-shetiyah*] before the sanctuary, on which the world is founded" (*Tanḥ. Qedoshim* 10). On the foundation stone at the center of the Temple, cf. "From the foundation stone
the world was created" (*b. Yoma* 54b). (*M. Yoma* 5:2 teaches that in the
Second Temple, the foundation stone was the replacement for the ark-
cover, the ark, and the cherubim.)

55   Thus Milik, the editor of the *Aramaic Book of Enoch* found at Qumran;
see Milik, *The Books of Enoch*, 37–38, n. 3. Others disagree with him; see
K. Coblentz Bautch, *The Study of the Geography of 1 Enoch*, "No one has
seen what I have seen" (Boston and Leiden: Brill, 2003), 6.

56   *2 En.* 23, 25–45, 52–63 in Kahana; 71 J:17–23, 28–37; 72A+J:1–6 in
Charlesworth. See discussion below.

57   Cf. the similar imagery in Deut 33:2.

58   *1 En.* 75:3–9; *Jub.* 4:17–18; 50:1-4.

59   That is, Sabbath, sabbatical year, jubilee year, seven holidays in the first
seven months of every year.

60   On Jubilees and the seven-based cycles of time observed from the days of
Enoch and Noah until the time of Abraham and his descendants, see
Elior, *The Three Temples*, 6–29, 82–87.

61   *Jub.* 8:19.

62   See 11QPs col. xxvii:2–1: *DJD* IV: *The Psalms Scroll of Qumran Cave
11(11QPs)* (ed. J. A. Sanders; Oxford: Clarendon, 1965), 91–93. See
also S. Talmon, *The World of Qumran from Within* (Leiden: Brill, 1989),
147–85; Elior, *The Three Temples*, 29–60.

63   Ezek 28:13-18. On the significance of the "shielding cherub," cf. "shielding the Ark of the Covenant of the Lord," attributed to the cherubim in
1 Chr 28:18.

64 *2 En.* 19:2 in Kahana; 68:1 in Charlesworth.

65 See Dan 7:25 and J. Collins, *Daniel: A Commentary on the Book of Daniel* (Minneapolis: Fortress, 1993) ad loc. Cf. Talmon, *The World of Qumran from Within*, 147–85.

66 There are variant readings on "south" or "east"; see comment in Charlesworth on v. 25.

67 *2 En.* 23:37–45 in Kahana; 71–72 in Charlesworth.

68 *Jub.* 4:26. In contrast to the three familiar places—the Garden of Eden, Mount Zion and Mount Sinai—the fourth place, referred to as "the mountain of morning" (*har haboqer*), "the mountain of the east," "the mountain of the south," or "the mountain of incense" is not identified consistently. The terms refer to a mountain located within the Garden of Eden, at whose top is an altar on which incense is offered; it is the celestial model of the terrestrial Temple to be built opposite it on Mount Zion.

69 The *heikhalot* literature connects the crown of Torah received by Moses and the crown of priesthood received by Aaron with Mount Sinai: "[T]he privilege of Aaron son of Amram, a lover of peace and pursuer of peace, who received the crown of priesthood from before Your glory on Mount Sinai" (P. Schäfer, ed., *Synopse zur Hekhalot Literatur* [Tübingen: Mohr Siebeck, 1981], par. 1); "[A]ll the storehouses of wisdom were opened to Moses at Sinai so he might learn [it] in forty days, as he stood on the mountain" (Schäfer, *Synopsis*, par. 388). It associates as well the mountain with the tradition of the chariot ("and the chariot within it on which the Holy One blessed be He descended on Mount Sinai" [84R]).

70 A parallel tradition in the Dead Sea Scrolls describes in exalted terms the dramatic encounter on Mount Sinai among God, Moses, and the angel of the presence. See Elior, *The Three Temples*, 149–50; and see the text itself: D. M. Gropp et al., *DJD* XXVIII, *Wadi Daliyeh*, II, *The Samaria Papyri and Qumran Cave 4 XXVIII Miscellanea* (part 2; Oxford: Clarendon, 2001), 213–14.

71 See Isa 8:18; Mic 4:7; Ps 74:2; "Joel 4:17.

72 Cf. *DJD* XIII, p. 12.

73 *Jub.* 18:13. See M. Segal, "Jubilees," ch. 9. The seven generations elapsed from the time of Abraham to that of Moses: Abraham, Isaac, Jacob, Levi, Qehat, Amram, Moses.

74 *Jub.* 17:15-17, 18:1-19. The Prince Mastema is mentioned in the scrolls; see *Community Rule* III 17–24; cf. Vermes, *CDSSIE* 101; cf. 4QBer. frg. 6, 1–11 (*DJD* XI 57–58); 4Q495 frg. 2, xiii, 9–12 (*DJD* VII, 55).

75 For a comparative analysis of the account and dates mentioned in it, see M. Segal, "Jubilees," 168–78. Cf. *Exod. Rab.* 15:11: "And in it [that is, in the month of Nisan, during which the exodus from Egypt took place] . . . and in it Isaac was born, and in it Isaac was bound." In *Jewish*

Antiquities I:226, Josephus cites a tradition tying the site of Isaac's binding to the site on which the Temple is to be built: "[O]n the third [day], when the mountain was in view, he left his companions in the plain and proceeded with his son alone to that mount whereon king David afterwards erected the temple."

76   On the fourteenth of Nisan as the time of the crucifixion, see John 19:31, stating that the crucifixion took place on Friday, the fourteenth of Nisan, and the eve of Passover, when the paschal sacrifice was offered. On that time in the early eastern Christian tradition and on the time of the crucifixion on a Friday that fell on the fifteenth of Nisan in the three synoptic gospels, see Yuval, *Two Nations,* 60–61, 210, 229. On the identification of the paschal sacrifice with Jesus, the Lamb of God, see Yuval, 73.

77   See Sh. Spiegel, "From the Legends about Isaac's Binding: A Piyyut by R. Ephraim of Bonn on the Slaughter and Resurrection of Isaac," in *Alexander Marx Jubilee Volume* (New York: Jewish Theological Seminary of America, 1950), 471–547 (Hebrew); and *The Last Trial: On the Legends and Lore of the Command to Abraham to Offer Isaac as a Sacrifice* (trans. with an intro. by J. Goldin; new preface by J. Goldin; Woodstock, Vt.: Jewish Lights Publishing, 1993). Spiegel cites legends telling of Abraham actually killing Isaac; and while those legends, derived from tannaitic midrash, postdate the New Testament, it is possible that they preserve earlier traditions. Yuval takes an opposing view, maintaining that these legends represent a Jewish effort to present Isaac as a substitute for Jesus as one who is killed and resurrected. See Yuval, *Two Nations,* 57, n. 62.

78   O. Limor, *Holy Land Travels: Christian Pilgrims in Late Antiquity* (Jerusalem: Yad Yitzhak Ben-Zvi, 1998), 122, 159 (Hebrew).

79   Y. Yuval, *Two Nations,* 23, fn. omitted.

80   Yuval, *Two Nations,* 38; A. Limor, "Christian Sanctity—Jewish Authority," *Cathedra* 80 (1997): 31–62 (Hebrew).

81   Yuval, *Two Nations,* 23–24.

82   See *Qumran Cave 4, V: Miqsat Maase Hatorah, DJD* X: "we have separated from the mass of the peo[ple]" (Vermes, *Complete Dead Sea Scrolls,* 227). The beginning of MMT sets forth the House of Zadok's priestly calendar of Sabbaths regulating service in the Temple, expressing the view of the scroll's writers of what was most important and most urgent.

83   *Pss. Sol.* 8:22 (J. H. Charlesworth, ed., *The Old Testament Pseudepigrapha* [2 vols.; New York: Doubleday, 1985], 2:660).

84   *Pss. Sol.* 17:4-6 (Charlesworth, *The Old Testament,* 2: 665–66).

85   *Pss. Sol.* 11:1 (Charlesworth, *The Old Testament,* 2:661).

86   Sir 51: unnumbered verses between 12 and 13 designated "Heb. Adds."

87   Sir 24:10-11.

88   2 Sam 24:16-25; 1 Chr 21:15, 18-30.

89   Kahana: the place of Aravna.

90   *2 En.* 71:29-35 in Charlesworth, vol. 1; cf. ch. 23 in Kahana.

91   *2 En.* 72:1; cf. ch. 23 in Kahaha. I corrected "Edem" to "Eden."

92   Ch. 23 in Kahaha, v. 5.

93   Vermes, *Complete Dead Sea Scrolls,* 501.

94   *DJD* XXIII, 229. See F. Garcia Martinez et.al., eds., 11Q13 in *DJD* XXIII, *Qumran Cave 11* (Oxford: Clarendon, 1998), 225–26 (Hebrew); 229–30 (English).

95   11Q13; *DJD* XXIII, 229.

96   11Q17; *DJD* XXIII, 270.

97   *DJD* XXIII, 230.

98   4Q522 frag 9ii: 3–9 *DJD* XXV, *Qumran Grotte 4 XVIII Textes Hebreux* (Oxford: Clarendon, 1998), 55–56. See the discussion of this passage, 57–62, and the article by its editor, E. Puech, "La Pierre de Sion et l'autel des holocautes d'apres un manuscript hébreu de la grotte 4 (4Q522)," *Revue Biblique* 99 (1992): 676–96. The translation in the text is by the present translator; cf. *DJD* XXV, 55–56.

99   4Q394 3 7ii 6 *DJD* X (Vermes, *Complete Dead Sea Scrolls,* 224; brackets indicating reconstruction omitted).

100 M. Baillet, ed., *DJD VII* (Oxford: Clarendon, 1982), 143–44; (Vermes, *Complete Dead Sea Scrolls,* 365; brackets omitted).

101 *2 En.* 21:4; 23:37-46 in Kahana; 67:2-3; 68:5; 71:35; and 72:69 in Charlesworth.

102 *1 En.* 33:3-4; 75:2-4; 82:6-7; *Jub.* 4:17-20, 21-25; *2 En.* 18–21 in Kahana; 68:1-5; and 72:69 in Charlesworth.

103 *2 En.* 23 in Kahana; 68–72 in Charlesworth.

104 Views are divided on the transfer of Isaac's binding from Nisan to Tishri. See P. R. Davies, "Passover and the Dating of the Aqedah," *Journal of Jewish Studies* 30, no. 1 (1979): 59–67.

105 See 1 Chr 5:27-41; 6:35-38; Ezra 7:1-5; cf. D. W. Rooke, *Zadok's Heirs: The Role and Development of the High Priesthood* (Oxford and New York: Oxford University Press, 2000).

106 See Elior, *The Three Temple,* 1–28, 201–31.

107 Vermes, *Complete Dead Sea Scrolls,* 305–6.

108 Cf. Ps. 133:3 in MT, which reads "mountains of Zion" rather than "Mount Zion."

109 On the Enoch literature, see above. On the *heikhalot* literature, including *3 Enoch,* see G. Scholem, *Major Trends in Jewish Mysticism* (New York: Schocken, 1954), 68ff.; idem, *Jewish Gnosticism, Merkabah Mysticism and Talmudic Tradition* (New York: Jewish Theological Seminary, 1960), 41–42; D. R. Halperin, *The Faces of the Chariot, Early Jewish Responses to Ezekiel's Vision* (Tubingen: Mohr, 1988).

Chapter 18

1 Suetonius, *Vesp.* 4.

2 Suetonius, *Vesp.* 4.

3 "The endurance of the Jews lasted till Gessius Florus was procurator. In his time the war broke out. Cestius Gallus, legate of Syria, who attempted to crush it, had to fight several battles, generally with ill-success. Cestius dying, either in the course of nature, or from vexation" (Tacitus, *Hist.* 5). Similarly Suetonius comments, "The rebellious Jews . . . murdered their governor, routed the governor of Syria when he came down to restore order, and captured an Eagle" (*Vesp.* 4).

4 Josephus, *War* 4.30–35.

5 Josephus, *War* 4.491.

6 Josephus, *War* 4.497–98.

7 Suetonius, *Galba* 16.

8 T. E. J. Wiedemann comments on the rapidity of the succession: "The Senate formally recognized Otho as the man who controlled the imperial household and the empire at a meeting held on the same evening [as Galba's death]" ("Nero to Vespasian," in *CAH* 10: *The Augustan Empire, 43 B.C.–A.D. 69* [2nd ed.; Cambridge: Cambridge University Press, 1996], 268).

9 Suetonius, *Otho* 10–12.

10 Suetonius, *Vesp.* 8–9.

11 Suetonius, *Vesp.* 8.

12 Suetonius, *Vesp.* 9.

13 Suetonius, *Vesp.* 10.

14 Suetonius, *Vesp.* 8.

15 It is possible that the levy for the temple was in fact introduced by Nehemiah and retrojected back into the Exodus account to legitimize it by giving it both antiquity and Mosaic authority. This suggestion is supported by the fact that the amount levied by Nehemiah, one-third of a shekel, was less than the amount stipulated in Exodus. This amount seems to accord poorly with general principles of inflation.

16 *M. Seqal* outlines the mechanics of collecting the temple tax: when it was to occur, what currency could be used, who was liable to the surcharge, and so on.

17 H. Danby, ed., *The Mishnah* (Oxford: Oxford University Press, 1933), 154, n. 3.

18 See Suetonius, *Dom.* 12.2.

19 M. D. Goodman, *The Ruling Class of Judaea* (Cambridge: Cambridge University Press, 1987), 232.

20 Suetonius, *Vesp.* 8.4.

21 Many scholars suggest that this figure is not accurate and emend the amount to 4,000 million sesterces. It is not sure whether the error is due

to exaggeration on the part of Suetonius (*Vesp.* 16.3), or the result of a later textual corruption. For a discussion of the amount more realistically being put at 4000 million sesterces see Griffin, "1: The Flavians; I: Vespasian," in *CAH* 11: *The High Empire A.D. 70–192* (2nd ed.; Cambridge: Cambridge University Press, 2000), 26.

22 Suetonius, *Vesp.* 16.

23 B. Levick, *Vespasian* (London: Routledge, 1999), 99–101.

24 Griffin, "1: The Flavians; I: Vespasian," 75.

25 Suetonius, *Dom.* 12.2.

26 Thompson's claim that "the rigorous administration of the fiscus Iudaicus under Domitian involved a witch-hunt for so-called Jewish tax-evaders and a spate of prosecutions of alleged evaders," is overdrawn. Especially since the accent falls more heavily on the Jewishness of the nonpayers, rather than upon the evasion of the fiscus. L. A. Thompson, "Domitian and the Jewish Tax," *Historia* 31 (1982): 329.

27 Pliny, *Panegyricus* 90.5.

28 Griffin, "1: The Flavians; III: Domitian," in *CAH* 11: *The High Empire A.D. 70–192* (2nd ed.; Cambridge: Cambridge University Press, 2000), 71.

29 Pliny, *Pan.* 42.1; 36.1; 55.5; 37–38.

30 Frontinus, *Aq.* 11.118.

31 See Griffin, "2: Nerva to Hadrian, I: Nerva," in *CAH* 11: *The High Empire A.D. 70–192* (2nd ed.; Cambridge: Cambridge University Press, 2000), 93.

32 Pliny, *Pan.* 37–38.

33 After F. W. Madden, *History of Jewish Coinage and of Money in the Old and New Testament* (London: Quaritch, 1864). This image is taken from Madden.

34 E. M. Smallwood is representative of scholars who suggest that the vigorous execution of the tax under Domition was aimed at Gentile proselytes to Judaism, or those who had adopted some Jewish customs. See his "Domitian's Attitude toward the Jews and Judaism," *CP* 51 (1956): 1–13.

35 Thompson, "Domitian," 331.

36 M. D. Goodman, "Nerva, the Fiscus Judaicus and Jewish Identity," *JRS* 79 (1989): 40.

37 Goodman, "Nerva," 42.

38 Arrian, *Epict. diss.* 2.9.20.

39 For the centrality of the temple and associated pilgrimage festivals, see J. C. VanderKam, *An Introduction to Early Judaism* (Grand Rapids: Eerdmans, 2001), 204–8.

40 It is, of course, incorrect to draw too rigid a contrast between these pairings. Both temple and synagogue coexisted prior to the destruction of the temple in 70 C.E., and even after the fall of Jerusalem, the rabbis

devoted considerable attention to cultic and sacrificial rites in the Mishnaic discussions.

41   The exact dating of the crucifixion of Jesus is notoriously difficult. See R. E. Brown, "Appendix II: Dating the Crucifixion," in *The Death of the Messiah*, 2:1350–78.

42   The major challenge to the validity of redaction criticism has been mounted by Richard Bauckham, "For Whom Were the Gospels Written?" in *The Gospels for all Christians: Rethinking the Gospel Audiences* (ed. Richard Bauckham; Grand Rapids: Eerdmans), 9–49.

43   For a response to Bauckham and a defence of redaction criticism, see D. C. Sim, "The Gospel for all Christians? A Response to Richard Bauckham," *JSNT* 84 (2001): 2–27.

44   G. D. Kilpatrick observes that "The section has traces of Matthean diction in προσῆλθον, τί σοι δοκεῖ, κῆνσον, ἄραγε, ἀνοίξας, στατῆρα, ἀντί" (*The Origins of the Gospel according to Matthew* [Oxford: Clarendon, 1946], 41).

45   Stories unique to Matthew's gospel that show a significant interest in Peter include Matt 14:28-31; 15:15; 16:17-20; 17:24-27; 18:21.

46   W. D. Davies and D. C. Allison note, "The story of the person who loses a piece of jewellery or a key in a lake or an ocean, only to regain it later through catching a fish and cleaning it seems to be at home in all times and place" (*Matthew*, 2:743). They cite examples from Greek, rabbinic, Christian, and modern sources.

47   U. Luz is strident in his assertion that "It is out of the question that the text, vv. 24-27, comes from the time after the destruction of the temple and deals with the problems the church faced in the times of Domitian with the fiscus Judaicus" (*Matthew 8–20* [Minneapolis: Fortress, 2001], 415). Instead he argues "that at issue is the Jewish half-shekel or double drachma tax for the support of the temple and not a civil Roman tax" (414).

48   W. Carter, "Paying the Tax to Rome as Subversive Praxis: Matthew 17:24–27," *JSNT* 76 (1999): 5–6.

49   The point is persuasively made by Goodman. He states, "The incentive to make such a declaration was presumably the freedom to carry on religious practices without odium, what Tertullian described, rather enviously, as *vectigalis libertas* (*Apol.* 18), freedom of worship bought at the price of the Jewish tax. Such privileges as avoiding court cases on the Sabbath and escaping charges of impiety for publicly boycotting civic cults were worth two denarii a year" ("Nerva," 42).

50   See in particular the discussions in Davies and Allison, *Matthew*, 3:692–704. A. J. Saldarini, *Matthew's Christian-Jewish Community* (Chicago: University of Chicago Press, 1994).

51   D. Garland, "The Temple Tax in Matthew," in *SBLSP 1987* (ed. K. H. Richards; Atlanta: Scholars, 1987), 201.

52 Suetonius, *Dom.* 12.2.

53 On the dicussion of whether the community's relationship to the synagogue was intra- or extramuros, see G. N. Stanton, "The Origin and
Purpose of Matthew's Gospel: Matthean Scholarship from 1945 to
1980," *ANRW* 2.25.3:1889–51.

54 R. Bauckham, "The Coin in the Fish's Mouth," in *Gospel Perspectives* 6
(eds. D. Wenham and C. L. Blomberg; Sheffield: Sheffield Academic,
1986), 237–44.

55 The phrase "the kings of the earth" (Matt 17:25), places the tax in question in a civil, rather than a religious context. This should be seen as cor-
roborative evidence for understanding the Matthean story as referring to
the fiscus Judaicus, and no longer to the temple tax.

56 W. D. Davies suggests that Matt 17:22-23 raises the question of "what
the attitude of Christians should be to Rome." The question of the payment of tax is part of this wider issue and offers a survival strategy for the
community. See his *The Setting of the Sermon on the Mount* (Cambridge:
Cambridge University Press, 1964), 391.

57 Carter, "Paying the Tax," 28.

58 Although some scholars have attempted to reconstruct the post-Gospel
history of the community, such reconstructions are methodologically
extremely weak. See D. C. Sim, *The Gospel of Matthew and Christian
Judaism: The History and Social Setting of the Matthean Community*
(Edinburgh: T&T Clark, 1998).

59 Pliny the Younger, *Ep.*, 10.96–97.

60 F. W. Beare, *The Gospel according to Matthew: Translation, Introduction,
and Commentary* (San Francisco: Harper & Row, 1981), 372–73.

61 *CPJ,* 228. The ostraca from Edfu that refer to the Trajanic period are
documented in *CPJ*, 194–229. Ostraca referring to receipt of the *fiscus
Judaicus* collected under the Flavian emperors are documented in *CPJ*
160–93. No ostrakon from Edfu makes reference to Nerva.

62 It is difficult to date the reference accurately. Origin lived between 185
and 254 C.E. It is likely that the epistle was written at some time in the
second quarter of the third century.

63 Origin, *Ep. Afr.* 20 (14).

64 Luz draws attention to the widespread nature of this misconception:
"Contrary to a widespread misunderstanding, the emperor Nerva did not
abolish this special tax but only the Fisci Iudaici calumnia, that is, the
fact that one could be forced to pay it on the basis of a denunciation"
(*Matthew 8–20*, 414).

65 Julian, *Ad Communitatem Iudaeorum,* 51 in *Julian* (ed. W. C. Wright; 3
vols.; LCL 157; Cambridge, Mass.: Harvard University Press, 1923),
3:176–81.

66 The most probable date is 362 or 363 C.E., because of Julian's reference
to the Persian campaign (see section 398).

67 Julian, *Ad Communitatem Iudaeorum*, 51.396–98.

68 *Ad Communitatem Iudaeorum*, lines 2–3: "had to contribute an untold amount of money to the accounts of the treasury."

69 *Ad Communitatem Iudaeorum*, line 1: "In times past. . . ."

70 *Ad Communitatem Iudaeorum*, lines 5–6: "when a tax was about to be levied on you again I prevented it."

71 *Ad Communitatem Iudaeorum*, lines 1–2: "by far the most burdensome thing in the yoke of your slavery. . . ."

72 *Ad Communitatem Iudaeorum*, line 17.

73 Constantius reigned for the period 337–361 C.E., following the death of his father Constantine I. It was under the reign of Constantine that Christianity was adopted as the religion of the imperial household, and consequently its popularity spread.

74 As Wright notes, "Julian like Epictetus, always calls the Christians Galilaeans because he wishes to emphasise that this was a local creed, 'the creed of fishermen,' and perhaps to remind his readers that 'out of Galilee ariseth no prophet'; with the same intention he calls Christ the Nazarene'" (*Julian* 3:313).

75 *Ad Communitatem Iudaeorum*, section 398.

76 Julian was killed in battle during the Persian campaign in 363 C.E.

77 Suetonius, *Vesp.* 16.

78 See T. Rajak, "Was There a Roman Charter for the Jews?" *JRS* 74 (1984): 107–23.

79 Carter, "Paying the Tax," 26–30.

80 Julian, *Ad Communitatem Iudaeorum*.

81 See Julian, *Against the Galileans*.

82 After praising the Roman inclination for philosophy and geometry, he mocks the story of the tower of Babel as an explanation of linguistic diversity. He concludes by exhorting readers to see the obviously fallacious nature of the account. "Then do you, who believe that this so obvious fable is true, and moreover think God was afraid of the brutal violence of men, and for this reason came down to earth to confound their languages, do you, I say, still venture to boast of your knowledge of God?" (Julian, *Against the Galilaeans*, 134D–135D).

Chapter 19

1 Significant parts of this article were originally published as "Paul et ses exégètes juifs contemporains" in *Recherches de Science Religieuse* 94, no. 3 (2006): 413–41 and are used with permission from the editor. In that article, I did not originally deal with Paul's religious experience, and so this represents, at the same time, an entirely new dimension of the study. Hurtado, *How on Earth*.

2   Jonathan D. Brumberg-Kraus, "A Jewish Ideological Perspective on the Study of Christian Scripture," *Jewish Social Studies* 4, no. 1 (1997): 122–52. His own work is with the Gospel of Luke: "Conventions of Literary Symposia in Luke's Gospel with Special Attention to the Last Supper" (Ph.D. diss., Vanderbilt University, 1991), and a book, tentatively entitled *Memorable Meals: Symposia in Luke's Gospel, The Rabbinic Seder, and the Greco-Roman Literary Tradition*, which is eagerly anticipated. He describes this phenomenon as the "Jesus-is-Jewish, Paul-is-goyish" trope.

3   Stefan Meissner, *Die Heimholung des Ketzers: Studien zur jüdischen Auseinandersetzung mit Paulus* (ed. Martin Hengel and Otfried Hofius; WUNT, 2/87; Tübingen: J. C. B. Mohr [Paul Siebeck], 1996).

4   This is supplemented by her article, "What Scholars Are Saying about Paul: What It Means for Jews," *The Reconstructionist* 51, no. 5 (1986), a more popular article based on her Ph.D. dissertation.

5   In the volume *Pauline Studies: Essays Presented to Professor F. F. Bruce on His 70th Birthday* (eds. D. H. Hagner and M. J. Harris; Exeter: Pater-noster Press, 1980).

6   (Grand Rapids: Academie Books, 1984).

7   Jonathan D. Brumberg-Kraus, "A Jewish Ideological Perspective on the Study of Christian Scripture," *Jewish Social Studies* 4, no 1 (1977–1998: 122–52, as noted above.

8   Pamela Eisenbaum, "Following in the Footnotes of the Apostle Paul," in *Identity and the Politics of Scholarship in the Study of Religion* (eds. Jose Ignacio Cabezon and Sheila Greeve Davaney; New York: Routledge, 2004), 77–98. See her article, "Is Paul the Father of Mysogyny and AntiSemitism?" *CrossCurrents* http://www.crosscurrents.org/ eisenbaum.htm. Also she has graciously shared her more recent, unpublished paper for the SBL Annual Conference in San Antonio with me.

9   See John Gager, "Scholarship as Moral Vision: David Flusser on Jesus, Paul, and the Birth of Christianity," *Jewish Quarterly Review* 95 (2005): 60–73.

10   *The Religious Imagination: A Study in Psychoanalysis and Jewish Theology* (Indianapolis: Bobbs Merrill, 1968).

11   *Power Struggle: An Autobiographical Confession* (New York: 1974; new ed.; Lanham, Md.: University Press of America, 1986).

12   This subject was offered at Heidelberg, Marburg, Leipzig, and Berlin. See Meissner, *Die Heimholung*, 76–77.

13   See the fine analysis of Schoeps's work in Daniel Langton, "Modern Jewish Identity and the Apostle Paul: Pauline Studies as an Intra-Jewish Ideological Battleground," *JSNT* 28.2 (2005): 217–58.

14   *Philo of Alexandria* (New York: Oxford University Press, 1979).

15   As quoted in Meissner, *Die Heimholung*, 86.

16 Samuel Sandmel, *The Genius of Paul* (Farrar, Straus & Cudahy, 1958; rev ed; Philadelphia: Fortress, 1979), 21.

17 See Langton, "Modern Jewish Identity," 217–58.

18 Sandmel, *The Genius of Paul,* 33f. See Meissner, *Die Heimholung,* 89.

19 Segal, *Rebecca's Children.*

20 (New Haven: Yale University Press, 1990).

21 (New York: Doubleday, 2004).

22 Daniel Boyarin, *A Radical Jew: Paul and the Politics of Identity* (Berkeley: University of California Press, 1997). 1.

23 *Carnal Israel: Reading Sex in Talmudic Culture* (Berkeley: University of California Press, 1995).

24 David Biale, *Eros and the Jews: From Biblical Israel to Contemporary America* (Berkeley: University of California Press, 1997).

25 Howard Eilberg-Schwartz, *God's Phallus* (Boston: Beacon Press, 1995).

26 Daniel Boyarin, *Unheroic Conduct: The Rise of Heterosexuality and the Invention of the Jewish Male* (Berkeley: University of California Press, 1997).

27 See, as always, the excellent work of Stefan Meissner on each Jewish writer on Paul (*Die Heimholung,* 131).

28 See Meissner, *Die Heimholung,* 133.

29 Susan A. Handelman, *The Slayers of Moses: The Emergence of Rabbinic Interpretation in Modern Literary Theory* (SUNY Series on Modern Jewish Literature and Culture; Albany: State of New York University Press, 2006).

30 See, e.g., Rom 9:6; 1 Cor 14:36; 2 Cor 2:17, 4:2; Phil 1:14; Col. 1:25.

31 See, e.g., the intriguing *parvum opus* of Wayne Meeks, *Christ Is the Question* (Knoxville: Westminster John Knox, 2006), 85–91.

32 Daniel Boyarin, *Dying for God: Martyrdom and the Making of Christianity and Judaism* (Stanford: Stanford University Press, 1999).

33 Daniel Boyarin, *Borderlines: The Partition of Judaeo-Christianity* (Philadelphia: University of Pennsylvania Press, 2004).

34 Mark D. Nanos, *The Mystery of Romans: The Jewish Context of Paul's Letter* (Minneapolis: Fortress, 1996). It won the National Jewish Book Award for Jewish-Christian studies in 1996.

35 (Peabody, Mass.: Hendrickson, 2002).

36 Pinchas Lapide and Peter Stuhlmacher, *Paul, Rabbi and Apostle* (trans. Lawrence W. Denef; Minneapolis: Augsburg, 1984).

37 Nanos, *Mystery,* 4. Daniel Langton reads this phrase as saying that the New Testament is a Jewish book. That would be a very naive statement, as parts of the NT are written by Gentiles for Gentiles. But extolling Christian adherence to Jewish Law is not the only criterion for deciding whether a scholar is on the right track. There are other reasons for appreciating Nanos's scholarship as well.

Chapter 20

1 Walter Bauer, *Orthodoxy and Heresy in Earliest Christianity* (ed. Georg Strecker; trans. Robert Kraft and Gerhard Krodel; Philadelphia: Fortress, 1971), which is a translation of his second German edition, *Rechtgläubigkeit und Ketzerei im ältesten Christentum* (BHT 10; Tübingen: Mohr Siebeck, 1934). Though Bauer's thesis has taken a number of hits since its publication, it remains a watershed as it altered the scholarly conversation concerning early Christianity in several ways, primarily in recognizing the diversity of early Christian development and identity and, in corollary, the need to identify and value provenance of a given writing and/or group.

2 Helmut Koester, *Introduction to the New Testament: History and Literature of Early Christianity* (2 vols.; New York: de Gruyter, 1982), 2:207.

3 My own baptism (as an undergraduate student) into NT Christology and the Jewish character of and influences on early Christianity came at the "hands" (i.e., by reading) of Hurtado, via his *One God, One Lord*, and Segal, via his *Rebecca's Children*. Since that time, I have been further informed and shaped in these areas of study through many of their other fine works and am grateful for their offer of friendship and collegiality. I am additionally indebted to Larry, as one of his postgraduate students in NT at Edinburgh, for the offering of his knowledge and skills during that period and for his mentoring as a scholar then and now. As is further fitting for this occasion, this essay was (in an earlier form) one I read in my first Society of Biblical Literature presentation in the "Early Jewish/Christian Relations" unit in 1996, in which Larry was also presenting, and one I later submitted to him and the University of Edinburgh as part of my postgraduate application. With much appreciation and respect, then, I submit this essay (modified a good bit!) to honor both Larry and Alan.

4 The body of literature known as the *Hellenistic Synagogal Prayers* was originally discovered within the *Apostolic Constitutions* (*Apos. Con.*), which is a manual of ecclesiastical life that contains Christian liturgy, instruction, exhortation, and models for living the Christian life. These prayers are found in books 7–8 of the *Apos. Con.*(7.26.1–3 to 8.41.2–5). K. Kohler was the first scholar to have noted these prayers in his "The Origin and Composition of the Eighteen Benedictions with a Translation of the Corresponding Essene Prayers in the Apostolic Constitutions," *HUCA* 1 (1924): 387–425. He further claimed that these Prayers are one of the sources that underlie the *Apostolic Constitutions*. While there is no extant evidence for these six prayers existing as a collection independently of the *Apostolic Constitutions*, their inclusion in the *Apostolic Constitutions* as a collection and the final compiler's reliance on and inclusion of materials from a number of other identifiable sources, such as *Didache*, *Didascalia*, and the

Apostolic Tradition, lend credence to the notion that they may well have existed independently as a collection. Further, since all of these other noted sources found in the *Apostolic Constitutions* are from the second through third centuries C.E., these prayers are usually assumed to have existed in their current form (i.e., with the Christian interpolations) during this same timeframe, with a Jewish *Grundlage* preceding it—likely something akin to the current form of the prayers minus the Christian interpolations.

Finally, when citing passages from the prayers, I will use notations from the *Apostolic Constitutions*. However, in the main text of this essay, I will continue to refer to it as "*HSP5*" or simply "the Prayer." Citations of the text from *HSP5* come from David A. Fiensy and D. R. Darnell, "*Hellenistic Synagogal Prayers,*" *OTP* (vol. 2; ed. James H. Charlesworth; New York: Doubleday, 1985, 682–84). On the text of the Prayer, see also David A. Fiensy, *Prayers Alleged to Be Jewish: An Examination of the Constitutiones Apostolorum* (Chico: Scholars Press, 1985), 74–79; and F. X. Funk, *Apostolischen Konstitutionen* (Frankfurt: Minerva, 1970). Also, I am grateful to have access to an early draft of a commentary that Pieter W. van der Horst and Judith H. Newman are writing on early Jewish prayer texts in Greek (including *HSP5*), forthcoming in the series *Commentaries on Early Jewish Literature* (Walter de Gruyter in Berlin).

5   W. Bousset, in his "Eine judische Gebetssammlung im siebenten Buch der apostolischen Konstitutionen," in *Nachrichten von der Koniglichen Gesellschaft der Wissenschaften* (Gottingen: Philologische-historische Klasse, 1915), 438–85, held that the *Hellenistic Synagogal Prayers* were composed somewhere in the Diaspora. Other scholars have cited the provenance to be in Alexandria, but no support is given for this hypothesis. Strong external evidence testifies to a Syrian provenance. Primary in this argument is that the *Didache* and the *Didascalia*, two of the main sources evident in the *Apostolic Constitutions*, have a Syrian provenance. It is also posited that the Apostolic Constitutions, based on these observations and others, originated in Syria. For additional support for a Syrian provenance for the prayers, see David A. Fiensy, "*The Hellenistic Synagogal Prayers*: One Hundred Years of Discussion," *JSP* 5 (1989): 26.

6   E. R. Goodenough, *By Light, Light* (New Haven: Yale University Press, 1935), 339. Fiensy is the only scholar who has brought serious critique to the theory of "clumsy" Christian redaction posited by Goodenough. Fiensy holds that the Christian elements in the prayers do not necessitate a conclusion including Christian redactional activity, not because of a challenge to how distinctively or authentically Christian they may be. Rather, Fiensy uniquely contends that the prayers originated within a Christian community; on this, see David A. Fiensy, "Redaction History and the Apostolic Constitutions," *JQR* 72 (1982): 293–302. However persuasive this argument may or may not be for the prayers as a whole,

it does not apply to *HSP5* because even he concedes this Prayer's unde-
niable Jewish origin.

7   A more in-depth examination of the Christian additions in *HSP5* will be
the subject of the second part of this essay.

8   This parallelism was first detailed by Kohler, in his "The Origin and
Composition," and receives further discussion in Fiensy, *Prayers Alleged
to be Jewish*, 129–64. For the text of these benedictions, see Sabbath and
Festival Prayer Book, The Rabbinical Assembly of America and the
United Synagogue of America, 1946. Since there is hardly any ancient
evidence for these benedictions and, as with much of ancient Jewish
liturgy of the period, they seem to have been fluid in form, there is
almost no way of knowing what they originally would have looked like.
Therefore, it is necessary to cite them from a modern source, while still
being attentive to possible anachronistic assumptions and/or readings.

9   *Sabbath and Festival Prayer Book*, 22.

10 *Sabbath and Festival Prayer Book*, 30–31.

11 Marcel Simon, *Verus Israel* (New York: Oxford University Press, 1964), 53.

12 Fiensy, "Redaction History," 302.

13 For references to "the iron furnace," see Deut 4:20, 1 Kgs 8:51, and Jer
11:4. Also, see Gen 11:3; Exod 5:7-8, 14, 16, 18-19; and Jdt 5:11 for references to "bricks" in relation to the labors of the Israelites in Egypt.

14 Additionally, van der Horst, in his forthcoming commentary with Judith
Newman, argues that the phrase "our fathers," for the Exodus generation,
is an indicator of the Prayer's Jewish origin (see, specifically, the section of
the commentary on *Apos. Con.* 7.36.3).

15 For references to the "hand of Pharaoh" in the HB, see Exod 18:10 and
2 Kgs 17:7. See Exod 3:8; 14:30; 18:9-11; Judg 6:9; and 1 Sam 10:18
for references to the "hand of the Egyptians." Finally, in the same vein,
God's power in the release of the enslaved Israelites is designated to be
done by his "right hand" or "hand." All citations from the Bible, unless
otherwise noted, are from the NRSV.

16 Learning from the prior conversations on "normative" Judaism or
Christianity, it need not be posited that any one of the Jewish traditions
in the Prayer is more significant or indicative of the community that produced it than another. Rather, taking the observations at face-value, we
first affirm that they are different but also that they all still are Jewish,
even if the confluence of Jewish traditions has no evident point of comparison in our knowledge of the known communities in that day.

17 Marianne Thompson, in her essay in this volume entitled, "Jesus: 'The
One Who Sees God,'" also notes this passage and emphasis in Philo
within her argument concerning John's claims about the uniqueness and
superiority of Jesus—as the one who sees God—in the Gospel of John.
All of the references to Philo come from the Loeb Classical Library.

18   Samuel Sandmel, in his *Philo of Alexandria* (New York: Oxford
      University Press, 1979), 59, notes that, according to Philo, the quality of
      sight "is not here meant to be perception by the eyes, but by the mind;
      such 'sight' is the highest point to which man can advance." For addi-
      tional works on Philo and "seeing God," see Segal, *Paul the Convert*,
      52–53; Birnbaum, *The Place of Judaism in Philo's Thought*, 61–127; and
      Bockmuehl, *Revelation and Mystery*, 69–75. For references to the one
      "who sees God" or "seeing God" as a definition for Israel, see *Alleg.
      Interp.* 3.38, 186, 212; *Posterity* 92; *Prelim. Studies* 51; *Names* 81; *Dreams*
      2.174; *Abraham* 57; *Rewards* 44; and *Embassy* 4.

19   See the section on *Apos. Con.* 7.36.4, within the treatment of *HSP5*, in
      the forthcoming commentary on Jewish prayer texts in Greek by van der
      Horst and Newman.

20   Other demographic, geographical, and sociological observations enable
      us to make additional claims concerning the significant Jewish influence
      on early Christianity. The pervasive presence of the Jewish population,
      during the first two centuries C.E., was unique to Syria among the
      Diaspora communities, as noted by Josephus: "The Jewish race, densely
      interspersed among the native populations of every portion of the world,
      is particularly numerous in Syria, where intermingling is due to the prox-
      imity of the two countries" (*Jewish War* 7.43—Loeb translation). On
      this, see also Adolph von Harnack, *The Expansion of Christianity in the
      First Three Centuries* (New York: Arno, 1904), 8. It is also noted that
      Edessa and Nisbis were important points in the interchange of commerce
      on the "Silk Road," which connected the Roman Empire with the East,
      thus linking Syria and Palestine economically and otherwise; see David
      Bundy, "Christianity in Syria," *ABD* 1:971 and Arthur Vööbus, *History
      of Asceticism in the Syrian Orient: A Contribution to the History of Culture
      in the Near East* (3 vols.; Louvain: Universitätis Catholicae Americae,
      1958), 1:5–6. Finally, much of the early Syrian literary evidence reveals
      a distinct Jewish-Christian theology. Gerd Lüdemann, in his, "The
      Successors of Pre-70 Jerusalem Christianity: A Critical Evaluation of the
      Tradition," in *Jewish and Christian Self-Definition* (ed. E. P. Sanders; 3
      vols.: Philadelphia: Fortress, 1980), 1:253, after citing that Jewish
      Christianity, which was modeled after early Jerusalem Christians, was
      regarded as heretical in the Diaspora, notes that "the situation in Syria
      was different." Likewise, Georg Strecker, in an appendix to Bauer's
      Orthodoxy and Heresy in Earliest Christianity, argues in support of Bauer's
      thesis. Strecker claims that the Jewish-Christianity present in the region
      of Syria, as revealed in the *Didascalia*; *Kerygma Petrou*; and by the
      Ebionites, stands as a parallel, but distinct, stream of development to the
      "great church" and was in existence prior to this orthodoxy. The argu-
      ment proposed by Strecker not only invites the reader to consider the
      Jewish influence in early Syrian Christianity but also to recognize its

formative presence. Finally, Stephen Wilson, in his *Related Strangers: Jews and Christians 70–170 C.E.* (Minneapolis: Fortress, 1995), 224, somewhat reluctantly admits that Jewish-Christianity in Syria is a viable option by posting an unexplained disclaimer that, "it is conceivable that Syrian Christianity toward the end of the first century was in some way influenced by the remnants of an originally small, now inactive, Jewish sect—though this is to assume a lot." The Jewish portrait of early Syrian Christianity is not as sketchy as Wilson intimates.

21 Koester, *Introduction to the New Testament*, 2:207.

22 The three sections of *HSP5* that contain Christian redaction are *Apos. Con.* 7.36.1, 2, 6. The date of the Christian redaction can most likely be placed in the third or fourth century C.E. The date of redaction surely predates the fourth-century compilation of the *Apostolic Constitutions* and postdates the second- and third-century sources which underlie it.

23 Wilson, *Related Strangers*, 223.

24 Wilson, *Related Strangers*, 224.

25 James A. Charlesworth, "Jewish and Christian Self-Definition in Light of the Christian Additions to the Apocryphal Writings," in Sanders, *Jewish and Christian Self-Definition*, 2:28. Charlesworth lists four types of Christian additions to the pseudepigrapha. First is the minor addition of a genitival phrase such as "through Christ" or "of Christ." Second is the insertion of at least a paragraph into the writing at some point. Third are the pseudepigrapha that have received significant Christian additions either at the beginning or the end of the work. Fourth are the pseudepigrapha, which are preserved only after massive rewriting.

26 Charlesworth, "Jewish and Christian," 31.

27 Echoes of the Johannine emphasis on Jesus as the wisdom of God in creation (e.g., John 1:1-5) are obvious at this point.

28 Charlesworth, "Jewish and Christian," 33. Other early Christian accounts of similar events in the life of Jesus, which are located in some type of confessional formulae, can be found in Rom 1:4; 4:24; 8:34; Phil 2:5-11; Col 1:15-20; 1 Tim 2:8; 3:16; 1 Pet 1:21; 3:18; *Barn.* 5:6; *Ign. Eph.* 18:2; *Ign. Trall.* 9:1; and *Ign. Smyrn.* 1:1-2.

29 See van der Horst and Newman's forthcoming commentary, within the treatment of *HSP5*, on *Apos. Con.* 7.36.2. It could well also be argued that, since immediately following this liturgical confession we find a thanksgiving for the Lord's providential guidance in leading the Israelites out of Egypt through the Red Sea, and for giving them the Law, it is implied that Christ, as the wisdom of God, was an active agent in each of these events. However, while that remains a possible conclusion, it may also stretch an implication too far.

30 The term "clumsy" has developed its own tradition history within the analyses of the Christian additions to HSP5; on this, see Goodenough, *By Light, Light*, 339; Simon, *Verus Israel*, 54; and Wilson, *Related Strangers*, 101.

31 On Jewish traditions concerning personified attributes and the early worship of Jesus, see Hurtado, *One God, One Lord*, 41–69.

32 Fiensy, *Prayers Alleged to Be Jewish*, 183.

33 Simon, *Verus Israel*, 54.

34 Wilson, *Related Strangers*, 101.

35 Once the reader looks beyond the surface animosity of Eusebius toward the first of these groups, this account reveals a group with liturgical practices seemingly similar to those present in *HSP5*, at least in the remembrance and celebration of both the Sabbath and Lord's Day.

36 See Christian Mauser, "προέχω," *TDNT* 6:692–93.

37 The larger arguments into which the earlier quotes (in this section) by Fiensy, Simon, and Wilson fit all stress the discontinuity between the Lord's Day and Sabbath, with προέχω often the linchpin in their argument for Christian supersessionism.

38 See this section of his and Judith Newman's commentary on *HSP5*.

39 For references in Philo to the one "who sees God" or "seeing God" as the true Israel, see *Alleg. Interp.* 3.38; 3.186; 3.212; *Posterity* 92; *Flight* 208; *Prelim. Studies* 51; *Names* 81; *Dreams* 2.174; *Abraham* 57; *Rewards* 44; *Embassy* 4; and *Heir* 78.

40 On this last point, see Fiensy, *Prayers Alleged to Be Jewish*, 217–20.

Chapter 21

1 This brief study of Matthew 5:21-26 is offered as a tribute to Larry Hurtado and Alan Segal, two exceptionally fine scholars from whose work I continue to learn. I am grateful to the editors of this volume for inviting me to be among the contributors, and to Carey Newman, the director of Baylor University Press, for extending the due date for the submission of this article. Research on this article began while I was a visiting research scholar at North-West University in South Africa and was completed upon my return to the University of Miami in Coral Gables, Florida.

2 See, e.g., H. J. Holtzmann, *Die Synoptiker* (3rd ed.; HKNT 1.1; Tübingen and Leipzig: Mohr [Siebeck], 1901), 209–10; Pierre Bonnard, *L'Évangile selon Saint Matthieu* (CNT; Neuchatel: Delachaux & Niestlé, 1963), 64; Josef Schmid, *Das Evangelium nach Matthäus* (RNT 1; Regensburg: Friedrich Pustet, 1965), 98–99; Robert Guelich, *The Sermon on the Mount* (Dallas: Word, 1982), 189–90; Davies and Allison, *Matthew*, 1:517, 519; Ulrich Luz, *Matthew 1–7: A Commentary* (CC; Minneapolis: Augsburg, 1989), 280–81; John P. Meier, *The Vision of Matthew: Christ, Church, and Morality in the First Gospel* (New York: Crossroad, 1991), 245 n. 20; Donald A. Hagner, *Matthew 1–13* (WBC 33A; Dallas: Word, 1993), 114–15; and Wolfgang Wiefel, *Das*

Evangelium nach Matthäus (THKNT 1; Leipzig: Evangelische Verlags-anstalt, 1998), 105.

3 The first biblical homicide was, of course, a fratricide occasioned by anger (Gen 4:1-16, esp. 4:5-6). Important texts in the Torah dealing with homicide include Gen 9:5-6; Exod 21:12-14, 29; Lev 24:17; Num 35:16-34; Deut 19:11-13. For a recent discussion of homicide in ancient Near Eastern law and the biblical text, see Pamela Barmash, *Homicide in the Biblical World* (New York: Cambridge University Press, 2005).

4 For the purposes of this essay, it is not necessary to address issues of authenticity and the history of tradition in regard to the three units of material in Matt 5:21-26. As far as Matt 5:22 is concerned, Matt 5:22b and 5:22c may well be secondary additions to 5:22a, but if so, they are certainly pre-Matthean. For the minority view that 5:22b and 5:22c are original components of the unit, see Robert Guelich, "Mt 5,22: Its Meaning and Integrity," *ZNW* 64 (1973): 39–52; for the majority view that they are secondary expansions, see Beare, *The Gospel according to Matthew*, 147–50, and Georg Strecker, *The Sermon on the Mount: An Exegetical Commentary* (Edinburgh: T&T Clark, 1988), 67.

5 Compare *Did.* 14.2 and see the discussion of Kurt Niederwimmer, *The Didache* (Hermeneia; Minneapolis: Fortress, 1998), 197–98, who also (p. 9) calls attention to the free quotation of *Did.* 14.2 and 15.3 by Ps.-Cyprian, *De aleatoribus* 4. See also Hans Dieter Betz, *The Sermon on the Mount* (Hermeneia; Minneapolis: Fortress, 1995), 224.

6 Assignment of Matt 5:25-26 to Q is the more common solution. See, e.g., Helmut Koester, *Ancient Christian Gospels: Their History and Development* (Philadelphia: Trinity Press International/London: SCM Press, 1990), 146, 168, 327. For a reconstruction of Q 12:58–59, see James M. Robinson, Paul Hoffmann, John S. Kloppenborg, eds., *The Critical Edition of Q* (Hermeneia; Minneapolis: Fortress/Leuven: Peeters, 2000), 394–99.

7 My use of the traditional name "Matthew" for the author of the first gospel is conventional, not a matter of conviction. For discussions of the authorship of this anonymous gospel, see the standard commentaries.

8 For a survey of ancient works *On Emotions* in general and on particular emotions, especially anger, see John T. Fitzgerald, "The Passions and Moral Progress: An Introduction," in *Passions and Moral Progress in Greco-Roman Thought* (forthcoming).

9 Although Matt 5:21-22 is broader than the household, Jesus' use of "brother" in discussing the victims of anger reflects the social reality that the household was often the setting for angry outbursts. On domestic violence in antiquity, see John T. Fitzgerald, "Domestic Violence in the Ancient World: Preliminary Considerations and the Problem of Wife-Beating," in *Animosity, the Bible and Us: Some European, North American, and South African Perspectives* (forthcoming).

10   See Ludwig Edelstein, "The Philosophical System of Posidonius," *AJP* 57
      (1936): 286–325, esp. 305, who makes this statement regarding the
      Stoic philosopher Posidonius of Apamea (Syria).

11   Alternatively, it is possible that the joining of 5:23-24 to 5:21-22 is pre-
      Matthean; see Strecker, *Sermon on the Mount*, 67, and Guelich, *Sermon
      on the Mount*, 189, who both mention this option as a possibility.

12   As is occasionally noted (see, e.g., A. H. McNeile, *The Gospel according
      to St. Matthew* [London: Macmillan, 1949], 62, and Davies and Allison,
      Matthew, 1:517), John uses the idiom "to have something against some-
      one" in Rev 2:4, 14, 20 to describe the relationship of the offended to
      the offending party. In this case, moreover, the offense is clearly specified
      (2:4, "you have abandoned your first love;" 2:14-15, some hold the
      teachings of Balaam and of the Nicolaitans; 2:20, "you tolerate Jezebel").
      See also Mark 11:25 and compare Acts 24:19. See also Joachim Jeremias,
      Abba: Studien zur neutestamentlichen Theologie und Zeitgeschichte
      (Göttingen: Vandenhoeck & Ruprecht, 1966), 104, who reaches a simi-
      lar conclusion (but without reference to anger) by appealing to various
      Syriac versions that indicate that the brother is holding on to the mem-
      ory of an offense that he has suffered at the sacrificer's hands. Thus, to
      the extent that anger is contextually implied in 5:23, it is the offended
      brother who is now angry, not the one sacrificing. The latter had previ-
      ously been angry, and it was his anger that has left the brother with hurt
      feelings. For the brother as angry, see also Schmid, *Das Evangelium nach
      Matthäus*, 99; Robert H. Gundry, *Matthew: A Commentary on His
      Literary and Theological Art* (Grand Rapids: Eerdmans, 1982), 86; Daniel
      Patte, *The Gospel According to Matthew: A Structural Commentary on
      Matthew's Gospel* (Philadelphia: Fortress, 1987), 79; and Luz, *Matthew
      1–7*, 280. For the view that the sacrificer is angry, see Hagner, *Matthew
      1–13*, 117.

13   On the concept and terminology of reconciliation in the ancient world,
      see esp. Cilliers Breytenbach, *Versöhnung: Eine Studie zur paulinischen
      Soteriologie* (WMANT 60; Neukirchen-Vluyn: Neukirchener, 1989).

14   In both the second and third units, the one called upon to take action is
      the one in the wrong. Therefore, "the brother [who] has something
      against you" in the second unit is parallel to (but not necessarily identi-
      cal with) "your opponent" in the third unit. This depiction is in keeping
      with the standard ancient paradigm of reconciliation, according to which
      it was the responsibility of the offending party to reconcile the offended
      one and bring the conflict to an end. See John T. Fitzgerald, "Paul and
      Paradigm Shifts: Reconciliation and Its Linkage Group," in *Paul Beyond
      the Judaism/Hellenism Divide* (ed. T. Engberg-Pedersen; Louisville:
      Westminster John Knox, 2001), 241–62, 316–25, esp. 248–50.

15   The first and third units are linked terminologically by the appearance of
      judicial language in each. Thus the two-fold mention of κρίσις ("judg-

ment") in 5:21-22 is picked up and continued by the two-fold reference to the κριτής ("judge") in 5:25. In addition, the solemn pronouncement that introduces Jesus' teaching in 5:22 (ἐγὼ δὲ λέγω ὑμῖν, "But I say to you") is echoed in the similar statement at the beginning of 5:26 (ἀμὴν λέγω σοι).

16 For the purposes of this study, it is not necessary to decide whether Matthew or Luke preserves the more original form of the dominical saying. For the view that Matthew's version is the more original, see *inter alia* Siegfried Schulz, *Q: Die Spruchquelle der Evangelisten* (Zurich: Theologischer Verlag, 1972), 421; Luz, *Matthew 1–7*, 281; and Joseph A. Fitzmyer, *Luke*, 2:1002. For the view that δὸς ἐργασίαν ἀπηλλάχθαι ἀπὸ τοῦ ἀντιδίκου σου was the reading of Q, see Dieter Zeller, *Die weisheitlichen Mahnsprüche bei den Synoptikern* (FB; Würzburg: Echter, 1977), 64. Robinson, Hoffmann, and Kloppenborg, *The Critical Edition of Q*, 394, 396, 398, offer a mixed text of Q that draws on the versions of both Matthew and Luke.

17 See LSJ 176, s.v. ἀπαλλάσσω (B 8), where Plato, *Leg.* 768c and 915c are cited, but in both cases "reach a settlement" (LSJ's "settle a dispute") appears to be the meaning (as R. G. Bury's translation in the LCL suggests). In Apollodorus, *Neaer.* 48 (= Ps.-Demosthenes, *Or.* 59.48), however, since ἀπηλλαγμένοι ἦσαν picks up the διαλλαγαί ("terms of reconciliation") and διήλλαξαν ("they reconciled," "settled their quarrel") in *Neaer.* 48, the meaning is "they were reconciled." See also *Neaer.* 46, where the two parties pledge to be "friends."

18 So also the TNIV, which omits "with you" and gives simply "try hard to be reconciled." For the view that the term means reconciliation, see I. Howard Marshall, *The Gospel of Luke: A Commentary on the Greek Text* (NIGTC; Grand Rapids: Eerdmans, 1978), 551. For interpretations that involve reconciliation, see also Walter Grundmann, *Das Evangelium nach Lukas* (THKNT 3; Berlin: Evangelische Verlagsanstalt, 1963), 273–74, and Eduard Schweizer, *The Good News According to Luke* (Atlanta: John Knox, 1984), 218. Norval Geldenhuys, *Commentary on the Gospel of Luke* (NICNT; Grand Rapids: Eerdmans, 1951), 369, appears to interpret the saying as an allegory, referring to the necessity of reconciliation with Christ before appearing before God as judge. Finally, see also Fitzmyer, *Luke*, 2:1002, who gives "to be reconciled of him" as the literal meaning of the Greek words.

19 See, for example, GOODSPEED, KLEIST, and BDAG 96 (s.v. ἀπαλλάσσω): "lit., get rid of him"; and WILLIAMS ("to get entirely rid of him"). See also MOFFATT ("to get quit of him"). Abbreviations used are found in *The SBL Handbook of Style* or are listed here:

JPS   Jewish Publication Society

KLEIST   James A. Kleist, trans., *The New Testament*, Part I: *The Four Gospels*

RHEIMS   The Douay-Rheims Translation of the Latin Vulgate
TNIV   Today's New International Version
WILLIAMS Charles B. Williams, trans., *The New Testament: A Translation in the Language of the People.*

20 For a rendering along these lines, see J. A. Findlay, "Luke," in *The Abingdon Bible Commentary* (eds. F. C. Eiselen, E. Lewis, and D. G. Downey; New York: Abingdon, 1929), 1022–59, esp. 1046 ("to be rid of"); the MLB ("to be freed from him"); the KJV and RHEIMS ("be delivered from him"); the ASV, WEYMOUTH, and Alfred Plummer, *The Gospel According to S. Luke* (ICC; Edinburgh: T&T Clark, 1901), 336 ("be quit of him"); and John Nolland, *Luke 9:21–18:34* (WBC 35B; Dallas: Word, 1993), 713 ("to be released from him"). See also Holtzmann, *Die Synoptiker*, 375, who notes that Luke lacks Matthew's connection with reconciliation and translates "seiner los zu werden."

21 For this point, see esp. Günter Klein, "Die Prüfung der Zeit (Lucas 12, 54–56)," *ZTK* 61 (1964): 373–90, esp. 383–84.

22 For the correlative formulation of ἀπαλλάσσω with ἀπό, see Xenophon, *Anab.* 7.1.4: "he intended to part company from (ἀπαλλάξοιτο . . . ἀπὸ) the army at once;" Plato, *Leg.* 868d: "the wife must be separated from the husband (ἀπαλλάττεσθαι . . . ἀπ᾽ ἀνδρὸς) and the husband from (ἀπὸ) the wife" (trans. Bury, LCL); and Josephus, *A.J.* 10.24: "the removal (ἀπαλλαξάσης) of the rest [of the enemy] from (ἀπὸ) Jerusalem" (trans. Marcus, LCL). The idea of "separation from" is also found in Luke's only other use of the verb ἀπαλλάσσω (Acts 19:12), where it indicates the departure of diseases from people (ἀπαλλάσσεσθαι ἀπ᾽ αὐτῶν τὰς νόσους, "the diseases departed from them") and is used in conjunction with exorcisms (τά τε πνεύματα τὰ πονηρὰ ἐκπορεύεσθαι, "the evil spirits came out of [them]"). The same is true of the two additional occurrences of ἀπαλλάσσω in Codex Bezae (D). In Luke 9:40, which concerns the exorcism of an unclean spirit and where NA[27] and UBS[4] read ἐκβάλωσιν ("cast out"), D reads ἀπαλλάξωσιν ("set free," "release" the boy from the evil spirit). Similarly with the curing of the sick in Acts 5:15, D adds the statement ἀπηλλάσσοντο γὰρ ἀπὸ πάσης ἀσθενείας, "for they were being set free from every disease."

23 For συναλλάσσω as a verb for reconciliation, see BDAG 964–65. In Acts 7:26 Moses comes upon two men who are fighting (μαχομένοις) and attempts to reconcile (συνήλλασσεν) them by bringing them to peace (εἰρήνην). That goal is utterly foreign to the context of Luke 12:58; see esp. 12:51, where Jesus declares that he has not come to bring peace (εἰρήνην) but rather division (διαμερισμόν). See also Luke 12:52-53, which dilates upon the idea of contentious divisions by focusing on the household as the locus of conflict. For familial discord as an occasion for

persecution of Christians and an impetus for domestic violence, see John T. Fitzgerald, "Early Christian Mission Practice and Pagan Reaction: 1 Peter and Domestic Violence against Slaves and Wives," in *Renewing Tradition: Studies in Texts and Contexts in Honor of James W. Thompson* (eds. M. H. Hamilton, T. H. Olbricht, and J. Peterson; Princeton Theological Monograph Series; Eugene: Pickwick, 2007), 24–44.

24 See, for example, 1 Cor 7:11, "but if she does separate (χωρισθῇ), let her remain unmarried or else be reconciled (καταλλαγήτω) to her husband" (NRSV).

25 Robinson, Hoffmann, and Kloppenborg, *The Critical Edition of Q*, 394, omit ἴσθι εὐνοῶν from their reconstruction of Q 12:58, preferring δὸς ἐργασίαν ἀπηλλάχθαι ἀπ᾽ αὐτοῦ. If this is correct, it means that Q 12:58-59 was a piece of sapiential instruction concerned with settling a case out of court and had nothing to do with reconciliation. Matthew should thus be credited with adding ἴσθι εὐνοῶν and thereby introducing the idea of friendship and reconciliation.

26 Already in Herodotus 5.24 one finds the two terms associated, with εὔνοος as an adjective modifying φίλος: "the most precious of possessions is a wise and well disposed friend." The verb εὐνοέω occurs together with ὁμονοέω, another term from the *topos* on friendship, in the LXX of Dan 2:43, οὐκ ἔσονται δὲ ὁμονοοῦντες οὔτε εὐνοοῦντες ἀλλήλοις. For the use of both terms and their cognates in the friendship *topos*, see John T. Fitzgerald, ed., *Greco-Roman Perspectives on Friendship* (SBLRBS 34; Atlanta: Scholars Press, 1997), 274 (s.v. goodwill, harmony/concord).

27 For Philo, see Gregory E. Sterling, "The Bond of Humanity: Friendship in Philo of Alexandria," in Fitzgerald, *Greco-Roman Perspectives*, 203–23, esp. 209. For Josephus, see *A.J.* 17.37 and compare *B.J.* 1.569–570.

28 The best comprehensive treatment of friendship is by David Konstan, *Friendship in the Classical World* (Key Themes in Ancient History; Cambridge: Cambridge University Press, 1997).

29 For this rendering, see the CEV, NASB, RSV, NASB, The Translator's New Testament, and WEYMOUTH. The New Century Version renders it similarly with "become friends." For this translation, see also Max Zerwick and Mary Grosvenor, *A Grammatical Analysis of the Greek New Testament* (2 vols.; Rome: Biblical Institute Press, 1974), 1:12; Gundry, *Matthew*, 86; Davies and Allison, *Matthew*, 1:519; and Hagner, *Matthew 1–13*, 117. See also Walter Grundmann, *Das Evangelium des Matthäus* (6th ed.; THKNT 1; Berlin: Evangelische Verlagsanstalt, 1986), 158 ("Freund sein"), and Joachim Gnilka, *Das Matthäusevangelium* (2 vols.; HTKNT; Freiburg: Herder, 1986–88), 1:150, 152, 156 ("sei Freund").

30 Note the translations in Walter Bauer, *Griechisch-deutsches Wörterbuch zu den Schriften des Neuen Testaments und der früchristlichen Literatur* (ed.

Kurt Aland and Barbara Aland; 6th rev. ed.; Berlin: de Gruyter, 1988),
654 (s.v. εὐνοέω): "sei deinem Gegner schleunigst *wieder* Freund"
(emphasis mine), BDAG 409 (s.v. εὐνοέω): "make friends quickly with
your opponent," and *EDNT* 2:80 (s.v. εὐνοέω): "make friends again."
See also Alexander Sand, *Das Evangelium nach Matthäus* (RNT 1;
Regensburg: Friedrich Pustet, 1986), 113: "bemühe dich, wieder Freund
zu sein."

31   Also noted *inter alia* by Gundry, *Matthew*, 86.

32   Strecker, *Sermon on the Mount*, 68, correctly notes that Matthew's ἴσθι
     εὐνοῶν "picks up the foregoing διαλλάγηθι" of 5:24. Gnilka,
     Matthäusevangelium, 1:152, also notes the connection and argues
     (1:157) that reconciliation is the central concern of the pericope. See also
     Betz, *Sermon on the Mount*, 226, who rightly notes that "the verb εὐνοέω
     ('be well disposed,' 'make friends with someone') indicates reconcilia-
     tion," and Grundmann, *Das Evangelium des Matthäus,* 152, who argues
     that both the second and third units advise reconciliation.

33   See, for instance, LSJ 401 (s.v. διαλλάσσω, III) and 899 (s.v.
     καταλλάσσω, II); G. Abbott-Smith, *A Manual Greek Lexicon of the
     New Testament* (3rd ed.; Edinburgh: T&T Clark, 1937), 109 (s.v.
     διαλλάσσω, 2) and 236 (s.v. καταλλάσσω); BDAG 521 (s.v.
     καταλλάσσω).

34   C. Spicq, *TLNT*, 2:262.

35   On the close relationship between reconciliation and friendship, see also
     Fitzgerald, "Paul and Paradigm Shifts," 257–59, and "Paul and
     Friendship," in *Paul in the Greco-Roman World* (ed. J. P. Sampley;
     Harrisburg: Trinity Press International, 2003), 319–43, esp. 334–37.

36   See, for example, Aristophanes, *Lys.* 1091 (διαλλάξει ταχύ); Josephus,
     B.J. 3.496 (διαλλάξει ταχέως). See also Isocrates, *Or.* 4 (*Paneg.*) 94.

37   Note esp. Josephus, *A.J.* 7.259: Once Absalom was dead, the Hebrews
     who had fought on his side blamed themselves for their actions, because
     they "had not appealed to David to abate his anger (ὀργῆς)" and to
     "show himself friendly (εὐνοϊκῶς) toward them."

38   This is why Adolf Deissmann, *Light from the Ancient East* (4th ed.;
     London: Hodder & Stoughton, 1927), 189 n. 15, translates the appeal
     διαλλάγηθι ἡμεῖν (literally, "be reconciled to us") in *PGiss.* 17 (early
     second century C.E.) with "be no more angry with us." The LCL trans-
     lation of this papyrus by Hunt and Edgar, on the other hand, points to
     the connection of reconciliation with friendship: "be friends with me."
     For a discussion of this papyrus, see Fitzgerald, "Paul and Paradigm
     Shifts," 250–51.

39   See esp. Adele C. Scafuro, *The Forensic Stage: Settling Disputes in Graeco-
     Roman New Comedy* (Cambridge: Cambridge University Press, 1997),
     esp. Part 2 ("Reconciliation and Its Rhetoric") and appendix 2 ("Private
     Arbitrations and Reconciliations in Athens"). She notes (p. 181) that

almost all such plays end harmoniously, "as if 'reconciliation' is the harmonious note on which the playwright must have his players leave the stage."

40   Scafuro, *The Forensic Stage*, 131–35.

41   For examples of amnesia clauses and grants of amnesty as well as concessions intended to facilitate reconciliation, see Scafuro, *The Forensic Stage*, 121–22, and Fitzgerald, "Paul and Paradigm Shifts," 256, and "Paul and Friendship," 336–37.

42   Scafuro, *The Forensic Stage*, 34.

43   On compensation as a "gift," see Scafuro, *The Forensic Stage*, 135.

44   Scafuro, *The Forensic Stage*, 130, 133.

45   The phrase is that of Victor Bers, trans., *Demosthenes, Speeches 50–59* (The Oratory of Classical Greece 6; Austin: University of Texas Press, 2003), 151.

46   Conventional morality (criticized by Jesus in Matt 5:43-48) called for one to help friends and harm enemies; see esp. Mary Whitlock Blundell, *Helping Friends and Harming Enemies: A Study in Sophocles and Greek Ethics* (Cambridge: Cambridge University Press, 1989). J. O. Burtt in the LCL clearly understood the import of the Greek terminology in this passage and rendered it "to treat each other as friends in future."

47   For texts that have this general meaning (such as Aeschylus, *Ag.* 41, where Menelaus is the "adversary" or "enemy" of Priam), see BDAG 88, s.v. ἀντίδικος. Note esp. Josephus, *A.J.* 13.412–13: "they said . . . they were now being slaughtered at home like cattle by their foes (ἐχθρῶν), and . . . that if their adversaries (ἀντίδικοι) were to be contented with those already slain" (trans. Marcus, LCL).

48   That is, Epicurean logic.

49   Literally, "the one on the outside (ὁ μὲν ἔξωθεν)." The reference is to someone who is not a member of the Epicurean community. Compare 1 Tim 3:7, where οἱ ἔξωθεν ("outsiders") is used of non-Christians. See also Iamblichus, *VP* 35.252, where οἱ ἔξω is used of those who are "outside of the school," that is, non-Pythagoreans.

50   The best critical edition is currently that of Giovanni Indelli, ed. and trans., *Filodemo: L' ira* (La Sculoa di Epicuro 5; Naples: Bibliopolis, 1988). For col. 31.11–24, see pp. 87–88. A new edition, with the first English translation, is in preparation by David Armstrong for the Society of Biblical Literature's Writings from the Greco-Roman World series. My translation is a modified version of that offered by Armstrong in his " 'Be Angry and Sin Not': Philodemus versus the Stoics on Natural Bites and Natural Emotions," in *Passions and Moral Progress in Greco-Roman Thought* (forthcoming).

51   The Greek term for "courage" was literally "manliness" (ἀνδρεία), the quintessential quality of the "man" (ἀνήρ), and anger was defended by many people in the Greco-Roman world as a spur to courage and other

virtues. This is one of the ideas attacked by Seneca in his *On Anger*. See, for example, *Ira* 1.13.5: "No one is ever made braver through anger, except the one who would never have been brave without anger. It comes, then, not as a help to virtue, but as a substitute for it" (trans. Basore, LCL).

52 The danger of a friend becoming an enemy was a widespread concern in Greco-Roman discussions of friendship; see Fitzgerald, *Greco-Roman Perspectives*, 272 (s.v. "former friends as enemies"). For this concern in a Jewish author, see Sir 6:9; 37:2.

53 See Fitzgerald, *Greco-Roman Perspectives*, passim. The financial aspects of friendship took various forms, including gifts, loans, and guaranteeing loans to a third party; see, for example, Sir 29:1-20, which not only deals with loans (vv. 1-7), alms (vv. 8-13), and giving surety (vv. 14-20) for friends and brothers (v. 10), but also recognizes that lending and borrowing can lead to enmity (v. 6). While fully cognizant of the problems and dangers of becoming surety for another's debts, Sirach views the practice as the mark of a good man (29:14). Proverbs, by contrast, is particularly opposed to it (22:26-27) and even joins the injunction against it to the admonition not to become friends with an angry person (22:24-25). See esp. Prov 6:1-5 LXX, where prompt action (compare Matt 5:25) is advised in cases where an individual has become security for a friend (φίλον: vv. 1 and 3) and, as a result, has fallen into the hands of an evil (v. 3) enemy (ἐχθρῷ: v. 1).

54 Betz, *Sermon on the Mount*, 228.

55 The translation is that of Herbert Danby, *The Mishnah* (Oxford: Oxford University Press, 1933), 172. The passage cited by Rabbi Eleazar is Lev 16:30, which he understands to mean "clean before the Lord" but not before the unappeased fellow. On Eleazar ben Azariah (Azaryah), a second generation Tannaite of priestly descent who for a short period of time led the rabbinic academy at Yavneh, see Tzvee Zahavy, *The Traditions of Eleazar ben Azariah* (BJS 2; Missoula: Scholars Press, 1977), esp. 131 and 312. A slightly different version of Eleazar's exegesis of Lev 16:30 appears in the halakhic midrash on Leviticus; see *Sifra, Aharé pereq* 8.1–2 and Zahavy, *The Traditions of Eleazar,* 131–32.

56 Irving Greenberg, *The Jewish Way: Living the Holidays* (New York: Touchstone, 1988), 188.

57 Greenberg, *The Jewish Way,* 206.

58 Greenberg, *The Jewish Way,* 206.

59 I have dealt with this passage and the tradition connected with it at some length because most commentators who mention the text do so only in passing and make no reference to the later tradition. Those who refer to *m. Yoma* 8.9 include Sherman E. Johnson, "The Gospel According to St. Matthew," *IB* 7:296; Krister Stendahl, "Matthew," in *Peake's Commentary on the Bible* (eds. M. Black and H. H. Rowley; London: Thomas Nelson,

1962), 769–98, esp. 776 (§679d); Schmid, *Das Evangelium nach Matthäus*, 99; David Hill, *The Gospel of Matthew* (NCB Commentary; London: Marshall, Morgan & Scott, 1972), 122; Robert H. Smith, *Matthew* (ACNT; Minneapolis: Augsburg, 1989), 98; Charles H. Talbert, *Reading the Sermon on the Mount: Character Formation and Decision Making in Matthew 5–7* (Columbia: University of South Carolina Press, 2004), 71; and John Nolland, *The Gospel of Matthew* (NIGTC; Grand Rapids: Eerdmans, 2005), 233 n. 147. On some of the differences between the Mishnaic text and Matt 5:23-24, see Ernst Lohmeyer, *Das Evangelium des Matthäus* (ed. W. Schmauch; 4th ed.; KEK; Göttingen: Vandenhoeck & Ruprecht, 1967), 121 n. 2, and Grundmann, *Das Evangelium des Matthäus*, 157.

60 The same concern with the sinner obtaining forgiveness from both God and humans is reflected in a parable attributed to R. Jose the Priest, a disciple of Yohanan ben Zakkai (*m. Avot* 2.8). His parable was occasioned by a question posed by Valeria, a female proselyte, who was puzzled by the apparent contradiction between Deut 10:17 (where God does not lift his countenance, viz., in forgiveness) and Num 6:26 (where he does lift his countenance and forgives). Jose solves the dilemma by telling the following parable: "It is like a man who lent his neighbor a 'maneh' and fixed a time for payment in the presence of the king, while the other swore [to pay him] by the life of the king. When the time arrived, he did not pay him, and he went to excuse himself to the king. [The king, however,] said to him: For the wrong done to me, I excuse you, but go and obtain forgiveness from your neighbor. So also here: one text [Num 6:26] speaks of offences committed by a man against God, the other [Deut 10:17] of offences committed against his fellow man" (*b. Roš. Haš.* 17b; the translation is that of Francis Martin, ed., *Narrative Parallels to the New Testament* [SBLRBS 22; Atlanta: Scholars Press, 1988], 129). The crucial difference, of course, is that in Jose's parable the king (God) forgives the debtor before the latter has gone to the lender.

61 The idea of debt links this part of the Lord's Prayer to Matt 5:26 ("until you have repaid the last penny").

62 Commentators on Leviticus who relate Lev 5:20-26 MT (6:1-7 NRSV) to Matt 5:23-24 include Gordon J. Wenham, *The Book of Leviticus* (NICOT; Grand Rapids: Eerdmans, 1979), 112; and John E. Hartley, *Leviticus* (WBC 4; Dallas: Word, 1992), 85–86. Talbert, *Reading the Sermon on the Mount*, 71, mentions Lev 5:14-16 but not Lev 5:20-26 MT.

63 Jacob Milgrom, *Leviticus 1–16* (AB 3; New York: Doubleday, 1991), 330, is right on target when he says that "a basic legal and theological postulate of the Priestly legislators is that man can seek reconciliation with God only after he has made the required restitution (to the sanctuary or to man)."

64   Intentional sins were usually inexpiable, especially in cases involving (as here) perjury, which was such a serious offense against the name of Yahweh that the Decalogue condemned it in no uncertain terms (Exod 20:7; Deut 5:11), as did Jesus (Matt 5:33; on perjury, see John T. Fitzgerald, "The Problem of Perjury in Greek Context: Prolegomena to an Exegesis of Matthew 5:33; 1 Timothy 1:10; and *Didache* 2.3," in *The Social World of the First Christians* [eds. L. M. White and O. L. Yarbrough; Minneapolis: Fortress, 1995], 156–57; and "Perjury in Ancient Religion and Modern Law: A Comparative Analysis of Perjury in Homer and United States Law," in *The New Testament and Early Christian Literature in Greco-Roman Context* [ed. J. Fotopoulos; NovTSup 122: Leiden: Brill, 2006], 183–202). But Lev 5:20-26 MT (6:1-7 NRSV) provides an important exception to the rule. Jacob Milgrom, *Leviticus: A Book of Ritual and Ethics* (CC; Minneapolis: Fortress, 2004), 51, notes that the law here allows intentional sins "to be expiated through sacrifice so long as the sinner feels guilt for his or her actions." Consequently, "repentance converts an intentional sin into an unintentional one, thereby making it eligible for sacrificial expiation."

65   Restitution and the payment of a fine are not optional, as Num 5:5-10 (a supplement to Lev 5:20-26 MT (6:1-7 NRSV) makes clear. For that reason, Baruch A. Levine, *Leviticus: The Traditional Hebrew Text with the New JPS Translation* (The JPS Torah Commentary; Philadelphia: The Jewish Publication Society, 1989), 33, translates 5:23 MT (= 6:4 NRSV) as follows: "When one has thus sinned, thereby incurring guilt, he *must* restore that which he got." He comments: "This corresponds to the formulation in Numbers 5:7, where the verb *ve-heshiv*, 'he must remit,' expresses what the criminal is *required* to do, not what he may prefer to do."

66   For the hypothesis that the Philippians' understanding of friendship was utilitarian and that Paul was seeking to correct it, see John T. Fitzgerald, "Philippians in the Light of Some Ancient Discussions of Friendship," in *Friendship, Flattery, and Frankness of Speech: Studies on Friendship in the New Testament World* (ed. J. T. Fitzgerald; NovTSup 82; Leiden: Brill, 1996), 141–60, esp. 157–60.

67   For a discussion of Matt 5:23-26 in terms of sapiential admonition, see Zeller, *Die weisheitlichen Mahnsprüche*, 62–67.

68   Mary Ann Tolbert, *Perspectives on the Parables: An Approach to Multiple Interpretations* (Philadelphia: Fortress, 1979), 102.

69   See, e.g., W. C. Allen, *A Critical and Exegetical Commentary on the Gospel According to S. Matthew* (ICC; New York: Scribner's, 1907), 50, and Luz, *Matthew 1–7*, 280–81. For the possibility that the joining of 5:23-24 and 5:25-26 is pre-Matthean, see Eduard Schweizer, *The Gospel According to Matthew* (Atlanta: John Knox, 1975), 115. For the view that the Sermon on the Mount as a whole is pre-Matthean, see Betz, *Sermon on the Mount*, 44.

70   For both the theory and the reality of strife between friends, see Alfons
     Fürst, *Streit unter Freunden: Ideal und Realität in der Freundschaftslehre
     der Antike* (Beiträge zur Altertumskunde 85; Stuttgart: Teubner, 1996).
     On the theme of friendship and homicide, see Plato, *Leg.* 865a and esp.
     Elizabeth S. Belfiore, *Murder among Friends: Violation of Philia in Greek
     Tragedy* (New York: Oxford University Press, 2000).

List of Contributors

Richard Bauckham is professor of New Testament Studies and Bishop Wardlaw Professor in the University of St Andrews, Scotland. He is a fellow of the British Academy and a fellow of the Royal Society of Edinburgh. His recent books include: *God and the Crisis of Freedom: Biblical and Contemporary Perspectives* (2002); *Gospel Women: Studies of the Named Women in the Gospels* (2002); *Bible and Mission: Christian Witness in a Postmodern World* (2003); and *Jesus and the Eyewitnesses: The Gospels as Eyewitness Testimony* (2006).

Helen K. Bond studied at the Universities of St Andrews, Durham and Tübingen. She is senior lecturer in New Testament language, literature and theology at the University of Edinburgh, where she has taught since 2000. She is interested in the historical, political, and social background to the gospels, particularly the passion narratives, and the life (and execution) of Jesus of Nazareth. Her publications include *Pontius Pilate in History and Interpretation* (1998), and *Caiaphas: Friend of Rome and Judge of Jesus?* (2004).

David B. Capes chairs the department of Christianity and philosophy at Houston Baptist University. His books include *Old Testament Yahweh Texts in Paul's Christology* (1992), *The Footsteps of Jesus in the Holy Land* (1999), *The Last Eyewitness: The Final Week* (2006), and *Rediscovering Paul: An Introduction to His World, Letters and Theology* (2007). He serves as the senior theological review editor for The Voice, a joint project of Thomas Nelson and Ecclesia Bible Society. Since the early 1990s he has been active in interfaith dialogue in Houston and cohosts a weekly radio show called "A Show of Faith" on 950 AM KPRC Houston.

Maurice Casey is emeritus professor of New Testament studies at the University of Nottingham. His main interests include the use of Aramaic to help us to see Jesus' life and teaching in its original context. His publications include *Aramaic Sources of Mark's Gospel* (1998), and *An Aramaic Approach to Q* (2002). He also has a specialist interest in the origins and development of New Testament Christology. His publications include *From Jewish Prophet to Gentile God: The Origins and Development of New Testament Christology* (1991). Both interests are combined in *The Solution to the Son of Man Problem* (2007).

April D. DeConick is the Isla Carroll and Percy E. Turner Professor of Biblical Studies in the department of religious studies at Rice University (Houston, Texas). She specializes in early Christian history and theology, noncanonical gospels, and gnostic and mystical traditions. Her books include *Seek to See Him: Ascent and Vision Mysticism in the Gospel of Thomas* (1996); *Voices of the Mystics: Early Christian Discourse in the Gospels of John and Thomas and Other Ancient Christian Literature* (2001); *Recovering the Original Gospel of Thomas: A History of the Gospel and Its Growth* (2005); and *The Original Gospel of Thomas in Translation, with Commentary and New English Translation of the Complete Gospel* (2006). She has also edited the collection of papers, *Paradise Now: Essays on Early Jewish and Christian Mysticism* (2006).

James D. G. Dunn is emeritus Lightfoot Professor of Divinity at the University of Durham, where he taught from 1982. Previously he served on the faculty of the University of Nottingham. He has authored over twenty monographs, including *Baptism in the Holy Spirit* (1970), *Jesus and the Spirit* (1975), *Unity and Diversity in the New Testament* (1977), *Christology in the Making* (1980), *Jesus, Paul and the Law* (1990), *The Partings of the Ways* (1992), *The Theology of Paul the Apostle* (1998), *Jesus Remembered* (2003), *The New Perspective on Paul* and *A New Perspective on Jesus* (2005), and commentaries on Romans, Galatians, Colossians and Philemon, and Acts. His doctoral pupils teach in many different parts of the world. He is married to Meta (they have three children) and functions as a local preacher in the Durham Methodist circuit.

Rachel Elior is John and Golda Cohen Professor of Jewish Philosophy and Jewish mystical fellow and visiting professor at University College

London, the University of Amsterdam, Oberlin College, the University of Michigan, the Oxford Center for Hebrew and Jewish Studies, Case Western University, Yeshiva University, Tokyo University, and Princeton University. She is the author of numerous works on Jewish mysticism and Hasidism, though not all have been published in English. Her publications include *The Three Temples: On the Emergence of Jewish Mysticism* (2005) and *The Mystical Origins of Hasidism* (2006).

Eldon J. Epp teaches in history and philosophy of religion at Harvard University. He is Harkness Professor of Biblical Literature (emeritus) and dean of humanities and social sciences (emeritus) at Case Western Reserve University. From 2003–2004 he served as president of the Society of Biblical Literature. His publications include *Studies in the Theory and Method of New Testament Textual Criticism* (1993, 2003), *1 Peter: A Commentary on First Peter* (1996), and *Junia: The First Woman Apostle* (2005).

John T. Fitzgerald is associate professor in the department of religious studies at the University of Miami. He has also served as visiting professor at both Brown University and Yale Divinity School. With Wayne Meeks he has edited *The Writings of St. Paul: Annotated Texts, Reception, and Criticism* (Norton 2007). In addition he has edited several monographs including *Friendship, Flattery, and Frankness of Speech* (1996), *Greco-Roman Perspectives on Friendship* (1997), and *Philodemus and the New Testament World* (2004).

Paul Foster is lecturer in New Testament language, literature and theology at the University of Edinburgh. He has published a study treating the debate concerning the social setting of the Matthean community, *Community, Law and Mission in Matthew's Gospel* (2004). His other publications include an edited volume of the *Apostolic Fathers, The Writings of the Apostolic Fathers* (2007), and various articles on noncanonical gospels, second century Christianity, and wider New Testament themes.

Paula Fredriksen is a William Goodwin Aurelio Professor of the Appreciation of Scripture at Boston University. Her publications include *From Jesus to Christ* (1988), *Jesus, Judaism, and Christian Anti-Judaism: Reading the New Testament after the Holocaust* (2002), *On the Passion of the Christ: Exploring the Issues Raised by the Controversial Movie* (2006) and forthcoming *Augustine and the Jews: The Story of Christianity's Great Theologian and His Defense of Judaism* (2008).

Charles A. Gieschen is professor of exegetical theology and chairman of the department of exegetical theology at Concordia Theological Seminary in Fort Wayne, Indiana. He teaches and writes in the fields of Second Temple Judaism and early Christianity, especially in the area of early Christology. In 1998 he published *Angelomorphic Christology: Antecedents and Early Evidence*. He is associate editor of *Concordia Theological Quarterly* and is on the American editorial board of *HENOCH: Studies in Judaism and Christianity from Second Temple to Late Antiquity*.

Larry W. Hurtado is professor of New Testament language, literature and theology and director of the Centre for the Study of Christian Origins at the University of Edinburgh. Prior to this appointment, he taught at the University of Manitoba. His major publications include *One God One Lord: Early Christian Devotion and Ancient Jewish Monotheism* (1988), *Lord Jesus Christ: Devotion to Jesus in Earliest Christianity* (2003), *How on Earth Did Jesus Become a God?* (2005), and *The Earliest Christian Artifacts: Manuscripts and Christian Origins* (2006).

Jonathan Klawans is associate professor of religion at Boston University, where he has been on the faculty since receiving his Ph.D. from Columbia University in 1997. Among his publications are *Impurity and Sin in Ancient Judaism* (2000) and *Purity, Sacrifice, and the Temple: Symbolism and Supersessionism in the Study of Ancient Judaism* (2005). In addition he has articles and reviews in journals such as *AJS Review, Harvard Theological Review, New Testament Studies*, and *Religious Studies Review*.

John R. Levison is professor of New Testament at Seattle Pacific University. He earned his Ph.D. from Duke University in 1985. His publications include *Portraits of Adam in Early Judaism: From Sirach to 2 Baruch* (1988), *The Spirit in First-Century Judaism* (1997), *Texts in Transition: The Greek Life of Adam and Eve* (2000) and *Return to Babel: Global Perspectives on the Bible* (1999). He has also coedited with Louis Feldman, *Josephus' Contra Apionem: Studies in Its Character and Context with a Latin Concordance to the Portion Missing in Greek* (1996). He is co-chair of the pseudepigrapha section in the National Society of Biblical Literature and a member of the Society of New Testament Studies. He serves on the editorial board of the *Journal for the Study of the*

Pseudepigrapha, and last year he became the founding editor of a new academic book series called *Ekstasis: Religious Experience from Antiquity to the Middle Ages.*

Marianne Meye Thompson is professor of New Testament interpretation at Fuller Theological Seminary. She is author of *A Commentary on Colossians and Philemon* (2005), *The God of the Gospel of John* (Eerdmans, 2001), and *The Promise of the Father: Jesus and God in the New Testament* (2000), and coauthor of *Introducing the New Testament* (2001).

Troy A. Miller is dean and assistant professor of Bible and theology in the School of Bible and Theology at Crichton College (Memphis, TN). He holds a Ph.D. in New Testament language, literature, and theology from the University of Edinburgh and specializes in late Second Temple Judaism, Paul, and early Christian identity formation. His thesis is titled "The Emergence of the Concept of Heresy in Early Christianity" and he serves as a theological review editor for The Voice project.

Carey C. Newman became the director of Baylor University Press in 2003. Before that he served as editor of academic books for Westminster John Knox Press. His publications include *Paul's Glory-Christology: Tradition and Rhetoric* (1992), *Jesus and the Restoration of Israel: A Critical Assessment of N. T. Wright's Jesus and the Victory of God* (1999), and *The Jewish Roots of Christological Monotheism: Papers from the St. Andrews Conference on the Historical Origins of the Worship of Jesus* (1999).

Pheme Perkins is professor of New Testament in the theology department at Boston College. She holds a Ph.D. in New Testament and Christian origins from Harvard University and specializes in the Johannine writings, New Testament theology and gnosticism. She is an associate editor for the *New Oxford Annotated Bible* and the *New Interpreters Dictionary of the Bible* and has published a number of books including, *Gnosticism and the New Testament* (1993); *Peter, Apostle for the Whole Church* (1994); *Ephesians* (1997), and *Abraham's Divided Children: Paul and the Politics of Faith* (2001).

Alan F. Segal is professor of religion and Ingeborg Rennert Professor of Jewish Studies at Barnard College, Columbia University. His books include *Two Powers in Heaven: Early Rabbinic Reports about Christianity and Gnosticism* (1977), *Rebecca's Children: Judaism and Christianity in the*

Roman World (1986), *Paul the Convert: The Apostasy and Apostolate of Saul of Tarsus* (1988), and *Life After Death: A History of the Afterlife in the Religions of the West* (2005).

Adela Yarbro Collins is the Buckingham Professor of New Testament Criticism and Interpretation at the Yale University Divinity School. Before this appointment she served on the faculties at the University of Chicago and the University of Notre Dame. Among her publications are *Cosmology and Eschatology in Jewish and Christian Apocalypticism* (2000), *The Beginning of the Gospel: Probings of Mark in Context* (1992), *Crisis and Catharsis: The Power of the Apocalypse* (1984), *The Apocalypse* (1979), and *The Combat Myth in the Book of Revelation.*